FIELDING

china

PEOPLE'S
REPUBLIC
OF CHINA

1993

BY
RUTH LOR MALLOY

FIELDING TRAVEL BOOKS
℅ **WILLIAM MORROW & COMPANY, INC.**
1350 Avenue of the Americas, New York, N.Y. 10019

Text design by Marsha Cohen/Parallelogram

ACKNOWLEDGMENTS

Many people are responsible for this book: travelers who took the time to share their experiences and impressions with us: hotel officials who talked not just of their businesses but of the problems and joys of living and working in China; business travelers on airplanes; and tourists in hotel coffee shops or trains.

I am also particularly grateful to travelers and friends, and travel professionals who gave a great deal of time in sending information or relating their experiences for the *Travel China Newsletter,* its hotel evaluation book, and this book: among the many are Joan Ahrens, Rich Baker, Ann Beatty, Fred Braida, Karen Chan, Charles Christensen, Sister Theresa Chu, Rob Corbett, Robert Dalton, Mr. and Mrs. G. Douglas, Frank Edmead, Betty Jean Elder, Midori Ijima, Peter Gilmartin, Holly Gibson, B. Goodland, Hilary Harding, Edna Harvey, Bill Hinton, Katherine Chi'iu Hinton, Adi Ignatius, Dennis Jones, Robert Joyce, Ken Keobke, Larry C. Kinard, John Kohut, Loren Lyle, Linda Malloy, Valery Plummer, Jenni Sheldon, Norman Shulmann, Sheridian J. Smith, John Stark, Milt Stern, Willy Thorogood, Paula Timmerman, Ross Wilmot, Lilian Wong, Xu Lijun, Xu Xin-Jian, Zhong Ying, Herta Zieman, and the Happy Hour at the U.S. Consulate (Guangzhou).

A special thank you goes to Environment Canada and Caroline Walker and her students Gen Li, Li Mi, and Gen Jie at the Sichuan International Studies University in Chongqing.

What could we do without the input of seasoned travel professionals and airlines like Air China, Japan Air Lines, and China Eastern Airlines, Arunas Travel Co. (New York), Bestway Tours & Safaris (Vancouver), Canadian-China Society, Canada Swan International Travel (Vancouver), China Educational Tours (Boston), China International Travel Service (H.K.), China Travel Service (H.K.), China Youth Travel (H.K.), Chinapac International (Vancouver), Kim Chui, China-Orient Tourism Council, Maria Flannery of Conference Travel of Canada (Toronto), Carole S. Goldsmith (Portman Hotel), Guo Feng Corporation (New York), Wendy Hughes, Gerry Kerr of Inter-Pacific Tours International (New York), Lucy Izon, Helga Loverseed, Orient Flexi-Pax (New York), Jo-Anne Ondrus of Pakistan International Airlines, Gloria Copeland (Trinity Travel, Toronto), U.S. China People's Friendship Association, and Steven Powers (Yangrima Trekking and Mountaineering, Nepal).

I also wish to thank the Chinese missions in Toronto and Washington, and the Chinese tourism officials who shared their time and knowledge, and the foreign embassy officials and foreign residents in China who spoke frankly and anonymously.

Who financed the research? Basically, the buyers of *Fielding's People's Republic of China* and the subscribers to *Travel China Newsletter*. A great deal of help came from the China National Tourist Office in New York, CYTS Tours Corporation, and from the National Tourism Administration of China.

In some cities or provinces, I was hosted or assisted by CYTs, China Travel Service, China International Travel Service, municipal foreign affairs departments, or the provincial tourism administration: Beijing, Datong, Guangdong, Guizhou, Hangzhou, Hohhot, Jiangmen, Shanghai, Taishan, Xian, Yunnan, and Zheijiang. The names of dedicated and very informative officials and guides who come to mind immediately are: An Yong Yi, Bao Wei Ming, Cao Xu Dong, Chang Shi Ling, Chen Qing, Chen Xiao Zhen, Chen Ying, Chi Jiugui, Deng Pei Qin, Deng Zhou-li, Fang Dan Ling, Fu Chuanwen, Fu Keping, Gu Duohao, Guo Wanlian, He Zhi Yong, He Wen Kan, Ho Yi Hsing, Hsu Ho-ping, Huang Ai Hong, Huang Jian Yong, James Kang, Lee Fusheng, Li Jian Qing, Li Run Ying, Lin Feng, Lin Ze Ping, Liu Bing, Liu Kezhi, Song Jin-Lin, Song Xiao Ping, Sun Dan, Michael Sun, Wang Bin, Wang Dian, Wang Min, Wang Zheng Yuan, Wu Bin, Wu Bo, Yang Cheng, Xu Chun Shen, Xu Zhen Hua, Yang Jian Cheng, X. G. Yang, Yin De Juan, Yuan Xiao Ge, Zhang Nan, Zhang Jun, Zhang Jun Ling, Zhang Keli, Zhang Xiao Jun, Zhang Xing Ji, Zhou Dayan, and Pei Quan Zhu. But there are many others. Appreciation is also due the Hong Kong Tourist Association.

Especially helpful hotels have been Holiday Inn Asia-Pacific and Swiss Belhotel; in **Beijing:** Airport Movenpick Radisson Hotel, Beijing International, Chang Fu Gong, China World, Exhibition Center, Friendship, Holiday Inn Crowne Plaza, Holiday Inn Lido, Jianguo, Jing Guang New World, Olympic, Palace, Ramada Asia, Regent/Beiwei, Tianlun Dynasty, Traders, Yanshan. **Guangzhou:** Holiday Inn City Centre, Garden, Novotel Jiang Nan. **Hangzhou:** Dragon, Shangri-La. **Hong Kong:** Conrad. **Jiangmen:** Crystal Palace. **Lhasa:** Holiday Inn. **Shanghai:** Cherry Holiday Villa, Garden, Olympic, Portman, Hilton International, J. C. Mandarin, Sheraton Hua Ting, Yangtze New World, **Shenzhen:** Century Plaza, Forum, Guangdong, Nan Hai, Oriental Regent. **Taishan:** Taishan. **Xi'an:** Dynasty, Holiday Inn, Jianguo. There are also many more.

Though she was unable to work on this edition, my appreciation goes to Priscilla Liang Hsu, who co-authored the 1987 edition and whose touch is still evident in this one. My gratitude also goes to Bob Orchard, publisher of the *Travel China Newsletter* and the *Guide to China's Hotels,* for his optimism and support. Acknowledgment is due my editor

Randy Ladenheim-Gil and Fielding Travel Books for giving me the opportunity to travel in China and help in its modernization.

Most of all, this book would not have been possible without the cooperation of my family, especially my husband Michael Malloy (who has no interest in China travel).

To all go my thanks, and the thanks of our readers.

Ruth Lor Malloy

UP-TO-DATE
INFORMATION

The logistics of tourism everywhere are constantly changing, especially in China, where new hotels are opening at a furious pace. Yet information about these hotels and the new regulations is difficult to obtain, frequently discovered only upon asking.

Because travelers need information on China as current as possible, we offer the benefit of our resources at a discount to owners of *Fielding's People's Republic of China* for one time only.

For a six-month introductory subscription to the *Travel China Newsletter* with the latest information and changes that have come to our attention, *please send the following coupon and US$20 (or equivalent)*. Yearly subscriptions are regularly available for US$87.

This newsletter has been published monthly since September 1987. You might want to request copies of the six editions prior to your China trip.

GOOD FOR A SIX-MONTH TRIAL SUBSCRIPTION

of Ruth Lor Malloy's newsletter
on China's tourism and hotels,
to be used with the 1993 edition of
Fielding's People's Republic of China.

Coupon valid to December 31, 1993

Date of your trip: _____

( ) When do you want your monthly subscription to end?

Please check information needed.

( ) Information **not already** in this book on hotels in China, including telephone numbers, addresses, descriptions, evaluations, and current price of at least a standard double in F.E.C.s—where these are available. Noted will be the hotels that have informed us in writing that they will reconfirm reservations by telex.

( ) Latest information **not already** in this book on visas, customs, credit cards, and currency; new flights, travel from Hong Kong, cities open to foreign visitors, important new tourist attractions with evaluations (if possible). Also travel tips, important address changes, etc.

( ) Latest prices: A sampling of prices for food, film, hotel laundry, taxis, souvenirs, C.I.T.S. service charges, etc.

( ) Travel brochures

Photocopies or facsimiles of this coupon will be ignored.

Please send US$20 to Blendon Information Services, Suite 1, 126 Willowdale Ave., Willowdale, Ont., M2N 4Y2, Canada.

Name: (please type or print) _____

    Address: _____

_____

CONTENTS

DESTINATIONS · · · 181

INTRODUCTION

WHY GO TO CHINA?

—Because it is historically and culturally one of the richest countries in the world, and many of its ancient buildings have been restored for all to enjoy. It is not a sterile theme park. It's real.

—Because China has some of the world's most spectacular natural scenery, unique national minorities, and other beautiful people.

—Because what is happening now to the Chinese people is vital and exciting—a recent openness to the outside world which you, the foreign visitor, can encourage. Here is a drama of immense importance to human history—will China, with its tremendous population of more than one fifth of mankind, achieve its goals of modernization by the year 2000? Can she do this with a minimum of social damage before any more adverse reaction to current policies takes place?

—Because the banquet food is rarely duplicated anywhere. Where else can you get dishes shaped like phoenixes or swans or rabbits? And today the art of the great master chefs is being passed on.

—Because you can see for yourself its time-honored handicrafts being made; for example, 45 balls within balls, each intricately carved and free-moving.

—Because you can experience a culture very different from your own, and yet in many ways similar.

—Because foreigners have influenced and are still influencing China's development and traces of that history can still be found and studied.

—Because if you are of Chinese ancestry (in this life or previous lives), you can look for your roots and especially help in the development of your ancestral land.

—Because China is available for the first time in recent history to tourists, and who knows when it may be closed to tourists again?

BACKGROUND

China is a country that has infuriated yet tantalized the rest of the world for centuries. Its arrogant indifference, the wealth and divine right of its emperors have intrigued generations of curious people everywhere. In more recent years, its fanatical adherence to an alien ideology has continued to mystify. Then, people around the world were asking, ''Is

1

it becoming capitalist?'' And in early 1989, "Is it becoming democratic?''

China started out as a nation over 2200 years ago. The thousands of years of relative isolation since then allowed the Chinese to indulge in and develop their unique Confucian-based culture until the 19th century. At that time, more advanced technology and greed encouraged many European countries and Japan to grab power and territory in China. The Chinese reacted to foreign victories with bewilderment, various anti-foreigner rebellions, and then, in 1911, with a republican revolution. After a period of embarrassing national disintegration, first under the war lords and then during civil war and Japanese invasion, the country was finally reunited in 1949 under the Communists.

The Chinese people, up until very recently, have been 80% agricultural. Attachment to land has colored their behavior. Their religion, their loyalties, and their efforts have always been based on pragmatism, family, and ancestral lineages. The wishes of the individual were subordinated to the system and in most cases still are.

Before 1950, China's economy stemmed primarily from a feudal system, land rented to peasants in return for a percentage of the crops. Landlords ideally had responsibility for the welfare of their serfs, on whom they were largely dependent for their wealth. Although the system was abused frequently, owning land was the goal of millions.

In 1949, heady with victory, the Communist leaders embarked on a series of programs following religiously the theories of Mao Zedong, the man who had led them to power. But the Chinese leaders were pragmatists first. When something didn't work, they tried something else.

The Communists started out with a land-to-the-peasants program, and then to collectivization, to communes, and to communes with private plots. During the Cultural Revolution, private plots were abolished, to be reinstated and encouraged later. In the 1970s, it was apparent that even that system was not meeting the needs of the people.

In the early 1980s, an economy largely based on the family replaced that of the communes. Most counties adopted the Responsibility System, whereby rural inhabitants rent land or machines. The government received an agreed share in the produce while villagers kept or sold the surplus. Anybody could also work on projects such as handicrafts, livestock, and vegetables, which they could sell for their own gain. These you will still see in "free markets." Families and collectives opened up hotels, restaurants, and factories. It would seem that China had almost come around full circle, with the government replacing the feudal landlords. But had it?

Under the new economic system, the government no longer determined all that was grown or produced and how much; the market affected most production directly. Many peasants had been working furiously and were making more money than they ever had before. Many villagers had higher incomes than most salaried city dwellers.

China was thus undergoing another revolution. For the first time, many villages were earning less than 50% of income from agriculture.

The revolutionary slogans of nationalistic self-sufficiency and personal sacrifice of the fifties and sixties gave way to international cooperation and modernization and some people getting richer faster than others. A mind-your-own-business attitude replaced the "Serve-the-people" slogan of the Cultural Revolution. This has now degenerated to a "So-what's-it-got-to-do-with-me?" mood.

The new economic policies also included, and still do, the opening up of the country to foreign investment. A concerted effort to attract foreign money has been made in the coastal areas, with a series of regional development zones extending from Dalian in the north to Beihai city in the south, and especially in Shenzhen, Guangzhou, Shanghai, Dalian, and Tianjin. Here foreign investment particularly is being encouraged, and harbors, roads, and telecommunications added to or improved. Factories, office blocks, hotels, and workers' quarters are shooting up everywhere. Many of these and other areas have or will soon have International Direct-Dial (IDD) telephones and international airports. Beijing, Hangzhou, and Shanghai have video telephone services.

The effects of the new economic policies are apparent everywhere, as you can see by the many construction cranes and satellite dishes wherever you go. Fiber-optic cables and digital satellite services are being installed. Cellular phones have been introduced. And 10% of the population, especially children, are said to be overweight. A battalion of private souvenir merchants greet you at almost every tourist attraction. Groups of former peasants have built hotels, roads, playgrounds, libraries, and schools in their own villages. In many areas, you can see a great deal of new peasant housing, some of luxury size. You can find U.S. name-brand clothing like Oleg Cassini, Victoria's Secret, and L.L. Bean in fashionable street markets and hotel stores. Of these, some are genuine factory overruns.

You could see the relaxing of the puritanical Maoist ethic in the new freedom to enjoy life. Instead of saving their money for the development of the country or spending on more than one child, people were eating out in restaurants, and couples were ordering bigger and more elaborate wedding feasts. People were buying videos, color televisions, washing machines, refrigerators, and mopeds. A few private citizens even bought cars and trucks!

Life became less serious. Lively dance parties were held in every city. Many men and women wore high-heeled shoes and sunglasses, and the women added some glamour to their lives with permanent waves, lipsticks, and colorful dresses. Billiard halls, discos, and state lotteries seemed to be popular everywhere. And Chinese tourists flocked everywhere in China, a few even traveling outside the country.

Whereas anything foreign was considered counterrevolutionary before, visits of musicians like Paul Simon and John Denver, innumerable foreign symphony orchestras and dance groups, and artists like Robert Rauschenberg helped stimulate an interest in foreign culture. New also was the more mature approach to history, some credit being given to the help of the Nationalists in fighting the Japanese invaders, for example, and nude paintings started appearing in art exhibitions.

After decades of drabness, China began to look more cheerful. It was a nice change.

But the new economic policies had other results. People became aware of what was going on in the outside world. Students and government officials traveled to Europe, Australia, and North America. Thousands of teachers arrived from abroad spreading democracy along with foreign languages. Young people working in tourism or selling in free markets made more money than their parents, especially if the parents were working for the government. The importation of luxury goods like television sets, video machines, and Mercedes Benzes depleted valuable foreign exchange. The attitude that nothing Chinese was good and everything foreign was good began to permeate the thinking.

New classes of wealthy farmers and merchants, and oppressed laborers developed. A "floating population," tied by registration to smaller communities, moved to the cities hoping for more lucrative work. Beijing now has over two million, and *The Wall Street Journal* estimates a potential 100 million nationwide, with an annual increase of seven million. The children of these people are not getting schooling or disease immunizations. Nor are these people being overseen by work units and villages for birth control and criminal behavior.

In the 1980s, previously suppressed individualism surfaced, out of greed, necessity, or a growing self-confidence. The press became more frank and printed real news, not just what the government wanted people to hear. For students, the new attitudes extended to politics, and demonstrations. The leadership, once benevolent on many levels, became nepotistic and corrupt (with lavish state spending on banquets, foreign cars, overseas trips, and other perks). Inflation started getting out of control.

And then in 1989, hundreds of thousands of student demonstrators arrived in Beijing's Tiananmen Square asking for the end of government corruption and a say in their own student government. They flaunted foreign symbols and shouted defiant foreign slogans. Demonstrations also took place in other towns and cities. Plans for the historic visit of the president of the U.S.S.R. at the same time were thwarted because of the students. The leadership was divided on how to react.

What emerged was a reversion to old ways watched by the world on television. Like a traditional, autocratic Chinese father who "lost face" in front of a guest and realized his authority was disintegrating, the Chinese leadership regressed to brute force. An estimated 300 to 3000 people were killed in Beijing on June 4, some innocent bystanders, some unarmed demonstrators, some civilians angry at the government, some soldiers, some rioters. Over 450 military vehicles, police cars and public buses were destroyed.

Student leaders were arrested. Looters and rioters were executed. (See "Milestones.")

As a result, tourism almost disappeared. Many foreigners were evacuated. Business negotiations were cancelled. Countries abroad gave preferential immigration treatment to students and political refugees from China. They imposed economic sanctions in protest and disillusionment.

Today, China is still recovering from the consequences of that one night and a plethora of other problems. The leadership has lifted martial law in Beijing and is still eager for foreign investment and tourism. But it has been imposing more political education, more political movies, and study meetings. The press is again dull and obedient.

The problems include the worldwide recession, the disruptions of the Gulf War, and record droughts and floods. The shortages of raw materials and energy have forced a cutback on production. There has been the flap about prison labor and the lack of protection of intellectual property. Many Chinese people have had to tighten their belts again. Many are taking second jobs or selling in the free market.

Foreign businesspeople are now back. International sanctions have lifted. The economy continues to grow, especially in the countryside, and China has an international trade surplus. Government leaders are still talking of economic reform and openness to the world. They are expanding economic reform and opening free-trade zones. And plans for the controversial Yangtze River dam have been resurrected.

They are trying to cut down on government subsidies in some food items, and in health care. They are trying to eliminate the unprofitable government enterprises that have been taking up one-third of the national budget.

But *guanxi* is still important, and bribery exists on all levels.

They are persisting in developing the infrastructure—the electrification of railways and the building of superhighways and nuclear power plants. China is developing good relations with all its neighbors, like both Koreas, Vietnam, India, Laos, and Russia—rebuilding the train and trade links with Hanoi, for example. It is opening more doors with Taiwan. It is a crucial time to visit because what happens now will determine China's future direction. One finds people ignoring or just paying lip service to government regulations, unhappy with dwindling incomes and frustrated aspirations. Its 1990 census revealed that it has

1,160,017,381 people, considerably more than it had expected and planned for. One finds many intellectuals, afraid of another suppression, trying to leave the country. But many people are speaking freely with foreigners in spite of government pronouncements to the contrary. We suggest you use discretion in talking politics, human rights, and arguing the western point of view, unless you want the publicity of being booted out of the country.

The atmosphere is not as bad as before or during the Cultural Revolution. Under most circumstances, that kind of fear does not exist and one can make friends with Chinese people without endangering them.

There are so many questions for you to ask: What about social security? Free health care? What is being done about AIDS, and illegal drugs? Legal rights? What has happened to the thousands of people who complained about corrupt officials? And what has happened to people who have used their positions for personal gain? What do they do with their money? Buy condos in Florida? What is the effect of the hundreds of thousands of satellite television dishes now proliferating in the country? Is there really a lucrative market in old Chinese postage stamps? Does the historic selfless idealism of the Communist Party still exist? What is happening about air pollution? Where is the garbage going? Are Shanghai and Xi'an really sinking? What do the Chinese feel about the fall of Communism and the disintegration of the Soviet Union? What was China's position on the Persian Gulf war? To whom besides Myanmar and Pakistan is China selling arms now? Is China selling babies? Will private business overtake that run by the government? What is socialist democracy? Have students been executed for demonstrating? Will things loosen up again? Will prosperous Guangdong rebel against political domination from Beijing? Is China ready for democracy? Will it develop more democratic institutions? What will happen after the passing of Deng Xiaoping? Perhaps you can find some answers to these questions when you visit China.

TOURISM

China has charmed or infuriated its tourists. Some have stomped away vowing never to return again. But many have stomped away and come back.

Those who hated it obviously weren't prepared. They complain about the difficulty in getting around, smelly toilets, substandard hotels, the crowds, and the lack of service.

Those who liked it saw beyond the problems. Attitude makes a difference.

The successful visitor is one who likes challenges, who approaches every new situation with humor and flexibility. Being stranded with heavy luggage and no porters in a train station is an opportunity to make friends! It might take a while, but eventually someone will come along to help, especially if you look approachable or ask.

China has a lot to offer visitors, and this makes up for the obstacles. Its people are generally affable and delightful.

China wants tourists. She needs friends and the foreign exchange they bring. The national government, which oversees tourism, keeps trying to make money. It is attempting to enforce minimum hotel rates. At the same time, it wants a good reputation for China. Visitors now have a choice of excellent, world-class hotels all the way down the line to dumpy ¥15-a-bed hostels.

In the early 1990s, tourist arrivals exceeded 1988 figures, mainly because of a dramatic increase from Asia, especially Taiwan. These guests, however, were attracted to the cheaper hotels. Because North American groups did not return in 1988 numbers, and because many new top hotels were opened, the better-quality hotels did not do so well.

Today, the quality of most facilities is very good. Desperate for business, hotels have been upgrading services, some offering free half-day tours or breakfasts, or lowering prices. China is also building highways, superhighways, airports, and ship quays. She is trying to raise standards of service by having airlines and travel agencies compete with each other for business. She is upgrading more tourist attractions. Over 700 destinations are now open to foreigners. This covers all of the important tourist attractions in the country.

Many new joint-venture hotels have opened, and some Chinese-managed hotels have reached good Western standards. In a few cases they have better than Western standards with smoke alarms in each guest room, easily monitored by an attendant on each floor. Great restaurants are now available. Communications have improved tremendously. In large part, tourism income has been used to develop the industry. But in some cases tourism is still held back by people in the industry who do not yet fully understand just what foreign visitors need. The biggest problem has been the domestic airlines, which need to learn a lot about public relations and computers. (It is still not easy to get a plane schedule in China, but one can now book about 30 destinations in advance in China or through Air China abroad.) Airport ground services need a lot of work. Sometimes flights are cancelled at the whim of the pilot, or airline staff might give the wrong flight time on the telephone. Another major problem is the lack of porters or luggage-carrying facilities for individual travelers at 95% of China's train stations. English-language capability has improved but still leaves much to be desired. And while public toilets have improved considerably in airports and at many tourist attractions, stinking, clogged, dirty toilets still can ruin a good meal.

And someone can still make a killing leasing out carpet-cleaning equipment, if he or she could convince Chinese managers of the need.

With occupancy down, some hotels can no longer afford expatriate staff and some foreign management companies have pulled out. Standards will probably deteriorate unless business picks up.

Until hotel occupancy improves, individual travelers should be able to pay about US$60 for top-quality hotel rooms, especially if there is a price war. Do ask for a discount. One should shop around and haggle, and especially look for newly opened hotels. Ask hotel representatives at airports.

Prepaid group tourism is still the easiest way to go but individual travel is becoming a lot easier, and can be cheaper than a group tour. In early 1992, people flying Dragonair could get a room for $22 in the Holiday Inn Downtown or $38 at the Holiday Inn Lido, both in Beijing.

Generally, it was possible to get clean, comfortable, though less luxurious, accommodations for $40. Below $20, one could expect plumbing problems, filthy carpets, and rats in no-star hotels.

Telexes and travel agencies make reservations easy, and hotel drivers can pick up checked luggage at airports. After tourism picks up, individual tourists can also get reasonably priced city tours in a few cities. China prefers groups. Government travel agencies charge outrageous prices for packages for individuals because groups are more efficient.

But China is not ignoring the persistent numbers of those individual travelers either, and many on-their-own adventurers have been happy about their experiences in China. These people still cheerfully network among themselves about the best of the cheaper hotels and how to avoid C.I.T.S.'s unsatisfactory tours in Tibet. A frontier atmosphere of pioneering and sharing exists among individual travelers—even among jaded business people who have been traveling in China for years.

Flights and passenger ship routes have increased over the last year. Airlines flying into China include Air China, Air France, Aeroflot, All Nippon Airways, China Eastern, Dragonair, Finnair, Japan Airlines, LOT, Lufthansa, Malaysia, Northwest Airlines, Pakistan International Airlines, SAS, Singapore Airlines, Swissair, Thai International and United. Land routes are open from Hong Kong, Macao, Mongolia, Nepal, North Korea, Pakistan, and the C.I.S. China is also working on opening its border with Burma, Laos, and Vietnam.

A shortage of staff with international experience means that service is not up to Bangkok or Hong Kong standards—though it can come close. Hotels are furiously training staff, and attempting to fire the hopeless. They are fining workers or giving bonuses, depending on performance and volume of business. Some hotels are allowing attendants to keep tips (though tips cannot be asked or waited for). The resulting polite and eager service is impressive.

The government has started awarding "stars" to hotels, with one to five stars for maintenance, service, facilities, food, etc. Tourism administrations in each city should have a list of hotels, restaurants, and shops approved for foreign visitors. Some cities have started telephone Tourist Hotlines to help with any problems and to accept complaints.

Many hotels now have public relations departments, and you should call on them for help if you have problems. But many tours still cannot guarantee their hotels. In far-off Tibet, except for the Holiday Inn, it's first come, first served. Sometimes guides are sent a day ahead to make sure there are enough rooms. Some prepaid tourists without vouchers have had to pay hotels twice.

The furious pace of hotel construction will probably continue into the early 1990s, although a halt has been called on many proposed projects. The range spans from huge palaces fit for visiting heads of state to tiny temple hostels for pilgrims.

Keep in mind that while new hotels might be very beautiful, they can deteriorate quickly. We have tried to grade hotels, but six months later the quality might be completely different. A renovation then brings the facilities back up to higher standards. (The *Travel China* newsletter publishes evaluations sent in by recent hotel guests regarding the state of hotels used.)

In the Chinese-managed hotels, total renovations are made every two to four years, but in the meantime, soft drinks and spit get hopelessly ground into beautiful wool carpets. On the other hand, the foreign-managed hotels try to practice perpetual maintenance.

The top joint-venture hotels have raised the level of expectations for all hotels. Where before tourists were happy to get a tacky room with a private bath, and then, later, an air-conditioner and television set, today's visitors expect a refrigerator and spotless rugs too.

One must keep reminding oneself that the standards of China's hotels have risen considerably since the days of no shower curtains and no coffee shops, less than a decade ago.

There has been another reform of the travel agencies. Currently, only the head offices of China International Travel Service, China Travel Service, CYTS, China International Sports Travel, provincial overseas tourism corporations, and a restricted number of branches are authorized to sell tours from abroad.

And there is a wide range of prices for services now. Travelers should shop around. The price of a trip to the Great Wall and Ming Tombs ranges from ¥12 to ¥150 depending on the travel agency, the bus company, or the hotel. Some agencies charge ¥20–¥43 to book plane tickets, yet some hotels will book tickets for free. A guide for two people per day from C.I.T.S. ranges from ¥40–¥167, depending on the city.

China's airlines have shown improvement, but are still not up to international standards, especially in their domestic operations. If one plane breaks down, the whole system stops functioning. And one still needs to have a ticket stamped to reconfirm. No telephone reconfirmations. Payment in China can only be made in cash, not by credit card. (In China, you might have to buy tickets from Air China or C.I.T.S. even if you are flying on a foreign airline.) They are adding many new planes, opening convenient booking offices, and building or expanding airports. But some planes are small and uncomfortable (especially for big foreigners). Some planes have broken seat belts and luggage bins that fall open. Cabin crews are not always careful about safety checks (but service is improving). If you have a choice of planes, study a flight schedule and pick the newer, faster planes. In 1990, Chinese airlines carried over 16 million passengers.

If you can't get a booking, you can try flying stand-by after you arrive in China, pleading emergency. The success rate of stand-bys is very high unless you happen to hit a busy travel period.

There are still delays. Those waiting for such flights are rarely given progress reports or announcements about free meals in English. Do ask about these if you find yourself waiting. There seem to be fewer delays now. New airports in Chongqing and Xi'an can be used in all but thickest fogs.

We still suggest that tours spend more time in fewer cities to minimize time in airports. Beijing, for example, has very interesting side trips—like Chengde within four hours' train ride. Henan, Jiangsu, and Shandong are ideal provinces for driving around.

Stewardesses smile more frequently now, and give the impression of wanting to help. (You should have seen them before.) They are dressing more smartly these days; they used to wear baggy khaki uniforms. Food on flights is usually below U.S. standards, but improving. And safety spiels and seat-belt checks are becoming more common.

The development of new domestic airlines has been slow. Of the non-CAAC airlines, the two most prominent have been Shanghai Airlines and China United Airlines, the latter a joint venture with the airforce. CUA uses military planes, pilots, and airports. All domestic airlines charge the same prices and have the same general regulations as CAAC (such as baggage allowances and refunds).

China is also buying more and better passenger trains, and improvements have started to show. Some travel agents have chartered coaches for their own clients and these should be clean and air-conditioned. The Shanghai Hilton can book, clean, and cater train coaches to international standards. Special air-conditioned tourist trains now ply between the likes of Beijing and Chengde. A luxury train trip along the Silk Road has been organized by Conference Travel of Canada. Jiangsu has tour buses with toilets.

There is exciting news about the possible start of passenger service, in 1992, of the railway from Rotterdam to Lianyungang on the east China coast through Germany, Poland, the C.I.S., and, in China, Xinjiang, Gansu, Shaanxi, Henan, Anhui, and Jiangsu provinces.

Taxi service has improved. Shanghai taxis now have meters marked with telephone numbers if you have complaints and we were able to get a ¥25 refund because our driver got lost. Shanghai is one of the cities working on a much-needed subway. Public sightseeing mini-buses traveling regular routes have appeared. These are more expensive than regular buses but cheaper than taxis.

The improved economy has also meant new problems like traffic jams and shortage of parking spaces. Many cities have now built elevated highways, and superhighways. But be prepared for delays.

The variety of goods on sale for tourists has also improved, both in quantity and quality. Clothing styles are better than before but China comes nowhere near surpassing Hong Kong as the place to shop for international fashions. Factory overrun clothing made for the North American market are very good buys, but the range of colors and sizes is limited. Jewelry has also proliferated, previously banned by the Cultural Revolution. China Travel Service has opened "Duty-free stores," selling imported motorcycles, microwave ovens, and computers to those with foreign currency and passports.

But problems have arisen here too. Pilfering in hotel rooms is on the increase, so lock your valuables away. Strong padlocks have disappeared between hotels, though usually nothing else is missing. People now have to watch their purses and wallets in crowded areas.

At least one hawker on a boat on Guilin's Li River has tried to pass fake pearls off as real. And some private merchants have become so aggressive, they've scared foreign customers away. One of the worst places is at the Terracotta Army in Xi'an, where little children have been exploited to charm tourists out of their money. And women hard sell their "beautiful" jackets with tears in their eyes.

In Xi'an, too, I bargained one merchant down to "ten" and then he insisted it was "ten U.S. dollars"! And we heard about two guides who kept for themselves, the ¥300 fine collected from a tourist for video-taping the Banpo Museum.

One can now rely more on credit cards, but plastic money is still not as common as in other countries and should not be counted on completely. Take traveler's checks and cash. The Bank of America has opened branches in Shanghai.

A recent trend in several cities has been the development of theme parks with reproductions of ancient buildings. The classic novel *Dream of the Red Chamber (Mansions)* seems to be a favorite. Shenzhen's *Splendid China* is a delight. Resort complexes with golf courses are being built, and have even opened in that most hallowed of spots, the Ming Tombs north of Beijing. Whole streets have been renovated or created in Song, Ming, or Qing architecture.

Tourist attractions are being developed and improved. Adventurous travelers should aim for festivals. While frequently badly organized, with a shortage of hotel space, these are well worth the inconveniences for the costumes, rituals, dances, fireworks, and sports competitions. Take lots of film. Exact dates for festivals of the national minorities are very difficult to obtain and frequently only decided a month or so in advance.

There seems to be more awareness of the hazards of cigarette smoking. It is now forbidden on domestic flights, and in some train coaches. A handful of joint-venture hotels have no smoking areas in restaurants and some rooms. But smoking is still very common.

Tourism information is becoming easier to obtain: Information desks have opened at some airports, the government has finally started a twice-a-month tourism newspaper, the National Tourism Administration has published a good booklet on Festivals and C.I.T.S. has one on hotels. Some C.I.T.S. branches have sent representatives to North America who should be able to answer questions about their provinces.

Going on a group tour doesn't eliminate all the problems. But it does mean someone else has to deal with them, and that "someone else" should also be able to find you a clean toilet.

Shortages of trained, experienced staff with a good command of the English language plague all sectors of the industry because it has expanded too quickly. Experienced tour guides have moved on to other positions, and recent group tourists have complained of inexperienced guides, although most are excellent. It is very important to take a list of what you want to do and see. Otherwise, some guides will take you shopping (to stores where they get commissions). Make a list as you read through this book. Deciding whether or not to tip, and how much to tip, is still a problem for travelers. A few tour guides are cheating. They greet each new tour group with "It's my birthday today, but because you needed help, I decided to come in and help you." Don't fall for it! Guides who accept commissions have been fired and blackballed from other tourism jobs.

Many new tourism institutes and courses have been started, but it takes time to produce competent graduates. Students have also been sent to the U.S., Australia, and Europe for tourism training.

We are still hearing stories like the one about the hotel that charged more for a single room than a larger double. About the Canadian who rode a public bus from Kunming to Dali. Her neighbor kept reaching over her and spitting out the window, refusing to change seats. And another Canadian who was told half an hour ahead of time that she had finally got a train ticket from Datong to Beijing. Then at the station, C.I.T.S. urged her to crawl under the train because there was no time to climb down and up the underpass.

Most of the horror stories happen to individual travelers trying to save money, but one traveler with a reserved paid plane ticket, took it to C.I.T.S. to be confirmed. She was told that she could not get on the flight for five days even though it was booked for two days away. She had to argue and insist. Eventually, she won. But this kind of frustration was repeated every time she went to get a ticket. She finally learned to say to the clerk, "Is your wife a good cook and do you have an extra place in your house to sleep in? Because if I don't get on that flight, I'm going to have to stay at your place."

But the ordinary Chinese on the street were very friendly and helpful. That and the challenge and adventure made it a good trip.

The big questions for tourists: Is China safe? What if there is another upheaval?

At this writing China is safe. And should there be any question, one can consult one's government or the *Travel China Newsletter* for last-minute advice. If disturbances do erupt again, please feel confident that in 1989, tour guides acted professionally. They avoided danger and got their guests out of China safely. No tourists were injured. No tourists were detained (except in Beijing, where they defied martial law orders against taking photographs in Tiananmen Square.) Some hotels acted admirably, the Palace in particular, checking people out and in to make sure they were safe.

CNN and/or BBC and foreign newspapers are available in the top hotels. No one gives political lectures to tourists unless asked. Strangers we met on the street invited us home to dinner. And my relatives were not afraid to invite my Canadian friend to a restaurant near her home. We felt no tension and the smiles are still there. An American teacher in China recently stated, "I do not feel I am helping the Chinese government by teaching English to students who do not support their government."

The same can be said of any visitors to China. One goes to enjoy the people.

NOTE

Fielding's People's Republic of China was written for all tourists in China: those on their own and those on escorted tours. It is for business people, foreigners living there, Overseas Chinese and Hong Kong, Macao, and Taiwan Compatriots—anyone wanting to make the most of opportunities in this fascinating country. This guide has been designed to help visitors plan their trips, and to give them an idea of what to expect. It should help you orient yourself, travel around China independently, and make decisions about where to stay, how to get there, and what to do and see. For those on escorted tours, it should give a broader picture of the places you are visiting and the options you have. You should not allow yourself to be at the mercy of tour guides.

Here also are as many Chinese characters as we could get for the names of restaurants, stores, and tourist attractions. You can communicate by pointing to them so non-English speakers will know where you want to go. The names of hotels are in pinyin romanization, so you can attempt to say them.

Over 700 cities, counties, towns, and villages are now available to foreign tourists. We have presented what we feel are the most important. Many of the minor destinations are listed as side trips from the larger cities, especially provincial capitals.

Since we couldn't put over 700 names on one map, we have put the names of many of the cities mentioned in this book on maps of the six tourist regions. After each city name in "Destinations" is the region. If you want to find out what other places of interest are in the area, consult that particular map as well as the text on the provincial capital.

China is now producing a great deal of travel literature of its own. We encourage you to supplement the information here with what is available in China, especially the Cartographic Department maps and the China City Guides series.

Please do not consider any guidebook as the only source of information about a country. A guidebook should stimulate your interest as well as give you a lot of essential facts. So please ask many questions in China about what you are experiencing. Only then will you learn, and in learning, enjoy.

Fielding's People's Republic of China is one in a series of 11 China guides written by Ruth Lor Malloy since 1973 under a variety of titles. Each one has been updated, expanded, and improved over its predecessor. The 1987 edition was the only one written in collaboration with Priscilla Liang Hsu.

Pinyin spellings: In 1979, China adopted the pinyin system of romanizing its language based on the Beijing pronunciation. This was no easy decision since the language is monosyllabic and the word *ma,* for example, can have at least four totally different meanings depending on the tone. China's recent published literature in English has been using this system. However, many older history books were written in the old Wade-Giles romanization, and in China itself, many historical names like Chiang Kai-shek and Dr. Sun Yat-sen can be found in either form of romanization. We have used the spelling most commonly found now in China.

We have also tried to include the English terminology and new spelling for place names because you will hear both. This might look cumbersome, especially with the Chinese characters; however, we hope all this effort will be helpful to you. The names of dynasties are in the new spelling. A glossary and charts are in the "Quick Reference" section to help straighten things out.

In cases where both the old and new spellings are used, the operative one is the new spelling.

Important to know is that pinyin is phonetic and that "X" is like *sh* as in *she,* "Q" is like *ch* as in *cheek,* "Zh" is like *j* as in *jump,* and "Z" like *z* as in *zero.* See also *How to Pronounce Chinese Letters* in "Quick Reference."

Another confusing area has been whether words like Hong Qiao should be together as one or separated into two words. The tendency now is to combine place names into one word even though they can be very long. Shijiazhuang, for example, would be easier to pronounce if separated into Shi Jia Zhuang, but is found written both ways.

Avoid confusing the provinces Hunan and Henan, Jiangxi and Jiangsu, Shaanxi and Shanxi, Hubei and Hebei, and the cities Jilin and Jinan, the many Hengshan Mountains, and Taishan (in Guangdong) and Taishan (in Shandong). And there is still no standard translation for important place names; for example, Lingyan Si in Jinan has been translated Magic Cliff or Intelligent Rock Temple in different pieces of Jinan tourist literature. It could be difficult to figure out just what is being described.

The imperial dating system has always been used in China: "in the fifth year of the Emperor Hongwu." We have compromised here by giving specific dates and/or the dynasty name or the number of "years ago." Dynastic identification is important because it puts events into context. Some dynasties are more important than others and we hope you will gradually learn them and not have to turn to the "Quick Reference" every time they come up.

From the second Sunday in April to about the second Sunday in September, China is on daylight savings time. Be sure to clarify exact departure and arrival times of trains, ships, and planes.

Note also that the information in this book is as accurate as could be compiled at press time. The situation in China is so fluid that changes will have taken place by the time you visit. When in doubt, ask. And should you find things different, please let us know so we can make changes for future editions. A handy form is in the back of the book.

The travel agencies, hotels, restaurants, and other enterprises listed here free of charge *should* be able to help you. As far as we can see they are reliable, but a mention in this book is not necessarily a recommendation. They are listed to show your options.

Finally, to avoid having to carry a book as heavy as this, cut out the pages you think you'll need in China, and staple each section. Carrying "Beijing" and "Useful Phrases" is a lot easier than carrying the whole book in Beijing.

Have a great trip!

THE BASICS

WHERE IN CHINA?

First of all, you must decide where in China you want to go. China is full of choices. It is a big country, the third largest in area in the world. It has huge mountains and small mountains, deserts and tropical rain forests, and the second lowest saltwater lake in the world. It has 5000-year-old neolithic sites and pandas in the wild. Among its many ethnic minorities are the Tibetans, who live on the roof of the world and have fascinated people for centuries with their unique customs and religion.

No other country has such variety and vitality, and such a long, continuous history. No other country has such a wealth of temples, pagodas, ancient palaces, gardens, mountains, and elaborate tombs. China has so many valuable cultural relics that one can actually get indigestion from seeing a fraction of what it has to offer.

Careful choices are important if you want to be continually thrilled and surprised. The third set of 500 unique *arhats* can get very boring unless you know what to look for.

The ideal is to take several two-week trips rather than one trip a month long. This gives you a chance to do some digesting and reading in between. Many visitors, unfortunately, have to take longer trips, their perceptions dulled by fatigue toward the end.

Keep in mind your physical capabilities. The most strenuous places to visit are the Silk Road, Inner Mongolia, and, especially, Tibet.

To help you plan your itinerary, make a list of your priorities. If you want to join an existing group tour, see if you can find one that fits. Here are some suggestions. Take one city from any of the following groupings in which you are interested. Take two cities if you want to see more of any particular item. Yes, the hard part is choosing; China has over 700 places open to visit! You have to study a long menu.

If time and money are short, try to confine yourself to one tourist region, such as North China or West China. Staying in one area is cheaper and less time-consuming than hopping all around the country. Currently, you could lose one day (or more) every time you fly.

General interest

For details, see "Destinations." If you can only visit one city, it must be Beijing. Then, in order of priority, Xi'an, and Suzhou, Hangzhou, or Kunming.

Ancient capitals: Best to visit are Xi'an and Beijing; then Luoyang, Chengde, Chengdu, Nanjing, and Shenyang; and finally Anyang, Hangzhou, Kaifeng, Datong, and Suzhou. Well-preserved imperial palaces still only in Beijing, Chengde, and Shenyang.

The Great Wall: See "Great Wall."

Impressive city walls: Nanjing, Lugouqiao (Beijing), and Xi'an.

Imposing imperial tombs: Ming dynasty—better near Beijing, but also the first one in Nanjing and a minor one in Guilin. Qing dynasty—most impressive in Zunhua, but also in Shenyang and Yixian (see "Zunhua"). Qin, Han, and Tang dynasties in Xi'an. The famous Qin Army Vault Museum is visited from Xi'an. Song dynasty near Zhengzhou, but not worth making a special trip.

Important Buddhist sites: Xi'an (including Famen Temple, where they found a finger bone believed to be that of Prince Gautama, the founder of Buddhism), Luoyang, and Beijing. Impressive temples with 500 arhats are in Beijing, Suzhou, Chengdu, and Kunming. The most important Lama temples are, of course, in Tibet, but there are also some exciting ones in Chengde and Beijing. The *Four Sacred Buddhist Mountains are Putuo Shan (Ningbo), Jiuhua Shan (Hefei), Wutai Shan (Datong), and Emei Shan, with many old temples. For **martial arts fans,** Shaolin Temple is reached from Zhengzhou.

Cave temples: The best are in Luoyang, Datong, and Dunhuang. Also impressive: Dazu, Lanzhou, and Leshan.

The *Four Important Taoist Temples: Baiyun Monastery in Beijing, Qingyang Monastery in Chengdu, Taiqing Monastery in Shenyang, and Shangzhen Monastery in Suzhou. For the mythology, there's Yantai, Qingdao, Lushan, and Yueyang.

Important Confucian sites: Best is Qufu, hometown of the sage. Beijing has the second largest temple, now the city museum.

Most important cities with Jewish history: Kaifeng and Shanghai.

Important mosques: Guangzhou, Quanzhou, Beijing, Hangzhou, Yangzhou, and Xi'an. Also Silk Road.

*Traditional Chinese evaluation.

Neolithic site museums: Xi'an, Lanzhou, and Zhengzhou. Many being opened elsewhere too.

Shang dynasty sites: Zhengzhou and Anyang.

Foreign imperialist history: Very little in museums, but much European architecture in Tianjin, Shanghai, Wuhan, Beijing, Harbin, and Qingdao. Some in Xiamen and Guangzhou (Canton). Among the 46 treaty ports were also Zhenjiang, Ningbo, Fuzhou, Xiamen (Amoy), Nanjing, Jiujiang, Shashi, and Chongqing.

Best ancient history museums: Beijing, Shenyang, Xi'an, Zhengzhou, and Wuhan.

24 cities of historical or revolutionary importance protected by the State Council: Beijing, Chengde, Datong, Nanjing, Suzhou, Yangzhou, Hangzhou, Shaoxing, Quanzhou, Jingdezhen, Qufu, Luoyang, Kaifeng, Jiangling, Changsha, Guangzhou, Guilin, Chengdu, Zunyi, Kunming, Dali, Lhasa, Xi'an, and Yan'an.

Most important revolutionary sites: With good museums—Beijing, Yan'an, Shaoshan, Nanchang, and Jinggang Shan.

Other unusual structures worth seeing: Hengshan for the Temple in Mid-air; Lhasa for the Potala; Shibaozhai (see Yangtze Gorges); Leshar.

Memorable boat rides: The Yangtze Gorges, the Li River from Guilin, Lancang River (Yunnan), and the Grand Canal.

Limestone formations: Very impressive caves in Guilin, but also good at Yixing, Nanning, and Zhaoqing. The Stone Forest at Kunming is celebrated.

Seaside resorts: Beidaihe, Qingdao, Sanya (Hainan), Shenzhen, Weihai, Yantai, and Zhuhai.

Impressive Movie Sets: Wuxi (Tang Palace), Xi'an (Qin Palace), and Zibo (Spring and Autumn Period Palace).

Dinosaurs: Zigong, Sichuan.

Best classical Chinese gardens: Summer Palace and Beihai Park in Beijing, the Yu Garden in Shanghai (very crowded), and many gardens in Suzhou, Wuxi, and Hangzhou.

Gorgeous mountain scenery: Guilin—tame; Lushan Mountain, Chengde, and Jinggang Shan—a little rough, but you can drive around there; Taishan Mountain (a 4-hour climb, but cable cars available); Huang Shan (cable car), Emei Shan (cable car), and Hua Shan—very rugged. Then there are the Himalayas in Tibet and Xinjiang!

Last Emperor: Puyi lived in Beijing, Changchun, Fushun, and Tianjin. Manchu dynasty palace and tombs in Shenyang.

Camel and pony rides, and yurts: Inner Mongolia, and Silk Road.

*Three Most Eminent Halls: Tian Kuang Hall in Tai'an; Taihe Hall in the Imperial Palace, Beijing; and the Dacheng Hall in Qufu's Confucius Temple.

*Five Great Mountains: Taishan, Hengshan (Hunan), Hengshan (Shanxi), Huashan, and Songshan.

Theme Parks: Dream of the Red Chamber in Shanghai and Beijing; Splendid China in Shenzhen.

For Those with Special Interests

Musicians should be interested in the bronze chime bells in Wuhan and the Chinese musical instruments factory in Suzhou.

Plant lovers can visit botanical gardens: Lushan, Guangzhou, Nanjing, Hangzhou, etc.

Hot-air ballooning and gliding: Anyang has both. See "Important Addresses" (misc.) for parapente/paragliding.

Sports: **Mountaineering**—Several peaks, including Qomolangma (Everest) are open. **Skiing**—Not well developed yet, but lifts near Harbin and Jilin. **Scuba diving**—In Hainan. **Golf**—Zhongshan, Zhuhai, Tianjin, Beijing, and Shanghai. **Sailboarding**—Qingdao, Xiamen, and Qinhuangdao.

Steam locomotives: No more factory but festival in Datong. Museums in Datong and Shenyang. Real working steam engines in An shan, Jilin, Shenyang, Changchun and Harbin, narrow-gauge train trips, Kunming.

Performing Pandas: Shanghai Acrobats and Circus. Wuhan Acrobats. Fuzhou zoo.

Pandas in a wildlife preserve: Wolong, near Chengdu; Baishui-jiang Nature Reserve in Gansu province; Shennonjia in Hubei. Most numerous in Chengdu Zoo.

Sister Cities: Many foreign cities have "friendship links" with specific Chinese cities, and you may want to include yours in your itinerary. For example, Melbourne and Tianjin, Edinburgh and Xi'an, Toronto and Chongqing, Chattanooga and Wuxi. Ask your city hall.

Wheel-chair-confined travelers: Hotel rooms with lower sinks, etc., for wheelchair-confined travelers: in *Beijing,* the China World, Holiday Inns, Hong Kong-Macao, Palace, Sara Shangri-La; in *Dalian,* the Holiday Inn; in *Fuzhou,* the Lakeside; in *Guangzhou,* the Garden and Holiday Inn; in *Guilin,* the Novotel; in *Shanghai,* the Garden, Hilton, Holiday Inn, and Westin; in *Xi'an,* the Garden, Holiday Inn, Hyatt, Sheraton, and Sofitel. Ask about these when you book.

As a rule of thumb:
—The cradle of Chinese civilization was along the Yellow River (Zhengzhou, Anyang).
—The Silk Road went west from Xi'an. See *Silk Road.*
—The western imperialists controlled areas along the Yangtze River, and also Changsha. They were active on the east coast between Liaoning province and Hainan Island. The Japanese controlled Northeast China, then known as Manchuria, and, later, most of urban China.
—Most national minorities live mainly in the west, north, and southwest parts of China, especially Guangxi, Yunnan, Guizhou, Sichuan, Xinjiang, Tibet, and Inner Mongolia. Turkish-related Moslem minorities live primarily in Xinjiang, Qinghai, and Gansu.
—The earlier migrations of Chinese to America and Australia in the 19th and early 20th centuries originated from Guangdong province; the migrations to Southeast Asia originated largely from Fujian, but also from Guangdong.
—**The 15 Coastal Cities** chosen for accelerated development are Beihai, Dalian, Fuzhou, Guangzhou, Lianyungang, Nantong, Ningbo, Qingdao, Qinhuangdao, Shanghai, Tianjin, Weihai, Wenzhou, Yantai, and Zhanjiang. **Special Economic Zones:** Shenzhen, Xiamen, Shantou, and Zhuhai. The Yangtze and Pearl river deltas—including Guangzhou—part of southern Fujian province—including Xiamen, Zhangzhou, and Quanzhou—and the Liaodong and Shandong peninsulas are also S.E.Z.s.
—**Free Trade Zones**—Pudong (Shanghai) and Tainjin. But so far, no shopping.
If you want to avoid crowds, head for areas away from the tourist track, like Changsha, Guiyang, Jingdezhen, Nanning, Quanzhou,

Shaoxing, Taishan, Weihai, Yangzhou, Yantai, Xiamen, Xuzhou, Zhaoqing, Zhengzhou, Zhongshan, and Zibo. These have enough for at least one day's sightseeing, but you could spend a week just exploring by bicycle if you're interested in lifestyles, looking for glimpses of old architecture, and getting chatty with the natives. Taishan (Guangdong) still has most of its old buildings, but come quickly, before it's all replaced by highrises.

WHEN TO GO?

If you care about the weather, the best time to visit is May–June or September–October, but these, of course, are the times when most people like to travel. If you go then, you could run into crowds and delays, even if all reservations are confirmed. You could also try April or November and hope for good weather. Do consult each city listed under "Destinations." South China is chilly but fine in January. Kunming has spring temperatures most of the year.

It is important to remember that the Chinese do not heat their buildings as warmly as foreigners do in winter. South of the Yangtze there is no heat at all, except in tourist hotels, even though it can be very cold. Some low-priced hotels do not have any heat at all. If the cold bothers you, avoid Northeast China, Inner Mongolia, Northwest China, Tibet, Qinghai, and any mountains in winter, especially around the lunar new year (around late January or early February). Even in Guangzhou at that time you need a top coat and a sweater. Avoid the lunar new year especially in Guangzhou and Fujian, as hotels and trains are full of Overseas Chinese visitors and prices are at their highest, and some tourist attractions are closed. Industrial pollution is particularly bad in winter too. But most tour agencies and hotels give discounts in such low seasons! Avoid the first few days of the trade fairs in Guangzhou.

The hottest time of the year is usually July and early August. Traditionally, the "three furnaces" of China are Nanjing, Wuhan, and Chongqing. Almost all hotels, but few other buildings, are now air-conditioned. Most tourist buses and many taxis are air-conditioned. This is the time to put mountain or seaside resorts at the end of a hot tour.

In late spring, April–May through the summer, rain and high humidity make south China (including Guangzhou and Guilin) quite oppressive, but the greenery is lush and beautiful. Inner Mongolia and the Silk Road have a problem with sandstorms in spring and autumn.

As a rough gauge, China extends from the same latitude as James Bay in Canada to south of Cuba. Beijing is at almost the same latitude as Philadelphia, and Guangzhou as Havana. Take altitude into account: the higher, the colder. Winter begins in mid-November.

Wise tourists who are healthy and not afraid of the cold could plan trips in the winter even in the north. New-fallen snow transforms any city into a wonderland and makes red pavilions and curved gold roofs intensely beautiful. (It also makes roads slippery, and traffic slow-moving.)

Winters in Beijing are about the same as in Philadelphia and Toronto, only the air is drier. Precautions like long underwear should be taken because of the lack of heat in many buildings (which sometimes seem colder than being outdoors). Beijing also has a strong wind from February on, which brings more shivers. Take a nose mask because of the pollution.

Winter is a good time to visit south China, Guangzhou, Hainan Island, and Yunnan.

Other things to consider when planning dates:

—If you are interested in visiting schools, factories, and offices, avoid vacations and holidays. People wanting to do business should avoid the national holidays.

—If you want to see a festival like the Third Moon Market or the dragon boats, consider those dates. See "Quick Reference."

HOW TO GO?

Take your pick. The group tour is *not* the only way to go, but it could be cheaper and has less hassles for all but the tour guide.

Groups and Individuals

On a prepaid tour This is the easiest way to visit China. Just book with a good travel agent and most of your problems are solved. You can choose one of the set tours offered by a travel agent or you can have one custom-made. The average size of a tour is 20 people or less. Of course, the fewer people you have, the more expensive the rate per person can be.

China prefers prepaid tours. They use scarce staff interpreters more efficiently and are given preference. Even groups of four pay-as-you-go individuals run the risk of being downgraded or having their reservations canceled in favor of a full-scale prepaid tour group.

By ordering and paying in advance, groups, rather than individuals, are more likely to get what they want. For example, a group can book a helicopter in Sichuan to go to Jiuzhaigou, and do the trip in a day. A party of two could also book the helicopter, but if it isn't already going there, the rate for two would be prohibitive to all but the richest tourists. Some of the tours listed in this book, such as cooking and taiqi lessons, are not generally available to one or two individual tourists, but a group can book them, and if there is space left over, then the individuals who happen to be there at the time might be able to pay their share and tag along.

By hiring a professional tour leader, tourists do not have to bother about getting permits for non-open destinations, making reservations, and all the annoying and time-consuming things you will see in the chapter on getting around.

Basically all prepaid tours are treated the same in China except for the quality of the hotel. You can choose between standard or the more expensive "deluxe" rooms. If the price of the same tour still differs from one agency to another, it could be because (1) all meals or more restaurant meals are included (rather than hotel meals); (2) there is an orientation session on China, and perhaps a full-time guide, who has more than a superficial knowledge of Chinese history and culture; (3) more than one agency is getting a commission; try to book from the wholesaler; (4) one agent is getting a bigger commission; (5) a luxury tourist ship rather than a ferry is guaranteed on the Yangtze, and that ship's facilities are of the highest quality—lectures, briefings, and side trips. Ask if it has 70 or 180 passengers if you care; (6) the tour operator has better connections in China or flies Air China.

Ask about refunds if you are stuck in an airport for three days. Ask about tipping—will you be asked for tips for guides and drivers in each city? Will you have to spend hours discussing what to give the national guide? Do you have a national guide? (This is important as groups have been abandoned at the airport and their planes have been cancelled. What happens then?)

Prepaid tourists can usually choose what they want to see in each city from a set list. You have to pay extra for any "optional tours." Some tourists complain of the time spent in making group decisions; others are happy to have a choice. If you just want to see China, a general-interest tour is ideal. If you want to visit schools, several factories, or hospitals, better take a special-interest or Friendship Association tour. Or you could make sure schools, factories, or hospitals are included in your tour.

Group tours are also flexible insofar as you can choose to avoid most of the group activities. If you want to sleep in a different hotel from the one assigned, you can. But you might have to pay extra. Just be sure to tell your group leader so no one will look for you.

But you usually have to travel from city to city with the group, or at least in and out of the country with it. Each group has one "group visa" and individual passports are not stamped at the border. The only way you can leave the country without your group is to have a new visa stamped in your passport.

Some group tourists have been able to acquire individual visas once inside China. Overseas Chinese tour groups are usually given individual visas in the first place so members can visit relatives after the tour is over.

Tour groups can be fun if you have the right people. But a tendency does develop to look inward toward your own group, and to regard the Chinese as "them" as opposed to "us." As soon as group members start joking about the "natives," you've crossed the line and have truly become a group tourist. If you are visiting China to meet Chinese people and learn about the country, you do have to make an effort to break free from your groupiness and dependence. Do venture out into the streets alone. Lounge in parks especially on Sundays. A lot of students are waiting to practice their English on you. You might even be invited to someone's home.

Luggage for foreign tour groups is not usually opened by Chinese Customs, but that of Overseas Chinese might be. The total weight of group luggage to be flown is usually added together and averaged.

On a cruise   Among the cruise lines that have included China are Cunard, EuroLloyd, Pearl Cruises, Princess, and Royal Viking. You usually pay extra if you want a guided tour at ports of call. See also "Yangtze Gorges" and *Fielding's Worldwide Cruises* by Antoinette DeLand.

On a minipackage   Travel agents offer prepaid packages that could include only travel tickets, hotel accommodations, and breakfast. You sightsee on your own or, *if available,* book sightseeing tours locally. It is an ideal compromise for business people and those who want the flexibility of scheduling their own time, as well as the assurance of a place to sleep. Minipackages are available for many cities. You can also buy a "join-in" package.

As a pay-as-you-go traveler   Many foreigners, especially those with time to spare, have traveled China happily and successfully on their own. Some backpackers have loved it, not minding the dormitory accommodations and delays. Backpackers should take along the Lonely Planet guidebook and the *Travel China* newsletter. Travelers with bigger budgets have an easier time. They can be met by their hotels at the airport if so requested. Most hotels have travel desks, and bookings are made with less difficulty now. If a group tour is not scheduled in a city, you can always hire a taxi.

On-your-own traveling is not, however, as easy in China as in Europe. If you can't speak Chinese, you can get around with this guidebook. See also "Getting Around."

As a traveler of Chinese ancestry   C.I.T.S. guides do not usually know anything about places in Fujian or Guangdong, where many Overseas Chinese (O.C.) have relatives. However, C.T.S. doesn't have as many English-speaking staff members.

An Overseas Chinese is anyone with a Chinese surname, face, or the address of a relative and/or an ancestral village in China, and either a foreign or Chinese passport. But there are no more discounts just because you're Overseas Chinese.

You can take in duty-free many kinds of gifts for relatives.

It is possible to live with relatives in China or have relatives stay with you in your hotel. It is also possible to take part in special camps and seminars offered by the Overseas Chinese Association in some counties in Guangdong province. Xinhui county has been giving free room, board, and travel in the county, and courses for two weeks, mostly but not exclusively for young people with roots in the county. Taishan gives courses, but it charges. These are great introductions to China and the area where you might have relatives. Courses could be on language, cooking, painting, medicine, music, dance—and are given in English.

You could write the Overseas Chinese Association in your county for information, or try a Chinatown travel agent, a family association, or a county association. You can probably find these in any large Chinatown, New York City, San Francisco, Los Angeles, Toronto, and Vancouver. A Chinese consulate might have information. See also "Special for Overseas Chinese."

As a Hong Kong, Macao, or Taiwan Compatriot   Hong Kong and Macao Chinese who have reentry permits to Hong Kong or Macao can enter China the same way Americans enter Canada. They can just buy a ticket and get on some means of transportation. But no more travel discounts unless you pass for a local Chinese.

On business   The usual procedure here is to communicate with a trade officer at a Chinese mission abroad, your mission in China, or your own government's department of trade. They will all probably tell you to contact a Chinese trading corporation, some of whom have representatives in North America. If the Chinese are interested in what you want to buy or sell, they will send you an invitation that will give you a visa from a Chinese mission.

Business people can usually take their spouses and travel individually in China, not just for negotiations, but afterward as tourists. You can discuss the logistics with your host trading corporations or deal with a Chinese travel agency once in China. You should tell your host unit the quality of the hotel you want because your host unit might assume you want to save money. The unit might also automatically book you into a hotel with which they have connections (which may not be up to your standards). It is embarrassing for a unit to make changes after you arrive. You can also take time off from a prepaid tour to visit a trading corporation. See also "Special for Business People."

As a foreign student, scholar, or foreign expert **Helpful Publications:** *Education in the People's Republic of China, U.S.-China Educational Exchanges* by Linda A. Reed; *Teaching in China,* National Association of Foreign Student Affairs (NAFSA); *China Bound: A Guide to Academic Life and Work in the PRC* by Karen Turner-Gottschang; *A Relationship Restored. Trends in U.S.-China Educational Exchanges, 1978–1984;* William Goede's *Love in Beijing,* a collection of short stories about foreigners living in Beijing's Friendship Hotel; Mark Salzman's *Iron and Silk,* about teaching in Changsha from 1982–84. **Foreign exchange** students studying in China are usually there as the result of an agreement between governments or educational institutions. Information on these exchanges can be obtained from the Council on International Exchange of Scholars. In Canada, contact the Chinese Embassy.

Most exchange students are already university graduates and stay up to two years. The home government pays transportation to and from China and gives spending money. The Chinese government pays tuition, the cost of accommodations, and a small stipend. It is possible to save money and also to travel around the country during vacations.

Some universities and colleges abroad have bilateral arrangements with their counterparts in China, and information can be obtained from schools in your home country.

"Self-supporting" foreign students are also accepted at an increasing number of schools in China; prospective students can apply directly. These students should be aware that academic credits for courses studied in China may not be equivalent to those studied in their home countries. Tuition depends on the school and has been about US$1600–$2500 for the Masters program, living expenses US$1.50–$6.00 a day.

Foreign students have lived in guesthouses in rooms sometimes described by students at Beijing University as "cold and small" with little if any privacy. Many have hot tap water only two hours a day. Students at some other universities might fare better. Food is usually of higher standard than that of Chinese students, but with less meat than in the foreigner's home country.

Students learn a great deal about China and the Chinese language. Courses and teaching methods in Chinese institutions, however, are not as rigorous as in Western countries. Students do get closer to Chinese people than most other foreigners.

Chinese missions abroad and foreign missions in China should have information on studying in China. See also the American Institute for Foreign Study for Chinese language study.

Scholarly visits are also arranged by government agreement, but much is being done privately now, bilaterally between institutions or directly by scholars themselves. In the United States the U.S. Information Agency, for example, sponsors the Fulbright program, which makes it possible for a limited number of American scholars to teach American studies in Chinese universities. U.S.I.A. also finances the National Program, which helps American scholars and professionals lecture and do exploratory research in China for one to three months.

The Committee on Scholarly Communication with the People's Republic of China (C.S.C.P.R.C.) has developed programs with the Chinese Academy of Sciences, the Chinese Academy of Social Sciences, the State Council on Education, and the Chinese Association for Science and Technology.

The C.S.C.P.R.C.'s activities include a program for American graduate students, postdoctoral students, and research scholars to carry out long-term study or research. This is in affiliation with Chinese universities and research institutes. There are also short-term reciprocal exchanges of senior-level Chinese and American scholars, bilateral conferences, and an exchange of joint working groups in selected fields.

Contact also the Center for International Education, and the United Board for Christian Higher Education in Asia. The British counterpart is the British Academy.

People who are going to China in other capacities can also make valuable professional contributions in China. Specialists and professionals can give lectures or demonstrations to their Chinese counterparts if invited to do so.

If you're thinking of getting financial compensation, forget it. If you're thinking of helping China in exchange for a deeper insight, as well as business or academic contacts, do offer to lecture—if you have anything worthwhile to say, that is. Don't expect anything more than a "thank you" and, if you're in business, probably a tax write-off for part of your expenses (if you can convince your tax people that you were actually making business contacts in China).

Many *teachers* hired by China specialize in a foreign language with one- or two-year contracts. The great need is for English language teachers and teachers of middle-level technology and managerial skills. In recent years, there have been more than 9000 foreign teachers working in China.

Long-term *experts* usually have at least a Masters and three years' teaching experience. They should receive a contract giving them their transportation paid from home and back, as well as home leave, after the first year and then every other year, for a month or so. The stipend ranges depending on the schools. It has been ¥7000–¥10,000 a year. Thirty to fifty percent of one's salary can be taken out of China in foreign currency. Certain categories of experts also receive free accommodation, free medical care, transportation to and from work, and a month's vacation in China. The salary for foreign experts is frequently ten times that of local teachers, so no complaints, please.

Foreign *teachers* (as differentiated from *experts*) are usually locally hired and do not get the same benefits as experts. Some money-strapped colleges have hired native English-speakers without any teaching qualifications who just drop by. They give them only room and board, and try to help them find financing through North American religious or government organizations. *Teacher-students* occasionally teach part-time and study part-time. In Guilin, one American student was teaching English for ¥30 RMB an hour plus a meal in a hotel, for a total of six hours a week.

Foreigners working in China have been advised by one teacher assigned to Nanjing "to know how to say 'no,' since the Chinese will often pile work on them. I would also suggest, if possible, getting advice from someone who has taught in China prior to one's assignment, and bringing as many teaching materials as possible, including textbooks. Warm clothes for winter and a commitment from the university about sufficient heat for housing are essential. . . . Some foreign experts have had a terrible time with the cold." Ask any branch of a China Friendship Association for the names of teachers with experience in China who can share their experiences with you.

Among the organizations hiring teachers for China or who can direct you to those in the market are the Amity Foundation, Bureau of Foreign Experts of the State Council on Education, China Educational Exchange, China People's Association for Friendship with Foreign Countries, NAFSA, U.S.-China Friendship Association, the United Board for Christian Higher Education in Asia, United Nations Volunteers, World Teach, and teachers federations. Canadians should contact Canadian International Development Agency (CIDA), the Ontario-Jiangsu Educational Exchange, WUSC, and the Canadian Council for International Education. The Great Britain-China Center has a list of organizations. Evangelical Christian groups are sending teachers but not missionaries.

Contact also the education officer at a Chinese consulate.

As a consultant   United Nations Volunteers are also looking for other skills besides teaching. The Association of Universities and Colleges of Canada has been looking for Human Resources development specialists. The China Educational Exchange wants physicians and agriculturalists. Many foreign and Chinese organizations recruit experts to China in connection with their own projects. The foreign companies offer the most money and usually the best living conditions.

The Canadian Executive Service Organization, Toronto, sends recently retired Canadians to work as volunteer consultants to industry, institutions, and governments in developing areas such as China. Other countries and some companies probably have similar programs.

Many foreign workers and students get taken on sightseeing tours for free, but more likely at much cheaper rates than regular tourists.

While some foreigners live without (horrors!) a refrigerator and air conditioning—and the minimal heat gets turned off on March 15 no matter what the weather—some live in good hotels. Either way, many are pleased with the experience. Some are not. Working in a developing country is the best way to learn how most of the world has to live and how very privileged those in the developed world are.

As a casual student Many provincial travel and tourism offices are now offering courses in cooking, martial arts, acupuncture, and other Chinese arts, but primarily for groups. Several colleges and universities offer six- to eight-week Chinese language courses.

One should not expect to learn Chinese or any other language in eight weeks. Nor can one learn taiqi in a day. It would be better to start learning such skills before you go to China, and expect polishing from the short course.

As a job hunter Tourists can try to pick up a job while traveling in China, but don't count on it. If you want to live in any particular place and are an experienced teacher, you could start by asking C.I.T.S. or any college or university if teachers are needed locally. If English is your native language and you have any idea about teaching, you could also ask any about-to-be-opened hotel or a tourism school if they want an English teacher. Many places want English teachers but do not have the foreign exchange to pay a "foreign expert." But again, don't expect to earn very much money. If that's not your line, talk with business people about job possibilities. Good English-speaking secretaries are in short supply. But check out work regulations and income tax for foreigners first. Local hires might be paid Chinese-level salaries.

For medical treatment Some provincial travel and tourism agencies, for example Wuxi, offer tour packages for treatment in Chinese sanitariums, but you can book directly. Just do not expect North American standards. Some hotels have *qiqong,* acupuncture, or no-smoking clinics.

As a property buyer Foreigners and Overseas Chinese can now buy resort, residential, and business property in some Chinese cities. Contact a Chinese mission or the municipal office in the city of your choice. Many Overseas Chinese have retired in China.

On a convention Many cities can now handle hundreds of convention visitors. Some hotels have simultaneous translation facilities. Contact the China Council for the Promotion of International Trade (C.C.P.I.T.) or any travel agent specializing in China for information.

As a journalist Contact a Chinese mission or Xinhua, the New China News Agency, if it is represented in your country. You could also contact the Information Office of the Foreign Ministry, Beijing, or the China National Tourist Office.

As a guest   This is great, but local residents and even government corporations may not know all the tourist attractions you want to see. One visitor to Harbin desperately wanted to find the locomotive·museum, but local friends never heard of it. One host ministry insisted on finding a museum's director (presumably to avoid the ¥1 admission fee and to show its hospitality). This cut down on time available to visit the museum. Another guest was put in a dumpy government guest house (where his host had connections) and couldn't change to a better hotel without embarrassing his host.

We suggest you make your wishes known to your hosts in plenty of time for them to make arrangements or find out.

Special tours   The important thing to remember is that C.I.T.S. and C.T.S. tours are set up primarily for tourists. They cannot be expected to understand the needs of travelers primarily interested in meeting Chinese Christians, for example, or doctors wanting to meet their counterparts in China. The needs of doctors and scientists can be met by some of these Chinese travel agents if you tell them exactly what you want, preferably with names and addresses. Give them plenty of time in advance. Or you could contact the Foreign Affairs Department of the Chinese Academy of Sciences yourself. Mountain climbers should contact the Chinese Mountaineering Association, and school groups, CYTS. Sports teams wanting to play Chinese teams, or individuals wanting a ski package or parachuting should go through China International Sports Travel Service. For religious groups, see also ''Religion.''

If you have any other questions, it might help to consult an experienced travel agent, a Chinese mission, or a China Friendship Association. Yes, you can write an organization in China directly with a good chance of getting a reply—but don't count on it.

In dealing directly with China, the best way to communicate is by Telex or Fax. Letters can take up to three weeks from North America. They do arrive more quickly if addressed in Chinese with the postal number (code) if possible, and are answered more quickly if written in Chinese. If you telephone China, be sure to have a Mandarin-speaking person with you in case no one understands English at the other end of the line.

For Addresses, see ''Important Addresses and Information.''

Should You Take Your Children?

I took my five-year-old for a five-week visit in 1973, my seven-year-old to visit relatives in 1978, and my nine-year-old on a group tour in

1979. I even took a reluctant teenager on an eight-destination tour. I was glad I did, but then, this depends on the child. A year later, the teenager went back to China on her own with her school to work on a commune!

I did not use a baby-sitter because the younger children accompanied me to evening movies and theatrical performances. Chinese dance dramas are easy for a child to understand, and acrobats and puppets are fun for all ages. The younger children did find the traditional operas boring, so unless you're sure of lots of action, skip them.

I would not take a child just to be left with a Chinese-speaking baby-sitter unless the child understood Chinese.

At communes and factories, many willing hands kept the children amused while grown-ups talked. The children were interested in seeing how things were made. Guilin, with its caves, mountains, and boat trip was ideal.

The Chinese love children and are intrigued by those different from their own. You may have to protect children with blond hair and blue eyes, for instance, from being overly fondled. Tour-bus drivers bought mine popsicles; cheeks were pinched. In restaurants they disappeared with waiters to be shown off to the cooks.

Two of them became sick with bad colds, but doctors took care of them. They were well in a couple of days, missing only one day of the tour. Two of them lived with relatives. The seven-year-old had a ball learning how to bring up water from an open well, washing his own clothes by hand, and tending a wood cooking fire. It took awhile to adjust to the smelly outhouses, but he managed.

The neighborhoods where we lived with family were full of other children, and in spite of initial shyness and the language barrier, they made friends. Strangers on the street and in buses would stop and try to talk to them. Barriers of formality melted right away, and I'm not the only one who has gotten a room in an overcrowded hotel because "my child is very tired."

Food was a problem. One lived only on scrambled eggs and *char siu bow* (steamed barbecued pork buns). Hamburgers and milk are now easier to find. Baby food in jars for infants and disposable diapers have arrived at Friendship Stores, but may not always be available at the time and place you want them and are very expensive.

Some hotels do not charge for children sharing their parents' room.

Should You Go If Your Health Is Fragile?

Things to consider: A prepaid group tour is usually strenuous, with lots of stairs to climb, and a packed schedule—unless the group agrees to a slower pace. Most hotels but not restaurants have elevators. Chinese guides are very considerate of older people.

Things can be easier for pay-as-you-go individual travelers who can do things at their own speed. But in no circumstances do we recommend traveling alone.

So far we have only heard of a few hotels set up for handicapped people, with wider bathroom doors and bars near toilets. A lot of helpful hands are available, however. And many hotels have ramps.

Chinese hospitals are adequate, and some doctors have Western training and excellent Western standards. But most facilities are at least 30 years behind what you're used to, and communicating with nurses could be difficult.

Could you be left behind alone by your group in a hospital and in a city where you have no friends, no language skills, and at your own expense? How would you feel about that?

Disabled travelers should contact organizations that specialize in travel for people with allergies, diabetes, wheelchairs, epilepsy, etc., like Mobility International U.S.A., P.O. Box 3551, Eugene, OR, 97403, tel. (501) 343–1284 (Voice and TDD). MIUSA publishes *You Want to Go Where?* (a 60-page booklet on China), and *Those Interested in Disability Issues in China.* Also contact Holi-Asia Tours, tel. 1 (800) 553–3533. See our chapter on local customs and emergencies.

CHOOSING A TRAVEL AGENT

You should consult a travel agent experienced with China. Do not hesitate about bothering agents. They make their money from commissions. Sometimes a travel agent will discount, especially if you buy packages. And yes, you can save money organizing your own tour group. The more people you have, the cheaper it is, but also the more headaches.

In dealing with a travel agent, consider seriously the following, especially if these apply to your situation.

How long have they been sending people to China? How many people did they send last year? If the answer is more than three years, and in the hundreds, you should be okay. They should have established good relationships with tourism officials in China so you will get the best rooms and services for your money. The Chinese do their best for people they know and trust.

We have found that many tours from North America are cheaper than flying to Hong Kong or China and booking tours from there.

The cheapest flights are probably through Chinatown agencies. We suggest you contact Air China, get a quote from its major wholesalers, and see if your own travel agent can match it. For individual travelers, does the agent know enough to advise you what to do if your guide doesn't meet you at the airport? Would the agent know the prices and quality of cheaper hotels? Whether or not the city has tour groups you can join on the spot? The cost of taxis?

A recent development in the U.S. has been the **China-Orient Tourism Council (COTC),** a non-profit association of tour operators, airlines, and hotels involved with China. There is also the China Master Agents program, which trains and certifies travel agents as specialists in China travel. China Master Agents must have at least three years' experience and be recommended by other COTC members. Not all experienced agents belong to this program, but it is a good place to start.

For prepaid tours with set itineraries especially

How many of your desired destinations are offered? How many days will you have in each place? Does the price include the Dazu sculptures in Chongqing, for example, or do you have to pay extra?

Do the dates fit your own schedule, weather preference, and Chinese holidays?

What is the price? Why is it different from another organizer's with the same cities and same number of days? What are you paying for? Usually the price includes visa fee, group transportation (be sure you establish if this is from your home or from your first point in China), hotel accommodation (double or single occupancy?), one or three meals and beverages a day, sightseeing, group transfers, transporting one piece of luggage (maximum 20 kg per person?), and admission tickets to tourist attractions and cultural events. Does the price include all the taxes and service charges along the way? Will you be traveling with a guide-interpreter? (Groups of over six people qualify for an escort in China.)

Are the hotel rooms "standard" or "deluxe," and do you get a refund if a deluxe room is not available? Are the trains soft or hard class? Are the airplanes first or economy class?

Price quotes do not usually include passport fees, laundry, hairdressing, taxis, postage, long-distance telephone calls, excess baggage, medical, and other expenses of a personal nature. Nor do they include insurance for expenses for changes in the itinerary, or prolonged tours "due to unforeseen circumstances." Ask about those "unforeseen circumstances." These could include plane cancellations, overbooking, arriving at the airport after the plane leaves, illness, or accident. Who pays for these inconveniences? Tour escorts have been known to pay for minor "extras," but will you be expected to pay on the spot or at the end of the tour for any substantial changes? If not, get it in writing. Ask about these, health insurance and cancellation insurance. Do you need evacuation insurance? What about compensation for delays? Evacuation insurance should be considered if you are in questionable health or traveling alone. Is China's insurance included in the price, and if so, what are the benefits?

What is the minimum group size required before the tour is cancelled? Are promised hotels guaranteed, and what happens if there is a change?

What language will the guides speak? For example, a tour booked in Japan may only have Japanese-speaking guides, while some tours booked in Hong Kong are in English. Or a tour might be in Beijing dialect and you expected Cantonese.

Do you get a group visa or an individual visa? Some tours allow longer time for individuals to visit relatives or negotiate business, etc.

How many people are in the group? How old? Sexes?

How much is the deposit and when do you pay in full? Are departures guaranteed? What refund do you get if the tour is cancelled? Should you buy cancellation insurance? What happens if you have to leave partway through the China portion? Will you get a prorated refund? Do you get a refund if a hotel lacks all the services described in its brochure? What hotels do you get? (Check these hotels in "Destinations" to see if that is what you want.) If you want an evaluation, check the *Travel China Newsletter*.

Will you be able to see everything you want? What happens if the tour operator goes out of business?

Does the tour operator offer the Yangtze Gorges tour on a regular public ship or on a luxury, air-conditioned tourist ship? Which would you prefer? See "Yangtze Gorges" and "On a prepaid tour" earlier in this chapter.

All tours are subject to changes in itinerary by the Chinese, so don't blame your travel agent. These changes should become less frequent as China acquires more hotels, trains, and airplanes. Prices, too, are subject to change.

Travel agents   China National Tourist Offices, now in New York City, Los Angeles, Tokyo, Sydney, London, Paris, and Frankfurt should be able to answer travel questions. Some representatives of C.I.T.S. branches are now in North America, and should be able to answer questions and make bookings for their own tours. If you can't find an experienced agent, here are some suggestions. Most of these can also make arrangements for individuals.

Australia *Helen Wong's Travel.*

U.S.A. *Abercrombie and Kent:* uses the top-of-the-line cruise ship *Bashan* on the Yangtze; *Arunas Travel Co.:* Mostly professional, semi-professional, and special-interest group tours as well as custom tours for FITs. Scuba-diving tours; *Asian Pacific Adventures:* can get you to festivals in Yunnan and Guizhou; *Backroads:* bicycle tours; *China Educational Tours:* All tours custom designed and marketed to educational institutions, museums, professional organizations, and community groups. Also administers semesters abroad for colleges, short-term residential programs for secondary schools, colleges, and professional schools; *China*

International Travel Service Inc. (Guangdong): can book some confirmed domestic flights in China and Hong Kong-to-China charter flights. It can set up exhibitions, special tours, and help issue visas for the Trade Fair in Guangzhou; *Elderhostel* has tours with good seminars for seniors. *InterPacific:* general tours and super-saver specials; *Mountain Travel:* overland tours in Tibet; *Orient Flexipak:* has general tours and super-saver specials. *Sino-American Tours:* One of the more aggressive operators. For leisure, business, and independent travelers. Some hotel reservations; *U.S. China Travel Service* is a branch of China Travel Service (H.K.), and is able to book fixed-schedule air charters between Hong Kong and major cities in China. Specializes in general, deluxe, cruises, and individual tours.

Canada *Bestway Tours* and *Safaris/Sitara Travel* (for entry from Pakistan and the Silk Road); *Canada Swan International:* bargain Beijing packages, Korea sales agent for Yangtze River cruises; *China Travel Service (Canada)* has general, custom, academic, youth, deluxe, and individual tours; *Chinapac International:* general tours and special Taishan Grand Prix and Weifang Kite festival packages. *Conference Travel of Canada* (among the cheapest for general tours); *Tour East Holidays.*

Hong Kong See "Getting There."

Nepal *Yangrima Trekking and Mountaineering.*

New Zealand *Globe Trotter Tours NZ LTD.*

United Kingdom *Hann Overland* has adventure tours.

China Friendship Associations all over the world can give information on travel to China and their own study tours. Some of these associations can organize tours for individuals. They also entertain visiting Chinese delegations and students, teach English, collect books for China, show movies, and provide lecturers on China. They can give you an idea of organizations who send people to China. Addresses can usually be obtained through the Cultural Affairs Officer at a Chinese mission. Among these are the Australia-China Friendship Society, the Federation of Canada-China Friendship Associations, the Great Britain-China Centre, the New Zealand-China Friendship Society and the U.S.-China Peoples Friendship Association. The Chefoo Schools Association organizes tours for alumni back to the old school in Yantai and Lushan.

See also "Getting Around" and money-saving travel tips in "Budget."

BEFORE YOU GO

BOOKING INTO CHINA

Book as much of your itinerary as possible beforehand. Complex international bookings are not as easy to make in China as in other countries. Trains, buses, and ferries can be booked into China by travel agents in Hong Kong. Some domestic trains can be booked by C.T.S. in Hong Kong if paid for 5 to 12 days in advance. Bus tours can be booked from Pakistan; the ferrys from Japan and Korea; trains from Europe. A travel agent should be able to handle everything. You do have options, even when booking a tour.

If you have over three days, you can book in Hong Kong after you arrive (except before the lunar New Year holidays). If possible, get as many visas as you need before you leave home. Getting a Chinese visa there takes less than one day, but you have to pay more for the speed.

Ask your agent if the international flights are nonstop. Do you care? Is there an extra charge for stopovers? A day in Paris? You've always wanted to see Kyoto! Budget airport taxes, taxis, and a hotel. Is going via Hong Kong really the cheapest? Maybe it's better via Karachi, Singapore, or Bangkok. How about entering China at Urumqi? How about around-the-world fares?

By air Every travel agent has a computer with the current schedules of every major airline in the world. In some cases, you pay less through an agent because a good one should know about cheaper flights like the excursion fares, off-season discounts, and charters of *all* airlines. On the other hand, each airline understandably prefers to sell you space on its own planes. Some travel agents can also discount off published fares.

A travel agency can tell you when airlines fly between China and the other places you want to go. It can also tell you which ones have direct flights and which have the shortest flight time. (Finnair claims the shortest time from the east coast to Beijing: less than 16 hours in two shifts. Cathay Pacific has leg rests in Economy and BBC news. United should have three flights a week now. Northwest necessitates a change in Tokyo.) Airlines do not fly all routes daily; some fly once a week. So you must plan your schedule carefully. Give your agent a list of stops you want to make before and after China, and how long you want to spend in each place. Suggest several options. Your agent should be able to work out a satisfactory itinerary. See also CAAC in "Getting Around" and "Introduction."

Airlines now fly direct, with no, one, or two stops, from the following cities to China, unless otherwise indicated. Because of reciprocal arrangements, at least one airline of another country could also fly the same route.

Addis Ababa to Beijing
Alma-Ata to Urumqi
Bagdad to Beijing
Bangkok to Guangzhou; Beijing; Kunming and Shantou
Belgrade to Beijing
Berlin to Beijing
Bucharest to Beijing
Cairo to Beijing
Frankfurt to Beijing
Fukuoka to Shanghai; Beijing; Dalian
Geneva to Beijing
Helsinki to Beijing
Hong Kong to China. See Getting There.
Irkutsk to Shengang
Islamabad to Beijing
Istanbul to Urumqi; Beijing
Jakarta to Xiamen; Beijing
Karachi to Beijing
Kathmandu to Lhasa (no winter service); later maybe to Beijing
Khabarovsk to Harbin
Kuala Lumpur to Guangzhou; Beijing
Kuwait to Beijing
Los Angeles to Beijing; Shanghai
London to Beijing
Manila to Guangzhou; Beijing; Xiamen
Melbourne to Guangzhou; to Beijing
Moscow to Beijing
Nagasaki to Shanghai
New York to Beijing; to Shanghai
Osaka to Shanghai; Beijing
Paris to Beijing; Shanghai
Penang to Guangzhou; Xiamen
Pyongyang to Beijing
Rangoon to Kunming
Rome to Beijing
San Francisco to Shanghai; Beijing

Sharjah to Beijing; Shanghai; Urumqi
Singapore to Guangzhou; Beijing; Xiamen; Shanghai
Stockholm to Beijing
Surabaya to Xiamen; Beijing
Sydney to Guangzhou; Beijing
Tokyo to Beijing; Dalian; Shanghai
Toronto to Beijing; Shanghai
Vancouver to Shanghai; Beijing
Warsaw to Beijing
Zurich to Beijing

By ship: Regular passenger ships sail from Hong Kong. These are not luxurious, but they are adequate. A ferry now plies between Kobe, (Japan) and Shanghai, and between Inchon (Korea) and Weihai, and Inchon and Tianjin.

By land: The only land routes that have been open to west China are from the C.I.S., Nepal, and Pakistan, with possible delays in the latter two due to mountain landslides. See ''Silk Road.''

North Korea, Mongolia, and several Russian border points have opened in the east.

By train from Moscow and Ulan Bator (Mongolia), to Beijing, from Pyongyang, Korea, to Beijing, and from Hong Kong to Guangzhou. A train line should start soon from Hanoi. Chinese officials have been talking about a railway line through northwestern Xinjiang province linking up with the C.I.S. railway system across the border, due to be open to passengers in 1992. See Regent Holidays (London) and China Railexpress Travel Service.

By bus from Hong Kong and Macao to various points in Guangdong and Fujian provinces and from Pakistan. By tour bus from the C.I.S. to Kashgar.

For travel via Hong Kong, see ''Getting There.''

BOOKING DOMESTIC TRAVEL

You should try to book domestic flights as early as possible before leaving for a trip to China. It can be done three months before in North America. If it can't be done, you will have to take a chance and book them after your arrival, or go on standby.

Flight schedules that are a great help in planning trips have been difficult to obtain in China. They do exist in English and it might be easier to get them from Air China in the U.S. or Hong Kong.

Public buses, trains, and ferries inside China can only be booked in China itself. You could speed the process by contacting a Chinese travel agency or your hotel (at a fee).

FORMALITIES

Passport. If you haven't got a passport valid for your trip and preferably three months afterward, get one. You can't travel without it. Give yourself plenty of time to get a copy of your birth certificate, photos, etc.

A **China tourist visa** can be obtained from any Chinese consulate in five working days or less, if you pay extra. Travelers to Tibet need to have a prepaid tour. (See Lhasa.) A frequent traveler can obtain a double-entry visa. A Chinese passport holder living abroad does not need an entry visa, but might have difficulty leaving China afterwards.

Transit visas are not necessary if you stay less than 24 hours and remain inside the transit lounge of the airport. You must have a visa for your next stop, and a confirmed plane reservation out. In an emergency, visas can be obtained at some ports in China. Emergencies include last-minute invitations, invitations to provide scientific or technological consultations, and visits to seriously ill patients or to make funeral arrangements. The ports include Beijing, Dalian, Fuzhou, Guangzhou, Haikou, Hangzhou, Kunming, Sanya, Shanghai, Shenzhen, Tianjin, Xiamen, Xi'an, and Zhuhai. Shenzhen and Zhuhai can issue 3-day visas on the spot. Zhongshan can issue regular visas on the spot.

Hong Kong travel agents can usually acquire a visa in 24 hours or less (for a service charge). Tourist visas from the Visa Office of China's Foreign Ministry are cheaper. See "Getting There."

Travel agents usually obtain one visa for a prepaid group tour of nine or more, but you have to enter and leave China with your group unless arrangements are made inside China. You do have to give your travel agent your passport number and other such information.

Overseas Chinese with Chinese passports do not need any visas at all for entry or exit. Nationals of South Africa, the Vatican, Israel, and South Korea can enter China in approved tour groups. Some individuals have entered after getting special permission from China.

A **Visa Application Form** requires one photo and the following information: name; nationality; sex; date of birth; place of birth; type and number of passport. Valid until . . . ; occupation; place of work; telephone number.

Also asked are: home address; telephone number; purpose of journey; host unit in China.

The host unit can be C.I.T.S., but it could be whatever Chinese agency is organizing your trip, the hotel where you have a confirmed reservation, or a friend in China who has invited you.

The form goes on to ask intended date of entry; duration of stay in China; places to visit in China; accompanying persons using the same passport (name, sex, date of birth, relationship to applicant); relatives or friends in China (to be filled in only by persons visiting relatives or friends; you will need their name(s), nationality, occupation and place of work, and relationship to applicant).

Sometimes, especially if booking by mail, a photocopy of the first four essential pages of your passport is required.

Overseas Chinese will win Brownie points if they add their Chinese name in Chinese. **In case of unexpected delays,** give yourself a few more days in China than you think you need.

Your visa will admit you to any international airport or seaport in China and to any of the cities currently open to foreign visitors without a travel permit within the time limit mentioned. Be sure you know the expiry date and how long you may stay. If you want to stay longer, you can apply in China for an extension.

Other visas may be required for countries in which you will be traveling. They are not necessary for countries where you change planes, as long as you stay in the transit section of the airport. They may be necessary for train travel, such as through the Democratic Republic of Germany, Poland, the C.I.S., and Mongolia, all of which have missions in Beijing. It can be difficult getting a Mongolian visa because its embassy keeps irregular hours. But do you want to spend precious time there getting visas? Consult your travel agent, who can obtain visas by mail or courier. Individual visas are processed more quickly and cheaply if you take your passport to a country's mission yourself.

Shots. You will need a certificate of immunization only if you are in a cholera or yellow fever area just prior to visiting China. Otherwise, no shots are required for China for short-term travelers. Long-term travelers should consult their embassies in China especially about Encephalitis B and Hepatitis B. However, if you are going to be living in the countryside, endemic areas, or any place where hygiene is minimal, consult the health department in your home city. At press time health departments in some North American cities were recommending immunization against typhoid, tetanus, polio, and hepatitis A. A health certificate is required for people residing in China for over a year and includes an AIDS test. Best get one before you leave home. In south China, once-a-week pills against malaria are recommended wherever mosquitos are thick at night. Most tourists do not have to worry about this, but those going off-the-beaten-track should think about it. The health department or your travel agent should know if immunization is required for the other countries you will be visiting.

Plan your budget   See "Local Customs and Emergencies" and "Budget."

Chinese customs regulations   Check through the customs regulations in "Important Addresses and Information" to see what you can and cannot take into China, especially video camera and tapes.

Hotel reservations   Your travel agent can take care of reservations in top hotels, but if you want to do it yourself, phone your airline or the relevant hotel reservation system. For example, for the Sheraton Hotel in Beijing, phone Sheraton's toll-free number or the Sheraton nearest you. See ''Budget and Hotel Quick Reference.'' Reservations can be made now at top, and some medium-priced hotels through some North American travel agents or directly by telex or fax with those hotels (cheaper). Reservations are recommended during high tourist season, festivals, or trade fairs. These tourist hotels usually telex an answer to a request for a reservation if asked. Some medium-priced hotels, however, will telex an answer only if there is no room. Hotels for backpackers and other medium-priced hotels do not usually accept reservations and will not answer.

   If you are traveling without a guide in a prepaid group, make sure you have vouchers for rooms and meals.

Write ahead to people   you want to meet, giving yourself at least 30 days for an answer if by mail. Do ask for their telephone numbers so you can call when you arrive. Most people could arrange their schedules to fit yours. Chinese friends and relatives should also be able to take time off with pay from their jobs to visit and even sightsee with you. If you receive no reply, it could mean they are not interested, or you have the wrong address, or they are terrible letter writers. Sorry, I can't decide for you.

   China does go through occasional xenophobic periods and your Chinese friends might get into a lot of difficulty explaining your relationship to them. Immediately after the Tiananmen Square massacre, many Chinese intellectuals were fearful of contacting foreign friends. If you get replies welcoming you to China, then you can make plans to meet. If you have only a couple of days in their city and do not know your exact itinerary ahead of time, you could telex them after you arrive in China. See ''Local Customs'' on looking up specific Chinese citizens.

   Overseas Chinese in particular may want to write to ask what their relatives would like you to bring them. Don't be surprised if they ask for a refrigerator, video, and motorcycle. If you cannot afford these, take a less expensive present and they will (or should) be happy to see you anyway.

   Usually, Chinese relatives just want you and your foreign passport for use as a courier. Only Overseas Chinese with foreign passports can import certain desirable goods duty-free. Hong Kong, Macao, and some travel agents in North America too, are set up for such shopping. You can either bring the goods in with you (the store or a travel agency supplying the transport), or you can just pay and carry the receipt and have it stamped by Chinese Customs officials at the border. It depends on the availability of the "gifts" in China. Your relatives can pick up the goods later in an Overseas Chinese store in China. I have never had trouble being reimbursed and I have carted sewing machines and bicycles on the train from Hong Kong! **But make sure reimbursement and in what terms are understood.** You have already saved them 30–50%! See Money Changing in "Getting There."

At this stage, Overseas Chinese should start collecting the names of relatives, particularly of ancestors, born in China. The name of your ancestral village is essential. Usually you should refer only to your father's family. No one cares about maternal lines! The names should help people in your village place you. The welcome if they can establish a connection is better than if they can't. The names, of course, should be written in Chinese. Take as much documentation as you can: a letter in Chinese from your family association, your father's or grandfather's old passport, and a map of where they lived in the village.

Overseas Chinese in particular should use both their Chinese and English names on correspondence and refer to themselves by the Chinese one, especially if they travel with C.T.S. The Chinese remember Chinese names more easily. If you don't know how to write your name in Chinese, learn. If you don't have a Chinese name, get one. It doesn't have to be legal, but it will make things easier for you as you travel around China. Just be sure you know how it is pronounced in both your family dialect and *pu tung hua* (standard Chinese).

Overseas Chinese whose families might have property in China should think about registering deeds if they have not already done so. It takes at least three months and lots of red tape to prove ownership. You could start proceedings during a visit. With the development especially of Guangdong and Fujian provinces, property values are going up. I discovered that my grandfather's old two-story, black-brick house a few blocks from the main street in Xinhui was worth about ¥50,000 to ¥60,000 RMB. Village property is probably less. You will lose it if you don't register.

If you sell property, the money will be in RMB, which you cannot repatriate. You could use it on trips in China, or for scholarships, for family, or business investments in China.

In case of emergency, inform people at home how you can be reached in China. Give **copies of your itinerary,** with your tour number and travel agent, to key people. If there is any possibility of unrest in China or you're an American staying over six months, or a Canadian over three, send a copy to your consulates in China, so they will know where to contact you. If you are with a C.I.T.S. tour, your friends can telephone the C.I.T.S. branch wherever you are in China and ask that you be told to telephone home. Friends should also mention your country as in "United States group" and the name of your national guide if possible—especially in cheaper hotels. The tour number and itinerary are important to help locate you. The mission of your country in Beijing, Shanghai, or Guangzhou might also be able to help. If you are traveling on your own without a set itinerary, an advertisement could be placed in *China Daily* asking you to phone home. This means you have to read *China Daily*. Outside of the big cities, it arrives several days late.

If you are not on a prepaid tour, it is best to schedule a **mail pick-up** at your embassy, or at one of the big hotels (whether or not you are staying there). Ask at the desk or look for a bulletin board. American Express now has client mail service in its Beijing office.

Get telephone numbers in case you lose your credit cards and travelers checks. Also leave your **passport number** with whomever does your banking, in case money has to be cabled to you through the Bank of China. Photocopy the essentials of your passport and credit cards in case of loss and carry this copy with you in a separate place as you travel. Take extra **passport pictures** in case you need them on the trip.

Since letters could take up to 15 days to reach you, quicker if by "express" or courier, it is best to tell friends not to write unless your trip is longer than that.

Consider buying **health insurance** in case of serious illness or accident, and **travel insurance** in case you lose anything. Many people already are covered by travel or health insurance if their tickets are bought with certain credit cards or through certain plans at home. Hospitalization in China costs about ¥300 a day, which you have to pay before you leave. Ask about the China-issued insurance you pay for with your tour.

Medical evacuation insurance could lend you money for the hospital, bring a relative to stay with you should you be in for a long time, and arrange for your repatriation.

The most active evacuation services in China for North Americans are SOS and Europ Assistance (Travel Assistance International), both with 24-hour accessible offices in Beijing and a network of offices or contacts around the country. SOS is strictly medical assistance. Europ Assistance should be able to help with other kinds of emergencies too, like lost passports, forgotten prescription drugs, etc. Asia Emergency Assistance is Singapore-based.

IAMAT is free and has a list of Western-trained, English-speaking doctors in several Chinese cities. Fees for their doctors seem to exceed the going rates, but you pay nothing if you don't have to use them.

Essential up-to-date information If you are wondering before you go if China is unsafe to visit due to floods, earthquakes, war, or civil disturbances, phone the U.S. State Department in Washington, D.C. (202) 647–5225; or consult any American consulate abroad (American

Citizens' Services). Airline computer reservation systems or passport agencies in the U.S. should also have this information. The State Department's Bureau of Consular Affairs also has a booklet, ''Tips for Travelers to the People's Republic of China'' (#044–000–02205–2, U.S.$1 from the Government Printing Office). In Canada, phone External Affairs (613) 992–7531.

Learn some Chinese   If nothing else, learn to read numbers. Then at least you will know dates in museums and street numbers.

If you're going to live with friends or relatives and they're Cantonese, Fukienese, or Shanghainese, they probably speak this dialect at home. If you're traveling around China, however, it would be more practical to learn Mandarin, *pu tung hua,* which is understood all over the country.

The same Chinese characters are also understood throughout China. The characters used today have been simplified since 1950, and Chinese people living abroad do not usually know the revisions unless they have kept up with the changes. Just make sure that your teacher gives you the new script and the pinyin romanization. The new script is used in ''Useful Phrases.'' It might be good to memorize some of these phrases so you can communicate.

As in any country, the more of the local language you learn, the cheaper your expenses will be. In the meantime, use the ''Useful Phrases.'' The standard of English spoken in China is improving daily, but it is still poor.

I don't speak much Chinese but traveled alone and had a good time even without an interpreter. Unlike the French, the Chinese try very hard to understand attempts to communicate. Draw pictures and try charades. Point at the characters in this book. At hotels, look for individual travelers, especially in restaurants, many of whom are lonely and delighted to make friends. Some of these speak Chinese and could interpret for you.

The more you try to speak Chinese, the more friends you'll make, and the more you'll enjoy China.

Learn about China   To get the most out of your trip, learn something about China before you go. There is a dizzying list of good books on China. Here are only a few suggestions. See ''Bibliography'' for details.

The more you know about most countries, the better you will enjoy going there. A statue may be striking, but it becomes more meaningful if you know it's the ''warrior woman,'' made famous in American literature by Maxine Hong Kingston. A building in a park in Lhasa becomes the movie theater built by Heinrich Herrar where the German refugee showed the eager young Dalai Lama his first movies. A peaceful street in Beijing becomes the fortress for terrified foreigners caught in a noisy, life-death siege at the turn of the last century. A tranquil lake is the site of an American missionary compound during the Northern Expedition, its idealistic residents fighting the attempts of the U.S. Navy to take them to "safety."

Armed with background knowledge, you can also be sensitive to internal conflicts and avoid unwise activities like taking sides on human rights issues. You will be able to understand the people you meet—what do they really mean by inviting you to dinner? Are they just being hospitable? Or do they want you to help get the son into a school abroad? And how can you, too, develop your own *guanxi* (connections) so you can get what you want?

Books: If you know nothing about China, start out with a **general history** like Brian Catchpole's *A Map History of Modern China*, which is extremely easy to read (high-school level), half maps and diagrams, the rest text. You can graduate from that to *China, Yesterday and Today*, a paperback that you might want to take with you for background. This covers the history of China, its political life, agricultural policy, etc.

Good bedside reading and very informative are *The Wise Man from the West*, about Matteo Ricci's unsuccessful attempts to convert China to Christianity 400 years ago, and *Son of the Revolution*, an autobiography of a young Chinese who grew up on the wrong side of the political fence and married his American teacher. *Son of the Revolution* is imperative for anyone wanting to get an insider's look at today's system, how the various campaigns since Liberation have affected the kind of people that you will be meeting, and how some Chinese circumvent the rules and stifling bureaucracy.

Fascinating is the *Soong Dynasty*, about the Chinese Christian who was educated in America, and whose children controlled China's economy for several decades.

You might want to read about all the **cities** to which you will be going—in addition to this guide, that is. Write to a China National Tourist Office or provincial tourism administration for brochures. If those cities are ancient capitals, then look into dynastic history. Raymond Dawson's *Imperial China* is another book to carry along—a good index and lots of juicy gossip about the likes of Tang Empress Wu and her boyfriends. If you are going to Hangzhou, the classic is *Daily Life in China* by Jacques Gernet, with a map of the city in 1274—if you want to look for changes.

For Beijing, read any biography of the Ming or Qing emperors and that of Empress Dowager Cixi (Tzu Hsi) and *her* boyfriend. For Tibet, read Heinrich Herrar's classic *Seven Years in Tibet*. Behr's *The Last Emperor* gives more background than the movie.

Han Suyin's autobiographical trilogy *The Crippled Tree (1885–*

1928), A Mortal Flower (1928–1938), and *Birdless Summer (1938–48)* are good background for those periods. She grew up in Chengdu. Her earlier *Destination Chungking* is for those who will be going there too. It is set during the Japanese war when Chiang Kai-shek was her hero.

For **British involvement** in China, there's George Woodcock's *The British in the Far East,* about the bad, old, but interesting imperialists like Captain Charles "Chinese" Gordon. For **U.S. involvement,** there's John Fairbank's *The United States and China.* If you're interested in missionaries, try Pat Barr's *To China with Love* or Alvyn J. Austin's *Saving China—Canadian Missionaries in the Middle Kingdom, 1888–1959.* Sun Tzu's over 2000-year-old book *Art of War* was credited with inspiring the U.S. military during its Persian Gulf campaign.

For more **recent history,** Edgar Snow's *Red Star Over China,* not only relates the history of the Long March but has the only autobiography dictated by Mao. If you are concerned about human rights, get reports from Amnesty International, and since you might be arguing about Tiananmen Square, do read the Chinese versions obtained from Chinese missions abroad as well as western sources like Simmie and Nixon's *Tiananmen Square,* and Gargan's *China's Fate.* Recommended is Jonathan D. Spence's *The Search for Modern China.*

Then there are the **personal accounts** of people who lived in China, notably Chen Yuan-Tsung's *The Dragon's Village,* a good picture of land reform in a poor village in western China in the early 1950s. Jack Chen's *A Year in Upper Felicity* and Ken Ling's *The Revenge of Heaven* are both set during the Cultural Revolution. For more details on that painful period, Jean Daubier has published *A History of the Chinese Cultural Revolution* and Roxanne Witke has written *Comrade Chiang Ching,* one of the best books about Chairman Mao's widow. A recent best-seller has been Nien Cheng's *Life and Death in Shanghai.*

Among the modern **Western novels,** the Communists used to say that Pearl S. Buck romanticized China too much and did not make political analyses, but a lot of the flavor of old China is in *The Good Earth* and *Pavilion of Women,* if you can find them. *The Sand Pebbles* by Richard McKenna was better as a movie, but is worth reading or seeing. It tells of an American gunboat engineer and a missionary woman in Changsha and the Yangtze in 1925. (Remember Steve McQueen and Candice Bergen?) Or try a Chinese novel. Gu Hua's *A Small Town Called Hibiscus* is very good.

If you're interested in **Chinese arts and crafts,** I would take along Margaret Medley's *A Handbook of Chinese Art,* Michael Sullivan's *The Arts of China,* or C.A.S. Williams's *Outlines of Chinese Symbolism and Art Motives.* These are all excellent reference books, profusely illustrated, that will help you appreciate the architecture, symbols, mythology, and customs of China. But do keep in mind that Williams's was written before Liberation.

The glossy magazine *China Tourism* should inspire you. Updated travel information can be found in China Travel News, and Travel China. Also helpful and current is the *Travel China Newsletter*.

Chinese **periodicals** can usually be found in bookstores in many Chinatowns. In the United States, the best-stocked store for China books is China Books and Periodicals, Inc. Write for a catalog.

Many western periodicals now have their own correspondents in Beijing, and you should keep your eyes open for news reports about China before you go. China Daily, Beijing's English language newspaper, is printed also in New York City, San Francisco, and Hong Kong.

You can pick up the very good Cartographic Department **maps** and China City Guides after you get there. One exists for every major city. They are inexpensive and describe the tourist attractions in some detail. However, you may want to see where you're going before you get there, and China Books and Periodicals, and some travel book stores may carry them. Chinese publications are considerably cheaper in China.

Lecturers The China Friendship Associations can recommend lecturers, and some branches have copies of Chinese periodicals in their libraries. Talk also to old China hands, recently returned schoolteachers as well as travelers contacted through these groups.

Videos of tourist attractions can be borrowed from Chinese missions, and film festivals do show Chinese **films** occasionally, some of which are no longer available in China. *Ju Dou* was nominated for best foreign film in the 63rd Oscars. *Red Sorghum* is surprisingly frank, powerful, and fascinating. *Horse Thief* (set in Tibet) and *The Ballad of the Yellow River* are also tragic. For good historical background, look for some China-made joint-venture movies. Attempts have been made to depict authentic clothing, architecture, and lifestyles, and some have been photographed at the actual site. Try to find movies like *Power Behind the Throne*, *The Burning of the Summer Palace* (see "Beijing"), and *Shaolin Temple*. The Lu Xun classic, *The Story of Ah Q* was filmed in Shaoxing. You could try also to find *Marco Polo,* filmed for television in China or the book. Some 1980's Chinese movies were very good and did not drip with propaganda. Things have now regressed.

The only foreign-made movies I can recommend about China are *The Sand Pebbles* (although filmed in Taiwan), *The Last Emperor* (with great shots of the Forbidden Palace), and *A Great Wall* (about a Chinese-American family visiting relatives in China). *Bethune, The Making of a Hero,* is about the Canadian doctor who became a Chinese role-model. These are entertaining and essential for anyone wanting to see the emotional component behind the relics and scenery. The Sino-Canadian *The First Emperor* (shown on the museum circuit), is short but excellent, especially for those going to Xi'an.

Learn about your own country   This is indispensable in your prep-
aration for China if you want to see factories and schools there. Visit a
factory at home and take notes so you can compare with China's such
things as incentives to work, unions, employee benefits, maternity leave,
child care for working mothers, job security, automation, and so forth.

When was the last time you were in a school? Find out what subjects are taught at what level, how discipline is maintained, how many
students are in a class, and about "open" classrooms. What about teacher
qualifications, incentives to learning, and slow learners? Who makes the
decisions as to what subjects are taught? How many computers does the
school have? Audio-visual equipment? Take your notes with you, and
in China, ask similar questions, point by point. With good facts on
hand, you can also help to clear up Chinese misconceptions about your
country.

Helping out   If you are thinking of inviting **relatives or friends** to
join you as immigrants or students, it is possible but very difficult to do
so. Check before you go with the China desk in your government's
foreign office, or your country's immigration office. You can also ask
for information at your country's consulate in China. Sponsoring a student is not cheap.

Getting permission is a long process and you should not expect all
procedures to be completed during a short trip.

See also "Gifts" and "Special for Overseas Chinese."

Check your own Customs regulations   Best write for a booklet.
Find out what you cannot take back into your own country. Dried beef
and pork have been confiscated. The U.S. allows no fruit unless canned
or dried, but Agriculture Canada allows tropical fruit like fresh lichees
and mangoes, as they are not normally grown in Canada. Dried medicinal herbs are okay, but bulbs and roots should be inspected for soil.
Certain animal products are forbidden or restricted; for example, both
Canada and the U.S. allow no ivory, and no crocodile or alligator,
leopard, or tiger products, as these are endangered species. See "Endangered Species" at the end of "Local Customs."

One should also be warned about the poisonous lead level in some
Chinese glazes. Do not eat or drink regularly out of Chinese ceramics,
especially yellows, until you have them checked.

In many countries, coin and stamp collections, antiques (over 100
years old), and "works of art" (one of a kind—not factory-made copies)
are duty-free. Be sure to get a certificate of proof at time of purchase.

Some items may be duty-free but liable to sales tax and GST in
Canada. You will need to keep receipts for purchases in China. The red
wax seal on an antique is China's proof that the item is allowed out of
the country.

Before you leave your own country, register valuable items you will be bringing back with Customs, especially if these items look new. You will need serial numbers. Or you could carry an appraisal report for jewelry with photo, bill of sale, or Customs receipt (if applicable). This is to avoid a hassle with customs officials on your return. You don't want to pay duty on items you've had for years.

For the United States, obtain a booklet from the U.S. Customs Service. Americans are allowed a duty-free exemption of $400 every 30 days if you are out of the country over 48 hours. You must pay 10% on the next $1000 worth of goods, even though items like uncut gems are normally dutiable at 2.3%. If you are planning to do a lot of shopping, it would be wise to consult the Customs regulations and tax rates before you go. For example, the tax rate on carvings from Hong Kong is lower than the tax rate on carvings from China. You can mail gifts worth US$50 or less, but the receiver cannot accept more than one duty-free parcel in one day.

Canada has a duty-free personal exemption on $100 worth of goods after 48 or more hours' absence, and a duty-free exemption once every calendar year after seven days' absence of Can$300. On the next $300, you pay approximately 15%. These free exemptions have to be claimed on separate trips. You may send duty-free gifts from abroad to friends or relatives in Canada, each gift valued at no more than Can$40. These must not be alcoholic beverages, tobacco, or advertising matter. The cost of shipping, however, may exceed the cost of the duty.

Certificates of Origin, obtained at some Friendship Stores and factories, could mean a much lower duty rate on silk, for example.

For more detailed information, please contact your local customs office. It is easier to get the information before leaving. Diplomatic missions abroad do not always have the latest regulations.

Comparison shopping   If you are a serious shopper intent on bargains, I suggest doing some research and keeping notes.

First of all, many goods you can buy in China are available abroad, and one traveler sadly related how the painted eggs she bought there were the same price as the ones she found later in a Washington store. So look around at home, especially in local Chinatowns, where prices are usually cheaper than in fancy curio shops.

Hong Kong has gotten too expensive to make a special trip there imperative for serious shoppers.

WHAT TO TAKE

Besides the items mentioned in the last chapter, such as passport, ticket, money, gifts, reference books, etc., here are some more suggestions. But weigh each decision carefully. Do not take anything you're not going to use.

If you're going in a tour group, you're usually allowed one or two suitcases. You should also have a **carry-on bag** for overnight train rides (your big bag may not be accessible) and airplanes.

If you're not in a tour group, remember that China's domestic airlines have been very lenient about hand-carried luggage, though this might change. They have been strict about their limit on checked bags. (First class 30 kg, economy 20 kg.) Discounted fares have an allowance of 20 kg (first class) and 15 kg (economy). Economy carry-on bags should not exceed a total length, width, and height of 115 cm. (or 45 inches). Air China allows two pieces of luggage on trans-pacific flights, each not exceeding 32 kg., and the sum of each height, width, and length should be no more than 158 cm (or 62 inches). A weight limit of 35 kg usually applies on trains.

Also keep in mind the lack of porters. This is usually no problem with tour groups, but independent travelers should be prepared to carry their own luggage in some train stations, perhaps up and down a flight of steps, to a taxi. Porters and trolleys are available in some but not all train stations and airports. Even if you are being met, you may be embarrassed if your guide offers to carry your luggage. Consider a set of **luggage wheels.**

Consider also the strength of your bag. Visitors report that some bags have been damaged in handling or left out in the rain.

Money   Major credit cards are now accepted at all the top hotels, and many of the medium-priced hotels in big cities. In addition, some are accepted in top restaurants, and in many government-designated tourist stores for purchases. For cash advances, the Bank of China charges a 4% surcharge. The following are among those accepted in China: American Express, Visa, MasterCard, Diners, Federal, Great Wall. American Express seems to be the most useful, particularly with its free emergency check-cashing service. You can buy an airplane ticket with a credit card from only a few airlines, among them some Dragonair offices, Finnair, JAL, Northwest, United and Lufthansa. With an American Express card, one can purchase traveler's checks in a large number of cities at the Bank of China.

If you expect to do serious shopping, take some U.S. cash. Vendors and even some factories come down in price more easily for it (in private).

Careful travelers might want to also keep valuables in a **money belt** or **neck safe** while traveling. You will not be able to carry a purse or camera bag into some places, like the mausoleums of Chairman Mao and Sun Yat-sen or the vault of the Famen Temple. **Do not depend entirely on credit cards.** Especially if you are straying off the high-priced tourist track, take traveler's checks. Canadians should note that American Express can also arrange refund of lost traveler's checks at some banks. As most of the branches only stock US$ traveler's checks, the refund will be in US$ traveler's checks. It is always advisable for travelers to China to purchase checks in US dollars,'' says an American Express official, though I've rarely had problems with Canadian.

At press time, personal checks are not generally accepted. Checks of companies and embassies established in China are accepted if known to the person cashing the check; it takes five banking days to cable money to you in China, assuming everyone does his job right; you might ask your embassy to help you cash a personal check, but don't count on it. At this writing, the Hongkong Bank, and Bank of America have branches in China that could cash checks or change money. This is changing, of course, so check with your bank before you go. Most of the foreign bank branches will be in Shanghai or a Special Economic Zone. Many banks have representatives for liaison and consultation, but few can do actual banking.

This all means, of course, that you should take enough cash and traveler's checks. You get less Chinese currency for cash than for traveler's checks. We suggest you separate your valuables when traveling. For example, you could put part of your traveler's checks in a briefcase, part in your inside coat pocket. If you lose your briefcase, you still have some of your checks to tide you over. Most good hotels have safe deposit boxes.

Clothing   From mid-November to late March, north China, including Beijing, is bitterly cold, sometimes with snow. I even froze in Beijing one May; two sweaters and a top coat were barely enough. Many of the buildings are not heated and many foreigners complain of the cold in low-class hotels. A jogging suit is ideal for lounging and sleeping on trains.

The Chinese sometimes lend heavy, padded jackets to visitors who didn't anticipate the cold, but you should take along your own coat plus long thermal underwear and heavy slacks. Thermal socks, warm boots, and *hot water bottles* are in order, too, for cheaper hotels.

I suggest you do as the natives do: plan on layers of warm clothing and a lightweight top layer. This is better than one thick, heavy coat that would only be excess weight in the warmer south. Down coats and jackets, winter-weight wool or silk underwear are on sale in cold weather, sometimes at half the price you would pay at home. They are ideal if you are staying a long time. If you are also traveling to warmer climes or need room in your luggage for purchases, you might consider taking clothes you don't mind discarding when no longer useful.

The rainy season is March to May in the south, with rain or drizzle almost every day. After it starts getting hot, a trench coat or plastic raincoat will feel like a sauna. You could buy a cheap umbrella then. The Chinese sell plastic sandals, which are great for rain, but they may not have big enough sizes for Western feet.

All of lowland China is hot in July. Sundresses on foreign women in tour groups are common now in big cities. In smaller towns, especially if you are alone, please cover your shoulders. The more you deviate from what the Chinese wear, the more they will stare at and surround you, a most oppressive experience on a hot day or when you're tired.

Generally speaking, most Chinese women wear trousers, loose-fitting blouses, sweaters, and jackets in winter, and, increasingly, skirts or long shorts and blouses, always with short sleeves, in summer. For men, slacks and loose-fitting white shirts are worn in the summer even in offices. In winter, they wear layers of sweaters and Mao jackets or Western-style jackets. Everyone wears padded coats. Trench coats for cooler weather are in style for office workers now.

The new, with-it generation has been dressing more colorfully with even men in high heels. Jeans have been fashionable at dance parties. But styles might become conservative again. Much depends on the political climate.

At banquets, cocktail parties, embassy receptions, and other formal occasions, Chinese men, particularly high officials, show up in Western suits and ties, or well-tailored Mao jackets. Black-tie occasions are rare. Foreign men should dress equally well, but women should dress modestly, as Chinese women don't usually wear elegant clothes except on the highest levels of society. Please don't upstage your hostess. The Chinese like to see foreign women wearing traditional Chinese dress, but try not to look like restaurant staff.

If you are invited to dinner, you could ask your host if what you have on is all right. Should men wear ties? How fancy is the restaurant? Your host may be pleased you asked, and dress accordingly himself. Women should not hesitate to wear some makeup but again, don't overdo it, or you'll have other people at the table wondering if your eyelashes and hair are real. Does everyone in Australia have blue eyelids? Some younger Chinese women are beginning to wear makeup themselves. Go easy on the jewelry too. My mother had shampoos and sets in four hotels, and three were great. The fourth became great after she insisted the hairdresser do it again.

Wearing cosmetics, jewelry, and bright colors (except for children) has been frowned on from Liberation until recently. Doing so led to hours of interrogation and even imprisonment during the Cultural Revolution. People who wore them then were considered self-indulgent, bourgeois, and counter-revolutionary. People in tight trousers then sometimes had them torn off in the streets. Long hair was seized and shorn off. It is understandable why the older generation hesitates about changes.

At less formal banquets, with friends and family, in ordinary restaurants (as opposed to fancy hotels), many Chinese men and women wear loose-fitting shirts and trousers. Some might be coming from work or arriving by bicycle. Chinese officials have not been bringing their spouses to banquets, but this is changing.

For business, you should dress as you would in your own country if you want to show respect; otherwise dress casually. Most government offices are dumpy though this too is changing.

Tourists should dress for comfort, with good walking shoes. You will be on your feet a lot and climbing stairs. You may even climb rough stone paths, treacherous for high heels. Sneakers are ideal. Please, no short-shorts; you might be thought of as sexually promiscuous. The natives are going to stare at you anyway, even if you are Overseas Chinese, so if you want to minimize the attention and the effects of pollution, wear dark, conservative colors. White is the color of mourning, so brighten it up with colored ribbons or something.

One feels compelled to dress up, however, in the new international-class hotels, where the clothes of staff members look better than that of the average Chinese and government official. But some tourists do lounge around the fancy lobbies in shorts and Hawaiian shirts, so wear what you feel most comfortable in.

Laundry is done in one day at most hotels if in by 8 a.m. Not all hotels have dry cleaning. Don't expect high-class service except in the top hotels. The Chinese do an adequate job, but if your dress is special, they could ruin it. It would be wise not to take your most expensive clothes to China, and to wash delicate clothes like underwear by hand yourself.

You can take drip-dry clothing if you want to do your own laundry, and in some luxury hotels clothes lines are provided. I found that even lightweight clothes took two days to dry in humid Guangzhou, except in air-conditioning. In the humid south, too, anything but predominantly cotton mixtures were stifling hot.

Toiletries In the joint venture hotels you will receive at least North American quality shampoo, conditioner, bathfoam, and soap. The Chinese-managed hotels will probably give you a Chinese toothbrush, toothpaste, soap, and sometimes a few other goodies like combs and Chinese shampoo. Keep this in mind when you pack toiletries. You might not need to pack much shampoo.

I do suggest you take sanitary napkins or tampons if needed, as these are harder to find. If you're adventurous, you might want to experiment with Chinese brands. The lemon shampoo is acceptable. The ginseng toothpaste is weird, but it might improve your sex life. Sandalwood soap smells heavenly.

Finicky people have taken a disinfectant or scouring powder, but this is no longer necessary unless you're well off the tourist track. If you care about fine clothes, take a small plastic bag of detergent or a small bottle of Woolite. I frequently wash clothes with hotel shampoo.

There is no need to bring toilet paper. Just pick up a day's supply from your hotel. But individually packaged moistened paper towels for cleaning hands are imperative.

Shortwave transistor radios During the 1989 turmoil, travelers in China could only get news from foreign sources on sometimes jammed shortwave radios. News was also received on Cable Network News (CNN) directly from the U.S. in some of the hotels. Chinese government news sources were not enlightening. In the days following June 4, China Daily mentioned nothing of the tanks and killings. And shortly afterwards, CNN and foreign newspapers were stopped.

News from foreign sources resumed again, but one never knows when it will be stopped. Many hotels now get 24-hour BBC news on Star TV (H.K.) or intermittent CNN news. These are marked ''USTV.'' The hotels are supposed to do their own censoring. But as China owns part of the satellite used, if you want to keep abreast, we suggest you take a shortwave radio.

Photography See ''Customs Regulations.'' You can buy Kodak film, usually Kodacolor, in China, but you have more choice if you import your own supply. Kodak film is available all over the country, but the prices are cheaper if you pay in F.E.C.s. Besides the danger of counterfeits, the Kodak box is entirely in Chinese. Color print film can be processed in many cities, but the quality may not be as good as at home except in the top cities. If you're going to be in Hong Kong afterward, it is best to have films processed there, as prices are considerably cheaper than in America and Kodak stores are usually reliable.

Be sure to take extra camera batteries, flash cubes, video tapes, and Polaroid film if needed, since these are not readily available in

China. If you run out, Guangzhou and Beijing have some available in special stores, but the button-shaped batteries are hard to find.

Small amateur videocameras are allowed. Commercial sizes require special permission. Not all tourist attractions allow video photography, but more allow still photography.

Videocassettes might be erased by airport x-ray machines, so pack them in lead pouches. If declared, these cassettes might need an hour to a couple of weeks for screening with a charge of about ¥5 each by Chinese Customs. They are looking for pornography and religious materials. You could argue that your cassettes are for your own use, but you might be fined.

Maps and books See "Learning about China" in the previous chapter for books to take with you. Some foreign books are available in China, but titles are limited. Even if you are on an escorted tour, you may not get a knowledgeable guide. So take out the relevant pages of this book, stapling each city together for lighter carrying. Take along a domestic airline timetable (available from Air China in North America) especially if you're traveling on your own.

You can usually buy a good tourist map in English in each city. A Chinese-English dictionary is superfluous if you have a bilingual person with you most of the time. For wandering around on your own, I have tried to anticipate most needs in the "Useful Phrases" in this book.

Medicines and vitamins Take what you will need; exact Chinese equivalents may be hard to find. The Chinese do have antibiotics, cold tablets, and cough syrups. Chinese traditional medicines are frequently effective, so if you're adventurous, you might rely on those after you arrive. Many hotels have doctors. With Chinese painkillers, you might experience strange mood changes. A few Chinese pharmacists can fill basic Western prescriptions, but don't count on it. You may want to take PeptoBismol tablets (mild) and Immodium (serious) in case of diarrhea or upset stomach. Do read the directions. Do not take Immodium as a preventative as some travelers have done. Ask your doctor about Diamox for altitude sickness medicine for Tibet. If you are bothered by pollution or dust, take a nose mask (or buy a cheap silk scarf in China) like the Chinese do. I also take a few *Sleep·ezeD* pills to help regulate jetlagged sleep patterns.

Pills for protection against malaria are controversial. They might not be effective as the parasite develops a resistance to certain drugs within a very short time. China's malaria is chloroquine-resistant. Some of the new pills like Mefloquine hydrochloride/Roche have not been available in Canada. Please consult a knowledgeable doctor.

If you are going to a malarial area, we do suggest you wear long sleeves and trousers after dark (when these mosquitos bite) and use a good mosquito repellant. If you have flu-like symptoms after being bitten, do tell your doctor to check for malaria. It can be fatal.

Gifts are not essential, but if you are adhering to the "no tipping" policy, you may want to leave an expression of your appreciation or a souvenir of your visit for friends, or attendants who have given you extra-special service. See "Tipping" in "Local Customs and Emergencies."

So what should you give? Anything *not* made in China is usually acceptable. Ties, lipsticks and other cosmetics are fine.

Many Chinese now collect postage stamps, so start saving them from your own letters to give away. (There is a market for old used Chinese stamps.) Some people give novelties like those magnetic things you stick on refrigerators, unusual ball-point pens, or candy. You can give postcards or picture books with scenes of your city or country. Or something for their children like coloring books or children's books in English. Little boxes of Lego and matchbox cars are easy to pack.

Trade, commerce, and other officials dealing with Japanese and Hong Kongers have been accepting television sets and condos in Hong Kong (!) for several years now, and some were reported asking shamelessly for videos, computers, and "Benzes." North Americans do not give such gifts. There is no guarantee that an expensive gift will get you what you want, and the intent could prove counterproductive.

The danger is that from time to time, campaigns rage against corrupt officials who use their positions for personal gain. Chinese jails aren't as nice as those at home. And Chinese legal rights aren't the same either. Capital punishment has been imposed for accepting bribes.

Usually, inviting an official to a banquet to celebrate a deal, or to thank especially helpful people, is sufficient. Modest corporate gifts like portable metal business card cases, calculators, agenda books, "traveling offices," and lighters are fine. Some, but not all, Chinese appreciate hard liquor.

It is not imperative to take gifts to schools, and certainly not to factories and communes that you visit for a few hours. The factories and communes will make money from your purchases. But schools do not usually receive any material compensation for the disruption caused by visitors. If you want to leave a souvenir of your visit, give **general gifts** like books and pictures that everyone can enjoy. Giving to a few individuals may antagonize the others. One tour group collected ¥40 for a youth palace in Beijing. If you want to do the same, ask your host to buy some treats or equipment for the children.

Since people everywhere are studying English and other foreign languages, give **books.** Textbooks, good supplementary reading books, and objective histories of Asia would be great. *The Soong Dynasty* is easily read and enlightening. Agatha Christie is fun. Please, no sexy novels! Books from museums are great. C.I.T.S. guides have written to ask for "best-sellers," Chinese-English dictionaries and thesauruses. Books about your country are fine, particularly if you have a sister-city relationship with China.

"Talking books" on cassettes are good for learning English and are lighter to carry. Most guides and schools have access to cassette players. Since you may be carrying music tapes anyway for dance parties, you could give some of these as gifts just before you leave.

You could take **posters and educational materials** for schools, novelty toys like Frisbees, and unusual (for China) **sports equipment** like a boomerang, hockey sticks and pucks where there's ice, or a baseball and bat. As football has been seen on television in China, a football would probably be much appreciated. Don't forget to demonstrate their use. The Chinese already have basketball, Ping-Pong, and soccer. China is so short of teaching materials, especially in science, technology, and languages, that the Chinese should appreciate everything you can give them—educational movies (16 mm is okay), taped English lessons and, if possible, tape recorders to match. Books on space and the history of flying come immediately to mind, and any books in English about China. As souvenirs of a visit, a geological delegation might want to give labeled rock specimens; a solar energy group may want to give a simple model. North American videos have to be converted to work in China.

Group gifts are difficult to organize on general-interest tours, where you might meet your fellow travelers for the first time on a plane across the Pacific. So don't worry about gifts. But **special-interest** and **Friendship tours** are different. Again, it's up to you. You may want to write ahead to the schools where you will be spending *more* than just an afternoon. Ask what they need. If the gift needs duty-free customs clearance, give the institution your date and point of entry so the papers will be ready for you. Do not be surprised if you get a list of books worth US$50,000. Never mind; take only what you can afford. The Chinese are used to spending very little money for locally printed books; they think books are cheap everywhere. See Chinese Customs in "Important Addresses and Information."

Just don't be turned off by a request for expensive presents. In all fairness, the Chinese really do not know the value of money outside China. When you get there just say something like, "I'm sorry I could only get these. They are just a fraction of what I wanted to bring." That should satisfy them. If it doesn't, don't feel guilty. Don't encourage greed. You did your best. Besides, some cheap pirated foreign textbooks are now available in China.

For **guides,** surprisingly, the best gifts are reference books on *China*. Many get their spiels from old copies of *Nagel's* and you might want to leave behind this guide. Yes, guidebooks with lots of good photos from your own country are also important. China is eager to improve its services and would like to see what other countries offer tourists.

Officially, no one is allowed to ask for tips, but no one quibbles about inexpensive things. Guides will usually knock themselves out trying to help you anyway. You could pick up a carton of cigarettes (Marlboro Lights is a favorite), and pass packs around to **drivers,** but that would be encouraging cancer, wouldn't it! How about chocolate bars, or wouldn't that rot their teeth! What about cute novelties, oversized pencils, bouncing things for decorating their buses? You can give lipsticks and other cosmetics to women.

If you want to give expensive gifts to relatives, ask them about a telephone (plus expensive installation), videorecorder, air conditioner (plus electricity), electric water heater, and automatic washing machine. They would probably prefer foreign brands, but know the good domestic ones. These can all be bought in China.

If you are going to Lhasa, Tibetans appreciate photos of the Dalai Lama. But be aware that by passing these out, you may be construed as taking sides in an internal dispute.

If you are visiting **foreign residents** in China, do write and ask what would be best to take them, especially if they are living in isolated communities away from the big cities and fancy hotels. Many are teaching English, so as many relevant books as you can possibly carry would be helpful. They also appreciate hard-to-get snack foods: cheeses, popping corn, Cheese Curls, instant coffee and tea bags, and Mom's homemade cookies. Around your holiday times, take traditional spices, condiments, and treats like cranberry sauce, Christmas spices, Sunkist oranges, Delicious apples, the makings for minced meat and pumpkin pies. China has all kinds of fruit, a limited variety of vegetables, and many meats, but there's nothing like goodies from home. If you are flying to the north from the south, pick up some tropical fruit, like litchis, cheaper in Guangzhou.

Ice Breakers. I think bringing bags of balloons and passing one each to little children on the street is fine. I am not happy about passing out ball-point pens because sometimes children end up fighting for them.

Museum pieces. The next suggestion is entirely my own, so don't blame anyone else for it. So many things were stolen from China by looting foreigners in the old days that as a gesture of friendship and support for the current policy of openness to foreigners, some visitors may want to return Chinese relics if they have any. These, of course, must have historic value. The British once returned a sword belonging to one of the Taiping princes. It is now in the Taiping museum in Nanjing. I think old photos of foreigners in China (against recognizable Chinese backgrounds), important old documents, and missionary clothes and old military uniforms would be most welcome. A museum official in Zhen-jiang said she was eager to get anything like that.

You really should write ahead of time to the Bureau of Historical Relics in Beijing *and* directly to the museum in the city relevant to the relics. Give details and ask if they would be interested in receiving the relics as a gift. Keep in mind that China has a problem of too many historical objects, but something unique and significant would be appreciated.

Your next problem is getting gifts into China without paying duty. See *Customs Regulations* in "Getting There."

Business Cards   These are essential for anyone doing business in China. Best have them printed before you arrive, preferably with the Chinese on the back side. Best also take a one-page introduction in Chinese of your company and business. A few of the top hotels do print poor quality cards within 24 hours and rent typewriters and computers by the day or hour (very expensive).

Miscellaneous   If you're fussy about coffee and tea, take your favor-ite brands, powdered cream, sugar, and a spoon. Many imported goods like Nescafe and Listerine are now available in the big cities, but cost considerably more than where they're made. Buying Cup o' Noodles may not save you money, but at least you are assured of cleanliness. Having disposable chopsticks would make washing utensils unneces-sary. TV popcorn, which can be made in a wok, is great for parties. Most Chinese have never eaten popcorn. Most hotels provide cups and a big thermos of hot water daily or free on request. Take prunes if traveling makes you constipated. A jackknife is handy for cutting fruit for snacks and a flashlight imperative for caves, museums, dark houses, and late-night walks. (Drivers of motor vehicles do not always turn headlights on at night, and many streets have ditches and potholes with no warning signs.) Cheap jackknives and flashlights can be bought in China too. You can sometimes borrow a hair dryer or an iron from a hotel. If you take your own, consider "Voltage" below. Wake-up calls in top hotels have been pretty reliable, but in other hotels, you probably need an alarm clock.

Take a money belt or neck safe to hold valuables if you will be sleeping on boats or trains. Note that money belts worn outside your clothing can be easily cut and stolen. If you're fussy about your ciga-rettes or liquor, take some duty-free in with you. China has some for-eign cigarettes and liquor, but they may not be your favorites. Cocktails and beer are not served on domestic flights. Visitors are usually pleased with the local beer, but find the wine very sweet. In many hotels you now find ice (made from boiled water, I hope). Chinese brandy and vodka have been described as "outstanding." But these are all a matter of taste. Yes, Coca-Cola is available locally, but not all varieties.

Take granola bars, hot chocolate mix, instant cereal, things to munch on, and a can opener, but not too much unless you want to save money. Most hotels have Western-style coffee shops. You may get tired of Chinese food. Carry snacks on domestic flights in case of delay. Some airports have no restaurants. You can buy crackers, cookies, instant soups, candy, American instant coffee, etc., in China.

During the rainy season you might be bothered by mosquitoes, if, for example, you're staying with a family or in an isolated rural guesthouse. Also take insect repellent then. Hot water bottles are great for hotels that have little or no heat in winter.

For people who want to do unusual things, and are not on a whirlwind tour, yes, take your paints, or if you want to be able to say you ice-skated in China, take your skates. Take your alpine skis or at least your boots if you're going to Jilin or Harbin in winter. (You can rent small sizes there, too.) Take cross-country skis if you're staying any length of time in snow country, the northeast. Some hotels have swimming pools, tennis, and squash. For people expecting to rent bicycles, take old identification cards or anything else with your photo. You are asked to leave a passport as a deposit and anyone can take yours by error; these make good substitutes. The only scuba diving is in Sanya on Hainan Island. Some Hong Kong dive shops are tied in with the sport in China, so you can get information from them before you go.

If you're backpacking, or going to isolated, less developed places, the following have been suggested by Louise Lore, a veteran: "Youth hostel sheet, towel, daypack (for biking especially), mouth masks (to keep out dust), folding cup (or buy a cup with cover in China), chopsticks, rain cape, plug for electrical appliances, small water bottle, tea strainer, throat lozenges, cough medicine, flashlight, rucksack, and luggage wheels.

"If you're going to Tibet and staying in cheap hotels, take flea powder, scouring pads, and medicine for altitude sickness. The medicine should be recommended by a doctor as you have to take some precautions with it. If you're going on the bus to Lhasa, take all your own food, long underwear, and winter clothing, even in summer."

If you're big on bicycling and staying any length of time, buy a bicycle in China or take one in with you. Chinese bicycles usually have one gear but a few have ten. You can sell it when you leave if you want.

If you're staying at cheaper hotels where anyone with a key can go into your room, you may want a rubber wedge to ensure your privacy when you're inside.

For mailing packages in China, pick up cloth bags available in a few Chinese post offices and take needle and white thread. Packages have to be inspected before mailing at the post office. Only a few hotels and stores have packaging services.

Take extra passport pictures for visas, a birth certificate or other legal documents, in case your passport is lost. Take photocopies of the essential pages of your passport, including your China visa. Pack these separately.

We suggest you carry essential medicines in more than one container in different bags.

Your luggage should be locked and will probably have to endure a lot of punishment. Some bags have been left out in the rain, some have been slashed. Your bags should have your name, telephone number, and address outside and in. (Take along an extra luggage tag in case yours disappears.) For shoppers, we suggest a folding bag for bulky purchases like tablecloths, carpets, and porcelain vases or buy another suitcase there. Cheap.

Think of everything you need before you go and try to be as self-sufficient as possible. If goods are sent in by mail, a hefty duty may have to be paid at a hard-to-find government office.

Voltage   Chinese appliances are 220V and have either two-, or more commonly, three-pronged plugs (with straight or slanted prongs). Many hotels have transformers for electric razors. Some but not all hotels have adapters. No need for electric kettles. You may want to pick up 220V electronics in Hong Kong.

GETTING THERE (AND BACK)

The prepaid traveler with a human guide does not have to worry about logistics. Read the sections on *Border Formalities, Adjusting Your Watch,* and *Leaving China,* but just glance at the rest of this chapter in case your guide disappears. (It's happened!)

The do-it-yourself traveler does have to read most of it.

Via Hong Kong   While many travelers go directly from their own country into China, many more enter China via Hong Kong. This is because flights from North America and Britain can be cheaper to Hong Kong, and South China is not much farther. Tours and flights bought together in North America, however, could be less expensive than buying a flight in North America and a tour in Hong Kong. Do check.

Because hundreds of thousands of Hong Kong Chinese and many foreign residents travel to China yearly from Hong Kong, competing travel agents there have developed a high degree of expertise. They are usually the first to upgrade services. Many have direct connections with individual tourism officials in China with whom they share a common language. Hong Kong is also loaded with professional China watchers, China-related banks, and experienced business people who can give advice. But we are getting close to 1997, when Hong Kong reverts back to China, and some people are thinking of leaving. One does get the feeling that some Hong Kong businesses are more concerned with making a buck than with giving service that will bring customers back. If this is the case, complain to the Hong Kong Tourist Association (H.K.T.A.), which does care.

While its prices have risen over the years, Hong Kong is still one of the bargain cities of the world, with its tax-free and duty-free jewelry, cameras, watches, and radios, and its relatively cheap shoes and clothes. It is a good place to stock up on camera film, video tapes, snacks, down coats, dried-food gifts for relatives, and locally published China guidebooks. Books published abroad and cosmetics are more expensive in Hong Kong. But a good selection of China books is available. Pre-Qing antiques can be bought here but not legally in China.

Quality and everyday goods from China can be found in stores like Yue Hwa, China Products, and Chinese Merchandise Emporium, which should have up-to-date lists of what Overseas Chinese can take into China duty-free. They will even pack and ship purchases to the railway station or provide a truck into China if you give them a couple of days' notice. You can also purchase coupons for duty-free goods to be picked up in China. (You can buy these coupons in North America at some Chinatown travel agencies too.) These coupons must be stamped later at the Chinese border by Customs officials when you enter China. Prices in these stores are "fixed," but they will give you a 10% discount card if you ask. (Try the Overseas Chinese Service Department, usually on the top floor.)

There are also duty-free stores in China where you can buy televisions and computers for relatives. This saves a lot of carrying.

Avoid money changers. You get better rates at banks.

Hong Kong was taken from China by the British during and after the Opium Wars. Urban areas are extremely crowded because of the refugees from China. You can feel some of the flavor of old China there, especially in isolated island villages or in the New Territories—the tiny temples, colorful incense-smoked festivals, elaborate weddings with brides dressed in red, and funerals with wailing mourners clad in sackcloth and white. It is a good introduction to the contrasts of new China next door, and it might be good for you to talk with refugees from China—why did they risk their lives to leave? Welfare agencies can help you contact them, or just ask around. China is beginning to practice again many of the old Chinese customs you will see here—but not so elaborately. A glimpse of traditional China can be seen in the Middle Kingdom theme park (good history lesson) and the exquisite Sung Dynasty Village. These are better organized than anything similar in China.

From Hong Kong to Guangzhou, times subject to change: Three **hovercrafts** daily 8:40, 8:50, 9 a.m. (Zhoutouzui); 9:45 a.m. (Huangpu), and **catamarans** (at 8:15 and 8:45 a.m.) make the 3-hour trip. These are recommended because the maximum 68 passengers each means shorter queues; however, you can't see much of the scenery.

Overnight ferries, either the *Xing Hu* and *Tien Hu,* leave Hong Kong and Guangzhou nightly at 9:00 p.m. No sailings on the 31st of any month. The trip is comfortable in air-conditioned deluxe cabins (2 and 4 passengers), though some people have found the cabins stuffy and the bathrooms badly maintained. No announcements are made in English. The early morning arrival means you've saved a night in a hotel room and you have a full day in China ahead of you.

All ships and hoverferries leave from the new China Ferry Terminal in the China Hong Kong City, on Canton Road. Ferries dock at Zhoutouzui or in Huangpu (Whampoa), on Guangzhou's south shore.

Customs and immigration sometimes take over an hour to clear if they have 500 or so passengers.

Because the ships are on a river, stability is good except during typhoons. Seasickness is not usually a problem.

Four air-conditioned **through-trains** leave Hunghom Railway Station in Kowloon (near East Tsimshatsui hotels) daily at 8:18 a.m., 9:03 a.m., 12:28 p.m., and 2:28 p.m. for the 2¼ hour ride to the main railway station. Best buy tickets in advance, but you can also buy them at the train station on the day of departure—if any are left.

Frequent **electric trains** zip to the border at Lo Wu where passengers line up to walk through two customs buildings. This way is cheaper than the express train, but not recommended unless you like waiting in railway stations, or standing on trains or in lines. No toilets are on the Hong Kong trains, which leave Hunghom railway station in Kowloon or Kowloon Tong MTR Station. An electric service all the way to Guangzhou is now operating from Shenzhen to the new Tonghe Railway Station in Guangzhou, closer to the Ramada Hotel. Be sure to get the name of the railway station so people meeting you will not be confused.

Flights leave for the 35-minute trip to Guangzhou several times a day. A **bus** departs daily.

April to September, daylight savings time means Hong Kong is one hour later than China.

Other destinations from Hong Kong   By air (Monday is 1, Tuesday is 2, etc.), also subject to change.

Either CAAC or regular charter flights (book through CTS or CITS) or Dragonair (booked abroad through Cathay Pacific): Beijing (daily); Changsha (1, 4); Chengdu (3, 6); Chongqing (1, 4, 6); Dalian (1, 3, 6); Fuzhou (daily); Guilin (daily); Hefei (1, 5); Haikou (daily); Hangzhou (daily); Jinan (2, 5); Kunming (daily except 4); Meixian (1, 5); Nanchang (2, 5); Nanjing (daily); Nanning (2, 5); Ningbo (3, 6); Qingdao (1, 3, 4, 6); Shanghai (daily); Shantou (daily); Shenyang (1, 4); Tianjin (daily); Wuhan (1, 2, 4, 6); Xiamen (daily); Xian (4, 7); Zhanjiang (1, 3, 5); Zhengzhou (3, 5, 7).

By ferry:

—to **Haikou** five times a month, taking about 18 hours each month.

—to **Ningbo** twice a month taking 55 hours.

—to **Sanya** twice a month.

—to **Shanghai,** about every five days on the S.S. *Hai Xing,* S.S. *Shanghai,* or S.S. *Jinjiang,* a 2½-day voyage. See also ''Shanghai.''

—to **Shantou** daily (less than two hours).

—to **Xiamen,** on the M.S. *Jimei* (2, 5 taking 22 hours).

—to **Zhuhai** (about an hour), **Shekjou** (about one hour), **Jiangmen** (about four hours). Frequency at least three times a day.

Ferries also go from Hong Kong to Guanghai (Taishan taking 3.5 hours), Zhaoqing (taking 12 hours in the wake of Matteo Ricci), Zhongshan (less than two hours), etc.

Depending on the class, going by ship could be the cheapest and most direct way to get to these cities from Hong Kong. Buses could be cheaper, but are not as comfortable. Avoiding Guangzhou saves time and hassle too. Services are basic. Lineups to disembark start early.

On the overnight ships, no regard for sexes is considered in the assignment of cabins, but you might successfully protest. Meals are usually very early. On the bigger ships, the pools may be unswimable.

By express buses: regularly to **Foshan, Shantou, Guangzhou, Quanzhou, Xiamen, Haikou, Zhaoqing, Zhanjiang,** and **Fuzhou.** Some routes may have an overnight hotel stop. A double-decker city bus goes between Hong Kong and hotels in Shenzhen, at least twice a day.

Generally:

As services are continually being improved and opened to more cities, it is helpful to ask travel agents here for up-to-date information. Hong Kong Tourist Association (H.K.T.A.) can give you addresses. It has offices conveniently located at the Star Ferry pier in Tsimshatsui, Kowloon, and Basement, Jardine House, 1 Connaught Place, Central.

Most **Hong Kong travel agents** listed here should be able to book some or all of these routes, the Trans-Siberian train, domestic flights in China and from Beijing to Pyongyang. Most can book group tours with English-speaking guides, and guaranteed departures for a minimum of two passengers. They can make arrangements for individual travelers, get visas, and book tickets by mail before you arrive. Phone around for quotes. Cheaper outbound airfares are advertised in Hong Kong newspapers, but at your own risk.

A few Hong Kong travel agents, but not those listed here, have given the industry a bad name because of unreliable service. Worse are the ones who take your money and disappear. The following have been in business for years, and I have used some of them myself. If any of them fail you, please let me know and I will certainly take them off the list in future editions. Tell us also if you have found others reliable.

If you try a travel agency on your own, make sure it is a member of the Hong Kong Tourist Association. If it does anything questionable, then you have the association to intercede for you. Always telephone first for information and tell the agency where you got its name. Having learned of it through this book, they are answerable for any mistakes to me. They should do their best for you. You in turn are adding to my influence with them. This is a lesson in Chinese *guanxi*.

Since the price of visas, tours, and train tickets can vary from agent to agent, do also ask about prices and services. It would be advisable to book long group tours one to three months in advance, but you still might be able to get a tour after your arrival in Hong Kong. Hong Kong agents need two passport photos, 1 or 2 application forms, and your passport for a China visa. Send a photocopy of the passport if done by mail.

American Express International.

China International Travel Service (H.K.)

China Travel Service (H.K.), the granddaddy of them all, is especially helpful for overseas Chinese. With an office in the railway station, it can help you ship heavy luggage to China.

China Youth Travel arranges regular travel and special tours for professional groups like medical doctors, lawyers, and teachers. It also arranges seminars with university students and scholars, summer camps, cycling expeditions, cultural studies, and performing arts troupes. Can book YMCAs in Hong Kong. Good for budget travelers. Tied with CYTS in China.

Hong Kong Student Travel Ltd. Budget and deluxe prices. Has own hostel.

Time Travel Services has been my own favorite for budget travelers. General agent.

Travel Advisers Ltd.: In business since 1932. Cargo handling.

Zhuhai Tours (HK) Ltd. Can book hotels and golf courses in Zhuhai and Zhongshan. Tickets and hotel vouchers can be picked up at MTR Travel Services Centre and C.T.S.

The **Visa Office of the Chinese Ministry of Foreign Affairs** issues visas at the cheapest prices. This is not a travel agent, but the equivalent of a Chinese consulate.

Via South Korea A 480-passenger ship leaves Inchon on Wednesdays and Saturdays at 16:00 and arrives in Weihai, Shandong, the next morning at 9:00. A 640-passenger ship sails every five days between Inchon and Tianjin (758 km in about 32 hours). Chinese visas are obtained at the dock in China.

Via Macao This Portuguese territory on the other side of the Pearl River delta can be reached after a 50-minute jetfoil or 20-minute helicopter ride from Hong Kong. It is also a free port, its prices lower than Hong Kong's because rent and labor costs are less. But its shopping selection is not as vast. Noted for its gambling casinos and good Portuguese food, it might be closer than Hong Kong for some ancestral villages.

The Portuguese traders lived in Macao from the 16th century, but went seasonally to Guangzhou to trade. Macao will revert back to China in 1999.

Travel Agencies in Macao can arrange taxis and air-conditioned bus rides to Guangzhou and other points in the province. Duty-free stores here can even provide you with a truck (at a price) to take large items like refrigerators to relatives in China. C.I.T.S. Zhuhai Branch and China Travel Service have offices here. One can walk across the border.

Via Nepal   Current information comes from the Holiday Inn in Lhasa, and Yangrima Travels in Kathmandu. Because of the political situation, only tours prepaid a month in advance can enter Tibet. In the early 1990s, it took 7 working days to get a Chinese visa in Kathmandu. Journalists were not allowed.

Flights have been sporadic, but one should be able to fly to Lhasa from Kathmandu from April 1 to the end of December on Tuesdays and Saturdays (China Southwest Airlines) and Thursdays from July to the end of October (Royal Nepal—RNAC). One should aim for the Chinese flight as Royal Nepal (RNAC) has a reputation for cancelling if the plane isn't full. The Chinese want the foreign exchange and give preference to its own tickets. For Everest, sit on the left side from Kathmandu and the right from Lhasa.

By road, the problem has been landslides because of rains between June 15 and September 15. From Kathmandu to the border is 114 km. (at the best of times 4 to 4½ hours). Most of the slides happen before Barabise at the 52 km. mark (from Kathmandu), the 54 km. mark, and the 100 km. mark. In China, landslides are common 13 kms. from the border. Porters on the Nepal side can carry luggage over the slides for less than US$10 each. They have been known to disappear around corners, so keep up with them. Be prepared to hike several hours yourself.

From Zhangmu at the border, travelers switch to Chinese-owned landcruisers and buses, with the most expensive tours usually getting the best. Do get a multiple-entry visa in North America for Nepal if you are returning to Nepal and spending some time there. (See also Lhasa.)

Via Pakistan   In addition to Pakistan International Airline's two flights a week to Beijing, entry from this country can be made by land. The best source of information on this spectacular Himalayan route has been **Bestway Tours & Safaris** (Vancouver). China visas can be obtained in Islamabad in three working days. The Karakorum Highway and border posts at Sust (Pakistan) and Pirali (China) are usually open daily May 1 to October 31 for foreign tour groups. Before and after that time nothing is dependable because of snow. The rains in July and early August frequently set off landslides, so that period should be avoided. Public minibuses and tours are available and individual travel is possible but not easy. You need ingenuity and flexibility. Motion sickness might be a problem. Women have traveled this route successfully. We suggest couples, not alone.

One can try to fly to Gilgit (Pakistan) from Islamabad. The weather does not always cooperate and people who are bumped off an aborted flight get first chance at flying the next possible day. Be prepared for delays. The alternative is rough road for 14-18 hours from Islamabad to Gilgit. Sitara Travel can help you. The weather is most reliable in September and October.

From Gilgit, there is a public bus (about 350 Rps.) leaving at 9 a.m., taking about six hours (189 miles) to the border. One can also get a car. There should be Chinese buses on the other side to Taxkorgan-Tashkurgan. From the border at Khunjerab to Chinese Customs and Immigration at Parali is about 31 miles. If you want to pay more to be sure of transportation, you can ask C.I.T.S. to meet you with a vehicle at the border.

Two small, cheap guest houses are in Taxkorgan, the Pamirs and the Traffic. Altitude 3200 meters or over 9000 feet; 53 miles north of Pirali. From here to Kashgar (175 miles, 9 hours), public buses only budge when full. You could hitchhike.

The highest point on the road is about 16,000 ft. at Khunjerab-Kunjirap Pass. The temperature ranges from −4° C to 30° C in summer. We suggest you read William Dalrymple's *In Xanadu. A Quest,* about his 1986 visit before the road was finished, and Diana Shipton's *The Antique Land,* about her life in Kashgar in 1946–48.

Besides the scenery, the advantage of this route is its proximity to what used to be Gandhara, the area between today's Peshawar and Taxila, where Chinese pilgrims came in the Tang dynasty to learn about Buddhism. The ruins of monasteries, the influence of Alexander the Great, and the superb collections of Greco-Indo art in museums here point to the development of Chinese Buddhist sculpture.

Via Southeast Asia   There are plans for opening the Vietnam border (train and plane), Myanmar and Thai borders (road), and Laotian border (boat) to foreigners, so do ask.

Border Formalities Anywhere in China   Have ready for inspection your passport, Health Declaration, and Entry forms at your first point of entry in China.

Chinese Customs will want to see your Baggage Declaration form in duplicate at the international airport when you disembark. If you are in transit to a Chinese city that has no international airport, you do have to clear Customs before you change planes. Give yourself plenty of time. If you are taking in any duty-free gifts to China, necessitating a stamp on a receipt, have that ready too. You surrender the copy of your Baggage Declaration form when you leave China. The Baggage Declaration form asks what Chinese and foreign currencies you are taking into China. Probably no one will count your money. If you declare only U.S. dollars, you can pay for duty-free goods in China only with U.S.

dollars, and you can take only U.S. dollars and F.E.C. legally out of China when you leave.

Everything you mark down—gold and silver ornaments, camera, tape recorder, video and movie camera—should be declared on the way out. Outgoing Customs once asked to see the wedding ring and camera I declared upon entry. If they think you left something in China, you might have to pay duty on it. If something is stolen in China, get a police report.

If you declare recorded videotapes upon entry, you may be delayed as Customs officials screen them. You will also be charged about ¥5 for reviewing each tape. If you don't declare recorded videotapes, and they are found on you, you will be fined and the tapes confiscated. Chinese Customs is looking for pornographic and religious materials. If they find any, you could argue the videos are for your own use. Good luck! In some Customs offices, there is a "Green Channel" if you have nothing to declare.

You should declare any large gifts you are going to leave in China. Unless you are Overseas Chinese on your first trip of the year to visit relatives, you will probably have to pay a very heavy duty.

Keep the Baggage Declaration and Departure Card in a safe place. You will need them on the way out.

Immigration   In most cases, you will have to line up to have your passport stamped by immigration officials. If the whole group has one group visa, then that will be stamped, and officials will take a quick look at each passport. If you are considered a VIP, you will be taken into a comfortable waiting room where you can make your own tea while you wait for immigration and health authorities.

Customs regulations   At this writing, Customs searches of foreigners and Overseas Chinese were rare, and of Compatriots occasional. See regulations in "Important Addresses and Information."

Money changing   Facilities to change money legally into Chinese currency exist at border points, tourist stores, the Bank of China, and at major hotels. Change only what you think you need for three or four days at a time. Small quantities can be changed back to foreign currency easily, but only 50% of what you originally exchanged, provided you've kept receipts. Before you go to isolated places like Xigaze, Jing Hong, and Kaili, ask about money changing. Frequently, this is only done in banks, not open on Sundays, early mornings, or evenings—so get enough changed before you go.

You will be given **Foreign Exchange Certificates** (F.E.C.s), which are different from *renminbi* (R.M.B.)—people's currency. There is a small service charge for traveler's checks and a lower exchange rate for cash. You will need your passport number and, in some cases, your passport to change money. The F.E.C.s must be used in *some* stores, hotels, taxis, and restaurants. They were introduced to control the illegal exchange of foreign currency. Chinese citizens are allowed to use them. Foreigners are not allowed to buy or sell foreign exchange except at designated exchange agencies at the official exchange rate quoted for the day.

F.E.C.s can be taken out of China, but not R.M.B.s. But in very remote places, people do not know or trust F.E.C.s and prefer R.M.B.s!

In Guangzhou, and especially in Shenzhen, Hong Kong currency has been accepted in stores or by street peddlers. However, using foreign currency is illegal, and there are periodic crackdowns. Local Chinese value F.E.C.s so they can buy otherwise hard-to-obtain items like bicycles and TVs at Friendship Stores. Some enterprises try to purchase F.E.C.s so they can buy equipment abroad without government red tape. People need foreign currency to go abroad.

To avoid getting change in local currency (R.M.B.), keep a lot of small bills on hand. You can spend R.M.B. in most stores and even some hotel restaurants, but do not keep too much of this currency as it is not as valuable as the F.E.C.s. Some stores will refuse it from foreigners. In markets and some stores, prices may go up if you offer R.M.B.s. Even some post offices ask for F.E.C.s.

Foreigners have been arrested and deported for illegally selling F.E.C.s. Foreign Exchange Certificates are labeled as such in English. R.M.B.s are usually dirtier, with no English.

For a list of acceptable traveler's checks and credit cards, see "Budget."

Getting from your arrival point to your hotel   Top hotels now have vehicles that can meet you at airports, bus, ship, and railway stations if you let them know you are coming. In most cities now, **taxis** are also available in these places, except after about 8 p.m. In some cities, very aggressive touts might compete for your fare. Please don't encourage such uncouth behavior. Usually there is a cheaper taxi stand outside with drivers waiting in line.

Another new development for China is the overcharging taxi driver preying on new arrivals who don't know local prices. If your taxi has no meter, settle on a price for the trip (not per passenger) before you go. Make a point to take down the odometer reading when you get in and when you arrive at your destination. For the per kilometer rate, see "Budget" in "Quick Reference." If the fare seems exorbitant or doesn't tally with your calculations, ask a staff member at the hotel for the price, or take down the license number of the taxi and complain to the police, taxi company, and the local Tourism Administration. If that fails to satisfy you, write to *China Daily* and the governor of the province.

For some cities, the distance from the airport to the hotel is listed in this book with the hotel, so you will have a rough idea of the charges.

To be perfectly fair, most taxi drivers are honest, but . . .

There is also an airport bus after every flight to the Air China office in town. This must be grabbed quickly before it disappears. If you must telephone for a taxi, be aware that it has to come from a taxi station and you will be charged from that point.

If you neglected to make hotel reservations, or otherwise need help, look first to see if there is a C.I.T.S. branch or hotel representative wherever you are. If not, telephone C.I.T.S., C.T.S., or one of the hotels listed in ''Destinations.'' You could also take a chance and go to a hotel directly. Some cities have touts trying to grab customers for inconveniently located hotels. See also ''Getting Around.''

Your passport   Keep it handy for registering at hotels, buying travel tickets, checking in at airports, applying for an alien travel permit, and sometimes changing money. Otherwise keep it locked up in a safe deposit box or in a pouch around your neck. If you are staying in China a long time or there is reason for an evacuation or worried parents, do register with your embassy or consulate. It is responsible for your safety.

Adjust your watch to the local time   All China is in the same time zone, though this may change in Xinjiang. See ''Quick Reference'' about Daylight Savings Time.

Once settled in your hotel, lie down or go to a coffee shop or bar and relax. You are now in China! Soon you will be ready to tackle the country and make use of the rest of the information in this book!

Leaving China   Reconfirm your flight at least 72 hours before departure. You can telephone your airline yourself unless you are flying a Chinese airline. While Air China says one can reconfirm international flights and flights from Beijing, Guangshou, and Shanghai by telephone, my own experience is different.

If you telephone, get a reservation number so that you can locate your reservation in person later. You can avoid the bother and frustration of going to the ticket office by asking your hotel or a travel agent to reconfirm for you for a very small fee. Ask what time you should check in at the airport.

Make sure your visa has not expired or you will be detained.

If your flight is very early in the morning, book transport and breakfast the night before. Some airports have restaurants. After you arrive there, be prepared to pay the airport tax required for all international flights, including those to Hong Kong.

You can change your money before or after Customs clearance if you have your foreign exchange receipts. At Customs, complete the blanks in your Baggage Declaration Form and hand it in. If you've lost it, you may be asked to fill out another, pay an "administrative fee," or be waved on. Just put down what you think you brought in and make sure it is less than you've marked on the form previously. Probably no one will check it against your original, especially if you don't look like a smuggler. You need your departure form completed for immigration, which would be at your last airport in China. If you are leaving China by land, the rules might be different; for example, you clear Customs at the Qinibah Hotel in Kashgar if you leave for Pakistan by bus.

Your next big hurdle is Customs in your own country. Have receipts ready. If you know the rate of duty, list the goods with the highest rate first on your declaration form. The Customs officials might just dismiss the little "souvenirs." Do report unaccompanied luggage so these will be exempted too. Show your Certificates of Origin if you are over your duty-free limit. Since much depends on the whim of each individual officer, you may not have trouble at all. On the other hand, undeclared dutiable purchases, if found, may be confiscated, and fines imposed.

The onus of proof that an article is an "antique" or "work of art" is on the owner of the goods. A Customs officer might not accept your certificate or receipts. Depending on the country, you probably have the right to appeal any decision.

HOTELS

HISTORY

The hotels of China **toward the end of 1978** were run by municipal service bureaus to provide travelers with not much more than a place to bathe, sleep, and eat. Many hotels were subsidized. One of the managers said then that he preferred Chinese guests because foreigners were too fussy: "Americans should learn from the Japanese not to complain!"

In some cities, especially during high tourist seasons, the demand for rooms exceeded supply. In the early 1980s, tour groups for Beijing were put into Tianjin hotels, or 50 km away in Hubei province. Some business people attending the Canton trade fair slept in hotel lobbies in 1979. Yet other cities had a surplus of rooms.

For many hotels, room reservations for groups could not be made very much in advance, and individual bookings could be canceled if Chinese officials wanted the rooms too. In addition, the revolutionary attitude was roughly, "If people are comfortable, they will become counter-revolutionary or revisionist. So don't let them be comfortable." Fortunately, this point of view has almost gone, but keep in mind that not all that much time has passed since this attitude was prevalent.

You can imagine what kinds of hotels resulted. Few, if any, were built during the early and mid-1970s. After the fall of the Gang of Four and the rise of Deng Xiaoping, the situation changed.

TODAY

Chinese tourism officials have been trying their best to attract tourists to China. While most hotels are still owned by some government agency or other, the building of many new hotels has resulted in good old-fashioned capitalistic competition. Pleasing the visitors has become important! Standards have risen! Chinese guests sometimes get displaced to make room for foreigners!

Each province or city state has a tourism administration that now regulates hotel prices and standards. While the tourism administration also owns and operates some of these hotels, it does have a mandate to make sure hotels are of good enough quality for foreigners. By the time you get to China, the local tourism administration should have a list of acceptable hotels, some with a plaque to that effect. If you have any complaints, you can take them up with the tourism administration. It is in a position to take hotels off its recommended list, and help get satisfaction.

The hotels you will use today are a world apart from the hotels of even the early 1980s. They still are not perfect, but are considerably better, the regular hotels very adequate, and those of international standard very good. Most hotels are now officially government-rated one to five stars, with five the top.

Foreign investment in the form of joint ventures both in the construction and in the management of some hotels has given China several hotels of international deluxe standard. A few hotels are being built solely by foreign interests. The big chains have been getting involved. Hilton, Holiday Inn, Hyatt, Ramada, Sheraton and Sofitel are companies that have already appeared on the sides of beautiful new buildings.

Some staff members have been sent on training programs outside China, and regular training programs take place on the job. Many hotels have also imported foreign executives and managers.

This does not mean that all joint ventures are of international standard. Some of the new hotels have deteriorated because of poor management. It does mean that in the early 1990s, foreign tourists are being billeted wherever possible in a standard Chinese hotel, or, if they choose to pay more, in a better hotel, possibly of international "deluxe" standard (if one of these is available). They can also choose, as backpackers will tell you, to live cheaply in a shared dormitory. But C.I.T.S. won't book you into those!

Hotel rooms are frequently classified from bottom to top: standard/moderate; superior; deluxe. "First class" is usually below superior and might even be the same as standard. Hotels with standards deemed unacceptable to most foreigners are being phased out as better ones open. At the turn of the decade, the rate of construction was still continuing, but it should stop soon. A surplus of deluxe hotel rooms has already become apparent.

Brand-new hotels may not yet have their acts together in regard to services, but at least the rooms will be in pristine condition. There is a tendency for Chinese partners to insist on a "soft" opening even before all facilities are ready, and you may find yourself in a hotel with only a restaurant, the lobby, and a block of rooms. A lot of hammering and the hint of better things after the "hard" or "grand" opening may be annoying. The *Travel China Newsletter* will try to keep you informed of hotel quality.

NOTE · · · Many hotels now have Public Relations Departments. Should you have problems, try the "Gong Gong Guan Si" during office hours. Almost all tourist hotels have someone on duty somewhere who speaks English.

Hotel Stars

These are a good but not absolute indication of architecture, decoration, equipment, hygiene, maintenance, management, service quality, and facilities (but not location). To qualify, hotels must also receive letters from satisfied guests. Do write your opinions, good or bad.

Each of the following items begets a certain number of points. Each star rating has a minimum number of points. Three stars does not mean that every hotel so graded has special guestrooms for wheelchaired people, for example. (They might only have a wheelchair.)

One to three star ratings are given by the local or provincial government, but three stars must also be approved by the national government. Four and five stars are determined by the national government.

Only hotels fully opened for one year are formally rated, and a plaque should be prominently displayed. Each successively higher rating incorporates the best criteria of the ratings below it.

Foreigners are not supposed to stay in a hotel with less than one star because the standards are terrible—but many of them do.

Among the criteria:

One Star must have air conditioning, coffee shop, dining room, at least 20 guest rooms, cleaned daily. Of these, 75% must have private baths. It must have central heating, a lobby with information and reception desk, postal service, 12-hour a day cold and hot running water.

Two Stars must have at least 20 guest rooms, 95% with private baths, and 50% with telephones. 16-hour cold and hot running water. Western and Chinese breakfast available.

Three Stars must have at least 50 beautifully decorated guest rooms with dressing table or desk, drawers, closet; carpet or wood floor; bedside panel; 24-hour cold and hot water; 110/220V outlet; telephones in every room with international direct dial (IDD); mini-bar and refrigerator; color TV sets, in-house movies, two TV channels broadcasting twice a day, programs not to end before midnight, and music; writing materials; sunproof curtains; bed turn-down service.

They must have single rooms and suites, western and Chinese dining rooms (with English speaking attendants and the last order no earlier than 8:30 p.m.), 16-hour coffee shop, banquet hall or function room, buffet breakfast and bar service (until midnight), and 18-hour room service with doorknob menus.

They must also have elevator service, public telephone and washroom, equipment and service for disabled people, disco, massage, beauty parlor, barber, bookstore, reading room, 12-hour a day foreign exchange, safe deposit boxes, store, film developing, facilities to send telegrams and telexes, store luggage, 24-hour laundry and drycleaning service, wake-up calls, shoe polishing, and taxis. They should be able to mend articles of everyday use for guests. They should accept credit cards (including American Express, Diners' Club, MasterCard, and Visa).

They must have an emergency electricity supply for the public areas, medical services, 16-hour a day doorman, and message service. On duty 24-hours a day should be a luggage porter, checkroom service, guest reception, and managers on call. An assistant manager should be in the lobby 18 hours a day.

Available should be a price list, tourist map (English-Chinese), flight and railroad timetables. China Daily and China Tourism News should be on sale (or free).

Four Stars Rooms should be soundproof, luxurious and spacious with low-noise toilet, and have hair dryers available. Guest and service elevators, background music, health club, swimming pool, sauna, business center, greenhouse, 24-hour doorman, reservations accepted through fax/telex, and onward reservations in China for guests. Guest reception and assistant manager in lobby 24 hours. Laundry returned within 24 hours. 24-hour room service. Restaurants should provide two kinds of Chinese food with the last order no earlier than 9:00 p.m. Bar service to 1:00 a.m. 24-hour coffee shop. Breakfast and dinner buffet. Clinic. Business center with photocopying, typing and translation services. Ticketing agency with city tours. Babysitting.

Notes on no-star hotels. These can be very dirty, with no private baths, no English, no heat and no air conditioning. A few might have rats, bedbugs and cockroaches. They might have mosquito nets. Shake out mosquitos before using, and tuck the net under the mattress after you get inside so that none can enter.

Some of these have attendants who snarl at guests, are reluctant to carry luggage, answer bells, or give any type of service. A few might be firetraps with stairways locked or blocked. Few have good bedside reading lamps. One Canadian woman was interrupted at 2 a.m. by the attendant with a male friend who wanted to sell her some souvenirs. But the staff is usually sweet and helpful.

Notes on one- and two-star hotels. These can be acceptable if you are not fussy. The English and service are not very good, but you might be surprised. An attendant can go to the bank for money changing, or take cables to the post office. Most can get plane or theatre tickets, or have someone run out to the street for a taxi. You can frequently borrow adapters (for electric razors), portable electric heaters, fans, hair-dryers, and irons. Some also have in-house television (in Chinese) and you can request special programs.

Most have shower curtains, and one day laundry service, in by 8 a.m. and back by 6 p.m.

The air conditioning and heat might not be adequate. Most have good bedside reading lamps. But the carpets will be stained and badly laid.

Sometimes gates are locked after 11 p.m. While most hotels over three stories have elevators, sometimes these are turned off at night, so if you're dependent on them, ask for the hours of service. In either case, bang and wake someone up.

Western breakfast selections might be limited to greasy fried eggs, orange juice, toast, and coffee. The Chinese breakfast would probably be better.

Attempts to make a reservation by telex or letter might just end up in a pile of unclaimed mail. Few staff, if any, can read English. Just take a chance and show up, or telephone on arrival. Some hotels charge the guest if the hotel has to telex back. This is understandable, considering the cost of telexes and the low room rate.

A few of these hotels might have roaches, but I have never experienced bed bugs. A few might also have smelly and clogged public toilets, and poor plumbing in the rooms.

In some of these hotels, standards might differ according to floors. Foreigners are usually given the best rooms, which might be three-star quality. But the foreigners might want to take something cheaper with no stars.

In areas recently opened to foreigners, local people are not used to western standards of hygiene. Some will spit or stub out cigarettes on carpets. If a room is mostly used by local people, the hotel won't bother to do more than mop up.

Notes on Top Hotels

In many cities and hotels, you should be able to receive television news in English from abroad. essential for keeping up. Many hotels have a video library with relatively recent movies in English. Top hotels like the Shanghai Hilton can do things like hire, clean, and cater a railway car from Shanghai to Suzhou. The Holiday Inn Guilin can cater a boat on the Li River.

Currently, we have found no hotel in China of five-star international standard, though some might be given five stars by the Chinese. Some hotels are very, very close. Lack of fluent English and the inability to anticipate the needs of world-class travelers are the main problems. This should change with time. Poor quality workmanship is another deterrent.

Reservations are usually guaranteed until 6 p.m.; if you give your credit card number, you can arrive later than that. Sheraton will only hold a reservation until 4 p.m. Some reservations can be made through hotel representatives abroad. If they tell you there is no room, you might still get a room by telexing directly to the hotel.

Some hotels have their own fleets of Mercedes limos or Toyota vans that make regular runs to the airport or city center. At least two hotels have Rolls Royces. Some hotels have been inviting guests to cocktail parties once a week, or upgrading frequent guests, or giving the 6th night free. Some have executive floors with concierges, free continental breakfasts, and fast check-in.

Some hotels have non-smoking areas in coffee shops and non-smoking rooms or floors.

Laundry can be so expensive in these hotels that you might want to buy underwear, tee shirts, and dress shirts, inexpensive at free markets and Friendship Stores.

The danger of a luxury hotel, in China as elsewhere, is its great economic disparity with the life of the ordinary citizen. The cost of one night in such a hotel could be the equivalent of at least four months' salary. The extravagance can be seductive, especially in contrast to the drabness and modesty of life outside. Your attitude to China could become like your attitude to Disneyland, whose purpose is to transport and amuse you in a world different from your own. You could become like the lonely Dalai Lama looking at the masses from the Potala in Lhasa through a telescope.

If you went to China to learn about China, you have to make a great effort to do so if you stay in a luxury hotel.

Generally

Beds are usually firm and good. Rooms for standard groups usually have twin-size beds, too small for couples. Some beds are too short and narrow for tall foreigners. Be sure of an extra blanket before the attendant goes off for the night.

Checkout time is usually noon with 50% of the room rate charged if you stay until 6 p.m.

Chinese Customs. While some hotels may look like North American hotels, don't be surprised to find staff sleeping in the lobby, and occasionally on the dining room tables.

Cleanliness. Top joint venture hotels clean and redecorate whenever necessary. Chinese-managed hotels give a lick and a promise and then redecorate every three years or so. In between the first spill of Coca-Cola and the redecoration, one has stained carpets.

Discounts. You should always try for one, especially if occupancy is down. You just might get one. Sample dialogue. "Look, I'll tell all my friends to come here." "I'm booked at another hotel but I heard you were cheaper." "I'm an Overseas Chinese," and "Okay, but how about including breakfast?" "Can I speak with the sales manager, please?"

Giveaways. Chinese hotels of lower stars might just provide Chinese toothbrushes, toothpaste, combs, shower caps, and low-quality soap and slippers. The top hotels probably provide western quality soap, shampoo, conditioner, and body lotion. They might have shoe cleaners, detergent, shoe horns, and better quality slippers (ask before you take them home). Most hotels have tiny sewing kits.

Keys. There are different room key systems. In the lower ranks, you might not get a key at all. An attendant will open and lock your door for you. Sometimes keys are left for guests to pick up on hooks at the attendant's desk on each floor. Sometimes you can pay a refundable deposit and get your own key.

At the other end of the scale, you might get a key card, customized just for you. This you can stick in a door slot to open. You can discard this card after you leave the hotel.

In many hotels, the key comes with a card to put into a wall slot to activate the electricity. If there are two people in a room and one wants to read and then sleep while the other goes bar-hopping and there is only one key, there might be a problem about the lights. Stick a comb or folded paper in the light slot.

Locks. Even some three-star hotels do not have double locks on their guestroom doors. An attendant could barge in on you at any time after just a token knock.

Restaurants. Those in hotels are usually the best in town, especially for western food. Hotel restaurants are usually cleaner too.

Security. Most top hotels have excellent security, the more high-tech the higher you go. You don't usually see anyone but hotel guests and staff on guest room floors. No unregistered guests can stay in rooms after 10 or 11 p.m. (This is not always enforced in poorly managed hotels.) Hotel thefts are rare, especially in the three stars and up range, but don't leave tempting valuables unlocked and in sight. Use the safe deposit boxes. Pilfering by hotel staff is rare but on the increase. Items taken recently have included perfume, a sweater, shoes, a flashlight, cigarettes, and film.

If you are on a lower floor, make sure your windows are locked.

Smoke alarms are usually in every room, sometimes monitored by an attendant. Fire extinguishers should be on every floor, and firehoses on higher floors. And most rooms have fire exit maps in English on their doors. One should always check fire exit signs anyway.

Sports. Hotels on all levels could have bicycles for rent, ping pong, badminton, and billiards. Attendants at swimming pools are not necessarily trained lifeguards, and you should supervise your own children. One should also personally check the cleanliness of a pool. Many of the top hotels have imported fitness equipment. And you can ask about taiji (taichi) groups you can join at 6 a.m. in the parks. Some hotels have aerobics.

State guest houses can be palatial, some villas fit for queens. They are usually in large gardens with lots of privacy. Rooms are frequently big, with high ceilings. The service, service facilities, and maintenance, however, are not as good as the joint-ventures.

Suites. Some of the top hotels have fancy two-story duplexes, or studios (which can be an office by day). Even medium-range hotels might have incredible luxury suites with gold-plated fixtures, antiques, and jacuzzis. Three people traveling together should ask about a suite. They could be less expensive than you think.

Most hotels have theme suites: French, imperial Chinese, rural Chinese, Indian, Japanese, art deco. Some hotels have Chinese rooms for the same price. Ask for them. They're more interesting than the usual U.S. clone.

Surcharges. On the higher levels, even Chinese-managed hotels add a surcharge of 5 to 15%, even on telephone calls and meals. Part of this is municipal tax.

Telephones. In most hotels, there's a telephone in every room. You can make local calls by dialing "0" or "9" and then the number once you get the dial tone. If it is not a dial phone, tell the operator what number you want. To reach an outside line, say "wai xian" (why she-an). To ask for the service desk, where there just might be someone who speaks English, say "fu wu tai" (foo woo tie). Local calls are usually free. To get other rooms in most hotels, just dial the room number unless otherwise notified.

Not all hotels will have IDD capability in every guestroom. You might have to call the operator or go to a desk in the lobby. If there is no IDD, you can still telephone abroad from your room. You might have to book the call at the service desk, and pay a service charge beforehand. Or an attendant might come knocking on your door afterwards. Until IDD is introduced, it might take at least 30 minutes to a couple of days to make a call abroad from an isolated town.

Some hotels might only have one or two IDD lines, in which case you have to keep trying. At top hotels, your calls will be on your bill. There will also be a service charge, even for collect calls not completed. The more expensive the hotel, the higher the service charge, and you might want to ask the rate first.

Tips. Asking for these is forbidden. According to the regulations, any tips received should be passed on by the receiver to the hotel, or to the total staff to share at staff parties, etc. This does not always happen.

Water for drinking. Hot, boiled water is provided in thermoses in all hotels, either automatically, or free on request. Sometimes, there is a flask for cooling, or you can cool it yourself in the cups provided. We strongly suggest you **DO NOT DRINK WATER OUT OF THE TAPS,** not even in the top hotels. One should get in the habit of not drinking tap water in China.

Some hotels have electric kettles that turn themselves off upon boiling. Because this does not give enough time to kill all the bacteria in the water, we urge you not to use non-potable water in these. Many hotels also provide ice cubes, hopefully made of boiled water.

Wheelchairs. We have found very few rooms with wider doors, lower sinks, and bars beside the toilets, for travelers confined to wheelchairs. These are listed at the front of this book and are mainly in expensive hotels. Usually the clothes racks are too high. Most hotels have ramps from the street for luggage, but some of these are too steep. But hotels have lots of willing hands. If they have a companion helping, people in wheelchairs can get around; but they cannot expect the same facilities (like sidewalk ramps) as at home.

Workmanship is generally bad in China. One cannot expect people who have never seen a western hotel to know that paint shouldn't be slopped on top of marble and bare holes left in bathroom floors. But hotels do function in spite of this.

Evaluating hotels is very difficult. You could help us rate them for future editions by telling us about your experiences and using the form in the back of this book. We hope to send around our own examiners, but we need your suggestions too. Future generations of readers will be grateful. Your opinions should filter back to China.

Hotel Chains. Some hotels are owned by chains and some hotels are only managed by them. Still, one can generalize about these chains even though some of their properties are not as good as others.

The top in China are the Hilton, Okura, Peninsula, Shangri-La, and Singapore Mandarin. The Holiday Inn Crowne Plaza, Hyatt, Sara, and Westin are also near the top. The Dynasty, Holiday Inn, Lee Gardens, New World, Nikko, New Otani, Ramada, and Sheraton are very good and dependable, with excellent services. Macau CTS hotels are less luxurious but good.

The Equatorial looks good, but we have found management problems.

Novotel is in the moderate price range, good but not luxurious. Chains and Vista International are also moderately priced and good, but we have found dirty carpets and grubby walls.

Of the Chinese-managed groups, the Jin Jiang runs the range from the pretentious Jin Jiang Tower (Shanghai) and the very good Kunlun (Beijing) down to the dumpy, roach-infested Overseas Chinese Hotel (Shanghai). The China Friendship Tourist Hotel Group also ranges from one or two good properties down to poor ones. The C.T.S. Hotel Corporation owns the high-ranking Holiday Inn Lido, as well as the disreputable Shuixiu in Wuxi.

FOOD

BACKGROUND

The infinite number of Chinese dishes, flavors, textures, and methods of cooking makes eating Chinese food especially exciting. The most famous cooking styles are Beijing, Cantonese, Shanghai, and Sichuan, but others also exist, including vegetarian.

Chinese food is usually chopped up in thin, bite-size pieces, making knives unnecessary at the dinner table. The thinness is deliberate for quick cooking, using a minimum of fuel. Chinese food can also appear whole, like fish or pork hocks, but these are cooked so they can be easily separated by chopsticks. When poultry is cooked whole, it is chopped up before appearing at the table. Sometimes the bones are splintered, so be careful. This is done purposely so the food inside the bones can be reached.

Chinese ingredients reflect the many periods of famine in Chinese history. Everything possible is eaten; nothing is wasted, not even chicken feet, duck tongues, jellyfish, and sea slugs—all of these famous delicacies.

The Chinese food served to most prepaid groups is usually adequate. It is not the best, but it is usually tasty and filling. If you want to eat better, you have to pay more for specialty restaurants. If food is most important to you, take a gourmet tour.

THINGS TO REMEMBER
ABOUT RESTAURANTS IN CHINA

Restaurants until recently were generally dumpy and tacky, a reflection of revolutionary attitudes. The new economic policies have given China many new or renovated eating places, some very striking joint ventures in the gaudy Hong Kong style, and even a branch of Maxim's de Paris. International-class hotels can import ingredients and executive chefs. Some families and factories have also started restaurants, competing with much better food and service than state-run establishments. The current make-a-profit-or-quit policy has forced improvements everywhere. At the same time, provincial and city-state tourism administrations are now also regulating restaurants. They should have a list of restaurants deemed fit for foreign tourists and should you have a complaint, contact the local tourism administration. Each restaurant should have a plaque that says it's been approved. All of these mean good eating is possible for everyone, especially in the big cities.

Many foreigners will automatically be put into **private dining rooms** in restaurants. These are less colorful and cleaner than eating with the masses, and usually cost a bit more. Sometimes these rooms have to be paid for in F.E.C.s. However, you won't be stared at, can make a reservation, and can enjoy a meal free of smoke, unless your party creates its own.

Many state-run restaurants receive guests until 6 p.m. and then rush them out at 8:30 or 9 p.m. so the staff can go home. If you want to linger, choose a privately owned restaurant or coffee shop in a hotel.

Ordering   Menus in hotels and restaurants for foreign visitors are usually in English and Chinese. Many restaurants have a menu in English, too, so ask for one if you don't get it. Every hotel restaurant has an **a la carte menu** where you choose individual dishes. Some restaurants have a **fixed menu** too. You don't usually get to see the fixed menu. You have to ask about it. The fixed menu is served to prepaid tour groups, who do not need to worry about ordering. Individuals can order this, too, and it is the easy way out.

Food on the fixed menu is relatively inexpensive and you get more variety for one or two people. Just say *feng fan* or *bao chan*.

In one hotel, lunch for one, *feng fan*, was steamed meatballs, curry chicken, spicy hot beef, greens and mushrooms, two steamed buns with sweetened black bean filling, egg custard cubes and tomatoes, clear soup with bits of meat and vegetables, white rice, and fresh watermelon. Of this I could only eat one third. While this was the most luxurious of the *feng fan* meals I had, most of the others were varied and filling. Menus change every day.

Gourmets avoid fixed menus because the food is not always freshly cooked. Gourmets also avoid **Chinese food buffets** for the same reason. But buffets, with their large number of different dishes, are good introductions to new foods. If you like something, you can ask the name, and order that dish again.

Every restaurant has its **specialties**—dishes the chefs are especially good at. So ask about these too. They will probably be a little more expensive than most on the menu but are usually worth it. Aim also for **local or regional dishes**—fresh seafoods if you're near an ocean. Seafood reaches Beijing frozen, so try for something else there. Meals in the countryside are usually excellent because the vegetables come right from the garden to the wok.

It is best to eat with a large group of people to get a greater number of different courses. Ten is ideal for a table, and you may even get a private room thrown in. When ordering, choose one poultry, one pork, one beef, one fish, one vegetable dish, one soup, and so on. Calculate one course for each person, then rice, noodles, or buns, and one more course. For example, two people should order three courses plus a starch; five people should order six courses plus a starch or two. This will give you variety and abundance. If you find you are getting too much, order less next time.

If you need more courses, start the rounds again. If you've already chosen chicken, then choose duck or goose. If you've ordered fish, then take shrimp or cuttle fish. Vary the tastes and textures: sweet, pepper-hot, salty, steamed, deep-fried, poached or boiled, roasted, baked in mud—the choice is endless.

Don't feel that every meal should be a banquet. The danger in China is overeating.

For popular restaurants, it is always best to reserve a table and even order meals ahead of time by telephone, especially for **banquets.** Restaurants for the masses won't take reservations. Ask the service desk at your hotel to make reservations for you, telling the restaurant how much you want to pay **but also approving the dishes** suggested. One restaurant suggested bears' paws, a local delicacy and an endangered species, which no one ate. Most of the cost went into that one dish!

Elaborate banquet dishes should be ordered at least 24 hours ahead of time, and a hefty charge is levied if you cancel.

Don't look for **chop suey or chow mein** with crispy noodles, or fortune cookies—those are American dishes. China has fried noodles, but they are not the same as in the United States. But then again, with the new economic policies, anything could show up!

Please be aware that some wild animals used by the Chinese as food are, or may soon be, on the **endangered species** list. Please avoid them. Tell your host in advance that you don't want them and why. See "Local Customs."

Careful travelers have found that many restaurants make "mistakes" in calculating the bill (in favor of the restaurant). We suggest you write down all you ordered with prices and check this against the tab later. Corrections are usually made cheerfully. Sometimes menu prices are quoted in F.E.C. but because of a large local clientele, are translated to R.M.B. on bills. Check out this possibility before calling the manager.

Special diets: If you do have special food preferences, let your guide know.

If you have an upset stomach, order rice congee, which is rice cooked to a gruel consistency and flavored with salted egg, fermented bean curd, or whatever. Congee is easy on the stomach. Avoid fried dishes, spices, and dairy products. Eat dry crackers, arrowroot biscuits, and apple sauce.

If you have cankers in the mouth, try *hung pean* (chrysanthemum

HOW TO USE CHOPSTICKS

The bottom stick is held firmly by the base of the thumb and the knuckle of the ring finger. The top stick is the ONLY one that is moved and is held by the thumb and the index and middle fingers. The tip of the top stick should be brought toward the tip of the bottom one. Keep the tips even.

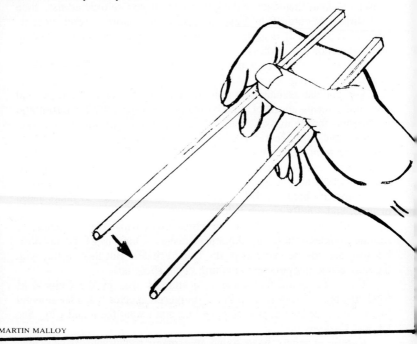

MARTIN MALLOY

tea). It comes already sweetened with sugar in one-cup packages at Friendship Stores and is an old Chinese remedy.

People on general-interest tours should not expect special diets. Salt-free and diabetic diets are impossible then. Chinese cooking uses more salt than Western cooking. You could, however, go on a tour organized especially for people with the same restrictions. Vegetarians usually manage on a general tour if they don't mind meat sauces. Vegetarian restaurants exist, but these are not on the daily tourist route. Moslem restaurants also exist. So far, we haven't found any kosher restaurants.

Desserts Foreign Friends will be offered Western-style sweet pastries and fresh or canned fruits. If you're in Guangdong in May or June, ask for fresh lichees—or buy them in markets. Look for pomelo, especially in Guilin or in Sichuan in season. It's a sweet grapefruit with a thick rind. Try Hami melon on the Silk Road. China also has ice cream, sweet red beans, sweet almond paste, and deep-fried crystallized apples and bananas. Aside from fruit, the Chinese do not have much of a tradition for desserts. You might want to try a coffee shop in one of the fancy hotels afterward.

Beverages Most prepaid meals for Foreign Friends include Chinese soft drinks, beer, and tea. Canned fruit juice, foreign-brand soft drinks, and liquor cost extra. Overseas Chinese pay extra for all drinks except for tea. Coca-Cola and Pepsi have bottling plants in China. The dreaded orange soda is being replaced in some cities by good, fresh or reconstituted juices.

Tea drinking is an art in China. Some springs are famous for their tea-making qualities. If you go to Hangzhou, try *long jing* tea there. A favorite tea in hot weather is *po li*. *Keemun* is good in the wintertime and when you've had greasy food. *Lu an* should help you sleep. *Oolong* is the most common tea in south China, while most foreigners like *jasmine*, the sweet-scented tea with bits of jasmine flower petals in it. Jasmine is said to heat the blood and should be balanced at the same meal with *po li*.

Every Chinese has a personal list of the four most famous green teas. *Long jing* (dragon well), *yun wu* (mist of the clouds), *mao hong* (red straw), and *bi lu chuen* (green spring) are probably among the most popular.

Dairies are beginning to open up, but in most places only UHT or canned **milk** is available. A shortage of refrigerator trucks hampers the distribution of fresh milk.

The Chinese consider the best **liquors** to be: *Mao tai*, made from sorghum and wheat yeast, and aged five or six years in Guizhou province. It is very potent and usually served in tiny goblets; *Fenjiu*, mellow and delicate flavor from Shanxi province; *Wuliangye*, five-grain spirit from southern Sichuan, with a fragrant and invigorating flavor.

The best Chinese-style **wines** are: *Yantai red wine* from Shandong, *Chinese red wine* from Beijing, *Shaoxing red wine* from Zhejiang, and *Longyan rice wine* from Fujian. If you get to any of the above places and have to bring a gift back for a Chinese friend, a bottle would be appropriate. Knowledgeable foreigners recommend Chinese-made Dragon seal wines.

Qingdao **beer** is the favorite. It is made from barley, spring water, and hops from a German recipe. Five Star Beer has been designated by the government for state banquets. Foreign beers are increasingly available. Laoshan is the most famous **mineral water.** In Moslem restaurants, take your own bottle, as alcohol is not served.

Breakfasts Foreign tour groups in two-star hotels are usually given Western breakfasts with greasy eggs. You also usually get lightly toasted bread, coffee, and fruit or canned juice. Three-star hotels now have good Western breakfast buffets.

You can opt for Chinese breakfasts if enough people in the group want them. Chinese breakfasts differ regionally: *dim sum* or rice congee with peanuts, pickles, and salted or 1000-year-old eggs in south China. In the north, you could get lots of different buns, or "oil sticks," which are like foot-long doughnuts, deep-fried and delicious but hard to digest. You dip these in hot soy milk. In Shanghai you might get gelatinous rice balls with sugar inside, or baked buns with sweet bean paste inside. They are great.

Western food is now advertised in most tourist hotels, but I have rarely found it as good as Chinese. Bread is cut thick and is usually white. Sometimes "Western" food is one Chinese meat-and-vegetable course with bread instead of rice. Excellent Western food is more consistently available in four-star and up joint venture hotels, and some restaurants. Some of these hotels also have delicatessens where you can buy cold cuts like salami and pastrami. Some restaurants in Northeast China have Russian food.

Local Chinese seem to prefer Chinese food and have rejected invitations to Western meals "because of too much meat." It could also be because of lack of familiarity with knives, forks, and Western table manners.

Courtesies Group tours in particular should be punctual at meals as the food is usually ready on time, and in family style all dishes may even be sitting at the table getting (ugh!) cold.

Guests of honor are traditionally given seats where they face the door. You might have fun speculating on the reason. Left-handed people have a problem and should sit where clashes with right-handed chopsticks can be avoided.

In many restaurants, damp hot or cold towels are distributed at the beginning of meals to refresh guests as well as to clean. One can wipe faces and backs of necks, as well as hands with them. Sometimes towels are distributed during the meal, too, and always at the end.

If tea or bowls or calling cards are to be passed, to be polite, use both hands and bow.

Chinese food is usually served on large platters, which ideally arrive one at a time. The food comes hot off the wok at the peak of its perfection and should be eaten immediately. Time is allowed before the next course arrives steaming, to take what is desired of the current dish.

In families, diners pick what they want with chopsticks, and should be careful not to spread their germs to food left on the platter. Chopsticks are great for reaching across tables, keeping fingers clean, and hitting naughty children. Outside of families, spoons should be used for serving, and if no convenient "lazy Susan" exists, then the platters on the table are relocated from time to time so that all can reach. Don't be shy about asking for serving spoons.

To begin eating after guests express admiration for the beauty of the food, Chinese hosts put the best morsels on the plates of the people around them. You could do this, too, after the first round if you want. Since you put your own chopsticks into your mouth, you could use the clean other end of your chopsticks for serving. The host usually invites guests to start eating. Or groups of friends could declare a moratorium on such formalities and have everybody dig in. *Hei fai* means "Raise chopsticks!"

Do not be embarrassed about slurping or even burping. This indicates that you are enjoying your meal. If you don't have enough room on your dish for bones and other discards, just leave them neatly on the table itself. Less-polished Chinese will spit them on the floor!

Good restaurants do not make their guests stand up and serve their own beverages. Getting your own rice from a big pot away from your table is only expected in families or very informal restaurants.

In very fancy restaurants, an attendant distributes every course and guests do not help themselves. Individual plates are removed and replaced with clean ones after most courses. The host usually invites guests to start eating.

Giving a banquet is the accepted and most important way to return hospitality or to show gratitude for a favor. If your guide persists in refusing your invitation to eat with you, he may relent and join you the day before you leave as a farewell gesture.

You may want to throw a banquet for some of your Chinese colleagues and people who have been particularly helpful. Discuss your guest list with one of the Chinese involved so you won't offend anybody important by leaving them out. If your guide is invited, be sure he knows. Discuss spouses and times and seating arrangements, but don't be offended if spouses don't show up. The venue is important because some restaurants are more prestigious than others.

Toasting Chinese people do not like to drink alone. Toasting at banquets is a complicated art, and you are not expected to know the finer points. Just do what you do at home. Stand up, give one or two sentences, make sure everybody else is joining you, and drink. *Gan bei!* means "Empty your glass!"

The first toaster is usually the host, who gets the ball rolling. A frequent toast is to the friendship of the people of your country and China, and the health of friends and comrades present. The next toaster can tell a funny story and then, perhaps, talk about your sadness about leaving China and the new friends you have made, or wishes that you will all meet again in your country.

Toasts might continue all evening, and so might the meal, or at least until the restaurant turns out the lights. If the banquet is extremely large, the host might circulate to all the tables, drinking toasts at each one. On smaller, less formal occasions, the Chinese may want to drink you under the table. Be alert; they may be putting tea in their own glasses. You may want to try that yourself after awhile.

I have been to banquets where I haven't touched a drop of liquor. I can't get *mao tai* past my nose—it's so strong. Chinese hosts are not usually offended, especially if you toast with tea or soft drinks. If you don't want to drink so much liquor, try to divert your fellow diners. Try exchanging songs—but not drinking songs or games. It may be the only occasion when you'll hear the national anthem of China. You could also turn your cup or glass upside down to signal to the waiter that you've had enough.

If you want to stop eating and your host keeps piling food onto your plate, just lay down your chopsticks. Thank him politely but don't eat anymore. They shouldn't feel offended.

Recently, as an austerity measure, the lavishness of top-level state banquets was curtailed officially to four courses and a soup, and one and a half hours. This might be the beginning of a trend, but then again, it might not be. Banquets are part of the culture.

Eating with the People

You can eat quite well for comparatively little money if you're willing to try food stalls and restaurants and sections of restaurants for the masses. The standard of cleanliness and speed of service, however, are not generally as high as in hotels and restaurants for tourists. The cigarette smoke may be suffocating. It is customary to share tables with other diners in busy restaurants.

Payment is made when you order (so you can't stomp out impatiently). Some finicky eaters take their own chopsticks and spoons to places like this, but as far as I can see the dishes are scalded, and if the food is freshly cooked, there should be no problems. The soup sterilizes the utensils (you hope), but you can also scald them yourself with tea. Usually a spittoon waits nearby for the discarded tea. We highly recommend James D. McCauley's *The Eater's Guide to Chinese Characters* if you are eating off the tourist track.

Dumpling and noodle shops are better for speed (if the lineup isn't too long). The food can be good too. Foreigners are frequently pushed to the head of the line. A knowledge of Chinese isn't necessary because you can point.

Fast food stalls, mobile canteens, and cafeterias are recent innovations and are multiplying quickly. Some serve instant noodles.

Outdoor night markets are a new, adventurous attraction for gourmet as well as budget foreigners. Just make sure the food is steaming hot and utensils scalded.

Food Streets first started in Hong Kong, but are also proliferating in China. They seem to be run by hotels so are cleaner and more foreigner-oriented than other restaurants. The food is usually light and prices are reasonable: noodles, fried rice, side orders of barbecued duck, cuttle-fish, etc. We paid in R.M.B.

At **restaurants for the masses,** it is best to take a Chinese friend who can help you order and possibly get you cheaper rates. You can also use the ''Useful Phrases'' or the *Regional and Special Dishes* below if no menu in English appears.

To eat:
—*mantou,* the plain steamed roll, either take bites off while holding with chopsticks or fingers, or break apart and stuff pieces with bits of meat. You can also dip it in the sauces. *Jiao zi* are the small stuffed ravioli-like pastries in soup; *bao zi* are steamed dumplings and may have beans, or meat and vegetables inside. The names get confusing.

—*white rice,* which is served in bowls, put the bowl up to your mouth and shove the rice in with chopsticks. More genteel people might want to pick up chunks with chopsticks;

—*1000-year-old eggs,* you usually have to either acquire a taste or close your eyes and think of something else; they are best eaten with pickles and are delicious;

—*shrimps with shells left on,* take a bite of half, then, with your teeth and chopsticks, squeeze out the meat. You may want to use your fingers to shell them. Cooking shrimps with their shells retains most of the yummy flavor;

—*two- and three-foot-long noodles,* lean over your bowl and pick up a few with chopsticks. Put the noodles in your mouth, biting off pieces and leaving the rest temporarily in your bowl. Don't worry about slurping. The Chinese like long noodles because they symbolize longevity;

—*ice cream,* ask for a spoon.

To avoid an upset stomach and intestinal parasites, do not drink water out of faucets. Steer clear of ice, popsicles, ice cream (except in tourist restaurants), watermelon, and any other fruit with lots of ground water. Don't eat anything raw unless imported, or carefully washed and then peeled. Animal and human manure is used in China as fertilizer. Local people develop immunities. Most bottled drinks are fine.

Be careful on ferries and small boats. Dishes are frequently washed in river water and not always scalded carefully afterward. Some people take disinfectants like tincture of iodine. Two drops in a liter of water kill all germs in contact with them in 20 minutes. When cooking your own food as in Mongolian Hot Pot, be careful that the utensils you use on raw meat or fish are not the same utensils you put into your own mouth. Just sterilize your own utensils in the hot pot.

Other tips The secret of eating a Chinese meal is finding out first how many courses you will be getting. Banquet meals usually have a copy of the menu on the table. If there are 12 courses, take no more than one-twelfth of what you would usually eat in a meal from each plate; otherwise, you will be too full to eat any of the later dishes. Also take your time. You can't rush through a big meal. Some famous banquets have taken days.

Fish is usually the last formal course in some places. If you happen to be eating with superstitious fishermen, don't turn a fish over to get at flesh on the other side. It means their boat will turn over!

Do not worry about "Chinese restaurant syndrome." Its symptoms are an increased pulse and a tight feeling around the sinuses. This "syndrome" is a result of the large amount of monosodium glutamate put in Chinese food in America. Cooks in China use a little, but not so much. You can ask them to leave out MSG or salt or chilis or anything.

Among the beauties of a Chinese meal is the variety. If you don't like one thing, you might like something else.

On prepaid tours, you might want to talk with your escort about the overabundance of food when meat for the common man is so limited—if, indeed, this bothers you.

To best enjoy a meal, never ask what a particular morsel is.

Even-numbered days are more auspicious than odd-numbered days. Restaurants may be busier with wedding parties then.

Menus in English are by translators, not public relations people. Some dishes may sound absolutely terrible, but are really very good. Don't let a name like "frog oil soup" throw you.

Preserved fruit is delicious, but do not eat too many at a sitting as they are full of preservatives.

Another new development are the **health restaurants,** with dishes made from Chinese herbal medicines. I've found them in Chengdu and Beijing, but if you look, they should be in other cities too. Lots of ginseng, sea horses, deer antlers, and things best left unmentioned. Some foods to combat high blood pressure; other foods good for pregnant women. These are indeed for the adventurous eater because of their unusual flavors, and they can be very delicious.

If you are invited to a restaurant by nonofficial Chinese friends, don't be surprised if they ask to buy F.E.C.s from you. Most of the top restaurants are paid in foreign exchange.

If you invite average Chinese people to dinner, be sensitive that a meal in a tourist restaurant is a real treat. Normally, they cannot afford it. Since they get little meat, do order more for them. Do encourage them to take the leftovers home. They may be too polite to ask.

See also "Useful Phrases" and "Destinations." For some prices, see "Budget."

SOME REGIONAL AND
SPECIAL DISHES ....

Beijing (a.k.a. Peking or Northern) Dishes 北京

Light, with few sauces; roasts; lots of garlic, leeks, and scallions; flour-made buns, rolls and meat dumplings, baked, steamed, fried, or boiled in soup. Salty.

Smoked chicken/duck	熏鸡／鸭
Crispy duck	香酥鸭
Peking duck	北京烤鸭
Sweet-sour fish/pork	糖醋鱼／肉
Deep-fried shrimp toast	炸虾托
Chicken and cucumber salad	凉拌三丝
Stir-fried pork with bean sprouts (served with pancakes)	京酱肉丝
Chinese cabbage with black mushrooms	冬菇白菜
Pan-fried onion cake	葱油饼
Hot and sour soup	酸辣汤
Pan-fried dumplings with minced pork	生煎小包子
Steamed bread rolls	银丝卷
Assorted meat soup in casserole	什锦砂锅
Shrimp with popped rice	虾仁锅巴
Apple/Banana Fritter	拨丝苹果／香蕉

Cantonese (a.k.a. Guangdong or Southern) Dishes 粤菜

Quickly cooked in peanut oil; crisp vegetables; somewhat sweet; starches in the sauces. Uses a lot of oyster sauce or fish sauce in cooking or poured over boiled vegetables. Many dishes are steamed to preserve natural flavors. Really exotic banquet dishes are dog, monkey, and snake. Please, no pangolin and other endangered species!

Crisp-skinned roasted goose/pork	烧鹅／烤乳猪
Steamed chicken with green onion	葱油鸡
Cha-shiu (barbecued) pork	叉烧
Stir-fried diced fish/filet	松子鱼／炒鱼片
Shark's fin in chicken and ham soup	鱼翅羹
Steamed live fish	清蒸鱼
Quick-boiled fresh shrimp	白灼虾
Stir-fried beef in oyster sauce	蚝油牛肉
Cantonese stuffed bean curd	酿豆腐
Sauteed fresh Chinese vegetable	炒新鲜蔬菜
Assorted meats in winter melon	冬瓜盅
Bird's nest in coconut milk	椰奶燕窝羹

Dim Sum 点心

These small fried or steamed pastries are for breakfast or lunch and sometimes ordered from a menu (classier), or chosen from a trolley brought to your table. You can ask the trolley attendant to take off any cover to see inside if you want. Your bill is usually calculated from the number of baskets or plates on your table.

The variety of dim sum has been more extensive in Hong Kong than in China except at the famous Panxi Restaurant in Guangzhou. Chicken feet, known as Phoenix feet, are delicious! Honest!

Har gau: smoothly wrapped shrimp dumpling	虾饺
Shui mai: minced pork and shrimp dumpling	烧卖
Cha shiu bau: barbecued pork buns	叉烧包
Tsun guen: deep-fried spring roll with pork, mushrooms, chicken, bamboo shoots, and bean sprouts	春卷
Ho yip fan: steamed fried rice wrapped in lotus leaf	荷叶饭
Pai gwat: steamed pork spareribs	排骨
Gai chuk: steamed chicken in bean curd wrapping	腐竹包鸡
Daan tart: egg custard tart	蛋挞

Fujian Dishes 福建菜

Lots of seafood and light soups, suckling pig, and nonfat spring rolls. You may recognize Filipino dishes like *lumpia* and *lechon*, originally from this province.

Five spices roll	五香卷
Fried fish slices	炒鱼片
Fried pig's kidneys	炒腰片
Spareribs in sweet-sour sauce	糖醋排骨
Fish with Brown Sauce	红烧全鱼
Fried straw mushrooms with pork	草菇肉片
Fried shrimps in sweet-sour sauce	糖醋虾
Fried razor clams in sweet-sour sauce	糖醋鲜蚌

Shaanxi Dishes 杭州菜

(From the Dongya Restaurant in **Xi'an**)	
Assorted cold dishes in the shape of a phoenix	凤凰拼饼
Four small cold dishes	四围碟
Sea cucumber in the shape and color of hibiscus	芙蓉海参
Crisp fried duck	香酥鸭
Mushrooms with the Three Delicacies	口蘑三样
Fried fillet of chicken	炸鸡排
Shark's fins with three kinds of slices (pork, bamboo shoots, and chicken)	三丝鱼翅
Fried fish shaped like grapes	鸡丝拉皮
Steamed carp	清蒸鲤鱼
White fungus with pineapple	菠萝银耳
Cakes and pastries	点 心
	冰 淇 淋

Shandong Dishes 山东菜

Abalone with green vegetables on shell	鲍鱼青菜
Fresh scallops with shell	鲜带壳干贝
Roast prawns	烤大虾
Conch with fire	火螺
Steamed sea bream	馒头
Sweet and sour croaker	酸甜黄花鱼
Three Delicacies Soup	三鲜汤
Toffee Apples	拔丝苹果

Shanghai Dishes 沪菜

From central China; Suzhou, Yangzhou, Wuxi, etc. foods are variations. Longer cooking in sesame oil, neither sweet nor salty. Can be very ornamental. Borscht is on the menu of most of Shanghai's restaurants because of all the White Russians who once lived in Shanghai.

Smoked fish	熏鱼
Deep-fried shrimp balls	炸虾球
Vegetarian vegetables	素什锦
Sauteed fresh bamboo shoots	红烧冬笋
West Lake fish	西湖醋鱼
Chicken with cashew nuts	西湖醋鱼
Scallops with turnip balls	干贝萝卜球
Won-ton (dumplings) in soup	虾仁馄饨
Beggar's chicken	叫化鸡
Sauteed egg plant	红烧茄子
Lion's head casserole	红烧狮子头
Sweet sesame dumplings	芝麻汤园

Sichuan (Szechuan) Dishes　川菜

Some dishes are highly spiced, peppery hot, and oily. Formal banquet cooking is more bland.

Smoked duck with camphor and tea flavor (not spicy hot)	樟茶鸭
Stir-fried chicken with hot pepper	宫爆鸡丁
Spicy stir-fried prawns	干烧明虾
Stir-fried shrimp with peas	碗豆炒虾仁
Stir-fried squid with/without hot pepper	金钧鱿鱼
Bon-bon chicken	棒棒鸡
Dry-fried string beans	干煸四季豆
Steamed spareribs (or pork) coated with rice powder	粉蒸排骨
Steamed fish with fermented black beans	豆豉鱼
Mo-po bean curd	麻婆豆腐

Suzhou Dishes　京菜

Sauteed shrimp meat	清炒虾仁
Squirrel Mandarin fish	松鼠桂鱼
Stewed turtle	清蒸元鱼
Stir-fried eel	生炒鳝贝
Fried crisp duck	香酥肥鸭
Water-shield soup with floating Mandarin duck	鸳鸯莼菜汤
Snow-white crab in shell	白雪蟹斗
Pickled duck	苏州酱鸭

Vegetarian cooking has had a long tradition in China and was first documented 2000 years ago. It developed with Buddhism, which forbids its adherents from killing animals, and restaurants are frequently found near Buddhist temples. Distinctively Chinese are dishes that imitate meat in taste, texture, and looks. While this does not encourage reverence for life as taught by Buddha, it does make it easier for some Buddhists to become vegetarian.

The following are some suggested dishes from the Ju Shi Lih Restaurant near the Lama Temple in Beijing and should give you an idea of what is available. Sorry, no calligraphy available yet.

Hors d'oeuvres
Water chestnuts and bean curd
Mushrooms and bamboo shoots
Shrimps (actually carrots, cucumber, bamboo
shoots, mushrooms, radish)
Black and white fungi
Sea crab (actually potato, radish, mushroom,
bamboo shoots)
Roast duck (actually bean curd)
Sweet and sour pork (actually locust seed)
Fish ball soup (tomato and celery)

GETTING AROUND

If you have someone taking care of all the logistics, read this only for reference in case your guide doesn't show up. The following is how things were at press time. Since then, the Chinese have probably made improvements.

NOTE: · · · A cancellation fee is always charged when you make changes in travel arrangements.

It is always best, no matter where and how you go, to have your destination written in Chinese so you can ask for directions. At least carry the name of your hotel in Chinese in case you stray from your tour group.

Always carry a wad of toilet tissue with you.

If you are traveling overnight by hard-class train, or by ferry (not a luxury tourist ship), take your own mug, soap, chopsticks, and towel.

The low tourist season is mid-November to mid-March, at which time many hotel prices are discounted and life is easier for individual travelers. But individual travelers should still expect difficulties, such as missing trains because you can't find the right platform. Few, if any, signs exist in English.

Formalities With your visa, you are allowed to go to any of a wide range of cities and counties in China without further formalities. You may have to get an **alien travel permit** to go to other places even if just traveling by road between open cities. You can only go to Lhasa if you have a prepaid tour. Ask a travel agent in China especially if you are going off the main tourist road. But some provinces have no restrictions; among these are Fujian, Guangdong, and Shandong. Jilin is 99% open, and Liaoning is almost all open.

Foreign travelers who have inadvertently (or deliberately) wandered into a restricted area have been detained by the police, sometimes questioned most impolitely, and put on the next bus out. You might be put in jail and deported. Or nothing might happen. It is a matter of who you are, enforcement, and being caught. Read *Xanadu, A Quest*.

Getting visas and visa extensions: If your visa has expired, you will probably be detained when you try to leave the country. Visa extensions can be acquired from the Foreign Affairs Department of the Security Police in one or two days. Be sure you take your passport and a few *yuan*.

Information For information before you leave home, see "Before You Go." You can also contact any China National Tourist Office in North America, Europe, or Australia for brochures and maps, or write directly to the provincial or city Tourism Administration in China. You can also get a wide range of literature from bookstores like China Books and Periodicals.

After arriving in China, please note that China has been producing a large number of maps, guidebooks in English, and a twice-a-month tourism newspaper. The Cartographic Department maps are very helpful as they include maps of important tourist attractions in many cities. Jinan's, for example, also shows Taishan Mountain and Qufu (with diagrams of the Confucian Family Mansion and Confucian temple). These maps list major hotels, tourist attractions, restaurants, stores, and important telephone numbers. The China City Guides series is excellent for background. Like the maps, one exists for most major cities. They are inexpensive and worth buying if you want to wander around on your own. Some cities also have public transportation maps. The China Travel & Tourism Press has a lot of good information in English.

Many tourist attractions now have relatively inexpensive, knowledgeable **on-site guides** paid by the hour. A few of the important tourist spots have English-speaking guides, but most speak only Chinese. Some tourist attractions also have freelance guides, who may know very little about the site and speak poor English. Test them and decide on a fair price beforehand if you want to hire them. (Try ¥5 an hour first.) You could also eavesdrop on someone else's English-speaking guide.

Diplomatic missions are not travel agencies, but some of them have libraries with books about China. The U.S. consulates have current travel advisories with up-to-date information on health problems, natural disasters, shortages of hotel rooms, and civil disturbances. Consulates should also have important addresses like those of doctors and pharmacies.

Fellow travelers are great. Most love to share their experiences. (Few people at home really care about the little important details.) You can find them on trains, in airport waiting rooms, in hotel elevators, at tourist attractions. They will tell you what they found worthwhile to visit and what was not. Don't be shy about asking.

Foreign residents are also great. Diplomats don't have much time for tourists except for emergencies and unforeseen circumstances, but you could try them. But foreign students and experts frequently meet in good (but cheap) hotels for support. Try the Hangzhou Hotel (Hangzhou) coffee shop or the Jinling Hotel (Nanjing) some evenings. They may look down on tourists, but if you invite them to dinner they should be able to give you a lot of good tips, such as where you can buy Jordache jeans for ¥25.

Hotels, if they are three stars and up, are usually very helpful. Try assistant managers, corcierges, or public relations. Some hotels organize their own tours. Hotel telephone operators and business centers in good hotels can usually find telephone numbers.

National, provincial and city tourism administrations
The National Tourism Administration is the body directly under the State Council responsible for the study, promotion, coordination, and supervision of tourism in China. It has information offices in Frankfurt, London, New York, Los Angeles, Paris, Sydney, and Tokyo.

National policies get handed down to provincial and city (i.e., Beijing, Shanghai and Tianjin) tourism administrations to handle. So if you want information about tourism in Jiangsu province, for example, you ask the Jiangsu Tourism Administration.

Tourism administrations regulate tourism in their areas, the pricing and quality of hotels, restaurants, travel agencies, taxis, stores, etc., approved for foreign tourists, and the behavior of tour guides. It is to these provincial and city tourism administrations that you can address complaints about the services of establishments approved for foreign tourists. They have the power to punish or take away licenses of these establishments or tour guides if they violate regulations. This authority is a recent development of the late 1980s and may not work perfectly everywhere. But do be aware they can help you. Each one should have a promotion department with English-speaking staff.

Provincial Overseas Tourism Corporations, Beijing head offices of C.I.T.S., CYTS, and C.T.S., etc., and a few others are the only agencies permitted to sell China tours abroad.

Travel agencies
should make traveling easier, but not all services are cheap or available. Commissions are usually added to the ticket price. You will find travel agencies in many hotels better than the government travel agency for English speaking. PARA, the main government travel agency for English-speaking foreigners, is China International Travel Service. China Travel Service, along with CYTS and China International Sports Travel, are also government agencies. Other agencies are frequently arms of government departments. They are all government-regulated and are probably honest, though not necessarily efficient or helpful. Prices are not always the same. They each have different connections and they try to underprice each other. They should be able to meet you at airports, buy travel tickets for you, reserve hotel rooms

and sightseeing tours, confirm flights, obtain travel permits, etc. They should be able to find guide-interpreters and also book individual travelers on mini-packages and group tours. Tour prices for one or two people are high, but some travelers have found that going 2 or 3 to a taxi is cheaper than taking city tours. Prices should go down if you wait and more people join your group tour. Ask also about "Join-In Tours."

Ticket-buyers should always double-check the number of tickets you are buying, and times and dates. The efficiency of any ticket seller or travel agency depends on its individual representatives. Some clerks have also been rude, especially when harassed and tired; others have been pleasant and polite.

For group tours, in the event arrangements are cancelled, C.I.T.S. has made substitutions, rather than refunds. For example, when CAAC cancelled a flight and passengers had to go by train instead, it made up the difference with another day's sightseeing and meals. In one case, where a national guide could not be provided, group members were given beautiful tablecloths instead. One group discovered that a day's delay in arriving in China meant one less day in Beijing. A change of flight time cut another half day off its stay in Xi'an and added a day in less interesting Chongqing.

We have had no significant feedback yet as to the quality of service of travel agencies other than the ones named in this section. They have smaller staffs and fewer branches, but they might try harder. We do know that some agencies are better at getting plane tickets, while others are better at getting train tickets.

Quality of service is uneven. Top guides as well as duds are in every agency. Branches in one city might be excellent but terrible in another. Agencies compete with each other, steering you toward their own hotels and tours. **China International Travel Service (C.I.T.S.),** in Chinese popularly known as Guo Li, is the largest and most experienced travel agent for foreigners. It has 149 branches and a staff of over 10,000, of whom 4000 are guides. Its standard of English is the best. It usually has an office in or near every tourist center. In a few small cities, notably in Guangdong and Fujian provinces, it is represented by China Travel Service.

For more information on C.I.T.S., see "The Basics," "Before You Go," and "Getting There."

China Travel Service (C.T.S.), popularly known as Zhong Li, has over 300 branches, 18 subsidiaries, over 33,000 staff members, and 109 hotels. It handles more visitors than C.I.T.S. Most of its clients, however, know Chinese and can manage largely on their own. It handles mainly Taiwanese, Hong Kong, and other Overseas Chinese visitors. Its tours also take Foreign Friends.

C.T.S. can do all the things C.I.T.S. does for travelers. It can also arrange permission and transportation to one's ancestral village and ship gifts to relatives. It can help you locate long-lost relatives. It does have fewer English-speaking guides than C.I.T.S. It does not appear to be as efficient as C.I.T.S. with individual arrangements.

CYTS's main task is to receive groups of young people, but it also takes care of older people. It has a total of 50 branches with over 1000 guides, and is represented in every province. Tour prices are a little cheaper than C.I.T.S.'s because of student discounts and less luxurious accommodations. Sometimes young people are put into school dormitories normally used by foreign students. CYTS, which is owned by the China Youth Federation, can arrange informal sports competitions with Chinese youth.

China International Sports Travel Co. handles formal international sports competitions and demonstrations, motorcycle tours, and television rights to international sporting events in China. It is under the All-China Sports Federation, but you don't have to be a professional or even a serious athlete to go this route. It has over 30 branches, with representation in every province. Among its offerings are tours by horseback on the Silk Road and in Mongolia, trekking in Tibet, and overland tours from Pakistan or Hong Kong to Beijing. It also has ski, sky diving, hot air ballooning, scuba, and martial arts packages. See also ''The Basics.''

Chinese Railexpress Service is especially good about train travel and can arrange a super luxury train. It would be among the first to know about the Euro-Asia Land Bridge. Offices are in railway stations.

Guides The people who escort foreign visitors are guide-interpreters, ''guides'' for short. Most are graduates of universities or foreign-languages institutes, with three or four years of foreign-language training at this level.

Training has been on the job, usually learned by accompanying an experienced guide for several months. But some agencies have been so short-handed at times that guides with little English and training have been used. The Department of Education is now responsible for staff training, and prospective guides are currently spending four years learning a language, Chinese history, geography, and art history.

Guides must now pass an exam before they can wear an official badge with their photo. They could lose their badge (and their job) for accepting commissions from stores. If you are on a group tour of several cities, you might get a national guide who stays with you during your whole stay in China. At each city you also get a different local guide and, at some tourist attractions, an on-the-spot guide.

If there is a shortage, you may not get a national guide.

For most visitors, your Chinese escorts will be the only Chinese people you can get to know with any depth. Guides are open about discussing their salaries and their training, especially if they like you. You could ask them questions, like how much money do they make? Do they get bonuses? How much is their rent? What happens if a tour group misses a plane? Who pays? How do they feel about Tiananmen Square?

You might notice your guide getting kickbacks or gifts from the stores and factories to which they take their tours. This is against regulations, and the guide can be fined and the store can lose its license. In any case, visitors intent more on seeing China than on shopping or eating should make their wishes known.

One important question is, can guides accept tips? Officially, they are not allowed to ask for gifts or money, nor to accept them, but they do. A guide could get into trouble for accepting a tip. It really would be better if you wrote a letter to the manager of the guide expressing how good (or bad) the guide was. The guide could get a bonus for it. See *Gifts* in "What to Take" and *Tipping* in "Local Customs."

In over two dozen trips to China, I have only met three guides who were not competent. But some travel agents are complaining that guides are getting lazy. You should make them work by asking a lot of questions.

Guides might be reluctant to be alone in the hotel room of a visitor of the opposite sex.

Please be patient when a guide is speaking English. If it is painful to listen to, keep muttering to yourself, "This is better than nothing." A confusion over numbers is one of the most common translation problems. The Chinese think in terms of ten thousands rather than thousands. Do not mistake sixteen for sixty, seventeen for seventy, either. Ask your guide to write down big or important figures for you. When you are using an interpreter, speak slowly. Phrase what you want to be translated simply, one sentence at a time.

Also remember that unlike Greek tour guides, Chinese guides are not scholars. Their knowledge of traditional Chinese culture is frequently limited to the few books they read.

Yes, you should take *Fielding's People's Republic of China* with you, as otherwise you might not get background information. You might want to take only the pages relevant to your trip.

Guides are not usually allowed to eat with you. At mealtimes, they can be found in a staff dining room. They also stay in your hotel overnight. It is good insurance to ask where they can be reached.

TRANSPORTATION

Flying Buying tickets is not always easy and you may have to resort to flying stand-by, showing up at the airport ticket counter pleading emergency. Because many travelers book more than one flight in order to assure themselves a seat, keep trying if you don't succeed. Rumor has it that seats are saved until the last minute for VIPs. If you have a choice of flights, choose the shortest flying time. You will more likely get a newer plane with bigger seats and a more comfortable flight. Aim also for the earliest flights. Delays become compounded as the day progresses. Tickets have to be paid for not later than 12 p.m. (noon) the day before scheduled departure time. Credit cards are still not accepted but some ticket offices have facilities for cash advances from a credit card. (You do have to pay 4% more.) All reservations have to be reconfirmed not later than 12 o'clock noon two days before the flight (72 hours prior to departure for international passengers. It also continues if you stay for more than 72 hours in the city of departure) or you risk being bumped off your flight. This was not my experience in 1991 when flights were full. The ticket might have to be stamped and your passport seen. Travel agencies should be able to do this for a fee, but are not always able. If there is any doubt, **reconfirm.** When you reconfirm, ask for the check-in time. It is best to arrive at the airport early in case of overbooking or planes taking off ahead of schedule. We suggest 1½ hours for domestic flights; 2 hours for international. Check-in stops 30 minutes before flight time. It is very difficult to get accurate flight departure information over the telephone. Give yourself extra time to get to the airport in rain or snow.

Most planes get booked from the front and there may not be room for all the carry-on bags. Planes have left early, but more often late. Some planes have been delayed for days.

Do not expect luggage carts (except at international airports) or porters. Be prepared to carry your own bags.

We suggest you carry some snacks, and a good book. You may find lots of time to kill and nothing to eat. If you are traveling without a national guide, take along the telephone number of the local branch of a travel agency. If your flight is cancelled, at least you can telephone for help.

In some airports, you have to go through Security before checking in. Then you line up under a sign with your flight number and city in English. Make a note of other people in the line so you can reassure yourself later that you are getting on the same plane. Sometimes there are queue jumpers and shoving.

The clerk should look at your passport and take your checked bags and give you your ticket, baggage stubs, and boarding pass. You then have to go through Security; show your passport, boarding pass, and ticket.

Airport waiting rooms all have an information desk with a clerk who might know some English. Because boarding announcements are not always audible or in English, check frequently with Information. I would look out the window for my plane; the plane number is painted on the fuselage and should be mentioned on the pass. I would also double-check by looking for other people with the same color boarding pass and trying out my few words of Mandarin. Some people take a friendly interest in foreign travelers and will tell you when to board the flight.

Many airport waiting rooms are filled with smokers.

If a flight is late, insist on a progress report; if very late, free food. Meal announcements have not been in English, so keep your eyes open. If the plane is postponed overnight, also insist that the airline arrange a hotel room and transportation there and back.

Be prepared to walk to your plane no matter what the weather, and to be pushed by other travelers. Usually no effort is made at orderly boarding.

Until recently, CAAC has been the only airline operating domestically in China since Liberation. In pre-Liberation days, it was originally known as China National Aviation Corporation. In 1949 it became the Civil Aviation Administration of China (CAAC), and now the General Administration of Civil Aviation of China. All of its financing has been government.

The aviation industry in China is currently being restructured. CAAC is overseeing the organization of several new airlines. CAAC will continue to manage civil aviation generally in China, including safety standards and airports, licensing and international relations.

The state airlines are regional subsidiaries of CAAC, and will be run by former CAAC personnel with CAAC planes and facilities. With their IATA code, they are: Air China (Beijing) CA, Northeast Airlines (Shenyang) CJ, Northwest China Airways (Xi'an) WH, China Southern Airlines (Guangzhou) CZ, Southwest Airlines (Chengdu) SZ, China Eastern (Shanghai) MU, Xiamen Airlines (Xiamen) MF, and Xinjiang Airlines (Urumqi) XO. While all airlines have to follow strict safety regulations and be under the administration of CAAC, differences in quality of service are apparent.

The most prominent of the other new airlines are China United Airlines (with military planes) and Shanghai Airlines. CUA flies to 23 cities, among them Chengdu, Fuzhou, Hangzhou, Suzhou, and Wuxi. Shanghai has a good reputation. Many airlines have been buying new planes recently.

The first of the non-state airlines has begun service to Beijing, Anyang, Zhengzhou, and Huiyang (Shenzhen). It is named Zhongyuan (Central China) Non-Governmental Air Co. With about 23 new airlines coming into operation, there might be a bit of confusion. It would help other travelers if you send us the date, flight number, plane number, and route of your flights. We are trying to decide which airline is best, and your input would be helpful. We suggest you avoid small airlines with old planes.

One schedule for all CAAC affiliates is available. It comes out twice a year, in November and April and has been found on sale in some airports. It is much easier to get at Chinese airline offices abroad. In China, local travel agents should also be able to make bookings for the smaller airlines and regular provincial charters.

One should be able now to make reservations through Air China or China Eastern in North America or in any of the following cities, for flights for many cities including Beijing, Changchun, Chengdu, Dalian, Guangzhou, Guilin, Haikou, Hangzhou, Harbin, Kunming, Nanjing, Qingdao, Shanghai, Shantou, Shenyang, Tianjin, Wuhan, and Xiamen. You should be able to make reservations 15 days to three months before a flight. Ticket offices are open in some airports but only for that day's flight. You may still have to wait until you arrive at other destinations to buy onward domestic tickets.

In the early 1990s, Chinese airlines fly Boeing 707s, 737s, 747s, 757s, 767s, A310 and A300 airbuses, Dash 8s, Shorts 360s, MD-80s, MD 11s, Twin Otters, 146 B Aerospace, Chinese-made planes (Yuns and MD-82s), and new and old Tupolevs, Ilyushins, and Antonous on **domestic flights.** Announcements are usually made in *pu tung hua* and English. Security at airports usually leaves much to be desired.

Most flights have only economy class, but a growing number also offer first class. Hot food has been served on some flights, but food is usually cold and no alcoholic beverages are available. Some overhead luggage racks are open and allowed to be overstuffed. Call the attendant if you think the goods will fall on your head. Be sure to confirm delays with more than one official before you go back into town or whatever. Flights have taken off without all their original passengers because of conflicting information.

With competition and more and bigger planes, domestic services should continue to improve. Recent travelers on some domestic flights have found stewardesses giving safety spiels, and checking seat belts (but not badly stowed carry-ons). Lights have been dimmed properly on night takeoffs. But the quality of service and safety is uneven. Sometimes no crew members objected if passengers stood in the aisles during takeoff. Don't expect world-class service yet.

CAAC has booking offices in some hotels.

The following **regulations** have been in effect in China but are subject to change and should apply to all airlines. If any domestic airline loses your luggage, you get R.M.B ¥40 per kg for full fare-paying passengers, and R.M.B ¥25 per kg for discounted passengers, unless you have declared a higher value beforehand.

If any domestic airline is responsible for unscheduled overnight stopovers, hotel accommodation will be arranged by the carrier free of charge. (But you might have to insist.)

If any domestic airline cancels a flight, you get a full refund. If a passenger asks for a refund 24 hours before flight departure, the cancellation fee is 20%; if within 24 and 2 hours before flight departure, the cancellation fee is 20% of the original fare.

If the cancellation is within 2 hours of flight departure, the cancellation fee is 30%. If you fail to cancel before flight time **there is a 50% refund.**

Refunds can only be made at the place of purchase or a place approved by CAAC.

There is no smoking on domestic flights.

The 20 kg (for economy class) and 30 kg (for first class) free baggage allowance for full-fare passengers seem to be *strictly enforced.* (An allowance of 15 kg for economy and 20 kg for first class is allowed on a discounted fare. There is no allowance for infants paying 10% of the adult fare.) Carry-on baggage should not exceed 5 kg. or volume exceed a total of 45 inches, length, width, and height but frequently does.

No babies under 10 days of age and no pregnant women almost due are allowed to fly. An infant under two not occupying a separate seat and accompanied by an adult is charged 10% of the adult fare. Children 2–12 are charged 50% of the adult fare.

Helicopter service is available in some cities depending on demand.

Air China operates **international flights** almost the same as other international airlines, but with minimal services. Flights have cheap headsets, nice gifts, unenthusiastic cabin crews, and alcoholic drinks in first class, beer in economy. On its New York-Beijing run we had two Chinese movies (with English subtitles) and two U.S. movies. The Chinese movies were a good opportunity to see Chinese attitudes. China Eastern should start North American service soon.

Reservations will be canceled unless reconfirmed on flights wholly within Europe. Full refunds on international tickets are made if you cancel before check-in time.

An airport tax in China is charged on all departing international flights, including those to Hong Kong. Exceptions are diplomats, transit passengers, and children under 12. Passengers holding international tickets with confirmed space on the first connecting flight should get free meals and hotel accommodations provided by CAAC within 24 hours after their arrival at the connecting points.

We suggest that you avoid sitting beside toilets.

If you are trying to make connecting flights in China, give yourself plenty of time. You have to clear Immigration and Customs first.

Foreign airlines also fly to China but have no domestic services.

Some but not all can sell seats on their own planes in China. United Airlines, Lufthansa, etc., will accept credit card payments for tickets. Some, like Canadian Airlines, have different dimensions for carry-on luggage (22″ x 14″ x 9″ or 56 x 36 x 23 cm) and are more strict than the Chinese about enforcing them.

Trains China has a vast network of railways, linking every provincial and regional capital except Lhasa to Beijing. And even that omission is being remedied. Railway lines have been burgeoning and many are being electrified. Diesel is in the process of replacing steam. Service has improved, with air-conditioned express tourist trains between Nanjing and Shanghai, Hangzhou and Wuxi, Shenyang and Dalian, Jinan and Qingdao, Shenzhen and Shaoguan, Beijing and Chengde, Guizhou and Anshun, etc.

Tickets can be obtained through hotels or travel agencies (usually for a service fee). Since the travel agencies cannot always be counted on to buy tickets for individual travelers, especially during high tourist seasons, you might have to go to the railway station and buy them yourself. In some big cities, special ticket windows are provided for foreigners, but be prepared for frustration and arguing. Lineups can be long, especially for hard class. Best buy your tickets at least six days in advance. Scalpers around train stations and in some coffee shops can buy tickets for you with a big markup. While this is illegal, everybody does it; but some scalpers might not be seen again. One pays upon receipt. Some foreign travelers have been successful using cheaper tickets bought by Chinese friends because conductors "don't care." Travelers have boarded trains using platform tickets and then bought tickets from the conductor on the train. This, however, is risky, as space may not be available. If you don't want to spend your time waiting in line and going back and forth, try your hotel or the Railexpress Travel Service at the station.

Train schedules for all Chinese trains should be available in three–star hotels, or at foreigners' counters in railway stations. Be sure to give yourself plenty of time to find your train; platforms are not marked in English, but the train number is posted. The destination of each coach should be marked on its side.

Like travel on overnight ferries, men and women are assigned berths without regard to sex even in soft class. If this arrangement bothers you, ask for another compartment. The Chinese are used to such travel and are not embarrassed. Tourist groups usually sort themselves out. I have never heard of sexual harassment on a train in China, so don't feel nervous. One can get used to sleeping in one's clothes and washing with strangers of the opposite sex nearby.

If you're *desperate* and can't wait for roommates to leave, change your clothes in the toilet room. You could also ask your roommates to wait outside your compartment for a moment while you change, undress under the covers, or wait until the lights are out. Businessmen wearing suits might look a little wrinkled next day, but who cares? Wrinkles aren't all that important in China.

To protect valuables, do not use your purse as a pillow. Things have been stolen that way. Put your valuables in a money belt around your waist or around your neck UNDER your clothes. Tie your camera to your arm.

Toilets look like they've been hosed down and not scrubbed. On coaches reserved for foreign tourists, you can be quite sure of toilet paper and soap (in a common soap dish). Soft-class travelers on some trains now have a choice of a Western toilet seat or a squat.

A washroom in each car offers several sinks with running water. Many prepaid tourists wait until they arrive at their hotels before washing. However, sometimes on arrival early in the morning hotel rooms have not yet been vacated, and tourists are frequently taken sightseeing or to breakfast instead.

All soft-class berths and some hard berths on express trains have been air conditioned. No smoking is allowed in some coaches. Baggage might be checked for inflammable and dangerous articles. The 35 kg weight limit is occasionally enforced. Luggage is frequently pushed in and out of train windows.

Do not discard your ticket. You might be asked for it again at the exit gate of your arrival station.

Trains are special express, express, regular, and suburban. Passengers could have a choice of hard- and soft-class seats and hard- and soft-class berths. The most comfortable are in the middle of a coach, away from noise and wheel vibrations. When you buy your ticket, state your preference.

Prepaid tourists usually travel **soft-class berth,** which can be almost the same price as going by plane. The berths are the height of bourgeois comfort if you have air conditioning. Compartments usually have clean slipcovers with lace doilies, lace curtains, a 16″ by 24″ table with a lamp and potted plant, an overhead fan, four porcelain mugs (for tea), and sleeping spaces with bedding and towels for four people on two uppers and two lowers. The bedding might not be fresh. An overhead loft stores large suitcases, but you have to rely on strong arms to get them up there and down. Train conductors are usually very helpful and friendly. An attendant keeps refilling the thermos of hot water and sweeping the floors.

It is best to take a small overnight bag if you are sleeping on the train, unless you want to do acrobatics or limit your leg room. Most group luggage is stored at one end of the car and may not be easily accessible.

Ask the conductor to lock your door when you go to the dining car. The plug for the fan (if you have one) and the switch for the loud-speaker are frequently under the table.

Dining-car food is edible and, on some trains, surprisingly good, but simple. Passengers usually give their orders to a steward beforehand and are notified when their food is ready.

Six people share one compartment of **hard-class berths** in the same amount of space as "soft." Berths are padded, however, and tiered in threes with even less privacy, the middle berth being the best.

Hard class is noisy and dirty, with frequent clearing of throats and spitting on the floor. You also cannot turn off the loudspeaker, which starts at 6 a.m. every morning. The coaches are mopped frequently. Sheets and warm blankets are provided, but if you get on between the two terminals, these may already have been used. Passengers can eat in the dining car, but can also buy food from vendors at train stations or circulating on the train itself. Don't expect gourmet fare! In fact, food from vendors can be downright unappetizing, like a box of rice with pork (including the skin, with hair left on). It might be best to bring your own instant noodles if you're on a tight budget. Steaming hot water is available in each car. Hard-class seats are very crowded and some travelers have ignored "no smoking" signs.

Accommodations can be upgraded after the train is underway if space is available. The conductor is usually in the middle coach.

Long-distance buses   Air-conditioned buses and mini-buses speed along many routes. Ask about the kind of bus you will be taking be-cause some buses are small, hard-seated, and very crowded, with little luggage space except on the roof. They can be uncomfortable for big foreigners, especially if you have to stand or squat. We have also heard horror stories of windows impossible to close in freezing weather, and carbon monoxide poisoning because of bad maintenance. So check your bus before you commit yourself. On some routes, you do have a choice of new buses. Not all highways are paved. Still, buses are good for seeing the countryside and meeting people—but you have to be young in spirit, strong, and adventurous. You usually book ahead of time at a bus station, Overseas Chinese hotels, or ask C.I.T.S. We strongly urge you to take your own food. These buses do stop at dumpy restaurants with a busload of travelers, and one can't expect service immediately. As soon as the driver is finished, the bus leaves. Toilets are usually primitive. Jiangsu province has some tour buses with their own toilets.

Long-distance ferries   Overnight ships between Hong Kong and Chinese ports usually have small, comfortable, but not luxurious cabins. See "Getting There." For boats on the Yangtze, see "Yangtze Gorges." For small one-class ships, see "Jiangmen." Some ferries have good reputations; some are filthy. Standards are uneven. Take a supply of seasick pills if you're susceptible. Take your own mug, towel, chopsticks, and soap on overnight trips.

Accidents have occurred because of overcrowding.

By road   Some but not all roads are being opened to foreigners. The problem is military zones. Four- to six-lane highways are being built. #107 goes from Beijing to Shenzhen, #312 from Shanghai to Yining (Xinjiang.) Tour groups of self-drive jeeps and cars are available from Xi'an or Qufu to Urumqi (still a rough trip). Studies are being made that should allow foreigners to bring their own jeeps and boats (for touring the Yellow River).

Some youth travel agencies have tours by bus in Fujian and Guangdong, a great way to see the country. One can take a group tour by motorcycle or bicycle, but these tours are not cheap. A truck carrying spare parts follows behind, picking up tired bikers.

Some adventurous bikers have traveled from town to town on their own. Please be aware of the problems. Roads might not be paved. If you get into an accident, you might not be able to communicate. You might not be able to get bicycle parts. You might secure only substandard accommodations. No guide books have yet been found for this kind of travel. You might have to get alien travel permits for some areas. Do check for licenses if you want to attempt individual travel by motorcycle. Police in China hassle motorcyclists.

For safety's sake, we urge you not to travel alone. If you do, let us know what happens so we can pass on information to other travelers.

It is possible to hire a **taxi** to take you from city to city, but you have to pay the return fare if you leave it at a city other than its home base. Always ask ahead of time for the approximate fare and distance and if you need an alien travel permit. See "Budget."

Hitchhiking has been and may have to be done. Backpackers have hitched rides with truck drivers. On-your-own tourists in isolated spots like the cave temples near Dunhuang (with only two public buses a day) have been able to get rides on tour buses (sometimes free). It's a matter of luck. If you have connections with foreign experts, etc., you might be able to use staff cars for much lower rates than taxis. Read *In Xanadu, a Quest.*

Porters. A big problem is lack of porters at bus and railway stations, ferry quays, and airports. Some places have them, but one never knows. Some freelance porters may be available, but they might also disappear with your luggage or not get you to your train on time. When you notify people you are coming tell them you need a porter or be prepared to carry your own luggage, especially if you arrive by bus or train. You can give your baggage checks to hotel drivers to claim at airports.

LOCAL TRANSPORTATION

Bicycles can be rented from hotels and bicycle-rental shops.

Some rented bicycles have fallen apart. Be sure to check the brakes, tires, bell, lock, etc. You will probably have to leave a deposit or some identification, but try not to leave a passport. Clerks have accepted old student cards, expired driver's licenses, anything with a photo. Guard your receipt carefully. Always park in a supervised parking lot; otherwise your bicycle may disappear, to be found again at a police station, you hope. Make a note of what it looks like, the license number, and the place where you have left it. Finding it quickly again among hundreds of identical bicycles may otherwise be a problem. Most cities have bicycle lanes, and some have streets forbidden to bicycles.

If you are staying any length of time in China, you might want to buy a Chinese bicycle and sell it when you leave. China makes a lot of bicycles, including 10-speed ones.

Officially all bicycles should have bicycle licenses, but most foreign riders have had no trouble riding without one. Some people have taken their own bicycles into China hoping to travel around the country, but only a few have been able to do this, and some have had to leave their bicycles behind because of the hassles. (To ship a bicycle by train means having to go to the train station a day ahead of time and, at the other end, spending time finding it.) Spare parts for foreign makes are also a problem.

Motorscooter rickshaws for two or more are cheaper than taxis and could take lots of luggage, but they are not comfortable, with much swerving and bouncing. Prices are often fixed and paid in advance at a stand.

Bicycle rickshaws built for two cost very little or a lot (in tourist areas), but you can only go short distances. Please consider the driver and get off and walk up steep slopes. Bicycle rickshaws are ideal for leisurely sightseeing in places like Hangzhou. They are on the increase even in Beijing. And please don't ride them in heavy motorized traffic since they can be dangerous. Do agree on a price in advance, especially in tourist towns, where revolutionary morals have given way to market forces. Make sure the price is for the ride, not for each person. If the driver demands something exorbitant, just hand him what is fair and walk away. If the price is right, he won't scream at you.

Taxis are normally found outside most tourist hotels, at railway stations, airports, passenger-ship quays and places frequented by visitors. If these places don't have taxi stands of their own, their service desks should telephone for a taxi for you. If you are not near any of these places, you can still ask someone to help you telephone for a taxi. See "Useful Phrases." Taxis can be flagged on the street in a few cities.

Taxis are not always easy to find. If you have several stops to make, it is usually better to hire a taxi by the half day or day, and have the driver wait for you. Or you could pay by the meter (or odometer) with a charge for "waiting time." Always check rates before you go. Usually you need not pay for a meal for a driver if you are near his home base, but you might invite the driver to a meal if you are a long way away. Restaurants and hotels have sections for staff if you don't want to eat together.

If you need a taxi early in the morning or for a full or half day, it is best to make a reservation at the taxi stand the night before. Taxi companies also have buses for larger groups.

Not all taxis have meters, and drivers have been known to cheat. While most drivers are honest, a few have added unused "waiting time" in Chinese to the receipts, or just charged higher rates. Taxi drivers without meters should calculate fares according to the distance per taxi, not per passenger. See "Budget" for recent per kilometer rate. (See *Getting from the Airport to Your Hotel* in "Getting There" for other tricks.) It would be wise to ask the price before you go and *make a note of the odometer reading before you start*. Ask for a receipt. You can usually pay for taxis in R.M.B., but you stand a better chance of getting one if they know you have F.E.C.s.

If you feel a driver is cheating you, don't pay, and ask *cheerfully* for someone to call a policeman. Hotel and C.I.T.S. staff members should know the distance from the airport, and between tourist attractions. If you have already paid, get a receipt, take the driver's name and license number, and complain to the manager or dispatcher at his/her taxi stand or to the local tourism administration. Ask your consulate for advice. Some cities have a taxi complaint office. Letters to *China Daily* have resulted in penalties for the driver and apologies from the taxi company.

Another ploy is to pay what you consider the proper fare, get out, and leave. If the driver follows you, then reconsider your calculations and negotiate a settlement.

Some drivers charge extra because they have to pay the touts who bring them customers. Try to avoid the middle man. Some drivers will give you R.M.B. instead of F.E.C.s in change. Drivers who cheat are a new phenomenon and should be discouraged.

Public tour buses are available in a few cities around railway stations offering relatively cheap transportation to some tourist attractions with a detailed commentary in English. Cheaper still are bus tours for Chinese people, a good bargain if you take along a guide book. Best take your own lunch to save time eating in restaurants, and make sure you know how long your bus is staying at each stop. Write down the bus number so you can find it again.

Shuttle buses are available at a few hotels. These go to airports, Friendship Stores, and perhaps a few tourist attractions.

Public city buses are usually very crowded, especially during the early-morning and late-afternoon rush hours, and all day Sunday. But they are cheap and are often your only means of transportation. Try them if you are athletic or adventurous. Hotel personnel can tell you which bus to take. Some cities have bus maps in English. Or you can take a map with you and point. Fellow passengers are usually friendly and helpful. Some set routes have public mini-buses. They are more expensive than a bus but cheaper than a taxi.

As in all crowded places, beware of pickpockets.

Subways are in Beijing and soon in Shanghai, Tianjin, and Guangzhou, and maps are available. Walk down the stairs, pay your money (cheap), and choose your platform. Signs should be in pin-yin.

Public ferries and tour boats. China has some real antiques crossing harbors and rivers. They are cheap, but avoid them if they look too crowded and tippy. (Fatal accidents with tour boats have recently been blamed on overloading and drunken crews.)

Something has to be said about **walking** because of all the bicycles. Crossing streets can be dangerous. Try to let a native upstream run interference. Cross at lights. Some cities have overpasses—use them!

COMMUNICATIONS

Services have greatly improved in the last few years and are still developing.

Postal services are generally reliable, and eventually all mail will be sorted by postal code, except for mail from abroad, which is translated by the post office, all mail must have postal codes. Delivery is faster if the addresses are marked in Chinese. China now has express service to a couple of hundred Chinese cities and about 70 countries.

Sending parcels is a problem. You have to use an international post office rather than one at your hotel. All packages are inspected, even those sent inside China. China customs is looking for more than two cartons of cigarettes, pornographic literature, used clothing, explosives, and antiques. Most post offices insist that packages be wrapped and sewn in white cloth or sealed in regulation boxes. A few post offices will even provide this service on the spot for about ¥1 per box or bag. Some, but not all, post offices are asking for receipts to show you paid for your goods in F.E.C. We managed to send off some purchases for which we had no receipts claiming "used clothing." Better still, ask your hotel to mail packages for you.

Some small city post offices will accept only airmail packages. In Foshan I tried to mail a 4-kg beaded curtain to Canada. I finally mailed it by surface from Guangzhou.

Surface mail to North America can take six weeks to three months. Registration and insurance are cheap and recommended—if you have someone in the city to follow up should packages get lost. Airmail takes about 7 to 10 days. Post offices are asking for payment in F.E.C.s.

Courier service is available. EMS (Express Mail Service) is available through the post office. DHL, UPS, TNT, and OCS, contacted through hotel business centers, have services between China and overseas. They have very strict rules about sending goods.

Telephones: Local calls from hotels are easy except when everyone else wants to use the few lines available. Some circuits are busier than others. Over 500 cities now have International Direct Dial (IDD). A few places like Shanghai Center have "call forwarding" and "conference call" facilities. Cellular phones are very expensive and rare, but increasing.

As a general rule, Chinese citizens do not have private telephones yet (though the situation is improving). Sets are available in most stores, urban neighborhoods, factories, and offices, with a small sign in Chinese about seven feet from the ground by the door. Cheap. Each village usually has at least one telephone in the village office. China is currently putting a lot of effort into improving telecommunications, but in the meantime, one can, for example, leave a message asking your friends to telephone you at your hotel. Be sure to give your room number.

The easiest way to call long distance and overseas is at your hotel. See "Hotels." These calls can also be made at a Post and Telecommunications office, which might be cheaper. Some hotels and airports have public telephone booths that can accept calling cards for overseas calls.

Direct dial between Chinese cities, and international direct dial are usually easy, once you get a direct dial line. Just don't try when everyone else is trying to use it. Direct dial is much faster (20 seconds) than operator-assisted calls, which might take from three minutes to a couple of days (in remote towns). For the local international operator, call 103, or in Beijing 115 on any telephone. You can then make a collect or AT&T calling-card call. AT&T also has a "USA Direct" service from a growing number of cities, including Beijing, Guangzhou, Hangzhou, Shanghai, and Shenzen. Dial 108–11. One can also dial the city code for these cities and then 108–11 to make the U.S. connection from other Chinese cities. AT&T has "USA Direct" telephones in some hotel lobbies and airports. See "Destinations."

Don't forget the time difference. New York City is 13 hours behind China during the winter months, and 12 or 13 hours during daylight saving months. Thus in winter, 8 p.m. China time is 7 a.m. New York or Toronto standard time, 12 noon Greenwich Mean Time, or 4 a.m. San Francisco time. See "Quick Reference" for time zones and Chinese telephone codes.

Holiday Inn's Teleplan means cheaper hotel service charges for telephone calls. Ask about it.

Telex service is usually instantaneous and reliable, but we suggest you ask for an answer in China because, for example, telexes requesting reservations have been ignored in some hotels. Not all telex services are available 24 hours a day. Many hotels have telex services. You could save money typing your own telexes because of service charges.

If you expect a telex in your hotel in China, best give your room number as part of your address. And for double insurance, keep looking for incoming telexes in the telex pile. Ask Reception.

Cable is cheaper and slower and might not be reliable. You usually book them through post offices.

Fax is not as efficient as telex, as it is dependent on overused telephone lines, but the Chinese are acquiring more of them. Sometimes fax machines are turned off at night, which is daytime in North America.

Travelers on their own aiming for travel without stress (but not backpackers). Hopefully, by the time you read this, you should be able to:

1) book as many domestic flights as possible from outside China three months before arriving in China. Because new flights are frequently added, try again later if you can't book any particular leg of your trip.

2) make reservations in hotels during high tourist season in the main tourist and business cities. You could take a chance in smaller, less important places, and arrive without one at other times. No. 1 and 2 can be done through a travel agent or Chinese airline. High season is June, August, September and October.

3) telex your hotel before you arrive to meet you with transport giving flight number, or train and coach numbers. Someone at your destination should hold up a sign with your name or the hotel's name on it. A few hotels do not charge for picking you up. If you have less than three days, you could also ask the hotel or travel agency to reconfirm or book the next stage of your travel.

4) consult your hotel travel service or a travel agency about your next travel plans, reconfirming plane tickets or booking train tickets, and repeating no. 3.

5) for your day of departure, book a taxi and if there are no porters, ask if the driver can carry your luggage to the train platform or check-in counter. If the driver cannot and you have loads of luggage, ask the hotel or a travel agency to help you.

6) avoid much hassle by booking mini-packages along the way through travel agents. Be sure to obtain vouchers.

Backpackers or anyone else trying to travel on a shoestring and carrying their own luggage:

1) should first and foremost be flexible, assertive, resourceful, polite, and patient. You should expect to do only a percentage of what you want to do, and make the most of standing in queues.

2) should not expect to make reservations in cheaper hotels, which usually take people on a first-come basis. Some train stations and airports have hotel-booking offices or C.I.T.S. who can refer you to hotels. And if you arrive at a hotel that is full, the clerks should be able to refer you to another hotel.

3) can save money sleeping in hotel dormitories, riding public buses, and eating in open-air food stalls. CAAC has an airport bus downtown that could go near some of the cheaper hotels. Try to ask fellow passengers to point out a suitable hotel if you don't know of any.

4) should look to CYTS or your hotel to recommend other hotels and make hard-class train or ship bookings. If they can't or these services are too expensive, you have to do it yourself.

5) should consider taking overnight ships between cities (to save on paying for a hotel bed).

6) should not expect a high standard of English or service or cleanliness or 24-hour hot water in cheaper hotels.

7) should network with other foreign backpackers.

Yes, you can do it successfully and cheaply.

LOCAL CUSTOMS AND EMERGENCIES

DOES "YES" MEAN "YES"? Well, usually. Cultural differences do create misunderstandings. For example, a memorandum of understanding in trade means there is reason to believe that negotiations can begin in earnest. It does not mean, as many foreigners have sadly discovered, that a contract has been signed. The official dealt with might be overruled by his superior. Also, if a Chinese nods and says "yes, yes," he could be just trying to please you. He may not understand a word you are saying. So be wary. Ask a question that needs a full sentence in reply. For the same reason, a Chinese might give you dates and spellings and swear they are right. But what he means is that it is the best information he has and if you press him, he will check—but if you don't, he won't bother.

Chinese people are very polite in their personal relationships with friends or business acquaintances—people they will see again and again. They try not to hurt feelings, yours or their own. If you make a mistake, the very polite ones will not point it out to you. If you do something they do not like, they might ask someone senior to you to talk to you about it. My aunt was asked to criticize me when my nieces thought my clothes were a little too risque.

But Chinese people may not seem polite at times, especially crowds, or clerks in government stores. But if someone introduces you properly, most Chinese will prove to be extremely hospitable and helpful. The shop girl who ignores you is probably afraid of you or bored and unfulfilled by her job. Don't take it personally.

Once I caught my knee in the door of a crowded bus and got a bruise that lasted for weeks. At the time, my cousins laughed while I felt like crying. It was just their way of reacting—probably embarrassment, not knowing how else to react. Just don't feel offended.

DOES "NO" MEAN "NO"? Well, sometimes. You will have to judge for yourself when a negative decision can be challenged.

You might hear "mei you" often. It means "there isn't any." Some foreigners have challenged it successfully at airline ticket offices by standing firm, smiling, asking for the manager, and refusing to budge until they get a ticket. Basically it means "please disappear," and when you don't disappear, something has to be done.

By protesting to a hotel clerk who said there was no room, I did get a bed in a dorm. This does not mean you should try to argue every time you are told "it is not possible," or that "your safety cannot be guaranteed." It could mean (1) language is a problem and they do not understand your request; (2) they don't want to be bothered trying; (3) they don't want too many people going there, but if you insist, they'll let you go; (4) there is genuine concern for your safety; (5) you really aren't allowed to go.

Arguing is an art too. Do not lose your temper or you've lost the battle. You should argue as much as possible in their terms. For example, one single traveler was put, as is the custom, in a small banquet room in one hotel for meals. There were no other foreign guests and the room was dingy and depressing. Two requests to move into the main dining room with the Chinese guests were refused. Single Traveler decided to go to a restaurant instead, pointing out to her guide that it was her problem. She said she was willing to pay for the hotel meals too, but she just couldn't bear eating alone under the circumstances. She was allowed to eat with the others.

Note: Sometimes no answer is a "no."

ASK QUESTIONS An official of the Overseas Chinese Travel Service once told me the only advice he had for visitors was, "Ask questions." It is good advice. For some reason, the Chinese do not volunteer much information. It might have something to do with their own lines of communication. So when in doubt, ask!

APPLAUSE You will frequently be greeted by applause as a sign of welcome or appreciation at institutions and cultural performances. It might even happen on the streets. Applaud back.

CRITICISMS AND SUGGESTIONS You may be asked for these and see many booklets in hotels, train dining cars, and restaurants with this title. If you have any criticisms and suggestions, do give them. But don't go on about how things are done in North America. Much doesn't apply to China. Criticisms should be helpful in the context of a developing country. Criticisms and suggestions are considered seriously, especially now that China is trying to improve her tourist facilities. Yes, mention that the bathroom floor is filthy. Go further than that and ask the attendant to clean it. If an attendant has been particularly helpful, write it down. She may get a bonus because of it.

TIPPING is officially forbidden. Travel agents encourage tipping because they want top service for present and future clients. Attendants and guides do accept tips and make more money than doctors, university professors, and government officials. Is it fair? The turn of the decade is an era of transition and new rules are developing. We suggest you tip only for services above the call of duty. Do not tip the attendant who fixes your broken toilet. That is his duty. Avoid tipping in hotels that add a percentage for service. While staff may not necessarily get the service charge, you have already paid additional for their service. In some hotels, tips are accepted "as a token of friendship" and shared among all the staff. As for tour guides and drivers, tip only those who have been exceptionally good, and no more than suggested in our "Budget" section. Miserable hours have been wasted arguing about tips and gifts.

Asking for tips is strictly forbidden. If there is any doubt about tipping, phone the local tourism administration or the manager of C.I.T.S. Some attendants and guides will actually refuse tips. They should be thanked profusely and perhaps given a modest "souvenir" instead.

GOOD MANNERS at home are good manners anywhere. Don't litter. Don't take "souvenirs," especially from historical places, such as a rock from the Great Wall. Don't pick flowers in parks.

In most other Asian countries it is fashionable to be late. Not so in China, where groups of children may be outside in the rain waiting for your car so they can applaud as you arrive.

Traditionally, Chinese conversations, even business conversations, start out with something innocuous: a discussion of the weather, of the calligraphy or a painting on the wall, or whatever. A mood of friendliness is set first. Then comes the business.

It is true that Chinese people themselves may not be polite in crowds. They may surround your bus and stare at you, crowd around when it's hot and ignore your pleas for help. But it is their country and just because you paid a lot of money to visit, it doesn't mean you can be rude.

Also, when you are using an interpreter, don't forget to look at the person with whom you are actually conversing.

JOKING ABOUT POLITICS AND SEX Many visitors are warned not to joke about sex or politics, particularly Chinese politics. With the older generation, to joke about sex is considered crude, and you condemn yourself when you do it. To joke about politics or even to argue about it is to show lack of sensitivity. Politics is taken very seriously in China. People are put into jail because of it, lose their jobs, waste years of schooling, and spend long hours in meetings discussing political implications. Some young people, however, might find such humor refreshing.

BEGGARS   Yes, there are a few. Use your own discretion. As I would in New York City, I would ask them why they have to beg, and then decide whether or not to give. Or I might take them to the closest restaurant and give them a meal. Or ignore.

FLIRTING   You may be tempted to flirt with a cute Chinese citizen of the opposite sex. Friendliness is appreciated, but anything beyond that used to and still may mean an interview with the Security Police, where you are asked why you insulted a Chinese citizen. It could also mean a fine or deportation. This puritanical attitude is much less strict now, but you will notice that even handholding is not too common especially in smaller towns. Casual dating is certainly frowned on. Friendly embraces common abroad are unusual even upon greeting a Chinese friend of long standing. (Chinese people overseas do it—but not in China.) You will probably be considered uncivilized if you indulge in too much display of affection in public, even with your own spouse. Older Chinese will be embarrassed. But things are changing.

It should take a month to get permission for marriages between Chinese and foreigners, if all goes well.

Foreigners are fined heavily (over U.S. $1000 in at least one case) if caught with an unrelated and unregistered Chinese of the opposite sex in a hotel room.

WILL YOU BE FOLLOWED?   Most probably not, unless the Chinese have a special reason to watch you. They might catch some foreigner selling foreign currency illegally to show they mean business. A foreigner is conspicuous. If you do anything wrong, your movements could be easily traced.

PHOTOGRAPHY   China is now like most other countries regarding photographs. At one time I couldn't even take a photo of my five-year-old on a public boat.

Today you can take pictures out of airplanes, on and off boats—everywhere except inside police stations, military installations, and certain museums, which, like ours, find they cannot sell their own photos if cameras are allowed. The Chinese also feel that flash photography damages relics. They charge a fee or confiscate your film. A recent exception was during martial law in 1989. Some tourists taking photos and videos of the demonstrations in Tiananmen Square were detained. Shortly after the massacre, a busload of tourists who had taken pictures of the square while passing, had their film confiscated.

Out of courtesy, please do ask people for permission to photograph them close up. Would you like someone to stick a camera in your face without permission?

If your camera breaks down, look for a Kodak agent, who might be able to repair it for you. Telephone Kodak in Hong Kong at (852) 3202843 for an address.

IF YOU GET INTO TROUBLE   Chances are these things won't happen, but just in case . . .

Earthquakes   The main danger here is collapsing buildings. If you don't have time to get outside into the open, away from falling debris, dive under a desk, table, or bed, or take shelter in a doorway. If the building falls down around you, at least you might have some protection. As soon as the shaking stops, which is usually after a few seconds, rush outside by stairway (not elevator).

Typhoons   This Chinese word meaning "big wind" is the Asian word for hurricane or tropical cyclone. These usually originate east of the Philippines and may hit China anywhere along the Pacific coast from April to November. They usually last for a maximum of three days and you should stay inside substantial buildings on high ground. The danger is falling debris, as well as strong winds and rain. Airports will probably be closed.

If you run out of money   Ask your embassy to cable home for some, or telephone collect. It usually takes five banking days. Borrow if you can from fellow travelers. You can get cash advances, with a 4% service charge, or free check cashing from the Bank of China with some credit cards. Some airlines take credit cards. The U.S. embassy gives small emergency loans, but very reluctantly. Bank of America should have a branch in Shanghai by now.

If you lose your traveler's checks   Take your receipts to the Bank of China. American Express also has courier refund, tel. Hong Kong (852) 8859332; 24-hour refund service available at Sheratons in Tianjin and Beijing, or Holiday Inn Lido (Beijing). If you neglected to get a collect telephone number for lost credit cards, you could phone a friend in the city where you got the card to have it cancelled and reissued.

If you lose your passport   Talk to your guide about it. Inform the local police and contact your embassy. Diplomatic offices are in Beijing, but U.S. consulates are also in Chengdu, Shanghai, Shenyang, and Guangzhou. Be sure you have your passport number somewhere in your luggage. If you're on a group tour, your tour escort should have a note of it and can give you a document so you can travel to other cities in China to get a new passport. C.I.T.S. should be able to help you if you are on your own. You need evidence of citizenship, like a birth certificate and two passport photos. Some U.S. consulates now have instant passport photo machines. Your embassy could give you a temporary passport within one or two hours. With this document you can get a Chinese visa so you can leave China.

Losing a passport creates a lot of trouble and additional expense, as it probably means staying a couple of extra days or leaving your tour group. Guard yours carefully.

Hostile crowds The May 1985 soccer riot in Beijing proved that this could happen. Anyone looking like the victorious Hong Kong Chinese was singled out for threats and abuse. But riots by soccer fans of defeated hometown teams can happen anywhere in the world, and did that year. Remember Brussels? This is not a Chinese phenomenom.

If you *think* you're surrounded by hostile people, try smiling. Chances are they're just curious or even jealous. Ignore them or try to make friends. Speak to individuals quietly, in English if you don't know Chinese. Someone may understand. Above all, act friendly and cool. Shouting obscenities is counterproductive.

If you are convinced the crowd is hostile, try to find out why. The Chinese do not get angry at foreigners just because they are foreigners. Even Japanese people, the hated invader for so many years, are received politely here. Hostility could be caused by something you have done. It used to be taking pictures of the wrong places and superstitious people but this is rare now. It could be an argument with a rickshaw or taxi driver. Try not to lose your temper; keep cool, polite, friendly. Call for the police. Apologize if you need to. If someone is drunk, just leave.

Demonstrations Don't be afraid of them. They are usually orderly except in Tibet, where demonstrators and bystanders have been shot without warning by police. Avoid demonstrations there, please. The blond wife of one foreign correspondent used to wave at marching demonstrators with a big, friendly grin on her face during times less friendly to foreigners. Participants used to be so surprised by this, they'd break step, stare, and grin back. If a policeman asks you to move on and not take photos, do as he says, or accept the consequences.

Recent demonstrations against African students should not discourage other Black people from visiting China. I have never heard of any unpleasantness against Blacks in general. Chinese people stare and occasionally titter at all foreigners. Please let me know if you find anything different. During the 1989 democracy demonstrations, foreigners were treated with respect by the students and caution by the military. I don't know of any foreigners hurt, nor generally the target of violence.

Car and bicycle accidents If your car accidentally injures anyone, do what you should in your own country. Give first aid, and then arrange to get the victim to a doctor or a hospital quickly. Otherwise, stay where you are. Do not get involved in arguments. Wait until the police arrive. The police will take statements, and if you are found to be in any way responsible as the driver or even as a passenger (were you distracting the driver?), you may be liable to a fine or payment for damages. The fine would be to remunerate the family of the injured or deceased for the rest of his productive years. There is a standard formula. If the accident is serious, contact your embassy. There have been cases where a Chinese was found at fault and his work unit paid for a broken windshield. There have also been cases of drunken diplomats causing traffic accidents. Many were asked to leave China. Since most tourists will not be driving, car accidents are not really a problem, but bicycle accidents might be.

Breaking the law If you are accused of breaking a Chinese law, try to contact your embassy as soon as you can. Do not expect the rights that you would have in your own country, like to bail or even to see a lawyer. China has only recently rewritten its civil law, which says that foreigners cannot be arrested without a warrant from the People's Procurate or the People's Court. Minor violations could mean detention and deportation. More serious violations like "burglary of scarce industrial materials" have meant the death penalty for Chinese citizens. Taking bribes worth ¥58,000 has meant life imprisonment. An American who fell asleep while smoking set fire to a hotel, resulting in the deaths of ten people. He was sentenced to 18 months' imprisonment and ordered to pay ¥150,000 compensation. Just don't do anything illegal! China has relations with Interpol. Anyone found guilty of producing or trafficking 1500 grams of opium or 100 grams of heroin could be jailed for life or receive the death penalty. Illegal possession of drugs could mean seven years' imprisonment.

Journalists must get permits before interviewing students and reporting on activities in universities.

What if you get hurt or sick? China has been among the healthiest and cleanest countries in Asia. But standards seem to be slipping.

There have been reports of typhoid, malaria, plague, and rabies, usually in isolated rural areas far off the tourist routes, though a few cases of rabies have shown up in Shanghai. Venereal diseases are back after being absent for decades, but are still rare compared to other Asian countries. One hears occasionally of encephalitis, hepatitis, cholera, and intestinal parasites. Avoid wading in lakes and rivers in central China's Yangtze River area because of schistosomiasis.

You can find out about these and about malaria areas from the

World Health Organization. If you are bothered by mosquitoes in China, use the net above your bed, or ask for one if there isn't any. You can also burn incense coils that keep mosquitoes away. Use insect repellent. Wear long sleeves and pants when you go out at night. Check for malaria if you have flu-like symptoms within a year afterwards.

Chinese medical facilities are good for common ailments. Many Overseas Chinese go to China for acupuncture and even Western medical treatment. If visitors are sick, it is usually the common cold or an upset stomach (see "Food"). Some visitors have also had hernias, heart attacks, and cancer. Your guide or the service desk at your hotel should be able to direct you to a doctor. Hotels frequently have medical clinics on the premises.

If you become ill at night, try the attendant on your floor. Some attendants sleep in a room close to the service desk. If you have a language problem, point to what you need in the "Useful Phrases."

In emergencies, knowledgeable foreign residents say **taxis are quicker to get than ambulances.** In Beijing, however, if you telephone 120 and inform the dispatcher that the patient has had a heart attack, the ambulance should arrive with a defibrillator. "120" is also used for ambulances in some other cities as well. See "Destinations."

You will probably be given a choice of Western or traditional Chinese medicine, or both. Chinese herbal medicines are frequently effective, but one of my kids had to be bribed with lots of candy to drink his herbal tea, it tasted so awful.

Chinese medical facilities might look grubbier than those in the West. An examination with medicines for an upset stomach at a hotel clinic at this writing costs from ¥5 to about ¥35. The foreign in-patients' section of Capital Hospital in Beijing charges about ¥300 a day. Since the Chinese have recently upgraded some facilities especially for foreigners, prices for foreigners are higher than for local people.

If a foreigner is treated the same way as a local Chinese, the charges are lower, similar to that for a local person.

The Chinese are concerned about the health of their guests. They frequently check whether you have enough clothing on. If you complain about your health too much, you might get a doctor even if you don't request one.

It must be pointed out that most tour organizers state emphatically that tours to China are rugged. They are not for invalids or people with respiratory or heart conditions because of dust and air pollution.

It is true that the Chinese are especially nice to older people, and many people want to see China before they die. A few people of Chinese ancestry want to be buried in China and the easiest way they can do this is to die there.

But for the rest of you, here are some things to consider:

Do take it easy. If you feel tired, cut out excursions and rest instead. You don't have to climb mountains, or if you do climb steps to the cable car, go slowly; or wait at the bus with the bus driver, who is usually very nice. You can teach him English or walk around on level ground and enjoy the view, or develop your own theories about the antics of Chinese tourists. Have someone help you up the Great Wall so you can say that you were on it. You don't have to go out to the theater in the evening. You can stay in your hotel and try to fathom Chinese television. Operas are frequently on television too.

Facilities for treating emergencies in China are not as sophisticated as in many other countries. Do not expect elaborate life-support equipment, or to be up walking the day after a broken hip.

The Chinese do not store O-negative blood in their blood banks because Chinese people do not have it.

Take any essential medicines with you. Do not count on a prescription made out to a pharmacist in the U.S. being filled in China, especially if it uses brand names.

If you do go to the hospital, you might have to take your own mug, plate, towel, soap, and a friend. The staff and other patients may not speak English. Standards are not the same as in America. In one of the best hospitals in China, beds were only changed once a week. One Canadian patient found that even a spilled bed pan didn't change the rules. (She got bed sores.)

In case of very serious ailments, contact your consulate. You may have to be evacuated outside of China for treatment.

In the event of a death? The Chinese contact the relevant embassy, which in turn tries to get in touch with next of kin. An embassy can make arrangements for repatriation if desired. Goods belonging to the deceased and death certificates might be released to next-of-kin *only* after the bills are paid.

SMOKING The smokers in China still hold power, but the handwriting is on the wall. Smoking is now forbidden on domestic flights, in some train coaches, the Beijing subway station, and some railway stations. Some hotels are beginning to have no smoking areas in coffee shops, and on some floors. They should be encouraged. Smoking is forbidden in elevators, and some hotels have signs forbidding smoking in bed.

The Zhuhai Hotel (Zhuhai) has a "Give-Up Smoking Clinic" where patients inhale a concoction of 30 different Chinese herbs for 30 minutes a day for three days. By the end of the third session, patients no longer want a cigarette. But the Zhuhai Hotel itself has no "no smoking" areas.

SPITTING Campaigns in some cities have taken place from time to time against this unhealthy, disgusting habit many people have of spitting in public. It is a reflection of rural society. Fines in Beijing have averaged ¥.42 and have been successful in curtailing spitting for a while, at least. The Chinese believe that swallowing phlegm is unhealthy, but haven't acquired any alternatives yet. One American successfully hands tissues and plastic bags to people with whom she is traveling.

LOOKING UP SPECIFIC CHINESE CITIZENS   Yes, you can usually visit friends and relatives in China, even while on a group tour or business trip. As a courtesy to your hosts or sponsors in China, do inform them if you want to take time off from the planned schedule. You might ask when the best time would be. In recent years, local Chinese could go to your hotel, but they may be interrogated by hotel staff. Previously they had to make application outside the building stating the reason for their visit and showing their identification cards.

Some front-office clerks are rude to local Chinese. Some local people may feel uneasy about entering a hotel, particularly a fancy one. Many are glad of the opportunity to see inside and brag to their friends that they ate there or at least had a photograph taken inside. If they are reluctant, however, to go there, you could arrange to meet in a restaurant, a park, or their home. You could take them on sightseeing trips with your tour group (for a fee). This will give you time to visit with friends without missing the attractions.

Your chances of going to the home of a friend will depend on the political climate at the time. It could also depend on how embarrassed some Chinese are about the modesty of their lodgings, and whether or not they can afford a taxi or elaborate meal for you. Previously, anyone who hosted foreigners in their homes was grilled later as to what the relationship was, what was talked about, etc. In the early 1980s, only a few appointed workers in each work unit were allowed to fraternize socially with their resident foreign expert. After the 1989 turmoil, many people still seemed very open to receiving foreign guests in their homes, but some did not. So do not insist if local Chinese friends are reluctant to take you home.

Making contact may be a problem until telephones become more common. If you've sent a letter, telegram, or cable earlier and your friend hasn't shown up, you may have to go to the home or work place. If you are worried about making trouble for your friend, ask someone less conspicuous than yourself to go and inquire.

When you do make contact, it is always better to visit friends alone, as they may be uncomfortable about talking openly if anyone else is around. Do not persist in asking questions that a Chinese seems reluctant to answer. Do not expect any spontaneous rap sessions, though you may get some now. I once asked a friend in the early '80s what happened to his family during the Cultural Revolution and was bluntly but politely told it was none of my business. In the mid-'80s, however, new friends quite openly complained about hauling manure on farms and sweeping floors in factories then.

Be sensitive and play along if people whisper to you. Don't say aloud, "Why are you whispering?" They are afraid someone is listening! It is hard to get over the terrors of the Cultural Revolution, and human rights today still are not like those in your own country. If they want to bring a friend to your meeting, it may be because they want a witness that they are not conspiring with you against the government. Or they might want you to help their friend.

Overseas Chinese have a freer time talking with Chinese citizens. Chinese people generally are not open about discussing their deepest feelings and problems with even close friends. Nor will Chinese people easily discuss their sex life. It once took six months of living together before one Chinese roommate confided to me how unhappy she was about her parents.

CHINESE HOSPITALITY   This can be very lavish and people may go into debt to show how happy they are to see you. It is always appropriate to take a gift when you go to a Chinese home. Especially welcome are cigarettes (Marlboro Lights are a current favorite), unless the family is religious. Novelties, souvenirs from abroad, and presents for children are fine.

But don't insult them by being overly generous. It is all right, however, to give their children money (about ¥10 each) if you are a relative or a close friend. Otherwise, it is insulting. If you have time for a return banquet, that would be the easy way out.

If you are accompanied by a Chinese friend or relative, avoid buying anything in a store because he may want to pay for it. The salary range for most people is quite low. Of course, rent is low. A Chinese doesn't have to pay exorbitant medical bills if he is sick, and most pay no income tax. But he has to save a long time to buy what you wouldn't think twice about paying for. Hospitality may demand that you be given a gift. Be gracious and suggest something inexpensive like a poster if you are asked.

I have visited many homes—of peasants, officials, workers, and professional people. By Western standards, most are crowded. One professional couple with two children might have a small apartment with two tiny bedrooms. Poorer families might share a kitchen and bathroom with several other families. In only rare cases will there be room for overnight guests, especially in the cities. Toilets may be the squatting kind. In smaller communities you may find a container of earth or a bucket of water for covering or flushing.

In rural areas, you might have to sightsee on foot or on the hard back ends of bicycles, since there may not be any other means of transportation. It is a real adventure!

IF YOU'RE INVITED TO A WEDDING   In old China, a gift of money in a red packet was the accepted thing to give. Money is still much appreciated. But gifts to help set up a new household are most frequently given now; porcelain tea sets, locally bought videos (machines made for the U.S. cannot be used here), blankets (preferably red, for happiness). In some places, giving a clock is bad luck. It implies a time limit on the marriage. Something imported from a foreigner would give you more *guanxi*. Some Friendship Stores may have gift certificates. Wedding invitations usually mean a banquet, but do ask. You could say something like "I've never been to a Chinese wedding before. Tell me what to expect." Budget ¥50–¥75 for casual acquaintances. See *Banquets and Toasting,* in "Food."

GIFT GIVING   One usually gives a gift upon first meeting the recipient unless it is inconvenient. For example, if the recipient is in a long reception line, it might be difficult. But you could mention in passing that you have something for him or her, and ask where you can leave it. The most important person receives the best gift, and gets it first. It is important not to give too expensive a gift. Some recipients may feel they have to reciprocate. Officials are forbidden to accept expensive gifts, samples, trial uses, etc.

RELIGION   Chinese people tend to be very pragmatic, worshiping whatever gods might answer their prayers. Religions were encouraged, tolerated, or persecuted depending on the times. In the early Tang, Buddhists were killed. But Buddhism later flourished, with imperial encouragement.

It has not been unusual for the same person to give support to several different temples and churches at the same time, and especially to worship one's ancestors. One owed one's life to ancestors and depended on them for good fortune even after they had passed on. It was one's duty to keep ancestral spirits happy. See Confucianism under "Qufu."

Christianity really suffered because of its relation to the unequal treaties following the end of the first Opium War in 1844. Many Chinese questioned the Christian preaching of only one way to salvation. Some foreign missionaries had to close their eyes to ancestor worship or they wouldn't have made many converts. Because of this backing by the foreign powers, Chinese Christians tended to become an elite group, at times appealing successfully to their foreign protectors even if they got in trouble with Chinese law. This, of course, caused much resentment.

Dr. Sun Yat-sen, the father of the Chinese republic, was a Christian, but as a Chinese nationalist he criticized missionaries as lackeys of foreign imperialists. Missionary motives were sometimes misunderstood, and some of these fears led to such incidents as the Tientsin Massacre (see "Tianjin"). Many missionaries were attacked more because they were foreigners caught in the growing nationalism of the era than because of what they taught.

Some Chinese Communist leaders were influenced by missionary schools. Mao Zedong (Mao Tse-tung) himself once edited the Christian-sponsored *Yale-in-China Review*. Some Christian ideals can be found in his teachings.

In 1950, the hysteria of the Korean War led the Chinese to consider Westerners, including many Christian missionaries, as "enemy aliens." Some were jailed and almost all were expelled. After all, Americans and Canadians were killing Chinese soldiers in that neighboring country. Americans and Canadians reacted similarly during World War II to Japanese people on our west coasts. Even locally born Japanese people had their property confiscated and were shoved off to internment camps. The Chinese also overreacted against all foreigners and those influenced by them, with accusations of spying and sabotage, jail, executions, or deportations.

The Communists also felt that foreign imperialism would continue as long as Chinese Christians maintained their dependency on foreign missionaries. After Liberation, the Christian churches were encouraged to be independent of their foreign roots, and the Protestants set up the Three-Self Patriotic Movement.

The Catholic church, however, officially opposed the rulers of new China. Most of the bishops not jailed fled. When those Catholic leaders who remained nominated new bishops to meet the pastoral needs of more than 100 vacant dioceses, the nominations were ignored by the Vatican. When Chinese leaders went ahead with consecrations, these new bishops were initially excommunicated, their consecrations regarded as irregular. This left resentment in the minds and hearts of Roman Catholic leaders in China seeking to meet the needs of loyal adherents. The situation has begun to improve. Chinese Catholics still celebrate mass in Latin. Some bishops are choosing to celebrate mass in Chinese. And the consecrations are now recognized by Rome.

During the Cultural Revolution, churches and temples were destroyed or closed by the Red Guards as part of the movement against the "Four Olds." The youthful revolutionaries and Mao ignored the constitution, which said that "Citizens enjoy freedom to believe in religion, and freedom not to believe in religion and freedom to propagate atheism." Many church buildings became apartments and factories. The Catholic Cathedral in Guangzhou was used for storage.

In 1978–79, the government encouraged the rebuilding of temples and churches, returning deeds to them and paying overdue rents. People and factories who had taken over the buildings had to be relocated before the buildings could become places of worship or tourism again, a time-consuming process. Some Christians actually continued to tithe even while the churches were closed and later brought these treasures to their newly opened gathering places.

Today the Chinese constitution simply says that all Chinese citizens have freedom of belief. Over 8000 churches and over 20,000 meeting points across China were flourishing at press time, a few having to open Saturdays as well as Sundays to accommodate the many worshipers. Some Christians worship corporately in their homes. While some foreigners have questioned the authenticity of the "state-recognized" versus the "house" Christians, Chinese believers do not regard these as two different categories. It may simply be a matter of convenience or accessibility. Some Christians attend both the small family fellowships and the large general congregations.

Foreigners wanting to contact Protestant groups should ask for the Three-Self Patriotic Movement 中国基督教三自爱国运动 . Catholics should ask for the Chinese Catholic Patriotic Association 中国天主教爱国会 . Don't let the word *Patriotic* bother you. It doesn't sound as chauvinistic in Chinese. You should also consult with the national headquarters of your own church or national church organizations. Some may have China committees and full-time China-watchers who should have the addresses of churches in cities you will be visiting and can give you advice. And when you get there, *worship* with them, even though you do not understand the words. And please do not disturb the service with a camera, or by being late, or by leaving early, as many tourists have done. Church services are not tourist attractions.

Chinese Christians, particularly those in isolated places, will probably be delighted to have you join them. At least one foreign churchgoer was asked to sing once it was known that he was a soloist in a choir in Canada. Please restrain yourself from being overly generous. To encourage materialistic values in a spiritual movement could dilute its spiritual strength. The Chinese want to be self-reliant. Donations with no strings attached can be made to the Amity Foundation, a Christian-inspired people's organization devoted to health, education, and welfare projects in and beyond the Christian community.

Recently, a group of foreigners were arrested for proselytizing. It is illegal for foreigners to do so. You could ask Christians in China if they want foreign missionaries. As for smuggling in Bibles, those days are over. The United Bible Society has given a modern press to the Amity Foundation, which is helping the churches publish their own literature. Since 1981, the China Christian Council has printed over 1.1 million copies of the Bible. The China Christian Council recently said there are now 6375 Protestant churches and 16,868 family meeting points, with over 7 million Protestant Christians and 10 to 20 million enquirers. In 1988, two Protestant bishops were installed. It was the first such event since 1955.

There are also about 3.6 million Catholic Christians, 1000 large Catholic churches, and 10,000 chapels. Between 1980 and 1985, about 130,000 adults were baptized. Eleven seminaries are now open and about 12 convents with 200 women under formation. In 1990, several Roman Catholic clergymen with ties to the Vatican were arrested.

There are also now more than 3600 Buddhist temples open for worship with over 30,000 monks and nuns.

See also *Religious Buildings* in "What Is There to See and Do."

PEOPLE'S FEELINGS   If you read Chinese history, particularly the history of imperialist times from 1840 to 1949, you should be struck by the lack of sensitivity foreigners had for the Chinese people. As a result, the Chinese started hitting back in whatever way they could. They demonstrated; they stoned churches; they murdered individual foreigners. Of course, they were desperate people then, pushed to extremes, but let's not provoke incidents.

Please dress modestly and save your jokes for the privacy of your own rooms. Someone who speaks English may hear you and be offended. Be aware if your driver is blocking a road, causing people pulling heavy loads to go around your bus. Your driver is trying to please *you*. Tell your driver to move somewhere else.

FORMS OF ADDRESS   "Attendant" is the best translation for all service personnel like waiters, room boys, and chambermaids. If you have to get their attention, you can call them "fo wu yuan." Ask your guide what he/she wants to be called. Some have English names.

You can call your guide "mister" or "miss," and if you feel comfortable with it, you can call him/her what the Chinese call each other: *lau* (as in "loud") plus surname, or *xiao* (like "show" as in "shower") plus surname, no matter the sex. *Lau* means "old" and *xiao* means "small." *Lau* is not derogatory in China and refers to anyone over forty.

Relatives are referred to and called by their relationship to you, like "Second Aunt Older Than My Father," or "Fifth Maternal Uncle of My Grandfather's Generation" (two Chinese words for each of these). Your relatives will tell you what to call them.

Chinese names have surnames first. Chou En-lai would be Premier Chou. You rarely address a person by his given name, except children or relatives.

GOVERNMENT   Communist. Officially at the top is the National People's Congress. (See *Great Hall of the People*, "Beijing.") The State Council is the executive organ accountable to the Congress and is similar in makeup to a cabinet. The Communist Party is now again involved in almost every facet of life, after voluntarily withdrawing in the late 1980s. It blamed the 1989 demonstrations on the lack of political education of the people.

GUANXI "Relationships," "influence," "pull," "connections." This is an important part of Chinese life. Schoolmates, teachers, relatives, workmates—people who know each other well have a stronger and longer hold on each other than in the West. *Guanxi* is related to merit and to helping each other. Strangers are politely accepted, but with reservation, until they have proved themselves trustworthy, friendly, and useful.

The government has spoken out against the excesses of *guanxi* because it isn't fair to people without connections.

DEMOCRACY These movements are not new. Writing criticisms and complaints in public places has occurred from time to time in China for centuries and was especially popular during the Cultural Revolution, when they were used for political debates and attacks on "capitalist roaders." The institution was protected by the constitution.

Late in 1978 the writing of big character posters on Democracy Walls flourished unhindered. Four months later, the right to "speak out freely, air views fully, hold great debates, and write big-character posters" was restricted. Taboo were criticisms of socialism, the dictatorship of the proletariat, party leadership, and the ideas of Marx, Lenin, and Mao.

In 1979 foreigners could visit Democracy Walls, talk with anyone who wanted to talk to them, and accept any leaflets. But some of the Chinese were arrested and charged with passing state secrets to foreigners. In December 1979, however, wall posters were curtailed. In September 1980, these rights were deleted from the constitution because they were "easily abused by careerists and schemers . . ."

In 1989, a million people supported student demonstrations for democracy in Beijing, and more elsewhere in the country. They were brutally suppressed. If you're thinking of encouraging dissident movements, just because you believe in democracy, please ask yourself a few questions first. Can China afford an American-style opposition now? Would political unrest upset China's program of feeding her tremendous population and furthering her goals of modernization? Do the dissidents represent a sizable majority? Has China ever had a Western-style democratic government? What is needed, if anything, to prepare the Chinese people for democracy? Can there be democracy without changing the paternalistic family structure?

If you want more information on this subject, Amnesty International and Asia Watch do have reports and the Western press does watch this carefully, sometimes too carefully.

IF A CHINESE asks for help to visit, study in, or emigrate abroad, use your own judgment. In some cases it is possible but not easy. If you're willing to go to a lot of trouble, so be it. But don't make empty promises that will cause great disappointment later. Check with your embassy regarding regulations.

If a local Chinese asks for foreign currency in exchange for regular Chinese currency, this is illegal. Do not break a law just because you have been given a lavish meal.

You could say you have no time to find places to spend R.M.B. They might offer to pay for your purchases or taxis in R.M.B. in return for F.E.C.s. This is so borderline, in terms of the law, that I would do it for friends. You might want to do it privately, too, but keep in mind that exchanging money at par is not to your advantage.

Be aware of the status of drivers in China. Until Chinese people do their own driving, keeping a driver happy is very important. You may find drivers sharing your table at mealtimes.

If Chinese officials visit you in North America, even on business, please be sensitive of foreign exchange. Inviting them to dinner might be better than giving a gift, so they can save on their *per diem* and buy exactly what they want to take home. They might ask to use your phone to call China. Don't be afraid to say no if you can't afford such a call.

FIRECRACKERS are allowed to be exploded in China, but usually in designated places. Many Hong Kong Chinese, forbidden to set them off at home, go berserk when they celebrate in China. Local Chinese are increasingly setting them off noisily at weddings, birthdays, and grand openings. It is not machine-gun fire!

ENDANGERED SPECIES China and many other countries are parties to the Convention on International Trade in Endangered Species of Wild Fauna and Flora (CITES). Any species or products of a species on its lists could be seized by the Customs Department of any of the signatories, unless you have a permit to carry them. The details of the regulations usually can be obtained from your government wildlife service. See "Important Addresses." The much-publicized Save the Panda campaign is an expression of this concern.

Locally, however, Chinese officials are lax about restricting the sale and eating of many endangered or threatened species, notably wild animals like pangolin (scaly anteater) and giant salamander. Coats of spotted cats have been found for sale in Friendship Stores. But the killers of a panda have been executed.

Even while passing through Hong Kong, you risk confiscation of garments and ornaments made of parts of certain animals, like turtles.

The problem is knowing what is or is not on the list. When in

No! No! You may have trouble taking this spotted cat jacket back to your home. It was on sale in the Guangzhou Friendship Store, and is held by Wu Hsiu-yi of C.I.T.S.

doubt, don't eat or buy products made from any **wild animals,** especially spotted cats, alligators, and birds. But some deer and game birds, for example, are grown commercially in China, and therefore can be eaten.

Among the other Chinese species listed by the Convention are: Himalayan argali, Tibetan brown bear, golden cat, dhole (wild dog), gibbons, Przewalski's horse, langur, macaque, and wild yak. Among the birds are the relict gull, crested ibis, and some varieties of cranes, storks, pheasants, and egrets. Avoid any elephant parts.

A copy of this photo of a spotted-cat jacket on sale in the Guangzhou Friendship store was sent to the U.S. Federal Wildlife Permit Office. An official replied, "Such an article of clothing cannot be imported into the United States."

The Canadian Wildlife Service replied, "To import a garment made of leopard cat skins, you must be in possession of a CITES export permit issued by the Government of China. On import, the foreign export permit must be surrendered to Canada Customs. Any attempt to enter the coat without the foreign CITES permit could, at the very least, result in seizure."

The authority allowed to issue CITES permits in China is:

The People's Republic of China Endangered Species of Wild Fauna and Flora Import and Export Administrative Office, Ministry of Forestry, Hepingli, P.O. Box 100714, Beijing; tel. 4214180 or 4213061. Branches also in Fuzhou, Guangzhou, Shanghai, and Tianjin.

SHOPPING

The most important things to remember about shopping in China are:
  —guides are not allowed to accept commissions from stores.
  —there are stores approved for foreign visitors where goods are "guaranteed," prices reasonable and fixed by the local tourism bureau or administration. If customers have solid evidence of misrepresentations about the merchandise, they should be able to get their money back. Customers can also appeal to the tourism bureau for mediation. Payment is usually in F.E.C.s. for foreigners, but not always.
  —there are privately operated stores and peddlers with whom you should haggle as prices are negotiable in R.M.B. or F.E.C.s. You can usually differentiate these from government stores because the clerks are more aggressive, and should you start to move away they will ask how much you want to pay.
  Haggling is imperative in these stores unless you want to pay three or four times the going rate. Start at one quarter what the clerk is asking. You should haggle in all free markets. Check Friendship Stores for current prices and try to beat them. Don't expect guides to be on your side; some have been scolded or beaten for telling tourists the price is too high. Prices fall quicker if you show them F.E.C.s. or U.S. cash.
  —There are fakes and misrepresentations, plastic pearls being passed off as real, substitutes being passed off as jade or pearls, counterfeit U.S. cigarettes. Your "approved" stores should be okay. Be careful in other stores.
  —There are stores that accept R.M.B. You have to figure out which currency is to your advantage as even "10% discount for F.E.C.s." might not match the black market rate.
  —An American size 9 doesn't mean a thing in China. If you are buying for yourself, you should try on clothes. If you are buying clothes for someone else, you should have their measurements.
  —Wool products will probably shrink if washed in hot water.
  —In some cases, a local U.S. consulate might be able to help you if the goods shipped to you are not what you ordered.
  —One should check clothing carefully for flaws and sizes.
  —Many foreign companies have clothes made in China. Some factory overruns are found in hotel and factory stores, and local markets like the Hua Ting in Shanghai and the Xiu Shui Dong Market in Beijing. We have found Oleg Cassini (in a Nantong hotel), L.L. Bean (in

a Nanjing hotel), Victoria's Secret (in a Lanzhou hotel), Yves St. Laurent (in a Shanghai street market), and Land's End (in a Wuxi hotel). Some styles had not yet reached North America. But sizes and color ranges were very limited. Do not expect exchanges except in government stores.

—If you have bought more than your duty-free limit, it might save you money if you had a Certificate of Origin. This could reduce the duty you have to pay on certain items. Certificates are available from some government stores when you make purchases.

—The export of antiques from Tibet is forbidden. Your purchases there could be seized.

NOTE: · · · Not all stores can crate and ship goods outside of China. Ask before you buy.

Take your own bag or basket for shopping in markets.

Save your sales slips so you can argue with Customs officials if need be in your own country. Receipts will be in Chinese with English numerals, so make a note of what each refers to.

Clothing and other items imported from elsewhere for sale in China are, of course, cheaper in the country of origin. Some of what you see may have been made in Hong Kong.

When comparing Chinese prices with those elsewhere, don't forget to include the sales tax at home, the rate of duty, and the shipping costs if these apply. In China you pay no additions to the asking price.

Several kinds of outlets should interest foreign shoppers:

FRIENDSHIP STORES were originally set up so that foreigners wouldn't have to buck curious crowds while shopping. But now anyone can shop there. At least one Friendship Store serves every city. Some accept RMB from foreigners. Don't ask, just hand it over. Prices are about the same or slightly higher than other Chinese stores, but the goods are of better quality there, and some items are unavailable elsewhere.

In addition to arts and crafts, many larger Friendship Stores have textiles, television sets, radios, watches, bicycles, sewing machines, cosmetics, herbal medicines, food, jewelry, thermos bottles, camera film, jackknives, flashlights, cashmere sweaters, silk blouses and shirts—just about anything needed by visitors and relatives of visitors. Friendship Stores usually have locally made goods for sale. The best stores are in Guangzhou, Beijing, and Shanghai. Be aware that some privately run stores are using the ''Friendship'' name and reputation, but they are not government Friendship Stores with guarantees.

ARTS, CRAFTS, AND ANTIQUE STORES These may or may not be government-owned. The quality of goods is sometimes better than that of Friendship Stores. These can be found in hotels or on shopping streets, some selling only for F.E.C.s and others for R.M.B.

FACTORIES Every arts and crafts factory has a showroom where visitors can buy. Prices are not always lower than elsewhere. Some showrooms are open all the time; others are open by appointment only. Aim for factories that have overruns from export orders.

DEPARTMENT STORES sometimes have arts and crafts, too. Visitors might find good buys in clothing, down, furs, novelties, etc. Pay with R.M.B.

FREE MARKETS are where farmers sell their excess produce, people with connections abroad sell foreign-made clothes, tailors solicit customers, and cottage industries sell handicrafts and baked goods. With no changing rooms, people buying jeans have to try them on over their own trousers. Many markets are in alleys under shelter.

Antiques have been sold in free markets but some antiques are not authenticated. Antique sections in free markets are closed down from time to time because of unauthorized sales of antiques. Look for the red wax seal. Great buys in clothes made for export are at the free market between the Friendship Store and the Jianguo Hotel in Beijing.

OVERSEAS CHINESE STORES are mainly for relatives of Overseas Chinese who receive foreign exchange. In these they can buy normally hard-to-obtain items. Some of these stores are called Duty-Free Stores and sell imported and locally made refrigerators, videos, microwaves, etc.

HOTEL STORES The best in clothing styles, fabrics, and antiques can usually be found in fancy joint venture hotel stores, but they are not cheap.

MINORITY HANDICRAFTS It is usually more meaningful to buy direct from the maker in her village. (Take a photo, her address and mail her a copy of the photo later if you want to make friends.) I once paid ¥25 for a baby's bonnet and then was told it took two months to make. I felt guilty for days after but she wouldn't have made even the ¥25 if I hadn't bought it. Embroidery is not mass-produced and can be very beautiful. There is not much to choose from but a good embroidered jacket from the Miao nationality (US$50 in Kaili) would probably sell in New York City for a couple hundred. Beautiful, large batik tablecloths in Dali were going for US$5 at the factory. Consider laundering before you buy. Some Miao skirts could lose their pleats and some jackets their paper or cardboard backing if washed.

HAGGLING   The possibility of bargaining down prices is better in China than in Hong Kong.

The secret is to know prices and not to buy anything the first time you see it. At free markets, there will be many stalls selling the same things. If you are asked what you want to pay, suggest a ridiculously low amount—a quarter of the price. Then walk away pretending you are not interested. The seller might counter with hand motions for you to give a higher bid and you could come up a bit. Start to move away again and look at the same thing in the next stall. It is a guessing game— the seller trying to decide how badly you want it, and you trying to decide the bottom line for the seller.

After you have gotten the price as low as possible, you could also ask a Chinese friend to try for less. Guides will do this for you, pay in RMB to get your FEC. Frequently guides cling to the shoppers to make foreign exchange, and ignore the rest of the group. Other members should complain.

WHAT TO BUY

China is famous for its **arts and crafts.**

Sometimes, but not always, your **best prices** in China are at the factories, where groups and anyone buying large quantities should get discounts. Your next best at stores in the same city or province as the factory. Sometimes demand has something to do with prices. Store managers do not always know how much to charge for an item, and so the same thing may have a different price in another store. Rubbings bought at temples where they were made might cost more than the same thing at the Friendship Stores. The only difference is a red souvenir seal on the temple-bought rubbing, but is it worth extra to you?

Compare prices in several stores. Price should not always be the deciding factor, though. You have to know quality to get good buys. Learn it by studying a lot of good art, and try your own hand at carving and painting before you go to China. Read books, talk with dealers like Hanart in Hong Kong, and even take courses. Go to museums in your own country that have displays of Chinese art. Many places in China make reproductions.

If you are a **serious shopper,** plan your trip so you can see how a favorite craft is made. Locally made crafts are listed under each destination in this book.

Telephone the factories first. If you are a "buyer" and have business cards to that effect, just telephone for an appointment. If you are an amateur without *guanxi,* you might have to make arrangements through C.I.T.S. (and pay). Not all factories are open all the time for tourists.

In the factory, you can study how the pieces are made, and ask about the most difficult techniques, the criteria of a good piece, and how to tell a phony from a genuine article. You can find out how to clean a piece and where the best materials are from. Will the wood or lacquer crack in dry, centrally heated homes? You should be allowed to handle some of the best pieces. Feel the weight, the surface texture. Compare these with the ordinary quality. For reproductions, study the originals in nearby museums. Remember also that handmade articles are each different—of course! So before you buy, check carefully, not just for flaws, but for the rendering that you like best.

Generally speaking, **consider** (1) the amount of work involved in the production—the finer, the more intricate something is, the better; (2) good proportions, lines, balance, and color; (3) how closely it represents what it is supposed to represent; (4) the quality of the material—will it chip? (soapstone breaks easily and is almost not worth buying); and (5) whether it will be a joy forever, or will you easily tire of it? Primitive art doesn't have to be well proportioned or intricate.

Remember, too, that government stores have a reputation for honesty. If they know something is better, usually they will tell you.

If you are looking for an **investment,** don't buy gold here. It is cheaper elsewhere.

Crafts can also be **made-to-order,** but most Chinese factories are not set up for easy ordering. The cross-stitch factory in Yantai can make good replicas of photographs, for example. These of course take a lot of time. The most difficult part of such an exercise is getting the idea of what you want over to the craftsman.

Most general tours include at least one handicraft factory and always one Friendship or Arts and Crafts store. Many cities also have handicraft *institutes* where new crafts are developed and craftspeople are trained.

If you are more interested in handicrafts than temples, it is best if you take an individual or special-interest tour. On a regular tour, the average tourist will be back at the bus waiting for you while you're still talking about texture or the iron content in glazes.

The destinations with the largest number of various handicrafts are Beijing, Tianjin, Shanghai, and Guangzhou.

Here is a list of some crafts and where they are made.

Bamboo: Guangdong (especially Huaiji County), Guangxi, Hunan and Hubei provinces

Brushes for Chinese painting: best from Huzhou, Jiangsu.

Batiks: Xi'an, Yunnan, Shaoyang (Hunan), Nantong, and Guizhou

Beaded curtains: Zhejiang province

Carpets: Tianjin, Shanghai, Qingdao, Beijing, Changchun, Urumqi, Kashgar, Weihai, Inner Mongolia. There is a difference between "hand made" and "hand knotted."

Cashmere sweaters: Hohhot, Baotou

Clay sculptures, painted: Tianjin, Wuxi

Cloisonne (metal base, wire designs filled in with enamel and baked): Beijing (best), Guangzhou, Shanghai, Xi'an (more expensive). Reject tiny holes in the enamel, uneven surfaces and broken copper wire.

Dough figurines: Beijing, Guilin, Shanghai. Peddlers used to make these for fascinated children who then promptly ate them. Today a chemical that makes the dough very hard is now added. For fine sculpture, this is your cheapest buy.

Embroidered or crochetted linens: best buys in Shantou, Guangzhou, Guilin, Nantong, Weihai, and also Shandong

Fans: Suzhou

Feather pictures: Shenyang, Qingdao

Food: best sweet vinegar from Zhenjiang, dried mushrooms from Fujian, dried tangerine peel from Xinhui *fa cai;* Hohhot, Yinchuan. Don't bother with cans or bottles. Go for the lighter dried things that are very expensive in North America.

Furniture: Good quality traditional Chinese furniture: Xi'an, Zhejiang

Furs: Shijiazhuang, Dalian, Tianjin, Beijing, Harbin

Glass, artistic: Chongqing, Dalian, Shanghai, Tianjin, Zibo in Shandong, Beijing

Glass snuff bottles: Beijing

Iron pictures: Wuhu, Anhu

Jewelry: Beijing, Guangzhou, Shanghai

Kites: Weifang, Tianjin

Lacquer: Yangjiang in Guangdong, Shanghai, Beijing, Xi'an, Shantou, Fuzhou, Yangzhou

Metal handicrafts: Jiangdu County in Jiangsu, Hangzhou, Shanghai, Chengdu, Zhangzhu in Jiangsu

Metal—swords and knives: Husaba in Longchuan County, Yunnan, Longquan in Zhejiang, Hohhot, Kashgar

Paintings and calligraphy: everywhere; peasant paintings from Xi'an, but some of our colors (gray) cracked when rolled

Paper—wood-block printing: Beijing (Rong Bao Zhai), Suzhou, Tianjin

Paper-cuts: everywhere. Transient peddlers used to make these on the spot and then sell them. For those mounted on colored paper: Hailun County in Heilongjiang; for multicolored ones: Yuxian County in Hubei; for large ones, about 2×3 feet: Foshan.

Paper New Year's pictures: Formerly of the kitchen god and the doorway gods, etc., these are now of cherubs and mythological characters. They are for posting around the house at New Year. Brighter, more cheerful colors than traditional art: Weifang in Shandong, Tianjin

Pearls: Zhejiang, Jiangsu for fresh-water; Hainan for cultured; Zhuji in Jiangxi is the country's largest distribution center.

Porcelain/Ceramics: most famous—Jingdezhen (blue and white, eggshell); Yixing (for purple, unglazed); Foshan (for Shiwan); Shantou (for multicolored and chrysanthemums in high relief); Liling in Hunan south of Changsha; Pengcheng County in Hebei (for the Cizhou kiln's "iron embroidery" ware); Longquan in Zhejiang, Hangzhou, Shaanxi, and Jingdezhen (for celadon, that porcelain attempt to imitate green jade). The finest porcelain is said to be white as jade, shiny as a mirror, thin as paper, and resonant as a bell. Poisonous levels of lead have been found in some Chinese glazes, especially yellows. We suggest you test anything you plan for food or drink before use.

Reproductions: of ancient porcelains: Jingdezhen; of bronzes: Hangzhou, Luoyang; of three-color Tang: Luoyang and Xi'an

Rubbings: Xi'an (best for calligraphy), Luoyang, Suzhou

Sandalwood: Suzhou

Shell art: Qingdao, Xi'an, Dalian

Silk: Guangzhou, Shanghai (best selection for ready-made garments but some factories are overpriced), Suzhou (very good selection), Hangzhou, Nanjing, Changzhou in Jiangsu; **brocade:** Shanghai; **double-faced silk paintings:** Zhangzhu in Jiangsu; **embroidery:** most famous schools—*Suzhou, Xiang* (Hunan—Changsha), *Yue* (Guangdong—Shantou), and *Shu* (Sichuan). Also of note: Shanghai, for **embroidered silk blouses; festival lanterns:** Beijing, Shanghai, Foshan, and Jiangsu, Fujian, Zhejiang, and Anhui provinces; **flowers:** Shanghai; **underwear:** Jiangsu and Zhejiang; tie-dyed **kerchiefs:** Xi'an; **scarves:** Shanghai

Stone carvings: Fuzhou in Fujian, Qingtian in Zhejiang, and Liuyang chrysanthemum stone carving in Hunan; **jade:** Shanghai, Beijing, Guilin, Xi'an. Jade can be nephrite (hard as glass, greasy look known as mutton fat, best pure white) or jadeite (wide range of colors, including emerald green; used more in jewelry, the more translucent the better). Since jade is very hard and thus difficult to carve, the most expensive is the most intricately carved and multicolored. The colors are cleverly worked into the design. Serpentine is not true jade but frequently passes as jade. It is softer. The Chinese use the word jade to mean a wide range of hard stones. Soapstone is cheap and breaks easily.

Straw: Fujian, Sichuan, Guangdong, and Shandong (Yantai) provinces

Tie-dye: Yunnan, Shanghai

Toys: one should hesitate about buying toys that could end up in a baby's mouth unless you know about the stuffing material or lead in the paint.

Tribal weaving and embroidery: the Miao in Guizhou province, and most places where national minorities live

Turquoise: Wuhan

Wood carvings: Quanzhou and Putian in Fujian, Changchun, Dongyang in Zhejiang (gingko wood), Fuzhou (longan wood), northeast provinces (azalea root), Wenzhou, Shanghai, Beijing. For **gilt camphor wood:** Chaozhou and Shantou. For **sandalwood fans** (smell before buying): Suzhou and Hangzhou

Wool needlepoint: Shanghai Arts and Crafts Studio; Yantai in Shandong

Favorite mythological and/or historical subjects of arts and crafts:

Poet Shi Yung—late Spring and Autumn Period. Knot on top of head. Sword on back.

Wei Tou—guardian of Buddhism and of the Goddess of Mercy.

Guan Yin—originally a god, but in recent sculpture, always the Goddess of Mercy. Depicted with children, or carrying a cloud duster (like a horsetail whip), or with many heads, or with a vase.

Princess Wen Chen—the Chinese princess who married a Tibetan king and took Buddhism to Tibet.

Scholar Dong Kuo—who was kind even to wolves. He once saved a wolf from a hunter and was admonished by the hunter that a wolf can't change its habits.

Li Shi-zen—Ming dynasty author of the classic book on medicinal herbs. Depicted carrying herbs in a basket, and a hoe.

God of Longevity—old man with peach.

God of Wealth—well-dressed man with scepter.

God of Happiness—man with scroll.

Laughing Buddha—sometimes with five children or standing alone with raised hands.

Eight Taoist Genii—see *Taoist temples* in "What Is There to See and Do?"

Fa Mu-lan—famous woman general who inspired Maxine Hong Kingston's *The Woman Warrior.*

Characters from classical Chinese novels—*Water Margin, Dream of the Red Chamber, Pilgrimage to the West.*

Favorite revolutionary subjects of arts and crafts:

Soldier O Yang Hai—usually shown on railway track pushing a horse. He was killed but the horse was saved.

Dr. Norman Bethune—usually the only foreigner depicted. Canadian doctor who worked with the Eighth Route Army until his death from blood poisoning in 1939.

Lu Xun—famous modern Chinese writer.

Soldier Lei Feng—PLA truck driver based in Shenyang who was always helping people selflessly and, like the Lone Ranger, anonymously. Killed in accident about 1964.

Antiques: As with such shopping elsewhere, you have to know your goods if you want a bargain. Antiques are not cheap, but Chinese antiques are usually cheaper there than in most stores in your own country. Actually your best buy for pre-Qing antiques is Hong Kong, but only if you know your stuff better than the person you're buying from.

So much has been smuggled out to Hong Kong that prices there are good. In China itself, you can get good buys in antiques in smaller communities like Qufu (which has a lot of old, ornately carved beds for sale). Antique stores and markets abound all over. So do fakes.

You have to prove to your own Customs people that what you have bought is a duty-free antique. Get convincing documents.

You can sometimes buy ''antiques'' in free markets, but nothing is guaranteed there. People are clearing out their homes of ''old'' things to sell and they don't know how old or how valuable they are. The usual rule is ''If you like it, and want to pay the price, then buy it.'' See also ''Before You Go.''

Officially, antiques made between 1795 and 1949 are not allowed out of China unless they have a red wax seal on them. Only one store is allowed to sell anything for export made before 1795 and that is the Yueyatang on Liulichang Dong St. in Beijing (tel. 330020). But in practice Customs officials rarely search the bags of departing visitors. You can have ''antiques'' checked and approved for export in the Beijing Friendship store, or ask C.I.T.S.

Novelties and miscellaneous: If your speed, like mine, is not in the $3000 carpet class, China does have a good variety of novelties, things distinctively Chinese to take back to your nieces and nephews and bridge buddies. Most of the following are obtainable from Friendship Stores, but some only from big department stores.

Acupuncture dolls: These are about ten inches high with genuine acupuncture needles and an instruction booklet (in Chinese) for do-it-yourselfers. If these are too expensive, try **acupuncture posters,** found in bookstores—cheap. **Health balls** to improve blood circulation and avoid arthritis.

Posters, postcards, and comic books are fun and cheap, and so is a **map** of the world showing China in the center, or of Canada and the U.S. in Chinese characters.

Books: There are some children's books showing Chinese characters with equivalent pictures, like our ABCs. If you're in a foreign-language bookstore, you'll find a great many books in English (cheap), all printed in China. They also make great souvenirs.

Museum reproductions: Some of these are quite good and not too expensive. Check out the retail store in any museum you visit.

T-shirts: marked ''Xi'an,'' ''Shanghai,'' or ''Shaoshan.'' Lots of cheap souvenir pins with the name of a touristy site. Then there are Chinese **kites,** traditional **baby bonnets** of silk or rayon trimmed with fur ears to make baby look like a tiger kitten, **Mao caps, plastic eggs**

with chicks inside, **folding scissors, stuffed animals,** battery-operated **toys,** do-it-yourself **acupressure machines.**

Cloisonne: comes in beads, bracelets, vases, thimbles, scissors, jack-knives, nail clippers, and pill boxes. **Silk** comes in ties and cute, cheap panties.

There are fancy gold-trimmed **chopsticks** from Fuzhou, and stone **seals** where you can have a rubber stamp made of your name in Chinese. Hong Kong visitors say these are cheaper in China.

Some visitors take back Chinese **wines** and **vodka** or Chinese **teas.**

Vests with appliques have been a hit with tourists to Xi'an, where they are cheaper than elsewhere in China, but consider laundering before you buy because of the paper backing. Now that people are free to market their handicrafts, a lot of new designs are being created. A lot of junk is being made too. If you buy the junk, the Chinese will only make more of it.

Chinese fiction is not written full of conflict, sex, and violence, the way some popular Western fiction is, but try some of the classics and Lu Xun if you want. Books make good gifts. China pirates Chinese translations of Western textbooks, but foreigners are not allowed to buy in those sections of the book stores. Book lovers must visit Liulichang in Beijing to look at samples of fine Chinese printing.

Tailors are not as good as in other places in Asia, like Hong Kong, and clothes take longer to make. But they are cheap! Don't bother having clothes tailored here unless a tailor is recommended by Western friends and you have a picture or sample of what you want made. Even Shanghai tailors have lost the art. See "Shanghai."

Furs, down coats, and leather jackets are bargains, but please, please, don't buy any endangered species. A Hong Kong furrier said the quality of the tanning of a lot of Chinese skins in general is not very good and might later stink when wet, so check carefully. See "Local Customs."

Live plants, birds, and animals: Check with your embassy. Usually these are not allowed into your country without specific certificates, not easily obtainable outside your country.

Cassettes: China has some fine musicians, and music lovers might like recordings. For names and titles see "What Is There to See and Do?"

Movies and slides of Chinese tourist attractions are available. The films are in 16 and 35mm and video cassette. The videos may have to be converted for use abroad; this takes a couple of days.

WHAT IS THERE TO SEE AND DO?

How Observant Are You?

By the time you've been in China a week, you should have some idea: (1) if the Chinese people are happy; (2) if the modernization campaign is succeeding; (3) who the premier is; (4) what the population is; (5) what kind of a government China has and how it functions.

You should also know: (6) the name of the capital; (7) the names of two provinces; (8) the names of two rivers.

And, one hopes, you would have looked at the inside of a Chinese home and chatted with some Chinese people besides your guide.

If you haven't done 80 percent of these, then think about why you came to China in the first place. Visiting China is a great opportunity to learn about another culture, another history, another way of life. It is a chance to speculate if China is going to affect your future: Will there be a war that would involve your country? Will its cheaper labor affect your economy? Will China's solutions to its problems help solve your country's problems? What is it doing about controlling the growth of its population? The energy shortage? Its ethnic minorities? Is it ready to become a democracy? Is there anything China can teach you about arts? Patience?

NOTE: · · · Visitors to China in previous years were given the impression that everything was going well in China. Yet later the Chinese themselves were saying that things were very wrong in several of the previous periods. So do evaluate what you hear critically. The person who briefs you is telling you the truth as he sees it. Do cross-examine pleasantly if he gives you information that just doesn't quite ring true to you. It may also be something you've misunderstood.

Things to Do

Checklist: To help you observe, especially when you have nothing to do on a train or bus, use this list. Make a check if you see any of these things:

1. a foot-operated water pump ( )
2. an electric water pump ( )
3. an earthen cone-shaped tomb ( )
4. a funeral ( )
5. a pregnant woman ( )
6. a satellite dish not attached to a hotel ( )
7. a village watchtower (mainly in south) ( )
8. a woman doing manual labor in high heels ( )
9. a fat child ( )
10. a city without a construction crane ( )
11. a mud sled with runners ( )
12. an old woman with tiny bound feet ( )
13. a wedding procession ( )
14. coal-dust bricks drying ( )
15. a brick kiln ( )
16. three kinds of wild birds, ( ), ( ), and ( )
17. a boy carrying a baby ( )
18. a statue of Chairman Mao ( )
19. criminals marching to be executed ( )

Survey citizens by age regarding ownership of color TVs, refrigerators, washing machines, private telephones, motorcycles, and videos.

Walk Go for a walk by yourself or with *one* friend and a copy of this book. Go early in the morning before breakfast when you are fresh (if you are fresh in the morning). Walk slowly without a camera, for cameras tend to separate people; they keep you from feeling, from savoring the waking of a world that is unlike any other on earth. Walk away from the main streets; explore the alleys.

Life swims around you; a woman brushes her teeth on the street. People line up doing the ethereal *taiji quan* exercises in slow motion. Most are following one leader. Join them and try it yourself. Usually they won't mind.

Look at the tiny houses, the charming paper windows, the carvings on the door hinges, the storefronts open to the street; wait—maybe they're tiny factories or homes with workshops in front. Go to a park; you might even hear some beautiful but very shy singers practicing. You might be asked to help a student practice his English. If the park is a historic monument, savor it slowly. There is no tour guide rushing you from place to place. Imagine how it looked 300 years ago when the common people and you were not allowed here. Think of the centuries of bustling human activity that took place here.

Go back to the street and watch the people riding to work on bicycles, buses, or trucks. Do they look harried, content, blank? Imagine yourself riding with them. Imagine yourself living in one of their apartments. Do you know enough about them to know how they feel?

Look for signs of Westernization. Any Coca-Cola ads yet? Any Western movies? Permanent waves? High heels? Is that bright-red billboard a Four Modernizations slogan? Or is it a poem by Chairman Mao? What are the sounds you hear? Traffic noises? The strains of "The East Is Red" on the loudspeaker or something from *The Sound of Music*? Listen to the language. It is tonal, like singing almost.

Look for old churches (Gothic-type windows) and temples. Was that bicycle cart an ambulance? Is that a woman pulling a heavy cart? Smile back at people who stare at you. Give them a cheery "Ni hao?" You might get a smile back. If you get lost, don't worry. See "Useful Phrases."

Visit a factory, any factory, just as long as it's not a handicraft factory where you'll get involved in discussions of artistic techniques and buying. C.I.T.S. or the service desk in your hotel can arrange the trip and a guide. Tell them you want to visit a worker's home and talk to some workers. You won't need the Chinese in the "Useful Phrases" if you have an interpreter, but these might give you some idea of what questions to ask first.

What is interesting about Chinese workers is mobility (or lack of it), job security, what happens if they don't like their jobs, housing, time off and vacations, social security, travel, work incentives before 1978 and now, what they think of as they bicycle to work, and how did they meet their spouses. How are young people today different from the previous generation? What are the incentives for a planned family? What if someone in the work unit absents himself too often? Workers' schools? Taxes? Do employees moonlight? Do employees have a say in personnel policies, hiring and firing, working conditions? What kind of information is kept in employee dossiers? How is the one-family-one child policy controlled? Communist party involvement? Is the person answering your questions a party member?

Who decides on what products to manufacture? Is the factory privately, collectively, or state owned? What is the difference? Do they have political meetings? How often? What about criticism–self-criticism sessions? What is the extent of recently introduced capitalistic practices? Are workers paid piecemeal or by salary? Does the contract system apply here, and if so how?

Learn about the manufacturing process and how different things are in China from your home country. Find out how the new economic policies have affected labor. Have the best and the brightest left to set up enterprises of their own?

Visit the countryside   Rural China has also changed dramatically lately. Formerly, the countryside was divided into "communes" and you might still hear the term used as it is a political unit. Communes are now "counties" again, and "production brigades" and "teams" are "villages," depending on location.

In addition to name changes, the average per capita income in counties has risen considerably since the early '80s, and living in a village now seems more appealing than living in a city. How have they done this? What percentage of the income is still agricultural? What is happening to the lifestyle? The birth-control program, with the economy based on the family? Since most of China is considered rural, developments here are very important. For a head start, read Hinton's *The Great Reversal—The Privatization of China.*

Some counties are more interesting to visit than others. The ones around Guangzhou offer shooting galleries, ox-cart rides, lion dances, and bicycle rentals! At harvest time, some villages will allow you to eat all the lichees/litchis and apples you want. You can learn a lot from the villages that preserve fruit, or grow jasmine tea, or silk worms. Around Beijing, you can see how Peking ducks are force-fed. Gardeners should have a field day learning about exotic vegetables. Have you ever seen rice growing before? Water chestnuts? Bamboo shoots, fungi, and *facai*? All are yummy ingredients you find in Chinese restaurants! Why does China have to import grain? Why is there a pork shortage?

But you can also look at the industries. Some counties produce transformers, cement boats, and arts and crafts, like Cabbage Patch clones. Look at the schools and facilities for children. Some counties have built swimming pools, zoos, and merry-go-rounds.

You will probably be given a briefing with the basic statistics. You could also ask: What about old-age pensions? What security is there if not children? What about the people who are not making as much money as the others? Is it a matter of luck, or are they not working as hard? Has anyone from here gone to university? Traveled abroad? Do young people still want to move to the cities? Why are some counties richer than others? Is any of the produce here exported abroad? Who decides what is grown? Housing?

Visit a school   Nursery schools are always entertaining. You have to be very hard-hearted if you aren't charmed by them. Count on half a day. In some nursery schools, visitors are involved in some of the children's games. In all nursery schools you will tour the classrooms, have a performance of songs and dances, and get a briefing with an opportunity to ask questions. Nursery-school songs are a good indicator of the current political atmosphere. At one time the children were singing songs about shooting down American planes. Recently, we found a five-year-old girl doing a sexy dance. (Of course we voiced objections to her teachers!) In more advanced schools, you may be expected to read an English lesson. Suggest that your reading be recorded so the children can hear it again and memorize your accent and inflections.

Chinese schools were closed during the Cultural Revolution, so that the students could "make revolution." After they were opened again, the curriculum placed more emphasis on politics than academics, even as a criterion for university entrance. How was this allowed to happen? What has happened to this generation of academically unprepared students? Is education going too much the other way now? Are students losing touch with peasants and workers? Do they still spend time working in factories? Why are only a few people going to university when China needs highly trained people? What kind of teaching aids do they have? How many students in each class? What about the slow learners? The exceptionally bright child? What scientific apparatus do they have? What prospects for graduates? Why have there been student demonstrations? Have the teachers been forbidden from receiving gifts from the students?

See also *Gifts* in "What to Take."

Offer to help, but only if the Chinese seem interested. (See also the section on visiting as a scholar in "The Basics.") This is not just for China's sake but also to give you a deeper experience in China. You may make some good professional contacts.

Two hours in a Chinese school will not tell you much about the education system, but struggling with an English class will tell you a lot more. If you are at a university and Chinese scholars start asking probing questions, then grab your chance. If you are in a tour group, make a date to meet them again. If you have brought along slides or pictures, tell them. If you are talking with a museum director and Chinese history is your field, offer to write the English titles on the exhibits or catalog their English-language library.

If you are already successfully helping hotel attendants with their English, and you're not on a tightly scheduled tour, offer to stay a few more days to make tape recordings or give more lessons. Hint that you don't have much money and can't stay too long. If the hotel management is sharp, they should grab the opportunity for a teacher in return for a room and maybe foreign experts' rates on food. This way they don't have to go through the red tape of getting a teacher. Student groups might offer to help plant trees with Chinese student groups if they're in China on tree-planting day in March or April.

Get off the well-beaten tourist track —it's safe. Just don't go anywhere there's a sign that says foreigners are forbidden. If anyone asks what you are doing, tell him. Just don't take photographs in police stations.

Actually, **police stations** are interesting. If you're lost, you might look for one to ask directions back. I once saw three teenagers locked in a cage under the stairs.

Visit a public market   The free market is where commune members sell the surplus from their private vegetable plots. You will see some women with three eggs or a couple of pounds of cabbage.

Look for an old map of the city you are in. The museum may have one you can copy. Follow the **old wall** or look for remains of gates. Follow rivers and canals. Figure out how the city was defended.

Learn Chinese   No, it's not all that hard to understand. Listen carefully as it is spoken. Some words reoccur frequently. Ask what these mean. You probably know some Chinese already. *Shanghai* means "above the sea." *Shang* is "above." When you get to Beijing, you will hear about Beihai Park, "North Sea Park." *Hai* again is "sea." As for *Bei,* also found in *Beijing,* it means "north." *Beijing* is "Northern Capital." *Jing* is the same "jing" as in *Nanjing,* "Southern Capital."

Learn your numbers and make the elevator operator grin. *Lou* as in "loud" means "floor." Reading numbers will help in museums. You only have to learn ten. The rest are combinations. See "Useful Phrases." Learn the polite things first: "good morning," "please," "thank you," and "good-bye." When someone asks you to help with English, ask him or her to help you with your Chinese. Exchange lessons with people you meet at English Corners, which are found in many cities in a designated park on Sundays. Ask C.I.T.S.

Visit museums   These can be deadly dull if you don't do it right. I have seen people hurrying past pieces that set my heart pounding, without batting an eyelash. You will get much more out of a Chinese museum (1) if you read something about Chinese history first; for a quick course see "Milestones in Chinese History"; (2) if you take a knowledgeable guide; and (3) if you are eager to learn things like the date of the earliest pottery, blue and white porcelain, weaving, writing, money, sewer pipes, paper, gun powder, metal implements, etc. It might excite you even more to compare these with the earliest in your civilization. Try to figure out how and why things were made. Trace their development. How did neolithic man get his fire? When did the Chinese first use fertilizer?

China is so rich in archaeology that most cities have good collections. These are lessons in history. The problem for foreigners is that most museums do not have titles in English. If you don't have a guide and have learned your Chinese numbers, at least you could look up the dates in "Milestones" and get a general idea of the period and what the relic might be. There is also a list of dynasties in the "Quick Reference'' section with the names in Chinese and English. Each gallery is usually labeled with a dynasty name and/or a date. You could try to figure from this too.

Chinese museums are usually set up chronologically from primitive to revolutionary times. City and provincial museums usually have relics found in the area. Some have exhibits of how things like bronzes were made. Most have excavations from ancient tombs, pottery figures of humans and animals, some of the most lifelike statues in China. Some of the most important pieces may not be original, but will be good reproductions. The originals are too valuable to expose to light and to the possibility of deterioration. You might notice that the lights are dim. It is deliberate. Take a flashlight.

Some museums have booklets in English. Some museums have been built over archaeological sites, a most exciting idea. You stand where you know people stood 6000 years ago and look at the remains of their houses, and where they stored their farm tools and buried their children. The skeletons are still there, excavated and protected by glass so you can see them. If you are at all psychic, you might feel some ancient vibes in a situation like this. Take your time. Meditate. I have a friend who gets visions sometimes if she holds a relic. She believes she sees the culture from which the relic came as if it were a movie.

Bronzes are not as well known abroad as Chinese porcelains or paintings. The museums in China are full of these ceremonial vessels, easily dismissed as uninteresting. They are, in fact, very exciting, the products of a highly developed technology with no peer anywhere else in the world at that time. Where else was there cast 800 kg of molten bronze into a one-piece bell over 3000 years ago? Just think of the logistics of doing it! How many men were accidentally burned to death in the process? Did they use cranes? How many finished bells were discarded when they did not produce the correct tone? Did anyone get beheaded for the mistake?

And then to bury the result! The economy must have been pretty solid to support this kind of extravagance. Or did the masses have to suffer for it? Confucius, who seems to have been sensitive to the needs of common people, looked back to the Zhou dynasty as a golden age of order and prosperity. Something about the bronze era must have been right.

Bronzes are uncensored history books cast in metal, said one enthusiastic scientist. On them have been inscribed the earliest script, like the family Bible of old, recording family names and important dates. Later, historical events were reported on them.

The shapes of the ritual bronzes were based originally on utensils of everyday use like two-level steamers and cooking pots. From bronzes, archaeologists have concluded that weapons and agricultural tools were basically of the same designs. No one seems to know if the bronzes

Gu—Wine goblet   Be—Ewer

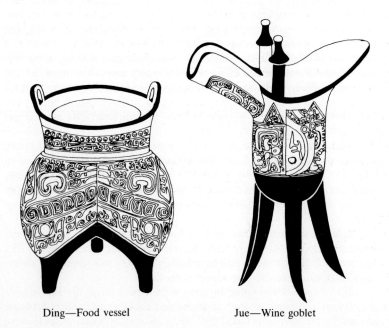

Ding—Food vessel   Jue—Wine goblet

themselves were used in daily life. They were usually found in tombs buried with the dead for the use of the spirits.

The Chinese cast this alloy of tin and copper from molds. Emperor Yu of the Xia Dynasty (about 21st–16th century B.C.) is believed to have ordered some vessels made by vassal states as tribute. Unfortunately, those bronzes were lost by the end of the Zhou dynasty and no solid evidence has since surfaced.

The oldest surviving bronzes are from the Shang dynasty, and one can trace the development of the art in China's well-stocked museums. The shapes of the legs, the decorations, the type of script. Even if you can't read Chinese, at least you can see the differences in style from dynasty to dynasty.

As you study them, note that the early thin-walled Shang pieces were relatively crude, with two-dimensional patterns and stylized boogeyman figures. Look for "ogres," serpents, dragons, and "nipples" (bosses) in bands. Later, the patterns covered the whole vessels in increasingly elaborate ways. Can you recognize cowrie shells, cicadas, birds, and braided rope motifs? Animal heads became three-dimensional and realistic. Animal statues like elephants and tigers started appearing. Bosses became coiled serpents. (Castings of human figures were rare.) Walls became thicker. The shapes of the legs developed from blades to dowels. Then gold or silver inlay came into being. More and different shapes appeared.

Bronzes were fashionable until the Han, after which the art died out. (See also *Provincial Museum* under "Wuhan" in Destinations.)

Some guides are steering tourists away from the revolutionary sections of museums, thinking they may not be interested. Do tell them if you are. It is good to see China's version of historic events. It may differ from what you have always heard. For this reason, Chinese history from 1840 on should be of tremendous interest. Did British soldiers really sack and rape in every city they captured? Was the British ship *Amethyst* acting cowardly or heroically? Did the missionaries deserve to be thrown out of China? Why do the Communists glorify the Christian-inspired Taipings and the fanatical Boxers? Was the Long March a cowardly or heroic act? Was the Great Leap Forward a mistake? Was the Cultural Revolution a mistake without any redeeming features?

Ask political questions   Don't be afraid to do this. If it is done in the right spirit, both the Chinese and you can learn a lot. Political discussions can get heated. Please keep the conversation friendly and relaxed. If you succeed in convincing them of your opinions or vice versa, it won't be because of shouting and red faces.

Do ask them why they think Richard Nixon is a hero, what is meant by "democratic centralism," what they think will happen if the Four Modernizations fail, and whether it was right to imprison novelist

Ding Ling (Ting Ling) and poet Ai Qing (Ai Ching) after the Hundred Flower Movement. If they look like they're uncomfortable with the question, don't pursue it. They may be under a lot of pressure to give the correct political answer and they may not know it. The better you know a person, the franker an answer you will get. And no answer will also give you an indication of the answer, if you know what I mean.

Go to cultural events   During and after the Cultural Revolution, at the instigation of Jiang Qing, wife of Chairman Mao, only eight operas were allowed to be performed, all with strong revolutionary messages. Since the end of 1976, many of the restrictions on entertainment were lifted. It no longer had to "serve the revolution." Some of it was actually frivolous. The pendulum has been swinging back and forth since.

Most movies are in Chinese. Look for historical dramas so you can see costumes and architecture, comedies about life in the factories, and cartoons. The *China Daily* has announcements about cultural events in Beijing and on national television. Some recent titles shown internationally are: *Evening Bell, Red Sorghum, Old Well, A Small Town Called Hibiscus,* and *People, Ghosts and Love.*

Chinese **television** consists primarily of documentaries, *kung fu* action thrillers, and tearjerkers. It also has news, sports coverage, commercials, boring political speeches, and educational broadcasts, such as language lessons. Occasionally it will have something especially good, like a visiting British ballet company or live coverage of historical events. Your hotel television may have closed-circuit programming with more of the kinds of programs you're used to.

The best **acrobats** are from Shenyang, Shanghai, and Wuhan, and foreigners usually find acrobats very entertaining. Also offered are **song and dance troupes** and **sports competitions.** I highly recommend exhibitions of **wushu,** the traditional martial arts.

Most tour groups will be taken to one or two cultural presentations. If you want to go to more, you can on your own. They are very cheap—usually less than four yuan. Tickets are frequently hard to get at the box office and must be booked in advance. See "Useful Phrases."

In Beijing, anyone can go to good movies, usually with English subtitles, at the International Club or the Great Wall Hotel. Take advantage of cheaper prices for western performers too. In almost every city, batches of seats for various kinds of performances are reserved for foreigners. You might be able to get some of these at your hotel service desk. China has ticket scalpers, too, at sometimes twice the going price.

Chinese traditional opera should be experienced at least once. It is very popular with older people, but not so much with younger ones, since it is sung in its own classical language. Your guide might not understand it except for the subtitles for the songs. The jabbering in the audience is usually a discussion of what is going on. Some cities have shorter performers for foreigners in comfortable theaters, occasionally with subtitles in English. To the uninitiated, traditional Chinese opera can be dull, with its many long monologues, its high-pitched singing, and its sluggish action. The villain is always known at the beginning. The chairs in the theater are frequently hard, and there may not be heat or air conditioning. The performance usually takes three hours, and the percussion instruments especially, are loud, as if to elevate the audience to a higher level of consciousness—but not as high as at a rock concert.

The stories are usually ancient, so a knowledge of history helps. Or they could be something out of classic literature, *The Dream of the Red Chamber* or *Pilgrimage to the West*. Some are based on modern history. Two books, published in China, should be helpful: Latsch's *Peking Opera as a European Sees It* and Wu's *Peking Opera and Mei Lanfang*.

Mei Lanfang was one of the greatest of the female impersonators. It is common to have a man play the woman's role, and vice versa. One opera company, the Shaoxing, has only female players. The male roles are extraordinarily well done. The makeup might throw you, but much goes into it: the temples taped to slant the eyes, paste-on hair pieces to reshape faces, and many colors to indicate character or specific roles such as the Monkey King, or the red-and-black-faced Zhang Fei. A face painted black is an honest but uncouth character; a white face shows a treacherous, cunning, but dignified person; a white patch on the nose indicates a villain. Red is for loyalty and sincerity; black for honesty and all-around goodness. Yellow is for impulsiveness and gold and silver for demons and gods.

It is always fun to watch the actresses in love scenes expressing themselves with delicate and reserved gestures. Note how they excitedly carry their tune to a higher and higher pitch within one breath.

Usually the staging, the costumes, and the acting are outstanding. The fighting scenes, if any, are breathtaking and graceful, like ballet. Cymbals and hollow wooden knockers punctuate the action, and somewhere in the orchestra is an instrument that sounds like a bagpipe. The audience frequently applauds a musician, especially the one playing the stringed *erhu*. Usually a good opera singer tries to keep his own erhu player for life. The costumes are handmade and artfully embroidered, depending on the character played.

The singing, ah yes, the singing takes some getting used to. It can sound like screeching and whining, and one wonders how long voices can last under that kind of abuse. But it takes many years of training to achieve such perfection.

Settings are usually simple and symbolic. The acting, too, is symbolic, and Chinese audiences know what every gesture, every move of the eyebrow means. Among the symbols: an old man and a girl with an oar are on a boat; a man lifting up his foot as he exits is stepping over

the high threshold of a door. Crossed eyes mean anger. Walking with hands extended in front means it's dark. A man holding a riding crop means he's riding a horse, or sometimes he *is* a horse. You should be able to tell the difference! A particularly well-executed swing of long hair (anguish) or prolonged trembling (fear) will elicit gasps of appreciation and applause.

With settings, two bamboo poles with some cloth attached is a city wall or gate. A chariot is two yellow flags with a wheel drawn on each. A couple of poles on either side of an actor is a sedan chair. A hat with two long, dangling pheasant or peacock feathers is worn by a high military officer, usually a marshal; a hat with wobbling wings out to the sides just above the ears belongs to a magistrate. Generals have flags matching their costumes and mounted like wings on their backs. The flags are distributed to identify imperial messengers.

After the performance, you may want to go backstage to see everything up close, and possibly makeup being removed. See "Useful Phrases."

Chinese opera dates from the Yuan, and blossomed into one of the most popular entertainment forms during the Ming for noble and commoner alike. For a largely illiterate population, operas were courses in history. For their entertainment value, they were performed at major festivals, weddings, funerals, births, promotions, etc., for human and ghostly guests.

China has many forms of traditional opera, the distinctions known to fans. The most popular are Beijing and Qunqi. Qunqi has more dancing movements and more melodic, mellow tunes. During a performance, one sees either a whole story or excerpts from several operas.

In the old days, operas were social events. As some went on for weeks, people came and left as they pleased, chatted with friends, ate and drank. The crack of watermelon seeds and the sipping of tea blended with the music, which spectators also sang if the tune was familiar. In addition to shouting approval and clapping, one also growled and swore when actors were less than perfect. The audiences sounded much like Elizabethan ones. In the old days, performers were considered little better than beggars and prostitutes in spite of many years of training and practice. Today, performers are considered cultural workers and are respected as artists.

Listen to music   Music lovers should be interested in hearing classical Western and contemporary Chinese and Western music. Among the best Chinese orchestras are the Shanghai Chinese Orchestra 上海民族乐团 , the Hong Kong Chinese Orchestra 香港中乐团 , Peking Central Folk Orchestra 北京中央民族乐团 , Beijing Central Philharmonic Orchestra, 北京中央管弦乐团, and China Broadcasting Symphony Orchestra 中国广播民族乐团

Among the most famous contemporary Chinese composers are Chou Wen-chung 周文中 (USA), Luo Jing-jing 罗京京 (Shanghai), Tan Dun 谭盾 (Beijing), Ma Sitson 马思聪 (USA), and Ju Hsiaosong 瞿小松 (Beijing).

You might also look for programs or cassettes that include popular compositions like the erhu concerto Manjianghong 满江红 ; The Butterfly Lovers 梁山伯与祝英台 for orchestra and violin; Reflections of the Moon on Two Lakes 二泉映月 , an erhu concerto; Lady General Mu Kweiying 穆桂英挂帅 , an orchestral work converted from Chinese opera.

Also recommended are: Li Sao (The Lament) 离骚 , an orchestral work; Willows in the Spring Breeze 春风杨柳 , light music; Tao Jin Ling 淘金令 , orchestral; The Swaying Plum Blossoms 梅花三弄 , pipa or flute; and Silver Snow in the Early Spring 阳春白雪 , pipa.

Then there are: The River Suite 江河水 , erhu solo; Moon and Lanterns 灯月交辉 , East China Silk and Bamboo Music recording; A Selection of Chinese Melodies on Traditional Instruments 中国民间器; Autumn Moon on a Calm Lake 秋湖月夜 , for piano and orchestra; and Pastoral Song 牧歌 .

The *erhu* 二胡 , *banhu, gaohu,* and *zhonghu* are stringed instruments held upright and played with a bow. The *pipa* 唢呐 and *liuqin* look and sound like mandolins, the *ruan* more like a banjo. The *yanggin* is like a dulcimer played with bamboo mallets.

Other Chinese instruments are the *kuchin* 唢呐 , *sheng* 笙 , bamboo flute 笛，箫, and *tseng* 筝 .

Night Life Dance parties and discos are fun, even if you sit on the sidelines and watch. They are more fun if you get up and dance. Some are organized at hotels. The one I saw in a small city (Yantai) took place in a large open courtyard, with a couple of hundred people, mainly men, but also some women and children. With the shortage of women, men were dancing arm-in-arm with other men. Some women, however,

The pearl-border

"T" pattern

Key pattern

These are favorites for the rims of cups and bowls.

The Dragon of Heaven

danced with each other. The music was a melange of fox trots, waltzes, tangos, cha-cha, and rock. It was great to see the Chinese letting loose after so many years of considering such activity bourgeois and frivolous. Many people say they dance for the exercise. The music was live. In some places, you can take your own cassettes. Quick, enjoy it, before dance parties get banned again!

Night markets are opening up all over where weather permits, for clothes and for some great cheap cooking. (See "Food.") Many hotels have started providing microphones for guests in karaoke bars along with high-tech monitors, a Japanese tradition. Guests can then perform with music, and some can be surprisingly good. Some can be terrible.

Nightclubs and North American–type bars have opened, some with live entertainment. And many hotels now have gym equipment, bowling alleys, and lighted tennis courts. On Friday evenings, many local foreign residents get together to celebrate TGIF. They are good sources of information. Contact your consulate for locations. Hotel coffee shops,

The cloud design

Cloud border

Still water

Sea waves; the little clouds over the angles represent the sea spray.

Decorative compositions of the hieroglyphic form of thunder.

Mountains and crags

Lightning and fire designs

bars, and many stores stay open late. Massages are great and serious. Men massage men; women massage women.

The days of going to bed at 9 p.m. because there's nothing to do are beginning to disappear.

Learn how to identify details of Chinese designs   You will see these everywhere in China: in palaces, temples, pagodas, museums, fancy restaurants, gardens, parks, on dishes, windows, and screens. Knowing what they are will help you recognize bits of Chinese culture abroad, too, especially on rugs, in textiles, in Chinese antiques, and in Chinese restaurants.

Illustrated are some of the more common designs. While their origins might be Taoist or Buddhist, Chinese symbols are primarily Chinese, taken over as part of the national culture, and not confined to any particular religion.

The Chinese Dragon is said to have the head of a camel, the horns of a deer, the eyes of a rabbit, the ears of a cow, the neck of a snake, the belly of a frog, the scales of a carp, the claws of a hawk, and the palm of a tiger. It has whiskers and a beard, and is deaf. It is generally regarded as benevolent but is also the source of thunder and lightning. The five-clawed variation was once reserved exclusively for the emperor. The flaming ball is said by some to represent thunder and lightning, by others, to be either the sun, the moon, or the pearl of potentiality. It is frequently surrounded by clouds.

The cloud design is now most frequently seen in blue as the lower border of a rich man's gown either in a traditional opera or a painted antique portrait.

This scepter is frequently about half a meter long and made of

The scepter of the supreme heavenly deity

The lion

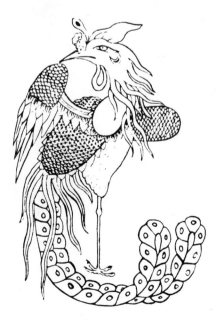

The phoenix

metal, stone, bone, or wood. It is like a magic wand and is frequently given as a gift, a symbol of good wishes for the prosperity and longevity of the recipient. The larger ones are found in museums.

The lion is not native to China. The design is unique to China because the craftsmen never saw a real one. Lions are frequently seen in front of buildings as protectors either playing with a ball (male) or a kitten (female). They are considered benevolent. The ball is said by some to represent the imperial treasury or peace. Others say it is the sun, a precious stone, or the Yin-Yang. Seen also on festive occasions as a costume for dancers, the lion is sometimes confused with the Fo dog, which is usually blue with longer ears.

The phoenix is said to resemble a swan in front, a unicorn behind, with "the throat of a swallow, the bill of a fowl, the neck of a snake, the tail of a peacock, the forehead of a crane, the crown of a Mandarin duck, the stripes of a dragon, and the back of a tortoise." Its appearance is said to mean an era of peace and prosperity. It was the symbol

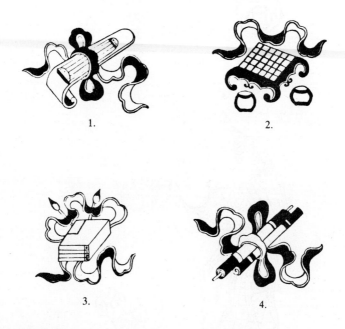

1.   2.

3.   4.

The intellectual elite was associated with these four symbols in ancient times:
1. The harp
2. The chessboard
3. The books
4. The paintings

a.

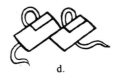

b.

c.

d.

e.

f.

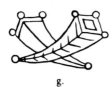

e.

f.

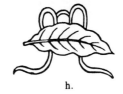

g.

h.

The eight precious things

a. The pearl
b. The coin
c. The rhombus (victory)
d. The books

e. The paintings
f. The musical stone of jade (blessing)
g. The rhinoceros-horn cups
h. The artemisia leaf (dignity)

1.

2.

These are only two of the many variations frequently seen. There is even a teapot in the *shou* design.

Character sign symbols

1. The round *Shou*
2. The long *Shou*, both meaning "long life"

used by the empresses of China and is often combined in designs with the dragon.

Below is but one of the many variations of the character for happiness. Sometimes it is circular and doubled, especially prominent at weddings.

The *Fu*, meaning "happiness"

The word for bat in Chinese is *fu*. So is the word for happiness. A bat is thus a symbol of happiness. These are everywhere: on the walls and ceilings of the Forbidden City, on the ceiling of the restaurant of the Peace Hotel in Shanghai. The peach is a symbol of longevity.

The bat   Bat and peach

Five bats, surrounding the character *Shou*

When five bats are combined with the longevity character, they mean the five great blessings: happiness, wealth, peace, virtue, and longevity.

Scepter, writing brush, and uncoined silver. Together, these are a symbol of success.

The three Fruits

These are fragrant fingers of Buddha, peach, and pomegranate. Together they mean happiness, longevity, and male children.

Prunus

Orchid

Bamboo

Peony

The prunus or plum blossom symbolizes beauty; the orchid, fragrance; bamboo is an emblem of longevity, and the peony means wealth and respectability.

Peach blossom

Lotus flower

Chrysanthemum

Narcissus

These are featured singly or combined in a set of four, since the peach blossom represents spring, the lotus flower is summer, chrysanthemum is autumn, and narcissus is winter. Frequently there are only one of each of these on a four-panel screen.

Among **other common symbols** are the *crane* (longevity), the *stag* (longevity and prosperity), and the *lotus* (purity and perfection). The Buddha is usually seated on a lotus.

Among the many **strange beings** are the two at the top two corners of many temple roofs, tails pointing to the sky. This is a *carp turning into a dragon.* There is also the *unicorn,* known as *qi-lin,* with the "body of the musk deer, the tail of an ox, the forehead of a wolf, and the hoofs of a horse." The male has a horn, but the female does not. It is a good, gentle, and benevolent creature.

The wooden *"fish,"* a red object found in most Buddhist temples, is a clapper, used for beating time while the monks chant the sutras. Some say that the monks dropped the sutras in water as the holy scriptures were being brought from India. A fish ate the sutras, so it was beaten to force it to regurgitate. Others say if you don't beat the fish, there will be an earthquake.

The *tortoise,* usually seen with a giant stele on its back, is one of the four supernatural animals, the others being the phoenix, the dragon, and the unicorn. Real ones are frequently kept at Buddhist temples, for they are sacred, an emblem of longevity, strength, and endurance.

Visit religious buildings   After sampling a few temples, you should be able to identify the various kinds just from a quick glance inside.

Confucian temples were in every sizable community. (For a history of Confucius, see "Qufu" in *Destinations*.) Everyone who passed by had to stop and bow respectfully before the gate, or be punished. Scholars came here both to worship the sage, for good luck, and to write examinations for the imperial civil service. Confucius was officially worshiped at the spring and autumn equinoxes. Try to imagine the burning of incense and the muffled clang of gongs, as processions of officials in long red gowns and caps arrived. The men kowtowed, their heads to the ground, in deepest reverence. They left offerings of food and wine on the altar. Musicians played ritual bells. Such ceremonies still take place in Qufu (and in Taiwan).

Confucian temples did not usually have statues, but simply tablets with the names of ancestors written on them. The walls were red. The south gate was usually left unbuilt until a son from the town passed the difficult examinations and became a Senior Scholar. Only a Senior Scholar and the Emperor could enter by the south gate. No women were considered for the examinations, but if Chinese opera plots are to be believed, some did successfully take them disguised as men.

Was Confucianism a religion or a philosophy? This question is frequently debated. While Confucius himself skeptically rejected the supernatural, Chinese people did and, in some cases, still do consider him a god. He is among the Taoist deities too. But he was primarily a teacher of ethics, of "right conduct," and good, stable government.

Many Confucian temples now are used as museums because Confucianism no longer has imperial patronage. The largest temples are in Beijing and Qufu.

Buddhist temples come in two basic varieties, of which there are infinite variations.

(1) Buddhist temples, surrounded by windowless walls, frequently have four fierce-looking, larger than life-size, human-type guardians after you enter the first gate. Each temple might have different names for these. Inside the first hall, visitors are greeted by the fat, laughing Buddha, *Maitreya,* or in Chinese, *Mi Lo Fu.* He is the Buddha still-to-come. Behind him is *Wei Tou,* the military bodhisattva, the armed warrior who guards the Buddhist scriptures. Wei Tou is probably comparable to the Indian god Indra.

Central in the main hall is the Buddha, a.k.a. the Enlightened One, Sakyamuni, or Prince Siddhartha Gautama. Also in this hall are usually statues or paintings of *bodhisattvas,* known in Chinese as *pusas.* These are saints who have gained Enlightenment but have come back to the world to help other people attain it too. A favorite bodhisattva is Avalokita, a.k.a. Guanyin (Kwan Yin, Kuan Yin), or the Goddess of Mercy, who may have several heads and arms and may be carrying a vase or a child. She is usually behind Sakyamuni, facing north. Guanyin started out as a male god in China until about the 12th century, when his followers preferred to worship him as a woman. He is still sometimes depicted as male. Said one guide, "Men believe he is male and women believe she is female."

Other bodhisattvas could be *Amitabha,* in charge of the souls of the dead, *Manjusri,* in charge of wisdom, usually with a sword in his right hand and a lotus in his left, and the Bodhisattvas of Pharmacy, Universal Benevolence, and the Earth.

Arhats, known in Chinese as *lohan,* are people who have achieved Nirvana. They are usually depicted in groupings of 16, 18, or 500, and are based on real Indian holy men. These are frequently seen in paintings, or as statues. Devout Buddhists should know each of them by name.

Gautama was the Indian prince, born in the 6th century B.C., who was brought up confined to a palace. One day, upon seeing the suffering of the outside world, he forsook his wealth and family. He was 29 years old then. For six years, he went searching for life's meaning. Finding it, he then preached his ideas for 45 years: the Four Noble Truths and the Noble Eightfold Path to Nirvana. These numbers now correspond to the circles on top of Buddhist stupas and pagodas.

Buddha taught that the source of all suffering is selfish desire, and one must stop all craving for it. Some sects believe in asceticism. The Chinese, Mongolians, and Tibetans follow the Mahayana school of faith and good works, which believes Buddha is divine and can answer prayers. You will see people in temples, smoking incense in hand, nodding to the statues or kowtowing on the floor. All forms of Buddhism aim at stopping the continuous cycle of reincarnation—but some adherents are more serious about this than others. Nirvana is the extinction of existence.

The swastika is a Buddhist symbol of good luck, later inverted and used by the Nazis. Most temples have live fish and turtles. Full-time Buddhists are vegetarians. Some Buddhist monks had pieces of incense burned into their skulls at their initiation, but this is no longer required.

The swastika, symbol of luck

Swastika border design

The swastika was a Buddhist good luck symbol of Indian origin long before the Nazis existed. You will find it on the bellies of some Buddhist statues and latticed on screens and windows in complicated variations.

An interesting study to make as you sightsee is of the clothing carved on buddhas. Some wear the plain, draped robes of Indian holy men, others the fancy, feminine Chinese court dress with jewelry. Buddhism arrived in China from India, but Buddhist art became distinctly Chinese. Can you date a statue from its clothes? The fatness of its face?

You will probably see many more Buddhist temples than Taoist and Confucian. You can also see and hear robed monks chanting prayers if your timing is right.

(2) **Lama temples** are expressions of the Tibetan and Mongolian form of Buddhism, into which have been injected elements of the early Tibetan religion called Bon. Some sources say that the dalai lama, who is considered both the temporal and religious head of Lamaism, is a reincarnation of Avalokita or Guanyin, or the god Chenrezi. The religion is riddled with superstition, demons, and an incredibly horrifying hell for sinners. All of these are reflected in the murals and statues of Lamaist temples. Lamaism is also divided into sects, the main ones being the meditative Yellow Hats and the sensual Red Hats.

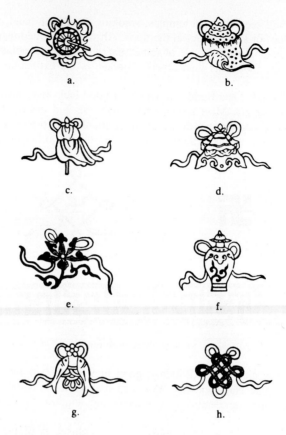

The eight Buddhist emblems of happy augury
a. The wheel of the law
b. The conch shell
c. The state umbrella
d. The canopy
e. The lotus flower
f. The covered vase
g. The pair of fishes
h. The endless knot

These temples are different from other Chinese Buddhist temples not only in their statues, but also in their architecture. Usually built on mountainsides, they have tall, narrow windows, flatter, less ornate roofs, and are usually decorated over the main door with a gilded wheel of Buddhist doctrine and two deer. Statues inside are frequently decorated

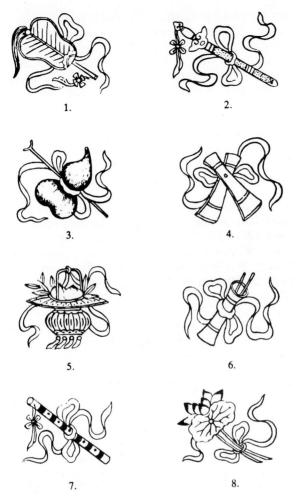

The attributes of the eight Taoistic genii

1. The fan
2. The sword
3. The pilgrim's staff and gourd
4. The castanets
5. The flower basket
6. The tube and rods
7. The flute
8. The lotus flower

with turquoise and coral, and many wear pointed caps. The best-known Lama temples are in Tibet, but important Lama temples are in Beijing, Chengde, Qinghai, and Inner Mongolia. A Lama temple also stands in Beijing's Summer Palace. See also "Lhasa" and "Chengde."

Taoist temples are identified by Taoist gods, among whom are Guanyin and Confucius, so don't get confused. Other gods and saints can be identified by the things they carry.

The Eight Taoist Genii or Immortals or Fairies were originally eight humans who discovered the secrets of nature. They lived alone in remote mountains (one of them in a cave at Lushan), had magic powers and could revive the dead. They are usually found together on a vase or in one painting, or as a set of eight porcelain pieces. Chung Li-chuan carries the fan to revive the spirits of the dead, Lu Tung-pin the supernatural sword, Li Tieh-kuai the staff, Tsao Kuo-chiu the castanets, Lan Tsai-ho the flower basket, Chang Kuo the bamboo tube, Han Hsiang-tzu the flute, and Ho Hsien-ku the lotus flower. Two are women.

Daoism (Taoism) was founded 1800 years ago by a sage named Lao Zi (Lao Tzu), whose message was conveyed to the world by a disciple named Mencius. It preaches that everything exists through the interplay of two opposite forces: male-female; positive-negative; hot-cold; light-dark; heaven-earth; yang-yin, etc. One wonders if Chairman Mao's theory of opposites and his emphasis on contradictions is related to this theory.

In the center of the dual Yin-Yang, the principles of being, surrounded by the eight trigrams of divination. The Eight Trigrams represent eight animals and eight directions. At eleven o'clock are the three unbroken lines of heaven; then clockwise, clouds, thunder, mountains, water, fire, earth, and wind. These are used in fortune telling. You may have heard of the I Ching.

Taoists try to achieve harmony out of the conflict of these forces through the Tao or the Way. Taoism is closer to nature than the other religions, its saints finding enlightenment after spending years meditating in caves. Over the years, it also has been diluted by superstition, its adherents believing in charms and spells, ghosts, nature spirits, and the worship of supernatural beings. *Feng-shui* geomancy, where man places his dwelling in harmony with natural forces, is an expression of Taoism.

Taoism was most popular in the Tang and Song, but declined in the Ming. Its most famous monasteries are in Beijing, Chengdu, Shenyang, and Suzhou.

Moslem Mosques are architecturally of two varieties and *visitors always remove their shoes* inside the great halls. The mosques similar to those in western Asia, with rounded, onionlike domes, are mainly in northwest China. Other mosques look like other Chinese temples, with curved roofs and ornate dragons and phoenixes (in spite of the prophet's teachings against making images).

In either style, there is a place for washing hands and feet before prayers. The main building is the Great Hall, which is frequently decorated with Arabic writing, arches, and flower motifs. Moslems pray five times a day, facing the holy city of Mecca in Saudi Arabia.

Moslems can pray anywhere, but the devout usually pray in a mosque if they can. Note the prayer rugs with designs woven into them indicating the direction in which to kneel. Carpets made in Moslem areas deliberately do not have images of animals or objects on them, in keeping with the commandment forbidding "graven images." Note also the disproportionate number of women worshipers, and in some mosques, separate sections for women. Ask about any Khomeni influences.

Moslems are followers of the Prophet Mohammed, who was born in A.D. 570. Known as Islam, his religion gives a different emphasis to the god of Judaism and Christianity. Old Testament prophets and Jesus Christ are considered honored prophets, but Mohammed was the last and the greatest. The holy book is the Koran, which teaches a strict code of behavior (no pork, no alcohol, no idols, etc.), and universal brotherhood of all believers. During the holy month of Ramadan, believers fast during the day.

Islam arrived in China in A.D. 652 during the Tang, with Arab and Persian traders who settled in Guangzhou, Quanzhou, Hangzhou, and Yangzhou. During the 13th century, many Moslem soldiers, artisans, and officials were brought to China to fight and work with Kublai Khan. The approximately 10 million Moslems in China are known as Hui, but Uygurs, Kazaks, Kirgiz, Ozbeks, etc., are also Moslem. Most Moslems live in the northwest. Friday is the holy day and mosques, which might otherwise be closed, are always opened Friday afternoons.

Besides those of the major religions, **other religious buildings** exist in China. Many of these are **ancestral temples** (*miao*), frequently one to a village. Many villages are each comprised of people with a common name and ancestor, so they only need one temple. Some of these temples were very elaborate and are used also as the village school. In ancestral temples, tablets with the names of the ancestors were kept in neat rows and worshiped with burning incense, gifts of food, and ceremonial bowing at least twice a year. The ancestors were informed of important family events like births and marriages, both verbally and in writing in a family history book. One worshiped ancestors in gratitude for one's life, but more so because the spirits of departed ancestors had to be kept happy so they could influence one's current fortunes. Many of these tablets were destroyed or hidden during the Cultural Revolution. When you go to a village, ask to see the ancestral temple.

Cave temples with frescoes and Buddhist statues were first built in India and spread with the Silk Road into China. Caves have always been conducive to meditation. There, one gets a feeling of security, like being back in a mother's womb. Dunhuang is the greatest for its paintings. The two at Lanzhou are noted for their strikingly dramatic sites and the richness of their sculpture. Important for carvings are also Datong and Luoyang.

Other cave temples listed as protected historical monuments by the State Council are at Anxi and Linxia in Gansu; Handan in Hebei; Turpan, Baicheng, and Kuqu in Xinjiang; Guangyuan, Leshan, and Dazu in Sichuan; Jianchuan in Yunnan; Gongxian in Henan; Guyuan in Ningxia; and Hangzhou in Zhejiang.

In old China, people worshiped any number of gods. They wanted to cover all possible bases. If a friend prayed successfully to one god for a baby boy, then other barren women tried that god too. It was not unusual for one person to have his children baptized as Christians, burn incense to a deceased grandfather, and then retire to contemplate in a Taoist or Buddhist monastery.

There are temples to the city gods. Fishermen worshiped the Goddess of Heaven, Tian Hou, who bears some resemblance to the goddess Guanyin. See "Quanzhou" for Manicheanism and "Xi'an" and "Quanzhou" for Nestorian.

Christian churches were most frequently built with gothic windows, as in Western architecture. Many Roman Catholic churches look like transplants from Europe. For more on Christianity in China, see *Religion* in "Local Customs."

Zoos are usually pathetic, but many have pandas. Beijing's is the largest. Animals do not have much space to roam.

Relax in a Chinese garden This is different from rushing through on a guided tour. Go back to one you especially like and just sit and absorb. A Chinese garden is not just a park or something attached to a building. It is an art form, the world in miniature, with mountains, water, plants, and buildings—a three-dimensional Chinese painting you can enter to try to experience infinity.

Gardens were built for a leisurely lifestyle in which poetry, philosophical contemplation, and the beauty of nature were of the utmost importance. Imagine *living* here! The ugly world of poverty and injustice was kept outside the high walls. "Above Heaven; below Suzhou and Hangzhou" probably referred more to the gardens than anything else.

Take your time exploring. Look at the integration of the buildings with nature, the pinpointing places of particular beauty by unusually shaped windows and moon gates. Absorb the tranquillity of the water. Look at the reflections. Think of poetry. The meaning of life. A garden takes time—infinite time.

Do a study—it is easy to get cultural indigestion. After the third temple, they could all look alike. But they don't! Take notes. Draw diagrams. Link up roof styles to dynasties and regions. Which ones have animals? And which animals? Are the roofs southern or northern?

Study the shapes of **pagodas**—those related to the Chinese *lou* and those related to Indian shapes. Is the shape distinctive to different dynasties? Do they all have an uneven number of stories? Which dynasties' are octagonal? Which pagodas have a different number of stories inside than outside?

Do a study of **tile faces** (wa dang) or eave tiles, for instance. These are the circular pieces of tile at the lower edges of a roof. Some have animal faces on them, some flowers, some Chinese characters. The designs were chosen in some cases as good luck symbols.

Find out details. Why do you have to step so high to get through some doorways and not others? Is it because of flood? Or because it blocks bad luck? What are the bumps on the head of some of the Buddhas? What do the different positions of Buddhist statues mean?

Who was China's most prolific graffiti artist? My vote would go to Qing Emperor Qianlong. Why is ''son of a tortoise'' one of the worst insults you can give?

Why have the Chinese placed so much emphasis on **calligraphy**? Why is it more than a means of communication, a very sophisticated art? Why is the calligraphy on one tablet better than the calligraphy on another?

Chinese people spend years mastering their written language. They first learn by copying the characters over and over again, an exercise in patience, perseverance, and discipline. For good calligraphy, writing legibly is not enough. One follows one of the four accepted basic styles with individual variations. One's calligraphy has to express one's personality and feelings, in tune with the content of the written message.

Chinese painting developed out of calligraphy, using the same materials and holding the brush in the same vertical way. Ideally, one needs an ink brush made of animal hair, rice paper, ink stick, and ink tablets. Students are taught to keep their backs, upper torsos, heads, and souls(!) in a straight line. The calligraphy you see on buildings, by Emperor Qianlong or whomever, was chiseled by someone else. Chairman Mao also was an excellent calligrapher.

Learn about **feng-shui** and the placement of buildings in harmony with the contours of the earth. Do all temples face south? Do all tombs face south? What role do pagodas play? Why are there screens in front of doorways and gates? How can you improve your own house to insure that good luck doesn't just go out your windows and doors?

Study the **different tomb styles**: Ming, Qing, Song, Han. How are they different?

Learn about Chinese **mythology.** Pick up a copy of *Old Tales of China—a tourist guidebook to better understanding of China's stage, cinema, arts and crafts.* Published by China Travel and Tourism Press, this inexpensive booklet in English relates many of the famous stories, some of which will help you understand Chinese opera plots. Try to figure out why these stories are so popular.

Read. Get immersed in old (and new) China. Read *Romance of the Three Kingdoms* while sitting on a cliff at Zhenjiang, overlooking the Yangtze, at the place where the widow of Liu Pei pined for her husband. Read *A Dream of the Red Chamber* while relaxing in the courtyard of one of the new reproductions of the setting. Read *Pilgrimage to the West* on a trip along the Silk Road. Translations of these books are cheaper in China, and if you have the time, will add immeasurably to your experiences there.

A Dream of the Red Chamber (a.k.a. Dream of Red Mansions) is one of the most popular novels published in China because it paints a vivid and convincing picture of how the rich (and their servants) lived during feudal times. Any Chinese over 35 years of age should know it. It is the story of a wealthy family, connected with the imperial court, who lived and declined during the Qing dynasty. The plot might move too slowly for Western readers, who probably will have trouble also remembering the Chinese names. (Make notes as you read it.) However, for details of lifestyles it is excellent, with descriptions of a funeral, impertinent bond servants, the visit home of daughter and imperial concubine Yuan-chun, etc. The sexual encounters are mentioned, and some are surprising, but they are not fully described.

Favorite among the characters is the bored, spoiled young hero Jia Pao-yu, who is surrounded by servants and is good at writing couplets. Sad to say, as the novel is popular largely because of its poetry, the poetry loses much in translation. Pao-yu is in love with his cousin, the beautiful Lin Tai-yu, but he is forced to marry someone else.

Attendants dressed as the characters inhabit the Red Chamber reproductions, known also as *Daguan Yuan* (Grand View Garden).

Learn about **China's minorities** (or nationalities). China has 56 different ethnic groups, 55 of whom are 8% of the population. These 91 million people live in areas totaling half of China. Yunnan province has 26 different nationalities. A nationality doesn't necessarily settle in one location. Often sub-branches are spread over several provinces, with different costumes and dialects. For example, the Miao nationality is found in Guizhou, Hunan, Yunnan, Guangdong, Guangxi, and Sichuan provinces. Miao women in Guizhou wear pleated skirts while those in Hunan wear pants. The color and designs of their turbans are also different. Great photos.

During festivals and market days, most of the minorities, especially the women, wear their distinctive costumes, which are usually decorated with fine embroidery, and, sometimes, heavy silver jewelry. Their hairstyles could indicate their marital status.

Some minorities are very musical, expressing more liveliness in their dances than the majority Han Chinese. Although the levels of their Chinese education and their economy is generally lower than average, their cultural heritage is rich and meaningful. Unusual courtship rituals are still practiced.

The festivals of the nationalities are usually worth experiencing. The Dai celebrate a watersplashing festival similar to that in neighboring Thailand and Burma. The Kazaks have a Horse Racing Festival, the Bai a Torch Festival, the Tibetans celebrate their New Year, etc. Mongolians have equally colorful sporting meets, with their distinctive wrestling, horses, and motorcycles. Facilities for tourists in minority areas are still modest but not impossible. Collecting minority weaving, jewelry, and musical instruments can be very interesting. Comparing customs can keep anthropologists and folklorists occupied for years.

We must warn you that some minorities here do have separatist aspirations, similar to those in other countries. We urge you to help reconcile differences rather than take sides.

Festivals have proliferated in the last few years. Some are nothing more than an excuse to sell something. But most are colorful, exotic, and especially great for photographers. People dress in their best. There are reproductions of historical events, Confucian rituals, and mythological stories. Many festivals are punctuated with fireworks, dragon dances, competitions, courtship rituals, parades, pageants, thousands of dancing school children, and special banquets.

Some are genuine folk festivals, religious worship, real horse and camel markets—badly organized for tourists but important for participants. These usually have just a vague schedule but arrangements for tourists should improve with experience.

Some festivals are so well organized, tourists travel with police escorts quickly from place to place.

We suggest booking a tour through a travel agency because festivals attract tens of thousands of people. As one of the crowd, you won't see much unless you're well over six feet tall, but if the travel agencies have organized something, you should be able to get a good seat and at least a sleeping space. Some dates are listed in ''Destinations'' and ''Quick Reference.''

NOTE · · · One should be aware that Chinese decorating is different from ours. Chinese decor might look ''busy'' to the westerner, with different wall paper on each wall, curtains that don't match, and a carpet that clashes. One should not look at it whole. One should look at the separate components, each one attractive by itself.

Furniture decorated by marble should be looked at the same way. Each piece is a picture, usually a landscape with mountains or rivers. If there are three pieces side by side, don't expect the lines to flow from one to the other. Look at them individually.

DESTINATIONS

Over 700 destinations are open to foreign visitors now, more than that if you count the smaller tourist sites available from major cities. For these, you do not need any permits to visit beyond your visa to China. For any other places, you need **alien travel permits.**

Listed here are the most important destinations. Mentioned under these headings, especially those of the provincial capitals, are minor destinations. The list here is alphabetical by pinyin, with alternative spellings in parentheses. Where the **Chinese characters** or **pinyin** for tourist sites and restaurants have been available, they are printed so you can ask taxi drivers and people on the street to help you find where you want to go. The words *Guesthouse* and *Hotel* are interchangeable and do not imply quality. The words *monastery* and *temple* are also interchangeable.

To locate any of these cities on a **map,** note the tourist region right after the name of the city; for example, "Northwest China." Look for the Northwest China regional map in the back of the book. For **shoppers,** we have listed items produced locally. These are usually cheaper and with more variety at the factory and in the province than elsewhere.

Don't jump to the conclusion that a temple "founded in 1250" means the buildings are over 700 years old. The buildings may have been rebuilt recently. (In a country that has had as many upheavals, air raids, and revolutions as China, it is amazing that so many great monuments have survived to this day.)

No other country has as many historic sites or as varied offerings as China. Chinese governments on all levels have selected some of the more important ones for renovation. This is a good indicator that the buildings are genuine and culturally significant. **An * means the site is protected as a historical or revolutionary monument by the State Council** of the national government.

(And please don't think that old is beautiful. Frequently the older the monument, the less developed and intricate.)

Hours given for stores and tourist sites are approximate, those in summer about an hour later than those in winter. **Schools, villages,** and **factories** are basically the same in the whole of China, and these are not mentioned in every destination unless there is something special about them. We do urge you to visit schools, villages, and factories wherever possible.

For those trying to learn Chinese:

ang = nunnery
bei = north
binguan = guesthouse
chan guan = restaurant
ci = temple
da lu = avenue
dong = east
fan dian = hotel or restaurant
ge = small pavilion
guan = pass
hai = sea
he = river
hu = lake
jiang = river
jie = street
jing = capital
ling = tomb
lou = multistoried pavilion big enough for people to live in
lu = road

men = gate
miao = temple, usually ancestral or Confucian
nan = south
quan = spring
sha = sand
shan = mountain
si = temple
ta = pagoda
tang = temple
ting = tiny pavilion usually in rural surroundings in which people can rest
xi = west
xian = county
yuan = garden
zhong = middle or central
zhou = city state (smaller than a province; larger than a city)

You will note some redundancy in names, such as Lu Shan Mountain, but those are for people who don't know Chinese, since such names are commonly used. It may appear cumbersome to put in the *pin yin,* the English, and the Chinese characters for place names, but in China some people will use the Chinese names and others will use the English, so the Chinese characters should help avoid confusion.

Sources differ sometimes as to historical dates and events, and *English translations* of site names. Please be flexible. Names like Han, Song, Ming, and Qing refer to dynasty, as "in the Ming," with Mongol the same as Yuan, and Manchu the same as Qing.

Correct telephone numbers have also been difficult to obtain. In some places more than one is listed because sources differed. If one doesn't work, try the other. Failing that, ask any English-speaking source like C.I.T.S., your hotel telephone operator, business center, or an embassy for an up-to-date telephone number.

Telephone numbers of **hotels** and **toll-free North American reservation numbers** are listed with recent prices in "Budget and Hotel Quick Reference." China **telephone codes** are under "Important Addresses."

The quality of a hotel facility in China frequently depends on the time that has passed since its renovation. It also depends on the room one gets. It is therefore impossible for us to grade Chinese-managed hotels. Recent evaluations by guests and staff surveys are available from the *Travel China Newsletter*.

Although we have been unable to obtain all information about all hotels, the following will give you an idea of what to expect. The number after the address is the postal code and must be used on all mail. The ''2*'' or ''3*'' etc., indicate the government's rating. See *Hotels*.

Many hotels have singles, suites, and dorms in addition to double rooms. Most hotels of 3* and higher will respond with a telex to a request for a reservation if so asked.

Hotels listed here are up to minimal standards except where noted. In some cases, we have listed the best hotels in a city even though they may not be very good.

The **restaurants** listed are those recommended by C.I.T.S. except in Beijing, Guangzhou, and Shanghai, where we have developed our own lists. Note that population figures for ''cities'' usually include several counties and municipalities. We have tried to give the figures for the main urban area where they were available. And some of the tours mentioned, especially those away from the main cities, are available only to tour groups booking in advance, not to individuals.

In trying to pack as much information as possible in this book, we have used the following abbreviations:

B.C.	Business center or capable of sending fax, telex, secretary for hire, photocopy, and typewriter rentals.
C.C.	Credit cards—American Express, Visa, Master-Card, and sometimes Diner's
Dist.A.P.	Distance from airport
Dist.R.W.	Distance from main railway station
H.K.	Hong Kong
IDD	International Direct Dial—might only be in the lobby.
J.V.	Joint Venture
Ren.	Renovated
H.K.T.V.	English-language broadcasts sometimes with CNN from Hong Kong.
USTV	Direct television transmission capability usually of BBC, CNN, or other U.S. stations. Hotels might have one or two channels, but might not be operating.
#	One of the state-designed cultural relics shops for certified antiques. (See Shopping.)
AT&T	Separate direct telephone line to the U.S. for AT&T cards and collect calls. Calls over three minutes usually cheaper.

ANSHAN 鞍山

Northeast China. 1½ hours by train, SW of Shenyang and still cold. Minimum in winter— ‾25°C; but maximum in summer is 34°C. Annual precipitation 715 mm, including snow. Urban population 1.2 million. Plane from Beijing Mondays and Thursdays.

Anshan was settled in the Yan State during the Warring States period. Its mines and smelting date back to the second century B.C. In 1395 (Ming), a city was built here; the ruins can still be seen. The Japanese colonized this area in the 1930s until 1945.

Today Anshan mines magnesite, talcum, white and green marble, and graphite, and has China's biggest iron and steel works. It is also known for **Mt. Qianshan** 千山风景区 , 44 square km of wilderness and jagged peaks, the highest 708 meters above sea level. Five Buddhist temples, one founded in the Tang but rebuilt in the Ming, and a Taoist temple add interest. It is 18 km SE of the main hotels.

The other main tourist attraction is **Tanggangzi Hot Spring Sanatorium** 汤岗子温泉 15 km south of Anshan. Arthritis, sciatica, and psoriasis are treated here. Modest hostel on the premises. A room was built for the Last Emperor, but he seldom used it. At Liaoyang, about 15 km NE, are some *Han and Wei tombs with murals, not yet open.

Fans can ride **steam locomotives** 38-km at the iron and steel complex.

Haicheng silk, ginseng, and Nanguo pears are specialties of the city. Tourism officials recommend the Anshan Roast Duck restaurant (May Rd.) and the Lao Zhen Xin (in the center of town).

HOTELS
Anshan Hotel (Binguan) ● *29 Shengli Rd., Tiedong District, 114002. Dist.A.P.15 km. Dist.R.W.1 km.* ● 1953; ren. 1987. Three stories, 132 rooms. IDD expected. Except for carpets, clean and well-maintained. This is the better hotel.

Victory Hotel (Shengli Binguan) ● *2 Xinhua St., Tiedong District, 114000, Telex 810032 SLHOT CN. Walk from free market, park.*

Near trolley line. Dist.A.P.15 km. Dist.R.W.2 km. • 1958, ren. 1987. 8 stories. Dorms, big rooms. Limited hot running water. Some rooms air-conditioned. Four-meter-high ceilings. IDD, no C.C.

CAAC, tel. 22139.
C.I.T.S. 29 South Shengli Rd., Tiedong, 114002; tel. 534403. Telex 810038 HAAH CN. Fax 532605.
C.T.S., 121 Section 1, Shengli Rd., Tiedong; tel. 24403.
China United Airlines, Iron and Steel Complex branch, Tuan Jie St., Dui Lu Shan, Tiedong Dist.
Friendship Store is in the Anshan First Department Store (May 1 Rd., Tiedong District). Open 8:30 a.m. to 6 p.m.
See also "Shenyang."

ANYANG 安阳

Northwest China. Northern part of Henan province north of the Yellow River on the Beijing-Guangzhou railway.

This city of half a million people is one of the oldest in China, founded in the Shang dynasty. For short periods in the 16th century B.C., it was a Shang capital. In the 14th century, the problem of flooding solved, it was made a permanent city, the capital for King Pan Geng (Pan Keng) of the State of Yin, and continued as the royal capital for some 270 years.

It was here that the oracle bones, an ancient means of divination, were later found. Here early writing was inscribed on tortoise shells and shoulder blades of oxen, and then cracked with heat. The direction of the crack foretold the future. Today the city is highly industrial, with an iron and steel works. Tourists might be interested in visiting its jade-carving, plaited-straw, and carpet-weaving factories. But its prime attraction is to students of archaeology and ancient and modern Chinese history. It is also exciting to people into air sports. Where else in China can you sightsee from a hot-air balloon or glider?

A one-day visit can include: the **Yin Ruins* 殷墟, 2.5 km from the Anyang Guest House. The ruins include palace foundations, royal tombs, and bronze and jade artifacts, and are inside a reproduction of a Shang Palace. Yin was the last capital of the Shang dynasty in the 11th century B.C. The Anyang Museum and the **Wenfeng Pagoda** 灵谷寺 are also important. The pagoda is unusual, as it appears to be larger at the top, with a dagoba (stupa) at the summit. Some excellent brick carvings of saints are close enough to the ground to be studied.

The Mausoleum of Yuan Shikai 袁林 (2.5 km from the Anyang Hotel) holds the remains of the ambitious, brilliant official of the Manchu court. Also a warlord, Yuan took over the presidency of republican China from Dr. Sun Yat-sen in 1913, declared himself emperor in 1915, and died of a heart attack in 1916.

Yuefei's Temple 岳飞庙 (22 km from the Anyang Hotel) is a memorial to the maligned national hero.

If you have more time, then you can take in the **Azure-cloud Palace Temple** 碧霞宫和大石佛 (60 km from the hotel) with the oldest and largest Buddha in the province. The **Red Flag Canal** 红旗渠, one of the Communists' earliest achievements, is 96 km away, a spectacular example of water management. Ask also about the first prison in China from the Shang dynasty, and the Yin-Shang (dynasties) festival, which has been held here in October.

If hot-air ballooning, sky-diving, or gliding are essential to your visit here, do make arrangements with the Anyang Aerial Sports School, Aviation Sports Association, or a travel agency before you go.

HOTELS

Anyang Guest House (Binguan) • *1 Youyi Rd. 455000, Dist. R.W 1 km* • 1959; renovated 1984.

C.I.T.S. 国际旅行社 , Anyang Guest House (1 Youyi Rd. 455000; tel. 2145.)

BAOTOU 包头

(Paotow) North China. Western Inner Mongolia. This mining and industrial city 2 km from the Yellow River is a 14-hour train trip or 1½ hour flight from Beijing, and three other cities. Its tourist attractions are mainly out of town. Take a scarf to cover your nose in case you encounter a sandstorm. The maximum temperature is 38°C, the minimum is ⁻30°C in winter! The average altitude is 1000 meters. Annual rainfall is a sparse 312 mm. The local tourist office points out 132 frostfree days a year! Prepare for cold weather except in summer.

The city was founded in the 17th century (Qing) on a neolithic site. At that time, people were encouraged to settle here to open up agriculture and defend the borders. The urban population is now about 870,000, of whom the Han are 90%, the Mongolians 2.5%, and the rest 21 other national minorities.

Of 1000 or so factories, visitors might want to see and shop at those producing leather and furs, porcelain, and arts and crafts. The **Baotou Carpet Factory** 包头地毡厂 is about 25 km from the main hotel.

If you only have one day, C.I.T.S. recommends the Wudangzhao Temple and a quick city tour. The city has over 40 archaeological sites, including the wall of the Zhao Kingdom and a Han dynasty town. The **Wudangzhao Temple** 五当召 is 70 km from the Blue Mountain Hotel and could be a rough trip. It is a massive 2500-room complex established in 1749 (Qing), once home to 1200 monks and covering about 50 acres. The largest lamasery in western Inner Mongolia, it contains statues, murals, and tankas typical of yellow sect Buddhism. More about Tibetan Buddhism under ''Lhasa'' and ''Chengde.''

If you have more time, the **Meidaizhao Temple** was originally built in the Ming. It is also known as the Sanniangzi Temple after the concubine of its Mongolian founder. She is buried here. A Han Chinese, she helped to bridge the differences between the two groups. The ***Tomb of Genghis Khan** 成吉思汗陵墓 was moved about 100 km south of Baotou to Ejinhoroq (Elinhoro) in 1954. It is in the shape of three yurts and has been restored. It contains ashes, said to be his. Pilgrims gather here to pay homage for one day in the third, fifth, ninth, and tenth lunar months.

Two new parks may be open by the time you arrive: the **Kongdulung Reservoir** 昆都仑水库风景区 , about 13 km from the hotel, and the **Nanhaizi Water Park** 南海子水上公园 , about 25 km.

In summer ask about the Nadam Fair: Seven days of horse racing, archery, and wrestling.

HOTELS

Blue Mountain Hotel (Qingshan Binguan) • *Qingshan district, 014030 Dist. A.P.30 km. Dist.R.W.7 km. Near government trade offices, and tourist shopping* • 1958; ren. 1988. Two stories, five buildings. Only Visa C.C. No IDD. B.C. Bicycles.

Baotou Hotel (Binguan) • *Kongdulung district 014010* • 1957; renovated 1983. This is the best hotel.

The hotels serve Chinese, Western, and Moslem food. Local delicacies include camel hump and camel paw and, of course, mutton dishes.

C.I.T.S. 国际旅行社 is in Baotou Hotel (tel. 24615).
CAAC 中国民航 (Donghe district; tel. 41404).

See also ''Hohhot.''

BEIDAIHE 北戴河

(Pehtaiho, Peitaihe; North Dai River) North China, Hebei, is a lovely seaside resort 5 hours by train via Tianjin due east of Beijing, and about 10 km south of Qinhuangdao; 7 trains a day each way serve Beidaihe. The town is 12 km from the railway station. An airport is at Qinhuangdao for the 50-minute air link with the capital. Air service also with Shijiazhang.

Beidaihe was built after the completion of the Beijing-Shanhaiguan railway in 1893. By 1949, 706 villas and hotel buildings had been completed, many of them for foreign diplomats and missionaries as well as wealthy Chinese. After Liberation, the Chinese government rebuilt some of the old buildings and added new ones as rest and recreation centers for its employees. The population is around 20,000.

The resort stretches along 12 km of hard, golden sand sloping gently out into the Bohai Sea. Swimming is good though there may be a few jellyfish. The beaches are divided by rock promontories. At the **Pigeon's Nest** 鹰角石 in the east, you can see Qinhuangdao across the bay and the best sunrise. At the **Tiger Stone** 老虎石 in the center, crab fishermen sell their catch in the summer.

Several swimming areas are attached to each of the hotels, manned by life guards and protected by nets. Each hotel has changing rooms on the beach with hot and cold fresh-water showers, open 8 a.m.–10 p.m. The swimming season is from May to September, depending on how cold you like your water. The hottest days are in August (maximum 36°C for a few days), but the high is usually 31°C, sometimes dropping to 24 or 25 at night.

A **Guanyin Temple** 观音祠 built in 1911 is on the grounds of the West Hill Hotel. The buildings were beautifully restored in 1979, the two statues and frescoes inside replaced after being destroyed by the Red Guards. The temple is about 1.5 km behind the hotel's service bureau, a nice morning's walk. The **Xiaobaohezhai Village** is also good to visit. It was one of the first in China to have pensions for its older citizens and one of the first with a birth-control program. It grows apples, peaches and pears for export, so an ideal time to visit is late August–September.

A good view of Beidaihe can be enjoyed from **Lianfengshan Park** 莲蓬山公园 . One can also rent bicycles, sailboats, and sailboards, and go sandsledding in nearby Changli county.

EXCURSIONS

Qinhuangdao—see separate listing.
Great Wall at Shanhaiguan—see ''Great Wall'' and ''Shanhaiguan.''
Mengjiangnu Temple and **Yansai Lake**—see ''Shanhaiguan.''

RESTAURANTS

Beihai Restaurant 北海饭庄 ● seafood
Kissling Restaurant 起士林餐厅 ● mainly European food
International Club 国际俱乐部 ● Chinese and Western food

HOTELS

The top hotel is the Jinshan, says the Beidaihe Beach Tourism Corporation.

Beidaihe Hotel for Diplomatic Personnel • *1 Baosan Rd., Beidaihe Beach, 066100. Fax 441807* • Open end of May to mid-October. Private Beach. No C.C. 1988. 2 stories, 185 rooms. IDD. Cheap.

Jinshan Hotel (Binguan) • *No. 4 Dongsan Rd., 066100. 3*. Telex 271053 JSH CN. Fax 442478* • 1986; 400 beds. Closed-circuit TV, radio, air conditioning, conference hall, ballroom, function room, open-air bar, beach, and several dining halls. Bicycles, gym, bowling, sauna, tennis, and pool.

C.I.T.S., 64 Minzu Rd., Qinhuangdao, 006000. Tel. 335974.

C.T.S., 4 Jinshan Zui Rd., Seaside. Tel. 41748.

NOTE: · · · Regular public buses between Beidaihe and the beach operate every 30 minutes from 6 a.m. to 6:30 p.m.

BEIJING

(Peking; Northern Capital) North China, surrounded by Hebei province on the northern fringe of the north China plain; 183 km west of the seacoast, about 44 meters above sea level, has mountains to the north, west, and east; 36 hours by train north of Guangzhou and 19 hours NW of Shanghai, it can also be reached by train from Ulan Bator and, beyond that, from Moscow. On almost the same latitude as Philadelphia, Beijing is about 4 hours west of Tokyo by air, 3 north of Guangzhou or Hong Kong, and 2 NW of Shanghai. The best time to visit is in the autumn. The hottest days are in July and August—up to 38°C for a week or so; the coldest are in January and February—down to ⁻20°C. Dust storms occasionally blow from December to late March, and sometimes into May. The winter air is heavily polluted. The government is trying to clean the air in its bid for the year 2000 Olympics. Annual precipitation is 683 mm, usually from June to August. Beijing has a chronic water shortage, which should be alleviated in the future by diverting water from the Yellow River. Population is 10.8 million (5 million urban); 5 million bicycles.

Beijing is the most important place to visit in China, not just because it is the capital but because it has a 3000-year history, from the Western Zhou, when it was known as Ji (Chi). Its most impressive historical monuments date from the 13th century. The museums here are the best in China, the temples among the most impressive. The palaces are the biggest and most elaborate. For most Chinese people, visiting Beijing has been and still is a lifetime ambition and, fortunately, many are now able to do it.

If you must pick only one city to visit in this country of thousands of outstanding ancient monuments, you, too, should choose Beijing.

The Liao (916–1125) were the first to build a capital here. They called it Nanjing, Southern Capital, as distinct from their old capital farther north in Manchuria. The name was changed again to Yanjing (Yen Ching) in 1013. In 1125, the Jin, a Tartar dynasty, overthrew the Liao and enlarged the city, calling it Zhongdu, Central Capital. The Mongols (Yuan), under Kublai Khan, overthrew the Jin and built a new capital called Dadu (Ta Tu). In 1368 the Ming drove out the Yuan and established their capital at Nanjing with Beijing, then called Peiping Fu, as an auxiliary capital in 1409.

Beijing became the main capital again in 1421 (Ming) and continued as the Qing capital into the early 1900s. In 1860, it was invaded by foreign, mainly English and French, troops. The foreigners completely destroyed the Yuanmingyuan Palace. The Boxers took over in 1900 and laid siege to the Foreign Legation section, but were repelled by an international military force while the Qing Empress Dowager fled temporarily to Xi'an. In 1928, the Nationalist government moved its capital to today's Nanjing, and Beijing became Peiping (Northern Peace). The Japanese held it from 1937 to 1945. When the Communists took over in 1949, it regained its old name and former position as capital of the nation.

Fortunately, the buildings of Beijing escaped the Pacific War relatively intact. During imperial times, no structures taller than the Forbidden City were allowed. In 1959, ten massive buildings were completed for the tenth anniversary of the founding of the People's Republic. Built in the heavy, plain Soviet style, these included the Great Hall of the People, the Museums of History and the Revolution, and the Palace of the Minorities. They are period pieces now.

In 1966, Beijing's Tiananmen Square was the setting for mass Red Guard rallies of over a million people. In 1976, the square was also the site of a clash between supporters of the Gang of Four and those of Premier Chou Enlai. In 1989, an estimated 300 to 3000 people were killed in or around the square in what the Chinese government called the quelling of the counter-revolutionary rebellion.

Beijing is centered around the Forbidden City and Tiananmen Square. The old foreign legation area was SE of these, between the Beijing, Xiqiao, and Capital Hotels. The few remaining European buildings there reflect that period of its history. The Chinese city was south of the Qianmen Gate on the southern edge of Tiananmen Square.

Beijing now consists of ten districts and nine counties. Rural villages raise the famous force-fed Beijing ducks. Over 2000 factories, mainly in the suburbs, produce iron and steel, coal mining, machines, basic chemicals and petroleum, electronics, and textiles.

The people of Beijing speak Mandarin or *pu tung hua,* the official national language, but they twirl their tongues more. They are predominantly Han, but you will see many flat, wide Mongolian faces too. Beijing people tend to be reserved compared to other Chinese. Don't be put off by this, for they are warm and friendly once they get to know you.

Beijing needs at least six days to cover its important attractions. Many individual travelers use public transportation successfully if they have plenty of time. Just avoid rush hours. Bus and subway maps are available in many hotels. The east-west subway line is 24 km long, each station in a different color marble. Trains operate every 3–8 minutes from early morning to late evening west from the railway station. Note the station at the south end of Tiananmen Square. The circle subway, a 16-km loop, completes the rectangle around Tiananmen Square and the Forbidden City and reaches near the Beijing Zoo and Friendship Hotel. There are two other lines, total 52 km.

A good, inexpensive introduction is the **Beijing City Bus Tour** from the Great Wall, Kunlun, Jinglun, or Jianguo Hotels, or anywhere else along its 16-stop, 45-km-long route. Each bus has an English-speaking guide on board and you can get off or on at any stop, seeing some of the main tourist attractions: the Friendship Store, Wangfujing St. (shopping), Drum Tower, and Lama Temple. Buses also stop at the Forbidden City; we recommend at least a day in that area. The bus schedule is on bright two-meter-high poles outside these tourist attractions. A non-stop trip takes 2½ hours. The last bus leaves the Great Wall at 2:30 p.m. It operates only if there is enough demand.

A relatively inexpensive **tourist bus** service run by the Beijing Motor Bus Company is recommended for those with a good guidebook or map. The human guides only give short introductions. Basically you're on your own. Regular tours go to the Great Wall, Ming Tombs, Fragrant Hills, Summer Palace, Tanzhe Temple, Yunshui Cave, Qing tombs, and Chengde (Jehol). These out-of-town tours can be booked south of Tiananmen Square on the same street as the Qianmen Kentucky Fried Chicken Restaurant, outside the Beijing Exhibition Center and at the Xinqiao Hotel. Cheap tours with English-speaking guides also go from the Qiaoyuan Hotel. C.I.T.S. has more expensive day tours booked from the Lido, Great Wall, and Jinglun hotels. These are less expensive than booking a tour for just one or two people through a hotel.

To help you plan your time so you can cover the most important sights, these groupings are suggested. The days can be interchangeable, depending on weather, train schedules, upset stomachs, traffic jams, and the hours a particular attraction is open.

DAY 1: Tiananmen Square, Imperial Palace, and Jing Hill. Lunch can be in one of the many restaurants (including Kentucky Fried Chicken) on Qianmen Xi Ave. (cheaper) at the south end of the square or at the Beijing Hotel Palace Tower, the World Showcase Restaurants (or Kentucky Fried Chicken take-out) between the Beijing Hotel and Forbidden City. There is a snack stand in the Forbidden City.

DAY 2: The Museums of Chinese History and the Chinese Revolution, Beihai Park and the Temple of Heaven. Tour of Dazhalan if you make arrangements first, and shopping at Liulichang. Lunch if you make a reservation on time at the Fang Shan (Imperial Kitchen) Restaurant (tel. 442573, Beihai Park). Also any of the "Day 1" restaurants.

DAY 3: Summer Palace, temples of the Western Hills, Fragrant Hill, ruins of the Yuanmingyuan, and Great Bell Temple. The temple is closed once a week, probably Wednesdays, so phone the tourist hotline first to make sure it is open. Avoid all but the temple if the weather is bad. Lunch at the Summer Palace (reservation needed at the Tingliguan there), or the Fragrant Hills Hotel.

DAY 4: Great Wall and Ming Tombs, but not on Sundays (traffic jam). Avoid in bad weather. Take your own lunch if you want, especially in pleasant weather. Most tourists visit the Great Wall at Badaling. If you want to get away from the commercialism and crowds, ask for Mutianyu or drive around the Genghis Khan military site.

DAY 5: Lama Temple (closed on Mondays), Confucius Temple/Capital Museum, China Art Gallery—half a day. Remainder and **DAY 6:** choice of arts and crafts factories, rural visit, shopping, cultural performances, or repeat visits to places where you wanted to spend more time but couldn't. Choice of other excursions.

As you can see, this is a very heavy schedule and you may have to squeeze your shopping and strolling into the evenings. One really needs more time. You can't enjoy details if you keep looking at your watch.

DAY 1

Tiananmen (Tien An Men) Square 前门城门 , 98 acres. Great for kite-flying in the spring. Try to imagine 1966 at the beginning of the Cultural Revolution when a million schoolchildren filled this square, chanting slogans and waving the little red book of quotations from Chairman Mao. The father of Communist China stood at the front of the gate to the north and acknowledged the screams and cheers of the youngsters. Besides giving them a vacation from school, he also gave them a mandate to travel around the country on the trains with room and board in each city—all free. Truckloads of shoes were swept away after the rallies. No one was able to retrieve lost shoes as the crowd surged wildly. Protests and rallies are still held here.

It will be hard for many foreigners to forget the much televised, idealistic young students demonstrating non-violently for democracy in 1989. The square was reopened to the general public early in 1990 but might be closed again—depending on the political climate. You can judge the political situation for yourself by what happens in the square.

No one is allowed to place memorial flowers without government permission, but sympathizers might "accidentally" drop a flower or two.

We suggest you read Chinese government accounts of the "turmoil" and western sources. They do not agree.

This square is bounded on the north by the Tian Anmen gate and on the west by the Great Hall of the People. On the east is the Museum of the Chinese Revolution and the Museum of Chinese History, and on the south one can't miss the imposing Qianmen (Chien Men) gate. In the center, from the north to south, are the Monument to the People's Heroes and the Chairman Mao Memorial Hall. Every May 1 and Oct. 1 the big portraits are displayed. They are, left to right, Marx, Engels, Lenin, and Stalin. Also prominent is Dr. Sun Yat-sen.

The **Great Hall of the People,** a.k.a. People's Congress Hall, built in 1959; 171,800 square meters. Three main sections include a 5000-seat banquet hall, a three-story, 10,000-seat auditorium, and lounges in the style of each of the provinces. This is China's equivalent of a parliament. To some observers, it is merely a rubber-stamp group of representatives. To others, the People's Congress is a forum for the opinions of the masses. It has been open Tuesdays, Wednesdays, and Saturday mornings for a small fee.

Qianmen Gate   天安门   is not open, but it is a magnificent, beautiful gate. To the south is Dazalan, a Chinese shopping area (see Day 2). The bus to the Great Wall can also be booked nearby.

Beijing's gates are marvelous. Each had a very specific purpose; for example, night soil could only go through the Andingmen in the north; prisoners to be executed plodded through the west gate, Xuanwumen. Departing soldiers marched through another of the north gates even if they had to fight in the south. The impressive Deshengmen (Victory Gate) can be climbed and may still have good contemporary art for sale.

Monument to the People's Heroes   人民英雄纪念碑   : If you had taken my advice and learned your numbers in Chinese, you would know the dates under each sculpture. Then if you looked up "Milestones in Chinese History" you would know that the sculptures here represent the burning of the opium and the Opium War, 1840–42; the Taiping Heavenly Kingdom, 1851–64; the Revolution of 1911; the May

4, 1919, demonstration against the Versailles Treaty and for the New Cultural Movement (such as literature in plain rather than the generally incomprehensible classical language); the May 30, 1925, Incident in Shanghai, a protest against foreign powers in China after a Chinese worker was killed by a Japanese foreman. Look also for the August 1, 1927, uprising in Nanchang and the Anti-Japanese War, 1937–45.

In April 1976, during the Qingming (Ching Ming) festival, when the dead are honored (in the old days "worshiped"), attempts by the Gang of Four to remove wreaths brought by private citizens in memory of Premier Chou En-lai were resisted by pro-Chou supporters at this monument. Hundreds were wounded and thousands arrested. This protest is now referred to as the April Fifth Movement against the Gang of Four, and encouraged pro-Chou politicians like Deng Xiaoping to attempt to overthrow them. In 1989, this statue was central to the student demonstrators.

The **Chairman Mao Memorial Hall** 毛主席纪念堂 was built in 1977. It has been open on Mondays, Wednesdays, and Friday mornings. Whether it remains open depends on the political climate. In this mausoleum rest the remains of China's great leader. The simple white building, with 44 granite columns and glazed yellow trim, is 33.6 meters high and 105 meters square.

Foreign and Overseas Chinese visitors line up separately from Chinese citizens, and the visit takes less than 30 minutes. As a token of respect, visitors are advised not to wear bright colors, especially red, but no one was stopped when I was there. No cameras or purses are allowed. One enters first the North Hall, where there is a seated, 3-meter-high marble statue of the leader. Then, quietly, two by two, you enter the Central Hall where Chairman Mao (1893–1976) lies in state.

Tian Anmen (Tien An Men; Gate of Heavenly Peace) is the second most famous structure in China. From its high balcony the imperial edicts were read, and this is where, on October 1, 1949, Chairman Mao Zedong (Mao Tse-tung) proclaimed the People's Republic of China. It is a symbol of old and new China. The country's leaders frequently appear here on national days to review the parades and festivities. It was built in 1651 and stands 33.7 meters high. The rostrum where Chairman Mao stood is open to tourists for ¥ 30.

Through the gate under Chairman Mao's portrait, to the left, is Zhongshan Park, the memorial park to Dr. Sun Yat-sen. To the right is Working People's Cultural Park. These two parks are great for 6 a.m. walks because of the magnificent walls, towers, gates, moats, and pavilions, and also because of the people limbering up for the day. You might hear some very beautiful voices resound off the walls from very shy singers hiding behind bushes and screens.

In the square between the two parks is a tiny white marble pavilion looking much like a Japanese lantern. In imperial times, if an official made a serious error, his black gauze cap was placed inside and he was taken out to be executed at the Wumen in front of the palace. Commoners were dispatched at the marketplace 7 km SW of here near the Qianmen Hotel.

*Gu Gong (Imperial Palace), a.k.a. Palace Museum or Forbidden City 故宫 : open 8:30 a.m.–4:30 p.m. (summer). No admittance after 3:30 p.m. Visitors usually enter by the Wumen (Meridian Gate) inside the Tian Anmen between the two above-mentioned parks, and head north. Because of the crowds wearing down the Forbidden City, a daily limit of about 25,000 tourists has been imposed. Foreigners might be exempt. An acoustiguide, a recording of Peter Ustinov giving details about a limited area, is recommended.

The Gu Gong was the home and audience hall of the Ming and Qing emperors. Many buildings here are as the Qing left them, minus relics now in the National Palace Museum in Taiwan. Many of the buildings are exhibition halls for historic treasures from all over China. Relics of the Last Emperor Pu Yi might still be seen, including his queue (which he cut off himself), his bicycle, and his cricket box. To walk at a leisurely pace from one end to the other takes about 30 minutes, but to explore it thoroughly takes at least a full day—some would say a week. And not all parts are open to the public!

The Forbidden City was originally built from 1406 to 1420 as the palace of the Ming emperors. It is on more than 720,000 square meters (178 acres) of land. Over 9000 rooms cover a total floor space of about 150,000 square meters. The surrounding imperial red wall is over 10 meters high. Only imperial palaces were allowed to have yellow ceramic roofs. (Commoners could only use gray.) This massive city was built by 100,000 artisans and a million laborers.

Toward the end of the Qing, 280,000 taels of silver were needed annually to maintain the palace, the money collected in taxes and rents from 658,000 acres of royal estates. During the Ming, 9000 ladies-in-waiting and 100,000 eunuchs (castrated males) served here. Some eunuchs became more powerful than the self-indulgent emperors. Sacked by foreign powers in 1900, the Forbidden City was restored and now maintains a permanent staff of painters and carpenters so that every 20 years all the buildings are renewed.

The city is divided into two major sections: the outer palace (for business) and the inner residential courts. Directly beyond the Meridian Gate are the five marble bridges "like arrows reporting on the emperor to Heaven." The River of Gold below is shaped like a bow. Note the gates; red was used only for important places like this. Each has 81 studs—nine times nine, an imperial number. Seven layers of brick line the courtyards, so no one could tunnel in from below. Note the white squares, on each of which a royal guard stood whenever the emperor ventured past.

Throughout the palace, huge caldrons of water stand ready for possible fires. On the north side, beneath the caldrons, are air vents to fan fires set in winter to keep the water inside from freezing. Note the lack of hiding places for possible assassins.

The first building is the **Taihedian** (Tai Ho Tien; Hall of Supreme Harmony) 太和殿 , the most stately of all the buildings. It is surrounded by incense burners, 18 bronze ones representing the then 18 provinces, and others in the form of a stork (longevity) and a dragon-headed tortoise (strength and endurance). Note the copy of an ancient sundial and the small openings on the side of the pavilion to allow air to circulate inside. The building was used for major ceremonies like the emperor's birthday, for imperial edicts, and for state affairs. Imagine the area in front of it covered with silk-gowned ministers and officials kneeling in rows. Imagine their heads to the ground in front of the hall while smoke poured from the incense burners and musicians played on the balcony. Can you see the child emperor being carried by palaquin above them to the highly carved throne? If you can't, try to see the Chinese historical movie *Power Behind the Throne* and the American movie *The Last Emperor*. Good books to read are *Inside Stories of the Forbidden City*, published in China, and E. Behr's *The Last Emperor*.

Each of the 18-meter-high cedar pillars was made from one piece of wood. Each of the floor tiles took 136 days to bake, after which it was immersed in oil for a permanent polish. The bricks are solid, about 5″ thick and 18″ square. The base and throne are carved sandalwood.

The **Zhonghedian (Hall of Complete Harmony)** 中和殿 was used by the emperor to receive his ministers, to rest, and to dress before he entered the Taihedian. The two Qing sedan chairs here were for traveling within the palace. The braziers were for heat, the four cylindrical burners for sandalwood incense. Note the imperial dragon symbols on the ceiling.

The **Baohedian (Hall of Preserving Harmony)** 保和殿 , the most decorative of these halls, was for imperial banquets and, during the Qing, the retesting of the top scorers in the national examinations. Note the ceilings and beams. Behind this hall, between the stairways, is a giant carving of dragons in one piece of marble from Fanshan county, 16.5 meters by 3 meters and weighing about 250 tons. Anyone caught touching this imperial symbol was executed. The carving and the timbers were brought here in winter by sliding them over ice made from water of wells especially sunk for the occasion. Nothing was too extravagant for the representative of Heaven!

Several buildings on both sides of these main halls were used for study, lectures, a library, and even a printing shop. Beyond this third hall are the **Inner Courts,** the three main buildings, similar to the three in the outer palace; the **Qianqinggong (Hall of Heavenly Purity)** 乾清 , where the emperors used to live and where deceased emperors lay in state. Here also Cixi (Tsu Hsi), the infamous Empress Dowager, received foreign envoys; the **Jiaotaidian (Hall of Union)** 交泰殿 , where ceremonies involving empresses took place (women were not allowed in the outer palace!); and the **Kunninggong (Palace of Earthly Tranquillity)** 坤宁宫 , which was a residence in the Ming and a shrine in the Qing. One of the Qing emperors used its eastern room as a bridal chamber. East of the Kunninggong is a hall where clocks from all over the world are exhibited, gifts from foreign missions. In the back of the inner court is the **Imperial Garden,** where a snack bar might save thirsty tourists. The imperial family sipped tea, played chess, and meditated in this beautifully designed garden. Can you imagine living here!

Then, continuing northward, one arrives at the back gate, where tour groups usually meet their buses. But you're not finished yet! Retracing your steps to the entrance of the inner court, turn left (east) at the Qianqingong, past the washrooms and the **Nine Dragon Screen,** and then turn left again. Here are several pavilions with exhibitions well worth seeing. One might have a stunning collection of gold artifacts—bells, incense burners, table service (with jade handles), and scepters. There are also precious Buddhist relics and the biggest jade sculpture in China, a 5-ton Ming statue depicting one of the earliest attempts in the Xia Dynasty to control the Yellow River. Look for paintings and antique jewelry, pottery and bronzes. Also notable north of this area is the 12″-diameter well in which the obviously thin Pearl Concubine was drowned by a eunuch after she incurred the wrath of the Empress Dowager in 1900.

A clean toilet is in this area near the jewelry exhibit.

In each building, look at the ceilings and the palace lanterns, the distinctive blue Manchu cloisonne, and the western clocks. Where were the imperial toilets? the kitchens? Think of the children who grew up within these walls and never set foot outside! Think of the eunuchs who gave up their manhood for a job that would benefit their families.

American Express has placed wooden signboards here with historical information.

Jingshan (Coal) Hill 景山 , outside the north gate of the palace, was originally the site of a Ming coal pile. It was built with earth excavated from the moats and is 43 meters high. It is now a park with a good view of the Forbidden City and the lakes to the west and north. As the Manchus were breaking into the city, the last of the Ming emperors hung himself on a locust tree located at the foot of the hill on the east side. A free market is outside the East Gate mornings.

DAY 2

The exhibits in the **Museum of the Chinese Revolution** 中国革命博物馆 have been about: the Opium War, the Taiping Heavenly Kingdom, the Sino-French War and the Sino-Japanese War, Tsarist Russian

Aggression, the Reform Movement of 1898, the Anti-Imperialist Movement of the Yi He Tuan, the Revolution of 1911, and the founding of the Communist Party, Chou En-lai, the civil wars, and the Japanese war. Recently, there has been an exhibit about the 1989 turmoil.

The **Museum of Chinese History** 中国历史博物馆 is China's best. It is divided into four sections: primitive society, slave society, feudal society, and semicolonial, semifeudal society. You can walk through without absorbing much in an hour, it is so large. You need at least a half day to do it justice. Please take it in short doses, especially if your feet tire easily. There is a lot to see! (See also *Visit Museums* in "What Is There to See and Do" and "Milestones in Chinese History.") Both museums are entered opposite the Great Hall of the People. The history museum is to the right.

Relics here start from 1.7-million-year-old pre-human teeth to 1911. They include a model of the cave where the Peking Man was found. Also on display are a 14th-century B.C. ivory cup inlaid with jade, a Shang bronze wine vessel with four protruding rams' heads, and a Western Zhou sewer pipe with the head of a tiger. Intriguing, too, are a model of a Warring States irrigation system, tomb figures galore, and a model of a first-century B.C. wheel used to operate a bellows to melt iron. Here, too, is the Flying Horse of Gansu, which people around the world waited many hours to see when it was exhibited abroad. No queues here!

There is also a model of a 1700-year-old drum chariot with a figure of a child on top, always pointing south, and another miniature drum chariot with a figure that beats a drum every 500 meters, a Yuan water clock, and some Yuan rockets attached to spears. I can only whet your appetite. It is best to take a Chinese-reading friend since there have been no signs in English.

The *Tiantan (Temple of Heaven)** 天坛 is about 5 km south of the Forbidden City. Think of the processions of incense-swinging priests, spear-bearing palace guards, and the palaquin bearers carrying the emperor—all marching from the palace unseen by anyone else. Setting eyes on the emperor was a crime punishable by death.

The temple is set in the middle of a 667-acre park with many pine and cypress trees, some over 500 years old. Give yourself at least 20 minutes for a quick look, an hour for a more thorough tour. The Temple of Heaven was built in the same period as the Forbidden City (1420), and ranks among the most famous structures in China. It was used a couple of times a year when the emperor, bearing all the sins of the Chinese people, humbled himself before Heaven and performed the rituals calculated to bring good harvests. The temple has two concentric walls, both round at the north and straight at the south, heaven being round and earth square, or didn't you know! The raised, 360-meter passage between the main buildings is the **Red Stairway Bridge.** To the north is the **Qiniandian (Hall of Prayer for Good Harvests)** with triple eaves, 38 meters high and 30 meters in diameter. The four central columns represent the four seasons. Around these four are two rings of 12 columns each, the inner symbolizing the 12 months and the outer the 12 divisions of day and night. Here, the emperor performed the rites on the 15th day of the first moon of the lunar calendar. All the columns are wood from Yunnan province.

South of this is the **Imperial Vault of Heaven,** originally built in 1530 and rebuilt in 1752. In this building without horizontal beams were stored the tablets of the God of Heaven, the Wind God, the Rain God, etc. Sacrifices were made on the circular Sacrificial Altar on the winter solstice. The surrounding wall has a strange echo effect. You can hear people talking softly beside it from an unusual distance. Also count the number of stone slabs on the floor, staircases, and balustrades. They are in multiples of nine.

*Beihai (North Sea) Park 北海公园 , open 7:30 a.m.–4 p.m., is only a few blocks west of Coal Hill. (Take bus 103 along Wangfujing St. from the Beijing Hotel if you wish.) If you are short of time, just head for **Baita Shan (White Dagoba Hill)** 白塔山 and then the **Nine Dragon Screen** (1756) on the opposite side of the lake. While the whole area is a historic site protected by the State Council, these are the highlights of a big, 168-acre park full of intriguing old buildings, the recently renovated **Jingxinzhai (Serenity Study),** winding paths, and interesting rocks, that could take a half day to explore. Rowboats are for hire and, in the winter, ice skating on the lake is an exotic experience (but bring your own skates). The Fang Shan Restaurant near the White Dagoba serves the same fancy, delicate dishes (well, almost!) once presented to the Empress Dowager. But you do have to make a reservation or risk going hungry.

In the 10th century (Liao), an imperial residence was built on the site and called Precious Islet Imperial Lodging. In the 12th century (Jin), auxiliary palaces were constructed here and a lake excavated, the earth used to build the artificial hills and the ***Round City** at the southern edge. Rocks from Kaifeng were also used. During the Yuan, the Qionghua Islet was expanded and the palace of Kublai Khan was made the center of the city. This palace is no longer standing. Also on the islet, the 35.9-meter-high, bell-shaped White Dagoba was first constructed in 1271 in the Tibetan style. The current stupa was built in 1731.

Also noteworthy is Kublai Khan's 3000-liter jade liquor container (1265) and the Jade Buddha in Chengguang Hall in the Round City on the mainland, by the White Dagoba causeway.

The Nine Dragon Screen on the north side of the lake is of glazed brick and is 5 by 27 by 1.2 meters. Successive dynasties added buildings to Beihai, and this park was also looted by the foreign powers in 1900. In the summer, there is a giant lantern festival.

Zhongnanhai 中南海 , south of Beihai, has not been generally open to the public because it contains the residences and offices of China's leaders. Very special tour groups have successfully requested a visit. The Guanxu (Kuang Hsu) emperor, who attempted to make modern reforms, much to the displeasure of the Empress Dowager Cixi, was imprisoned here during the winters when he was not at the Summer Palace. The historically important Pavilion of Purple Light and Fairy Tower were recently repaired. The south gate, brilliant red and fancy, is on Changan Avenue west of the Tian Anmen, too prominent to miss.

Now, if you have more time, the antiques, arts and crafts shopping center of **Liulichang** 琉璃厂 is nearby, a pleasant place to poke around. Built during the reign of Qing emperor Qianlong, it has recently been renovated in the old Qing style. See *Shopping*. The shopping area of **Dazalan** 颐和园 , just south of the Qianmen, is the market area for ordinary people. However, a huge, 3000-meter-long underground air-raid shelter (now a well-maintained underground tourist attraction, with arts and crafts store and a hotel) makes this special. The shelter has 90 entrances and can hold 10,000 people. Officials estimate the teeming streets above can be cleared in six minutes in an emergency.

Dazalan's underground is worth visiting, but arrangements must be made in advance by joining a tour. You can enter by a trap door in the floor of a clothing shop.

DAY 3

Summer Palace, Temple of the Azure Clouds, Temple of the Sleeping Buddha, and Fragrant Hill are all within 10 km of each other, 20–30 km NW of the Tian Anmen. Because of traffic jams, avoid Sundays here. If time permits, you can visit the Yuanmingyuan and Great Bell Temple too.

The **Yiheyuan (Garden of Cultivating Peace)** 仁寿殿 , a.k.a. **Summer Palace** (open 6 a.m.–5:30 p.m.). A visit to this 717-acre garden usually takes half a day. It is three quarters water. Originally built in the 12th century, it was expanded in 1750 for the 60th birthday of the mother of the Qianlong emperor and burned in 1860 by the British-French army. It was rebuilt by the Empress Dowager Cixi (Tzu Hsi) on the occasion of her 60th birthday (1895) and financed with funds meant for building the Chinese navy. It was badly damaged by the foreign powers in 1900. The existing buildings were restored in 1903.

The imperial court lived here every year, when possible, from April 15 to October 15, receiving diplomats and conducting business in the **Renshoudian (Hall of Longevity and Benevolence)** 大戏楼 . Empress Dowager Cixi, who was the power behind the throne from 1861 to 1908, lived in this hall near the **Deheyuan (Grand Stage)** , where she could indulge in her passion for theatricals. The stage floor is hollow so that "ghosts" could emerge from it. The Grand Stage is now a separate museum requiring an additional fee. It contains Cixi's jewelry and dinnerware, and wax figures of Cixi and two imperial concubines. Attendants are in Qing palace costumes, and you can have your photo taken with a live "eunuch" or wax figures. In the exhibition hall behind the stage is the 1898 automobile given to the emperor by General Yuan Shikai.

Twenty-eight ladies-in-waiting, twenty eunuchs, and eight female officials waited on the Empress Dowager. For lunch, she was offered 128 courses daily.

In the **Hall of Jade Ripples** 玉栏堂 , to the south of the main entrance, she kept the Guangxu (Kuang Hsu) emperor imprisoned every summer from 1898 to 1908 after he tried unsuccessfully to institute reforms to modernize China and to take his rightful power back. Note the walls around the compound. The rooms here and elsewhere are furnished as they were then.

The **Long Corridor** extends 728 meters along the lake to the famous **Qingyan (Marble) Boat.** The 1400 paintings here (count them if you don't believe it!) are a most spectacular display. To the north up the hill are the **Hall of Dispelling Clouds** 排云殿 , the **Tower of Buddhist Incense** 佛香阁 , and the **Temple of the Sea of Wisdom** 智慧海 , where the empress used to hold her birthday celebrations and religious services. The **Xiequeyuan (Garden of Harmonious Interests)** 谐趣园 was designed like the Jichangyuan (Garden) in Wuxi. Also on the hill is a Tibetan-style Lama temple. Crossing Kunming Lake is a 17-arch bridge and, on an island, the **Dragon King Temple** 龙王庙 .

A good restaurant is in the **Tingliguan (Pavilion for Listening to Orioles)** 听鹂馆 ; reservations essential (tel. 283955).

The Summer Palace Hotel is in the garden, near the Hall of Scalloped Clouds, an exotic experience if you don't mind being isolated. It is a long way from downtown. Accessible from the Palace is Suzhou St., reconstructed on its original site. Built in the 18th century, and destroyed in 1860 by foreign soldiers, it was the shopping area used by palace residents. Attendants in Manchu dress give demonstrations of crafts and music. Photos are best late morning and early afternoon.

Northwest of the Summer Palace is the **Temple of the Sleeping Buddha,** a.k.a. Temple of Universal Spiritual Awakening 卧佛寺 . This was first built in the Tang and reconstructed and renamed in the Yuan, Ming, and Qing. The lacquered bronze Sakyamuni, which was cast in 1331 (Yuan), is 5.33 meters long and weighs 54 tons. It is the largest bronze statue in China. The Buddha here is giving his last words to his disciples before his earthly death. Because he is barefooted here, successions of emperors have presented the statue with 11 pairs of huge handmade cloth shoes, which are on display in the same room. One can also stay in the temple overnight very cheaply.

The **Biyunsi (Temple of Azure Clouds)** 白云寺 is more impor-

tant than the Sleeping Buddha because of its stunning collection of religious statues and the Diamond Throne Pagoda. The Biyun was first
built in the Yuan as a nunnery. During the Ming, it was the burial place
for powerful eunuchs. In 1748, Emperor Qian Long (Chien Lung) ordered to be built the **Hall of Five Hundred Arhats** 五百罗汉堂 and
the **Diamond Throne (a.k.a. Vajra Throne) Pagoda** 金钢宝座塔 .
The 508 gilded, wooden arhats are life-size and strikingly beautiful,
each different, and protected behind dirty glass. How many are not sitting? Which have two heads?

In 1925, the body of Dr. Sun Yat-sen lay in state at this temple
until the completion of his mausoleum in Nanjing. A tiny museum is at
the spot. The unique 34.7-meter Diamond Throne Pagoda consists of
five small pagodas in the Indian style and has some excellent carvings
and towers, showing a great deal of Indian influence.

Xiang Shan (Fragrant Hill) Park 香山公园 , open 7:30 a.m.–
5:30 p.m., was a 150-hectare (384-acre) hunting ground for many emperors. A 20-minute chairlift to the top of the mountain now gives a
spectacular view of the area, especially in autumn, when the air is less
dusty and some leaves are red. Prepaid tour groups automatically jump
the queue because they have already paid the higher fee. The highest
peak here is 557 meters above sea level. The lift goes by a small Glazed
Pagoda, a Western-style mansion that was presumably the hunting lodge,
and a Tibetan-style temple, which you can inspect at closer range later.

Drop in at the **Xiang Shan (Fragrant Hill) Hotel** 香山饭店 for
coffee. See *Hotels* below.

If time permits on the way back to town, glimpse the **Yuanmingyuan** 圆明园 ruins. This Garden of Clear Ripples was built in an area
full of bubbling springs and was used as an imperial resort beginning in
the 11th century. It became the site of a major palace in 1690 and later
was rebuilt into a favorite 160-hectare palace garden by Qing Emperor
Qianlong, with buildings copied from Suzhou, Hangzhou, and Yangzhou. Sacked by Anglo-French forces in 1860 (after the Qing defeated
the foreigners at Taku and tortured their envoys), it was partially repaired only to be destroyed again in 1900. The foreigners wanted to
punish the emperor who loved it in revenge for the siege of the lega-
tions. The few remains of this ''Garden of gardens'' and ''Palace of
palaces'' can be glimpsed in twenty minutes if you are in a hurry to get
to the Great Bell Temple. Enough remains of the marble archways of
the Evergreen Palace to show the influence of the European missionaries
who helped design it early in the 1750s. Since the imperial families
favored the Yuanmingyuan over the Imperial Palace, they kept their
most precious treasures and books here. The 1860 burning took two
days and is documented in a good Chinese-made movie, *The Burning
of the Summer Palace*. One of the best accounts in English is Garnet J.
Wolseley's *Narrative of the War with China in 1860*. A small exhibition

near the entrance tells the story. The maze and some other buildings have been reconstructed.

You are rushing now to get to the **Jueshengsi (Temple of Awareness of Life),** popularly known as the Temple of the Great Bell 大钟寺 This temple houses over 40 different ancient bells. The most spectacular bell was cast in the reign of Emperor Yongle of the Ming (1403–25) in a clay mold, and weighs 46.5 tons. How would *you* have brought the bell here without a crane and truck? In 1733, the Chinese slid it on ice in winter or on wheat shells in summer and put it on a mound. After attaching the bell onto the beams, the mound was dug out and then the hall was built around it. The 220,000 amazingly handsome Chinese characters decorating it are Buddhist scriptures and prayers.

The other bells in the exhibit were for various purposes. In religious ceremonies they drove away worldly worries and attracted the attention of the gods. Some bells here announced the time of day and the closing of the city gates. Some were used in music rituals. (See also "Wuhan.") A small hall contains an exhibit on how the bells were made, unfortunately labeled only in Chinese.

DAY 4

Some people prefer to take their own box lunch to the Great Wall even though restaurants are available.

*Great Wall—see separate listing.

*Shisan Ling (Ming Tombs) 十三陵 , open daily 8 a.m.–4 p.m., are usually combined with a trip to the Great Wall at Badaling. They are a 50-km (1¾-hour) drive NW of the Tian Anmen. Avoid Sunday traffic jams.

These 13 imperial tombs were built from 1409 to 1644 and spread over 40 square km. Each tomb consists of a Soul Tower, a Sacrificial Hall, and an Underground Palace, surrounded by a wall. Approaching from the south, one sees a big, carved white marble archway, erected in 1590, beyond which are the Great Red Gate, ornamental pillars, and the Tablet Pavilion. The Sacred Way has 24 stone animals (lions, unicorns, camels, elephants, etc., 12 larger-than-life-size humans (military officers and government officials), and an army of enterprising hawkers (also an old China tradition) selling everything from furs, porcelain, and fruit to junk. The 400-year-old stone animals and figures cannot be mounted.

At least two of the tombs are open to visitors: **Chang Ling 乾陵** , the biggest and earliest, and **Ding Ling 定陵** , which has been excavated and can be entered. Ding Ling is the tomb of the 13th Ming Emperor Wanli, who ruled for 48 years, starting at age 10. The tomb was begun when he was 22 years old. It took six years and cost eight million taels of silver to build.

The underground palace consists of three halls, the central one with passages to annex chambers, totaling 1195 square meters. The marble doors each weigh four tons and were closed *from the inside* by propping two large stone poles against them. Note the two triangular depressions in the ground inside the door where the poles rested. Note also the blue and white porcelain jars with the dragons, which were half filled with oil when the tomb was opened. The oil was burned to create an oxygen-free vacuum inside.

In the central hall are three marble altars, two for the empresses, one for the emperor. Note the ''Five Altar Pieces'' and the porcelain lamp. The rear hall has the three coffins and plaster replicas of 26 chests. **Don't miss the separate museum,** which has on display some of the objects found in the tomb, such as the gold crown, headdresses, a jade belt, and a gold bowl. A 20-minute movie about the opening of Ding Ling is shown. The Ding Ling Restaurant nearby is better than the exotic Ming Yuan Hotel a few km away.

Enjoy the rural beauty, the vast, open spaces between the tombs, and the peace when you escape the 10,000-a-day tourists and peddlers. If you have time, you should also wander around the other tombs, which are not repaired and are usually free of tourists. These other tombs are not opened because of the high cost of careful archaeological excavation. Besides, no one knows where the entrances are because their builders were executed and no records have survived. The tombs and the Great Wall are best seen at dusk, when one feels the presence of ghosts. Seeing weeds growing on imperial terraces and birds making nests on once glorious beams is a good time to reflect on life and death. Think of the cracked roofs and fallen walls of the monuments you yourself have built.

But visit here soon. The Beijing Municipal Government and a Japanese firm have started work on a recreation complex with roller coasters, Ferris wheels, hotels, and camel-racing tracks. It is expected to be completed soon. An 18-hole golf course has already opened.

DAY 5

***Yonghegong (Lama Temple)** 雍和宫 : Count on at least 40 minutes. The Temple of Harmony and Peace was first built in 1694. This Mongolian-Tibetan yellow-sect temple is within walking distance of the Overseas Chinese Hotel 第二华侨饭店 It should not be missed. Beautifully renovated, it reveals pavilion after pavilion of increasingly startling figures, the largest in the back hall 18 meters high. This Buddha was carved from one piece of sandalwood from Tibet and the temple was built around it.

The steles are incised with Han, Manchurian, Mongolian, and Tibetan script. The statues in the main halls resemble those in most Buddhist temples, but some statues do wear the pointed Himalayan caps and white Tibetan scarves, a traditional gift. On either side of the symmetrical structure, however, the more typically Tibetan demons, human skulls, and tankas are displayed. Another admission ticket is required for the exhibition hall that shows many Tibetan silver utensils of very intricate craftsmanship.

The Yonghegong was built in 1694 as an imperial residence for Emperor Yongzheng, then still a prince. It was transformed into a Lama temple in 1744 during Qianlong's reign. Prayer wheels are for sale. Closed Mondays.

This temple was an attempt by Emperor Qianlong to unite the Han, Manchu, Mongol, and Tibetan nationalities into one country. He also took a Uygur princess from what is now Xinjiang into his court as one of his favorite empresses. For more on Lamaism, see also ''Lhasa'' and ''Chengde.''

The **Shudian (Capital Museum)** 首都博物馆 is in the old Yuan dynasty **Confucius Temple** 孔庙 , almost across Yonghegong Avenue from the Lama Temple. It is the second largest Confucian temple in China (the largest is in Qufu, the hometown of the sage). The exhibits on Beijing history, Qing armor, and the stone drums are worth seeing. Look for maps and relics of the old Yuan city too.

The **China Art Gallery** 中国美术馆 is open daily, 9 a.m.–5 p.m., closed on Mondays. It is near the Sara Hotel, and has changing exhibitions. See also *Victory Gate*.

For *your last day and a half,* assuming you only have six days, you must choose from the following. If you want to do more, then you have to stay longer or come back again.

—**Arts and crafts factories:** favorites are cloisonne and ivory and jade carving. Travel agents or your hotel can arrange.

—A **rural village or cooperative**

—Pandas in the **Beijing zoo**

—The **Cultural Palace of the Nationalities** 民族文化宫 (Fuxingmennei Ave.), for those who are interested in ethnic minorities. It houses exhibitions of the various ethnic groups when not used for commercial shows. Books and minority handicrafts for sale, but not much and very expensive.

—Shopping

—**Daguanyuan (Grand View Garden)** is a 100,000 square-meter theme park in southwest Beijing inspired by one of China's greatest novels, the *Dream of the Red Chamber*. The buildings are sometimes staffed by actors dressed in Qing fashions as characters from the beloved novel.

—The *White Dagoba Monastery* 白塔寺 at Miaoyingsi (Temple of Excellent Confirmation) in Xichang is Yuan (1271). During repairs made in 1978 after the Tangshan earthquake, archaeologists found more than ten relics inside dated 1753, from the Qianlong emperor. He was indeed a busy man.

—The **Residence of Mme. Soong Ching-ling** is interesting not only because she was an illustrious humanitarian, the respected widow of Dr. Sun Yat-sen, but here, the father of Emperor Pu-yi (the "Last Emperor") was born. Canadians might be intrigued by a copy of Margaret Trudeau's book in the library. (Read *Soong Dynasty*.) Tel. 444205.

—**Niujiu Mosque** 牛街回民区 : In the southeast part of the city, where about 10,000 Moslems live on Niujiu Street, this mosque is primarily for visitors with an interest in Islam and religious buildings. The mosque was founded in the Liao dynasty (A.D. 996) by the Arabian scholar Nasullindin and rebuilt and enlarged in subsequent dynasties. Although it is in classical Chinese architecture, the interior does have west Asian arches and Arabic writing. Note the curtained-off section for women. Tel. 557824. (See also "What Is There to See and Do.")

—*****Beijing Gu Guanxiangtai** (Ancient astronomical observatory) 古天文台 (Jianguomen Ave., near the Friendship Store and Jianguo Hotel) was built in 1442 (Ming) and has some instruments dating from 1437 to 1442. Good for a history of Chinese astronomy, with many Qing exhibits as well.

—**Beiyunguan (Temple of White Clouds)** 白云寺 , outside Fuxingmenwai, southwest of Beijing TV, is the largest Taoist Temple in China. Built originally in the Tang, it burned down in the Jin and was rebuilt in the Ming. During the Qing, it was enlarged. It has some striking incense burners and gilded statues, including that of Taishang Laojun, the initiator of Taoism. Open every Tuesday and Friday from 9 a.m. to 10 p.m. Attended by young men in Taoist robes and long hair. A visit takes about two hours. See *Taoism* in "What Is There to See and Do?"

The only nunnery open is the **Tongjiao Nunnery** (Zhen Xian Lane, Beixiao St., in the Eastern District). Established during the Ming, it now has 30 nuns. Public religious ceremonies are held once a week.

Among the recently opened tourist attractions is **Prince Gong's Mansion** (23 Lu Yin Jie), built from 1776 to 1785 and owned at one time by the great-uncle of the Last Emperor. Open daily. There's also the **Yunju Buddhist Monastery** with 14,000 stone tablets.

The **International Club** 国际俱乐部 (Jianguomenwai Ave., near the Friendship Store). Open 9 a.m.–9:30 p.m., has a coffee shop, and Japanese and Cantonese food (tel. 593482). Reasonable prices. Movies (U.S., Hong Kong, and Chinese) are shown most evenings (sometimes with English subtitles.) The swimming pool is open in summer. Tennis. Disco dancing. Bicycles are available at many hotels.

Walks: North of the Xinqiao Hotel and south of the Beijing Hotel for the old European architecture. This foreign legation area was under siege during the Boxer invasion, from June 13, 1900. On June 20, most foreign diplomats and missionaries and 2000 Chinese Christian refugees took shelter in the British Legation until the International Relief Force arrived on August 13. That British Legation building has been torn down to make way for a housing project.

The area around the Minzu Hotel, Drum Tower, and the Xi Dan Market toward the Forbidden City is full of old houses, antique doors, carvings, grinding stones used as steps, and fancy, carved stone door hinges. The back alleys with tiny houses and crowded courtyards with paper windows, are also fascinating.

The names of the alleys immediately around the Forbidden City are appealing. Nai Zi Hutong (Wet Nurse Lane) was the street where the new mothers who nursed the imperial babies lived. Flower Lane was for those who handmade all the silk flowers for the imperial ladies. There were also Goldsmith Lane, Laundry Lane, and Bowstrings Lane.

NIGHT LIFE AND CULTURAL EVENTS

The best of China is here: opera, ballet, symphony orchestras, movies, acrobats, gymnastics. (See also *Go to Cultural Events* in "What Is There to See and Do?" and check *China Daily*.) The Great Wall Hotel and the International Club frequently offer movies and ballroom and disco dancing. The most popular discos are at the Palace Hotel, Jing Guang, China World, and the Holiday Inn Lido. The larger hotels also offer cocktail lounges with live music. Pleasant, small, privately run Chinese bars have opened, but have also been periodically closed "for prostitution." Favorite ex-pat hangouts have been the Holiday Inn Lido, Jianguo, and Brauhaus in the China World. Many hotels have live entertainment in their lobbies. Frank's Place near the Chains City Hotel is a foreign-owned bar.

There is also **Beijing Opera** in the dirty, drafty, but cheap Ji Shang Theatre or in the more pleasant Liyuan Theatre in the Qianmen Hotel, tel. 3016688, every evening at 7:30. Sometimes with English titles. Interesting open-air night food market near the East Gate of the Forbidden City. In the summer, the Beijing Amusement Park near the Temple of Heaven has a recommended cinema-fountain show.

For Beijing opera, I prefer the **Lao She Teahouse** in the Da Wan Cha Bldg., 3 Qianmen Xi Ave., 50 meters west of Kentucky Fried Chicken. Tel. 546324. Look for the neon tea cup. After 7 p.m., it offers a variety show with top talent and including Beijing opera, magicians, and comedy acts. 1920's atmosphere with dirty floor and watermelon seeds. The talent transcends language.

Sunday Christian **church services** for foreigners (in English) have been held at 10 a.m. at the International Club.

DAY TRIPS

The **Tan Zhe Si** 潭拓寺 and **Hui Zhi Si** are only 6 km apart, so can be seen in one day, but they are not very exciting. Southwest of

Beijing, they make a pleasant excursion into the mountains. The Tan Zhe Si has its roots in the Tang. During the Yuan, the daughter of Kublai Khan is said to have resided at the Tan Zhe Si to try to atone for her father's sins. In 1888 a Qing prince retired here. After the 1911 Revolution many foreigners used it as a summer resort, and after Liberation it was a workers' health spa. The Ming temple bell here is over 400 years old.

Lugouqiao (Reed Valley Bridge) a.k.a. Marco Polo Bridge 芦沟 is 20 km SW of the city. Built in the 12th century, it is 250 meters long with 11 stone arches and 485 stone lions spaced along its railings, each one different. The bridge is named for Marco Polo because the Venetian explorer described it at length in his book. It is the site of the incident that touched off the Japanese war on July 7, 1937. The bridge was renovated in the late 1980s with the addition of a museum of Chinese resistance to the Japanese invaders, primarily photos. The museum is inside the quaint walled village.

*Zhoukoudian 周口店 (48 km south of Beijing) is where the Peking Man, who lived 400,000–500,000 years ago, was found in a cave in 1927. At least 44 skulls have been discovered there. A small museum has some relics, but many of the bones were lost during the Japanese war. A model of the area is in the Museum of Chinese History in Beijing.

Aviation buffs should be interested in the **Aviation Museum,** with its 151 planes. Ask about the 505 m **Beijing Sightseeing Tower** whose viewing platform is at 240 m.

See also "Zunhua" for Qing tombs.

For **overnight trips,** see "Chengde" (3 days), "Tianjin," "Shijiazhuang," "Beidaihe," "Shanhaiguan," and "Datong."

TRAINS TO RUSSIA

Check with the U.S. embassy first regarding travel through Russia. The better train is the Chinese one, leaving on Wednesdays via Datong. The Russian train leaves on Saturdays via Shenyang and Harbin. They take seven days to reach Moscow. Tickets can be bought at C.I.T.S. (Beijing International Hotel). However, give yourself at least two weeks in Beijing to get all the visas. You have to get a visa for your farthest point first, before you can get the others.

FESTIVALS

The week before and after the lunar new year, a temple fair takes place at the Temple of the Earth, the Ditan. Ice sculpture shows. Golden Autumn Festival at the Yuanmingyuan. Dragon boat races. Kite-flying contests.

SHOPPING

Beijing has the best shopping after Shanghai. The Beijing Tourism Administration has a list of shops approved for foreign visitors. Most stores are open 8:30 or 9 a.m. to 7 or 8:30 p.m. Available are goods from all over the country (at higher prices, of course). Made locally are cloisonne, lacquerware, jade carving, filigree jewelry, carpets, and woodblock prints. Also made locally are felt hats and track suits.

The main shopping street is the very crowded **Wangfujing Ave.** 王府井, along the east side of the Beijing Hotel. Resident foreigners check shopping bags at the desk under the international clocks of this otel while they go out for more. You might want to do that too. On this street are **Beijing Department Store** 北京百货公司 (on west side; tel. 556761), **Jianhua Fur Store** (#192; tel. 5127965), **Beijing Arts and Crafts** 北京工艺美术公司 (on east side; tel. 5127691), and the large **Xinhua Book Store** 新华书店 , with books in English as well as Chinese. The **Marco Polo Shop** at 86–88 (tel. 555380) specializes in jewelry. Primarily for tourists is the **Yuan Long Embroidery Silk Co.** (55 Tiantan Rd.) with a good selection of silk textiles as well as jewelry, carpets, embroidery, furs, and silk clothes. Tel. 754059, 753287. It has a branch at the China World Trade Centre and in the Grand Hotel. The CWTC also has a lot of upscale shops.

The largest collection of stores selling antiques and arts and crafts is **Liulichang** 兆龙饭店 (on both sides of Nanxinhua), the main street where the buses stop. Open 9 a.m.–5:30 p.m. (winter) or to 6 p.m. (summer). In 1277, glazed tiles were made here. In the Qing, it was a market with 140 shops selling the same sort of arts it does today, including reproductions of paintings, the Dunhuang murals, bronzes, and porcelains. Prices here might be better than the Friendship Store. It is less crowded too. Try the east side for tiny shops and more adventurous shopping. One shop here is allowed to sell pre-Qing relics. (See Shopping.) The # **Beijing Cultural Relics Store** is at 64 Liulichang Dong St., tel. 33601.

A very good market for export-quality goods is the Yong An Li Free Market, between the Jianguo Hotel and Friendship Store on Xiushui Dong St. A similar fashionable free market is west of Ritan Park. Haggle like mad for good buys. The Jianguo-Friendship Store area is less crowded than Wangfujing. It also has the very good **Gui You Department Store** (open 9:30–2:00) with prices cheaper than the Friendship Store.

Beijing Huaxia Arts and Crafts Shop (12 Dong Cheng Qu, Chong Nei Da Jia, tel. 544676, 541529; branch at 293 Wangfujing St., tel. 542489) is known also as the **Theater Shop** because of its theatrical costumes. Also secondhand goods (antique clocks, brass, furs, furniture, etc.). The **Beijing Jade Carving Factory,** tel. 757371 x210.

Friendship Store 友谊商店 (Jianguomenwai Ave. near the Jianguo Hotel; tel. 593531): One can buy any crafts made locally, plus furs, down coats, and even fresh flowers, etc. The Friendship Store can reset jewelry. Also has a snack bar and a supermarket. And a tailor here does a reasonable job in three weeks. Merchandise bought here can be easily customs-cleared and packed for shipping.

Marco Polo Shop 懋隆商店 (Temple of Heaven, near West Gate, and across from the Friendship Store; tel. 754940): arts, crafts, reproductions.

Antique markets are the privately run **Jin Song Antiques Bazaar** in the southeast of the city (100 shops) There's also the **Chai Wai,** beyond the northwest corner of Ritan Park, and the Hongqiao, close to the North Gate of the Temple of Heaven. If your purchases do not have a red wax seal, take them to the Beijing Arts Objects Clearance Office in the Friendship Store for permission to export, if you want to be legal.

RESTAURANTS

(See also *Food* under "Useful Phrases" and "Food.") Beijing food is much like Shandong's, but influenced by the imperial kitchens. It is usually salty (as opposed to sweet), but is not highly spiced. Sauces are less frequently used than in Cantonese cooking. Everyone must try Peking duck at least once! The best part is the crispy skin, which is dipped in sweet, dark brown *hoisin* sauce, seasoned with a green onion, and then wrapped in a thick pancake and eaten by hand. Worth trying, especially on those early morning walks, are the rolls, or the Chinese equivalent of doughnuts—the long, deep-fried "oil sticks" 油条 —dipped in sweetened hot soy milk (cheap). Also famous are the *baozhe* , meat dumplings either steamed or boiled in soup.

Mongolian food is local too, especially hot pot and barbecue.

Beijing is a gourmet's delight, with excellent food from all over the country and the world. The current "in" restaurants for foreign business people seem to be **Windows on the World** (28th and 29th floors, CITIC Building, 19 Jianguomenwai; tel. 5002255), the Chinese restaurant in the Shangri-la Hotel, the Sichuan restaurant at the Palace Hotel, and the Cantonese restaurant at the Tianlun Dynasty. Unique are the previously mentioned **Tingliguan (Pavilion for Listening to Orioles)** in the Summer Palace (tel. 2501955) and the **Fang Shan Restaurant** 仿膳 in Beihai Park (along the lake by the White Dagoba; tel. 442573). Their cooks were taught by the Empress Dowager's own cooks. The Imperial Hotel (tel. 752365) across from the north gate of the Temple of Heaven) also has good imperial food. Some popular restaurants, particularly the Fang Shan and the **Wangfujing Beijing Duck Restaurant** 13 Shuaifuyuan (tel. 553310) may require reservations well in advance. Resident foreigners dub this duck restaurant the "Sick Duck" because it is near the Capital Hospital. See *Day 1* above.

Some foreigners have celebrated their weddings with dinner on a boat in Kunming Lake at the Summer Palace, or enjoyed picnic suppers on the night of a full moon at the Ming Tombs. Another special and exotic experience is **Li Jia Chai,** a one-table ten-seat restaurant in a private home. In a lane full of tiny old Manchu houses it's across the lake from Soong Ching-ling's residence. Great imperial cooking and classy table settings. A reservation is required months in advance and a party of ten get priority (of course). Set menu. Please do not cancel without notice; the restaurant will have bought food only for you. This restaurant is very difficult to find, with no sign outside the gate. Have your driver telephone 6011915 for directions.

For budget travelers, there are the food stalls at night and the Hong Kong Food Center near the East Gate of the Forbidden City. For good noodles, try the Minzu Hotel and the Overseas Chinese Hotel #2. The Holiday Inn Lido's Jiang Tai Restaurant is great. Pizza Hut is at Dangzhimenwai St. near the new Australian and Canadian embassies, and Uncle Sam's is near the SCITE Tower. Fast-food Chinese restaurants are in the basements of the Jing Guang and the Tianlun Dynasty. The Tourism Food City is just east of the Peace Hotel. Minim's at 2 Chongwenmen Xi Ave. is not bad.

OTHER RECOMMENDED RESTAURANTS:

Donglaishun Moslem Restaurant • *between Palace Hotel and Wangfujing, 16 Jinyu Hutong* • Modest. Good Mongolian hot pot. Tel. 552092.

Mongolian Restaurant • *Meng Gu Kao Ru, Qian Men St.* • Modest. Choose your own ingredients.

Peking Roast-Duck Restaurant 北京烤鸭店 • *Hepingmen; tel. 338031* • a.k.a. Wall Street Duck to local foreigners because a wall was once beside it, of course. An old six-story restaurant.

Quanjude Peking Duck Restaurant 前门烤鸭店 • *32 Qianmen Ave.; tel. 5112418* • a.k.a. "Big Duck." Tends to mass-produce duck dinners for tourists, but it's good.

Ritan Park Restaurant • *southwest corner of Ritan Park, within sight of sign on top of CITIC Building; tel. 592648* • In a palace. Sichuan, Huiyang, and Imperial food. Moderate price. Not always good.

Sichuan Fan Dian 四川饭店 • *Rongxian Hutong, Xuanwumennei Ave.; tel. 656348* • Sichuan.

World Showcase Restaurants • *tel. 5129180* • Five outlets on Hua Long St. and Nan He Huan Ave., including the China Tea House (dim sum), between the Beijing Hotel and the Forbidden City.

For **Western food,** the top restaurants seem to be at the Jianguo Hotel and China World. Other luxury hotels also have very good restaurants with a wide variety of food, especially the Airport Movenpick, Grand, Holiday Inn Lido, Palace, and Shangri-La. The Movenpick has imported Swiss ice cream. For reasonably priced **Japanese** food, there's the Fortuna Building and the Baiyun at Youhao Guest House, 7 Houyuan'ensi; tel. 441036 X264. Lots of good Korean restaurants. For good **Thai** food in a beautiful setting, there's the Holiday Inn Lido. For vegetarian cuisine, see Food.

HOTELS

Beijing now has so many good hotels that we can't list them all. We are only mentioning those we consider important because of quality, location, and price range. We urge you to ask for discounts, as we expect prices will be soft in 1993.

The demand for hotel rooms seems to be catching up a bit with the supply this year, but with new hotels still opening, travelers are urged to haggle for the best prices. Beijing has many world-class hotels. The ones here were selected because of quality and location in a wide price range.

The most luxurious and classy hotels with top services are the China World and the Palace, almost a tie. China World's more spacious and quiet surroundings are appealing. The alley between the Palace and Wangfujing St. is so crowded, it could be dangerous. But the Palace is much closer to the Forbidden City.

The Shangri-La is also very good, except for its distance from Tiananmen. It is nearer to the Summer Palace and Western Hills. The Holiday Inn Crowne Plaza should be near the top soon.

The Grand is the only hotel with exotic Chinese decor in its rooms. It is very beautiful, but we have questions about its service. The closest hotel to the Forbidden City/Tiananmen, it has the best location. The sunset view from the 10th-floor bar shouldn't be missed.

In the second-best location for tourists and some business people within walking distance of the Forbidden City are the Tianlun Dynasty and Holiday Inn Crowne Plaza, both recommended. The Sara here was not open in time for my inspection but should be top quality. In the vicinity is the cheaper but adequate Peace Hotel, across from the Palace. The Haoyuan is east of the Tianlun.

All these hotels are handy to shopping on crowded Wangfujing, colorful street food markets, good restaurants, and bars.

The next best location, especially for business people but also for shoppers, is about 4 km east on Jianguomenwai Ave. around the

S.C.I.T.E. Centre/Noble Tower and Beijing Tourism Tower on the south side. On the north side are the C.I.T.I.C. Building, Friendship Store, International Club, and China World Trade Centre (CWTC). This less congested area is also within walking distance of the U.S. embassy, Ritan Park, and enticing shopping.

The Chang Fu Gong and Tianping hotels are on the south side of this main avenue, while west to east on the north side are the Jianguo, Beijing-Toronto, China World/Traders, and the much cheaper Guanghua. The CWTC is an expat community in itself with hotels, apartments, offices, and shops. It also has exhibition and conference centers, and the offices of several airlines, Bank of China, DHL, and American Express.

The Beijing International Hotel is between these two areas, within walking distance of the old railway station.

A little closer to Tiananmen Square is the Xinqiao to the southeast along the edge of the Old Legation Quarter. The Minzu to the west of Tiananmen Square is closest to the new CAAC booking office and the Xidan market area.

On the periphery of city center, but too far to walk from, are the good-looking Hong Kong Macao Centre, the flashy Jing Guang Centre (about 2 km due north of the CWTC), and more modest Chains City Hotel. Farther out is the Great Wall/Kunlun/Landmark Towers (in descending order of quality). This group is relatively close to other diplomatic areas, including the new Australian and Canadian embassies and the Agricultural Exhibition Centres. The Landmark here is cheaper with service to match. North of the Great Wall Hotel is the Kempinski in the huge Lufthansa Center.

In the vicinity of the Temple of Heaven in the south of the city are the Parkview Tiantan, the Rainbow, and the Beiwei.

The closest major hotel to the airport is the fancy Airport Movenpick Radisson. The Holiday Inn Lido/Grace/Yanxiang cluster (in descending order of quality) is about 30 minutes from Tiananmen and the next closest to the airport.

The SAS Royal is beside the China International Exhibition Center. The Exhibition Center Hotel is adjacent to the Beijing Exhibition Center in the northwest of the city. It is in the same general area as the zoo, hi-tech district, Shangri-La, and Friendship Hotels. The Fragrant Hills Hotel is beyond the Summer Palace, very far from downtown.

The Diaoyutai and new Hilton are in the central-western part of the city.

The best value for money appears to be Traders, and if you're a romantic, the Summer Palace Guest House. The Grand and the Diaoyutai are overpriced, but they are unique, special, and worth the splurge for one night.

Brand new hotels usually have an opening discount that might be better than older hotels of lower quality. Try the Hilton, Kempinski, SAS, and Sara.

For backpackers, there's the Beiwei, the Qiaoyuan (not so good), and the better Longtan. The Youth Hostel is now open.

Beijing Airport Movenpick Radisson Hotel (Guo Du Da Fan Dian) • *Xiaotianzhu Village, Shunyi County. P.O. Box 6913, 100621. Telex 210609 BAMRH CN Fax 4561234. Dist. A.P. 3 km. Dist. R.W. 25 km* • C.C. 1990. 12 stories, 423 rooms. Duplex suites. Outdoor pool, gym, and tennis—all due now. Pub. Movenpick restaurant. Shuttle buses. Deli. B.C. Executive floors. Non-smoking floors. USTV.

Beijing Grace Hotel (Xin Wan Shou Binguan) • *8 Jiang Tai Xi Rd., Chao Yang Dist., 100016. Fax 4361818. Telex 210599. BJGH CN* • C.C. 1990–91. 17 stories. 479 small rooms. USTV. IDD. Japanese, Continental, Shanghai, and Cantonese food. Budget travelers only.

Beijing Hilton International • *1992.*

Beijing Hotel (Fandian) • *33 Chang'an Dong Ave., 100004. 5* but without the class expected of such. Telex. 22426. BHCTL CN. Fax 5137842. Dist. A.P.30 km. Dist. R.W. 2 km* • C.C. Middle Wing (1915) and West Wing (1954) 300 rooms. Best is the East Wing (1974) ren. 1991. 583 large rooms with 3.6-m-high ceilings. Hair dryers. Dim reading lights. IDD. USTV. Good shopping. CAAC. Post office. Bank. Tea house. Spotted carpets. Mouldy grouting. Wide, dark halls. Poor food and English. AT&T.

Beijing International Hotel (Guoji Fandian) • *9 Jianguomenwai Ave. 100005. 4*. Telex 211121. BIH CN. Fax 5129972. Dist. A.P.28 km. Dist. R.W. 0.5 km* • C.C. Mainly tour groups. 1990–1991. 29 stories, 1049 rooms. Tennis, bowling. USTV. B.C., IDD. Italian and Korean food. Gym, indoor pool. Tennis. Supermarket. Florist. Air China and CITS offices. 24-hour coffee shop. Dark lobby. Narrow halls. Fast elevators. Problem with English. Managed by Jin Jiang Group (Shanghai). AT&T.

Beijing-Toronto Hotel (Jinglun Fandian) • *3 Jianguomenwai Ave., 100020. 4*. Telex 210012 JLH CN. Fax 5002022. Dist. A.P. Dist. R.W. 3 km* • C.C. IDD. USTV. 1984. Ren. 1989. 12 stories, 686 rooms. Glitzy. Small bathrooms. Wide twin beds. Indoor pool, gym, B.C. Aeroflot and Qantas offices. Managed by Nikko Hotels International.

Bei Wei • *In southeast Beijing next to Rainbow Hotel. Same company and address. 2** • 1954. 5 stories, 200 rooms. Only western breakfast. Modest. Backpackers only.

Chains City Hotel (Xin Shi Ji Fandian, formerly New World Tower) • *No. 4 Gonti Dong Rd., Chao Yang Dist., 100027. 3*. Fax 5008228, 5007668. Telex 210530. NWTBJ CN.* • C.C. 1989. 85 big rooms. 135 studios and apartments. Bit shabby. IDD. USTV. Shuttle bus. B.C. Managed by Chains International (H.K.)

Chang Fu Gong Hotel (Chang Fu Gong Fandian) • *26 Jianguomenwai Ave. 100022. 5*. Telex 222937. BCFGC CN. Fax 5139810–11. Dist. A.P. 31 km. Dist. R.W. 2 km* • Managed by New Otani International. C.C. 1990. 25 stories. 512 rooms. Japanese restaurant. IDD. USTV. Indoor pool, tennis, gym. B.C. Low bathroom ceilings. Molded plastic sinks. Lots of shops. Some notices in Japanese only. JAL.

China World Hotel (Guoji Mao Yi Zhong Xin) • *1 Jianguomenwai Ave., 100020. 5*. Telex 211206. CWH CN. Fax 5050828, 5053167/9. Dist. A.P. 33 km. Dist. R.W. 5 km* • CC. Managed by Shangri-La International. 1990. 21 stories. 743 rooms. Quiet elegance. Non-smoking floor. Gym. Squash. Tennis. USTV. Pool. Bowling. B.C., IDD. Deli. Drugstore. Bake shop. Florist. Japanese restaurant. Big bathrooms. Three phones per room. AT&T.

Diaoyutai State Guest House (Diaoyutai Guo Binguan) • *2 Fu Cheng Rd., 100830. 5*. Telex 22798. DYTSG CN. Fax 8013362. Dist. A.P. 35 km. Dist. R.W. 10 km* • C.C. Government guest house set on 42 acres of old imperial gardens (with waterfall, 2 red-crested cranes and at least 6 peacocks). Built 1959. 15 separate villas with individual rooms available. The beautiful villa #18 renovated for Queen Elizabeth II can be booked for about $20,000 per day. Has 26 rooms, indoor ponds, own waterfall, private elevator. Bldgs. #6, 12, and 16 ren. in 1990. Bldg. #10 used by Henry Kissinger ren. 1991. Bldg. #6 used by tour groups looked good. IDD. Bowling, pool, gym, tennis. No travel service. Planning USTV. High ceilings. Free beer and juice. #3 bldg. bit scruffy but generally good.

Exhibition Centre Hotel (Zhan Lan Guan Binguan) • *135 Xi Zhi Men Wai St. 100044. 3*. Fax 8021450. Telex 222395. BECH CN. Dist. A.P. 30 km. Dist. R.W. 14 km* • Quiet setting on own small lake. HKJV. CC. 1988. 7 stories, 250 rooms. USTV. IDD. B.C. Good service. Small, friendly hotel. Small gym. Building Thai restaurant.

Fragrant Hill Hotel (Xiangshan Fandian) • *Xiangshan Park, Haidian Dist. 4*. Telex 222202. FHH CN. Fax 2566794. 40 km from airport. Dist. R.W. 30 km.* • Great for hikers and conferences. CC. 1982. Ren. 1991–92. 3 and 4 stories. 292 large rooms with view of greenery. Soft beds. Beautiful, austere-looking public areas. Grubby carpets, poor maintenance but otherwise fine. Outdoor pool. Gym. B.C., IDD. USTV due soon. Architect I.M. Pei. Recommended in summer only.

Friendship Hotel (Youyi Binguan) • *3 Baishiqiao Rd. 100873. Fax 8314661. Telex 222362. FHBJ CN. In residential suburbs. Dist. A.P. 33 km. Dist. R.W. 16 km. (Can walk to Bai Shi Qiao (high tech street.)* • CC. Built 1954 for Soviet experts and now home for other foreign experts. 5- and 6-story buildings of different qualities. 800 rooms for foreign tourists. Large gardens. IDD. Pools, gym, tennis. B.C. Shuttle bus. Bowling due soon. #5 bldg. ren. 1990. # bldg. ren. 1987. #3 bldg. ren. 1990. Small rooms. Most 3*. #1 bldg. ren. 1990. 4*. Japanese, Russian, French, and Arabian style food.

Grand Hotel (Gui Bin Lou Fan Dian) • *33 Chang'an Dong Ave., 100004. 5*. Fax 5130048. Telex 210454. BHPTW CN* • Much better looking than attached Beijing Hotel. Separate Hong Kong management. Member Leading Hotels of the World. CC. 1989. 10 stories. 218 large rooms. IDD. In-room safe. Indoor pool. B.C. Sauna. USTV. Hair dryers. Small, dark lobby.

Great Wall Sheraton Hotel (Changcheng Fandian) • *Donghuan Bei Rd., Chaoyang Dist., 100026. 5*. Telex 22002. GWHBJ CN. Fax 5003398, 5001919. Dist. A.P. 25 km. Dist. R.W. 9 km. Near Chaoyang Golf Course* • CC. 1985. Ren. 1989. 1,004 rooms. 21 stories in central block. Wide twin beds. Indoor pool, Clark Hatch gym. Tennis, 24-hour B.C. Air China and C.I.T.S. IDD. USTV. Shuttle bus. French restaurant. Patterned after glitzy Dallas hotel.

Guanghua Hotel (Guang Hua Fandian) • *38 Donghuan Bei Rd. 100020. 2*. Telex 211234 GHHCN. Fax 5016516* • 1967. Ren. due 1992. Four stories. 100 rooms. B.C. No CC., IDD, or elevators. Rooms spacious but grubby. Quality of food uneven. Budget travelers only.

Haoyuan Binguan • *53 Shijia Hutong (Lane), Dengshikou St. 100010* • 1984. Maintenance needs work. Operated by the All-China Women's Federation. Lacking in most services. No English, not even on the gate. But charming, clean, and cheap. 17 hard-to-get units.

Holiday Inn Crowne Plaza (Wang Guan Jia Re Jiu Dian) • *48 Wangfujing Ave., 100006. Aiming for 5*. Fax 5132513. Telex 210676.*

HICPB CN. Dist. A.P. 35 km. Dist. R.W. 3 km. Near China Eastern booking office ● CC. 1991. 9 stories, 400 large rooms. Wide twin beds. Gym due soon. Indoor pool. Art gallery. Store sells ethnic handicrafts and original art. Executive floor. Non-smoking floor. Grill room. Cantonese food. USTV. Deli with coffee counter. B.C. Can rent golf course and cater picnics at isolated Ming Tombs.

Holiday Inn Lido (Lido Fandian) ● *Jichang Rd., Jiang Tai Rd. 100004. 4*. Telex 22618 LIDOH CN. Fax 5006237. Dist. A.P. 17 km. Dist. R.W. 15 km* ● C.C. 1984/85. Ren. 500 rooms 1989. Total 1029 rooms. World's largest Holiday Inn. Executive floor due 1992. IDD, USTV. Good supermarket. Bowling, gym, indoor pool. Squash, tennis. Pizzeria, deli. Pub. German farmhouse, Thai, and Mexican restaurants. Jiang Tai Restaurant serves cheaper Beijing food. Nonsmoking areas. Post office. Bank of China. Apartments, office block. Japanese, German and international schools on premises. Free shuttle bus. Air China. C.I.T.S. Video rentals. B.C. Spacious, attractive rooms. Wide twin beds. AT&T.

Hong Kong-Macao Centre (Gang Au Zhong Xin) ● *Gong Ti Bei Lou, Dong Si Shi Tiao, 100027. Dong Si Shi Tiao subway stop. About 2 km north of CITIC Bldg. Aiming for 5*. Telex 222527 HMC CN. Fax 5012501* ● CC. Managed by Swissotel. 1991–92. 18 stories, 496 rooms. Two executive floors. Medical and dental clinic. Gym and recreation center. IDD. B.C. In Derby Club, hotel guests can bet on horse races in Hong Kong's Jockey Club. Cantonese food. Hong Kong stores. Building outdoor skating rink. Philharmonic orchestra performs Sunday mornings.

Jianguo Hotel (Jianguo Fandian) ● *Jianguomenwai Ave. 100020. 4*. Telex 22439 JGHBJ CN. Fax 5002871. Dist. A.P. 30 km. Dist. R.W. 3 km* ● CC. Managed by Swiss-Belhotel. 1982. Ren. 1990. 4 and 9 stories. 386 rooms. Wide twins. Continental and Japanese food. IDD. B.C. Video rental. Photo developing. Indoor pool. Acupuncture. Gourmet food/bake shop. USTV. CAIL, Asiana, and Cathay Pacific airline offices. CITS booking office. Indoor pool. Gym due 1992. Little worn but okay. Service needs work.

Jing Guant New World Hotel (Jing Guang Zhong Xin) ● *Hu Jia Lou, Chao Yang Qu, 100020. 5*. Fax 5013333. Telex 210488. JGNWH CN* ● C.C. 1990. Glitzy lobby and bright public areas. 52 stories (not all hotel). 492 rooms. Indoor pool. Gym. B.C. Non-smoking floor. Yellow and black check taxis. Free shuttle. Sports Bar. Executive floors. Food Street. Flower shop. USTV. Managed by New World Hotels International.

Kempinski Hotel • *50 Liangmaqiao Rd., Chaoyang Dist. 100016* • CC. In large complex with office building, apartments, 6-story department store. 1992. 540 rooms. USTV. IDD. Indoor pool. Tennis, sauna. B.C. Lufthansa office with own print shop. Non-smoking rooms. Acupuncture. Patisserie. Deli. Parcel service. Bavarian and Mediterranean Restaurants. Fast Food.

Kunlun Hotel (Kunlun Fandian) • *2 Xin Yuan Nan Rd., Chaoyang Dist., 100004. 5*. Telex 210327. BJKLH CN. Fax 5003228. Dist. A.P. 25 km. Dist. R.W. 9 km* • CC. Jin Jiang Group. 1986–88. 28 stories, 978 rooms and office suites. C.I.T.S. Indoor pool, tennis. USTV. Revolving restaurant. Chicago-style grill room. Shanghai and Japanese restaurants. Rooftop helipad. Shuttle bus. B.C. and gym.

Landmark Hotel (Liangmahe Fandian) • *8 Dong Huan Bei Rd., Chao Yang Dist., 100026. 3*. Fax 5013506. Telex 210301. LTC CN. In same compound as Great Hall Sheraton* • CC. 1990. 15 stories, 490 cute rooms. 240 apartments. Charming decor. IDD. USTV. B.C. Claims biggest Karaoke bar in town. Small indoor pool. Gym. Sauna. Cantonese and Tang dynasty restaurant. Good shopping.

Minzu Hotel (Fandian) • *51 Fuxingmennei St., 100046. 3* Telex 22990. MZHTL CN. Fax 6014849* • Grubby. But clean in renovated sections. CC. (No Diners). 1959, Ren. 1991–92. 9 stories. 617 rooms. IDD. B.C. Japanese restaurant. No STV. AT&T.

Palace Hotel (Wangfu Fandian) • *Goldfish Lane (Jinyu Hutung), 100006. 5* Telex 222696. PALBJ CN. Fax 5129050. Dist. A.P. 35 km. Dist. R.W. 2 km* • Member Leading Hotels of the World and Preferred Hotels. Owned by the People's Liberation Army. Managed by Peninsula Group. C.C. 1989. 15 stories. 578 classy rooms. Duplex suites. IDD. Obtrusive security. French, Italian, Bavarian, and Japanese cuisine. Bank of China. B.C. Indoor pool and gym. Deli. USTV. Non-smoking floor. Rolls Royces. Acupuncture. Bathroom panic button. Rodger Craig beauty salon. Executive floors. H.K. drugstore. AT&T.

Parkview Tiantan Hotel • *1 Tiyuguan Rd., Chong Wen Dist. 100061. Fax 7016833. Telex 221034. TTH CN. Dist. A.P. 35 km. Near Temple of Heaven* • CC., B.C. Poor English. Hong Kong management.

Peace Hotel (Heping Binguan) • *3 Jinyu Hutung, Wangfujing St., 100004. 4* Telex 222855. PHB CN. Fax 5126863* • C.C. 1952. 1989. Ren. some rooms 1991–92. H.K. J.V. 500-room tower. 22 stories. Gym. B.C. IDD. USTV. Air China. Post Office. Beijing opera on request.

New East Building has spacious rooms. Old West Building has tiny rooms, small beds, and is not well maintained. Dirty.

Qiaoyuan Hotel (Fandian) • *Dongbinhe Rd., You Wai, Fentai Dist. 100057. South part of city. Dist. R.W. 10 km. Dist. A.P. 39 km, 1/2 km. from Yong Ding Men Railway station* • Desperate backpackers only. Poor plumbing and English. 318 dorms and rooms. Cheaper tours to Great Wall. ¥15 bed in dorm.

Rainbow Hotel (Tian Qiao Binguan) • *11 Xi Jing Rd., Xuan Wu Dist. 100073. 3*. Telex 222772. RBH CN. Fax 3011366. Dist. A.P. 35 km. Dist. R.W. 6 km. Less than 2 km. to Temple of Heaven* • C.C. Japanese J.V. 1991. 15 stories. 690 rooms. IDD. B.C. No STV. Japanese food and herbal food. Tea house. Gym.

SAS Royal Hotel • *6A East Beisanhuan Rd., Chaoyang Dist., 100028. Telex 211241. SASZH CN. Fax 4081385. Close to China International Exhibition Center in northeast Beijing.* • Reserve through SAS or UTELL. 1991–92. 374 rooms. IDD. USTV. Everything guaranteed to "work perfectly at all times." Executive floors. B.C. Grill room. Sichuan and Cantonese food. Indoor pool. Tennis. Squash. Gym. Deli and bake shop.

SARA Hotel Beijing (Hua Qiao Da Sha) • *2 Wangfujing Ave. 100004. Telex 210453. HQSR CN. Fax 5134248. Dist. A.P. 35 km. Dist. R.W. 4 km* • CC. 1991–92. 11 stories. 403 rooms, continental food, IDD, USTV, VCR players, gym, indoor pool, B.C. Deli. Bakeshop. French and Tex-Mex food. Grill room. Non-smoking rooms. 15 live performing Peking ducks. Same Swedish management as classy Golden Flower Hotel (Xi'an). Mini-bar goodies will be same price as hotel bars. No surcharge.

Shangri-La Hotel (Shangri-La Fandian) • *29 Zizhuyuan Rd. 100081. 5* Telex 222323, 222324. SHABJ CN. Fax 8418006. Dist. A.P. 38 km. Dist. R.W. 15 km. Close to Negociation Bldg.* • C.C. Managed by Shangri-La International. 1986–87. Ren. floor by floor 1992–93. 24 stories, 742 rooms. Hairdryers. 44 offices. Executive floor. Indoor tennis, indoor pool, qigong, gym. B.C. Non-smoking floor. USTV. Continental and Italian cuisine. Indoor tennis. Squash. Shuttle bus. The Chinese pronounce the name "Shang Gorilla."

Palace Guest House (Yiheyuan Binguan) • *Summer Palace, 100091.* • Book through a travel agency. Long walk from main gate. Modest hotel in spite of opulent setting. Poor English. Cheap.

Tianlun Dynasty Hotel (Tianlun Fandian) • *50 Wangfujing St., 100006. Aiming for 4* Fax 5137866. Telex 210575. TLH CN. Dist. A.P. 35 km. Dist. R.W. 3 km* • CC. Managed by Dynasty International Hotel Corp. 1991–92. 9 stories, 408 rooms. USTV. IDD. B.C. Gym and indoor pool. Bowling. Tennis. Mongolian barbeque. Bake shop. Personal room safes. Huge European-style atrium. Cantonese and Vietnamese cuisine. Food Street. Antique shop with reproductions from the Forbidden City. Executive floor.

Tianping Lee Gardens Hotel (Tianping Jiu Dian) • *2 Jianguomennan Ave. 100022. Aiming for 4*. Fax 5158533. Good location but difficult access* • Managed by Lee Gardens International. Owned by the Legal Exchange Association which offers free legal advice to guests. C.C. 1990–92. 423 large rooms and suites. IDD. Gym. Pub. Indoor pool. USTV. B.C. Executive floor. Pub.

Traders Hotel (Guo Mao Fandian) • *No. 1 Jianguomenwai Ave., 100020. 3*, aiming for 4*. Telex 222981. THBBC CN. Fax 5050818/ 0838. See China World above* • 1989. 298 rooms. Executive floors. Rooms designed for women. Non-smoking rooms. B.C. IDD. USTV. Guests can use facilities like gym and pool at China World Hotel and Trade Centre. Shangri-La International management. Excellent deal for business people. Comfortable, intimate with efficient services.

Xin Qiao Hotel (Fandian) • *2 Dongjiaominxiang St., 100004. 3* Telex 222514. XQH CN. Fax 5125126. Dist. A.P. 35 km. Dist. R.W. 3/4 km. 1954* • C.C. (no Diners). 1990–91. 6 stories, 329 small rooms. USTV. IDD. Cantonese, Russian, Shandong and Japanese food. Fast food. Natural hot spring water. H.K.J.V. Maintenance problems. Budget travelers.

Youth Hostel • *22 Banchang Hutong, Dongbinhe Rd., East District. On #20 bus route, north of Art Gallery* • 60 beds. No dorms. Garden style. Only hostel affiliated with World Youth Hostel Federation. Budget travelers only.

OTHER IMPORTANT ADDRESSES
Airlines:

Booking offices for all domestic airlines: 15 Changan Xi Ave. west of telegraph building (clock tower) and Zhongnanhai gate. Tel. 67017755. Bookings also at Beijing, Beijing International, Kunlun, Great Wall, Holiday Inn Lido and Xiyuan Hotels.

Aeroflot: CWTC, tel. 5002412.

Air China: domestic tel. 6013336; international tel. 6016667. Administrative offices tel. 5138833 × 3342.

Air France: CWTC, tel. 5051818, 5051431
All Nippon Airways: CWTC, tel. 5053311.
British Airways: SCITE Tower, tel. 5124070, 5124075.
Canadian Airlines International: Jianguo Hotel, tel. 5001956.
China Eastern: tel. 6024070. tel. airport 4562135.
China North: tel. 6024078; tel. airport 4562170.
China Northwest: tel. 6017589; tel. airport 4562368.
China Southern: tel. 6016899; tel. airport 4564089.
China Southwest: tel. 5054343, 6017590; tel. airport 4562870.
Dragonair: CWTC tel. 5054343, 4564466. Fax 5054347
Ethiopian Airlines: CWTC, tel. 5233285, 5050314.
Finnair: SCITE Tower, tel. 5127180
Japan Airlines, Chang Fu Gong Building, tel. 5130888.
LOT: CWTC, tel. 5052288, X8102.
Lufthansa: Lufthansa Center, tel. 4654488.
Malaysian Airlines: tel. 5052681-3
Northwest: CWTC, Fax 5051855, tel. 5052288, X8104.
PIA: CWTC, tel. 523274, 523542.
Qantas: Hotel Beijing-Toronto, tel. 5002481.
SAS: SCITE Tower, tel. 5120575.
SIA: CWTC, tel. 5052233
Swissair: SCITE Tower, tel. 5123555, 5123556.
Thai: SCITE Tower, tel. 5123881-3
United Airlines: SCITE Tower, tel. 5128888.
Xinjiang Airlines: tel. 6024083; tel. airport 4562803.

Airport 北京机场 : Plane inquiries: tel. 552515, 555531, X382.
Ambulance: tel. 120. Emergency Center at Gi Jou Chong Xin (near Qianmen Kentucky Fried Chicken on Qianmen).
American Express: West Wing L115D, CWTC, tel. 5052639, 5054406; telex: 210172 AMEXB CN; fax: 5052818.
Beijing Tourism Administration: Beijing Tourism Tower, 28 Jianguomenwai Ave., 100022; tel. 5058844. Fax 5258251. Telex 22489 BTTC CN (for information and brochures).
Canada-China Trade Council: Suite 1802, CITIC Bldg. 19 Jianguomenwai St. 100004; tel. 5126120. Telex 22929 CCTC CN. Fax 512–6125.
CITIC International Building: 19 Jianguomenwai Dajie; tel. 5002255.
C.I.T.S. Beijing Branch 中国国际旅行社北京分社 : For international trains, domestic flights, Beijing International Hotel, tel. 5120509, 5120503; also ground floor, Beijing Tourism Tower, (behind the Chang Fu Gong Hotel) 8:30–11:00; 1:30–4:30. Tel. 5158844. Fax 5158602.
C.T.S. and Overseas Chinese Travel Service 中国旅行社 : Beijing Tourism Tower, tel. 5158844. Telex 22052 BCTS CN. Fax 5158557.
CYTS: 23B Dong Jiao Min Xiang, 100006; tel. 5127770. Fax 5120571.

Telex 20024 CYTS CN. Behind the Capital Hotel.

Embassies: See also ''Useful Phrases.''

Australia 澳大利亚大使馆 : 15 Dongzhimenwai St., Sanlitun 100600; tel. 5322331.

Britain 英国大使馆 : 11 Guanghua Rd., Jianguomenwai 100600; tel. 5321961. Fax 5011977. Cultural Sections, tel. 5011903.

Canada 加拿大使馆 : 10 Sanlitun Rd., Chao Yang District 100600; tel. 5323031; telex 22717. CANAD CN. Fax 5324072.

C.I.S. : Dongzhimen Bei Zhong Jie #4 100600 (Open Mon., Wed., Fri., 9 a.m. to 1 p.m.), tel. 5321267, 5322051.

France 法国大使馆 : 3 Sanlitun Dong Rd., Chao Yang District; tel. 5321331, 5321332.

Federal Republic of Germany: 5 Dong Zhimen Wai St., Chaoyang District; tel. 5322161. Fax 5325336.

Indonesia: Sanlitun Diplomatic Office, Building B, 100600; tel. 5322238.

Japan 日本大使馆 : 7 Ritan Rd., Jianguomenwai; tel. 5322361.

Mongolia 蒙古共和国大使馆 : tel. 5321203, 5321810; fax 5321810; 2 Xiushui Bei Jie. (Open Mon., Tues., Thurs., Fri., 8:30–11:30 a.m.) Accepts only US$ for visas.

Myanmar: tel. 5321425, 5321488

Nepal: tel. 5321795, 5323251

Netherlands: 1-15-2 Ta Yuan Building for Diplomatic Missions, 14 Liang Ma He Nan Rd., 100600. Tel. 5321131. Fax 5324689

New Zealand 纽西兰大使馆 : 1 Ritan Donger St., Chaoyang District, 100600; tel. 5322731. Fax 5324317.

Pakistan: Dongzhimenwai, tel. 5322504, 5322695.

Philippines 菲律宾大使馆 : 23 Xiu Shui Bei St., Jianguomen-wai, 100600; tel. 5321872, 5324678 (Consular).

Poland 波兰大使馆 : 1 Jianguomenwai Baitan Rd.; tel. 5321235. (Open Mon., Tues., Wed., Fri., 8:30 to 11:30 a.m.)

Thailand: tel. 5321903, 5323955.

U.S. 美国大使馆 : Xiushui Beijie 3 (Chancery) 100600, tel. 5323431, 532831. Bruce Bldg., Xiushui Dongjie 2, 100600. (American Citizen Services), tel. 5323831, ext. 250. 17 Guanghua Rd. (Press and Culture), tel. 5321161.

Vietnam: tel. 5321155, 5321125.

Embassy office hours are usually 8:30 or 9 a.m. to 12 or 12:30 p.m.; 1:30, 2, or 2:30 p.m. to 5 or 6 p.m., Monday to Friday; Saturday mornings also. Summer hours are even more complicated: some are open only 7 a.m.–noon. Most embassies are north of the Friendship Store and International Club.

English Corner: Purple Bamboo Park near Capital Stadium. Sundays. Closed temporarily.

Europ Assistance, CWTC, tel. 5053191; fax 5053196.
Foreign News Agencies. Check number with relevant embassy.

ABC, Inc.: tel. 5322671.

Associated Press: tel. 5321510.

Reuters: tel. 5323517, 5321921.

British Broadcasting Corp.: tel. 5323777, 5323694.

Canadian Broadcasting Corp.: tel. 5321510, 5323754.

CBS: tel. 5322301, 5322472.

CNN: 5128635, 5128351.

Toronto Globe and Mail: tel. 5321661.

NBC, Inc.: tel. 5233153, 5233961.

New York Times: tel. 5233115, 5232658.

Time: tel. 5232669, 5231293.

Wall Street Journal: tel. 5323673.

Washington Post: tel. 5323464.

Police 警察 or **Fire** 火警 : tel. 550720, 552725, 553772.
Railway Station 火车站 : Jianguomenwai Ave. Train inquiries: tel. 554866, 755272. Tickets for foreigners tel. 5581032.
Sino-German Policlinic, Landmark Tower, tel. 5011983. Fax 5011944. Open 24 hours. Western-trained doctors.
SOS International Assistance: tel. 5003388–438, 5003419.
Taxis: Capital Car Company: tel. 863661, 557461 for buses or mini-buses and 444468 for cars.

Beijing-Shenzhen Travel Service, tel. 483846. Taxis with English-speaking drivers.
Telephone Operators

information: 114; Long-distance information: 116; Overseas operator: tel. 115. Direct Dial to U.S. (AT&T) 108–11; to Hong Kong 108–852.
Tourism Hotline (questions, complaints, compliments): 24 hours, tel. 5130828.

BOOKS ON BEIJING (See ''Bibliography'' for details)

Behr, Edward: *The Last Emperor.*

Bredon, Juliet: *Peking.* First published in Shanghai, 1919.

Haldane, Charlotte: *The Last Great Empress of China.* A biography of Cixi.

Lin Yutang: *Moment in Peking.* The story of a Peking family beginning in 1900 as the foreign forces are marching on Beijing.

Shimmie, Scott and Nixon, Bob: *Tiananmen Square.* 1989 Douglas & McIntyre.

Warner, Marina: *The Dragon Empress. Life and Times of Tz'u-hsi, 1835–1908, Empress Dowager of China.*

CHANGCHUN 长春

Northeast China. This capital of Jilin province (formerly Manchuria) is a 1½-hour flight NE of Beijing. It can also be reached by plane from 18 Chinese cities; or by train, via Shenyang and Harbin. It is noted mostly as an industrial city manufacturing automobiles (China's first plant), trucks, railway carriages, tractors, and textiles. The urban population is 1.6 million. Changchun is very cold in winter (lowest ⁻30°C) with lots of snow. There are ice carvings in the parks then. The summers are relatively cool with a high of 32°C. Average annual rainfall is 600–700 mm, mainly in the east, in July and August. About 150 frostfree days!

The city was founded in 1800. Invaded by Tsarist Russia in the 1890s, it became a Japanese concession in 1905 and the capital of Japanese-controlled ''Manchukuo'' from 1931 until 1945. It can be very attractive with its lovely broad avenues flanked by beautiful hospital and university buildings.

The province of Jilin borders on Korea and the Soviet Union. Its 24 million people include Koreans, Manchus, Hui, Mongols and Xibos. Settlements have been recorded since the Qin dynasty. It has developed a regional opera based on song-and-dance duets.

If you have only one day in Changchun, you must see the **Museum of the Former Palaces of the Last Emperor Pu Yi,** 10 km from the Changbaishan Hotel. From 1932 to 1945, Pu Yi lived and worked in this complex. He was head and then Emperor of Manchukuo. The Ton De Palace was actually used as one of the sets in the movie *The Last Emperor.* (The movie company put in the chandelier). Only one of Pu Yi's wives lived in this palace which was built for Pu Yi by the Japanese and now holds provincial relics. A good guide can tell you which rooms she lived in. Pu Yi himself lived in a neighboring building; he believed the Ton De Palace was bugged and used it only for receptions.

You can see the emperor's throne in the white trim building, the Qian Ming and his living quarters. Photographs of the emperor, his wedding, wives, parents, and English teacher are on display. The palace was looted after the Japanese surrender and Pu Yi was taken off to the

Soviet Union. After Liberation, an automobile factory used it as an office. A hall was built in 1963 to teach young people of the cruelty of the Japanese invasion, but this museum was neglected again during the Cultural Revolution. (Mao badges were produced here.)

A tunnel goes from here to the railway station, but it is not open to the public yet. This museum is open 8:30 a.m. to 5 p.m. in summer, and 8 a.m. to 4:30 p.m. in winter. Tourism officials say they can make arrangements for visitors to meet one of Pu Yi's widows.

In Changchun, C.I.T.S. recommends: the **Changchun Film Studio** 长春电影制片厂 , (tel. 53900, 53688), one of China's largest, and the **Changchun No. 1 Motor Vehicle Plant** 长春第一汽车制造 厂 , where you can watch a more labor-intensive manufacturing process than in America or Europe. You won't believe the wages! You can skate in the winter and swim in the summer in **Nanhu Park** 南湖公园 , the largest park in the city.

If you have more time, **Xinlicheng Reservoir** 新立城水库 in the suburbs has some sika deer, ginseng root, and is stocked with fish. The **Changchun Movie City** project has been put on hold because of cutbacks. It is a large theme park with movie sets, musical fountain, exhibition hall of movie props and trick photography, sedan chairs, and the like. The 480-square-km **Songhua Lake** 松花湖 is about 20 km SE of the city. The **Changbaishan Nature Reserve,** with tigers, deer, and sable is in **Antu County** about 300 km SE, with its own mythical monster and at least two hotels. See ''Jilin.''

Jilin has a Korean area and an **ancient Korean capital,** dating back 1400 years, with Korean festivals. It also offers a **white river expedition.**

For fans of **steam locomotives,** tourism officials boast that Jilin has no diesel engines stationed here (which says a lot about the air quality). In one of its forest areas is a narrow-gauge train which tourists can ride. Because it is hilly and engines have to work harder (and thus produce more photogenic steam, especially in wintertime), photos are good at the East Junction (Tong Har Tao Kao), 15 minutes by taxi from the Changbaishan Hotel. Another good site for photos is the South Bridge (Quan Ping Tao Quo—tram 53 or 54).

One of my most moving experiences in China has come at 6 a.m., in front of the palacial **Geological College** here, watching over a thousand people enjoying themselves **dancing** in unison.

FESTIVALS

Sept. 3 to 6, yearly. **Liberation Day.** Holiday celebrating the Japanese surrender.

Lunar third month, third day. **Mongolian festival** in Baicheng, 400 km from Changchun. For 5 to 6 days. Horse racing, archery, wrestling, dances. C.I.T.S. can arrange a tour. Hotel not very good.

A **Ginseng Festival** is held for three days, usually in August, in Fusong county at the foot of Changbai Mountain. In August-September is the Port Wine Festival (1993, 1995).

SHOPPING

Locally produced are: wine, ginseng, sable furs, deer antlers (aphrodisiacs), and frog oil (tonic). Tonghua and Changbaishan wines are made from wild grapes. Changchun produces carpets, embroidery, feather patchwork, mushrooms, azalea, wood carving, and bark pictures. The deer farm also has a retail shop. Please avoid furs from endangered species. I've found a leopard skin coat in this city. Store hours: 9 a.m. to 6 p.m. (winter) or to 7 p.m. (summer). The **Friendship Store** 友谊 商店 is at Zhi You Da Rd and Beijing St. See also "Jilin."

Jilin Provincial Antique and Curio Store 吉林省文物店 (7 Xi'an Rd.; tel. 22537); **Changchun Fur Factory** 长春市皮毛厂 (4 Lane 7, North Second Rd., north of railway; tel. 37765). **Changchun Wood Carving Factory** 长春木雕工艺厂(8 Xiangyang Rd.; tel. 24797).

RESTAURANTS

Chunyi Hotel Restaurant 春谊饭店 (in the hotel; 2 Stalin St.; tel. 38495). Try also the **Tianma Restaurant,** 15 Xinjiang St., tel. 882187.

Exotic specialties: houtou (golden orchid monkey head) mushrooms 猴头菇 , ginseng chicken 人参鸡 , thick deer antler soup (with sea cucumber, prawn, egg white, ham, and chicken) 鹿茸羹 , and frog oil soup 哈什蚂油汤 . Frog oil is said to be very nutritious and tastes better than it sounds. Please, no endangered species! And yes, you can get other dishes too!

HOTELS

C.I.T.S. says the Chang baishan is the best.

Changbaishan Guest House (Binguan) ● *12 Xinmin St. 130021. 3*. Fax 882003. Telex 83026 BOOTH CN, Dist.A.P.17 km. Dist.R.W.8 km ●* In attractive setting near park, hospitals, and university. T.R., no C.C. 1982. 12 stories, 268 rooms. 11th and 12th stories ren. 1987. Elevator old and slow. C.I.T.S. on premises. IDD.

Provincial Chunyi Hotel 省春谊宾馆 ● *2 Stalin St., 130051. 3*. Dist.A.P.16 km. Dist.R.W.100 meters ●* Centrally located. Front section built 1904 in two-story tsarist style. (It was known as the Railway Hotel then.) Back section built 1934 in 4-story Japanese style. 80 rooms, some with 4-meter-high ceilings. No IDD, no C.C. Should now have 24-hour hot running water. Standards barely adequate, but the ambiance of the 1930s is charming. Dorms.

CAAC 中国民航 *2 Liaoning Rd.; tel. 38189; Quanan Square, tel. 846525. Airport tel. 74501.*

C.I.T.S. 中国国际旅行社 ●*Fu 10 Xinmin St. 130021; tel. 882401; Telex 83085 CITSC CN. Fax 885069.*

C.T.S. ● *27 Beian Rd., 130051. Fax 861675.*

C.Y.T.S. ● *Tel. 861544.*

Jilin Overseas Tourism Corporation ● *12 Xinmin St. 130021; tel. 882401, 885069. Fax 885069 Telex 83028 CITS CN.*

Jilin Provincial Tourism Bureau ● *Fu 10 Xinmin St. 130021; tel. 885074. Telex 83028 CITS CN. Fax 882053.* ● Complaints and suggestions.

Ambulance, tel. 826458. **Police,** tel. 110.

Long Distance, tel. 113. **Tourist Hotline,** tel. 885074.

CHANGSHA (LONG SAND)

South China. Capital of Hunan province south of the Yangtze River. 95-minutes' flight SW of Shanghai, 1 hour NE of Guilin, and 2 hours south of Beijing and direct flights from Hong Kong and 22 other Chinese cities. On the main Beijing-Guangzhou railway line, 726 km north of Guangzhou. Population: 1 million. Coldest temperature is about $^-8°C$ in January; hottest about 30°C in July. Rainfall from 1250–1750 mm, mostly April–June.

Changsha, in one of China's main rice-growing areas, was a small town 3000 years ago. It was almost completely destroyed during the Japanese War. It is famous because Chairman Mao was born and lived nearby in Shaoshan. He studied for about five years at the Hunan Provincial First Normal School (1912–18). Yale started its mission in about 1904 and eventually established a medical school, hospital, and middle school. The Americans left shortly after Liberation.

Changsha is also known for its important Han excavation. Its embroidery is one of the four most famous in China.

The novel and movie *The Sand Pebbles* was set partly in Changsha during the Northern Expedition in the late 1920s. The hero was an engineer on an American gun boat, which sailed up the Yangtze through Lake Dongting and along the Xiang River. The movie is one of the few good Hollywood efforts on China.

Changsha is also the setting of a more recent book, Liang Heng and Judith Shapiro's autobiographical *Son of the Revolution,* a refreshing look at growing up in Communist China and beating the system. The excellent novel *A Small Town Called Hibiscus,* is set in the southern part of this province.

Hunan province's nationalities include Han, Tujia, Miao, Dong, Yao, Hui, Uygur, and Zhuang.

If you only have one day in this city, C.I.T.S. suggests the Hunan Provincial Museum and the embroidery factory and the Yuelu Academy.

Hunan Provincial Museum 湖南省博物馆 (Dongfeng Rd.; tel. 25123): Because this is the main tourist attraction, skip everything else if you are short on time. The 1972–74 excavations of three 2100-year-old tombs have overshadowed the revolutionary and other ancient collections in this museum. You must see these Han relics, important because of their excellent state of preservation and vast number. You may want to return to see the rest of the museum later.

The Han collection is in the white middle building on the right after you enter the gate. The three tombs were of Li Tsang, chancellor to the Prince of Changsha and Marquis of Dai, his wife, and his son. The son died in 168 B.C. The body of the woman, 1.52 meters long and weighing 34.3 kg, is incredibly well preserved, with flesh, 16 teeth, and internal organs. The lungs, intestines, and stomach were removed after disinterment and preserved in formaldehyde. They are all on display in the basement. An autopsy revealed arteriosclerosis, gallstones, tuberculosis, and parasites. Death came to her suddenly at age 50; there were undigested melon seeds in her stomach. The remarkable state of preservation is attributed to the body's being wrapped in hemp and nine silk ribbons, and sealed from oxygen and water in three coffins surrounded by 5000 kg of charcoal and sticky white clay. She died after her husband; maybe that is why her tomb is the largest and she is the best preserved of all. She probably planned it herself.

The 5000 relics include 1800 pieces of lacquerware, many of which needed only cleaning to appear new. Look for the ear cups for wine and soup, and a makeup box with comb, mirror, powder, and lipstick. She also had for her after-death use incense burners, clothes, silk fabrics, medicinal herbs, and nine musical instruments. Maybe she did use them! An inventory of the relics was written on bamboo strips, paper still being rare then. In the building to the left as you leave the marquess are the three coffins and a model of the tomb site. To the right is an arts and crafts and antiques store. Some reproductions are on sale. Open daily (except Sundays), 8–11 a.m. and 2:30–5 p.m. Exceptions made on request.

The **Han tomb site** 墓址 , only 4 km away in Mawangdui 马王堆 , is now just a large hole in the ground under a roof. One can see the pyramid-shaped hill, the neat, earthen walls, and staircase inside. Geomancy students can figure out the *feng shui*. Was it practiced then? Did the tomb face south?

The **Hunan Provincial Embroidery Factory** 湖南省湘绣厂 (285 Bayi Rd.; tel. 27219) is worthwhile, as you can see this ancient craft being performed and be amazed at the number of workers not wearing eyeglasses. Look for embroidery so fine it can be displayed from either side.

A tour of the city includes **Tianxin Park,** the highest point here, with a small section of the 600-plus-year-old city wall. Open daily, 6 a.m.–8 p.m. **Juzi (Orange) Island** 橘子岛 , 5 km long, is probably the "long sand" after which Changsha is named. In the middle of the Xiang River at Changsha, it is 300 meters at its widest. The island is inhabited, cultivated with orange groves, and stacked with reeds for making paper. It has a small sand beach for swimming and a place to change. Good for relaxing evening walks and bicycling. Open daily, 6:30 a.m.–9 p.m.; tel. 82152.

The **Hunan Normal School** (Shuyuan Rd.), outside the south gate of the city, has a small museum. Mao studied and taught here in 1913–18 and 1920–21. The current structure, built in 1968, is a copy of the 1912 school and reflects its European connections. Open daily for visitors, 8 a.m.–noon and 2–6 p.m.; tel. 31786.

Yuelu Hill 岳麓山 , on the western side of the Xiang River, is good for climbing and hiking. The Wangxiang Pavilion has a good view from the top. The **Lushan Temple** 麓山寺 was built in A.D. 268 and reconstructed last in 1681. The **Yuelu Academy** 岳麓书院 was one of the four major institutes of higher learning from A.D. 976 (Song), rebuilt last in 1670. The **Aiwan Pavilion** 爱晚亭 was built in 1792 (Qing). Open daily, from 8:30 a.m.–4:30 p.m.; tel. 82011. These are not very spectacular.

Wulingyuan is 400 km west of Changsha (7 hrs by bus; 22 by train). It is a 360-sq.-km forest close to Dayong county in the western part of Hunan province, full of beautiful hills, stone pillars, flowers and wild boar, monkeys and leopards. Six small hotels and several guest houses. Altitude about 500 to 1500 feet. Contact **C.T.S.,** Jiefang Rd., Dayong City. Tel. 233691.

Shaoshan   , is 104 km. SW of Changsha, a worthwhile 2½ hour trip by road, more by train. The countryside is lovely, with tea plantations, orange groves and rice field. This is the ***Birthplace of Chairman Mao,** a simple mud-brick farmhouse where the founder of the People's Republic was born on December 26, 1893. He lived in this charming, and apparently tranquil, village until 1910, when he left for studies in Changsha. He returned briefly several times, holding meetings and conducting revolutionary activities. The original house was confiscated and destroyed by the Nationalists in 1929, but after Liberation, it was rebuilt along the original lines. The house was shared by two families, the section on the left as you enter being the Mao's. It is very sparsely furnished. The dining room still has the original small table, typical even for large families. The master bedroom has portraits of his parents and the bed in which he was born. Another room holds original farm tools.

The **museum,** with ten large galleries, is a ten-minute walk from the farmhouse. It is full of exhibits depicting his life although Mao's deposed widow, the late Jiang Qin (Chiang Ching), and his unsuccessful assassin Lin Piao don't appear at all. One can also visit the family temple and stay at the modest **Shaoshan Hotel,** five minutes' walk from the museum. **C.I.S.** and **C.I.T.S.,** tel. 2444.

Also in the province are ''Hengshan'' Mountain, ''Shaoshan,'' and ''Yueyang,'' under separate listings.

ENTERTAINMENT

Local Huagu opera originated from provincial folk songs and ditties. The Hunan Provincial Puppet Show Troupe is well known.

SHOPPING

Made in the province are embroideries, porcelain and pottery, chrysanthemum stone, peach stone, and bamboo carvings, fans, firecrackers, lacquer reproductions, smoky quartz and bloodstone carvings, handicrafts from minorities, and duck-down clothing.

Hunan Antique Store 湖南省博物馆文物商店 (Jiucaiyuan, Wuyi Rd.; tel. 446822); **Hunan Arts and Crafts Shop** 湖南工艺品商店 (Xiangxiu Building, Wuyi Square; tel. 447656); **Zhongshan Rd. Department Stores** 韶山路百货商店 (213 Zhongshan Rd.; tel. 444621); **Shaoshan Rd. Department Store** 中山路百货商店 (Shao-

shan Rd.; tel. 224588); **Hunan Foreign-Languages Bookstore**
(Zhong Cai Dong Rd.; tel. 227238).

HOTELS

Huatian Hotel (Dajiudian) • *16 Jie Fang Dong Rd. 410001. Telex 982021 HTDJD CN. Fax 442270. Dist.A.P. 28 km. Dist.R.W. 1 km* • CC. 1990. 17 stories. 288 rooms. IDD. B.C. Pool. Gym. Disco. Conference hall. This is the best hotel.

Lotus Hotel (Furong Binguan) • *9 Wuyi Dong Rd. 410001. 3*. Telex 98153, 98132. Fax 445175. Dist.A.P. 30 km. Dist.R.W. 1 km* • CC. 1984; ren. 1990. 15 stories. 265 rooms. IDD. B.C.

Xiang River (Xiangjiang Binguan) • *2 Zhongshan Rd. 410005. 3* Telex 98131 XIANG CN. Fax 448285. Dist.A.P.22 km. Dist.R.W.5 km.* • Close to shopping and post and cable office. Near the former site of Mao's Teach-Yourself College; 1951, ren. 1988. Nine stories, 300 rooms. C.C. (no Diner's). IDD, B.C. CYTS and CTS. Bicycles.

OTHER IMPORTANT ADDRESSES

C.I.T.S. 中国国际旅行社 : 8 Wuyi Dong Rd. 410001; tel. 222250, 224855. Fax 441328; telex 98173 HLHCT CN.
C.T.S. 中国旅行社 : 21 Shaoshan Rd. 410011; tel. 430822, 446434. telex 98132 HLHCO CN; fax 443828. Complaints to G.M. tel. 43820.
CYTS: tel. 408283. Fax 441866.
CAAC 中国民航 : 5 Wuyi Dong Rd.; tel. 223820, 222560. Airport, tel. 449500. Information tel. 449540.
Dragonair, Lotus Hotel. Tel. 24855, 401688. Fax 446996.
Hunan Provincial Travel Bureau, 19 Wuyi Dong Rd., 410001. Tel. 227356, 228227. Complaints and brochures. **Human Overseas Tourist Corp.** Tel. 227356, 28227 for tours; telex 982058 OTCHN; fax 446996, 441378.
Ambulance: tel. 119 or 552056.
Fire 火警 : tel. 119.
Police 警察 : tel. 110 or 22351.
Tourist Hotline: tel. 809246.

CHANGZHOU 常州

East China, Jiangsu province, halfway between Shanghai and Nanjing on the Grand Canal. Population 600,000 urban. Flights from 4 other cities. Three hours by boat from Wuxi. Highest temp. 40°C; lowest minus 7°C.

Visitors to this 2600-year-old city can see Hongmei Park, *Tianningsi (Heavenly Tranquility) Temple (500 Tang arhats), Yizhouting Pavilion, and the 78.9 m.-high, 1000-year-old Wenbita (Writing Brush) Pagoda. 20 km SE are the 74-hectare ruins of Yancheng, the capital of Yan State (11th-century B.C.), with a small museum, ongoing excavations, and pearl farming in its moats.

A 1500-year-old comb factory still makes wooden and bamboo combs. One can buy "Palace Combs," one of the "eight famous hair decorations worn by imperial women." Cross-stitch embroidery. Good antique store near the Grand Hotel.

HOTELS

Changzhou Grand Hotel (Dajiudian) • *65 Yanling Xi Rd. 213003. 3*. Telex 381039 FAOCZ CN Fax 607701* • Downtown location. C.C. (no Diners.) This is the best in town. 1991. 17 stories. 360 rooms. Diet therapy restaurant with food to "prolong life and beautify women." B.C. Clinic. IDD. Next door to C.I.T.S.

Hotel Jiang Nan Chun (Binguan) • *39 Yin Bin Rd., 213001. 2*. Telex 361012 JNCCZ CN. Fax 601498 Dist.A.P.20 km. Dist.R.W. 5 km* • 1982, ren. 1988. Nine stories, 190 rooms. IDD, B.C., bicycles, C.C. (no Diner's). Garden. Suburbs.

C.T.S. and **C.I.T.S.:** 75 Yanling Xi Rd. 213003. Tel. 600481. Telex 361039 FAOCZ CN. Fax 607701. Branch in Changzhou Hotel. C.T.S. tel. 26739.
CYTS: tel. 601925.

Ambulance: tel. 609595
Police: tel. 110.

CHENGDE 承德

(Chengteh, Chengte, Jehol, Jehe.) North China, Hebei province, 250 km NE of Beijing. Urban population, 130,000. Coldest temperature—⁻19°C; hottest—35°C for a very short time each year. Most rain June and July. An express train leaves Beijing daily about 7 a.m. arriving at noon. You can leave Chengde daily about 1 p.m. arriving in Beijing at about 6 p.m. It should take three hours by road.

The Qing imperial summer resort here was built for Emperor Kangxi (Kang-hsi) from 1703 to 1790, not just to relax in, but to curry favor with the Mongolian nobles in the area. To help win them over, he built 11 Lama temples also. Chengde is well worth seeing, especially if you don't go to Tibet. It is one of the 24 historical cities protected by the State Council.

The **Imperial Summer Resort** 避暑山庄 covers an area of 5.6 million square meters, which is larger than the Summer Palace in Beijing. Most of it is surrounded by a 10-km-long wall.

In the last century a one-way trip took the Manchus 3–20 days by horseback, palanquin, or bumpy chariot.

Chengde oozes with history. The Qing court lived here from May to October each year. It was in a yurt here in 1793 that Lord Macartney of Britain refused to kowtow to Qing Emperor Qianlong (Chien Lung) and where the envoy was dismissed as a ''bearer of tribute'' from ''vassal king'' George III, his requests to trade refused. In 1860 the Manchu court fled to Chengde as Anglo-French forces approached Beijing. The death of Emperor Xianfeng (Hsien Feng) here in 1862 led to the rise of Cixi (Tzu Hsi), the Empress Dowager, as regent. Think of the plotting that went on as he lay on his deathbed. Cixi visited here again, by train, in 1900. In the 1930s, many of the buildings were looted and destroyed by the warlord Tang Yu Liu. The most important buildings have been repaired. Some of the ruins are intriguing and fascinating in themselves.

Sit in the hulk of the "Potala" at dusk and tell ghost stories as darkness falls.

You can see the main palace and garden in one day and five of the outer temples on a second day. If you rush and avoid the climb to the Club Stone, all the open temples and the summer resort can be covered in one full, hurried day.

The Imperial Summer Resort has nine courtyards. It is not as palatial as Beijing's Summer Palace, but it is worth seeing. The building to the right inside the second gate has a painting of the Macartney visit 马戈尔尼来访画片 and a hunting scene 木兰秋狄图 (with officials sporting animal head masks and imitating mating calls to attract the bear, deer, wolves, leopards, and tigers). To the left is the **Hall of No Worldly Lust but True Faith,** which is also called the **Nanmu Hall** 楠木殿 because of the scented wood from which it is made. You might get a whiff of it. The emperor received subjects and envoys in this ceremonial hall. On either side are waiting rooms, one for foreign visitors and one for relatives and tribal leaders. Among the exhibits in these and other halls are Manchu coats with sleeves shaped like horses' hooves, sedan chairs, an elephant dotted with pearls, brilliant blue kingfisher feather ornaments. In a hall displaying fine porcelain are Qing imitations of Ming vases.

The **Refreshing-at-Mist-Veiled-Waters Pavilion** was the imperial bedroom. On either side are the pavilions of the two empresses. The imperial bedroom has a "hollow wall" (seen from the back) where Cixi listened carefully as the emperor lay dying inside. As a result of her eavesdropping, she was able to seize power from her rival. Cixi lived in the **Pine and Crane Pavilion,** which was originally built for the mother of Emperor Qianlong.

The emperor used the two-story pavilion beyond to enjoy the moon 云山胜地 with his concubines. It has no interior stairs. The Qian Long Emperor studied in the pavilion, which now houses paintings for sale.

The garden is beautiful, and visitors should be able to rent ice skates and bicycles. The trees planted by the Qing are tagged with identification numbers. The two most influential emperors chose 72 scenic spots and wrote poems about each. Kangxi's poems have four characters; Qianlong's have three. Thirty of these places are still marked by pavilions from which you can see the view, including one on the top of the hill to view the snow 南山积雪 . There is even one to view the Club Stone.

Among the buildings counterclockwise around the lake is the **Jinshan Pavilion** 金山亭 , copied from one of the same name in Zhenjiang, and the **Yanyulou (Misty-Rain Tower)** 烟雨楼 , the latter built by Qianlong, a copy of one now destroyed in Zhejiang. It was used to watch the misty rain, of course, and to read.

On the flatland area here, Emperor Qianlong stooped to receive the equally arrogant Lord Macartney, the envoy from Britain. One of the scenes from the television movie *Marco Polo* was filmed in this garden—the one where Polo meets the Yuan emperor.

The walled garden on the **Changlang Islet** 沧浪屿 is a copy of the Changlang Garden in Suzhou. Some people collect postcards when they travel; the Qianlong emperor collected buildings!

Nearby on a side road is a herd of about 40 spotted deer 鹿场 . A herd was started here during the Qing because some of the emperors drank deer's blood as a tonic.

The two-story Imperial Library 文津阁 has a pond in front and few trees as a precaution against fire. It is approached through the rockeries. If you see tourists in front of the library staring into the water, it's because they are looking for the reflection of a crescent moon. Look for it yourself. The library is a copy of one in Shaoxing.

As a Chinese garden, this imperial summer resort is one of the best, a microcosm of the whole country with lake, grasslands, and mountains.

The **Outer Temples** 外八庙 , outside the walls, are a mixture of Manchu, Mongolian, Tibetan, and Han Chinese architecture with a similiar mix of artifacts inside. Once housing 1000 lamas or monks, they are now all museums. The steles usually have Manchu writing in front, Chinese behind, and Mongolian and Tibetan on the sides. If you are short of time, the Putuozongsheng and Puning are the most important to see. Otherwise, start with the *Pule 普乐寺 , which is also known as the Round Pavilion, as it was built in 1766 to resemble the Temple of Heaven. Inside is a statue of two hard-to-see copulating gods from the esoteric sect of Lama Buddhism. From this temple one can climb to the **Club Stone** 磬锤峰 , the giant, mallet-shaped stone, for a marvelous view of the palace, the temples, and Chengde city itself. Cable car.

The small **Anyuan Temple** 安远庙 is patterned after a temple in Xinjiang that no longer exists. Inside is a statue of Lu Du Mo, a female goddess. The **Puren** should be open for your visit.

Near the Puning Temple, one can get a Qing horse cart ride, or a room in a tiny hotel aimed at Chinese tourists. Inside the temple gate is a stele about Qianlong's suppression of a rebellion of the minorities. The *Puning Temple 普宁寺 contains a copy of the spectacular 1000-headed and 1000-armed Guan Yin, Goddess of Mercy, which should not be missed. Actually he/she has only 42 hands and arms, each representing 25. On each palm is an eye. The statue is 22.28 meters high. It is in the Mahayana Hall 大乘之阁 . The warlord stole the original.

The Puning Temple is patterned after the Sumeru temple in Tibet and is known also as the Temple of Universal Peace or Big Buddha Temple. Inside are a drum and a bell tower, a laughing Buddha, and four guardian kings. About 100 larger-than-life-size arhats remain of the original 508; the others were destroyed by fire. Only eight of the arhats are Chinese. The mural of the 18 arhats is 230 years old and original, remarkable for its preservation. Look for the big bronze cooking pot that fed 1000 lamas. The buildings in back are classic Tibetan style, with nothing inside. The number of buildings and stupas are symbolic—the center of the world was Sumeru Mountain, with four great continents around it.

The **Xumifushou (Longevity and Happiness) Temple** 须弥福寿 was inspired by the Xiashelumpo (Zhaxilhunbu) Temple in Shigatse, Tibet, and used as a residence for the sixth panchen lama. Dragons seem to scamper along the edges of the roof, most unusual for a Han temple. Built in 1780, it is the newest of the temples and commemorates Qianlong's 70th birthday, at which point he started to learn Tibetan. In the main building is a statue of the founder of Lamaism and behind him, Sakyamuni. The tentlike pagoda in the back is similar to the one in Fragrant Hill Park in Beijing.

The ***Putuozongcheng Temple** 普陀宗乘之庙 is patterned after the Potala Palace, home of the dalai lama, in Lhasa, Tibet. It was built from 1767 to 1771 for the 60th birthday of Qianlong and for the 80th birthday of his mother. The elephant symbolizes the Mahayana sect. (One elephant equals 500 horses.) The five pagodas on several of the buildings symbolize the five schools of Lamaism. Not to be missed is the **Donggang Zi Dian (East Hall),** where statues unusual for this part of China can be found. Please try not to show your insensitivity as an embarrassed guide explains what is happening under the yellow aprons. These are statues of the Red Hat sect of Lamaism, where sex with a person other than one's spouse was part of the religious ritual. In the opposite hall on the same level are other metal Buddhist statues. Another 164 steps lead up to the main building, which is decorated by Buddhas in niches—the 80 at the top representing Qianlong's mother's age. The six in front each symbolize ten years of Qianlong's life. Some birthday cake! The temple was built to commemorate the birthdays, as well as a visit by tribal leaders. This temple is the largest.

The **Shuxiang Temple** 殊象寺 should be open when you visit too.

A 300-meter-long **Qing dynasty-style street** 清朝一条街 should now also be open, with tea houses and souvenir and local product shops. Planned also are Qing horse-drawn carriages and sedan chair rides.

The **Jinshan Ling** 金山岭长城 section of the Great Wall is 110 km away. Officials here say it is better than Badaling, north of Beijing.

SHOPPING

The Friendship Store 友谊商店 is small, near the De Hui Gate. Gardeners of miniature plants might be interested in the cheap water stones, which absorb water and therefore can grow plants on top of them. But they are heavy! The area also produces silk, walnut walking sticks, and wood carvings.

RESTAURANTS
Found at almost every meal are the locally grown apricot kernels, usually sweetened and delicious.

HOTELS
The best hotel, says C.T.S., is the Yunshan, then the Diplomatic Missions, and third the Qiwanglou. Reservations necessary May through October.

Guest House for Diplomatic Missions • *Wulie Rd., Zhong Duan 067000; tel. Beijing 5324336* • 98 rooms. Health center. French and Russian food.

Qiwanglou Hotel (Binguan) • *1 East Rd., Bifongmen 067400. 2*.* • Built in ancient Chinese style, inside the palace grounds north of the main gate, used also for heads of state. 1987.

The 33 Yurt Hotel 蒙古包宾馆 • *Wanshuyuan 067000. 2*. Inside the palace grounds in the shadow of the* **Six Harmonies Pagoda** 六合塔 • 1987. Attendants wear Mongolian dress and the location should give you plenty of time to enjoy the garden in its different moods. 100 beds. Only for the adventurous. Standards not very high.

Yunshan Hotel (Fandian) • *6 Nanyuan Dong Rd. 067400. Dist.R.W. ½ km. 3*. Telex 27727 YSHCD CN.* • 1988. 12 stories, 230 rooms. Gym, sauna.

C.I.T.S.: Chengde, Beijing International Hotel, Beijing. Tel. 5126688 X 7503.
C.T.S.: 6 Nanyuan Dong Rd. 067000; tel. 227496, 228930; fax 228930.
Chengde Tourism Bureau: Zhonghua Rd. 067000; tel. 223502.
Ambulance: tel. 224343.
Police: tel. 223091.

CHENGDU

(Chengtu) Southwest China in central Sichuan province, slightly over 2 hours by air SW of Beijing. It can also be reached by a 21-hour train ride from Kunming with about 250 km of tunnels and a view of Mount Emei. Direct flights from 35 other cities in China and Hong Kong. A 4- to 6-lane highway cutting the trip between Chengdu and Chongqing from 10 hours to 6 is due 1997. Population is 1.6 million, urban. With an altitude of 500 meters, its hottest temperature is 37°C in July and its coldest may be ⁻3°C in January. The tourist season is April to November, with July and August uncomfortably hot. Annual precipitation about 1000 mm, mainly in July and August.

Chengdu has a history of over 2000 years. In the fourth century B.C., the King of Shu moved his capital here and named it Chengdu (Becoming a Capital). In the Han, after brocade weaving became successfully established, it was called "the Brocade City." During the Three Kingdoms, it was the capital of Shu. Many American, Canadian, and British missionaries and teachers lived here before Liberation.

Today it is the provincial capital and an educational and industrial center. Its industries include metallurgy, electronics, and textiles. The area grows rice, wheat, rape (for oil), chilis, and sweet potatoes. It also grows medicinal plants and herbs that are sold all over the country.

Chengdu has so much to offer, you need at least 5 days to cover it, preferably more. Travel agents suggest the following grouping based on regions, but you can plan your own schedule:

Day 1: Du Fu's Thatched Cottage, the Temple of Marquis Wu, and the River-Viewing Pavilion.

Day 2: Chengdu Zoo, Tomb of Wang Jian, Divine Light Monastery, bamboo-weaving, brocade, jade-carving, or lacquerware factory.

Day 3: Dujiang Irrigation project and Green City Mountain.

Day 4 and 5: Meishan, Leshan, and Emei Shan.

Day 6 plus: Jiuzhaigou

*Du Fu (Tu Fu)'s Thatched Roof Cottage 杜甫草堂 is actually a park with a replica of the modest residence of the famous Tang poet who lived here and wrote 240 poems during four years, from A.D. 759. A temple and a garden were first built as a memorial in the Northern Song. These have been replaced periodically, the pavilions here from the Qing. Statues, books, and art exhibitions are also found in the 20-hectare garden. Some translations here of Du Fu's poems in 15 foreign languages might help foreigners understand his importance. Open daily, 8:30 a.m.–6 p.m.; tel. 25258.

The Temple of Marquis Wu 武候祠 , in the southern part of the city, was originally built in the sixth century in memory of Zhuge Liang (Chuke Liang), a famous strategist and statesman, prime minister of Shu during the Three Kingdoms (A.D. 220–265). Here are tablets written during the Tang, larger than life-size statues, and the still unexcavated **Tomb of Liu Bei** 刘备墓 , the king of Shu, one of the heroes of *The Romance of the Three Kingdoms*. The current buildings are Qing and are open daily, 8:30 a.m.–6 p.m.; tel. 53297. The ***Zhuge Liang Memorial Hall** 诸葛亮殿 is also listed as a historical site under State Council protection.

The Wangjianglou (River-Viewing Pavilion) 望江楼 , in the southeastern part of the city, was once the residence of a Tang dynasty woman poet, Xue Tao. The park has over 100 varieties of bamboo. Sit in the ''Pavilion for Poem Reciting'' or the ''Chamber to Relieve Your Resentment.'' See if they inspire you, too, to poetry. Sit in them quietly for half an hour and breathe deeply. Open daily, 8:30 a.m.–6 p.m.; tel. 42552.

The 25-hectare **Chengdu Zoo** 成都动物园 is 6 km north of the city and boasts over 10 giant pandas, the largest collection of this endangered species in captivity anywhere in the world. It also has rare golden-hair monkeys among 2000 animals of over 200 varieties. Open daily, 8:30 a.m.–6 p.m.; tel. 31951.

Try for the ***Tomb of Wang Jian** 王建墓 (A.D. 847–918), the emperor of Shu in the 10th century, if you are more interested in history. Wang Jian captured not just Sichuan, but parts of three other provinces, and proclaimed himself emperor in 907. The 23.4-meter-long tomb is elaborate, with double stone arches and carved musicians. Open daily, 8:30 a.m. to 5:30 p.m.; tel. 21245.

The **Baoguangsi (Divine Light Monastery)** 宝光寺 should not be missed. It is 18 km north of the city at **Xindu** 新都 , and famous. Originally founded during the Eastern Han, about 1900 years ago, it was the site of a palace ordered built by Tang Emperor Li Huan. During the Ming, the monastery was destroyed by war, but it was reconstructed on its original foundation during the Qing in 1671. Pagodas, five halls, and 16 courtyards make it most impressive. The Tang pagoda is 30 meters high, 13 stories with a glazed gold top. The 500 arhats are from the Qing in 1851, each about 2 meters high, unique and vivid. The Stone Carved Stupa is also Qing, 5.5 meters high, in granite. Look for the 175-centimeters-high stone Thousand Buddha Tablet, carved on four sides in A.D. 450. Look also for the Buddhist scriptures written on palm leaves from India. Open daily, 8:30 a.m.–6 p.m.

You may want to skip the factory and go shopping instead. If you are on our 5-day plan, this is your last day in the city. If you dig museums, the **Sichuan Provincial Museum** 四川省博物馆 (Renmin Nan Rd.) is at your disposal. Learn more about the Long March through Sichuan or local history. Open daily, except Mondays, from 8:30 a.m.– 6 p.m.; tel. 22158.

There's another Buddhist monastery, the **Wenshu (God of Wisdom) Monastery** 文殊院 (Wenshuyuan St., Beimen; tel. 22378). Founded in the Tang and reconstructed in 1691, this temple has ancient paintings and a white jade statue from Burma, gilded Japanese scripture containers (Tang), and other treasures. Open daily, 8:30 a.m.–8 p.m. In the nearby **Cultural Park** 文化公园 is an old Taoist temple . Open daily, 8 a.m. to 6:30 p.m.; tel. 22378.

The ***Dujiangyan Irrigation System** 都江堰灌溉系统（灌溉工程） 1½-hours' drive NW (57 km) in **Guanxian county** 灌县（灌县） usually takes a full day. It was originally built in 256 B.C., the oldest such project in the country. Impressive because of its age and scope, it controlled floods and diverted half of the Minjiang River to the irrigation of the fertile Sichuan plain. This area has old temples, murals, and a swinging bridge. The 240-meter-long bridge over the river was first built before the Song, and most recently rebuilt in 1974, so don't be afraid to walk on it. The **Fu Long Kuan (Dragon Subduing Temple)** 伏龙观 houses a statue of Li Bing, the mastermind of the project. The

Erwang (Two Kings) Temple 二王庙 is a memorial to Li Bing and his son.

Near Dujiangyan is a **deer farm** 养鹿场 where you can buy Pilose Antler Juice "for aching back . . . impotence and premature ejaculation." Also near Dujiangyan and 90 km from Chengdu is **Qingcheng (Green City) Mountain** 青城山, one of the birthplaces of Taoism and still a Taoist center, with 38 buildings left of its 70 original temples, shrines, and grottoes. With some of its cliffs shaped like city walls (hence the name), this strikingly beautiful mountain rises up to 1600 meters. It was also a base for a peasant insurgency led by Zhang Xianzhong (Chang Hsien-chung), who captured Chongqing in 1644 and occupied Chengdu. Visitors can reach the **Jian Fu Temple** (Tang) by road. Guesthouses midway up and on top.

In the Han, one of the founders of Taoism, Zhang Daolin, put up an altar here for preaching. The **Cavern of Taoist Master Temple** was founded in 617–605 B.C. The building is from the Tang and contains a portrait of Zhang Daolin, stone carvings of the Three Emperors, Ming woodwork, and murals of the Eight Taoist Fairies. The mountain is full of legends.

Sansu Shrine 三苏祠 is in **Meishan County** 眉山县, 89 km south of the city. It was the residence of three famous literary men of the Northern Song and became a shrine during the Ming (1368–98). The current structures are Qing.

For *Leshan's Giant (Tang) Buddha and *Emei Shan Mountain, see separate listing.

Another excursion possibility is **Jiuzhaigou,** a "fairyland," opened in 1985. Located 500 km from Chengdu in Nanping county town, this is a 1½-day's drive. One can stay in the Jiuzhaigou Hotel. Three nights and two days are needed. Trips are usually by bus for two to five days.

This is a 60,000-hectare primitive forest with species earlier thought to be extinct. Naturalists should go wild with excitement here. It is the home of many wild, exotic animals like wild pigs, bears and snakes. The setting is full of forested hills, carpets of flowers, lakes and waterfalls, and even some legends.

Jiuzhaigou means "nine stockades canyon," three of which are about 2500 meters above sea level. Tibetans live in the area. The best time to visit is September and early October.

Wolong Nature Preserve 卧龙自然保护区, about 150 km from Chengdu, has many pandas in the wild, but tourists might not see any. There are more seen in the Zoo, above. Very rough road. Visitors stay in the Forestry Bureau hostel. Travel agencies can help tourists get permission. Naturalists estimate that there are now about 1000 pandas in the wild. Chengdu is building a breeding facility, with help from abroad.

Zigong, 240 km from Chengdu and Chongqing is famed for its Dinosaur Museum (with over 100 unearthed), salt museum, and its Lantern Festival (with giant dragon lanterns) for about 20 days before and after the spring festival. It is not easy to get to by public transport, and tours can be arranged for the festival. Tan Mu Ling Guest House (Binguan): 1985. 50 rooms.

Tours have been leaving from Chengdu by overnight train for the satellite launching center at **Xichang.** Ask also about the acrobatic monks at the **Douchan Hills.**

SHOPPING

Of the factories that can be visited, those of interest to visitors make bamboo weavings, brocade, Shu embroidery, filigree crafts, and lacquerware. The main shopping areas are **Renmin Rd. 人民路** , **Yanshikou 盐市口** , and **Chunxi Rd.**

Friendship Store 友谊商店 (519 Dong Da Zhong Rd.; tel. 27067).

Sichuan Antique Store 四川文物商店 (11 Shangyechang; tel. 22787).

Chengdu Arts and Crafts Shop 成都工艺美术品 (10 Chunxi Rd., Beiduan; tel. 26817). Branches in Jinjiang Hotel and airport.

Chengdu Fine Arts Company (440 Dong Da Xi Rd.; tel. 24184).

RESTAURANTS

Next to Cantonese, Sichuan cuisine is the most famous Chinese cooking in the world. Not all of it is spicy-hot, and dishes are toned down for tourists. Flower petals and herbs are used in such specialties as ''fried lotus flower,'' ''governor's chicken,'' diced chicken with hot pepper and peanuts, and ''smoked duck with tea fragrance.'' Try also the dumplings and Dan Dan noodles. See ''Food.'' The restaurants in the tourist hotels are best, especially the Minshan.

HOTELS

The top hotels have been the Minshan and Jin Jiang. New hotels, the 31-story Shudu Grand, the Chengdu Grand, and the 500 room Hong Kong J.V. Yinhe Dynasty are due soon. Major hotels should have USTV now.

Jin Jiang Hotel (Binguan) ● *36 Section 2, Ren Min Nan Rd. 610012. 3*. Telex: 60109 JJH CN. Fax 581849* ● Across from the Minshan Hotel and close to CAAC and C.I.T.S. head office and within walking distance of shopping and university. Dist.A.P.18 km. Dist.R.W.9 km. C.C. 1962, ren. 1992. 9 stories. 519 rooms. USTV.

Rooftop Garden Restaurant, Chinese and Western food. IDD. Bicycles. Hong Kong J.V. B.C., lots of stores. Booking offices for C.T.S., C.I.T.S., and C.Y.T.S. Clinic. Long dismal hallways. Should have pool and bowling soon.

The **Minshan International Hotel (Minshan Fandian)** ● *17, Section 2, Renmin Nan Rd. 610021. 3*. Telex 60247 MSH CN. Fax 582154. Across street from Jin Jiang.* ● C.C. 1987/1988. Ren. 1990. 21 stories, 337 rooms. Sichuan and health food restaurants; Western food restaurant joint venture managed by Windows on the World; English pub (with darts) and Food Street (for snacks). Outdoor swimming pool, sauna, and gym. Rooms tastefully decorated, good reading lights and furniture. C.T.S. IDD. USTV.

The **Chengdu Hotel** ● *Dongyiduan, Shudu 610066; 3*. Fax: 441603, Telex: 60164 CDHOT CN. Dist.A.P.20 km. Dist.R.W.8 km* ● In downtown industrial area. 1984, ren. 1987. 14 stories, 310 rooms, two buildings. C.C. (No Diners). IDD. B.C. Swimming pool, barber shop, gym, and clinic.

Foreign Guest House ● *Sichuan College of Education, Renmin Nan Rd., Section 3, No 24, 610016* ● Six stories, 36 rooms. No elevators. Good for budget travelers but inconveniently located.

OTHER IMPORTANT ADDRESSES

CAAC 中国民航 : Renmin Nan Rd., opposite the Jin Jiang Hotel; tel. 23038, 23087. Bookings also in Jinjiang and Chengdu hotels. Information, tel. 22304.
C.I.T.S.: 180 Renmin Nan Rd. 610016; tel. 679186, 28225. Telex 60154 CITSD CN. Branch in Jin Jiang Hotel.
C.T.S.: Jin Jiang Hotel; tel. 22630; cable 1278; Telex 60241 CITCD CN.
CYTS: tel. 22201, 29932.
Chengdu Overseas Tourist Corp.: No. 45, Shengxis huncheng St., 610000.
Dragonair: see C.I.T.S., tel. 679186, 22825. Fax 663794.
Provincial Travel Bureau Inspection: Renmin Nan Rd. 17, 610016.
Sichuan C.T.S.: Sichuan Hotel, 31 Zong Fu St., 610016. Tel. 24757, 29724. Telex 60241 SCCTS CN. Fax: 660963.
Sichuan Overseas Tourist Co.: 19 Second Section, Renmin Nan Rd., 610021. Fax 672970, 663794.
Sichuan Tourism Bureau: Ren Min Nan Rd., 610016. Tel. 671456.
Tibet Travel Bureau: Tibet Hotel, Renmin Bei Rd. (for tours to Tibet).

Tourist Hotline: tel. 28825.
U.S. Consulate: Jin Jiang Hotel, tel. 582222.

Z·M·Li

重 庆

CHONGQING
(CHUNGKING)

Southwest China. Southeastern Sichuan province on mountain-sides between the Changjiang (Yangtze) and Jialing rivers. A little over 2-hours' flight SW of Beijing. Overnight train ride from Chengdu. Flights from Hong Kong and 21 Chinese cities. Population: About 4.1 million urban. Highest temperature in summer, 40°C; lowest in winter, 6°C. Annual precipitation: 1000 mm. Chongqing is one of the "three furnaces" of China. Clear skies only in summer. Fog between November and March.

Chongqing has a history of 3000 years. It was capital of the Kingdom of Ba in the 12th century B.C. During the Song, it was named Chongqing, which means "double celebration." During the Qing, a 10-meter-high, 7-km wall was built around the city. Chongqing was one of the treaty ports open to foreigners, and foreign missionaries and teachers worked here before Liberation. Innumerable books have been written in English about this area.

In the late 1930s, during the Sino-Japanese War, the Nationalist government moved its capital here, and Han Suyin's book *Destination Chungking* reflects that period. Unfortunately, Japanese bombs destroyed much of the city, and few ancient relics survived the war. Zhou Enlai (Chou En-lai) lived here as he tried to work with the Nationalists against the foreign invader. The American (Stillwell, Hurley, Marshall, Wedmeyer) missions attempted unsuccessfully to get the Nationalists to work with the Communists. Read Theodore H. White's *In Search of History* for that period in the 1940s. The Communists took over the city in November 1949.

Today, Chongqing is crowded and industrial. It has very few bicycles because of the narrow, winding, and hilly roads. The houses clinging to the hillsides are fascinating. It is now primarily of interest to students of modern history. It is also the place where you can get a 2-day trip to the Dazu sculptures, and take a ship down the Yangtze through the gorges. A new highway between Dazu and Chongqing cutting the distance from 175 to 130 km. should be finished in 1994.

We strongly urge you to see **Dazu.** Or you can learn a bit about modern Chinese history at **Hong-yancun Revolutionary Memorial Hall** (a.k.a. Red Crag Village)　村革命纪念馆　(13 Hongyang Village). This was the office of the Communist Party and the Eighth Route Army between 1939 and 1946. It was also residence for Chou En-lai and other revolutionary leaders including, briefly, Mao Zedong (Mao Tse-tung). The opening of this office was greatly influenced by the kidnapping of Nationalist leader Chiang Kai-shek in Xi'an in 1936.

No. 50 Zengjiayan was the residence of some of the people working at Red Crag Village. The prison used by the Nationalists for Communist prisoners is at **Zhazi Cave,** at the base of Golo Mountain in the northwestern suburbs. Today it is an exhibition on the infamous **Sino-American Special Technical Cooperation**　中美合作所集中营展览馆, responsible for the tortured deaths (with U.S. help?) of many people who fell afoul of Nationalist government officials. Open daily, 8 a.m.–5:30 p.m.

For less recent history, there's the **Chongqing Museum** (Pipashan Zheng St., near Loquat Park), open daily, 8–11:30 a.m. and 3–6:30 p.m., with an excellent display of Ba relics and ship burials. If you want to go back farther than that, try the **Chongqing Museum of Natural History** 重庆自然博物馆　(Beibei District, 43 km NW of the city). Dinosaur bones were found in this region and some are on view here. Open daily, 8:30–11:30 a.m. and 3–6:30 p.m. In the same general vicinity is beautiful **Jinyun Shan,** known also as "Little Emei Shan," with its highest peak 1,030 meters. The **Jinyun Temple** was founded 1500 years ago and has relics from the Six Dynasties and the Ming. **Beiwenquan (North Hot Spring) Park** is below the temple. Its 10 hectares are pleasant and shady, with winding trails for strolling amid ancient Chinese architecture (if you don't care for a hot spring bath). The natural water temperature is 28–35°C. Open daily, 8 a.m.– 6 p.m.

For art lovers, the Sichuan Fine Arts Institute in Huang Kuo Ping District is well worth a visit. The institute is one of the best in China, with a teacher-student ratio of 1:2. It has an excellent three-story gallery with art for sale. Open daily, 9–11:30 a.m. and 2–5:30 p.m. (tel. 23423). The **zoo** is good, with one of the best panda houses in the world.

For those who just want to pass the time relaxing while waiting for boats, there's **Eling (Goose Neck) Park** 鹅岭公园 , between the two rivers. It has pleasant pavilions, ponds, and gardens. Open daily, 6:30 a.m.–8 p.m. **Pipashan (Loquat Hill) Park** 枇杷山公园 is the highest point in the city and was a former warlord's residence. Good view of the two rivers and the city. Monkeys and birds. Open daily, 6:30 a.m.– 10 p.m. Storytellers abound in the evenings!

Nanshan (South Mountain) Park 南山公园 , on the south bank of the river, is where George C. Marshall, the American mediator, and Chiang Kai-shek lived. The Nationalist leader lived in "Yun Xiu." A museum for General Joseph Stillwell is planned. Nearby is **Tu Hill**, the site of the residence of King Yu of the Xia, the first ruler to control the rivers (see "Chengdu"). Also close is **Laojun Cave**, where Lao Tzu, the founder of Taoism, lived.

An 800-meter-long **cable car** 缆车 goes across the Jialing River from Cangbailu Station to Jinshajie Station for a bird's-eye view of the area. (6 a.m. to 11 p.m.) Another cable car goes across the Yangtze.

Fengdu, 170 km east of Chongqing on the Yangtze, and an over-night boat ride, has a restored seventh-century city based on an ancient legend, a gathering place for ghosts. It has statues of demons and is considered Hell, with unique celebrations of the Qing Ming festival. There is a real village nearby.

For the "Yangtze Gorges" and "Dazu," see separate listings.

SHOPPING

Made in the province are umbrellas, silk, satin, bambooware, glassware, jewelry, knitting wool, and carpets. The **Artistic Lacquer-ware Factory** is at 118 Yuzhou Rd. 680041; tel. 810199, 810496. The **Painters' Village** is at No. 24 Hwa-Cun, Hualongqiao; tel. 52177 for woodblock prints and other arts.

Friendship Store 友谊商店 (People's Liberation Monument; tel. 41955); **Chongqing Gallery** 重庆美术馆 (Renmin Guesthouse; tel. 53421), paintings; **Chongqing Arts & Crafts Service** 重庆二艺美术

服务 (People's Liberation Monument; tel. 42797); **Chongqing Department Store** 重庆百货公司 (People's Liberation Monument, tel. 41484). The Chongqing Museum has a good gift shop.

RESTAURANTS

Sichuan food is famous. Not all of it is chili-hot. See *Sichuan Dishes* in "Food." The restaurants in the hotels are best.

HOTELS

The best is the Holiday Inn Yangtze. No. 2 is the Chongqing Hotel. All hotels here are adequate. The best for budget travelers is the Shapingba; for backpackers, the Ciyun Temple and the Huixian.

The Holiday Inn and the Chongqing Hotel have the best western food. No bicycles for rent. Jiangbei Airport is 30 km from downtown. The People's Hotel should improve soon with its new management.

Chongqing Guest House (Chongqing Binguan) • *235 Minshen Rd. 630010. 3*. Telex 62122 CQGH CN. Fax 350643. Dist.R.W. 5 km. Walk to all downtown attractions* • H.K.J.V. C.C. Became hotel in 1963. Ren. 1990. 9 stories. 358 rooms. B.C. Rooms for wheelchair guests. Building 8-floor tower with pool. IDD.

Chongqing Hotel (Chongqing Fandian) • *41–43 Xin Hua Rd. 630011. 3*. Telex 62193 CKHCL CN. Fax 43085. Dist.R.W. 5 km. Close to Chaotianmen Wharf* • H.K.J.V. C.C. 1987. Ren. 1992. 9 stories. 213 rooms. IDD. CITS. Gym. Karaoke. Disco. Beauty salon. B.C. Office tower. USTV.

Holiday Inn Yangtze (Yangzijiang Jia Ri Fandian) • *Dian Zi Ping, Nan Ping Xiang, Nan An District 630060. 4*. Telex 62220 HIYCQ CN. Fax 351884. Dist. R.W. 4 km. Near corporate head offices* • C.C. 1989. 21 stories. 379 rooms. IDD. Cantonese food. Sauna, gym. Disco. Mailing and packing service. B.C. Clinic. Rooftop lounge. Saturday-night show. Beauty salon. Shuttle bus. Best English. Rooms for wheelchair guests and non-smokers. USTV.

People's Hotel (Renmin Binguan) • *175 Renmin Rd. 630015. 3*. Telex 62127 CORMH CN. Fax 352076. Mainly for groups. Dist.R.W. 10 min. Great Temple of Heaven architecture. Near Chongqing Museum, Pipashan Park, municipal offices, and downtown* • H.K. management. C.C. 1953, became hotel 1987 (N.S. Building) and 1989 East Building. 7 stories. 248 rooms. IDD. CITS, CTS, CYTS. B.C. Sauna. Disco.

Shaping Grand Hotel (Shaping Ba Dajiujia) • *84 New St., Xiao-longkan, Shapingba 630030. 3*. Telex 62194 SCGH CN. Fax 663293. Dist.R.W. 10 km* • H.K. management. C.C. (No Am. Express.) 1988. 26 stories. 250 rooms, some dorms. French and Russian food. Roof garden. Disco. Pool. Clinic. IDD. B.C.

Yuzhou Guest House (Yuzhou Binguan) • *No. 3 Dapin Youyi Rd., Shapingba 630038. 2* Telex 62201 YZGH CN. Set in suburban garden 5 km from city. Dist.R.W. 15 min. On grounds of the Sichuan Academy of Traditional Painting, near Erling Park* • Japanese J.V. 1958, ren. 1986. 4 stories. 124 rooms. Pool soon. Disco. B.C. Only western food continental breakfast. Poorest English. May be too far out.

OTHER IMPORTANT ADDRESSES

Railway station 火车站 , and passenger quay 长江客运码头 .
CAAC: 190 Zhongshan San Rd.; tel. 52970.
Changjiang Cruise Overseas Travel Corp.: 4 Shaanxi Rd., tel. 47108, 41005 X 104. Fax 45942
Chongqing Overseas Tourist Corporation, C.I.T.S., and **C.T.S.:** all at 175 Renmin Rd. (Renmin Hotel) 630015. Tel. 350092, 350806, 352216. Telex 62126 CCITS CN. Fax 350095. Tel. C.T.S. 752126.
CYTS: tel. 350951, 352569.
First Aid Centre: Jiankang Rd.; tel: 51880.

DALIAN 大连

(Talien, a.k.a. Luda) Northeast China. This ice-free port near the southern tip of Liaoning province is an important industrial center. One of the Open Coastal Cities, it can be reached by train from Beijing or Shenyang, and also by plane from Tokyo, Fukuoka, Hong Kong, and 26 Chinese cities. A 375 km. toll highway joins it to Shenyang. It can also be reached by ship from Shanghai, Tianjin, Qingdao, and Yantai. Ocean cruise ships sometimes stop here. The urban population is 2.2 million. Dalian's hottest temperature (August) is 34°C, its lowest is ⁻21°C. The annual precipitation is 600–800 mm.

Known then as Port Arthur, Dalian was seized briefly by the Japanese in 1894, but was leased as a naval base for 25 years to Russia in 1898 in return for a loan to pay China's indemnity to Japan following the first Sino-Japanese War. Russia was also given the right to build a railroad connecting the base with the Trans-Siberian railroad. As the result of the Russian defeat by Japan in 1905, Japan took over the base until 1945.

Dalian is a very attractive city, with a lot of old tsarist and Japanese architecture and a high percentage of first-rate hotels. It also has 1800 km of coastline and a few beaches. Tourists might be interested in its **ornamental glass factory** 玻璃制品厂 , the centrally located **zoo,** and the harbor and its beautiful beaches. The best swimming beach is at the Bangchuidao Hotel. If the guard at the gate tries to stop you, telephone C.I.T.S. The second best swimming beach seems to be at **Tiger Park Beach** 老虎滩公园 . This beach is rocky and usually very crowded. You might try hiring a sampan to go to an outer island.

The **Natural History Museum** 自然博物馆 (3 Yantai St., in the north of the city), is only open a few days a week from 8 a.m. to 4 p.m.

Travel agents can arrange a visit to a worker's home, a commune, or a genuine wedding if given 20 days' notice. Best between May 1 and Oct. 1. It is planning a summer holiday center called **White Clouds Mountain Park** 白 云山公园 and bicycle tours, etc.

The old **Port Arthur** can be visited.

Snake Island, 25 nautical miles away, has an estimated 13,000 pit vipers and is a snake sanctuary. It supplied a research center studying the medical benefits of the venom. Snake museum in Lushun.

The **Economic and Technical Development Zone** is about 30 km from the city and has its own hotel, the *Silver Sail*. The Trade Fair building is downtown Dalian with a 248-room hotel of its own.

FESTIVALS

Temple Fairs: 8th to 18th day of the fourth lunar month. Locust Flower Fair in May, International Fashion Festival in Sept., and International Marathon Race in Oct.

ENTERTAINMENT

The Dalian Song and Dance Ensemble and the Dalian Acrobatic Troupe have performed internationally. Local foreigners get together once a week at their *Dabizi Julebu* (Big Nose Club), and visitors can join the Hash House Harriers on their weekly run.

The **English Corner** is every Saturday in Zhongshan Square. There should be a night market in the summer from 7 to 9 p.m. You can rent a tram car for a party.

Travel agents can arrange for scuba diving (water temp. 16° C to

22° C in summer), fishing, and mountain climbing. Lots of steam locomotives, best seen at Victory Bridge.

SHOPPING

Made here are shell pictures (said to be the best in China), fancy glass ornaments, and dishes.

Arts and Crafts Service Dept. (87 Puzhao St.; tel. 26281); **Antique Store** (229 Tianjin Rd.; tel.24955); **Dalian Department Store** (108 Zhongshan Rd.; tel. 23254) silk on 4th floor; **Dalian Foreign Languages Bookstore** (178 Tianjin St.; tel. 25472); **Friendship Store** (137 Sidalin (Stalin) Rd., tel. 234121); **Tianjinjie Department Store** (199 Tianjin St., tel. 26259).

RESTAURANTS

For seafood, of course: **Xun Ying Lou** • *Xiuzhu St.; tel. 230547.*

HOTELS

The top hotel for service is the Holiday Inn, for hardware the Furama. Third is the International. The Regent is also luxury standard. The centrally located Nanshan is an older hotel with good service and cheaper prices.

Bangchuidao Hotel (Binguan) • *Bangchuidao 116013. Telex 86236 DBCIG CN. Dist.A.P.22 km. Dist.R.W.10 km. In the southeastern suburbs* • 1961, ren. 1983. Seven villas of differing quality with 10 to 12 beds each, 100 to 500 meters from the beach. 260 rooms. Main building 6 stories. Villa No. 5 has 4-meter-high carved ceilings, gold-plated fixtures in bathrooms, and a jacuzzi. B.C., disco, tennis. Should now have IDD. Some travelers report a hot water problem.

Dalian International Exhibition Centre Hotel • *1 Jiefang St. 116001. Telex 86338 DIEC CN. Fax 806969* •

The **Dalian International Hotel (Guoji Jiudian)** • *9 Stalin Rd. 116001. 3* or 4*.; Telex 86363 DIH CN. Fax 230008. Dist.A.P.25 km. Dist.R.W.3 km* • C.C. 1987; ren. 1991. 27 stories, 380 rooms. hour room service. IDD. B.C. Chinese herbal medicine clinic, acuture to stop smoking. Gym, sauna, Karaoke bar. All-Nippon and gonair offices. USTV. Handy central location.

Furama Hotel (Fulihua) • *74 Stalin Rd. 116001. 4* or 5*. Telex 86441 FRAMA CN. Fax 804455. Dist.Harbor 1 km. Dist.A.P.14 km. Dist.R.W.2 km* • Close to shopping. Book through UTELL. C.C. 1988.

22 stories, 500 rooms. No relation to Furama in Hong Kong. IDD, B.C., office suites, free shuttle. Claims largest ballroom in northeast. Indoor pool, gym, whirlpool, and tennis. USTV.

Holiday Inn Dalian (Jiu Zhou Jia Ri Fandian) • *18 Sheng Li Square, Zhong Shan Ward 116001. 4*. Telex 86383. DJZH CN. Fax 809704. Dist.A.P.11 km. Dist.Harbor 1 km. Next door to R.W.* • *1989.* 23 stories. 394 rooms. C.C., IDD., B.C. Pub. Japanese food, health club, USTV. Tennis.

Nanshan Hotel (Binguan) • *56, Fenglin St., Zhongshan Dist. 116001. 3*. Telex 86446 DNSH CN. Fax 804898. Near Nanshan Mountain and children's playground. Dist.A.P.18 km. Dist.R.W.1.5 km.* • 25 villas built 1920 to 1932 with 4 to 6 rooms each. (#25 was headquarters for the Japanese commander of the Sept. 18 Incident.) 1985: 5-story main building, 93 rooms. IDD, health club, sauna, bowling. C.C. C.I.T.S. office, USTV.

Regent Hotel (Lijing Jiudian) • *12 Hutan St., Zhongshan Dist. 116013. 4*. Telex 86352 DLRH CN. Fax 282210. On a hill above souvenir stalls and Tiger Beach* • Better beach at Bang Chui Island 10 km. away. Dist.A.P.20 km. Dist.R.W.8 km. No connection with Hong Kong's Regent. 1988. 14 stories, 220 rooms. IDD, tennis, pool, business center. Rooms 2 to 13, 16 to 27 have seaview. Bicycles. C.C. USTV.

OTHER IMPORTANT TELEPHONE NUMBERS
Ambulance, tel. 331000.
Police, tel. 110.
All Nippon Airways, tel. 239744.
C.I.T.S. and C.T.S.: 1 Chongtong St., Xigang Dist. 116011, Tel. 335795. Telex 86485 DCITS CN. Fax 337631. C.T.S. also 1 Stalin Sq., 116011. Tel. 331258. Fax 337831.
CYTS: tel. 336541, 337248.
CAAC   : tel. 337090; airport 552071.
Dalian Overseas Tourist Corp., 1 Changtong St., Xigang Dist., 116011. Tel. 331080. Telex: 86460 OTCDL CN. Fax: 337831. Tours.
Dalian Tourism Bureau, 1 Stalin Sq. 116012. Tel. 332765.
Dragonair: Dalian International Hotel, tel. 238238 X601. Fax 230008.
Liaoning Tourism Administration: Business Management Dept., 113 Huange Nan St. (Suggestions and complaints.)

Railway Station 火车站 : tel. 203331.
Passenger Quay 客运码头 : tel. 229363, 234241.

DATONG

(Tatung) North China. Northern Shanxi. 10 hours by train from Beijing. From here one can continue by once-a-week train to Ulan Bator and thence onward to Moscow. The population is 300,000. The highest temperature in summer (July–August) is 37.7°C, the lowest (December–February) ⁻29.9°C. Rainfall is a scant 400 mm a year, mainly July–September. The best time to visit is May–October. Altitude 1000 m.

Founded during the Warring States, about 2200 years ago, this was a garrison town built between two sections of the Great Wall. The Northern Wei (386–534) declared it their capital and instructed monk Tanyao to supervise the carving of the Yungang Caves.

Datong is basically a coal-mining town, one of the largest open-pit coal producing areas in the world, with a 600-year supply at the current rate of production. The city is industrial and heavily polluted. Outside Datong are visible coal deposits, with all kinds of coal transport equipment blocking up the roads. Some of the equipment is the most advanced in the world. The mining may be ugly but it is worth seeing. Because the mining has unearthed some old burial grounds, Shanxi has an extremely large number of excavated tombs and neolithic sites.

Datong gained considerable publicity recently because Occidental Petroleum of the United States has a joint venture in open-pit coal mining close to the city.

Datong is most famous for the *Yungang (Yunkang) Grottoes, said to be the best-preserved, the largest, and the oldest sandstone carvings in China. They can be reached by Bus No. 17, about 20 km from Datong. Fifty-three caves here contain over 51,000 stone carvings of Buddha, bodhisattvas, apsaras (angels), birds, and animals. These statues range from 17 meters to a few centimeters high, and some of them still retain their original color. They were restored in 1976. The grottoes are at the southern foot of Wuzhou Hills, 16 km west of the city. They were built between A.D. 460 and 494 after a period of persecutions against the Buddhists supposedly led to the illness of Emperor Taiwu. The grottoes extend east-west for a kilometer. The Wei dynasty later moved its capital to Luoyang and built another set of grottoes there.

Although the exposed caves have suffered natural erosion as well as damage by man, they are nicely preserved and well worth visiting. The walking is easy, with no lighting problems. The best are at the Five Caves of Tanyao (Nos. 5, 6, 16–20), which include the largest statues. The large ears could mean long life or poverty (no earrings). Although Datong was not on the Silk Road, the carvings carry strong Indian, Persian, and even Greek influences. One can expect to spend at least half a day here, strolling from cave to cave. During tourist season, English-speaking guides are available for hire. There is a restaurant in the area for foreign tourists. Open 8:30 a.m. to 4:30 or 5 p.m.

If you only have one day to spend in the city, C.I.T.S. recommends the Yungang caves, Huayan Monastery, Shanhua Monastery, and the Nine-Dragon Screen.

The *Huayan Si (Huayan Monastery) 华严寺 , is the second largest temple in China. One can easily spend from 2 hours to a half day there, there is so much to see. It is in the SW section of the city, 3 km north of the main tourist hotel. Good antique store at temple, tel. 233629.

The monastery is well preserved and is separated into the Upper Huayan and the Lower Huayan. You pay two entrance fees. In the upper is the magnificent main hall, Daxiong Bao Dian, built in 1062 and rebuilt in 1140. It is 53.75 meters wide and 29 meters long. The beam structure, murals, five large Ming buddhas, and 26 guardians are most impressive. In the Lower is the main hall, the Bhagavan Stack Hall, built in 1038. Along its walls are 38 two-story wooden cabinets, housing the Buddhist sutras. The temple's exquisite 31 clay statues were made in the Liao. The **Datong Municipal Museum** has prehistoric fossils and cultural relics and is in the Municipal Exhibition Hall.

The *****Shanhua Monastery** 善化寺 , in the SW part of the city, was founded in A.D. 713. Surviving are relics of the Liao and Jin. The **Nine Dragon Screen** 九龙壁 , in the SE section of the old city, is almost 600 years old, and at 45.5 meters, larger than the two in Beijing. The morning is better for photographs. A nearby Christian church is worth a 10-minute visit.

If you have more time or special interest, the 67.3-meter-high *****Sakyamuni Wooden Pagoda at Foguang Temple** 佛宫寺释迦塔 may be worth the 1½-hour drive if you are interested in unusual pagodas. It is the tallest ancient woodframe structure in China. It was constructed in 1056 (Liao), with eight corners and nine stories. From the outside it looks like five stories. Local folklore says that the pagoda only sits on five of its six vertical beams. One of the beams is always "resting," and you can pass a piece of paper underneath it. Each beam takes its turn without having to hold any weight. Bring a piece of paper and test it for yourself. This pagoda is usually locked, but ask for permission to view the interior. 75 km south of Datong in Yingxian county.

The **Great Wall** 长城 is 40 and 150 km away. On **Wutai Mountain** 五台山 , 240 km south, are about 50 temples from the 5th century, three of them historical monuments also protected by the State Council. These are the *****Main Hall of the Nanchan Temple** 南禅寺 (Tang), the *****Foguang Temple** (Tang to Qing), and the *****Xiantong Temple** 佛光寺 (Eastern Han). The main halls of the Nanchan and Foguang temples are the oldest extant woodframe buildings in the world. Both have histories of over 1200 years and are worth the whiteknuckle trip through the mountains. Ask for the 3* Friendship Guest House. Wutai is one of the Four Great Buddhist Mountains of China. Visitors can hike on a paved path to the summit. Festival here in July. Dr. Norman Bethune's model hospital is also in this area.

Trips can also be arranged from Datong to **Hengshan Mountain**, 80 km south, for the **Xuankongsi (Temple in Mid-Air)**. See separate listing, "Hengshan Mountain." Visitors should be able to see 11th-century Liao dynasty tombs. For other places of interest in the province, see "Taiyuan."

In Datong there used to be a steam locomotive factory, but now there is only a museum with China's oldest (1882), and festival. You can also visit a brass products factory 铜器工厂(hot pots, plates, tea pots).

SHOPPING

Made locally are porcelain, brassware, knitting wool, furs, leather, silk dolls, and carpets.

Brassware Factory: 9 Nan Cang St.; tel. 232786.
Friendship Store 友谊商店 : 17 Nanguan Nan St.; tel. 232333.

FOOD

Look for people preparing "Knife-cut Noodles" on the street. Ask about the chefs who put noodle dough on their heads and slick it with a knife into a cooking pot.

HOTELS

IDD should arrive soon. No hotel has air conditioning or takes credit cards.

Datong Guest House (Binguan) • *8 Yingbin Xi Rd., 037008. Dist.A.P.50 km. Dist.R.W.13 km.* • 1958, ren. 1988. CTS here, tel. 522046. For backpackers only.

Yungang Hotel (Fandian) • *21 Yingbin Dong Rd. 037008. 2*. Telex 290013 DTQLS CN. Dist.A.P. 50 km. Dist.R.W. 10 km* • 1985; ren. 1991. 9 stories. 157 rooms. B.C. Considered the best hotel but don't expect much.

Ambulance: tel. 521001.
Police: tel. 110.
C.I.T.S. and **Datong Municipal Tourist Bureau:** Yungang Hotel, 037008, tel. 522265, 522046. Telex 290001 CITSD CN. Fax 522830. Office in Xiyuan Hotel, Beijing.
CYTS: tel. 522830, 521601, 521632 X624.
Datong Tourism Bureau: tel. 521601 X915.

DAZHAI (TACHAI) 大寨

North China. SE of Taiyuan in Shanxi province, Dazhai was a commune famous as a model because of its spirit of hard work and self-sacrifice. Up until 1978, you could frequently hear the slogan "In agriculture, follow Dazhai." In 1979, however, officials pointed out that while this spirit to struggle hard was correct, the slavish copying of Dazhai's example was not. Because every commune had different conditions, every commune had to improve its production in its own way. Dazhai was accused of falsifying its production figures.

DAZU 大足

Southwest China. About 175 km NW of Chongqing (3 to 4 hours by good winding road) in Sichuan province, this is usually an overnight trip. 280 km SE of Chengdu. Road and plane access from Chengdu. Population 780,000. Altitude 380 meters.

The **Dazu Stone Buddhist Sculptures** are considered by some connoisseurs as better preserved and of finer quality than Luoyang, Datong, or Dunhuang. Decide for yourself. About 50,000 of them are located in 43 places in Dazu County, most not readily accessible by car. To see both Beishan and Baodingshan takes about a day and a half. Since the carvings are in hilly surroundings, take time to enjoy the natural scenery and the nearby water reservoir too. Study details. Look for the mother sleeping next to a bed-wetting child, the village girl tending ducks, the funeral rites, the wedding, etc.

The most concentrated numbers are at *Beishan (Northern Hill) (Tang to Song), 2 km north of the Dazu Guest House. Under State Council protection are **Fowan, Guanyinpo, Foerfeng,** and **Yingpanshan**. From the car park, you have to climb nearly 400 stairs. However, the 25-minute climb is spread out along pleasant, shady trails and is much easier than expected (10 minutes downhill). The sculptures at *Fowan are grouped together like beehives. A couple of chambers are fenced with iron gates and locks. Although some of the sculptures have been damaged, the arrangement and the preservation of some are excellent. Take special note of the enchanting Goddess of Mercy of No. 125, and No. 113. The locked No. 155 and No. 136 are worth careful inspection. The pagoda, about 1 km away, is also full of sculptures and is a popular picnic spot with local students.

The first statue was carved here in A.D. 892 by Wei Junjing. It was then a military camp.

Also worth seeing and accessible in large numbers are the sculptures at *Baodingshan 宝顶山 (Song dynasty), 15 km NE of the Dazu Guest House. The ones here were basically done by one monk, Zhou Zhifeng, from 1179 to 1249, and centered on the theme "Life is Vanity." The daily life of people is well-illustrated with vivid facial expressions and body language. The work here is largely intact and the sculptures are huge. The Sleeping Buddha is 31 meters long, and some of the standing figures are 7 meters high. It is essential that you obtain a tour guide to explain highlights to you. To see this grouping takes only a few minutes.

The sculptures at *Xiaofowan 小佛湾 are in the Shengshao Temple near the entrance of *Dafowan 大佛湾 . Many tourists are only shown Dafowan, but other sculptures are close by. If you want to see more, do insist on it. Another group of sculptures, carved in the Song dynasty, are at Shimenshan, 23 km from the Dazu Hotel.

Also under State Council protection here are *Guangdashan, *Longtan, and *Linsongpo.

An excellent book on Dazu has been published by the Sichuan Provincial Academy of Social Sciences in English and Chinese.

You might be able to tell roughly when the sculptures were created because the Tang figures are simple, smooth, and more alluring. The Five Dynasty statues are meticulously carved with details. The Song statues are rather reserved but distinctive in personality and expression.

The largest statue is the Sleeping Buddha and the most famous a 1000-armed Goddess of Mercy 千手观音 , both at Baoding Hill. Beautiful is the face of the Hen Wife here. You may notice that many of the larger statues are bigger at the top and lean forward to make viewing easier from below.

Made locally are stainless steel tableware and bamboo carvings.

HOTELS

Dazu Guest House (Binguan) • *47 Gongnong St., Longgangzhen 632360. 1*.* • 70 rooms. Expanded in 1984. New air conditioning 1987. 140 beds. Better suited for business people.

Beishan Hotel (Binguan) • *632360 100 rooms.* Better, but not good. • Reservations for either from Renmin Guest House (Chongqing) or Jin Jiang Hotel (Chengdu).

C.I.T.S. and **C.T.S.,** 中国国际旅行社 : 47 Gongnong St., 632360; tel. 22245.

DUNHUANG 敦煌

(Tunhuang, Tunhwang) Northwest China. Western Gansu. One of the world's greatest art treasures, now protected by the United Nations.

Between the fourth and 14th centuries, more than 1000 caves were cut out of the cliffs 25 km SE of the city and filled with Buddhist carvings, gilt and colored frescoes, and murals. Known as the *Mogao Grottoes 莫高窟 or the **Thousand Buddha Caves,** 492 of these remain today in three or four rows on a 1½-km-long wall. The State Council has renovated murals like the **Feitian (Flying Apsaras)** fresco (Tang) and repainted over 2000 statues. Some of the statues in about 20 caves were repainted in the Qing. Note the intricately painted ceilings.

The most important cave is the **Cangjing (Preserving Buddhist Scriptures) Cave** 藏经洞 , now No. 17. Dating from the Jin to Song (or late Tang to Western Xia, depending on sources), a span of 600 years, this is where 40,000 important old documents were found, including the Diamond Sutra (A.D. 868), said to be the oldest existing dated printed book. It is now in the British Museum in London. Other important caves include #45 (clay figures), #158 (the 15.6-m-long Sleeping Buddha), and #96 both have 26- and 33-meter-high Maitreya Buddhas respectively. #130 (the 33-m-high Maitreya Buddha). #71 was recently restored. Entrance to some of these might require additional payment.

Many caves have stories. One of the most famous is outlined in a series of pictures about a woman who was badly treated by her husband. While returning to her mother, she encountered a wolf that killed her two children. After becoming a nun, she learned that her miseries were a punishment for mistreating her stepsister in a previous incarnation.

Some of the statues are damaged, many by Moslems in the distant past and a few by the Red Guards. Signs indicate which museums abroad have stolen the pieces originally here. Some of the colors are still original and vivid. The red might be from pig's blood or cinnabar. One could get a real feeling of history and mysticism here. Caves were used as temples because they were conducive to meditation and secure, like a mother's womb (perhaps symbolizing reincarnation). Tel. 2113 X 15.

The caves are a one-day trip at least. In recent years only a couple of enterprising noodle vendors and a seller of sickly sweet orange drink served visitors here, so better take your own lunch. Lots of souvenir shops though. As there are few Chinese tourists, public buses from Dunhuang city are infrequent, leaving the Dunhuang Guest House at 8:30 a.m. and 1:30 p.m., arriving at Mogao 30 minutes later. Make sure you find out what time the last bus leaves (probably about 4:30 p.m., but do check) if you have to rely on public transport. The caves are open from 8:30 to 11:30 a.m. and 2:00 to 5 p.m. Knowledgeable guides are available for hire on the site to show you around, and about five speak English. As with all cave temples, it is best to take flashlights to see what **you** want to see. (They can be rented.) And do not expect to see an entire mural as you would in a spacious museum. You have to piece each section together in your own mind. This fragmentation has disappointed some tourists. A heavy metal door protects each cave. The next scholarly international symposium should be held in 1993, organized by the British Library and the Chinese Academy of Social Sciences. A temple fair is held annually.

Cameras and bags are not generally allowed. Photography needs special permission in advance. Tourists cannot wander around the site without a guide. About 30 or so caves are available at any one time, of which you will see a fraction.

If you are anxious to see more, ask for special permission in advance.

Dunhuang can be reached by train from Beijing (27 hours). The train station is at Liuyuah, a 1.5 hour bus ride from the city. Some charter flights available in the summer only, also with Beijing, Xi'an and Dunhuang. Regular flights with Jiayuan and Lanzhou. The bus to Jiayuguan takes 6 hours.

Summers are hot; winters are very cold. The warmest is about 32°C in July, the coldest .4°C in December, but it can be 4°C in April and 9.5°C in May. The annual rainfall is only 36.8 mm. *The best time to visit is May, Sept., or Oct. The altitude is 1000–1200 meters. The caves are open all year-round.*

Dunhuang was an important cultural exchange center and oasis on the Silk Road. The old town is 250 meters west of the current one. Dunhuang was founded in 111 B.C. during the Han. From here, the road west splits into northern and southern routes and ended 7000 km away at the Mediterranean Sea. Dunhuang was a military outpost under the Tang. In A.D. 400, it became the capital of the Xiliang kingdom. An enemy army of 20,000 attacked the city and flooded it 21 years later. It changed hands several times. In 1227, Genghis Khan seized it, and in the Ming, it was a military headquarters. The ruins of the walls and a 16-meter-high tower can be seen in the old part of town. The population now is 15,000 urban and rural.

Visitors also can see the **White Horse Pagoda** 白马塔 (only a 12-meter-high dagoba in the desert and a 5-minute stop). It commemorates the horse of the Indian monk Fumoluoshi, which died here. The **Yangguan Pass** 阳关 (70 km south of Dunhuang) is just a wall now, of interest to people who like deserts or have a feeling for history. It was a military command post from the Han to the Yang, but the sands of the desert have inundated it.

The **Yumen (Jade Gate) Pass** 玉门关 (80 km NW of the city) has remains of the old wall. Jade used to be carried through here. These three sites are in themselves really not worth the hardship of getting here, but if you think of what went through here, the caravans of camels and merchants supplying the wealthy homes of Europe, and the envoys bringing tribute to the emperor, they can be emotional experiences. A recent Chinese movie *Dunhuang* makes an attempt to recapture the spirit of the era and could help you appreciate the relics here.

Dunhuang also has a carpet factory 地毯厂 , and the **Mingsha (Singing Sand) Hill** 鸣沙山 (5 km south), where once a whole army was buried during a sandstorm. Their ghosts are still heard from time to time playing military drums and horns! Here one can get a short camel ride to Crescent Moon Spring, climb sand dunes, and visit a folk custom museum.

20 km south of the city one can visit a movie set of old Dunhuang. Apricots, ju jubes, pears, melons, peaches, and wine grapes are grown locally. Made here are carpets and batik.

Dunhuang Hotel (Fandian) • *Dong Dajie, 736200. 2☆. Telex 72078 DHBGS CN. Dist.A.P.13 km. Dist.R.W.130 km* • 1980. 130 rooms. Larger rooms, lobby, and shop than Solar Hotel. No air conditioning in rooms. Only American Express C.C. Should have IDD soon. Best in town and quite good.

Solar or Sun Energy Hotel (Pai Yiang Neng Benguan) • *Dabai Jie, 736200. Fax 2121. Central location* • 1987. 73 rooms. No foreign exchange. C.C. Breakfast only. Western food available.

C.I.T.S.: 1 Dong Dajie, 736200. Tel. 2494. Telex 72194 DHLXS CN.
CAAC: tel. 2389
Dunhuang Tourist Bureau: tel. 2336.
Airport: tel. 2216.
Police: tel. 110.
Fire: tel. 119.
See also ''Silk Road.''

EMEI SHAN 峨眉

(Emei or Omei Mountain) Southwest China; 170 km SW of Chengdu in Sichuan, Emei Shan is one of China's four great Buddhist mountains. The base can be reached by train from the North Railway Station in Chengdu, or by bus to Emeishan City. From there one takes a bus to Baoguo Temple.

The climb to the summit and back can be done on foot in one day if you're energetic, or two days for the less agile. Along the 60-km stone path are 23 monasteries, intriguing caves, gushing waterfalls, magnificent views, and birds. Be careful of monkeys. They can steal food, scratch, and bite. Land Rovers drive to within 6 km of the peak at **Jieyin Hall** 接引殿 at 2670 meters. At that height, it can be very chilly, about ⁻20°C at the top in January. Hostels are at the base of and on the 3100-meter-high summit. Restaurants along the way. Guides available.

The best time to climb is from April to June and September to November. It may be too cold and slippery for climbing from December to March, but the mountain is beautiful. The rainy season is July and August.

Baoguo Temple 报国寺 , at the base, has a scale-model map of the mountain with lights. The temple originates from the Ming. **Wannian Monastery** 万年 (a.k.a. Samantabhadra Monastery), on the slope, dates from the 4th century. Its *bronze and iron Buddha images are Song to Ming. The bronze Samantabhadra on a white elephant is 7.4 meters high and weighs 62 tons. The beamless brick hall, roof, and square walls are said to be typically Ming.

HOTELS

Red Spider Mountain Hotel (Hong Zhu Shan Binguan) ● *614201. 2*. Fax 33788. Near the Baoguo Temple ● Dist.A.P. 130 km. Dist.R.W. 10 km* ● American Express and Diners C.C. only. 1935, ren. 1990, 1992. 3 stories. 180 rooms, 10 buildings. Largest in the city. IDD, B.C. Bicycles. C.I.T.S.

The **Southwest Jiaotong University Guest House (Keji Giaoliu Zhong Xing)** • *614202* • 1986. Three stories, 52 rooms.

C.I.T.S.: tel. 33888; fax 33788.
Hospital: The **Red Cross Hospital,** next to Hong Zhu Shan Hotel.

FOSHAN 佛山

(Fushan; Cantonese Fashan) South China, Guangdong province, about 25 km SW of Guangzhou. Population 365,000. China United flies between Foshan and Beijing, Nanjing, and seven other cities. It is a pleasant but not a world-class destination, interesting because of its prosperity, the Ancestral Temple, and Shiwan ceramics. Can also be reached by train.

Named "Hill of Buddhas" because a mound of Buddhist statues were excavated here, this is one of the Four Ancient Towns of China. The city is over 1300 years old and is famous for its handicrafts. In addition, it makes machines, electronics, chemicals, textiles, plastics, pharmaceuticals, cement, etc. It is famous for pottery, and has a 0.5-km-long street of ceramic and pottery stores. It is a good one-day excursion from Guangzhou accessible by superhighway.

Foshan Folk Art Institute 佛山民间艺术研究社 produces palace lanterns, T-shirts, and paper cutouts. It is a training institute for master crafts people in all fields. The **Shiwan Artistic Ceramic Factory** 石湾美术陶瓷厂 is one of the most famous porcelain factories in China; some of its works adorn the tops of temples in south China and Hong Kong. Its collection of maroon-robed *lohan,* with expressive, bulging eyes and unglazed faces, is well known.

The **Ancestral Temple,** now the **Foshan Municipal Museum** 祖庙博物馆 was originally erected in the Song (Emperor Yuanfeng, 1078–1085) and rebuilt in 1372 after a disastrous fire. Expanded and rebuilt after Liberation, the temple contains sculptures, ancient relics, and a 2500 kg bronze figure named Northern Emperor. Note the variety of decorations on the bases of the arches and the stone, wood, and brick carvings. Four of the statues are said to be made of paper, the others of wood or clay. The roof, decorated with Shiwan pottery figures, is one of the most elaborate in the country. A little gaudy, but artistically and culturally important.

The **silk factory** 丝织厂 is also open to visitors.

Air-conditioned bus with television goes from the station near the Foshan Hotel to Hai'an (from where you can get a ferry to Haikou on Hainan Island). Takes about 10 hours.

Nightlife: evening markets, nightclubs, disco halls, and amusement park. Best food in the Foshan Hotel and Golden City Hotel (tel. 227228).

Xiqiao Mountain is about 25 km away, a resort area with the 3* Xiqiao Grand Hotel (Dajiudian) at the base of a 400-m-high mountain. Primarily for hikers (3 lakes, 44 caves, 72 peaks, 207 springs, and innumerable waterfalls; 8 villages). Small Ming tower and Qing Taoist temple. Amusement park. Cable car. C.I.T.S., at White Cloud Cave, Nanhai County 528200; tel. 686799. The hotel has a pool and B.C.

SHOPPING

Locally made are cuttlebone sculptures, brick carvings, silk, lanterns, paper-cuts, etc. And of course the famous Shiwan ceramics.

HOTELS

We found the food very good at the Chancheng Hotel. HKTV in all these hotels. The best is the Foshan.

Foshan Hotel (Binguan) • *75 Fenjiang Nan Rd. 528000. 3* Telex 425016. Fax 368944, 352347. Dist. A. P. 8 km. Dist. R. W. 3 km* • Attractive downtown garden hotel. 1973. Ren. 1987. 8 stories. 214 rooms. Extension 1993–4. B.C. Outdoor pool. Gym. IDD. Japanese and Chaozhou food. C.I.T.S.

Foshan Overseas Chinese Hotel (Huaqiao Dasha) • *14 Zumiao Rd. 528000. 3*. Telex 425041 FSOCH CN. Fax 227702. Across street from folk art store. Dist. A. P. 8 km. Dist. R. W. 1 km* • C.C. 1962. 5 stories; 152 big rooms. IDD. C.T.S., B.C. Third best.

Golden City Hotel (Jin Cheng Dajiudian) • *48 Fenjiang Nan Rd. 528000. 3* Telex 425038 GCHFS. Fax 353924. Dist. A. P. 8 km. Dist. R. W. 3 km* • Downtown. Across from Exhibition Center, C.C. 1989. 19 stories. 180 rooms. IDD. Outdoor pool. Gym. B.C.

Ambulance, tel. 221000.
Police, tel. 110.
CAAC: tel. 32404.

C.I.T.S.: Foshan Hotel, tel. 223338. Fax 222347, 248944. Also, room 2812, North Wing, Liuhua Hotel, Guangzhou.
C.T.S.中旅社: O.C. Hotel, tel. 223828; telex 425041.
Foshan Tourism Bureau, 3/F, 103 Renmin Rd. 528000; tel. 285901, 222356. Fax 223098.

FUSHUN 抚顺

Northeast China. Eastern Liaoning, 50 km NE of Shenyang. It is one of China's biggest coal centers but is becoming best-known for the prison where the Last Emperor spent nine years, from 1950 to 1959. Urban population is 1.24 million. A new airport should be opening soon, between Shenyang and Fushun. Shenyang is one hour away by train. The temperature reaches a high of 36°C in summer and a low of ¯35°C in winter. Annual precipitation about 800 mm, with 153 frostfree days a year.

Built on a neolithic site, Fushun became a walled city in the Ming. In 1778, the town was rebuilt as a political and economic center. **Xingjing town (Hetuala)** in Yingbin county was built by the founder of the Qing dynasty. Over half of the population are Manchu, and you can see some of the old customs. The first Manchu capital was here in 1616. The last emperors of China were Manchu. **Yongling** (1598), 100 km from Fushun, has the oldest Qing tombs, those of the ancestors of the Qing emperors. A pagoda on **Mt. Gaoer** (5 km from the hotel) and a Guanyin temple below it date from the Liao (1088).

Tourists can also visit the 2 by 6.6 km **West Open Cast Coal Mine** 西露天煤矿 (10 km from the hotel) and the **Dahuofang Reservoir** 大伙房水库 (17 km from the hotel). An elaborate 1929-built tomb of Warlord Zhang Zuolin is at the foot of Mt. Tiebei on the reservoir. At **Soldier Lei Feng's** museum you can see how today's heroes are made.

The real interior of the **Fushun War Criminal Prison** was not seen in the movie *The Last Emperor*. The prison was opened for former Japanese inmates to show their families. It was originally built by the Japanese in 1936. About 900 Japanese prisoners, Emperor Pu Yi, 50

Manchu officials, and over 300 Nationalists were held here. The exhibitions and photos displayed inside are of these three groups, instruments of torture, bacteria warfare experiments, and the Japanese surrender. In 1988, officials were asked to put up signs in English.

A torture chamber, in the basement of the first building, is now used for storage. The building used for prisoners sentenced to death became a clinic in the 1950s. A photo of each prisoner is above his bedspace.

You can see the greenhouse where Pu Yi learned gardening, the room where his last concubine stayed 48 hours with him (and afterwards filed for divorce), and the room where he received his pardon. Arrangements can be made for tourists to sleep in the prison (or the air-conditioned prison guesthouse), and even on Pu Yi's bed. There were 11 other Manchus in his room at first; he was moved in 1952 because he didn't know how to tie his shoelaces. Note the chamberpot. Pu Yi also eventually learned to clean it.

SHOPPING

Amber and jet carvings. Gold and silver filigree, jade carving, artistic candles and artistic glassware are also made here.

RESTAURANTS

The best are in the Friendship and Fushun hotels.

HOTELS

The new section of the **Friendship Hotel** • *4 Yongning St., 113008. 2*. Telex 819014. Fax 26773. Dist.R.W.½ km* • should be the best in town. Four-story section built 1958, ren. 1989. Seven story section with dorms should be open now. No C.C. Small TVs, high ceilings. IDD.

Fushun Hotel (Binguan) • *1 Xiyi Rd. 113008. 2*. Telex 80388 FSHTL CN. Central. Dist.A.P.40 km. Dist.R.W.½ km.* • No C.C. 1960, expanded 1986. 5 stories, 216 beds for foreigners. No IDD. Small rooms and bathrooms, poor reading lights. CAAC booking office.

C.I.T.S.: Friendship Hotel, 4 Yongning St., 113008; tel. 23341. Telex 819023 FEXOF CN. Fax 26773.
Fushun Travel & Tourism and **Fujian Overseas Tourist Enterprise:** Foreign Affairs Office, Fushun Municipality, Yong'on Square 113008; tel. 29756.
Ambulance, tel. 119.
Police, tel. 110.
CAAC: tel. 2448.

FUZHOU 福州

(Foochow, Fuchou) East China. Capital of Fujian province on the east coast across from Taiwan, this city is over 2000 years old. Urban pop. 1.3 million. Flights from Hong Kong and 23 other Chinese cities. Buses from Guangzhou or a 37-hour train ride. Hottest temp. 39°C, July-August; coldest—0.8°C, February.

Opened to foreign trade in 1842, Fuzhou had British and American dockyards, and factories for making tea bricks. Once home to about 10 foreign consulates, its foreign cemetery was dug up and replaced by a school. The old British Community Church, never used by the Chinese, is now a warehouse. Across the street is a women's college looking for native English-speakers willing to teach English in return for room and board.

What you can see are **Gushan (Drum Hill)** 鼓山 , topped by a huge drum-shaped boulder in the eastern suburbs, at least 969 meters high. The **Yongquan Si (Surging Spring Temple)** 涌泉寺 was founded in A.D. 908 and has a white jade Buddha. Monks chant at 4:30 a.m. and p.m. for one hour. The **Qianfo Taota (Thousand-Buddha Pottery Pagodas)** 千佛陶塔 and the **Shuiyun Ting (Water and Cloud Pavilion)** 水云亭 , east of the Yongquan Si are both from the Song. Views from the 18 caves west of the temple are said to be famous. Several hundred inscriptions on the cliff are near the **Lingyuan Dong (Spirit Source Cave)** 灵源洞 . Over 100 of these writings are from the Song.

The city is also noted for its hot springs, with over a dozen in Fuzhou itself. The most famous temples are the plain-looking **Baita (White Pagoda)** 白塔 , on the west side of Yushan Hill, and the **Wuta (Black Pagoda)** 乌塔 , at the base of Wushi Hill, both in the center of town. The main hall of the *Hualin Temple 华林寺 , from the Song, is worth seeing. The **Jinshan (Gold Mountain) Temple** 金山寺 is snugly perched on an island west of the city.

The **Memorial Hall of Lin Zexu** 林则徐祠堂 , the official who burned the 20,000 chests of opium near Canton in 1839, is a small shrine with a statue of the national hero. Known also as a calligrapher and a poet, Lin was one of the first Qing officials to take an interest in things foreign. Because the British fired on China as a result of Lin's actions, the emperor exiled Lin to Yili in Xinjiang.

Most developed for tourists in the province seems to be Xiamen, with good hotels. Quanzhou is next, for some interesting things to see. Fuzhou seems to have less to offer. See separate listings.

For outdoor types, **Wuyi Mountain** 武夷山 , in the northwestern part of the province, is a summer resort (snow in winter) with 86 hotels, rafting through beautiful Guilin-type scenery, and a Song dynasty replica shopping street. It is aiming at 3 million visitors a year by 2000. It is a train trip to Nanping plus a 3 to 4 hour bus ride or a one-hour plane ride (three times a week) from Fuzhou or Nanjing (Thursdays and Sundays). C.I.T.S.: tel. (5098) 32258. C.T.S.: tel. 32981. The Wuyi Mountain Villa is rated 3*. Two-hour bamboo-raft-trips leave from Xingcun Village.

Aside from Wuyi, Fujian is mainly for those interested in maritime history, in Koxinga (museums in Xiamen and Quanzhou), and in the relics of Arab traders, Manichaeanism, and Nestorian Christianity. Some of its native sons have returned from Southeast Asia with wealth. They have built monuments, schools, hospitals, and temples. The religious buildings are uniquely flamboyant with cosmopolitan touches.

The Fujian dialect is distinct, neither Cantonese nor Mandarin. This language is spoken also by the majority on Taiwan, just across the straits. The weather is subtropical, and most of the province is mountainous.

ENTERTAINMENT

Disco at the **Hot Springs** Hotel. Night market near May 1 Square.

Festival of Goddess Mazu in April and May on Meizhou Island in Putian City, 108 km south.

C.I.T.S. recommends the Ju Chun Yuan (tel. 553038) and Beijin (tel. 522334) and Grand C.I.T.S. Restaurants (tel. 526813).

SHOPPING

Good lacquerware, cork carving, and Shoushan stone carvings are made and sold here.

Friendship Store 友谊商店 (May 4 Rd., tel. 550013.); **Fujian Antique General Store** 省文物总店 (Wuyi Dong Rd., tel. 556702). **Fuzhou Tourist Shopping Center; Fuzhou Carving Art General Factory** (Tel. 552373); **Bodiless Lacquerware Factory** (North of Wu Yi Rd., tel. 554411, 550661. For sightseeing as well as buying—no credit cards).

HOTELS

Hotels here are centered around the Foreign Trade Center (FTC) except the Lakeside and the nearby West Lake Guest House. The best-looking hotel was the classy new Lakeside (if you like modern, glass-walled high-rises). C.I.T.S. says it and the Hot Springs are best. The Foreign Trade Center Hotel and the Hot Spring Hotel seem better than the Overseas Chinese Hotel. The Dong Hu was scruffy and had smaller rooms, but handy to C.I.T.S. All the downtown hotels have hot spring water and all are convenient to shopping.

Donghu Hotel (Binguan) • *44 Dong Da Rd. 350001. 3*. Telex 92171 DHHFZ CN. Fax 555519. Dist.A.P.13 km. Dist.R.W.4. Dist.FTC ½ km* • T.R., C.C. 1984, ren. 1988. Ten stories, over 200 rooms. IDD. B.C.

Fujian Foreign Trade Center Hotel (Wai Mao Zhong Xing Jiudian) • *Wusi Rd. 350001. 4* Telex 92158 FTC CN. Fax 550358. Next door to FTC. Dist. A.P. 25 km. Dist. R.W. 3 km* • C.C. 1985, ren. 1991. 7 stories, 163 rooms. 5* addition with 250 rooms due 1993. IDD, B.C., attractive rooms, pool, tennis, and conference hall. Preferred by business people, though second best. USTV.

Hot Spring Hotel (Wen Quan Daxia) • *Wusi Zhong Rd., 350003. 4*. Telex 92180 HSHFZ CN. Fax 535150. Dist.A.P.13 km. Dist. R.W.4.* • Dist.FTC ½ km. C.C. Reservations through Utell. 1986, ren. 1989. 15 stories, 311 rooms. IDD. Outdoor pool, gym, tennis, bowling. B.C. Qigong. "Bubble" elevator. Large rooms with balconies, small closets, no drawers. Hair dryers.

Lakeside Hotel (Xihu Dajiudian) • *1 Hubin Rd. 350003. 4*. Telex 92255 FLHBC CN. Fax 539752. Dist. A. P. 14 km. Dist. R. W. 5 km* • C.C. 1988. 22 stories, 436 rooms. Gym, disco, pool, B.C., grill room. IDD. C.I.T.S. Rooms for wheelchair guests. Even-numbered rooms have lakeview. USTV.

Overseas Chinese Hotel (Huaqiao Dasha) • *Wusi Rd. 350001. 3* Telex 92123 FJKTS CN. Fax 550648. Dist.A.P.13 km. Dist.R.W.4 km.* • Across street from FTC. C.C. 1961, ren. 1988. 8 stories, 250 rooms. C.T.S. IDD, flourescent lights, thin drapes. Good furniture. Dorms.

C.I.T.S. and **Fujian Overseas Tourist Enterprise Corp.:** 44 Dongda Rd. 350001; tel. 555506, 552052. Telex 99201 CITS CN. Fax 537447, 555497. FOTEC: tel. 557755 X 85204, 535159. Fax 523456.
C.T.S. 中旅社 : Fujian Br., Wusi Rd., 350001; tel. 556304, 554215. Fax 553983. Telex 92123 FJKTS CN.
CAAC 中国民航 : May 1st Rd.; tel. 55113.
Fujian Medical College (Union Hospital), tel. 557896.
CYTS: tel. 555138, 555208.

Fujian Provincial Tourism Bureau: 24 Dong Da rd. 350001; tel. 553794.
Tourist Hotline: tel. 554153.
Police: tel. 110.
USA Direct telephone line: Fuzhoo Phone Center.

GRAND CANAL 大运河

The oldest and longest in the world, this canal was built in the Sui dynasty (A.D. 581–618) and originally extended 1794 km from Hangzhou to Beijing.

Today visitors can still take tour boats on parts of the canal, a trip that gives you an intimate look at the life on the water, in waterside houses, villages, and countryside. One can sleep on ferries too between cities to save on paying for a hotel room. But the water is dirty and the trip can be noisy as traffic moves on the canal all night.

At individual cities along the route, you can see parts of the canal. Wuxi has a 36.5-meter-long, two-storied "dragon boat" with flashing eyes. Tours mainly between Yangzhou and Suzhou.

GREAT WALL 长城

(Wanlichangcheng—10,000 li-long wall.) The Great Wall has been officially 12,700 Chinese li, or 6350 km, or 3946.55 miles long from Jiayuguan to Shanhaiguan. Some scholars, however, add another 1040 km all the way to Yalu River on the Korean border. The length depends on what you measure, there being many offshoots and parallel walls. It is in various states of repair.

The Great Wall was first built in shorter pieces, starting in the fifth century B.C., as a defensive and boundary wall around the smaller states of Yen, Chao, and Wei. The first Qin emperor (221–206 B.C.), who unified China for the first time, linked up and extended the walls from Liaoning in the east to Gansu in the NW as protection from the Huns and other nomadic tribes to the north. The wall was subsequently repaired and extended by succeeding dynasties, especially the Ming.

Originally built by slave labor, it has been called the world's longest graveyard because many of its builders were buried where they fell. It was designed, in places, to allow five horsemen or ten soldiers to march abreast along the top. It was almost a superhighway, considering the rough mountain terrain. A system of bonfires communicated military information to the emperor at a speed rapid for that period.

The best time to visit is after 2 p.m., when most of the tourists have left. Stay to see the sunset if you can.

The Great Wall is most frequently visited at ***Badaling (Padaling),** about 75 km (two hours) by bus NW of Beijing. It is extremely crowded. You still need to avoid the Sunday traffic jams. Usually the trip can be done by taxi in 4 hours if you don't linger. Most tourists now go from Beijing by tourist bus. Tourist buses leave Beijing daily at 8 a.m. and stop at both the Great Wall and Ming tombs.

Badaling is about 1000 meters above sea level. Here the wall averages 7.8 meters high, 6.5 meters wide at the base, and 5.8 meters wide at the top. Watchtowers are located every few hundred meters. Note the giant rocks and bricks of uniform size, the gutters, and the waterspouts. You can walk, and in some places climb, for several hundred feet in either direction or you can take a cable car. Skateboarding on the wall has been allowed, but is not recommended when it is thick with people, which is most of the time. Try first thing in the morning or late afternoon. A restaurant for eating and usually a shaggy Bactrian camel or pony for photographing are available. Taking a box lunch is recommended, especially in pleasant weather, so you can spend more time at the wall rather than waiting for service in a crowded restaurant. Or you can see a 15-minute movie with English subtitles on a 360° screen.

Also of note is the gate in the center of **Juyongguan (Chuyungkuan Pass,** about 10 km south of Badaling. It is built of finely carved marble and called ***Guojie (Cloud Terrace).** Originally the base of a tower built in 1345 (Yuan), the walls are decorated with carvings of Buddhas, four celestial guardians, and the text of a Buddhist sutra in Sanskrit, Tibetan, and four other languages. Currently, tours do not usually stop here except by request.

A 3-km-long section of the Great Wall is at **Mutianyu,** 70 km NE of Beijing in Miyun County. It is less crowded and is very beautiful, less commercial, with more rugged hills than Badaling. A 720-meter-long Swiss-built cable car can take you from the parking lot uphill to the base of the wall. You still have to climb the wall, but you can walk 40 minutes down 1100 steps back to the parking lot. Or take the cable car down.

One restaurant open now. All buildings tastefully built in Ming style. A road has been completed so that one can go from here to the Ming tombs. A third section is at **Simatai,** 140 km from Beijing and also in Miyun County. If you have time, drive to the Genghis Khan Military Headquarters reproduction with its wax figures. Impressive imperial yurt. Look at the Wall in this area. It is fascinating.

The *Great Wall has also been restored and opened to visitors at 3000-year-old Shanhaiguan (with cable car), over 40 km north from Beidaihe, and about 30 km from Qinhuangdao in the east. See separate listings. There is also a museum in the tower. Note the sign "The First Pass Under Heaven." The gate was built in 1381. Nearby, **Old Dragon Head,** is the place where the Great Wall meets the sea and is open to visitors.

The Great Wall can also be visited at **Jinshan Ling,** 110 km from Chengde in Hebei, and Huairou County (2 km long), 60 km NE of Beijing. The railway line from Beijing to Chengde crosses it. An 850-meter section is open in Jixian County, north of Tianjin, and another section is open near Datong. In the west, it can be seen in Ningxia at Yinchuan, and in Gansu at *Jiayuguan, its western terminal (Ming) where it is much narrower. Museums are at Jiayguan and Shanhaiguan. See "Jiayuguan" and "Shanhaiguan."

GUANGZHOU
(KWANGCHOW, CANTON)

South China; 125 km NW of Hong Kong in Guangdong province on the Zhujiang (Pearl River), a nonstop 2–3 hour train ride, a 3-hour hydrofoil ride, or a half-hour flight from Hong Kong. It is also linked by air with Bangkok, Jakarta, Kuala Lumpur, Manila, Melbourne, Singapore, Sydney and 58 cities in China. Guangzhou is a 36-hour train ride south of Beijing, and a 2 to 5 hour drive from Zhuhai on the Macao border. A super highway is also planned to link it with Shenzhen, Hong Kong, and Macao. All these should relieve the nightmarish situation every time there is a long Hong Kong holiday, when over 100,000 visitors try to get from Hong Kong to China and back. Tourists should especially avoid the lunar new year holiday (late January or early February), trade fairs, and Qing Ming (early April). Elevated highways and more bridges have been built to relieve some of the urban traffic congestion but parking and traffic jams are the price of prosperity. The weather here is subtropical. Coldest—about 0°C, January–February; hottest—about 38°C, July–August. Average rainfall: 1680 mm. Extremely humid summers. Best time to visit: October–February. The urban population is about 3.85 million.

Guangzhou is also known as the Goat City because five fairies came here supposedly in 1256 B.C., riding five goats from whose mouths the fairies drew the first rice seeds. The city was founded over 2000 years ago. In 214 B.C., the first Qin emperor set up the Prefecture of Nanhai here. It was the capital of the state of Nanyue during the Western Han, a dynasty that lasted 93 years, from 196 B.C. It is best known as the largest and most prosperous trading city in South China, a role it has played at least since the Tang dynasty. Arab traders started arriving over 1300 years ago. The Portuguese settled in Macao, 64 km away, in 1557. More recently, it was the site of the Canton Trade Fair, for 23 years China's main foreign trade institution.

Guangzhou is the capital of Guangdong, a province that has three Open Economic Areas (the Pearl River Delta, the Han River Delta—Shantou, and the Jian River Delta—Zhanjiang). Open areas extend along its entire coast and parts of its interior. Guangdong is the provincial "home" of many Chinese immigrants to Australia, the United States, Canada, and many parts of Southeast Asia. These people have contributed to the economic development of their adopted lands and have also brought or sent back expertise as well as money to their ancestral home. Many are playing a leading role in China's modernization program, and are largely responsible for Guangdong's economic boom.

Being a long way from the political center of China, the people here developed a rebellious, independent spirit. Guangzhou was the starting point or site of many important historical events:

—the fight against the importation of opium. Chinese officials burned 20,000 chests of it (1839); the struggle against foreign imperialism, at Sanyuanli, for example, during the Opium War in 1841;

—the movement against the Qing dynasty by the Taiping Heavenly Kingdom. Leader Hong Xiuquan (Hung Hsiu-ch'uan) was born about 66 km north of the city and was given the Christian tract that changed his life and China's history in Guangzhou;

—the campaign against the Qing in the early 1900s led by Dr. Sun Yat-sen, who was born south of the city in Zhongshan county near the Macao border. The fight was fueled by the failure of the Qing emperors to repel the encroaching foreign powers;

—the general strike against the unequal foreign treaties, starting in June 1925. It lasted for 16 months and almost closed Hong Kong;

—the Communist Revolution. Mao Zedong taught peasant leaders here in 1926 at the National Peasant Movement Institute;

—the Northern Expedition, whose officers were trained at the nearby Huangpu (Whampoa) Military Academy. Chiang Kai-shek was director; Chou En-lai was in charge of political indoctrination. In June 1926 this expedition to unify China and to assert Chinese nationalism started off from Guangzhou.

—an uprising against the Nationalists led by the Communists in December 1927.

Many foreign missionaries established schools and churches here after the city was opened to foreign trade and residence by the Treaty of Nanking in 1842. From 1938 to 1945, the Japanese occupied Guangzhou. The Communists took over from the Nationalists on October 14, 1948.

In recent years, Guangdong has been one of the main suppliers of food, water, and electricity for neighboring Hong Kong. It is rich in livestock, fruits, and vegetables. Guangdong has 11 institutions of higher learning, including Zhong Shan University, which is on the site of the missionary-founded Ling Nam University. There are 3200 factories producing heavy machinery, textiles (silk and ramie), petrochemicals, sewing machines, ships, and electronics.

Tourists would probably be interested in its **ivory-carving factory,** where about 50 concentric balls within balls have been made from one piece of ivory.

The city is divided by the Zhu (Pearl) River, which is crossed by five bridges, a tunnel and innumerable ferries to be avoided at rush hours. Most of the places of interest to tourists are located on the north side. A 35 km. long subway is planned for 1997, two lines totaling 43 km. There are two railway stations, the newer Tianhe near the Ramada Hotel serving some Shenzhen trains at press time.

While *pu tung hua* (Mandarin dialect) is understood by almost everyone, the language spoken in most homes is Cantonese.

If you only have one day, see the **Zhen Family Hall,** the **Han Dynasty Mausoleum Museum,** the **Temple of the Six Banyan Trees/ Flower Pagoda** (for exotic Chinese architecture), and the **Qingping Free Market** (for genuine local color). You could also decide on a garden (if you like plants), or an arts and crafts factory. Be sure to eat in one of the **garden restaurants,** have dim sum at the **Banxi Restaurant** or **China Hotel,** and a drink in the riverside coffee shop at the **White Swan Hotel.** If you have more time (at least a day), go to **Foshan** for the ancestral temple and ceramics (See "Foshan.")

Guangzhou is not noted as a prime tourist destination, but it has enough to do for two or three days.

Probably the most exciting recent development for Guangzhou has been the discovery in 1983 of a 2100-year-old imperial tomb now officially known as the **Museum of the Western Han Dynasty Mausoleum of the Nanyue King.** The second king of Nanyue ruled this region during the early Western Han (206 B.C.–A.D. 24). More than 1000 burial objects were excavated. Included in the find were a chariot, ritual bronzes, gold and silver vessels, ivory and lacquerware, jades, musical instruments, weapons, and tools. Human sacrifices, concubines, and servants were buried with him also. The relics are beautifully displayed, with English titles, at the actual site. Don't miss the video, in English, of the excavation. The museum is about half a block behind the China Hotel on Renmin Rd. towards the river. Tel. 6664920.

The **Guangdong Provincial Museum** 广东省博物馆 (Wenming Rd.; tel. 3332195) displays relics of local primitive society and is not as good generally as the Guangzhou Museum. The **Guangzhou Museum** 广州市博物馆 is in the **Zhenhai (Sea-dominating) Tower** in Yuexiu Park and is better organized (tel. 3330627). The original tower itself was built in 1380 to assert the power of the Ming dynasty. It was perhaps more impressive at the time. It has been rebuilt several times since then. Located at one of the highest points in the city, it has been used as a pleasure palace for high-ranking imperial officials and as a Nationalist hospital. Starting with prehistory, on the second floor, to revolutionary history, on the fifth, the exhibits include some interesting old clocks, ceramics, and a painting of the burning of the 20,000 chests of opium. For a city of this size and wealth, however, one would expect a better, larger museum, especially one about Overseas Chinese.

The **Zhen (Chen) Family Temple** 陈氏书院 (陈家祠)(7 Zhongshan Rd.; tel. 8841559, 8885259) is well worth a visit. It was built in the 1890s with nine halls and six courtyards of different sizes and has been used as a school. Its windows, doorframes, and pavilions are all lavishly decorated with intricate carvings and sculptures—almost too much for the mind to absorb at once. Take it in small doses. Because the army occupied these buildings during the Cultural Revolution, the artwork suffered very little damage. The Guangdong Folk Arts and Crafts Museum is located here now, and it is a good place to shop. Just don't let the bargains distract you from the ceramic opera scenes on the roofs and the charming carved mice eating the lichees on the pillars.

Shamian (Shamien, Shameen) Island 沙面 , in the Pearl River in central Guangzhou, became a British and French concession in 1859–60. It was then an 80-acre sandbank, later built into a European ghetto, much resented by the Chinese. The architecture reflects its European occupants, but, unfortunately, so many of the old buildings have been destroyed that its overall charm has almost disappeared. The island is joined to the mainland by bridges and now cars are allowed in certain areas. You can still find some of the old buildings, but it isn't the same as it was before the fancy **White Swan Hotel** was built in 1982. At the western tip of the island, this 31-story luxury hotel, built on reclaimed land, is among the top international-standard hotels in China.

The **Mausoleum of the Seventy-two Martyrs at Huanghuagang (Yellow Flower) Hill** 黄花岗七十二烈士墓 (Xianlie Rd.) is past the Garden Hotel and the Friendship Store on the road to the zoo. This commemorates an unsuccessful attempt to overthrow the Qing in 1911, led by Dr. Sun Yat-sen. Of special interest to visitors of Chinese ancestry, this 260,000-square-meter park was built with donations from Chinese

Nationalists' Leagues around the world. The stones in the main monument are inscribed in English with the names of the donors, among these Chicago, Illinois; Moose Jaw, Saskatchewan; and Lima, Peru. The miniature Statue of Liberty on top was replaced in 1987.

The **National Peasant Movement Institute** 广州农民运动讲习厅 (42 Zhongshan 4-Rd.; tel. 3331790) was a school for 327 peasant leaders from 20 provinces and regions. It was open only from May to September 1926 in an old temple. Mao Zedong was the director and Zhou Enlai a teacher.

The **Dr. Sun Yat-sen Memorial Hall** 中山纪念堂 (tel. 3332430, 333432). This is a theater seating over 4500, built in 1931 and expanded and renovated in 1975. This building is architecturally important because its huge hall is supported by four vertical concrete beams that branch out on top to form the octagonal roof. The modern technique and pure Chinese style, with its bright blue circus-tent-shaped ceramic roof, is unique. (For more on the life of Dr. Sun, see ''Nanjing.'')

The *****Guangxiao Temple** 光孝寺 (109 Sheshi Rd. and Guangxiao Rd.; tel. 3346775, 3333593) has the longest history in the city. It was founded on the site of the residence of the King of the Southern Yue Kingdom. The temple was built in A.D. 397 to commemorate the visit of the Indian monk Dharmayasas, and is the largest temple in South China. An iron pagoda dated A.D. 967 stands inside, historic, well preserved, but not beautiful. The present buildings are from the Five Dynasties to the Ming. The attractive Sixth Patriarch's Hair-burying Pagoda is a miniature of the Flower Pagoda. See also ''Shaoguan.''

The **Huaisheng (Remember the Sage) Mosque and Guangta (Smooth) Minaret** 光塔寺 (Guangta Lu; tel. 3331878, 3333593) is only of historical value. It is not the least bit attractive. Considered the oldest mosque in China, it was built in A.D. 627 by Arab traders. It is open daily. Visitors can climb its minaret, which has also been used as a lighthouse. The 26.3-meter minaret is said to be original. The tomb of the founding Moslem missionary, Sad Ibn Abu Waggas, is in the Orchid Garden.

The **Liu Rong (Six Banyan Trees) Temple** 六榕寺 (Liu Rong Rd.; tel. 3344926) was founded 1400 years ago. It was so named because the famous Tang poet Su Dong Po found six luxuriant banyan trees there in 1100. The present buildings were rebuilt in 1989. Its nine-story **Flower Pagoda** is 57.6 meters high and originally built in 537. It can be climbed for a good view and the exercise. Monks chant Tuesday and Friday mornings.

The **Shishi (Cathedral of the Sacred Heart)** 石室 (Yide Rd.; tel. 3336737, 8883724) was built in 1863–88. Its 57.95-meter Gothic spire was probably built deliberately taller than the pagoda nearby. Shishi means Stone House. It was closed as a church during the Cultural Revolution and used as a storehouse until 1979. Now it has been restored almost to its previous grandeur. Mass has been celebrated weekdays at 6 a.m. and Sundays and festivals at 6, 7:30, and 8:30 a.m. (See *Religion* in "Local Customs.")

The **South China Botanical Garden** (Guangzhou Botanical Garden) 华南植物园 (Longyandong, in the north of the city; tel. 7705626, 7705693) is a research institute of the Chinese Academy of Science. One of the world's largest botanical gardens, this 300-hectare garden is home to more than 2000 species of tropical and subtropical plants. Depending on the season, bring your own insect repellent. Ask about the Qinghua Garden in Shunde.

The **Orchid Garden** 兰圃 (Dabei Rd., west of Yuexiu Park and behind the Foreign Trade Center; tel. 6677255) is a delight for orchid lovers. It has over 100 species and 10,000 plants on five hectares.

The **Xi Yuan (West Garden)** 西园 (next to Dongfeng 1-Rd.; tel. 8889318, 8885867) specializes in *penjing*, miniature trees and landscapes, of the Lingnan School. 25,000 potted plants.

You can go directly to any of the **arts and crafts factories** and **Foshan.** See *Shopping* below. Crafts can also be seen at the Guangzhou Gold and Silver Jewelry Centre. Jewelry is a recently revived craft, having been discouraged since Liberation. The artisans are young. As with gems and jewelry everywhere, you have to know your products to get a good buy, but prices for small freshwater pearls seem to be good in Guangzhou.

The **Pearl River boat ride** 珠江游艇 with dinner can be arranged through hotels from April to October (7:30 p.m., 39 Pier, Xiti) but it needs work.

Guangzhou Zoo 广州动物园 (Xianli Rd.; tel. 7775574) is in the northeastern suburbs. It has 200 species, including pandas.

Yuexiu Park 越秀公园 (Jiefang Bei Rd., within walking distance of the China Hotel) is the largest in the city, on 92.8 hectares. There you can find the sculpture of the five goats, symbol of Guangzhou. **Liuhua Park** 流花公园 (Xicun Gong Rd.) was built in 1957–59; it is 800,400 square meters. Both parks are great for early-morning jogging.

Guangzhou Cultural Park 广州文化公园 (near the Nanfang Department Store on Xiti 2-Ma Rd.; tel. 8882488) covers 8.3 hectares. More pavement and less sylvan than other parks. Best avoided after 7 p.m. unless you want to see masses of people enjoying Chinese opera, puppet shows, acrobats, exhibit halls, basketball games, and roller-skating. The annual Lantern Festival and flower shows are held here.

A reproduction of a Han dynasty "city" has opened with wax figures in imperial period dress. (206 B.C. to 220 A.D.).

New areas being developed for tourism are Lotus Flower Hill (30 km. from Guangzhou), and the Yamen Fort (50 km. toward Hong Kong) and Dongguan, where Lin Zexu burned the opium. The **Huangpu Mil-**

itary Academy (1924) should be of interest to historians. Changzhou Island, Huangpu; tel. 4448083. The **Museum of Hong Xiuquan's Former Residence** (leader of the Taipings) is in Guanglubu Village, Huaxian County, 18 km from the city.

Another escape is a visit to a **village.** Many of the area villages grow and preserve fruit and olives for export, an interesting as well as delicious process to experience, as tourists are frequently given samples. Lucky are those who visit during the lichee season! (April to late June.)

Bicycles can be rented near the back door of the White Swan Hotel. The **English Corner** is on Shamian Island on Sundays and the Guangzhou Library on Zhongshan Rd. A golf course is due soon and the local Da Bei Disco offers an "English Night." Look on the apartment building bulletin boards at the China and Garden Hotels for announcements about the Hash House Harriers. The Holiday Inn City Center, China Hotel, and U.S. Consulate are TGIF hangouts for local expats.

Another favorite is Pimm's No. 1 Bar, across from the northeast corner of the Sun Yat-sen Hall at 21 Ying Yuan Rd. (tel. 3351247).

English-language interdenominational church services are held at the Garden Hotel.

Guangdong province has several other places to offer tourists, especially for those who do not want to travel too far from the Hong Kong border: golfing, mountains, rivers, tropics, national minorities, historical sites, arts and crafts and beaches. See also "Foshan," *Hong Kong* ("Getting There"), "Jiangmen," "Shantou," "Shaoguan," "Shenzhen," "Taishan," "Zhaoqing," "Zhongshan," and "Zhuhai."

FESTIVALS

Lunar second month, 10th to 13th day. Nanhai God Temple, Miaotou village, Huangpu. Tel. 7770927. Happy Festival with performing arts groups in autumn. Fine food festival during the autumn Trade Fair.

SHOPPING

Main shopping area around **Zhongshan 5-Road** 中山五路 and **Beijing Road** 北京路 . Locally made are carvings of ivory, jade, bamboo, and wood, painted porcelain (porcelain from Jingdezhen; handpainted here), and gold and silver jewelry. Shantou (Swatow) drawnworks and embroidery are famous, and are cheaper here.

Colored Painted Porcelain Factory 广州织金彩瓷工厂 (tel. 8881235, 8881919); **Daxin Ivory Carving Factory** 广州大新象牙工艺厂 (Tien Pin Zhar, Saho; tel. 7705556); **Daxin Ivory Carving Factory Sales Dept.** (415 Daxin Rd.; tel. 8882870); **Guangzhou Gold and Silver Jewelry Centre** 广州市金银首饰总汇 (199 Dade Rd.; tel.

3342320, 3337624). Export quality jewelry is at the **Guangdong Jewellery Import and Export Co.,** 54–58 Daxin, tel. 3336971. **Nanfang Jade Factory** a.k.a. Guangzhou South Jade Crafts Factory (15 Xiajiu Rd.; tel. 8889045, 8861040).

We haven't been able to check out any of these but for the serious adventurous shopper, there's the **Guangzhou Arts and Crafts Service Dept.,** 1/F, 59 Tai Nam Rd., tel. 3332258. It has showrooms around the city.

The **Chung Hwa Artiste-dress Factory** makes opera costumes, wedding dresses, etc., tel. 3330071. For the **Nan Fong Jade Carving Factory,** tel. 8887347, 8888040, the **Guangzhou Hand-painted Pottery and Porcelain Factory,** tel. 3330986; **Guangzhou Gold and Silver Wares Mfy.,** tel. 8883540, 8883993; **Guangzhou Palace Lamp Factory,** tel. 3334366, 3331735; **Hwa Nam Wood Carving Furniture Factory,** tel. 3330304; **Hung Mein Carving Factory** (screens, rosewood furniture, etc.), tel. 4447368; **Guangzhou Red Wood Furniture Manufacturing,** tel. 4447072.

Needless to say, you need someone who speaks Chinese to follow up on these leads, and some factories may be wholesale only. Do let us know how you make out.

One of the free markets here, the **Qing Ping Ziyou Shi Chang** 清平路自由市场 , has been selling antiques like old coins, water pipes, and old porcelain, with some reproductions. Qing Ping Free Market is also the largest herb market in the city (about five blocks), where you can find dehydrated lizards, snakes, plants, and weird-looking roots. Some live animals, too, including pangolins, an endangered species and civet cat. This market is not for the squeamish as they also have skinned barbecued dog dangling in the stalls. The market is not very clean, always crowded, but fascinating even if you don't want to buy anything. Within 20 minutes' walking distance of the White Swan Hotel, 6 a.m. to 6 p.m. As in all crowded places anywhere in the world, beware of pickpockets!

Huanghua Free Market and the **Xihu Night Market** are good for clothes, mainly T-shirts, jackets, and trousers. Prices for Hong Kong–made items can be about three to five times Hong Kong prices, so beware. Some locally made clothes, factory overruns, and seconds are reasonably priced here.

The Xihu market also has food stalls (mostly dirty and not well developed) but some foreigners love it. It is open to about midnight, and is near the White Swan and the Cultural Park.

China Hotel Friendship Store (Liuhua Rd.; tel. 6666888) is open 8:30 a.m.–9 p.m. Less crowded than the larger Friendship Store.

Friendship Store 友谊商店 (369 Huanshi Dong Rd.; tel. 3336628) is open 8:30 a.m.–9 p.m. Across from the Garden Hotel and next to the Baiyun. One of the largest in China; well stocked with goods from all over the country and especially Guangdong. It seems to cater more to local Chinese.

#Guangdong Cultural Relics Stores (696 Renmin Bei Rd., tel. 6678608. **Guangzhou Antique Store** 广州文物商店 (Wende Bei Rd.; tel. 3330175); **Guangzhou Porcelain and Pottery Shop** 广州陶瓷 (Zhongshan 5-Rd.; tel. 3330328); **Guangdong Arts and Crafts Service** 广东工艺美术服务部 33 (Dongshanshu Qian Rd.; tel. 7773606, 7766110); **Nanfang Dept. Store** 南方大厦商店 (49 Yanjiang Xi Rd.; tel. 8886022); **Yiyuan Art Shop** (Wende Rd.; tel. 3336497). Ask about the Xin Daxin Dept. Store.

Guangzhou Trade Fair is held annually from April 15 to April 29, and October 15 to October 29. Pickpockets as well as traders visit Guangzhou for the event, so be careful. One applies for an invitation through a Chinese corporation or the China Foreign Trade Center Group (117 Liu Hua Rd., 510014; fax 6665851). During the fair, you can buy a pass in its Dong Fang Hotel office. In the early 1990s, over 40,000 traders attended each fair.

RESTAURANTS

Guangzhou's **garden restaurants** are among the prettiest in China. The **Nanyuan** and **Beiyuan** are of traditional Qing dynasty China, small dining rooms surrounded by fish ponds, latticed windows, bamboo, and flowers. They rate a visit only for the Old China atmosphere. The **Banxi (Pan Hsi) Restaurant** is tops for food, specializing in *dim sum*. See "Food." A reservation here is mandatory for the fancy, private banquet rooms, especially the Reception Dining Hall with its traditional, redwood Chinese furniture and beautiful blue glass windows. This restaurant is set around a large pond and we found clean, yes, clean washrooms!

The restaurants in the top hotels are excellent, the Garden, China, Plaza, and White Swan for both Chinese and western food. The Baiyun and Dong Fang are good for Chinese. Try the "Drunken Prawns." Some opulent Hong Kong-style restaurants have also recently opened here. For lighter, cheaper food like noodles, congee, and dim sum, try China Hotel's **Food Street,** Garden Hotel's **Lai Wan Market,** Holiday Inn C.C.'s **Dai Pai Dong Food Alley,** and the Chinese restaurants in the Dong Fang.

Local foreign residents have mentioned the excellent Vietnamese restaurant across from the main entrance of the Banxi Restaurant, the **Hua Bei Restaurant** (corner Zhong Shan Wu and Jiefang rds.) for northern dumplings, and the Garden Hotel has a great **Pizzeria.** They also talk about the Japanese restaurant in the Equatorial Hotel, and the **Xin Yuan Garden Restaurant** on Jiefang Rd. (Cantonese). They liked the Canadian J.V. snack bar **Timmy's,** downriver from the Nanfang Dept. Store.

Guangzhou Restaurant 广州酒家 • *2 Wenchang Nanlu; tel. 8887136, 8884339* • One of the best, but very noisy. A little grubby and no parking. Huge, fancy branch across the river from the White Swan Hotel.

Nanyuan Restaurant 南园酒家 • *120, Qianjin Rd. (south bank of Pearl River); tel. 4449979* • One of the garden restaurants. A little far from the center of things.

Banxi (Pan Hsi) Restaurant 泮溪酒家 • *151, Long Jin Xi Rd. W.; tel. 8815718, 8889318* • Specializes in Dim Sum pastries.

HOTELS

The top international class luxury hotels here are still the Garden, China, and White Swan, with the Ramada a strong contender. Also good are the Dong Fang, Holiy Inn, and Plaza Canton (after renovations). The Landmark should be up there too. The Parkview has big suites for the price of rooms but lacks some services and looks a mite grubby. The Holiday Inn had the widest twin beds.

For the Trade Fair, the best location is across the street at the Dong Fang, China, or Equatorial. The Liu Hua and Parkview are not much farther away. This area is also the best for tourists. It is within walking distance of two big parks, the Orchid Garden, the Han Museum, the Six Banyan Tree Temple and pagoda, China Hotel Friendship Store, Zhenhai Tower (museum), C.A.A.C., C.I.T.S., and the main railway station.

The next best area for all visitors is about three kilometers east. Here are the Garden, Holiday Inn City Centre, Bai Yun Hotels, the new GITIC Hotel, the Friendship Store, and the Guangzhou World Trade Centre. The zoo is nearby.

The White Swan Hotel is relatively isolated on a historic island, but an elevated highway means only a 15-minute drive to the Trade Fair. It has the U.S. Consulate, and one can walk to the exotic Qingping Market. Also on the island are the cheaper Victory Hotel and a youth hostel.

Within steps of the Pearl River Bridge downtown are the Guangzhou and Landmark close to C.T.S., and shopping. The Ramada is in a less crowded area, far from anything but the river. It is the closest joint venture to the Tianhe railway station. The Plaza Canton is the only major hotel south of the river, 2.5 km from Zhoutouzui.

The White Swan has the most beautiful lobby. Its bar and coffee shop have the best view of the Pearl River, but the Ramada view includes a pagoda and the river. The Garden's lobby is the most elegant and the China Hotel has great Cantonese food. For the best gawdy Chinese atmosphere and good, relatively inexpensive food, there's the Dong Fang.

But its lower standard of English and service keep it from the top. Most big hotels here can receive English-language television from Hong Kong. All outdoor pools close in November for the winter.

Bai Yun Hotel (Binguan) • *367 Huanshi Dong Rd. 510060. 3*. Telex 44327 BYHTL CN. Fax 336498. Dist.A.P. 6 km. Dist.R.W. 4 km. Next to Friendship Store* • C.C. 1975; ren. 1990. 34 stories. Over 700 large rooms. 28th floor best. Film processing.

China Hotel (Zhong Guo Da Jiu Dian) • *Liu Hua Rd. 510015. 5*. Telex 44888 CHLGZ CN. Fax 6677014. Dist.A.P. 5 km. Dist.R.W. 1 km.* • During trade fair, deposit required for reservation. C.C. 1983; ren. 1990. 18 stories. 1200 spacious rooms. Executive floors. Shopping. Bank of China. B.C. Gym. Deli. Tennis. Bowling. Outdoor pool. Reservations through UTELL. Managed by New World Hotels.

Dong Fang Hotel (Dong Fang Binguan) • *120 Liu Hua Rd. 510016. 5*. Telex 44439 GZDFH CN. Fax 6662775. Dist.A.P. 5 km. Dist.R.W. 1 km* • 1961; ren. 1990, 1992. 7 stories. 1300 rooms. Charming but not classy. Karaoke. Beautiful Chinese garden. Photofinishing. Bowling. Golf putting range. Clinic. Tennis. Pool. Old wing larger rooms, high ceilings. C.I.T.S, H.K.T.V. AT&T. Thai, Japanese, and Indonesian food. Book through UTELL.

Garden Hotel (Huayuan Jiu Dian) • *368 Huanshi Dong Rd. 510064. 5*. Telex 44788 GDHTL CN. Fax 3350467. Dist.A.P. 6 km. Dist.R.W. 4 km.* • C.C. Telex reservation accepted during trade fair only with deposit. 1984–85. Currently renovating floor by floor. 30 stories. 1100 rooms. Clinic. B.C. Tennis. Outdoor pool. Non-smoking floor. Executive floors. Office tower. SIA. Five rooms for wheelchair travelers. Very fancy karaoke. Coffee house. Red Flag limousines. AT&T. Malaysian, Garuda, and SIA airlines. International school. Managed by Lee Garden.

Guangdong Victory (Shengli Binguan) • *54 Shamian St. 510130. 3*. (Shamian Island). Telex 441163. Fax 8862413* • C.C. In charming European building from last century. Became hotel in 1950s. Ren. 1989. 117 rooms. Dirty carpets and windows. Cracked dishes. Gym. B.C. Budget and romantic travelers only.

Guangzhou Hotel (Binguan) • *Hai Zhu Sq. 510115. 3*. Telex 44336 KCHTL CN. Fax 3330179. Dist.A.P. 9 km. Dist.R.W. 5 km* • C.C. 1968; ren. 1992. 27 stories. 441 rooms. B.C. and Karaoke bar soon. Poor reading lights and English. Bit musty. Little space for parking. Otherwise adequate, especially the 14th to 23rd floors. During trade fair, mainly Japanese traders stay here. English poor. AT&T.

Holiday Inn City Centre (Jia Re Wen Hua Jiu Dian) • *Huan Shi Dong Rd., 28 Guangmin Rd., Overseas Chinese Village 510060. 4*. Telex 441045 HICCG CN. Fax 7753126. During Trade Fair prefers deposit. Dist.A.P. 12 km. Dist.R.W. 4 km.* • C.C. 1989–90. 24 stories. 431 rooms. H.K.T.V. Exhibition center, gym, B.C., outdoor pool, 500-seat cinema. Bicycles. Two rooms for wheelchair travelers. Executive floor. Free shuttle bus. AT&T.

Holiday Inn Riverside • *Bin Jiang Xi Rd., 2–6 Hong De Rd. (510235.) Dist. R.W. 6.5 km* • 1993. 27 stories. 335 rooms.

Hotel Equatorial (Guidu Jiu Dian) • *931 Renmin Rd. 510010 Fax 6672583, 6672582. Telex 441168 EQUAT CN. Dist.A.P. 4.5 km. Dist.R.W.* • 1989–90. 310 rooms. Steamboat. Japanese, French and restaurants. Deli. B.C. Gym. Pool. Singapore J.V. English needs work.

Hotel Landmark Canton (Huaxia Dajiudian) • *Qiao Guang Rd. 510115. Aiming at 4*. Telex 441288 HLC CN. Dist.A.P. 10 km. Dist.R.W. 4 km. Beside Pearl River bridge* • C.C. 1991–92. 39 stories. 900 rooms. Hairdryers. Business studios. B.C. Gym. Helipad. Pool. Tennis. Karaoke. Chaozhou food. 1992–93. Renovating adjacent O. C. Mansion. Managed by C.T.S. Macao.

Liu Hua Hotel (Binguan) • *194 Huanshi Xi Rd. 510010. 3*. Telex 44298 GZLHH CN. Fax 667828. Dist.A.P. 4 km. Dist.R.W. 300 m. Near post office, CAAC, CITS* • C.C. 1972. 7 stories. 720 rooms. North bldg. ren. 1989. Spacious rooms. Rest looks grubby. Service and English poor. Chipped dishes. B.C. Shanghai Airlines. No USTV. Budget travelers only.

Parkview Square (Tian An Da Sha) • *960 Jie Fang Bei Rd. 510030. 3*. Fax 6671741. Dist.A.P. 6 km. Dist.R.W. 2 km. Next to park and across from Han museum* • C.C. 1989–90. Ren. 1992. 10 and 12 stories. 176 apartments only. Kitchenettes supplied for long-term guests only. Executive club. Gym, saunas. B.C. Food St. Chaozhou and Taiwan food. H.K. management.

Plaza Canton (Jiangnan Dajiudian) • *348 Jiang Nan Da Rd. C. 510245. 4*. Telex 441032 PLZCT. CN. Fax 4429645. 3 km south of Pearl River Bridge in residential area. Dist.A.P. 15 km. Dist.R.W. 9 km. Close to Zhong Shan University* • C.C. 1988–89. 28 stories. 450 rooms. French cuisine. B.C. Gym. Tennis. Outdoor pool. Owned by local farmers and managed by Traditional Investment Corp. (formerly Novotel).

Ramada Pearl Hotel (Ra Mai Da) • *9 Min Yue Yi Rd., Dong Shan Dist. 510600. Aiming for 5*. Fax 7767481. On 150 m. of waterfront. Dist. R.W. Tianhe 3 km. Dist.A.P. 14 km. Near Hai Yin No. 3 Bridge* • C.C. 1992. 25 stories. 400 rooms. Non-smoking floors. Gym. Shuttle bus. Golf-driving range. Squash, tennis, bowling, B.C. Office tower and apartments. Boating. Fishing. Indoor and outdoor pools. Hair dryers. Executive floor. Asian buffet.

White Swan Hotel (Baitian E Binguan) • *Shamian Island 510133. 5*. Telex 44688 WSH CN. Fax 8861188. Dist.A.P. 11 km. Dist.R.W. 7 km* • Member Leading Hotels of the World. C.C. H.K.J.V. 1982–83; part ren. 1988. 28 stories. 834 spacious rooms. B.C. Gym. Tennis. Squash. Pool. Rolls Royces. Grill Room. Japanese food. Good stores. Executive floor. AT&T. U.S. Consultate.

OTHER IMPORTANT ADDRESSES
Bank of China, Guangzhou Branch 中国银行 : 197 Dong Feng Xi Rd.; tel. 3338080. Branch in China Hotel.
C.I.T.S. 中国国际旅行社 : Open daily 8:30–12; 2 to 5 p.m. 179 Huanshi Rd. (next to main railway station); tel. 6678356. For tickets, tours and other services, office in Dong Fang Hotel, Room 2366, tel. 6669900 X 2366, 662427. Telex 44450 CITS CN. Fax 6678356.
C.T.S. 中国旅行社 : 2 Qiaoguang Rd. 510015 (Haizhu Square next to Huaqiao Mansion); tel. 2222811, 3336888. Telex 44217 CTS CN. Fax 3332247 or 472 Dongfeng Dong Rd. 510060; tel. 3339965.
CYTS: tel. 7773471, 7760105.
CAAC: Next to main railway station; tel. 6661803 (int.), 6662969. (dom.) Booking offices at the China, Dong Fang, Liu Hua, Overseas Chinese, White Swan, and Yuxin hotels.
   Airport Service Desk, Departure Lounge: tel. 6678901.
   Baiyun Airport: tel. 6678901, 6666123.
   Domestic inquiries: tel. 6662969.
   International inquiries: tel. 6661803.
Foreign Trade Center 外贸中心 : 117 Liuhua Rd.; tel. 6677000, 6661799. Shopping, supermarket, restaurants, Bank of China, bookstore.
Guangdong Provincial Travel & Tourism Bureau: 185 Huanshi Xi Rd., 510010; tel. 6677426, 6677410. Fax 6665039. Ask for list of stores, restaurants and hotels approved for foreign tourists. Contact Business Management Dept., tel. 6677422, with complaints and suggestions.
Hospitals (Clinics in Garden and Dong Fang Hotels.)

Guangdong People's Hospital 广东人民医院 : Zhongshan 2-Rd.; tel. 8885119, 7777812, 8884713.

Guangzhou First People's Hospital 广州第一人民医院 : Panfu Rd., 602 N. Renmin Rd. 333090; tel. 8886421. Use if you are near the Dong Fang. Entrance at rear to Pan Song Lou open 6 a.m. to 11 p.m. Use main gate 11 p.m. to 6 a.m.

The First Hospital Attached to Zhongshan Medical College 学院第一附属医院 : Zhongshan 2-Rd.; tel. 7778223, 7778314.

The Second Hospital Attached to Zhongshan Medical College 医学院第二附属医院 : Yanjiang 1-Rd.; tel. 8882102.

Japanese Consulate: Garden Hotel; tel. 3338999.

Malaysian Airlines, Garden Hotel, tel. 3358828, 3358838.

Passenger Pier for Hong Kong, Zhoutouzui 洲头咀客运码头（往香港）: tel. 4448218.

Railway Station 火车站 : tel. 7777112, 6661789.

Singapore Airlines: Garden Hotel, tel. 3338989 X1056.

Tourism Hotline: tel. 6677422.

U.S. Consulate 澳洲航空公司 : White Swan Hotel. U.S. Citizens Services: tel. 8882222.

USIA tel. 3354269.

GUILIN

(Kweilin; City of Cassia Trees) South China. In northern Guangxi, the first "province" west of Guangdong. 55-minute flight NW of Guangzhou and from 11 Chinese cities. Direct regular charter flights from Hong Kong. Guilin is connected by tourist train with Guangzhou (15 hours) by rail to Beijing, Kunming, Shanghai, Zhanjiang, and Nanning, and by bus to Wuzhou (boat to Guangzhou and Hong Kong). The weather is subtropical. Hottest—34°C in August; coldest—⁻3°C. Rainy season—February–May. Annual precipitation—1900 mm. The best time to visit is autumn, or late spring, when it is warm enough to ignore the rain. The scenery is best seen in the mist, which inspired centuries of landscape painters, or when the sun and clouds conspire to give you constantly changing pictures. From November until the February rains, the water in the river may be low. It has been dredged, and with a reservoir controlling the flow, boats should be able to use it year-round. Electricity shortages are severe here. Make sure your hotel has its own generator before you go in summer. Population is 400,000, 8% of whom are dependent on tourism.

Founded in 214 B.C., this prefecture is famous for its vertical limestone mountains rising above tree-lined streets, rice fields, and the meandering Li and Taohua (Peach Blossom) rivers. It is also known for its caves.

Guilin developed with the opening of the Ling Canal in 214 B.C. It was the provincial capital until 1014, and a command post for the Northern Expedition in 1926. During the Japanese war almost all of the city was destroyed, the Seven Star Cave alone sheltering 5000 refugees. Because about one third of the 10 million people living in the province are of Zhuang nationality, Guangxi is an "autonomous region" rather than a "province." National guides may not understand the local dialect.

The city itself, a favorite of honeymooners, is small, full of parks, and ideal for walking. The ground is level except for the sporadic mountains, each of which has a bright-red pavilion complementing nature, an invitation to climb.

You will want to spend a minimum of two days; three would be better. Guilin is one of the 24 historical cities protected by the State Council. Some of its houses are antiques and one should stroll through the past at leisure. Many tame mountains beckon climbers.

For those in a hurry, one morning could be spent at Diecai Hill, Fubo Hill, and Seven Star Park, and the afternoon at Reed Flute Cave and Elephant Hill. The Li River boat trip could be enjoyed on a second day or vice versa. The Ming tomb museum, the Guilin Museum (at Xishan Park), Gao Shan, a handicraft factory, shopping, just walking or cycling or the Ling Canal can fill up your third day.

Diecai (Folded Brocade) Hill 叠彩山 (3.6 km from the Sheraton Hotel) is the tallest in town at 73 meters. The peaks are named Bright Moon, Crane, and Seeing Around the Hill. Partway up past the ornamental arch is the Wind Cave with Ming and Tang poems and memorials on its walls. A good view of the area can be seen from the top.

Fubo (Whirlpool) Hill 伏波山 (2.8 km from the Sheraton Hotel), named after famous Han Marshal Ma Fubo, is 60 meters high. At the base is a 7½-ton iron Qing bell belonging to the temple originally here. To the right is the Cave of the Returned Pearl, where guides might tell you a dragon left a gift of a pearl for a poor family, who returned it: "This illustrates the honesty of working people." Nearby is a rock where Ma Fubo tested his sword, and a cliff with Tang buddhas. Partway up on the right is a pavilion with a view of the river.

Qixing (Seven Star) Park 七星岩 (2.7 km from the Sheraton Hotel) is about 10 square km. It contains a zoo, Camel Hill, and Seven Star Hill, its seven peaks positioned like the stars in the Big Dipper. With lots to see, you may want to return for a more leisurely look. Just think, you will be following in the footsteps of tourists from the Sui (581–618) dynasty! Seven Star Cave, on the west side of Potaraka

Hill, has three levels; visitors enter the middle one. It is bigger than Reed Flute Cave, 1 km long, 43 meters at its widest, and 27 meters at its highest. Colored lights highlight the grotesque limestone formations.

A forest of cassia trees blossom in spring and a 700-year-old stone replica of the Flower Bridge (Song) spans a stream. Originally built of wood but destroyed in a flood, the bridge was designed so that the water below reflects its arches to form a complete circle.

The "Cave for Hiding a Dragon" 龙隐洞 does look like it could snugly fit a dinosaur. The most famous of the stone Song steles nearby lists people meant for execution. The emperor sent copies around China (although paper was invented by then) and when the verdict was reversed, all but the stele in Guilin were destroyed.

Also on the west side of Putuo (Potaraka) Hill is the Yuanfeng (Deep and Windy) Cave, and on top, the Putuo (Potaraka) Temple (good view) and Guanyin cave.

Ludi (Reed Flute) Cave 芦笛岩 is 8–9 km from the Sheraton Hotel. One km long, this cave takes about 40 minutes to see. The temperature inside is a cool 20°C. The lighting is cleverly placed so that with a bit of imagination, the limestone formations resemble a giant goldfish, a Buddha, a wall of assorted vegetables, etc. The cave is named after the reeds that grow at the entrance.

Xiangbi (Elephant Trunk) Hill 象鼻山 (1.4 km from the Sheraton Hotel), located at the junction of the Li and Yang rivers, really does look like an elephant drinking. Shuiyue (Moon-in-Water) Cave is between the trunk and front legs. Elephant Eye Cave is where you would expect. The Samantabhadra Pagoda tops the hill.

The **Li River boat trip** is the other outstanding attraction in the area. Book with a travel agent or your hotel. The price is about the same. If you want to try for a cheaper trip, you could shop around for boats for Chinese tourists, which leave near the Sheraton. Be aware that the guides here speak only Chinese, the boats are not as clean, and there is no air conditioning.

Boats with air conditioning for foreigners leave from Zhu Jiang wharf, about 20 km. from the city. The ride from there to Yangshuo is 59 km. in 4 hours. Prices usually include lunch and the bus back to Guilin. If one has several friends to share a taxi, boat tours for individual travelers might be cheaper bought at Zhu Jiang than at a hotel. (Information from Guilin Tourism Motor Boat Co., 3 Fuxing Rd., tel. 445595, 443306.) Some people stay in Yangshuo to bicycle, but the hotels there aren't very good. The tour south to Yangshuo usually returns by land about mid-afternoon. The Li River, normally 50–100 meters wide, winds its way between some incredible rock formations, the highest about 80 meters. Pollution control has been upgraded on the river, but one still sees dishes being washed in the river.

Look for Crown Cave (shaped like the British imperial crown), a cock with tail up bending down to pick up rice, followed shortly by the U-shaped Ram's Hoof Mountain on the right. On the right is Conch Shell Hill, then a temple on a cliff.

On the way, look for large cormorants (real birds, not stone), usually seen sitting on fishing boats. If you're lucky you might even see them at work, fishing on behalf of people. You might want to also ask about a special tour to see the cormorants fishing at night.

A variation is a **two-day cruise** with stops at Daxu village, cave and minority cultural center. Overnight camping at Xinping in tents or simple hotel.

Yangshuo 阳朔 , the tiny town at the end of the boat ride, has a park, museum, good shopping, and an old temple. If time allows, you might be able to walk along the main street to the right of the landing. Behind Green Lotus Peak on the left of the landing is Jian (Mirror) Hill, so named because some of its cliffs are smooth. The museum is of the famous painter of galloping horses and Li River scenes, Xu Beihong, who lived there between 1935 and 1938. Several cruddy hotels are available if you want to stay overnight and bike, hike or rent a canoe (from Owen at the restaurant at Xi Jie 26). You can take the bus back the next day. The best is the (ugh!) Yangshuo Hotel.

Duxiu (Unique Beauty) Park was the site of the 1393-built mansion of Zhu Shouqian, grandson of Emperor Hongwu of the Ming. Destroyed during the Qing, and again during the Japanese war, it is now the site of the teachers' college. Today, only the original wall, its gates, and the steps remain.

Recently opened is the **Jingjiang Ming Tombs,** a good place to bicycle to. You pass old villages, water buffalo herds, mountains, and several intriguing Ming cemeteries, a total of 320 tombs in 100 sq. km. All persons buried there are descendants of the Ming emperor's family. A museum and several guardian statues of animals, servants and officials are at the unexcavated tumulus of the grandson Zhu Shou Qian Chi of the dynasty founder's older brother, who died in 1370 A.D. Much smaller and less elaborate than Ming tombs near Beijing, but worth a visit if you have the time. Open daily 9 a.m. to 5 p.m. The tombs are on the way to **Yao Shan (Broadcast Mountain),** which is 300 m. high with a road to the top. Nothing more than good views.

Lingqu (Ling Canal) dug in 214 B.C. to connect the Chang (Yangtze) and the Zhu (Pearl) rivers, is also of importance, an inland route to Guangzhou. It was a waterway until the 1930s and is still used for agricultural irrigation. It may be of interest to engineers and history fans. It has 18 locks and sections, and still can be seen starting about 66 km north of Guilin at **Xing'an County.** Ask about the Cassia Festival in March.

SHOPPING

Here you can buy locally grown oranges, pomelo, and mangosteens (luohan guo). Artistic pottery factory.

Guilin also produces bamboo and new and old-style wood carvings, woven and plated bamboo, dough figures, tablecloths, embroidery, down jackets, and batik. The main shopping area is along **Zhongshan Zhong Rd.**, where you will find the Guilin Department Store (open 9 a.m.–9 p.m.) and the **Arts and Crafts Center** at #109 (tel. 222116).

I haggled down the **Guilin Antique Store** (at 2 Shabu Bei Rd., tel. 228172) from ¥150 to ¥75 on one item and then found the same at Y35 at a market (without the red seal and customs certificate). The night market between the Universal and Sheraton has 100 stalls.

The best shopping is in Yangshuo for cheaper "antiques." There is no time between the boat and the bus to compare, dicker, and be invited into homes. You usually get about 20 minutes. Serious shoppers should give themselves two hours. Avoid ethnic earrings because they have big stems requiring big ear holes. The "silver" bells are great.

RESTAURANTS

Hotel restaurants are cleaner with better ambiance. Many hotels have Hong Kong chefs. We found the food particularly good at the Sheraton and the Holiday Inn.

Chinese food here is usually Guangxi or Guangdong (Cantonese). Food is served with chili sauce and fermented bean curd as condiments. You should like the beancurd if you like blue cheese. Mix a bit with your rice. The local rice wine, Sanhua, is made from a 200-year-old recipe. If you're desperate to try a local restaurant (not yet approved by the tourist office), there's Kowloon near the Osmanthus Hotel.

HOTELS

The top hotels here give good service. The best is the Sheraton, then the Holiday Inn, Royal Garden, and Gui Shan. The Garden is the most beautiful. The less luxurious Universal was also good, especially for its location and Cantonese food. The Plaza looked good. The Royal Garden and Holiday Inn had the widest twin beds.

The best located for tourists and business people were the Holiday Inn and the Ronghu on a lake, within walking distance of C.I.T.S., city hall, and tourist shopping. On the west bank of the Li River, also relatively central to these, are the Lijiang, Sheraton, and Universal. On the east bank are the Garden and the Gui Shan, less convenient for shops.

The Windsor Seven Star and Plaza are neighbors near the International Exhibition Centre one km from the river on the east side of town, nowhere near good shopping. The Garland is across from the railway station. The Park is pretty, but less conveniently located in the suburbs. The Hubin, Guilin, and Taihu are for backpackers.

Gui Shan Hotel (Guishan Dajiudian) • *Chuan Shan Rd. 541004. 4*. Telex 48443 GSHTL CN. Fax 444851. Suburban setting between two rivers, near Seven Star Park. Dist. A. P. 15 km. Dist. R. W. 5 km* • C.C. 1988. Ren. one building 1991. Attractive garden architecture. 5 stories, 4 connecting buildings. Could be long walk. 607 rooms. IDD. B.C. Outdoor pool. Gym. Bowling. Clinic. Bicycles. Tennis planned. Lots of shops. Managed by New World Hotels International.

Guilin Garland Hotel (Kaiyue Fandian) • *86 Zhongshan Nan Rd. 541002. 2*. Telex 48438 GLGAR CN* • Grubby. Expecting to renovate 1992. 15 stories, 300 rooms. B.C. Soft beds. Golden Mile Hotels management. Budget travelers only.

Guilin Park Hotel (Gui Hu Jiu Dian) • *No. 1, Luosi Hill, Laoren Shan Qian, 541001. 3* Telex 48498 GLPKH CN. Fax 222296. By Gui Lake next to Lao Ren Hill* • C.C. 1990. 5 stories, 270 rooms. USTV. Gym. Outdoor pool. Dim sum. Managed by Vista International.

Guilin Plaza • *20 Li Jiang Rd. 541004. 3* Telex 48449 PLAZA CN. Fax 443323. Dist. A. P. 15 km. Dist. R. W. 5 km. Dist. Zhishan Bridge 1 km* • C.C. (no Diners). Formerly Novotel. 1989–90. 13 stories, 300 rooms. B.C. services at front desk. IDD. Japanese and European food. Bicycles. Will have two rooms for wheelchair travellers. USTV. Pool. Sauna.

Guilin Royal Garden Hotel (Di Yuan Jiudian) • *Yanjiang Rd., 541004. 4*. Telex 48446 GLGDN CN. Fax 445051. Dist. A. P. 17 km. Dist. R. W. 6 km* • 1987, ren. 1989. Formerly Ramada. 7 stories, 335 spacious rooms, but smallish bathrooms. Good furniture and decor. Huge atrium garden coffee shop with nightly "national minorities" dance show. Rooms could be a long walk from elevators. Hairdryers. Outdoor pool. (8 a.m.–8 p.m.) B.C. IDD. Tennis. Japanese food. No ticketing service. Has packing service. 2 deluxe boats. Store with interesting minority crafts. Management consultant Dai Toh Corp. (Japan).

Holiday Inn Guilin (Jia Ru Binguan) • *14 Ronghu Nan Rd. 541002. 4*. Telex 48456 GLHCL CN. Fax 222101. Dist. A. P. 14 km. Dist. R. W. 3.5 km* • C.C. 1987. 9 stories, 259 rooms. Emergency flashlights. Small, intimate atmosphere. IDD. Cathedral ceiling and balconies in top-floor rooms. USTV. Bicycles. Can cater sunrise or sunset meals on nearby Broadcast Hill or on boat. Gym. Outdoor pool, B.C. Bake shop outside.

Hotel Universal Guilin (Huan Qiu Dajiudian) • *1 Jiefang Dong Rd., 541001. 3* Telex 48475 LHU CN. Fax 223868. Closest to Liberation Bridge. Dist. A. P. 14 km. Dist. R. W. 7 km* • C.C. 1989–90. 7 stories, 229 rooms. IDD. Dim sum. B.C. Italian restaurant. No ticketing service. Macau C.T.S. management. Suite 519 has great view.

Li River Hotel (Li Jiang Fandian) • *1 Shanhu Bei Road, 541001. 3** • Dark, dismal, and dirty.

Osmanthus Hotel (Dangui Fandian) • *451 Zhong Nan Shan Rd. 541002. Telex 48455 GLOSH CN. Fax 335316. Dist. A. P. 14 km. Dist. R. W. 1 km* • C.C. 1986 west wing, 14 stories, 214 rooms. IDD. B.C. Bicycles. Even-numbered rooms have river view. Little rundown. Soft beds. Pool.

Ronghu Hotel (Fandian) • *17 Ronghu Bei Rd. 541001. #5 and 6. 3*. Telex 48483 GLRHU CN. Fax 225390. Dist.A. P. 15 km. Dist. R. W. 4 km* • 8 buildings on large hilly grounds, total 488 rooms. #5 is 1986 Hong Kong J.V. Wintersweet Village. Rooms smaller than in #6. Beds a little soft. IDD. Japanese restaurant. B.C. #6, 1990. 200 rooms, B.C., and gym.

Other buildings are older, with high ceilings and old-fashioned decor but look clean. They are not as conveniently located. All poorly maintained.

Sheraton Guilin (Si Lai Deng Fandian) • *Bing Jiang Nan Rd. 541001. 4*. Telex 48439 GLMAN CN. Fax 225598. Dist. A. P. 20 km. Dist. R. W. 5 km* • C.C. 1989–91. Ren. 1991. 6 stories. 490 large rooms. USTV. IDD. B.C. services at front desk. CITS. Dragonair. Gym. Indoor pool. Beautiful atrium lobby. Garden with waterfall.

Windsor Seven Stars (Xing Jiudian) • *9 Lijiang Dong Rd. 541004. Next to parent Pine Garden Resort across from Plaza. 3*. Telex 48447 GLPGR CN. Fax 445893. Dist. A. P. 15 km. Dist. R. W. 5 km. Near Pagoda Hill and 7-Star Park in future downtown center* • C.C. 1990. 7 stories, 201 rooms. IDD. B.C. Bicycles. Pool. Shuttle bus. USTV. Gym due soon. Planning Moslem restaurant. Managed by Windsor Hotels International (H.K.)

OTHER IMPORTANT ADDRESSES
Telephone numbers are changing.
Guilin Airport 桂林机场 : tel. 332741.
CAAC 中国民航 : 141 Zhongshan Zhong Rd., tel. 233063.
C.I.T.S. 中国国际旅行社 : 14 Ronghu Bei Rd., 541001. tel. 233063, 225714. Fax 222936, 227205. Telex 48460 GLITS CN.

C.T.S. 中国旅行社 : 29 Xinyi Rd. 541002; tel. 226236; fax 226237. Telex 48472 GLERA CN.
CYTS: tel. 442366.
Dragonair: Sheraton, tel. 225588. Fax 225598.
Guilin Municipal Tourism Bureau Inspection Station., 14 North Ronghu Rd., 541001. Tel. 227191 (for compliments and complaints).
Guilin Overseas Tourist Corp., 14 North Ronghu Rd., 541001. Tel. 224214, 226234, 226232. Telex 48471 GLMTB CN. Fax 226230.
Ambulance: tel. 120.
Police tel. 110.
Railway Station三轮车站: Zhongshan Nan Rd.; tel. 333124.
Tourism Hotline: 226533, 227191.

GUIYANG 贵阳

Southwest China, in the central part of Guizhou province, of which it is the capital. It is joined by air with 15 Chinese cities and by charter flight with Hong Kong. It is also at the hub of railway lines with Chengdu, Nanning, Kunming, and Changsha. It has an altitude of 1070 meters. The western and central part of the province has an altitude of 1–2000 meters. The terrain is rugged, with karst formations, underground rivers, jagged peaks, dramatic valleys, and terraced rice fields. The annual precipitation is 900–1500 mm. The province is rich in minerals—aluminum, coal, iron, lead, gold, silver, zinc, etc. It has China's largest mercury deposit. It grows rice, corn, tobacco, cork, raw lacquer, and timber. The coldest in January averages 4.6°C. The warmest is June, with 24°C average. We suggest visiting in April because of the festivals, the terraces of golden rape, and spring weather. Guiyang's urban population is 800,000.

This area has been a part of recorded history since the Shang dynasty, about 3000 years ago. Today, out of a total population of 30 million, 26% are minorities: Miao, Buyei, Dong, Yi, Shui, Hui, Gelo, Zhuang, Yao. They contribute to the fascinating architecture and the over 100 lively festivals a year, many unlike those in other parts of China. These include bull fights, dragon boats, horse races, and Lusheng dancing.

Because this province has only recently been opened to tourists, people looking for the unusual will find it here but don't expect private baths and hot water everywhere. You'll be lucky to get a clean hotel room outside of Guiyang. New hotels are currently being built.

We found villages untouched by tourists, warm hospitality, a brilliant bouquet of ethnic clothing, elaborate welcoming ceremonies, totem worship, a coffin on a back porch to make its future inhabitant happy, and intriguing music. Miao music reflects their mountain home. We suggest you bring a tape recorder as well as lots of film.

Guiyang has karst caves, wild monkeys, some temples, a colorful Sunday market, and visits to Han-ized Buyei and Miao villages. It is a rundown city, dirtied by coal dust. But the province has a bird sanctuary, hiking, and mountain scenery.

The only real tourist attraction in the province besides the colorful minorities is **Huangguoshu Falls,** China's biggest waterfall. This is best seen after the rains from July to early October, when it is 76 m wide and 84 m high. In April, it is a trickle. This tourist area is reached from Anshun, southwest of Guizhou, by a 1½-hour tourist train twice a day. Public tour buses are at the Anshun station.

The falls are near Zhenning, 50 km from Anshun, and one can walk into the caves behind them. They are not as impressive as Niagara Falls, but are not as commercialized. A trip here can be combined with the Black Dragon Cave (840 m, relaxing boat trip inside; tel. [853] 23969 or 22615). Some world-class views of the countryside nearby.

Among the minorities near Anshun are the Old Han, whose ancestors were sent by the Qing to fight a Miao rebellion in the 18th century. They won and to this day, their lifestyle and clothing have not changed. About 2000 of them seem to live in a time warp. Also in the area are a batik factory and Chaiguan Village, with its masked peasant opera.

The Miao and Dong Autonomous prefecture is 300 km east of Anshun, in the southeastern part of the province. At **Kaili** 196 km. east of Guiyang, you will see women laden with silver jewelry and hear the unique Miao antiphonal courtship singing. The people here have not been Han-ized and retain most of their unique customs. **The Museum of National Minorities** is new, lacks titles in English and is opened only on request. Taijiang, 50 km. from Kaili is the center of the Miao culture, the source of the best embroidery. Dong architecture is unusual; their drum towers especially are a charming mixture of Chinese pagoda styles with flaming eaves.

The **Museum of Minority Festivals** is in Huangpin County, about 190 km east of Guiyang. **The Museum of Minority Architecture** (models) is in Zhenyuan, 270 km southeast of Guiyang. **The Museum on Marriage Customs** is in Xinyi, 400 km southwest of Guiyang. The last is the best of the three.

SHOPPING

Made in the province are embroidered vests, silver Miao jewelry, bamboo flutes, lacquerware, and batik (best in Anshun). The hotel in Kaili had a good selection of Miao handicrafts. Also produced here are Maotai (the most famous and most potent Chinese liquor), pears, oranges, kiwi fruit, and tangerines.

FOOD

Local food is frequently chili hot, but you can get a bland cook-for-yourself hot pot. Dog is a favorite, and sweet potatoes a staple. Please note that the giant salamander, a favorite of the Chinese gourmet, is an endangered species. Roasted bean curd and roasted corn are famous local snack foods.

HOTELS

Even in Guiyang, expect little if any heat in the winter and hot tap water only a few hours a day. We found no hotels with credit card facilities and not all hotels can change money. This should improve soon. Be prepared for a welcome drink poured into your mouth by a singing waitress, and anticipate contributing a song yourself. The best hotel in town is the Park, but don't expect much.

Huaxi Hotel (Binguan) • *Wei Zhai Huaxi 550025. Telex 66017 HXHTL CN. Isolated in countryside beside Huaxi Park, Dist. city center 17 km. Dist.A.P. 14 km. Dist.R.W. 18 km* • Large rooms and high ceilings. 1952. Ren. 1992. 22 buildings on 3.6-sq.-km grounds. Upgrading its Ping Shan Zhuang building to 3* soon with pool, gym, tennis, bowling. B.C. IDD.

Park Hotel (Guizhou Fandian) • *66 Beijing Rd. 550001. 3*. Telex 66075 GZPHL CN. Fax 624397. Dist. A.P. 39 km. Dist. R.W. 4 km* • Big rooms, best on upper floors. Elsewhere dirty carpets. Poor management. IDD.

Plaza Hotel (Jin Zhu Dajiudian) • *2 Yanan East Rd., 550001. 3*. Telex 66001 PLAZA CN. Fax 29276. Dist. A.P. 38 km. Dist. R.W. 4 km* • C.C. 1989–90. U.S.J.V. 22 stories, 175 rooms. Disco and karaoke. IDD. Pool expected soon. Gym, sauna. Poor management. Filthy.

In **Anshun,** there is the **Hongshan Hotel (Binguan)** • *Baihuang Rd. 561000. Tel. 23454, 23435. Dist.A.P. 7 km. Dist.R.W. 2.5 km* • Became hotel in 1982. 225 beds. No hot water. No heat. Soft beds. Thin walls. Dirty carpets. Renovations expected 1991, at which time it should improve and be the best hotel. C.T.S.

The **Nationalities Hotel (Minzu Binguan)** • *561000. Dist.A.P. 11 km. Dist. R.W. 3 km.* • 1986. 8 stories. Had 62 rooms for foreigners. Air conditioning. 24-hour hot water. Staff are minorities who can perform songs and dances. Ethnic food. Generally grubby.

In **Kaili,** tourists are put in the **Ying Pong Po National Hotel (Binguan)** • *53 East Ying Penpo Rd., 556000.* • Ren. 1989. Isolated on pleasant hill in residential area. Mosquito nets. Dirty. One hour heat at night in November! Not up to our standards but no choice. New tourist hotel due soon.

Guizhou Overseas Travel Co.: 11 Yanan Zhong Rd., 550001, tel. 523095, 523433. Telex 66065. GZITC CN. Fax 523095. (Sales).
Guizhou Provincial Tourism Bureau: 11 Yanan Zhong Rd. 550001,

tel. 523205. Telex 66002 GZFAO CN. Fax 523163. (Brochures, complaints, and compliments.)
C.T.S.: Jin Qiao Hotel, 38 Shifu Rd. 550002. Tel. 29525, 25510 or 7 Yanan Zhong Rd. 550001. Tel. 28388.
CYTS: tel. 525013, 623030.
CAAC: 264 Zunyi Rd.; tel. 523006.

HAINAN ISLAND 海南岛

South China. China's second largest island, 30 km off its southern coast, became China's 31st province in 1988. Hainan includes the Xisha, Nansha (Spraley), and Zhongsha Islands. Travelers can fly to Haikou or Sanya from Guangzhou, or to Haikou from Hong Kong (1 hour), and 11 cities in China. It can also be reached by ship from Guangzhou, Zhanjiang, or Hong Kong. An international airport is due in Sanya in 1992. The island is almost as big as Taiwan, with about the same latitude and climate as southern Cuba. Foreign oil experts have been visiting it for years, but it is only now in the process of being developed for tourists. Hainan is also being developed as a very special economic zone with more flexibility and openness than other SEZs in developing foreign trade.

The only worthwhile tourist attraction on this island is the southern beaches but world class resorts and facilities won't be ready for a while. In the meantime, Hainan has a frontier atmosphere, people out to make a fast yuan, an atmosphere less controlled than that of the rest of China.
While prostitution is illegal, it is pretty obvious. Massage parlors with private clinics on the floor below blatantly advertise treatment for venereal diseases. Male travelers might get telephone calls about "special services." This is a warning.
But Haikou can be pleasant and even now one can relax in Sanya and enjoy the beaches if you don't mind barely adequate hotels.
Hainan was first colonized by Han dynasty troops. From the Tang, disfavored scholars and officials were sent here to live in exile, a tropical Siberia. During the '30s and '40s, a Communist army detachment fought here, and after Liberation part of the island became an autono-

mous region because a large percentage of the population are tribal minorities: mainly Li and Miao, but also Hui. Many of these still wear their beautiful, distinctive dress.

It has not been overly developed and is short on electricity, water, and efficiency. The weather is tropical, with 2000 mm of rain a year. Visitors can be admitted to Hainan for 15 days without a visa.

The island produces tea, coffee, rubber, fish, sugar, coconut, and rice. Other industries are being developed. The population is around 6 million.

Haikou 海口 , with a population of 300,000 people, has the **Five Officials Memorial Temple** 五公祠 nearby, which commemorates some of the banished officials and the **Hai Rui Tomb** 海瑞墓 but nothing world class.

Two roads go from Haikou to Sanya. If you take the 296 km. central road, you can stop at the Feng Mu Deer Farm and then visit a Miao village. Modest hotel in Tongzha. If you go via the 321 km. eastern route, you can visit the Monkey Peninsula, 衡山 Overseas Chinese farm at Xinlong 华侨 (hotel) and stop at the Chao Yin Si Temple on Mount Dongshan.

Air-conditioned buses from the Overseas Chinese Hotel make a direct trip in about six hours. A new highway should be completed in 1992.

Sanya has a dive shop next to the Sanya International Hotel. (Tel. 74641. Telex 45091. Fax 72250.) One can also visit a pearl farm, 珍珠场 and the ''Ends of the Earth'' 天涯海角 . Moslem fisherpeople live in the area.

The best time to go is winter but even April was very pleasant. Mosquitos are a problem in the summer and one should take precautions against malaria. May is the time for lichees, 23 varieties of mangoes and jackfruit. Typhoons usually hit July to September but other times as well.

SHOPPING

Locally found are rubies and rose quartz. Locally produced are cultured pearls, fruit, and minority handicrafts.

FOOD

Local specialties include Wenchang-style chicken 文昌鸡 , Jiaji duck 加积鸭 , Hele crab 和乐蟹 , and Dongshan mutton 东山羊肉 .

The Haiwei Seafood Restaurant near the Monkey Peninsula is the only good restaurant in the vicinity. The restaurants in Haikou's top hotels are good.

HOTELS

Aside from the International and Jinling in Sanya, don't expect much outside Haikou, though good hotels are being built. In the capital, the top hotels, the Financial Centre and the Haikou Tower, are international class. The Haikou Hotel is second best. Top hotels should have USTV soon.

The Financial Centre and the Haikou are the best placed for business people.

Haikou Hotel (Binguan) • *4 Haifu Dado, 570001. Fax 72232. Telex 45060 HTLHK CN* • 1988. C.C. 10 stories. 184 rooms. Maintenance needs work. IDD. Pool. Health and business centres.

Haikou International Financial Centre Hotel (Jinrong Da Sha) • *33 Datong Rd., 570001. Telex 490058 HITFC CN. Fax 72113. Dist.A.P. 2 km* • C.C. 1987; ren 1991. 22 stories. 241 rooms. Pool. Bowling. Gym. B.C. IDD. Dragonair. Eastwest Enterprise management.

Haikou Tower Hotel (Tai Hua Jiu Dian) • *Binhai Rd. 570005. 3*. Telex 490050 TOWER CN. Fax 23966. Near bus station* • C.C. (no Diners). 1986; ren. 1991. Two-stories. 240 rooms. IDD. Tennis. Pools. Jogging trails. Wheelchair ramps. Good furniture. Bicycles. B.C. H.K.S.T.T. management.

Outside of Haikou:

Da Dong Hai Tourism Center (Da Dong Hai Liu You Zhong Xin) • *Sanya 572021. Dist. bus station 3 km. Dist. pearl farm 4 km* • On 3-km-long Da Dong Hai Beach. Tents (cheap). C.C. 3 stories. Badly maintained. No western food. No laundry service.

Jinling Holiday Resort • *Luling Rd., Sanya, 572021. Fax 74088.*

Longhai Hotel (Binguan) • *Yalong Bay. Accessible by public bus* • On a 7 km.-long beach. 1989. Six one-story, Korean modular buildings about 100 meters from the water. Another group of buildings 300 meters from the water. Low standards.

Sanya International Hotel (Guoji Dajiudian) • *Jiefang Dong Rd., Sanya 572000. Fax 32049. Dist.A.P. 5 km. On ocean and riverfront (but not beach)* • 1989. 220 rooms.

C.T.S., 17 Datong Rd., Haikou 570001; tel. 73288, 23623.
C.I.T.S., Da Dong Hai Hotel, Sanya 572000; tel. 74640, 72117; Haixlu Rd., Sanjiaochi (next to Haikou Hotel), Haikou, tel. 74640, 72117. Telex 45024 CITSHN CN. Fax 72187.
CAAC, 50 Jiefang Rd.; tel. 24614, 23515.

Dragonair: tel. 73088, 74099.
Hainan Provincial Travel Bureau, Sanjiaochi. Tel. 72287, 72288.
(Brochures, complaints, and compliments.)
Hainan Peoples' Hospital: Haikou, tel. 521001.
Hainan Tourist Corp., 6 Haifu Ave., Haikou, 570003. Tel. 72264.
Fax 73647.

HANDAN 邯郸

North China, south Hebei on the Beijing-Guangzhou railway line.

Handan was the capital of Zhao State during the Warring States, 475–221 B.C. In 198 B.C., it became capital of the prefecture. The *Xiangtangshan Cave Temple from the northern Qi (about A.D. 500) to Ming dynasties is in a coal mine. Its nine caves in the north contain 700 buddhas, those in the south more than 3500.

Cizhou pottery, a distinctive traditional style with strong flower patterns, is still made in Pengcheng, near Handan, at eight factories.

HOTELS

Handan Hotel • *74 Zhonghua St., 056014. Dist.A.P.15 km. Dist.R.W.3 km* • 1958, ren. 1988, 1989. Four stories, 280 rooms, IDD, no C.C. Business center, bicycles.

C.I.T.S., 66 Zhonghua St. 056014; tel. 26420. Telex 26290 HDPBL CN.

HANGZHOU
(HANGCHOW)

East China. Capital of Zhejiang province, Hangzhou is on the Qiantang River at the southern end of the Grand Canal on the east coast of China. It is 189 km SW of Shanghai and less than a 2-hour flight SE of Beijing. Flights from Hong Kong and 19 Chinese cities. Coldest weather is in January, a little below 0°C; hottest in July, with highs of 37°C. Annual precipitation about 1452 mm, mainly May–June. The population is 1.3 million.

Hangzhou is one of the most famous beauty spots of China, with its Xihu (West Lake). It is also of historical importance. Founded over 2200 years ago in the Qin, it began to prosper as a trading center after the completion of the Grand Canal in 610. It was the capital of the tiny state of Wuyueh (893–978), at which time the first dikes forming the lake were built. It was also capital of the Southern Song after 1127. The best source for a detailed picture of the city from 1250 to 1276 is Jacques Gernet's *Daily Life in China on the Eve of the Mongol Invasion,* essential for visitors who want to know a lot of history, to compare life then with today, and to look for old ruins. The city was seized by the Mongols under Kublai Khan in 1279 and visited by Marco Polo the next year when it was known as Kinsai. The Venetian explorer raved about the city, then the largest and richest in the world, its silks and handicrafts much in demand in China and abroad.

Hangzhou has been a famous resort for centuries, attracting famous painters, poets, and retired officials as well as tourists. It is also an industrial city now, with iron and steel, machine-making, basic chemicals, an oil refinery, and electronics. Tourists would probably be interested in its factories producing silk textiles, satin, brocades, sandalwood fans, scissors, silk parasols, and woven silk "photographs." Villages here grow the famous long jing (Dragon Well) tea and silk worms. These make a rural excursion especially worthy.

The center of the city is on the east side of **Xi Hu (West Lake)** 西. The 5.6-square-km lake was originally part of the Qiantang River until its outlet became silted up. It is now 15 km in circumference, with an average depth of 1.8 meters. The lake is now linked with the Qiantang River and is usually renewed with fresh water once a month. Just strolling around the edge of the lake is worthwhile. Many of the tourist attractions are close to its shore.

If a visitor only has one day to spend in the city, C.I.T.S. recommends a boat ride on the lake with stops at various famous sites. Then take in the Pagoda of Six Harmonies, Lingyin Temple, and a silk factory. Boats are available for hire at four different places around the lake.

One could also rent a bicycle (faster) from a hotel or the shop at the intersection north of the Children's Palace, or a pedicab. (See also "Getting Around"). That way in one day you can ride along Baidi Causeway with stops at the Autumn Moon on Calm Lake Pavilion, Wenlan Ge (next to Zhejiang Provincial Museum), Xiling Seal Engraver's Society, Tomb and Temple of Yue Fei, and Jade Spring. You can then explore Lingyin Temple. Then you can visit the Feilaifeng Grottoes across the stream from the temple and turn back to the Yue Fei Tomb and then south onto Sudi Causeway. Follow Nan Shan and then Hubin roads. Stop to enjoy Liulanwenying Park if only for its name, which means Park to See the Waving Willows and Hear the Singing of the Birds. Then back to the Children's Palace.

The best times to see the lake itself is in the mist, or in the moonlight, or just at sunrise before the sun makes strong shadows, and when the birds are singing in the willows. One of the favorite spots for viewing the lake, especially during the harvest moon, is at **Pinghuqiuyue (Autumn Moon on Calm Lake Pavilion)** 平湖秋月 at the southeastern end of **Gu Shan (Solitary Hill)** 孤山 . But don't expect to be alone.

On the islet also is the **Wenlan Ge (Pavilion for Storing Imperial Books)** 御书楼 , built in 1699 (Qing), and one of the seven imperial libraries. This one was especially built to store the Sikuzhunsu, a 33,304-volume Chinese encyclopedia ordered by Emperor Qianlong. Copied by hand, the encyclopedia took 10 years to compile.

The **Xiling Seal Engraver's Society** 西泠印社 was founded in 1903 and has its headquarters on a hillside here full of pavilions, towers, and a pagoda. Seal engraving is a fine art in the Orient, with several different styles. This society meets twice a year, gives many exhibitions, and publishes periodicals. The stone **Chamber to the Three Venerables** *Han San Lao Hui Zi* here was carved in A.D. 52. The island has a provincial museum and a restaurant, the Louwailou. (Tel. 21654).

Lively **giant golden carp** can be seen at **Huagang Park 花岗公园** at the SW end of the lake, beyond the Sudi Causeway. A Song official once had a vacation home here. The pavilions were built after Liberation. This 20-hectare park also has a restaurant and a tea house.

The 2.8-km **Sudi Causeway** is the more beautiful of the two causeways here, lined with grass, willows, and peach trees. No motor vehicles are allowed because of its hump-backed bridges. It's a pleasant bicycle or pedicab ride, but please give the driver a break. Get off and walk up those bridges.

The famous **Zig-Zag Bridge** is on the islet **Xiaoyingzhou (Three Pools Mirroring the Moon) 小瀛州** and can be reached only by boat. It is east of Sudi Causeway. Did you know that bad spirits have to move in straight lines? Stand on the bridge here and nothing can harm you. This islet was first constructed in 1607 (Ming) with mud cleared from the lake. Look for the "island in a lake and the lake in an island."

During the Moon Festival, candles light up the small pagodas, thus creating "Three Pools Mirroring the Moon." In June, this is a good place to enjoy water lilies and lotus flowers.

Everywhere around West Lake are exquisite gardens, some with artistically cobbled foot paths. The large mansions on the shore, once owned by the rich, are now hotels or resorts for workers. The 1.8 km **Baidi Causeway 白堤** in the north was first laid over 1000 years ago and is named after Bai Juyi, the great poet and governor of the Tang.

Visitors can also go by boat to **Ruangongdun Island** on the NW side of West Lake just south of Gushan Hill. **Huanbi Zhuang,** there, is an attempt to reproduce a Song dynasty village with period costumes, sedan chair rides, wine shop, music, and dance. Some tourists have found it fun, but serious students of Chinese history might find it too commercial. At the Mid-lake Pavilion is a 20th-century disco.

The ***Liuhe Ta (Pagoda of Six Harmonies) 六和塔** is on the north bank of the Qiantang River. Built in A.D. 970 (Song), it is 59.89 meters and 13 stories tall, octagonal, and made of brick and wood. It can be climbed for a good view. West of this temple is the shallow and clear **Nine Creeks and Eighteen Gullies,** which cut through the rugged but tranquil (few tourists) Yangmei Hill. Great for hikers, the paths wind for about 7 km. There are donkeys for rent nearby for the less ambitious.

The **Lingyin (Soul's Retreat) Temple** is 9 km from the city, west of West Lake. Founded in A.D. 326 (Jin), its Celestial Kings' Hall and 33.6-meter-high Buddha Hall are all that is left of the original 18 pavilions and 72 halls. Lingyin at one time housed 3000 monks. The statues have been replaced now. A seated Sakyamuni inside is 19.6 meters high. The temple guardian behind the Four Celestial Kings was carved from camphor wood during the Song. Lingyin is still one of the largest and most magnificent temples in China. Two restaurants serve vegetarian food, the one inside better than the one next to the temple.

Across from Lingyin temple is ***Feilaifeng (Peak that Flew from Afar)** 飞来峰 , named by an Indian monk after a similiar-looking Indian peak that must have flown here. The 380 carvings along the narrow, hilly trails are from the Five Dynasties to the Yuan.

A trip to a silk factory to watch the weaving and designing can be arranged. The **Dujinsheng Silk Weaving Factory** (215 Feng Qi Rd.) is about five minutes' walk from the Wanghu Hotel. Silk brocade pictures, cushion covers, fancy tablecloths, silk fabric. Closed on Sunday. The **Hangzhou Silk Printing and Dyeing Complex** 杭州丝织厂 (Gong Zhen Qiao; tel. 87824) is more interesting to see. A 15-minute taxi ride from the Wanghu Hotel, it is next to the Grand Canal on which the cocoons are transported. Here you can see the process of preparing the cocoons, spinning, weaving, printing, and dyeing. To make a shirt requires 500–1000 cocoons, depending on the thickness of the material.

The unpleasant part of a silk factory visit is the deafening noise of the weaving machines, but there are other things to see besides those machines. Do complain about the noise to the management.

It could take three or four days to cover all the important spots in Hangzhou. The 45-meter-high **Baochu (Precious Stone Hill) Pagoda** is on a 200-meter-high hill north of the lake, 2 km from the city. It was first built in 968 (Song) to pray for the safe return of the unjustly arrested Qian Hongchu, a successful effort. The pagoda, last reconstructed in 1933, is now filled with dirt and no one can enter.

The ***Tomb and Temple of Yue Fei** 岳飞庙，岳坟 is at the NW corner of the lake, next to the Shangri-La Hotel. He was a famous Song general who was unjustly executed in 1142. Public reaction forced a retrial 20 years later that reversed the verdict. A temple was built with statues of his four accusers kneeling for forgiveness before his grave. These four are spat on even today.

Yue Fei was also a calligrapher and poet who came from a family that valued patriotism. His mother tattooed his back with four characters to remind him of his duty to his country. His son was murdered on the day of Yue Fei's death. Their tombs are next to each other, but only contain their clothing. An exhibition hall illustrates Yue Fei's battles and shows his handwritten proposals to the Song emperor.

At the **Hupao (Tiger) Spring** 虎跑 you will find water that will not overflow from a full cup even though many coins are added to it. The high surface tension will also support a carefully placed Chinese coin, a trick that also works in Toronto, so don't be gullible. The spring is near the Hangzhou Zoo, about 6 km from the city SW of the lake on Hupao Road. A handy tea house is here. The well is named after a tiger in a monk's dream that dug successfully for water here. The monk woke up and excavated this well at the same spot as in his dream.

The **Longjing (Dragon Well)** 龙井, to the NW of Hupao, is another spring. The water here has a curious ripple effect when you stir it, especially on rainy days. This phenomenon is explained by the differences in the specific gravity of the rain water and the spring water, and is a good ploy to encourage business in wet weather.

Two km SW is **Longjingcun (Dragon Well Village)** 龙井村, where you can see the famous tea growing on hillsides. It is usually picked in late March or early April. Connoisseurs of good tea pay fabulously high prices for the best of the harvest, the most tender leaves, hand-picked before the spring rain. The quantity is also limited because only a few villages have the proper soil and water. The best Longjing Tea, when brewed, has a fresh, crystal-green color, a mild and pure fragrance, and a slight sweetness.

At the **Meijiawu Tea Garden** 梅家坞茶园, SW of Longjingcun, you can see the tea production process.

The third of Hangzhou's famous springs is **Jade Spring** 玉泉 (Yugu Rd., off the NW corner of the lake). It is for gold fish and flower lovers, as multicolored ornamental fish are bred here. It is inside the 200-hectare **Hangzhou Botanical Garden** 杭州植物园, which has 3700 species of plants, including 120 varieties of bamboo. Along with the Shanwaishan Restaurant, these are within walking distance of the Shangri-La Hotel.

A **cable car** 缆车 runs from 8 a.m. to 5 p.m. between **Beigao Feng (North Peak)** 北高峰 and near the Lingyin Temple, giving a good view of the lake. Visitors can also drive up **Wushan Hill,** east of the lake, the highest spot in the city. This has an 800-year-old camphor tree and a cave made for the Song emperor. Also accessible is **Yuhuang (Jade Emperor) Mountain** 玉皇山, overlooking the river at a spot where a Song emperor pretended to do manual labor. A **wax museum** on Wushan Hill has paintings and sculptures of local historical figures. Museums about tea, ceramics, traditional Chinese medicine and silk have recently opened.

Most temples are open from 7:30 a.m. to 5 p.m. in summer and from 8 a.m. to 4:30 p.m. in winter. Some parks close at 6 p.m. Ask about the special events: the marathon race (September), traditional medicine festival (May), Chinese calligraphy festival (March), bridge festival (October), and New Year's Eve.

Excursions can be arranged from Hangzhou. For Ningbo (about 150 km SW), Shaoxing (about 50 km SE), and Huangshan (200 km.) see separate listings. **Mogan Mountain** 莫干山, 700 meters high (about 75 km NW), is a well-known summer resort with over 300 hectares of waterfalls, bamboo forests, stone trails, ponds, and caves. Good for hiking and relaxing in beautiful surroundings. **Wuling Guesthouse 武陵宾馆** . The main town is now known as Wujitu, and Chiang Kai Shek's home was number one.

The large limestone **Yaoling Cave 瑶琳仙洞** is 120 km SW of the city, close to Tonglu County, and is 25 meters high and more than 1 km long, with many stairs. This is usually a one-day trip.

In **Tiantai,** about 100 km from Hangzhou, the **Guoqing Temple** is the home of the Tiantai Buddhist sect.

The **Tidal Bore of the Qiantang River 钱塘江观潮** is most spectacular on the 18th day of the eighth month (lunar calendar). In 1974 it reached a height of nine meters, but it is not usually that dramatic. Best seen at Yanguan town at Zhan'ao Pagoda 45 km from Hangzhou, or at Haining. Check with C.T.S., 1 Shihan Rd., tel. 557050 for dates and bus tours if you are in Hangzhou in late September or early October.

SHOPPING

Produced in the province are silk textiles, woven pictures, Dragon Well tea, silk parasols, mahogany and boxwood crafts, fresh water pearls, lace, Longquan Celedon, fans, woven bambooware, distinctive Tianzhu chopsticks, and stone and wood carvings. Hangzhou makes some fancy scissors that are useful souvenirs. The main shopping area is **Jiefang Rd.** and **Yan'an Rd. 延安路** . In addition to the above-named silk factory, some important places to shop are:

Zhejiang Arts and Crafts Service (Exhibition Hall, Wuling Sq.; tel. 550521); **Hangzhou Department Store** (739 Jiefang Rd.; tel. 22449 20891); **Hangzhou Friendship Store** (18 Hubin Rd., tel. 725410); **Hangzhou Silk Goods Store** (31 Hubin Rd.; tel. 24508); **Wangxingji Fans** (77 Jiefang Rd.; tel. 28255); **Zhang Xiaoquan Scissors Shop 张小泉剪刀店** (105 Yan'an Rd.; tel. 21860). The Zhejiang Guest House has a good-sized store.

RESTAURANTS

Food and ambiance in hotels are generally better. The Wanghu top floor is good for Chinese food; the Shangri-La for Western. For vegetarian food, try the restaurant inside the Lingyin Temple.

HOTELS

The top hotel here is the Shangri-La. #2 is the Dragon. #3 is the Friendship. Most hotels are within walking distance of West Lake, the main tourist attraction here. On or almost on the lake are the Overseas Chinese, Huagang, Shangri-La, and Wanghu. The Wanghu, Xin Qiao, and Friendship are closest to the shopping and business district.

The high tourist season here is May, July, and October. Reservations recommended all year round.

Dragon Hotel (Huang Long Fandian) • *11 Shuguang Rd. 310007. 4* Telex: 351048 DRAGN CN. Fax: 558090. Dist.A.P.12 km. Dist.R.W.7 km. Near Bao Chu Hill and Yellow Dragon Cave, but not West Lake.* • 1987–88. 6, 7 and 9 stories. 557 rooms. Chinese architecture. Courtyard gardens. Largest banquet hall in city. Tennis courts, swimming pool, IDD, C.C., gym. Shuttle service to lake and business district. Designed for groups. B.C. Dragonair. Problem with noise. Managed by New World Hotels International. USTV.

Friendship Hotel (You Hao Fandian) • *53 Pinghai Rd. 310006. 3*. Telex 35068 FRISH CN. Fax 773842. Dist.A.P.15 km. Dist.R.W. 3.5 km.* • 1986; ren. 1990. C.C. Good looking hotel. 23 stories, 220 rooms. West side has view of lake. Japanese J.V., B.C. Two discos. Small bathrooms. IDD.

Huagang Hotel (Dajiudian) • *4 Xishan Rd. 310007. 3*. Fax 772481. Telex: 35007 HUAJG CN. Dist.A.P.18 km. Dist.R.W.7.5 km. Near Huagang Park, 5 min. walk to lake.* • Main wing with lobby 1954, ren. 1989. North wing 1980, ren. 1987. Set in garden. Chinese architecture. 4 stories; 220 rooms. Beautiful wood carvings. Long dark hallways. Poor decor. Small TVs. B.C. Budget travelers only.

Overseas Chinese Hotel (Huaqiao Fandian) • *15 Hubin Rd. 300006. 3*. Telex: 35070 HOCH CN. Fax 774478. Dist.A.P.15 km. Dist.R.W.5 km. Two blocks from Wanghu Hotel.* • 1983. Main building 1958, ren. 1987, east building ren. 1989. 5 stories, 288 rooms. C.T.S. C.C., IDD, B.C., bicycles.

Shangri-La Hotel (Fandian) • *78 Beishan Rd., 310007. Telex: 35005/6 HOTCH CN. Fax: 773545. Dist.A.P.20 km. Dist.R.W.5 km. Walking distance to Solitary Hill Island and wharf for renting boats.* • East building, formerly the Xiling Hotel, renovated 1985. 7 stories. 156 rooms Chinese decor. West building opened 1956, ren. 1987. 6 stories, 199 rooms. More Western decor. The two buildings are joined by a covered walkway cooled by fans. Also three villas with 32 rooms. Total: 387 rooms. Managed by Shangri-La International. Convention center. 30 acre site. No disco. C.C. B.C., C.I.T.S. Fast food restaurant on grounds. Old world charm. IDD. Has brochure with walking and cycling tours. Bicycles. Planning pool and tennis.

Wanghu Hotel (Binguan) • *2 Huanchen Xi Rd., 310006. 3*. Telex 351029 OLWH CN. Fax 771350. Dist.A.P.14 km. Dist.R.W.4 km.*

Walking distance to Friendship Store, Bank of China and import-export corporation. ● Built 1986. Ren. 1990. C.C. 8 stories, 360 good rooms. C.I.T.S. and CAAC offices on premises. B.C. Photo-finishing.

Xin Qiao Hotel (Fandian) ● *176 Jiefang Rd., 310001. 3*. Fax 722768. Telex: 351028 XQH CN. Dist.A.P.12 km. Dist.R.W.2 km. 200 meters from lake. Near biggest department store and arts and crafts store.* ● 1987, ren. 1990. Hong Kong J.V. 20 stories; currently 351 rooms. Italian marble in lobby. Rooms have good furniture but poorly tailored drapes. C.I.T.S. Mainly Chinese food. Claims biggest disco in city. B.C.

Zhejiang Guest House (Binguan) ● *68 San Tai Shan Rd. 310007. 3*. Fax 771904. Telex 351044 ZSGH CN. Dist.A.P.20 km. Dist.R.W. about 6 km. Near Dragon Well Spring. (Bus 27 to city). Isolated and pretty rural setting.* ● C.C., 1978. Some buildings ren. 1988. Former private villa of Lin Biao, who never lived here. Six buildings on vast grounds, some with own dining rooms. The best is #3. 2 and 5 stories. 155 rooms. Dorms with no air conditioning. Basketball. Indoor pool. Large store. IDD. B.C. No disco. Budget travelers only.

OTHER IMPORTANT ADDRESSES

CAAC 中国旅行社: 160 Tiyuchang Rd.; tel. 552575, 554259. Airport: tel. 42160.

C.I.T.S. 中国国际旅行社 : 1 Shihan Rd., 310007; tel. 552888. Telex 351110 CITSH CN. Fax 556667.

C.T.S. 中国民航 : Overseas Chinese Hotel, 15 Hubin Rd.; tel. 774401. Telex 35070 HOCH CN. Fax 774978 or 1 Shihan Rd. 310007; tel. 557050.

Dragonair: Dragon Hotel; tel. 554488.

Hospital: in case of illness, ask for help at your hotel. Otherwise, try the **Zhejiang Hospital** 浙江医院 : Lingyin Rd.; tel. 21357.

Ambulance: tel. 767396.

Police: tel. 110.

Tourism Hotline: tel. 556631.

Telecommunications Services: Try your hotel first, but 24-hour service at Hangzhou Telegraph Office 杭州电报局 : Qingnian Rd.; tel. 23121.

Zhejiang China Travel Service: 1 Shihan Rd., 310007. tel. 557479. Fax 556746. Telex 351033 CTSZJ CN. Zhejiang Overseas Tourist Corp.: 2 Huancheng Xi Rd. 310006; tel. 776194. Fax 722837. Books tours from abroad.

Zhejiang Tourism Bureau: 1 Shihan Rd. 310007; tel. 556631. Telex 35031 HZT CN. Fax 556429 (complaints).

Zhejiang CYTS: 32 Wen Er St. 310012; tel. 888837, 882741, 880042. Telex 351097 ZYTS CN. Fax 887326.

HARBIN 哈尔滨

(Haerhpin) Northeast China. This is the capital of China's northernmost province of Heilongjiang, formerly part of Manchuria, a 1½-hour flight NE of Beijing or a 5-hour train ride from Jilin. Flights with Khabarovsk (Siberia) and 19 Chinese cities. Possibility of flights from Japan and Hong Kong. It has a population of over two million and is an industrial city 159 km from the Daqing oil fields, China's biggest. Its highest summer temperature is 36°C; its lowest in winter is ⁻38°. The winter is six months long, so take your longjohns. Wintertime, however, is brightened by the **Ice Sculpture Festival.** You can also bring skates and skis. Annual precipitation 250–700 mm, mostly June through August.

The area was first settled by people of the Nuzhen nationality in 1097. In the Yuan, the city was renamed Harbin. In 1898 it was opened as a port and became a Russian concession. Tsarist troops and police patrolled the Russian ghetto. From 1932 the Japanese occupied the area until the end of the war. You can see a lot of tsarist and Japanese architecture, although neglected, and cobblestone streets (in Dao Li District). The Northeast is not as developed as other parts of China.

Today, Heilongjiang numbers among its population Han, Manchu, Korean, Hui, Mongolian, Daur, Orogen, Ewenki, Kirgiz, Hezhen, and other nationalities.

If you only have one day here, C.I.T.S. recommends that you tour the harbor and along the Song Hua River, with its 10 km dike. From January 5 to February 25, visit the magical **Ice Sculpture Festival 冰灯 游园会** , about 8 km from the Swan Hotel. The show can take 2 or 3 hours if you can stand the cold. This international competition has attracted teams from Canada, Japan, Hong Kong, etc. Full of ice pagodas, bridges, giant lanterns, human figures, mazes, palaces, and children's slides, it is best seen at night with its twinkling lights.

Other attractions include a 2-km-long miniature railway for children 儿童铁路 (4 km from the Swan); in summer you can rent sailboats and sampans; in winter you can sail-sled on ice. Among the animals at the **zoo** you can find a Manchurian tiger, a red-crested crane, and a moose. The **Heilongjiang Provincial Museum** is supposed to have one of the best skeletons of a mammoth to be found in China.

Travel agents have bird-watching, gold panning, horse riding (Mongolian), and skiing tours. Bicycle tours go from Wuying-DafengNancha-Dailing to Langxiang. Steam locomotive tours are taken on narrow-gauge mining and logging trains and to the railway bridge near the International Hotel. China's biggest bird sanctuary 扎龙自然保护区 , the 210,000-hectare **Zhalong Nature Preserve** is near **Qiqihar,** 280 km away. Its cranes, storks, swans, geese, herons, etc., are best seen from April to September. The famous red-crested cranes are considered a symbol of luck. **C.I.T.S.** is at 4 Wenhua St., Qiqihar 161005; tel. 77010. Fax 87128. **Daqing** is a 6–hour train ride NW. The best hotel is the Daqing Hotel, 163000.

Also in the province is the **Taiyang Island summer resort,** another ice festival in Qiqihar, and **Jingpo Lake** in **Mudanjiang.** 90–minute flights or train to **Heihe** at the Soviet border are available from which you can make a day trip to **Siberia.**

Skiing here is an experience. It is not for serious skiers. Facilities are not well developed yet, though the province has two resorts with lifts.

ENTERTAINMENT

Leather-silhouette show. Annual Harbin Summer Music Festival.

SHOPPING

Fur hats, jackets, and collars: sable, mink, muskrat. Handicrafts include straw patchwork, horn carving, knitting, and ivory, jade, stone, and wood carving. Good to eat are its pine nuts. Lots of ginseng. Harbin No. 1 Department Store, 146 Diduan St., tel. 49291; Harbin Embroidery Factory, Arts and Crafts Bldg., tel. 225055 (for tablecloths); Tourist Fur Store, 88 Zhongyang St., tel. 49683.

RESTAURANTS

The most famous dishes are served in the International Hotel. There you can try moose nose and hazel grouse. Please, don't eat any endangered species! For those who want something less questionable, try monkey head–shaped mushroom. Russian food in hotels.

HOTELS

The top hotel is the International or Swan, the former better located for tourists. No. 2 is the Hepingcun Guesthouse. Some business people prefer the Friendship (postal code 150036. 3*). None are luxury quality.

International Hotel (Guoji Fandian) • *124 Dazhi St., 150036. Telex 87081 GUOLU CN. Dist.A.P.40 km. Dist.R.W.½ km. Walking distance of Friendship Store, antique store, Protestant church on Dazhi St., and museum* • C.C. 1937-built section has bigger rooms. 1980-built section 9 stories. IDD of sorts. 5th-floor lounge should be club for foreigners.

Peace Village Hotel (Heping Cun Fandian) • *107 Zhong Shan Rd., 150036 Telex 87079 HBHPC CN. Fax 220124. Near trade center, arts and crafts factory. Dist.A.P.37 km. Dist. R.W.4 km* • No C.C. 1986. 9 stories, 230 rooms. IDD.

Swan Hotel (Tian E Fandian) • *73 Zhongshan Rd. 150036. 3*. Telex 87080 TIANE CN. Fax 224895. Quiet location. Dist.A.P.45 km. Dist.R.W.5 km* • C.C. (no Diners), 1983; ren. 1990. 15 stories, 258 rooms. 24-hour bar. Soft beds. B.C., CAAC, IDD. Near C.I.T.S.

Ambulance: Tel. 120., 278118
Police: Tel. 110.
C.I.T.S.: 73 Zhongshan Rd. 150036. Tel. 222655. Telex 87034 HCITS CN. Fax 222476.
CAAC: 85 Zhongshan Rd.; tel. 222337. Also Swan and Tianzhi hotels.
C.T.S. Harbin: 57 Youyi Rd., Daoli Dist. 150010. Tel. 29857 Fax 344679. Telex 87124 HFP CN or 52 Hongjun St., 150001. Nangangju. Tel. 34679, 31476 X102.
C.Y.T.S.: tel. 31042, 31503.
Heilongjiang Overseas Tourism Corporation: 124 Dazhi Rd., Nangang Dist. 150001.: Tel. 221088. Fax 221088. Telex 87187 OTC CN. (Sells tours and arranges China-USSR visits.)
Tourist Hotline: Tel. 341441 X 331.

HEFEI (HOFEI) 合肥

East China. Capital of Anhui (Anhwei), a province that is about two-thirds north of the Changjiang (Yangtze) River. Anhui is famous for its dramatic mountains that have inspired poets, mystics, and painters for centuries. In the province live Han, Hui, She, and other nationalities. Flights from 13 cities and Hong Kong. Flights planned with Japan and Southeast Asia. Train service from Beijing (14½ hours); Nanjing (6 hours); and Shanghai (11 hours). Connected by expressway to Nanjing. Population 820,000. Its coldest weather in January is minus 1° C. Its hottest in July and August is 33° C. Because of its strategic location, numerous battles were fought here in the ancient past. Its tourist attractions can be squeezed into one day.

In **Xiaoyaojin** 逍遥津 , near the center of the city, during the Three Kingdoms period 1700 years ago, General Zhang Liao of the State of Wei fought against General Sun Quan (Sun Chuan) of the State of Wu. The site is now a park with three islets, on one of which is the tomb of General Zhang. Near the park is a zoo. Two km south of Xiaoyaojin, the **Lecturing Rostrum/Archery Training Terrace** 教弩台 is where Emperor Caocao trained Wei troops in using crossbows. These sites are marked with pavilions in traditional architecture. The **Mingjiao Temple** is on the terrace. This monastery was founded in the Tang. Destroyed in the 19th century during the Taiping War, its buildings were rebuilt by General Yuan Hongmo of the Taiping Heavenly Kingdom.

The **Temple to Lord Baozheng** 包公祠 , situated in a park in the center of the city, was built in honor of Baozheng, an honest and outstanding official of the Northern Song. He was a magistrate, prefectural head and vice minister of Rites. The **Provincial Museum** has a pleasant dinosaur garden. You might be able to squeeze in the China University of Science and Technology, and local opera too.

SHOPPING

Grown in the province are pears, pomegranates, grapes, kiwi fruit, and herbal medicines. Made are candied dates, tea, bamboo mats, and iron pictures. It is also noted for its four scholarly treasures: Xuan writing brush, Hui ink stick, She ink slab and Xuan paper. Try the Hefei Department Store, Anhui Provincial Arts and Crafts Store, and Gongnongbing Textile Shop. The Chenghuangmiao shopping center was built in the Ming style and surrounds the 900-year-old Town God's Temple.

RESTAURANTS

Anhui specialties are freshwater crabs from Lake Chao nearby and locally produced Gujing Gongjiu wine, once sent as tribute to the Ming emperors. Try cured Mandarin fish 腌鲜桂鱼 , stewed turtle　清炖马蹄, Fulizi braised chicken 符离集烧鸡 ，Wenzhenshan bamboo shoots and sesame cakes　向政山笋和芝麻糕 . Dishes are somewhat salty and slightly spicy hot, with thick soups. Try the **Anhui Restaurant** on Shouchun Rd. Tel. 252865.

HOTELS

Anhui Hotel (Fandian) ● *2 Meishan Rd., 230022.* ● Telex 90029 AHHTL CN. Fax 332581.

Luyang Hotel (Fandian) ● *Shushan Rd. 230061. 3*. Fax 332244. Dist.A.P.12 km, Dist.R.W.5 km. 2 km from city center. Telex 90032 LYH CN* ● Six stories; 1958, 1985. Should now have extension, tennis, swimming pool. Accepts American Express cards. Best hotel.

Daoxianglou Hotel (Binguan) ● *Jinzhai Rd. 400 Yan'an Lu Kou, 230061. 3** ● 400 beds.

Anhui Overseas Travel Corp., Anhui Tourism Administration, and **C.I.T.S.** Hefei Branch, are together at 4 Meishan Rd., 230022. Tel. 331707, 332017. Fax 332855. Telex 90024 AHPBD CN. The Corporation sells tours and has information about festivals and Buddhist events. A.T.S.: tel. 331038.

CAAC: 192 Jinzai Rd., tel. 331454, 332772.
CTS: tel. 52281.
CYTS: tel. 52950.

OUTSIDE OF HEFEI IN ANHUI

Huangshan (Mount Huangshan) 黄山 is reached from Hefei by plane or bus. The bus takes about 10 hours. See separate listing.

Jiuhuashan (Mt. Jiuhua) 九华山 , one of the Four Buddhist Mountains (alt. 1341 meters), is a day's trip by road. It has 78 Ming and Qing temples, 6800 buddhas, which were untouched by the Red Guards, and 99 peaks. Motor vehicles can drive up to 600 meters. Important are the Roushen Hall and Qiyuan Temple. In the **Baisui Gong (Buddhist Mummy Hall)** is preserved the 400-year-old cadaver of a monk. The Dongyan Hotel (Jiuhua St., tel. 242811) has 150 beds. Temple Fair on the 30th of the 7th lunar month for 10 days. Coldest mean temperature in January is ⁻3°C. Hottest mean temperature is 18°C in July. C.I.T.S. branch, tel. 202.

Wuhu 芜湖, in the southeastern part of the province, is where the Qing-yi River joins the Yangtze. It is slightly warmer than Hefei. On the railway lines from Nanjing and Hefei, it is the main foreign trading river port for the province and the fourth largest port on the Yangtze. It also produces those lovely pictures made of forged iron, usually painted black. It has a silk factory, Alligator Breeding Center, and the Dragon Spring Cave. Yangtze River boat tours. Hotels are the 260-bed Tieshan 铁山宾馆 3 Gensin Rd., 241000. 3☆. and the 32-bed Wuhu, 10 Renmin Rd., 241000. C.T.S. at 74 Jinghu Rd., tel. 83755.

Ma'anshan (Horse Saddle Mountain) 马鞍山 , south of the Yangtze near the eastern provincial border, has impressive stone outcrops into the Yangtze. This large industrial city is on the railway line between Nanjing and Wuhu. Yangtze River boat tours. The **Taibai Pavilion** was built at Caishiji (Rock of Various Colors) and has relics related to Li Bai, the world-famous Tang poet whose grave is at the foot of Qingshan. International poetry festival on the 9th of the 9th lunar month. C.T.S. at 22 Hubei Rd., 243000. tel. 72944.

Ma'anshan Hotel (185 beds) is on Xingfu Rd. 243021.

Near Bengbu, on the railway line between Beijing and Shanghai, is the ancestral home of the first Ming emperor, who proclaimed it a royal city. It contains among its tombs that of Tang He, who was one of the Ming dynasty founders. The *''ruins of the Imperial City of the Middle Capital and stone inscriptions at the Imperial Mausoleum'' here are now under State Council protection. It also has the Temple of King Yu. One of the first attempts at the ''Responsibility System'' was started herein 1978. Accommodations at the 118-bed **Nanshan Hotel** 南山宾馆 126 Xiangyang Rd. See ''Huangshan'' for Tunxi. Travel services are at 128 Zhongshan St., tel. 4150 and 161 Zhongshan St. 233000; tel. 41918. Telex 91207 ABMFA CN.

Tunxi 屯溪 C.I.T.S. says the top hotel is the Huaxi (tel. (559) 4312), then the Huashan (tel. 33529) and thirdly the Jiang Xin Zhou. **CYTS:** tel. 212771, 214228.

悬 空 寺

Z.M.Li

HENGSHAN (MT. HENGSHAN)

There are several of these Hengshans, not all the names written the same in Chinese. Of the two most worthwhile to see is **Hengshan** 山西恒山 in Shanxi province, 2 hours' drive on a country road SE of Datong. Along the way are remains of ancient beacon towers (see ''Great Wall'') and mud cave houses similar to those around Yan'an. Note the windows covered with folk art or paper cuts.

The main attraction here is the very breath-taking ***Temple-in-Mid-Air,** a.k.a. Suspending Temple 悬空寺. A marvel of cliffside architecture, the temple literally clings to an almost vertical mountainside, some of its 40 small pavilions supported by wooden poles and beams, some by manmade rock foundations, some by natural stone. A trip here is not for people afraid of heights nor for people over 180 lbs., as the walks are narrow and involve many steep stairs.

This temple was first built over 1400 years ago (Northern Wei) and rebuilt in the Tang, Jin, Ming, and Qing dynasties. Its clay statues are not well done so are probably not originals. The bronze and iron castings and stone and wood carvings are older. Lunch in Hongyun County town nearby.

Hengshan #2 湖南衡山 is in Hunan province, about 310 km south of Changsha, South China. It is one of the Five Great Mountains of China, with 72 peaks and about 20 Taoist and Buddhist temples. The most noteworthy of the temples is at Nanyue, occupying 98,000 square meters. First erected in 725 (Tang), it has Song and Ming architecture. A hotel and botanical garden are also on the mountain. One can drive from Hengyang to most scenic spots and especially to see the sunrise. Vegetarian food at the Zhusheng Temple.

HOHHOT (HUHEHOT) 呼和浩特

North China. The capital of Inner Mongolia (a.k.a. Nei Monggol) Autonomous Region can be reached by train or plane from 19 other cities. Flights soon with Ulan Bator. It is NW of Beijing in the south central part of the 1800-km-long province. The best time to visit is June through Aug. The highest temperature in Hohhot then is 30°C, but the nights are cool. The winters are very cold and windy, with a ⁻32°C low, and you need longjohns even in early May. The spring has sandstorms; the annual precipitation is between a scant 50 and 450 mm, mostly late summer and early autumn. The altitude is 1500 meters above sea level and it has from 90 to 160 frostfree days. The urban population is over 700,000.

Inner Mongolia is of historical and religious importance. The Mongols, one of the nationalities living here, united under Genghis Khan in

A yurt.

1206, and their descendents went on to conquer the rest of China and then parts of Europe in the 13th and 14th centuries.

The traditional religion, as reflected now in its monasteries and temples, is a distinctive branch of Buddhism known as Lamaism, and is related to that of Tibet.

Hohhot dates from the Ming, at least 400 years ago. It was called Guisui under the Nationalists. After Liberation it was renamed Hohhot (Green City), the name preferred by the natives. In the past, Nei Mongol has been a home for nomads. Today its population includes Han, Daur, Ewenki, Oroqen, Hui, Manchu, Korean, and, of course, Mongolian nationalities. The Mongolians are actually a minority. Hohhot looks like any other Chinese city except for the horse statues.

In summer, visitors can travel out from here, if they wish, and sleep in a yurt in the sparsely settled grasslands. You can drink tea laced with milk, butter, and grain, said to be very filling and great for cold winter days. It is too greasy for hot weather. Visitors can go to one of several rural communities located 90–180 km away, on roads cut through the rolling grasslands or prairies.

Real yurts are made of compressed sheep's wool with no windows unless you count the roof. They are shaped somewhat like igloos, and can be folded up and carried by camel. Eight people can put up a large one in 40 minutes. Visitors staying in yurts sleep on padded earthern mattresses. Everything smells of sheep. (Put a bag between you and the wall if the smell keeps you awake.) We found 1–3 people to a yurt very comfortable, and 6–8 very crowded. In our yurt, we could hear bugs eating the felt, but nothing really bothered us. A mosquito net brought by my companion kept out flying but harmless bugs one night. Most

Mongolians now live in houses but keep yurts around because they are cooler in summer.

Visitors must realize that many Mongols do not have toilets of their own and cannot be expected to know how to maintain and use ones that flush. Nor are they well organized or aware of foreigners' needs. In some yurt hotels, there is a separate bathhouse with running water and flush toilets (when the pump is working). The people are charming and wear their traditional costumes. The hospitable Mongols will even sing for you. We found the food barely edible, with tough fresh-killed mutton, fried millet, boiled millet, rice, boiled eggs, and cake. Do not expect hot pot or barbecue except in winter or in the cities. Take some snacks to fill up. Also soap. Each travel agency has a different hostel on the grasslands, some better than others.

One can visit Mongolian homes and an *aobo,* the rock mounds at high points where people worship, gather, and leave messages for each other. Mongolians now ride motorcycles much more than horses. Hohhot used to have many temples but they were destroyed during the Cultural Revolution. Among the survivors is the oldest **Dazhao Temple** 大召庙 (Ming) with a rare silver Buddha and many musical instruments, the **Xiaozhao Temple** 灵隐寺 and the Wutasi Temple. The **Wutasi (Five Dagoba Temple)** 五塔寺 was founded in the Ming. The tallest of its dagobas is 6.26 meters and they are made of glazed bricks carved with Buddhist symbols and inscribed in three languages: Mongolian, Sanskrit, and Tibetan. Behind the pagodas is a Mongolian astrological chart. The **White Pagoda** 白塔 on the eastern outskirts of the city at the Xilitu Lamasery is from the 10th century and is 40 meters and seven stories high. Inside are native tapestries. Ask also about the **Wudang Lamasery.** For more on Lamaism, see "Lhasa."

The **Tomb of Wang Zhaojun** 王昭君坟 is 10 km south of the city. About 2000 years ago, she was an imperial Han concubine, married off to a Xiongnu tribal chief to form an important political alliance. A bit of climbing. The **Great Mosque** 清真大寺 is in Chinese architecture. Hohhot also has the **Provincial Museum** 内蒙古博物馆 , with a highly recommended display on Mongolian lifestyle. For those serious about Mongolians, there is a Mongolia Society in the U.S.

FESTIVALS

The Nadamu festival takes place in Aug. 15–20 with ceremonies, competitions, and exhibitions in Hohhot and participants moving out to the banners afterwards. Each year could be different.

One year at Siziwang, about 100 km outside of Hohhot, was a demonstration of Mongolian culture with a parade, wrestling, archery, horsemanship, and traditional songs and dances. We ate Mongolian food, slept in yurts, used flush toilets, and visited Mongolian homes. Horses and camels were available for riding. Tourists outnumbered Mongolians.

At Xilinhot, 500 km from Hohhot, foreigners slept in yurts or in town and commuted about 40 minutes to the fair grounds carrying their own food. The 10,000 Mongolians attending slept in yurts, put up 200 booths to sell kitchenware, boots, carpets, and motorcycles, but no native clothes or jewelry. They wore traditional dress, and used muddy open-pit toilets with canvas covers. There were circus acts and real wrestling, archery, and horse-riding competitions with lots of chaos and no explanations, no dancers, and no horseback rides. Only a few foreigners attended.

One has to choose. Because of the crowds, we urge you to book a place through a travel agency and expect ''no star'' accommodations. We do think these will improve as organizers get more experience.

SHOPPING

Today, in addition to less exotic goods, Nei Mongol produces woolen textiles, cashmere sweaters, carpets, and tapestries. It also manufactures Mongolian-style boots, daggers with chopsticks, silver bowls, brass hot pots, cheap but fancy tweezers, wrestlers' jackets, saddles, stirrups, and felt stockings. Also available are antique bottles of jade or agate. Try the **Inner Mongolian Minorities Handicraft Factory** and **Minzu Shang Chang** (Nationalities Market), the **Hohhot Antique Shop,** and the **Hohhot Carpet Factory.** Shopping is better in Hohhot than in the grasslands.

FOOD

Meat, mainly mutton, but also beef. Notable are barbecued lamb, mutton hot pot, sesame pancakes, braised oxtail, beef kebab, ox tendon in egg white, camel hoof, and *facai* (the edible black hairlike algae that is a favorite in China.) Mongolian food is better in Hohhot at the hotels than in the grasslands.

HOTELS

The services of the Inner Mongolia seem to be better, but the location of the Zhao Jun is more interesting. The Zhao Jun, formerly a H.K.J.V., now seems to be sliding downhill. Both hotels need work.

Inner Mongolia Hotel (Nei Mongol Fandian) • *Wulanchabu Xi Rd., 010010. 3* Fax 27914. Dist.A.P. 16 km. Dist.R.W. 2.5 km. Dist. museum 1 km* • 1982–86. 20 stories. 250 rooms. Best floors 9–14. Shopping. IDD. Disco. C.I.T.S., C.T.S. Mongolian consulate. No air conditioning.

Zhao Jun Hotel. (Zhaojun Dajiudian) • *11 Xinhua Rd. 010050. 3*. Telex 85053 ZJHPT CN. Fax 668825. Dist.A.P. 15 km. Dist.R.W. 1 km. Dist. city hall 200 m* • C.C. 1988. 22 stories. 262 rooms. IDD. Chipped dishes. Badly laid carpets. Plumbing needs work.

Ambulance: tel. 42584, 663871.
Police, tel. 110.
C.I.T.S./C.T.S.: Inner Mongolia Hotel 010010; tel. 664233, 667924 X8932. Telex 85016 HTONM CN. Fax 661479. Overseas Tourist Corp.
CYTS: 9 Zhongshan Dong Rd. 010020; tel 663560. Telex 85094 CYTSI CN. Fax 664910. All agencies can sell tickets for the international train.
CAAC: Xilin Bei Rd., Minhang Lou.; tel. 24103.
Tourism Administration Inner Mongolia: 1 Xin Hua Rd., 010010. Tel. 665978.
Tourist Hotline: 665978.
See also "Baotou."

HUANGSHAN MOUNTAIN 黃山

East China in southern Anhui province. Huangshan is 120 km in circumference, and is one of China's most spectacular mountains. A climb has been described by one writer as "walking into an unending Chinese landscape painting." Huangshan can be reached by bus from Hefei. The airport at Tunxi, 75 km away, has links with 12 cities. Visitors can also travel by ship from Shanghai and Nanjing, to Chizhou or Wuhu, and then bus to Huangshan. The coldest is January, with a low of $-6°C$. The warmest is July, with a high of $20°C$. Annual precipitation is 2395 mm, mainly from June to September.

The highest of the 72 peaks, **Lian Hua (Lotus Flower)** 莲花峰 rises 1873 meters above sea level. To reach the valley before the final ascent to the top means climbing 800 stone steps cut into an 80° cliff, nose almost to rock.

One section of the second highest, **Tian Du (Heavenly Capital Peak)** 天都峰 (1864 meters), is a ridge less than a meter wide called "Carp's Backbone." Although iron chain railings exist to assure the unsure, some people resort to crawling to get across. This is just to say that Huangshan is for the very strong and adventurous, who will be rewarded by giant vertical peaks, pines (at least one over 1000 years old), hot springs (42°C), lots of streams, mist, magnificent views, and a great feeling of achievement—if you make it.

But there's hope. A **cable car** 缆车 , China's longest, is now operating to the North Sea Hotel from the Cloud Valley Monastery. C.I.T.S. advises no leather or plastic soles, or slippers. The climb is not easy. Take a walking stick, water bottle, and some food, and do not climb alone, here or anywhere else in the world.

If you only have one day, you have a choice. C.I.T.S. suggests taking a bus at 7:30 a.m. to Cloud Valley Monastery and then beginning to climb. At about 11 a.m. and 3000 stone steps higher, you will arrive at the **Beihai (North Sea) Hotel.** This place is noted for its strangely shaped pines and weathered rocks. The Refreshing Terrace should give you a view of a sea of clouds. Now you have to return the way you came, but if you stay here overnight, this is the best place to see the sunrise. If you do not stay overnight, you can retrace your climb (about 3 hours).

A second descent is via the **Jade Screen Tower** 玉屏楼 and the Heavenly Capital Peak. Hostels in each of these places serve Chinese and some Western food.

As with most mountains in China, paths are crowded with hikers during the summer at Huangshan. The end of April is said to be the most beautiful time, and hiking is good to the end of October.

A Ming village with over 100 temples, ancestral halls, pagodas, bridges, pavilions, and other relics collected from that period is planned for the foot of Purple Cloud Peak, 13 km from Tunxi.

SHOPPING

Paintings of Huangshan, Huangshan tea, bamboo and straw curtains. It is traditional to buy a special stone and find someone to carve your name on it.

HOTELS

Most hotels here are basic; with dirty blankets, dorms, poor service, and no private baths. C.I.T.S. says the Xihai is best, then the Cloud Valley Villa and third the Beihai, but don't expect much.

Cloud Valley Villa • *Cloudy Valley Temple, 242700. Telex 90078 AHHSZ CN.*

Xihai Hotel (Fandian) • *Xihai Scenic Area, 242700. Telex 90911 HSXHH CN. 3** • About 50 rooms. On mountain. Not much heat in winter. 20 min. walk from top of cable car. Hong Kong J.V.

North Sea Hotel (Beihai Binguan) • North Sea Resort, 242700. Telex 90908 AHTYH CN. 1700-meter altitude. 1958; renovated 1984. 112 beds.

Peach Spring Hotel (Taoyuan Binguan) • *3 Yanan Rd., Tunxi Dist. 245000. Telex 90915 CHB CN.* • 1979; ren. 1985. 134 beds. Pool, C.I.T.S. theater, dance hall.

OTHER IMPORTANT ADDRESSES

C.I.T.S. 中国国际旅行社 and **C.T.S.** 中国民航公司 : near Hot Spring, to the left of Peach Spring Hotel in Wenquan 245000; tel. 2206, 2371. Telex 90908 AMTYN CN.
C.Y.T.S.: tel. 214228. See also "Hefei."

JIANGMEN 江门

(Kiangmen; Cantonese Kongmoon) South China in Guangdong province on the Pearl River Delta, about 100 km south of Guangzhou. This old waterfront city can be reached by road or ship from Guangzhou or by daily nonstop 4-hour ferry from Hong Kong, and Macao.

This former foreign treaty port is also a cheap overnight passenger boat ride from Guangzhou, an interesting experience, to say the least. Several ferries leave daily from about 1 km east of the Overseas Chinese Mansion in Guangzhou. The night boat leaves before sunset, so you have a chance to see the never-ending river traffic, the maze of tributaries and canals, many lined with breakwaters, irrigation gates, and factories. If you're lucky, you'll have a full moon—and it's beautiful!

You sleep (if you can—it's somewhat noisy) 12 abreast on wooden platforms, softened only by straw mats and separated from fellow passengers by four-inch-high dividers. Upper and lower platforms line three sides of the room. You could have over 60 to 100 roommates, some of them curious, some friendly, but all discreet. A lot of women travel this way and I've never felt threatened. No privacy exists, not even for bathing, which is from a very public sink (with brown river water). The toilets, however, are in tiny, private cubicles, a hole in the floor through which you can see river water rushing by (and also your pants, if you don't hang on tight!) You can rent pillows and sheets and buy proletarian food. Boiled hot drinking water is available, but you should have had the foresight to carry your own mug and towel, like all the other passengers.

At dawn, or sometimes before, you find the boat entering a canal. Recent travelers have found a very boisterous group of taxi drivers bidding for their fare at the boat dock. Some travelers have succumbed to several hundreds of yuan worth of transportation but the city bus station is only 5 km away from the pier. From there, mini-buses can take you where you want to go for much less. Xinhui is 20 minutes away.

Jiangmen has East Lake Park (with rides), and a small Ming dynasty temple (Chen Bai Sha Temple, in honor of a famous philosopher). It has prospered in the last few years and now has many hotels, one of which has a revolving rooftop restaurant. Two fifths of the people here are Overseas Chinese or have Overseas Chinese relatives and therefore receive remittances from abroad.

Jiangmen City is made up of five counties: Xinhui, Heshan, Kaiping, Enping, and Taishan.

HOTELS

The newest, most modern hotel is the Crystal Palace. The East Lake is a good garden-style hotel. Both are close together in the suburbs, 5 km from the port and 2 km from the bus station.

Crystal Palace (Yin Jing Jiu Dian) • *22 Kong Kou Rd. 529051. Telex 459038. Fax 373001* • C.C. 1990. 214 spacious rooms. H.K.T.V. Attractive. Large pool. Good food. Gym. B.C. Bowling. Helipad.

East Lake Hotel (Dong Hu Binguan) • *Kong Kou Rd. 529051. 3*. Telex 45914. Fax 459038, 351010.* • C.C. 1973; ren. 1989. 3 stories. 182 rooms. Small rooms. Beautiful Azalea Villa opened 1990 with only suites. B.C. Pool. IDD.

C.I.T.S. • *13 Nonglin Rd. 529000; tel. 356562, 353384.*
C.T.S. • *15 Gangkou Rd. 529051; tel. 333611. Telex 45914. Fax 351010.*

JIAYUGUAN

Northest China. Western part of Gansu province in Hexi Corridor, eastern Gobi desert. Can be reached by regular flights from Dunhuang and Lanzhou and by more frequent chartered planes during the tourist season. Bus on 383-km paved road from Dunhuang, six or seven hours (lunch at Yumen Guest House in Anxi, stop at Qiao Wuan town—the 300-year-old mud ruins of an imperial scam, 100 km east of Anxi). Altitude 1600 m. Population 190,000. Hottest August, 34°C. Coldest January, −30°C. Best time to visit May–Oct. Sandstorms March–May, especially in Anxi. Strong winds Nov., Dec.

Jiayuguan is a pass at the western end of the Great Wall. The fort was first built in 1372 when the first Ming emperor had the wall repaired to keep out the defeated Mongols. Government and military officers were sent to develop the region and to protect commerce on the Silk Road. It covers over 33,500 square meters and has three imposing gates with fancy 17-meter-high towers. In addition to military structures, it has a theatre built in 1502, a reading room for officials, and a temple to the God of War. The God must have worked. The fort was never defeated. Six and one-half km from town. English titles.

The end of the Great Wall here is a mere trickle of its eastern magnificence, but it still fascinates. It does continue from here west for 7.3 km to the first beacon tower.

The **Wei and Jin Tombs** 魏晋墓群 (220–420 A.D.) are 20 km east of the city. One can be entered to see the famous bricks with delightful paintings of lifestyles and mythology. There is also a modest museum, well worth seeing. Jiayuguan also has a **Great Wall Museum** and a **glacier** (120 km away).

Jiuquan 酒泉 is 25 km away with a **Bell and Drum Tower** 鼓楼 originally built in 343 and renovated in the Qing. Han pagoda. Carpet factory. The "wine spring," the Western Han relic after which the city is named, has now dried out. The other city attraction is the **Luminous Jade Cup Factory**玉杯厂 where almost eggshell-thin goblets of "jade" are made. There is also the **Jiuquan County Museum** 酒泉博物馆.

Hotels

The best is the Great Wall. The airport is 13 km away. No IDD nor C.C.

Changcheng Binguan (a. k. a. Great Wall Hotel) • *16 Jianshe Xi Rd. 735100. Telex 72062 CCHZY CN. 3* •* Built like fort. On edge of town with great view of snowcapped Qilian Mountains. Close to museum. 1990–91. 5 stories. 150 rooms. Comfortable but don't expect too much. We found food uneven. Breakfast edible but unappetizing. Damp towels.

Jiayuguan Hotel (Binguan) • *1 Xinhua Bei Rd. 735100. 2* •* 5 stories, 65 rooms. C.I.T.S.

C.I.T.S.: tel./fax 26931. Don't expect much of this either.

JILIN (KIRIN) 吉林

Northeast China, in the center of Jilin province, 90 km east of the capital Changchun. Population nearly one million. It can be reached by rail from Beijing, Changchun, Shenyang, Harbin, Tianjin, etc. The airport is 25 km away with flights from 3 Chinese cities. Like the rest of the area formerly known as Manchuria, this also is extremely cold, with snow in winter and average minimum temperature December–February of ⁻24°C–⁻15°C.

By Chinese standards, Jilin is young, only about 300 years old. The Japanese took over in 1931, but were forced to leave in 1945. Tourist attractions include the **Deer Farm at Longtan Hill,** which produces antlers (for aphrodisiacs), ginseng, and sable. Also of interest are the ginseng gardens, the **Jilin Exhibition Hall 吉林展览馆** (with a 1770-kg meteorite, believed to be the largest in the world), and **Jiangnan Park. Songhua Lake 松花湖** is a 480-square-km manmade lake, and is 20 km from the city center. The Songhua River runs through the city and beautiful hoarfrost forms on the trees lining its banks in −20°C weather, celebrated with the Rime Festival. Ice lanterns in winter too.

Jilin has alpine skiing but facilities are not good (for example, electricity to run the lifts is not reliable). A 1800-meter-long ski chair lift services its 3.5-square-km "professional" ski area, with runs 3000 meters long. Skis can be rented. It is 16 km from the city at Fengman. Best skiing is December–February.

380 km SE of the city are the **Changbai Mountains,** their highest peak 2691 meters. An 800-meter ski slope is operating here now, but there are no lifts. Its crater is beautiful **Heaven Lake** with its own mythical monster. Changbai Mountain can be reached by road from Jilin and Yanji, by rail from Tonghua and tourist helicopter from Yangji. The other side is Korea. Visitors can also see **Arladi Village,** 70 km from Jilin, where Korean customs are still practiced.

FOOD

Local specialties include venison, frog oil soup, steamed whitefish, raw salmon and carp, and chicken and ginseng in earthenware pots.

HOTELS

The major hotels are along the Songhua River, but only the Milky Way comes close to satisfying the fussy. The Xi Guan is interesting because it has a villa once used by the warlord Zhang Zou Xiang. Big rooms and musty smells. Staying there should give you a feel for 1920s history.

Milky Way Hotel • *126 Songjiang Rd. 132011. 2*. Telex 84010 BYOOL CN. Dist.R.W.3 km* • C.C. (not Diner's). Hong Kong J.V. 1988. 15 stories, 200 rooms. Should have IDD by now.

Xi Guan Hotel • *155 Chuan Ying St. 132012. 2*. Dist.R.W.7 km* • No C.C. State guest house with several villas on 19 hectares. Huge rooms, 3.3-meter-high ceilings. White villa built 1953, expanded 1989.

CAAC: tel. 24260, 39772.
C.T.S. and C.I.T.S.: 4 Jiangwan Rd. 132001; C.I.T.S., tel. 459204. Telex 84007 FAO CN. Fax 453773. C.T.S., tel. 827790 X 313.
CYTS: tel. 829702, 54272.

JINAN (TSINAN) 济南

North China. The capital of Shandong is due south of Beijing, 15 km. from the south shore of the Huanghe (Yellow River), at the junction of the Beijing-Shanghai railway and the Qingdao-Jinan Railway. Jinan can also be reached by plane from 19 cities. It is on the main Beijing-Guangzhou train line, 6 hours from Beijing. The climate is temperate. Hottest in late July to early August, is 33°C; coldest in January, −6°C. Annual precipitation is about 700 mm, mainly in July and August. Population is 1.4 million urban.

Jinan dates as a city with a wall from the sixth century B.C., when it was made capital of the State of Qi. However, it was settled here more than 5000 years ago by neolithic cultures, the Dawenkou and the Longshan. It was named Jinan, meaning "south of the Ji River," a name that has been kept even though that river dried up centuries ago.

Jinan was a busy commercial center during the Tang, and Marco Polo wrote favorably of its garden atmosphere and its thriving silk industry after he visited it during the Yuan. It has been the capital since the Ming. It is now an industrial center producing trucks, textiles, and paper, and as a tourist destination, famous primarily for its springs, its Buddhist temples, and its proximity to Taishan Mountain and Qufu.

The excellent quality of the water in this "City of Springs" was first recorded 2500 years ago by a geographer. The Chinese kept records of pretty well everything! During the Jin (1115–1234), someone else listed 72 springs on a tablet. He missed a few. A 1964 survey mentions 108 natural springs.

The "springs" are not just holes in the ground spouting water. They are fountains, wells, and pools, and have been embellished with gardens, rockery, pavilions, and tea houses. The water was forced to the earth's surface here by a subterranean wall of volcanic rock. But unless you have a water fixation, a trip to one or two groupings will suffice. The performance of the water is seasonal because of the lowering water table. The best time seems to be after the rains in August and through the autumn.

The **Baotu Quan (Jet Spring)** 豹突泉 (tel. 22716), in the SW corner of the Old City, is said to be the best, with 16 fountains and the greatest amount of water, and is open from 8 a.m. to 5 p.m. It is in the center of a square pond, three separate sprays of bubbling water gushing almost a foot high.

The **Heihu Quan (Black Tiger Spring Park)** 黑虎泉 (tel. 20366) is another of the "four most famous springs." It is a 10-minute walk from the east side of Jet Spring. In this park the water gushes from the mouths of three stone tigers. Does it sound like the roar of tigers?

The third famous spring is the **Zhenzhu Quan (Pearl Spring)** 珍珠泉, tel. 615522. In the courtyard of the Pearl Spring Auditorium. The **Five-Dragon Pool** 五龙潭 completes the four most famous. It is outside the West Gate.

At this point head for the outskirts. Take in the **Qianfo (Thousand-Buddha) Hill** 千佛山 (tel. 611257), 2½ km south of the city. Here you find Buddhist images carved into the side of a cliff. Much climbing is involved to see the **Xingguo Si (Revive the Nation Temple)** 兴国寺, with 60–70 buddhas from 20 centimeters to over three meters tall, ranging from the Sui to the Tang. Look for three caves at the foot of the cliff and in the rooms of the west courtyard of the temple. There you find, yes, more buddhas.

In the **Yilan Ting (Pavilion of Panoramic View)** 一览亭, the tallest building around, you can get a good view of Jinan. On **Jueshan** you can see the 10-meters-high cave inside of which is a buddha head, seven meters tall.

West of Xingguo Temple about 3 km, is the **Yellowstone Cliff** 黄茅岗 a 40-meter-high rock around which were carved more Buddhas, and heavens!—flying devas—some of them nude! These were made during the Northern Wei, about 1600 years ago.

A stimulating time to visit this temple is on the ninth day of the ninth lunar month, when the hill is full of chrysanthemums and market stalls are set up.

If you have a half day left and your own vehicle, you can head to either **Liubu** 柳阜, 34 km south, or the **Lingyan Temple** 灵岩寺, which is closer. Both are important. Liubu has even more (210) and better Buddhist statues in five grottoes, most from the Tang, but some from the Song, Yuan, and Ming. In the **Qianfo (Thousand-Buddha) Cliff,** these range from 2.85 meters down to 20 centimeters high. Look for the Buddha called Blessing, ordered for Tang Emperor Taizong by one of his daughters.

The center of Buddhism for the province was at the **Shentong Si (Temple of Magical Power)** at the site of the current Tongtian Yu (Valley that Leads to Heaven). The **Long-hu (Dragon-Tiger) Tower** (Tang) has carvings of dragons, warriors, tigers, and devas. Are these devas (or good spirits) clothed? Look for yourself! The miniature pagodas are tombstones of abbots from the now extinct Temple of Magical Powers. Look for the one-story, 15-meter-high square **Simen* (Four-**

Door Tower) 四门塔 . At 1400 years of age, this is the oldest single-story tower of stone in the country. Note the thickness of the walls. A thousand-year-old pine protects its NE corner.

Only 3 km south is the **Jiuding (Temple of the Nine Pagodas)** 九鼎寺 . Here is the very unusually designed octagonal Nine-Spire Pagoda, probably dating from the Sui. Inside are murals from the Ming and Qing.

The remnants of a 12.6-by-10.7-meter platform, believed to be from the Tang is carved with dancers and singers holding musical instruments.

The ***Lingyan Si Temple** in Changqing county is one of the "four finest temples" in China. It was founded by a famous monk in A.D. 354 who was much moved by the beauty of the surroundings and whose sermons caused birds to listen, animals to stop, and even a rock nearby to nod in agreement. Hence the name. The current temple is from the Tang. The temple expanded in the Song when over 1000 monks studied and worshiped here. Surviving the centuries are the rock grotto from the Northern Wei, the Tang halls and pavilions, the Song clay images, and various rock carvings. Important to see is its **Thousand Buddha Hall,** built in the Tang, and repaired in the Song, Yuan, and Ming. Here are three large statues of Buddha, one of wood and two of bronze. The 40 painted clay arhats are very lively and about 102 centimeters tall. Northwest of this hall is the nine-story, 52.4-meter-high **Pizhi Pagoda** from the Tang, restored in the Song. The iron spire on the top is unusual, with its eight or nine Buddhist wheels chained together.

To the west is another cemetery with tiny dagobas marking the graves of monks, no two dagobas the same. This is the second best graveyard of this nature in the country. (See Shaolin Temple in "Zhengzhou"). Guess which dagoba belongs to the Tang dynasty temple's founder, Huichong? The most impressive one, of course! This 5.3-meter pagoda is similar to the square Four-Door Tower in Liu Bu, and decorated with dancers, devas (with or without?) and lion heads.

The **Shandong Provincial Museum** 山东省博物馆 (Wenhua Xi Rd.; tel. 20087), contains both historical and natural history relics. The history dates from neolithic times and includes Sun Bin's famous treatise on the art of war, written on bamboo about 2000 years ago. Also note the frescoes from Sui dynasty tombs, musical instruments, paintings from the tomb of the Prince of Lu (Ming), and musical instruments from the Confucian Family Mansion in Qufu.

You really need a couple of days to see **Taishan,** over 50 km away, and **Qufu,** the hometown of philosopher Confucius, 140 km south. Taishan is listed under "Tai'an." Both are very worthwhile. ***Linzi,** the former capital of Qi, is from the Zhou dynasty. In the province also are Qingdao, Yantai, Weihai, Weifang, and Zibo. See separate listings.

SHOPPING

Made in the province are human hair and silk embroidery and lace (Jinan Embroidery Factory); wool carpets, straw articles, kites, feather pictures (lovely) and dough modeling (yes, they do last!). The province also produces Qingdao (Tsingtao) Beer, the most popular Chinese beer. The main shopping area is Quancheng Rd. and also along Jin 2-Rd.

Shandong Antique Store (west of Department Store, 401 Quancheng Rd.; tel. 21185). Also 1 Gong Qing Tuan Rd., 3rd floor, phone 21435. The **Shandong Arts & Crafts** is at Jing Qi Wei Yi Rd., 250001, tel. 614082, 614081.

RESTAURANTS

Exotic local fare are cattail, lotus roots and lotus seeds from Daming lake, roast duck, winding-thread cakes, and monkey head mushroom.

HOTELS

The best hotel for tourists is the Qilu. The airport is 35 km from town. The glitzy Pearl and Minghu are better located for business people.

Foreign Students' Residence, Shandong Teachers' University (Shan Shi Wei Bin Lau) • *84 Wenhua Dong Rd. East 250014 (No. 18 bus from rwy. station to the main gate)* • Heat not regular. Some rooms air-conditioned. Budget travelers only.

Minghu Hotel (Dajiudian) • *366 Beiyuan Rd. 250033. Aiming for 3*. Fax 556688. Closest to International Trade Center. Dist. A.P. 4 km Dist. R.W. 2 km* • 1990–91. 22 stories, 273 rooms. C.C., B.C., USTV.

Pearl Hotel (Zhen Zhu Dajiudian) • *164 Jingsan Rd. 250001. Telex TEAJN 390028. Fax 615167. Next to park. Walk to city hall. Dist. A.P. 8 km. Dist. R.W.O. 5 km* • 1991–92. 24 stories, 200 rooms. C.C. USTV due. B.C. Gym. Very small driveway.

Qilu Hotel (Binguan) • *Qianfoshan Rd., 250014. 3*. Telex 39142 QLHJN CN. Fax 613524. Good view to the south of 1000 Buddha Hill in the suburbs. 5-minute walk to C.I.T.S. Dist.A.P.15 km. Dist.R.W.7 km* • C.C. 1985–86, ren. 1991 11 stories, 255 rooms. Tennis, B.C. Good standards. IDD, pool, gym, USTV.

OTHER IMPORTANT ADDRESSES

C.I.T.S.: 26 Jing Shi Rd., 250014; tel. 615858; telex 390001 CITSJ CN. Fax 616210.

C.T.S.: 26 Jing Shi Rd.; tel. 615858 X6107, 6411 or 2 Maanshan Rd. 250002; tel. 613931 X5104.
CYTS: tel. 25576, 25488.
CAAC: booking, 626 Jing 10 Rd.; tel. 664445; airport 554241.
China United Airlines: booking, tel. 23359.
Police: tel. 110.
Ambulance and Fire: tel. 119.
Shandong Tourism Bureau: 26 Jing Shi Rd. 250014; tel. 615858, 615859. Telex 39144 SDTJN CN. Fax 614284, 615870.
Tourist Hotline: tel. 43423.

JINGDEZHEN (CHINGTECHEN) 景德镇

South China. Northeast Jiangxi province NE of Nanchang. A must for porcelain lovers. It was from here that some of the best was shipped to Europe centuries ago, including the famous blue-and-white. It has been producing porcelain for over 2200 years and imperial porcelain since the Northern Song, over 980 years ago. Today Jingdezhen is still producing some of the best porcelain in China, a combination of the right clay, abundant pine wood for fuel, and easy transport (on the Yangtze). The city was founded in the Han and is considered one of China's Three Ancient Cities. Population 300,000. Altitude 200–500 m.

Jingdezhen has been reached by road, usually leaving Nanchang after breakfast and arriving about 4 p.m. It can be reached via Jiujiang, or by rail from Nanchang or Nanjing.

Visitors are usually taken to their choice of different factories, each with its own specialty: the *site of the Hutian Porcelain Kiln, dating from the Five Dynasties (white glazed) to the Song (celadon) and Yuan (blue-and-white). They can also see where the Kaolin clay is mined.

On Pearl Hill is the site of the Ming and Qing imperial kilns. The town itself is surrounded by mountains and the Chang River. The town also has a Pottery and Porcelain Exhibition Hall, the Ceramic Museum, and the Pottery and Porcelain College. Annual festival in October.

Jingdezhen Hotel (Binguan) • *3** • J.V. is on Lianhuatang and is the best in the city.
C.T.S.: and **C.I.T.S.:** 8 Lianhuatang St. 333000; tel. 222939. Fax 222937.

JINGGANG SHAN (CHINGKANG MOUNTAINS) 井冈山

South China. Mao Zedong (Mao Tze-tung) led his forces after the Autumn Harvest Uprising in 1927 to this 665-square-km mountain range in Jiangxi province near the Hunan border. Here the Communists established a base, carrying out land reform among the peasants. Forced to flee by the scorched-earth campaign of the Nationalists, the Communists embarked on the now legendary Long March to Yan'an in October 1934.

Mao's former residence, the **Jinggang Shan Revolutionary Museum** 井冈山革命历史博物馆, and other revolutionary sites are open to the public. These are mainly centered around the town of Ciping (Tseping) 茨坪. The battles against the Nationalists, who were trying to rid the country of the Communists, took place mainly in the five major mountain passes. These are Bamianshan, Huangyangjie, Shuangmashi, Tongmuling, and Zhushachong. A visit to any of these will show you how difficult it was to destroy the base.

The mountains are now being promoted as a tourist resort rather than a revolutionary monument. They are very beautiful, with steep cliffs and deep valleys in the south. One of many caves, the **Feilong Dong (Flying Dragon) Cave** 飞龙洞 can hold several hundred people. Its height ranges from 1 to 60 meters. Also of note are the **Youji Dong**

(Guerrillas Cave) 游击洞 and **Shuilian Dong (Water Curtain Cave)** 水帘洞 . Waterfalls are at Ciping, Liujiaping, Changping (130 meters high), and Longtan (Dragon Pool). The highest mountain is 1841 meters.

Larger in area than Lushan (also in Jiangxi province), a modern paper mill and bamboo handicraft factory are located here.

In Ciping 茨坪 are also a cinema, restaurants, hotels and library. At press time, it could be reached by a 2-day drive (about 300 km) from Nanchang in the north (overnight stop in Ji An) or by road from the south.

C.T.S.: 19 Hongjun Bei Rd., 343600, tel. 504.

JIUJIANG 九江

(Kiukiang, Chiuchiang, a.k.a. Xunyang) South China. Northern Jiangxi province on the south bank of the Yangtze River, where it bends south between Wuhan and Nanjing. It is bounded on the east by Poyang Lake and Mt. Lushan on the south. Accessible by train from Nanchang, by plane or by passenger boat along the Yangtze, this 2000-year-old city has been used as a port for the porcelain city of Jingdezhen since ancient times. It was also a treaty port and currently is comprised of two urban districts, ten rural counties, and Mt. Lushan. The population in Jiujiang is 47,000.

Of interest to visitors are the **Yanshui Pavilion** 烟水亭 in the middle of Lake Gantang, an 1840-square-meter island covered with gardens, halls, and pavilions; and the **causeway between Lake Gantang and Lake Nanmen** 甘棠湖和南门湖之间的长堤 , built in A.D. 821. Also important to see are the **Dasheng Pagoda** 大胜塔 in Nengren Temple and the **Xunyanglou and Suojianglou Pagoda.** Important also is the **Donglin Temple,** the birthplace of the ''Pure Earth'' sect of Buddhism (founded 1,500 years ago), and the **Boyang Lake Migrant Birds Preserve,** said to be the largest in the world (from Oct. to March).

The **Nanhu Hotel** (28 Nanhu Rd. 332000) is on the side of South Lake, with villas. The **Bailu Hotel** (Xunyang Ave. 332000) should be open now.

C.I.T.S., 28 Nan Hu Rd. 332000; tel. 221895. Telex 95063 IPTXB CN.
C.T.S., 77 Nanci Rd.; tel. 4015.

KAIFENG

Northwest China. Northern Henan on the Shanghai-Urumqi railway line, about 75 km east of Zhengzhou. It is 10 km from the southern bank of the Huanghe (Yellow River), and is highly recommended for its history and quiet, exotic charm. Population 620,000. Hottest July–early August 38° C, Coldest January minus 9. Rain 600 mm. mainly July–August. Dry, dusty, and windy in spring.

With a history of 2600 years, Kaifeng was the capital of several dynasties, including the Wei, Liang, Later Jin, Han, Later Zhou, Northern Song, and Jin. During the Song it was an important commercial and communications center, producing textiles, porcelain, and printing. It was sacked by Jurched tribesmen in 1126 and never recovered.

With 120 recorded Yellow River floods due to dams breaking near Kaifeng between 1194 and 1948, one wonders why Kaifeng exists at all. In 1642, during a peasant uprising, the Yellow River dike was destroyed by Ming forces so that the city was completely inundated and 372,000 people were killed. In 1938, the Nationalists destroyed the dam upriver near Zhengzhou to stop the Japanese and 840,000 people died.

Today, the riverbed, raised by centuries of silt deposits, is about 10 meters higher than ground level near Kaifeng.

Since Liberation, the Chinese have given top priority to controlling the Yellow River, and since 1984 the Chinese government and the United Nations World Grain Planning Program have worked together on an irrigation and warping project here.

Kaifeng is one of the 24 cities of historical importance protected by the State Council. It is laid out in the classic Chinese plan, and has a well-preserved but decaying earth Song city wall.

The 13-story *Tie Ta ("Iron Pagoda") 铁塔 was built over 900 years ago (Song) leaning towards the wind but it is now standing straight. At a height of 55.6 meters, it is actually of glazed brick. The **Xiangguo Temple** 相国寺 , built in A.D. 555, was rebuilt in 1766 after the flood. It has a famous thousand-armed, thousand-eyed Buddha of gingko wood. The **Longting (Dragon Pavilion)** 龙亭 is at the site of the Northern Song palace. The existing buildings here are from the Qing, the stone lions in front from the Song. Also worth seeing are the **Yanqing Taoist Temple** 延庆观 , **Lord Bao's Memorial Hall** (wax figures) on Bao-gong Lake, and the very fancy **Guild Hall of Three Provinces** 山陕甘 会馆. The **Yuwang Miao (King Yu's Temple)** 禹王台 was built in the Ming in honor of Emperor Yu, who tried to control the floods. The bottom of the **Pota Pagoda** 繁塔 was built in 977, the top in the Qing, after the original was destroyed. Except for the Yellow River, all important sites are inside or near the 4 × 8 km. long wall.

Kaifeng is also famous for its embroidery, and its Jewish community, the remnants of which still remain today. The stele with the history of the Jewish community was last seen outside the warehouse behind the museum, face to the wall. The museum is open 8 a.m.–4 or 5 p.m. with two hours for lunch. A famous painting of the ancient city, *Qing Ming Festival at the Riverside,* inspired the design of the Song Dynasty Village in Hong Kong. Its 400 m *Song Dynasty Street* is photogenic, a copy of the famous painting *River Scenes from the Qing Ming.* Song style food and entertainment in the Fanlou Restaurant.

Because of its size and compactness, Kaifeng can be seen in two days. Great for bicycling but you'll need more time.

Canadians in particular might be interested in the grave of Canadian Dr. Tillson Lever Harrison who died in Changqiu in 1947 after delivering three box cars of medical supplies under horrendous conditions through the Nationalists' areas to the Communists. It is in the Revolutionary Martyrs Cemetery with a stone almost 2 meters high. There is also a Tillson Lever Harrison Memorial School in the city, probably on the site of the old Anglican church where he was first buried.

Shopping is at **Xiangguo Temple Market's** 3000 stalls. For antiques, try the *Kaifeng Cultural Relics Shop, 23 Madao St., tel. 23262.

Hotels The Kaifeng and the Dongjing are the best, but neither is luxury standard nor well maintained. Their ranking depends on which is the most recently renovated. The Dongjing has the better setting and is garden style. The Kaifeng has the bigger rooms.

Dongjing Hotel (Dongjing Dafandian) • *14 Yingbin Rd. 475000. 2*. Telex 46110 KFFAO. Dist.A.P. 70km, Dist.R.W.2 km, T. R. 1988– 89* • Three stories, 200 rooms. Thin walls. Should have B.C. and IDD now. Attractive traditional-style garden. C.C. Bicycles.

Kaifeng Guest House (Binguan) • *64 Ziyou St. 475000. 2*. Dist.R.W.3 km, Dist.A.P.70 km* • 1974, ren. 1989. Three stories, 119 rooms.

C.I.T.S. and **C.T.S.:** Kaifeng Guest House 475000; tel. 23737. Telex 470503 KFFAO CN. Fax 23737.
Kaifeng Tourism Administration: Dongjing Hotel, 475000; tel. 33155 (complaints).
Ambulance: tel. 22261.
Police: tel. 32530.

KASHI (KASHGAR) 喀什（喀什噶尔）

Northwest China at the farwestern tip of Xinjiang province, about 164 km from the C.I.S. border. One of the highlights of a Silk Road trip because of its ambience, architecture, and extraordinary Sunday market, it can be reached by air (1085 km in 1.5 hours) from Urumqi or a 3-day bus ride each way. One can also go from here by land to Lhasa. It is also accessible by road, but not without a long, tiring, and sometimes spectacular journey from Pakistan (520 km) or the C.I.S. (164 km). Independent travelers are warned that getting from and to Urumqi might be difficult. Give yourself a couple of extra days. Flights are frequently cancelled. Population 280,000 urban and rural, 74% Uygur. Altitude 1289 m. Annual rainfall below 100 mm (take precautions against dust). Highest temperature in summer 40°C. Lowest in winter −24°C. Early May is fine. The end of September can be cold. Tourists go to Kashi for the Sunday market, a medieval crush of 100,000 Uygurs, Afghanis, Pakistanis, Kirghiz, Tadjik, and Mongols, blacksmiths, barbers, "dentists," and donkey carts. Here are traded peppercorns, mutton shish kebabs, pomegranates, grapes, cloth, bright felt carpets, jeweled knives, and boots, camels, and goats. Kettles are mended and bicycles repaired. This market is more for photographing than buying, and needs at least three hours. Most residents don't mind cameras. Go early to avoid the heat.

Government officials and hotels here keep office and meal hours by Beijing time, but some shops keep "Kashgar time," and others keep "Pakistan time"—which could mean a three-hour difference. Kashi is over 2000 years old and has been fought over by many contenders. In the mid-10th century, a Uygur-Turkish coalition, the Karahanid (Qurakhanid) Dynasty took over the area. Its leaders later converted to Islam and made Kashi their capital. Today it grows rice, wheat, fruit, and cotton. Like other cities of Xinjiang, it gives one a feeling more of west Asia than of China. It is the only city in China where women are veiled.

City centre is around the 1442 A.D. Idkah Mosque   ,
which holds 7,000 people. Nearby is a giant pomegranate, symbol of
the city (and fertility). Just sitting in this square is like watching a movie
of life and death in the Middle Ages. We saw a funeral. The carpet and
musical instrument factories are close by. Behind the mosque are streets
with old buildings, wrought iron balconies, and alleyways with mud
town houses like those in north Africa, and friendly natives.

Kashi was on the Silk Road and is a center of Uygur culture. It is
exotic, with many people wearing traditional national dress.

Visitors can see the huge **Abakhojia Tomb**   阿巴克和加麻扎
(Ming and Qing), the final resting place of 70 descendents of Muhatum
Ajam, an Islamic missionary. It is 3 km from the Kashar Hotel. A
museum is being built close to this hotel. The **San Xian (Three Immortals) Buddhist Caves** 三仙洞 are north of the city and difficult to
reach. Three rectangular holes high in the side of a cliff beckon the fit
and curious. Unless they have been recently repaired, the frescoes inside are not in good condition.

Recent visitors have seen the snow-covered Pamir Mountains from
Scholar Mohamed Kashgari's Tomb on the road to Pakistan.

Thirty km east of Kashi is the town of **Hanoi** 罕诺依 , abandoned
after the 11th century and now just a ruin. In the area, one can also
cruise **South Lake** 南湖 , but it is only a respite from all the dryness.
South of the city and east of the Sino-Pakistan Highway toward Afghanistan are 7719-meter-high **Mt. Kongur** 公格尔冰山 and 7546-
meter-high **Mt. Muztagta** 穆士塔格山 , part of the Pamirs. If you
keep in mind that Hunza in Pakistan and Kashmir in India are also to
the south, you will get an idea of the magnificence and isolation of the
area here. Think Himalayas!

Kashi produces gold and silver ornaments, leather boots, bronze-
ware, jewelry, rugs, jade carving, embroidered caps, daggers, and musical instruments made of apricot wood. The jewelry bazaar is on Zhiren
St. The Odali Bazaar sells daggers and caps. One can get around locally
by bumpy donkey cart. If you buy the fancy ''jewelled'' daggers, do
put them in your checked luggage if you're flying, or leave them with
the flight crew (for a fee.)

HOTELS

Generally poor with limited services. No IDD. At the Kashgar,
money exchange. The Seman's new section has an exchange desk. Many
backpackers eat at John's Cafe at the Seman.

Kashgar Hotel (Binguan) • *Tazriz/Tawuguzi Rd. 844000. Bldg.
#4 2*. Fax 23087. Closest to Sunday market. 4 km to town center* •
Set in large garden. Moslem dining room. Good hot water but terrible
plumbing. Amex C.C. only.

Qiniwak Hotel (Qinibah) • *93 Seman Rd. 844000. Fax 23087. Telex 79051 CITS CN* • The old British Consulate building is still there. 1990 addition, 5 stories and 140 rooms. Bigger bathrooms than Kashgar Hotel. C.I.T.S. nearby. Customs for travelers going to Pakistan cleared here. Read *The Antique Land* by Diana Shipton, who lived here in 1946.

Seman Hotel • *Seman Rd. 844000 2*. More central* • Three hours of water a day. Former Russian Consulate still here. Noticeboard for travelers. Bicycles.

C.I.T.S. at Qiriwak Hotel, Semar Rd. (tel. 3156, 3087). **C.T.S.** at Jiefang Bei Rd. 844000 (tel. 2217).
CAAC: tel. 2133.
See also "Silk Road."

昆明

KUNMING (A.K.A. KUNNANFU)

Southwest China. The capital of Yunnan province, which borders Vietnam, can be reached by train from Chengdu, Changsha, etc. and by plane from 20 Chinese cities, and from Hong Kong, Bangkok, and Rangoon. It is beautifully situated on the 330-sq.-km Dianchi Lake, China's sixth largest. Because of its altitude of 1894 meters and its subtropical location, it is blessed with the best weather in China, spring all year round, though some snow fell in 1991. The hottest temperature is 29°C in July and the coldest ⁻1°C in January. 1500 mm. of rain falls mainly from May to October. One of the loveliest times to visit is February, when the camellias are in bloom. Urban population: about 1 million.

Kunming is important to see because of its mountain scenery, its national minorities, the artistry and history of its temples and architecture, the Burma Road, and the Stone Forest. The weather is a big attraction.

In the province also are several unusual sights. These range from almost year-round snow-capped mountains to tropical jungles where elephants and monkeys roam. One third of its over 34 million people belong to 25 national minorities. Many of the groups, especially the women, still wear their distinctive clothes, even while working in the fields. Many still practice old customs—like the Dai **Water-Splashing Festival.** Kunming ranks in my books as the third most desirable tourist destination in China, after Beijing and Xi'an. One could easily spend two weeks in the province.

Kunming itself has a history of 2400 years. The region has always been considered remote and resistent to the central government. The Xiaguan area was part of the Nanzhou empire, which refused to submit to the Tang but was subdued by the Mongols in the 13th century and visited by Marco Polo. The narrow-gauge railway from Hanoi was built by the French in 1895 to 1904 and you can now ride it. Kunming was a French concession with a Catholic cathedral, convent, and French Club. The French wanted the province's tin, tungsten, and opium. It was also rich in hard wood, rubber, and rice. When Yuan Shih-kai proclaimed himself emperor in 1915, Yunnan rebelled. The Japanese wanted it as part of the first phase of their campaign to capture southeast Asia, a conflict in which the Vichy French tried not to be involved. The province was ruled during the Japanese War by warlord governors, one of whom, Lung Yun, an ex-bandit and opium king, was later overthrown with American help.

The city is completely surrounded by mountains. Sightseeing here can be a little rugged in spots. The **Dragon Gate** necessitates a climb of 200 stairs, but the effort is well worth it.

If you only have one day, you have to choose between a tour of the city or going to the Stone Forest. It is better that you stay at least two days, preferably more. Important in the city are the Western Hills, Golden Temple, Black Dragon Pool, Bamboo Temple, Yuantong Temple, Daguan Park, and Green Lake.

Xishan (Western Hills) 西山 are about 26 km from the hotels. They have the 14th-century **Huating Temple** 华亭寺 , the largest in the city. South of here is the **Taihua Temple** 太华寺 (Yuan), with the best view of the sunrise over the lake. The **Sanqing Tower**, 2 km farther south, was the summer resort of Emperor Liang of the Yuan. It has nine tiers, each about 30 meters above the other. On the top is the **Long Men (Dragon Gate)** 龙门 , with another great view of the lake. The stone corridors, chambers, paths, and intricate carving of the Dragon Gate were cut from 1609 to 1681.

The coppercast ***Golden Temple** 金殿 , NE of the city (11 km away), is 300 years old, 6.5 meters high, and weighs 200 tons. The **Qiong Zhu (Bamboo) Temple** 筇竹寺 18 km NW of the Kunming Hotel, has 500 life-size arhats carved in the Qing. These are very expressive and are worth a visit. The temple was founded in 1280.

The **Daguan Lou Pavilion** 大观楼 , across the lake from Xishan Hill (7 km from the Kunming Hotel), has a 180-character couplet at its entrance, the longest ever found in China. Composed by a Qing scholar, the first half praises the landscape while the second deals with Yunnan history. Also important is the **Black Dragon Pool** 黑龙潭 , with its Ming temple and tomb. The Heishui Shrine here may be from the Han. Nearby are the Botanical Gardens.

Yuan Tong Si 园通寺 , the only Tang temple in town, is on the same street as the Green Lake Hotel, a little over a kilometer away.

The **Stone Forest of Lunan** 路南石林 , one of the highlights of a Kunming visit, is 80 km SE of the city, and tourists usually stay in the adjacent **Stone Forest Hotel (Binguan)** Lunan County 652211. About 270 million years ago the area was covered with water. The limestone pushed its way out of the receding sea and rain continued to corrode the stone into these incredible formations. One fifth of the 64,000 acres is open to visitors. Here, too, are many steps and safety fences. The shortest of the two routes is 2½ hours long, and in this maze it's easy to get lost.

Near the hotel is a Sani nationality 撒尼族 village, and minority-type handicrafts are for sale. You can buy direct from the weavers. Groups of local dancers in national costume have entertained hotel guests in the evening with songs and dances. The Stone Forest is very commercialized, and peddlers can be a real nuisance.

The trip between Kunming and the Stone Forest itself is remarkable because of the hilly scenery, the eucalyptus trees, and the occasional native, brightly costumed.

If you have more time, a 2-hour boat cruise on 340-sq.-km **Lake Dianchi** can be arranged, but go only for the rest, as not much can be seen (except for Daguan Lou, fish farms, and people fishing with large triangular nets). There is a Provincial Museum 博物馆 and at the Institute for Nationalities 少数民族学院 is the only exhibit of minority clothing. At the institute, students perform minority dances on special occasions and carry out field studies to document the history and culture. Make arrangements through a travel agent well in advance as it is not generally open.

Along the west shore of the lake is Sleeping Beauty Hill and a series of swordlike hills. On the southern tip of the lake is **Jinning** county town, the birthplace of the famous Ming navigator Zheng He, who sailed to East Africa half a century before Vasco da Gama. The Memorial Hall to Zheng He 郑和纪念馆 is on a hill above the town.

Festivals worth experiencing, in addition to the water-splashing, include the **Yi Torch Festival,** in late July or early August in the Stone Forest, the **Third Moon Market** (usually April, sometimes May) in

Dali, and the **Horse and Mule Market Meeting,** around early April in Lijiang. Also ask about weekly minority markets. Lijiang's is especially mind-boggling. An arts festival with performances by most of China's national minorities has been held mid-February to early March annually.

A good detailed guide with photos is Patrick R. Booz's *Yunnan.*

SHOPPING

Blue and white batik, feather products, and tribal handicrafts (especially shoulderbags and clothes), tin and spotted copperware.

FOOD

Specialties include "Rice Noodles Crossing the Bridge" 过桥米泉 Yunnan ham, and crispy, dried goat's cheese. The adventurous could try snake, or congealed blood. Dai food includes grasshoppers. Try the hotpot at the **Chihua Yuan Restaurant.** The **Quanjude Restaurant** at 111 Yuantong Dong Rd. has ethnic dances and good food. The Kunming Ice House near the Kunming Hotel has cold beer.

HOTELS

The top hotel is the Golden Dragon of almost international luxury standard. The Kunming Hotel is second. Other hotels are far behind. The Green Lake however has a 4* Singapore J.V. addition due soon. Best for businesspeople and shops are the Golden Dragon, Camellia and Kunming.

Camellia Hotel (Cha Huan Binguan) • *154 East Section Dongfeng Rd., 650011. 1** • Favorite of budget travelers. No C.C. No IDD. No money exchange. 1985. Ren. 1989. 13 stories. Twice daily bus to Dali. Tours to Stone Forest. Bicycles. Dorms.

Golden Dragon Hotel (Jinglong Fandian) • *575 Beijing Rd. 650011. 3*. Telex 64060 GDHKM CN. Fax 31082. Dist.A.P.7 km. Dist.R.W.1 km* • Hong Kong management. 1988–89. Ren. 1991. 19 stories, 302 rooms, C.C., IDD probably 1990. B.C., bicycles, tennis, hot-spring swimming pool, gym. USTV. Dragonair.

Green Lake Hotel (Cuihui Binguan) • *6 South Cuihu Rd. 650031. Telex 64073 GLHTL CN. Cable 5046. Dist.A.P.15 km. Dist.R.W.8 km. Across street from park* • 1980. Ren. 1990. 5 stories, 160 rooms. C.C., B.C., bicycles. Has had problems with water pressure.

Kunming Hotel (Binguan) • *122–145 East Dongfeng Rd. 650031. Telex 64058 KMHTL CN. Dist.A.P.7 km. Dist.R.W.4 km* • 1958 sect. and 1982 sect. both ren. 1989; back section ren. 1991. Better. 450 rooms. C.C., IDD, B.C., bicycles. Good food.

Yunnan Travel & Tourism Bureau, C.I.T.S., and **C.T.S.:** 8 Heping Xincun, Huancheng Nan Rd., 650011; tel. 23316, 27259. Telex 64027 KMITS CN. Fax 29240 (for brochures and information). For complaints, tel. 35412. YTTB: tel. 32332, 34019. Near Golden Dragon.
C.T.S. and **Yunnan Overseas Travel Corp.:** 145 Dongfeng Rd. 650041. C.T.S. tel. 28522. Telex 64027 KMITS CN. YOTC tel. 64341. Telex 64135 KMCH CN. Fax 32508.
CAAC中国民航: 146 Dongfeng Dong Rd.; tel. 24270.
CYTS: tel. 31963.
Dragonair: tel. 33104, 33105 X20430. Fax 31082.
Tourist Hotline: tel. 35412.

Outside of Kunming you can go in two directions, southwest to Jing Hong or west along the Burma Road. Don't expect good hotels.

From Kunming to Jing Hong in **Xishuang Banna** region (pronounced She-Schwan-Ban-NA) is about a 24-hour drive on paved roads. Planes fly at least twice a week in an hour. This area has an elevation of 550 to 2300 meters, with tropical lowlands growing rubber. There is 1200 to 2000 mm of rain annually. Take precautions against malaria.

Jing Hong has about 30,000 people. Thirteen minorities inhabit this region. The few tourists usually go to the Water Splashing Festival, the Dai New Year, in April. Minority customs have remained largely intact, more so than in Dehong on the Myanmar border. It has been hard to find handicrafts for sale, but this should change as tourism develops.

Recent visitors explored a Dai village, market, and Buddhist temple (similar to some in neighboring Laos). They took a steamer ride on the Lancang River (which becomes the Mekong 30 km away in Laos). During the well-organized festival, they watched minority dances and demonstrations, dance dramas, and bamboo rocket competitions. Wa tribesmen sacrificed a bull. C.I.T.S. had a boat from which they could see the dragon boat races, about a km away. Foreigners were encouraged to sing at banquets. Take a water pistol and shower cap.

The water-throwing was confined to certain areas between 10 a.m. and 4 p.m. on one designated day. Tourists were taken to a park and loaned basins. As they walked back to their hotel, local youths came at them gleefully. It was a lot of fun. Instead of a few reverent sprinkles, it was a good-natured water fight. Do keep your valuables at the hotel and your camera in a plastic bag.

The Dai-style Yin Bing Dai Wei Canting Restaurant, Nan Feng Restaurant (Sichuan food), and the restaurant in the Jinghong Hotel (Di Er Jiao Dai So) have been good.

Hotels here are basic and modest. No western food. The best hotel has been the Xishuangbanna. The Banna Building Hotel has a good location on the main street but needed lots of work. Elevator only 8 a.m.–10 p.m. During the festival, rooms are in short supply.

Xishuangbanna Hotel (Binguan) • *6661000. Downtown location. Dist.A.P. 7 km. Dist. bus station 2 km* • 1956. 200 rooms. Few rooms air conditioned. Mosquito nets. Set in a garden, it had a lot of mosquitos, lizards, and cockroaches. The best villas were no. 5 and 7. Dorm for backpackers. Bicycles. No money exchange. C.I.T.S.

Tourism officials are working toward tours by ship from Jinghong into Thailand, Laos, and Burma.

About 3 hours by car **west** of Kunming along the Burma Road is **Chuxiong.** During festivals, many Yi people sing and dance from 9 p.m. to dawn in the center of town, conversing socially through music. The rhythms and energy level are amazing. A minorities fashion festival has also been held here. Chuxiong's tourist hotel is frequently a lunch stop for trips to Dali. If you're careful about hygiene, the roadside stalls along this road can provide memorable meals with congealed blood, pork kidney, squirming eels and chilis.

Further along the Burma Road, the hotels are barely adequate. Do not expect air conditioning, heat, IDD, money exchange, carpets, coffee shops, bars, 24-hour electricity or hot tap water.

Xiaguan is at an altitude of 1000 meters, the capital of Dali Bai Autonomous Preferecture. About a 12-hour 400-km drive from Kunming, it is at the southern tip of 41-km-long Lake Erhai. The highest temperature here is 29°C in June. The coldest, minus 3°C in December. There is 1200 mm rain, mainly May–August. Windy all year round but strongest November–March. There is a tea brick factory and a temple to the Tang general who failed to conquer Xiaguan. There are boat trips on the 2000-year-old man-made lake to see 3800-m-high Cangshan Mountain, snow-capped most of the year.

Public air-conditioned buses are crowded and crude and can be booked at the Camellia Hotel in Kunming. The best view is the side behind the driver. Public buses in Xiaguan stop running after 7 p.m., but you can usually hitch a ride on a horse cart. The Erhai Hotel here is adequate but it is more fun to stay in Dali.

There is a tendency to confuse the names Dali and Xiaguan. Xiaguan was the old term for greater Dali, and the name is still used. **Dali** is 10 km north of Xiaguan, an old walled town with marble factories and some of the best marble in China. Some houses are made of it. Look for a large obelisk erected by conquerer Kublai Khan in the 13th century.

Dali has the **Sanyuejie (Third-Month market)** 三月街 , the 15th to 20th day of the third lunar month, with caravans of horses and mules arriving to be traded. It is also an important market for traditional medicines. About 100,000 people take part in the market, from all provinces. Enlivened by races and, perhaps, gambling, the site west of Dali at the foot of the mountain is a former Nationalist execution grounds. The best hotel inside the wall is the Dali Guest House. No. 2 Guest House, the La La Cafe, Jimmy's Peace Cafe, and Tibetan Cafe have been are popular with backpackers.

Xizhou, just north of Dali, has especially remarkable Bai architecture, incorporating marble. Bai architecture is characterized with whitewashed walls and black trim. The much-decorated houses have courtyards in the middle and living quarters on three sides, with the entrance in a painted wall. The women's dress is basically white with red or black vests and a colorful bonnet. The women sing easily on request here. In addition to courtship rituals, the songs also relate local history, and are sung at work and during ceremonies such as weddings and funerals. The Tian Zhuan Binguan (hotel) here in Bai style is charming.

Shizhong Shan 石钟山 石窟 , near Jianchuan (a long, one-day excursion north), has a uniue Buddhist grotto reached by a steep 45-minute climb. It has a 1-meter-high female genitalia, which women rub for fertility and boys for courage. It also has some of the earliest Buddhist carvings in China—several styles, including some humans pictured with long curly hair, probably ancient foreigners. Indians, perhaps? At the base of this mountain lies an exotic old monastery.

Shibao Shan 石宝山 , nearby, also has temples and an annual singing contest in late August or early September by young people of many minorities. During the festival, thousands sleep under the trees or in temples, talents are discovered, and friendships and romances blossom. The singing is a courtship ritual. Currently, public transportation exists in this area, but roads are unpaved. Fish is the local specialty, but the cooking is not outstanding.

San Ta Si (Three Pagoda Temple) 三塔寺 , on the west shore of Lake Erhai, 4 km. outside the NW gate of Dali, was built in the Nanzhao/Tang period, over a 1000 years ago, and recently renovated. The view of the lake, the three towers (70 meters and 43 meters high), and the mountains behind are famous.

Butterfly Pool 蝴蝶泉 , on the northern tip of the lake, is a natural spring with one huge tree covering it. In May strings of different kinds of butterflies appeared.

Shopping is best at the various tourist attractions or factories: "silver" jewelry, embroidered purses, natural marble pictures, tie-dyed cotton. I've sewn a thick Bai embroidered flower onto my business suit.

Further north of Dali is **Lijiang** 丽江 in northwest Yunnan, about 700 km from Kunming, where the **Yu Long (Jade Dragon) Mountain** 玉龙山 rises spectacularly 6000 meters above sea level. Here the Naxi people still use hieroglyphic writing and wear sheepskin capes on their backs for warmth and to cushion heavy baskets. On the sheepskin are seven small embroidered moons to show how hard they work (until the moon and stars appear).

Some of the Naxi are matriarchal, with "walk-in" marriages. At age 14 the boys are put out of their homes and have to find girlfriends to sleep with. Without a girlfriend, a boy sleeps with the dogs. There are no marriages. They breakfast with their mothers. Children are supported by all males in the community.

Also important to see are the **Dabaoji Palace, Liuli Temple,** and **Dading Temple,** all in Ming architecture. The **Liang Guesthouse** (60 rooms) is in Naxi style.

Farther north of Lijiang, toward the Tibet border, is **Zhongdian,** considerably off the tourist path, with an altitude of 3000 meters. **Guihua Si,** on a hilltop there, was once a very prosperous Lama temple. During the Cultural Revolution it was totally destroyed except for the ruins of walls now standing, still an astounding sight. The main hall has been reconstructed and should soon make a visit to this remote area rewarding for those eager to be among the first. The scenery from Zhongdian to Xiaguan is especially great for bird watchers, and is full of lakes, forests, and mountain views. The temple has a simple inn.

Trips can be booked in Dali for Lijiang and Zhongdian, and we suggest you aim for the Sunday markets. You may need an alien travel permit. Tours also go this way to Tibet.

We recommend C. P. Fitzgerald's *Tower of Five Glories,* about his experiences in this area in the 1930s.

Dali/Xiaguan is usually an overnight stop on the **Burma Road.** This road extends 879 km from Kunming to Dehong on the Burmese/Myanmar border. It was first built from 1947 to 1949 by 160,000 Chinese and Burmese laborers. The United States financed it to supply China in her fight against the Japanese. Used by the Allies until 1942 when it was closed by the Japanese capture of Burma, it was extended and reopened from India to Kunming in 1945, and renamed the Stillwell Road after the U.S. general.

Unfortunately, there is nothing to mark this Sino-U.S. achievement, and local people seem to know nothing about it. It does have the only monument to the Chinese soldiers who fought in the Japanese war (near Tengchong), and the government is talking about building a museum near the border.

The drive south from Dali takes about 9 hours through mountains, its highest elevation 4000 meters. Many battles took place here. Tengchong has a huge rhododendron forest, the biggest tree 16 m high. It also has geysers.

Flights go from Kunming to Baoshan, 176 km from the border. Flights also go to the border, where one should be able to see the barter trade between the countries, and pigs sniffing for heroin. There is a jewelry factory. Chinese officials hope tours here can continue some day into Myanmar, Laos, and Thailand.

LANZHOU (LANCHOW) 兰州

Northwest China. Western Gansu province, of which it is the capital. Almost in the center of China, on the Yellow River, it can be reached by air from 23 Chinese cities including Beijing, Dunhuang, and Xi'an (500 km away. A shorter road from Xi'an with a 2.4 km. tunnel is due 1994.) Lanzhou is also serviced by train from Baotou, Urumqi, and Yinchuan.

Lanzhou is important as a stop on the Silk Road and as a gateway to two cave temples, the *Bingling Temple Caves and the *Maijishan Caves. Do not stop here unless you're interested in cave temples and have at least three days and the strength to climb. In any case, the infamous pollution here has been reduced by the growing use of electricity instead of coal.

Founded about 2200 years ago, Lanzhou was called the "Gold City" after gold was found here. At an altitude of 1524 meters, the coldest winter temperature is -7°C in January; the hottest, 23°C. Annual precipitation in the province is between 30 and 340 mm, the rain mainly in the SE. Sandstorms April–May.

With a population of over one million, the city is industrial, with petrochemicals, machine building, and smelting.

Gansu province today has a population of 23 million, including Han, Hui, Tibetan, Dongxiang, Yugur, Bonan, Mongolian, Kazak, Tu, Salar, and Manchu nationalities. The area was settled 200,000 years ago; 3000 years ago, the inhabitants started farming the eastern part of Gansu. The province is the setting for Yuan-tsung Chen's excellent autobiographical novel *The Dragon's Village,* a book based on her own experiences with land reform shortly after Liberation.

In Lanzhou, of mild interest is the **Baita (White Pagoda Park)** 白塔 on a hill on the north bank of the Yellow River. First built in the Yuan, then rebuilt and expanded in the Ming and Qing, it has seven stories and eight sides and is about 17 m high. Open 8:30 a.m.–5:00 p.m.

Five km from the Qincheng Hotel, the **Wuquan (Five-Fountain) Hill 五泉山** should be visited for its genuine temples, the oldest, the Ming Dynasty Chung Wen left untouched and spooky. Legend credits General Ho Qubing (Huo Chu-ping), in 120 B.C., with stabbing the ground with his sword after finding no water for his horses. Five streams of water appeared and have been flowing ever since. Other important relics to see are the Taihe Iron Bell, 3 meters high, weighing 5 tons, cast in 1202; and the Tongjieyinfo Buddha, cast in copper in 1370 and weighing nearly 5 tons. Open 8:30–5.

The **Yellow River cruise** is not special, but the **Provincial Museum,** Xijin Dong Rd., 5 km from the Qincheng Hotel, is well worth the trip for the famous 1800-year-old Galloping Horse of Gansu that toured the U.S. and Canada. It was found in Wuwei in the middle of the province. A replica of its original presentation is in the Qincheng Hotel. Also important are the 2000-year-old-wooden ''slips'' (documents of history and medicine) from north Gansu and 7000-year-old painted pottery. Open 9–11; 2–5. Closed Mon. Another good museum is in Guyuan near Pinoliang.

The elaborate fifth-century *****Bingling Temple Caves** (Pinglinghsi) **炳灵寺石窟** are 120 km SW of the city, near **Linxia.** Six hours each way. Tours can also visit a hydroelectric power station. Here are 183 caves and shrines with 694 stone Buddhist statues and 82 clay ones, the biggest Buddha 27 m high, the smallest only 25 cm. Like some other cave temples, this involves a lot of stairs. The statues range from Northern Wei to Ming, the youngest, at least 350 years old. The most spectacular is the Xiasi (Lower Temples) Open April–Nov., depending on the water level.

The *****Maiji Grottoes 麦积山石窟** , also Northern Wei to Ming, are 45 km SE of the city of **Tianshui 天水** , itself 350 km SE of Lanzhou. Tianshui was a trade distributing center on the Silk Road and has two temples, the Fuxi and the Nanguo, and is accessible by air.

At Maiji, there are 194 caves full of thousands of stone and clay Buddhist statues, and 1300 square meters of murals dating from the end of the 4th century to the 19th, a period of 1500 years. These caves are on a mountain, which rises almost vertically, and are reached by wooden staircases and protected by doors and windows. Some of the statues are completely unsheltered. One statue 15.28 meters high is from the Sui. The work on the mountain was done by craftsmen who piled blocks of wood up to the top and started carving while standing on them. As the artisans worked their way down, they gradually removed the blocks. The Maiji is better than Bingling.

Also near Tianshui, at **Dadiwan** in Qin'an County, is an on-the-site museum similar to that at Banpo in Xi'an. Its 1154-sq.-meter hall covers a 7000-year-old primitive village with painted pottery tripods, stone and bone artifacts, and ground paintings. Of the 200 houses so far discovered, one covers 600 square meters, the largest such building found so far in China.

If you have a chance, do see the authentic **Chinese dances,** inspired by the paintings in the caves, performed by the Gansu School of Dance in Lanzhou.

At Xiahe 8 hours southwest, it is a three-day trip by road to the Labrang/Labuleng Si Lamasery, the largest outside of Tibet, built in 1709. Best seen in July. Yellow sect. A beautiful but rough trip. Crude hotels. Ask about **Qingyang,** a village devoted to the making of those flat, stuffed, whimsical animals seen in stores here. Also in the province are Dunhuang and Jiayuguan. See separate listings and ask about the 6000 Roman troops (Han dynasty) who "lost" their way and ended up in Wuwei.

SHOPPING

Lanzhou produces a kind of honeydew melon, red dates, the best tobacco for water pipes, carved ink slabs, "jade" cups and bottle gourds. It also manufactures carpets, lanterns, and reproductions of ancient paintings based on the Silk Road murals. Some of its replicas of the famous Flying Horse of Gansu are made from molds directly from the original in the local museum.

Try the **Provincial Arts and Crafts Shop** (West Donggang Rd.) and the **Nanguan Department Store,** with its Friendship Store branch.

Museum reproductions and cloth animals at the **Tianma (Celestial Horse) Store.** (361 Tianshui Rd.). **Gansu Cultural Relics Shop,** 3 Xinjinxi Rd., tel. 36461.

FOOD

Roast piglet (delicious!), sweet and sour Yellow River carp, *facai,* steamed chicken, fried camel hoof (ugh), and fried sheep's tail. For snacks, try toffee potatoes and toffee melon.

HOTELS

The airport is 75 km from the city (with a terrible restaurant). The Jincheng is best. The **Lanzhou Hotel (Binguan)** is nearby and cheaper.

Jincheng Hotel (Binguan) • *363 Tianshui Rd., 730000. 3*. In the center of town. Telex 72121. BTHJC CN Fax 418438. Dist. R.W. 1 km* • *1982.*

Northwest Airlines: 256 Donggang Xi Rd.; tel. 23432, 20404.
C.I.T.S., C.T.S.: Gansu Overseas Tourism Corporation (sales) and Gansu Tourism Administration (brochures and complaints) are all at 361

Tianshui Rd., 730000.
C.I.T.S.: 209 Tianshui Rd.; tel. 26181, 26798. Cable 7139. Telex 72103
CTSLB CN. **C.T.S.:** tel. 27098. Fax 418457. Telex 72012 CTSGS
CN; **G.O.T.C.,** tel. 26188. Fax 24670. Telex 72160 GSOTC CN.;
G.T.A., tel. 418443. Fax 418443. Telex 72159 GTA CN.
See also "Silk Road."
CYTS: tel. 466724, 466723.
Tourism Hotline: tel. 26860.

LESHAN (LE MOUNTAIN) 乐山

Southwest China, about 170 km SW of Chengdu and 38 km. from
Emei Mountain. The long trip by road is preferable if you have
the time and want to see the Sichuan countryside, the architecture
of the farmhouses, and obnoxious truck drivers.

Leshan is a small 1300-year-old town. Warm rain from April through
June adds to the mystical atmosphere.

It is the home of the ***Dafu (Great Buddha) Temple** 大佛 . Here
sits a 58.7 or 70 meters (depending on sources) Buddha, started in A.D.
713 and completed 90 years later, believed to be the largest in the world.
From Leshan city, visitors could take a public bus to the front gate, or
arrive by ferry at the foot. The view from the water is better; otherwise
you can't see the temple guardians and if you look toward the Big Buddha from a distance, you should see an even bigger, more virile, reclining Buddha, head to the right, formed accidentally by the shape of the
hills and a pagoda. At the confluence of three rivers (Min, Dadu, and
Qingyi), the monastery buildings stand at Buddha's eye level.

This huge statue was built to offset the large number of serious
accidents on the river. Since statistics were probably kept before and
after, it would be enlightening to know if, indeed, the statue was worth
it.

Two guest houses fringe the head of the Buddha. Caves, bare floors,
and Chinese beds.

The **Wuyou (Black) Temple** 乌尤寺 can be reached in 15 minutes by footpath from the Dafu Temple, or by 336 steps from where the tour buses stop. It has a good museum for its tiny size.

HOTELS

Leshan is 30 km from a railway station. The closest airport is Chengdu. No hotel has IDD. C.I.T.S. says the Jia Zhou is tops, followed by the Jiu Ri Feng. A new three-star hotel, the Nushen (Haitang Rd. 614004), should open soon.

Jia Zhou Hotel (Binguan) • *19 Bai Ta Rd., 614000. 2*. Telex 32419. Good location across river from the Great Buddha* • 1953, second bldg. 1987, ren. 1988. 13 stories, 296 rooms. B.C., bicycles. IDD. Planning pool and sauna. Originally a Canadian mission before Liberation. Near shopping, park, and boat to Great Buddha Temple.

Jiu Ri Feng Hotel (Binguan) • *614000. 2** • At Buddha's head. 99 rooms. Dorms.

Ambulance: tel. 23631.
Police: tel. 22174.
C.I.T.S. and **C.T.S.** 国际旅行社 23 Boshui Rd. 614000; tel. 22154.
Leshan Tourist Bureau: 23 Boshui Rd. 614000; tel. 23968 (complaints).

LHASA 拉萨

Northwest China. The fabled capital of Xizang (Tibet) has been open to travelers (except during times of civil unrest) only on prepaid tours even of one person. These can be arranged by Holiday Inn Lhasa or any travel agency. Occasionally, these restrictions have not been enforced, but don't count on it. Because tourists have complained of guides with little knowledge and poor English, please take this guide book with you or get something more detailed, like Elisabeth B. Booz's *Tibet*. Contact U.S. missions in China, especially the consulate in Chengdu, or the Sales Manager, Holiday Inn Lhasa for current information, especially on important Tibetan anniversaries when there may be demonstrations. Travelers without permits risk getting turned back at the Lhasa airport. Lhasa is north of Bhutan and Bangladesh and almost due south of Urumqi. It is reached by daily flights from Chengdu and Kathmandu up to three flights a week. But not all winter. (See also Getting There Via Nepal.) Lhasa's Gonggar airport can now accommodate 747s. More routes are expected soon. You can go by daily bus on a prepaid tour from Golmud (1155 km) with an overnight stop in Amdo or wherever the driver wants to sleep. About 30 hours' driving time (and the possibility of snow in the passes, even in June. Wear warm clothing and take motion sickness pills, and your own food. No toilets on bus.) Travelers have been going by land from Kathmandu, Chengdu via Chamdo, Kashi, and Chengdu via Yunnan province. Road conditions are very poor, however. You should expect delays due to landslides and bumpy roads most of the year round. The altitude is about 3607 meters. Most tourists visit April–October, but Holiday Inn insists the winters are sunny and beautiful, and pilgrims gather in Lhasa for festivals.

Tibet is generally safe for visitors except those who get involved in local politics. We also suggest you avoid getting close to the many stray dogs here.

Tibet is one of the more exotic places to visit in China, virtually a country in itself, with an area about the size of France, Spain, and

Greece combined. It is isolated by the highest mountains in the world. It is important to see because of its unique culture, its celebrated monasteries, and its magnificent scenery.

This is colorful National Geographic land: you can see prostrating pilgrims, fierce-looking tribesmen, people spinning prayer wheels on the street, a great variety of tribal dress, yaks, maroon-robed monks, unusual handicrafts and architecture, great mountains, and smiling, friendly natives most of whom don't mind having their photo taken when asked. Best take a long lens. The essentials of Lhasa can be covered in two hurried or three less hurried days if you are in good shape.

While visiting Tibet is no longer an experience just for the adventurous few, it is still not for the weak. The average altitude in Tibet is over 5000 meters (very hard on the skin, so take some good sunscreen). Usually it takes about two days to decide whether or not you'll be sick, and two weeks to feel at home. Bottled oxygen is available in the hotel rooms and on some tour buses. Just don't push yourself too hard. Taking it easy is difficult, as a lot of climbing is involved just to sightsee. Do not go if you have asthma or other pulmonary problems. In addition to the altitude and dust, the temples are full of incense smoke and are lit by butter lamps—all of which might make breathing difficult. Qualified doctors may not be available.

Since all food, energy, and most building materials have to be imported by truck or plane, the cost of accommodations and sightseeing is higher than in other parts of China for the same quality. You should bring your own flashlight, drinking flask, medicine for altitude sickness, and alarm clock.

Spring and summer days can be very dry with lots of dust blowing. A nose mask and goggles are helpful. Only light clothing needed in summer for Lhasa, but warmer clothes are needed for higher altitudes. Winter days can be warm with highs of 20–25°C and you can get a sunburn. But the nights can be cold. The best time is September to November.

The hottest temperature in Lhasa is 27°C in July and August; the coldest, −15°C in December and January. The annual precipitation is about 500 mm, mainly from June to September. Some of the hotels are not well heated in winter. (Take a hot-water bottle!)

Tibetans are nomads, or farmers raising barley, yak, and sheep. Tho-tho-ri Nyantsen, 28th king of Tibet, introduced Buddhism into the country in A.D. 233.

In the seventh century, the king of Tubo conquered the other tribes and made Lhasa his capital. He also invaded neighboring Sichuan, and although he was repulsed, his request for a Chinese wife was granted. His marriage with Tang princess Wen Cheng and his interest in Tang culture introduced much Chinese culture into Tibet. Among the innovations were silk, paper, and the architecture of the palace he built for her. His marriage to a Nepalese princess also meant Indian influences. Tibetan script is basically Indian. Both princesses promoted their own brands of Buddhism. The Tibetan kingdom subsequently expanded to include parts of Yunnan and northern India.

In 779, Buddhism became the state religion. The Mongols invaded Tibet in 1252 and adopted Tibetan Lamaism for themselves and propagated it to help control their subject tribes in other parts of China. Some lamas became very powerful during the Yuan. Kublai Khan appointed a lama as king, but maintained overall power himself. This system has continued with varying degrees of Chinese enforcement ever since. Qing Emperor Qianlong (Chien Lung) was one who especially asserted his authority.

The Jesuits were the first western missionaries to arrive in Tibet in 1624. During the lifetime of the fifth Dalai Lama, the office of Dalai Lama became political as well as religious. The first British mission arrived in 1774 and a British military expedition (Younghusband) forced the Dalai Lama to flee to Mongolia from 1904 until 1909. In 1910, the Chinese again asserted their control and the Dalai Lama retreated for a time to India. In 1911, the Tibetans repelled the Chinese. The British tried to maintain some control here, but gave up in 1947 after India became independent.

The Chinese People's Liberation Army arrived in 1951. An abortive uprising by some Tibetans in 1959 forced a large number of Tibetans to flee to India. The current Dalai Lama, the 14th, has been there ever since. In 1964, Tibet was made an Autonomous Region within China. In the last few years, the Chinese have made attempts to train Tibetans to replace Han administrators. The 2.09 million Tibetans here are over 95% of the population. Do you agree that there could also be about 300,000 Chinese soldiers in Tibet?

Recently, some Tibetans demonstrated for independence and several people were killed. The current Dalai Lama was awarded the Nobel Peace Prize. China accused the U.S. and other countries of interfering in its internal affairs.

As you move around the region, be sensitive to the feelings of people. I have been appalled by the loud talking of my Chinese guide during Tibetan prayers. Walk clockwise around temples. If you hand a picture of the Dalai Lama to a Tibetan, make sure no Han Chinese is around because this could bother him or her. Hold the photo (postcards are great) in both hands, put it to your forehead and then bow your head as you hand it over.

The Dalai Lama is god, and you might be asked "Dalai Lama picture?" in every monastery. One could have given out 40 in the Potala alone. However, having pictures of the Dalai Lama in your possession could be interpreted as support for Tibetan independence. Some foreigners have been arrested for getting involved in this dispute.

Tibet's Buddhism is different from that of the rest of Asia, aside from Mongolia and northern China. It believes strongly in reincarnation and a vicious, torturous hell for sinners, which is reflected in its art. It is full of demons and human skulls, witchcraft and magic, much influenced by the pre-Buddhist polytheism of the Tibetans. It has also many pre-Hindu influences and much recitation of spells. You might hear the chant *Om Mani Padme Hum,* which means "Hail to the Jewel in the Lotus," a mantra that helps the individual communicate with the eternal.

At the same time, Lamaism has many mystical elements, and a highly developed theology.

The goal of Buddhism is the end of continuous reincarnations.

At one time, a quarter of the male population of Tibet were monks, and the theocracy was such that no matter how cold it was, on whatever day spring was proclaimed by the Dalai Lama, everybody had to change into summer clothes!

Like other religions, Lamaism is divided into sects: the two main ones here are the Red Hats, where sex with a person other than one's spouse was part of the ritual, and the Yellow Hats, which is more strict about celibacy and other traditional Buddhist monastic practices. The Dalai Lama is head of the Yellow Hats.

Fascinating are the stories of how the successive Dalai Lamas were chosen—babies recognizing objects used by themselves in their previous incarnations. The current incumbent is from a peasant family from Amdo, at that time in Qinghai province. The Dalai Lamas are earthly incarnations of the four-armed God Chenrezi, and when each incarnation dies, his spirit takes on the body of another Tibetan child at birth. Disputes have arisen over who is the real reincarnated Dalai Lama, and the issue is politically very sensitive. To the chagrin of his followers, the current Dalai Lama has said there should be "no more Dalai Lamas," and "there is no need to preserve this institution . . ." Lamas are very learned monks or recognized reincarnations of previous lamas or monks.

Among traditional Tibetan customs is the giving of a *hada,* a long silk scarf, as a token of esteem and good luck. The sticking out of the tongue is a sign of respect. At one time, Tibetans practiced polyandry, brothers sharing one wife because of poverty. Every summer a festival celebrates the annual washing and cleaning.

Tea is drunk with yak butter and salt and tastes more like beef broth. It does seem to give much needed energy for survival and is said to be good for colds. The proper way to drink it is to lightly blow the top cream away from you and allow it to settle on the sides of your tea cup. The thicker the cream, the more generous the host. Fresh, hot yak milk has been described as sweet and "heavenly" and has a higher fat content than cow's milk. Often barleylike flour is added to the milk or tea to form a dough. Chang (tsang), a barley wine, is another favorite drink offered to guests.

The remains of the dead are frequently cut up by funeral workers at dawn to feed vultures, a 1000-year-old tradition. Tibetans now believe these birds take the spirits to heaven. Those who cannot afford this expensive rite, like beggars or victims of serious illnesses, are fed to fish—which is why Tibetans don't eat fish. Burial in the ground is for the very poor and unfortunate, such as criminals or victims of murder. High lamas are covered in butter and cremated.

Tourists are forbidden from seeing the birds at work, because the families of the deceased fear the tourists will scare the birds away.

Look for the *tangkas* hung on monastery walls. These are the scrolls used by itinerant preachers to illustrate the teachings of the Buddha. Look for prayer wheels, with a written prayer inside, which adherents spin in the belief that each rotation sends a prayer to Buddha.

Tibet has 50 monasteries open, including seven for nuns, with 3000 men in residence and 138 women. Forty-three more religious buildings are under repair and another 80 will be restored. All this work is being done by the central and local governments, which also maintain the monasteries and the monks. At Liberation, Tibet had 2770 monasteries.

The most important buildings in Lhasa are the Jokhang Temple, Potala Palace, Sera Monastery, and Drepung Monastery. Ask about a bronze bell with Latin inscriptions in one of Lhasa's temples. It should be from 17th c. Catholic missionaries.

Getting Around. Group tourists need not worry but in your spare time you may want to go out on your own. This small city is flat and most hotels rent out bicycles. Public buses are infrequent; jeep-type vehicles are expensive (almost three times the taxi-rate in any other Chinese city). Monastery hours keep changing so check at your hotel, but the Potala was open mornings 9 a.m. to 12:30 p.m., Mon. and Thurs.

To travel to other parts of Tibet, ask your hotel, C.I.T.S. or other travelers. Most hotels have bulletin boards with notices.

Transfers. CAAC's bus from the airport has been meeting people on the runway and can stop at the Holiday Inn before it arrives at the Tibetan city and walking distance to the inns there.

The ***Potala Palace** 布达拉宫 cannot be missed. It is 3.5 km from the Holiday Inn and 1 km from the Jokhang. It dominates the city from its lofty cliff. Groups get driven up to the entrance. Individual travelers climb 300 meters. The only toilet is near the east entrance. In spite of its 13 stories, there are no elevators. If you follow the crowds and go into every open doorway, you should be able to see everything worth seeing in three hours. No signs in English or arrows. And there are a lot of stairs.

Originally built in the seventh century by Songsten Gampo, the Potala was the official residence of the Dalai Lama, the religious and secular head of Tibet. The first Dalai Lama lived from 1391–1474. The Potala has 1000 rooms, 10,000 chapels, and the tombs of eight Dalai Lamas, some gold-plated and studded with diamonds, turquoises, corals, and pearls. The largest tomb is 14.85 meters high. More than 200,000 pearls cover the Pearl Pagoda. The tombs are not always open so ask about them. Additional payment is worth it. Every room has a helpful monk-guide. And the discerning have been able to take photos without payment.

The building was destroyed and rebuilt several times, the latest structure dating from 1642. Among its 200,000 statues are those of King Songsten Gampo and his Chinese wife.

Every wall is covered with murals. Noteworthy are those in the Sishiphuntsok Hall. In the West Big Hall, the murals record the life of the Fifth Dalai Lama, including his meeting with Qing Emperor Shunzhi in Beijing in 1652.

The palace is 400 meters by 350 meters, and is made of stone and wood, its walls between three and five meters thick. The White Palace was built during the time of the Fifth Dalai Lama (1617–1682) and the Red Palace afterward. From the 18th century, with the construction of the Norbulinka (Summer Palace), the Potala was used only in winter. Can you imagine a child growing up here? The current dalai lama was brought here at the age of two. Think of him flying his kite from the Potala's roof and exploring the city and its people with a telescope!

The *Jokhang Temple 大昭寺 , a.k.a. Juglakang, is the most important Buddhist temple in Tibet. It is 4.5 km from the Holiday Inn and is the heart of the city. It was built in the mid-seventh century, also during King Songsten Gampo's time. It has been expanded several times since. Note the Nepalese and Chinese features. Princess Wen Cheng brought with her from China the seated statue of the child Sakyamuni. The Tibetans believe that the statue was made by the Buddha himself. The Great Prayer Festival is held annually here from the 3rd to 25th of the first month of the Tibetan calendar. Currently being renovated.

The temples here are full of worshipers, some prostrating themselves 500 times a day and donating yak butter to feed the lamps.

The *Sera Monastery 色拉寺 in the northern suburbs 10 km from the Holiday Inn and 4 km from downtown, was built in 1419. It was extended in the early 18th century, and is one of the four major monasteries in Tibet, at its height housing 10,000 lamas and monks. The 18 sandalwood arhats and four Heavenly Kings here were gifts from the Ming emperor. Look also for a gold statue of an 11-faced Guan Yin, the Goddess of Mercy.

The *Drepung Monastery 哲蚌寺 , a.k.a. Daipung, is in the western suburbs 6 km from the Holiday Inn and 10 km from the Jokhang. One can climb to the roof for the view of the valley. Financed by the same nobleman who built the Sera, the Drepung was founded in

1416 and extended several times. It is one of the four major monasteries. Among its treasures is a white conch and a gilded Buddha. Inside the abdomen of the statue in the main hall are the remains of a master translator named Dorjidak. At one time, this monastery also had a population of over 10,000 monks and lamas.

If you have more time, **Norbulingka Park** 罗布林卡 was the summer residence of the Dalai Lamas, with 370 rooms. It is 4 km from the Potala and set in a 100-acre garden. Kalsang Podang, the first building, was originally erected in 1755. The New Palace for the 14th Dalai Lama was built in 1954–56. It is also full of statues and murals. The murals are of Princess Wen Cheng and her marriage to the king, the three worlds, and Buddha preaching under a banyan tree. The bedroom is as the current Dalai Lama left it to flee to India. In the 1940s, the German mountain climber Heinrich Harrer set up a movie theater for the Dalai Lama in this park.

An exhibition of tangkas is usually in one of the temples in the back. If you don't like the toilets, go over to the Holiday Inn nearby.

One can also learn about Tibetan medicine and ride a yak-skin raft. The ***Ganden Monastery**, 60 km east, is listed as early Ming to Qing. At least 10 buildings have been restored. Less than 100 monks live there now. At one time, it had over 8000 monks. This is a one-day trip as is that to Lake Yamdrok Yamsto. The ***Royal Tibetan Tombs,** from the seventh century, are at Chonggye/Qonggyai in Lhoka/Shannan prefecture, about 180 km SE. Hotel in Zedang. The **Yumbulakang** palace, built in 228 b.c. by the first Tibetan Kings, is on a hilltop.

Shigatse/Xigaze is about 225 km (9–13 hours) west of Lhasa over a 3000-meter-high pass. The road is currently being shortened to five hours. The ***Tashilhunpo (Zhaxilhunbu) Monastery** 扎什伦布寺 there is the most important of the religious buildings in that city. It was founded in 1447 and was the home of the Panchen Lamas, the reincarnations of the Buddha of Eternal Light. Only religiously have the Panchen Lamas been equal to the politically superior Dalai Lamas. However, the Chinese consider the Panchen Lama a political equal. This is also a very sensitive and controversial point.

At one time, the Tashilhunpo had a population of 3800 monks. Today there are about 600. This monastery also has many halls and chapels, and statues of the 18 arhats. The Hall of the Buddha Maitreya Champa/Qiangba was built from 1914–18 with a 26.7-meter statue of the Buddha in gold and copper inside. The gold-plated reliquary of the fourth Panchen Lama is 11 meters high and is decorated with precious stones. The tenth Panchan Lama died here in 1989.

You can probably hear the lamas chanting in the Grand Chanting Hall from 8 a.m. to 11 a.m., from 1 p.m. until 3 p.m., and 6 p.m. to 9 p.m. A market of Tibetan handicrafts is nearby.

Zhangmu, on the Tibet side of the Nepal border, is now open to

tourists, with a 100-bed guesthouse. The trip takes three days. Tingri/
Dingri County at the foot of Mount Qomolangma (Everest) and all
mountains in Tibet are expected to be opened gradually to foreigners.

Several Lhasa tour agencies now offer **treks** in Tibet, and prices
for these are higher than similar treks in other countries. Mountaineering can be organized through the Chinese Mountaineering Association.

Highly recommended is Heinrich Harrer's *Seven Years in Tibet,*
about his adventures there in the 1940s, a good picture to compare with
today's Tibet. Harrer, a German, taught the Dalai Lama English and
was his cameraman. A sequel tells of Harrer's recent return trip. Also
recommended are the classic *Tibet and Its History* by Hugh E. Richardson, and Peter Fleming's *Bayonets to Lhasa.*

ALTITUDE SICKNESS

If you only have two days, it may not be worth visiting Lhasa
because of the altitude. About 60% of new arrivals get a headache. If
you are one of the small minority afflicted with severe altitude sickness,
you could spend much of your time in bed.

You won't know you are susceptible until you get to about 8–
9,000 ft. One can travel successfully in high altitudes 20 times and get
it on the 21st. It seems to hit the young and strong more than the old
and weak. Young people have passed out checking into hotels. Jumping
onto a bicycle upon arrival is a no-no.

The symptoms are severe headache, dizziness, insomnia, nausea,
vomiting, and difficulty in breathing. People who make a gradual ascent
by road rarely get it, if at all. People who fly in are prone. So are people
with colds, breathing difficulties, poor health, and heart disease. Pregnant women should stay below 3,600 meters, says the Himalayan Rescue Association in "Hints on High Altitude" circulated by the Holiday
Inn.

It is better to let your body adjust naturally. Avoid smoking, alcohol, and sleeping pills. Move about in slow motion. **Drink over three
liters of liquid a day.** Get plenty of bed rest especially if you feel any
of the symptoms. Open your windows. Breathe deeply. Relax. Do not
panic.

Some hotels have oxygen in the rooms. This will give relief but
will retard the time it takes the body to adjust. Some people have found
aspirins helpful. Some have successfully taken the diuretic Diamox
available in North America by prescription only. Most doctors will not
prescribe it because they don't know its effect at high altitudes. With a
few people Diamox has caused vomiting, confusion, and of course uri-
nation. Discuss it with a mountaineering club or travel agency doctor
before you go. You have to start taking it a day before you arrive.

In very severe cases of altitude sickness, the only recourse is evacuation to a lower altitude and you may not get a plane out for days.

FESTIVALS

October–November the Gods Descending Festival. November–December the Fairy Maiden Festival (Jokhang Temple). December Tsong Khapa's Festival. January–February Tibetan New Year. February–March Great Prayer Festival (Jokhang). February–March Butter Lamp Festival. July Giant Tangka Festival (Shigatse). August Shoton (Tibetan Opera) Festival. Some have been cancelled even at the last minute.

SHOPPING

Tibetan boots, rugs, saddle blankets, jewelry, temple bells, prayer wheels, woolen blankets, etc. Look for the market around the Jokhang Temple, the Barkhor (bazaar). There one can also buy Nepalese-made Tibetan tangkas which are finer than Tibetan ones, at several times the price of those in Nepal but cheaper than in North America, at Syamukapu International, tel. 214327. (Using the front gate of the Jokhang as 6 o'clock, this upmarket store is at about 10 o'clock.) Tangkas and original art can also be bought at the Tibet Art Gallery at the foot of the Potala (bus stop). Not cheap, but cheaper than North America. Unmounted prints of Tibetan tangkas are a great buy for about Y 12 and have been found in the Holiday Inn and at the Potala.

FOOD

Except for the main hotels, restaurants here are generally dirty and the food not good. Few vegetables. If you are going outside of Lhasa, we suggest you stock up on cup noodles, granola bars, peanut butter and crackers, etc. before you arrive.

Tibetan (Yak meat and cheese), Moslem (mutton or lamb), or Chinese.

HOTELS

Telex is more reliable than Fax, but the phone system is being improved.

The best hotel is the Holiday Inn Lhasa Hotel (with the best English), then the Tibet Hotel. These two are within walking distance of each other and the Norbulinka. The Himalaya is okay, cheaper and closer to the Jokhang, but the bathrooms and English need work. Aside from the Holiday Inn, few hotels honor reservations. You might have to send a scout a day ahead to secure rooms. Hotels outside of Lhasa can be downright crude. Ask about money-changing facilities there too.

The cheaper Tibetan inns are within walking distance of each other and the central Jokhang Monastery in the old Tibetan city and have been off limits to foreigners from time to time. The best of these are the **Kirey** and **Banak Shol.** No Tibetan inn has western toilets. Few rooms have private baths and most have cheap dorms too. Most had concrete floors and lots of flies. Some offered free laundry service. Usually only one telephone and one television for everyone. The clientele (mainly young people) necessitated the sign in one inn, ''Do not shit in the shower.''

Banak Shol 八郎学旅社　● *11 Beijing Dong Rd. 850001. Dist.A.P.90 km* ● 1984. 3 stories, 106 rooms. Bicycles, dorms, no C.C. Western-style toilets. Has good level of English. Two washing machines. Iron. Offers good map of city. Largest bulletin board.

Holiday Inn Lhasa (Lhasa Fandian) ● *1 Minzu Rd. 850001. 3*. Fax 35769 or 25796. Western suburbs. Dist.A.P. 96 km. Telex 68010 HILSA CN* ● 1986. 468 rooms and suites in five and seven story buildings. Sichuan and Himalaya restaurants. Western coffee shop. C.I.T.S., CYTS, and Tibet Tourist Corporation. C.C., clinic. Superior and cheaper economy rooms. City and out-of-town tours one can join if enough demand. Write for worthwhile newsletter.

Tibet Hotel (Xizang Binguan) ● *93 West Beijing Rd. 850001. Behind the Holiday Inn. 2*. Telex 68013 TGSIH CN.* ● This exotic hotel has more upmarket Tibetan flavor than any other hotel, but service is poor. 1986. Coffee shop and teahouse. Clinic. Beauty parlor. Swimming pool with cold water, bathing suits for sale.

C.I.T.S. 中国国际旅行社　: Beijing Xi Rd. 850001. tel. 22980. Telex 68009 ZMLAS CN or 68012 ITSLT CN; write for the dates of festivals so you can plan your trip to include them. Offers trekking.
CAAC 中国民航　: Jiefang Rd., No. 12, Lhasa; tel. 22417, 23772.
C.T.S.: tel. 23877, 22980.
CYTS: tel. 10891, 24173. Telex 68017 CYTST CN.
Nepalese Consulate: 13 Norbulingka Rd., tel. 22880.
Tibet Tourism Administration Bureau: 208 Beijing Xi Rd., 850001. tel. 23857. Telex 68012 ITSLT CN. Office in Tibet Hotel, Chengdu.
China Tibet Sports Travel, 6 Linkhor Dong Rd., 850000. Tel. 23775. Telex 68109 TIST CN. Fax 26366.

LUOYANG 洛阳

(Luoyang; North Bank of Luo River) Northwest China. 2 hours by train west of Zhengzhou and infrequent air connections with 5 Chinese cities. An 8-hour train ride east from Xi'an. About 25 km south of the Yellow River. Hottest temperatures: July–August—39°C; coldest: January–February—$^-$12°C. Generally mild. Altitude: 145 meters above sea level. Urban population about 1 million. Quiet, provincial atmosphere starting to wake up.

Luoyang is important because of the Longmen Grottoes, the White Horse Temple, the Ancient Tomb Museum, and because it was an imperial capital for many centuries. It is one of the 24 cities of historical importance protected by the State Council.

Luoyang was first built in the 11th century B.C. From 770 B.C. it was the capital at one time or another of the Eastern Zhou, Eastern Han, Wei, Western Jin, Northern Wei, Sui, Tang, Later Liang, and Later Tang dynasties. Moves were frequently made here because of drought in Xi'an, a city that was preferred. Because there are hills on three sides, it was relatively easy to defend, and whoever wanted to control western Henan had to take Luoyang. Consequently, many battles were fought in this area and many treasures were buried to save them from the soldiers. Luoyang was one of the earliest centers of Buddhism, from the first century A.D. During the Tang, it was the biggest city in China. It declined later because the capital moved away.

Luoyang people will proudly tell you that the Silk Road actually started from Luoyang and not from Xi'an, as is commonly supposed. "Knowledgeable merchants always came here for silks," they say. "It was cheaper."

The older, eastern part of Luoyang is more interesting than the newer sectors. Today, there are over 400 factories manufacturing everything from truck cranes to ball bearings. Tourists might be interested in its arts and crafts factory, which makes palace lanterns and reproductions of three-color Tang porcelains and Shang bronzes.

Area farms grow cotton, corn, winter wheat, a little rice, sesame, sorghum, sweet potatoes, apples, pears, and grapes. They also raise yellow oxen, goats, and donkeys. The city is also noted for its peonies, first grown in the Sui! Flower lovers should aim for the Royal City (Wangcheng Park) between April 15 and 25.

The following can be covered in one day if you don't dawdle.

The *Baima Si (White Horse) Temple 白马寺 , 25 km from the Friendship Hotel, was founded in A.D. 68 after second Han Emperor Mingdi dreamed that a spirit with a halo entered his palace. His ministers convinced him that the spirit was the Buddha, so he sent scholars to India to bring back the sutras. After three years, the famous Indian monks Shemeteng and Zhufalan arrived here with the scriptures, having made the last part of the trip on a white horse. The emperor put the monks up in his resort, the Cold Terrace, at the back of what is now this, the first Buddhist temple in China. There they translated the scriptures into Chinese. Both monks died in China and were buried in the east and west corners of the grounds beyond the moon gates.

None of the buildings here are original, though the red brick foundation of the Cold Terrace is Han; none of the others are earlier than Ming. The State Council lists them as Jin to Qing. Tang Empress Wu made one of her favorites the abbot here.

In the main hall to the right of Sakyamuni is Manjusri, the Bodhisattva of Wisdom, carrying the sutras, and at Sakyamuni's left, Samantabhara, Bodhisattva of Universal Benevolence. In the next hall are 18 clay arhats, each with a magic weapon, the oldest statues here (Yuan). One is Ceylonese, one Chinese (the Tang monk Xuan Zang who went to India), and the rest Indian. Inside the back halls are statues of the two monks, the Pilu Buddha (Sakyamuni), and drawers where the sutras are kept.

The **Qiyun (Cloud Touching) Pagoda** 齐云塔 nearby is in the Tang style, first built in 1175. Only the base with the darker brick is original. It was repaired in the Northern Song and Jin dynasties and has 13 stories. You get a strange echo effect if you stand either north or south of the pagoda and clap your hands.

The **Luoyang Municipal Museum** 洛阳博物馆 has 2000 pieces on display and roughly 50,000 in its collection. Relics include historical maps of the city. The first imperial city is where Royal City (formerly Laboring People's Park) is now. The *Han and Wei city was east of the White Horse Temple; the Sui and Tang cities were on both sides of the Luo River; two mammoth tusks found right in town in 1960; double boilers used 3700 years before the British used double boilers; a crossbow with a trigger (476–221 B.C.); iron farming tools (Han); figures from the tomb of a Northern Wei prince, including a band with one musician falling asleep; *original* three-color Tang horses and camels from which the copies are made. Study these carefully for comparison if you want to buy reproductions. Tel. 37107.

*Longmen (Lungmen) Grottoes 龙门石窟 : China has 19 important ''cave temples'' and Longmen is among the top three. Although predating these caves and built also by the Wei, those at Datong are said to be better preserved, more elaborately colored, and bigger. The stone at Longmen, however, is better. The grottoes are 20 km south of the city from the Friendship Hotel and extend north along the Yi River for about 1000 meters. They were not touched by the Red Guards, but the heads and hands of some were damaged at the beginning of this century. The buses stop by a 303-meter copy of a famous Sui bridge built of only stone and cement in 1962. Tel. 35431.

Work on the caves began about A.D. 494, when Emperor Hsaio Wen of the Northern Wei moved his capital from Datong to here. Work continued at a great pace from then until the Tang. A few statues were added during the Five Dynasties and Northern Song. There are 1352 grottoes, over 750 niches, and about 40 pagodas of various sizes. They contain more than 100,000 Buddhist images, ranging in size from 2 centimeters to 17.14 meters.

Compare the dress of the statues. Some are clothed in the plain robes of Indian holy men; others wear female Chinese court dress, sometimes with jewelry, a later development. One can guess that wealthy, devout worshipers wanted to clothe their gods in the best fashions of the day. This practice is much like that of medieval European religious art, which also ignored the mystical preachings of its teachers. The narrow, regular pleats are characteristic of the Northern Wei. The Tang statues tend to have rounder faces. While it is said that the gods could change their sex at will, the feminine faces are because, as one adherent said, "We want people to look at the face of Buddha. Since women's faces are more attractive than men's, the statues are made to look more feminine."

The **Wan Fo (10,000 Buddhas) Cave** actually has 15,000 Buddhas on the north and south walls. It was completed in A.D. 680 (Tang). Note the musicians and dancers at the base. The back wall has 54 bodhisattvas, each sitting on a lotus flower. Outside the cave is a Guanyin with a water vessel in her left hand and a whisk in her right. There used to be two lions here, but they are now said to be in the Boston Museum of Fine Arts. The **Guyang Cave** was the earliest, built around A.D. 494 (Northern Wei). The cornlike design represents a string of pearls. The ceiling is covered with Buddhas, lions, and tablets.

Fengxian Temple 奉先寺 , the largest and most spectacular, was completed in A.D. 675. The main statue (17.14 meters) is the Vairocana Buddha (i.e. Sakyamuni). If you look carefully, on the left side of the face are traces of a five-centimeter crack extending from the hairline to the chin. This was repaired recently. The square holes around the statues were used to hold the roof structure that was taken down when it was found that sunlight was good for limestone. Behind the smaller disciple to Sakyamuni's right is an imperceptible cave large enough to hold 400 people and from which climbers used to negotiate the top of the head. Fortunately, this is now blocked. On Sakyamuni's far left is Dvarapala, whose ankles are worn black and smooth by individuals trying to embrace them in return for happiness.

During imperial times, the common people had to look at them from afar, and in later periods, peasants broke pieces off the statues to make lime fertilizer.

The **Tomb of Guan Yu (Kuan Yu)**关林庙 —or at least that of his head. Guan Yu was one of the heroes of *The Romance of the Three Kingdoms,* and he is also known as the Chinese god of war. His tomb, between the grottoes and the city, was built in the Ming. He was beheaded about 219 A.D. One of the buildings has a moving statue of recent vintage. Tel. 37001.

Outside of the city is the **Tomb of Liu Xiu.** He was first emperor of the Eastern Han 1900 years ago. A visit could be combined with a trip to see the bridge across the Yellow River. The **Luoyang Ancient Tombs Museum,** with 22 Han and Song tombs, is 7 km from the city, near the airport and is worth a visit. Tel. 38678. It has 22 substantial tombs (displaced by new construction), all but one 15 meters underground. These are from the Han, Tang, Ming and Qing dynasties, some genuine, some reproductions. Tourists keen on tombs can compare the dynastic differences. Cool in summer, and dark. Take a flashlight. Children would love it. An imperial Wei tomb is next door.

The **Folk Customs Museum** is charming if you have a good guide explaining the symbols on tiny women's shoes, embroidered headbands and children's clothes. It has a special display of birthday and wedding customs and religious influences. The tombs and folk customs museums are not on the regular tour and must be asked for if you are interested.

SHOPPING
Store Hours: about 8 a.m.–6 or 7 p.m.; some 9 a.m.–7:30 p.m.

Friendship Store   : Reproductions, along with brushes, chopsticks, artificial flowers and inkstones, all made locally; **Arts and Crafts Store** 郎娌孖工 / 半美 : Sells palace lanterns and reproductions of Shang bronzes, artistic tiles. Tang horses and camels, made upstairs. Tel. 36428.

Luoyang Cultural Relics Shop, 17 Zhoungong Rd., tel. 35486.

HOTELS
The best hotels are the Peony and East Wing of the Friendship. Third is the Garden.

Friendship Hotel (Youyi Binguan) • *6 Xiyuan Dong Rd. 471003. Western part of Luoyang. Telex 47011; Dist. A.P. 15 km. Dist. R.W. 7 km.* • Two 4-story wings. 1956 325 rooms. West Bldg., ren. 1990. 2*.

Kung Fu Monk, Pagoda Forest, Shaolin Temple, Zhengzhou.

Lushan Mountain in Jianxi Province.

Miao nationality children, Hainan Island.

Five Pagodas Temple in Hohhot.

Lunan Stone Forest, Kunming.

Great Buddha in Leshan, Sichuan Province.

Garlic Market. Burma Road near Dali, Yunnan.

The Great Wall.

The Potala Palace, Lhasa.

PHOTO COURTESY OF C.I.T.S.

Qin Army Vault Museum, Xian.

Temple of Heaven in Beijing.

Song Dynasty Street, Kaifeng.

East Bldg. ren. 1987. 3*. In residential district. Pool, gym. Bicycles. Dorms. IDD.

Garden Hotel (Hua Yuan Jiu Dian) • *Nanchang Crossroads 471003. 2*. Half km east of Friendship Hotel and near large park* • C.C. 1989. 5 stories. 143 rooms. B.C. Disco. Bicycles. Dorms. IDD soon.

Peony Hotel (Mudan Dajiudian) • *15 Zhong Zhou Xi Rd. 471003. 3*. Telex 473047 LYPH CN. Fax 413668. Dist.A.P. 15 km. Dist.R.W. 4 km. City center.* • 17 stories. 196 rooms. H.K.J.V., IDD. 1990.

OTHER IMPORTANT ADDRESSES
Ambulance: tel. 23252
Police: tel. 35153
C.T.S. and **C.I.T.S.:** Friendship Hotel. 6 Xiyuan Rd. 471003; tel. 23701. Telex 47011 CITSL CN. 413901. C.T.S. tel. 412667.
CYTS: tel. 21212, 23455.

LUSHAN 庐山

(Mountain of Straw Huts) Part of Jiujiang City, South China. 40 km south of the port of Jiujiang, the closest airport. Overlooking Poyang Lake and the Yangtze River. Weather: Hottest—32°C (rare) at noon in July; coldest—⁻16°C in January. Snow from the end of November through February. Best time to visit is June–October. Lots of mist and rain, especially April and May—great for mood photographs but not for view. Altitude: 1094–1400 meters. Annual precipitation: 1916 mm. Population: About 9000 in Gulin. About 10,000 summer tourists in one day. The mountaintop tourist belt is about 8 by 4 km.

Primarily an old mountain resort, highly recommended as an escape from the heat or as a rest stop near the end of a tour. It is great for hiking and is a beautiful place to visit, with enough religious, historical, and folkloric aspects to make it interesting.

Legend says that the seven Kuan brothers lived on the mountain as recluses during the Western Zhou (11th century–771 B.C.). Because they were worthy men, the emperor sent an emissary to invite them to the capital to help govern the country. When the agent arrived, he found only empty straw huts. Hence, the name. The mountain was visited by the Jin poet Tao Yuan-ming (365–427). Its peach blossoms inspired Tang poet Bai Ju-yi. The first Ming emperor is supposed to have escaped an enemy here with supernatural help.

But it was not until after the last half of the 1800s that a resort was developed. About 100 hotel buildings and villas were completed and used by wealthy Chinese, government officials, and foreign missionaries. Most of these people were carried by sedan chair up a steep, 9-km path. People still climb this path from the base in about 2 hours from Lianhuadeng (Lotus Flower Hole). Chiang Kai-shek also visited Lushan when he wasn't campaigning against Mao Zedong at nearby Jinggang Shan. He lived in Building No. 180 in the East Valley.

During the Cultural Revolution, Lushan was closed, and parts were destroyed by the Red Guards. Foreign tourists were first encouraged to come in 1978, and now it is also a stop for some of the Yangtze boat tours. Lushan's views of the plains and the Yangtze are breathtaking. It is full of lovely trees, hills, pavilions, and old Tang pagodas and temples. It has a printing plant, a hydroelectric power station, and a few small factories.

Lushan is divided into an East Valley and a West Valley, with a tunnel at Gulin. Taxis are available. A tourist bus leaves downtown Gulin near the entrance to the city park whenever full. (Tel. 282037.)

Flower Path Park 花径公园 has a flower and Chinese *bonsai* exhibit. The miniature trees that inspired the Tang poet are here. A natural rock formation beside the lake and the highway looks like two ends of a bridge over a ravine, with a little imagination. The story goes that before he became the first Ming emperor in 1368, Zhu Yuanzhang escaped from his rival at this spot. A dragonfly completed the bridge, making it possible for Zhu, but not his enemy, to cross.

Grotto of Taoist Immortal 仙人洞 : Beyond the moon gate to the right is a cave about 30 feet wide, deep, and high, where Lu Tung-pin, a famous monk, studied Taoism so successfully that he became one of the Eight Taoist Immortals, the one with the supernatural sword. Note the formation over the mouth of the cave, shaped like Buddha's hand.

Big Heavenly Pond 大天池 : The water in this pool maintains the same height (it is said) through rain or drought, and is thus said to be "made in Heaven." The pavilion behind the pond is on the site of a temple, built to commemorate the spider who saved Zhu Yuanzhang's life by spinning a web to cover him while Zhu was hiding in a well from his rival.

The monks who lived in this temple were Taoists who tried to achieve immortality through study and meditation. As a test, they jumped off Dragon Head Cliff. If you look down, you can probably guess why they were never seen again. The climb down to Dragon Head Cliff (by no means the bottom) is about 170 steps, but the view is worth it. On the way, look for a carved step that was probably part of the old temple.

Hanpokou (the Mouth that Holds Poyang Lake) 含鄱口 , named after the shape of this pass in relation to the lake, is the best place to see the rising sun. The lake is one of China's largest and is 20 km away.

The **Lushan Botanical Garden** 庐山植物园 is a short walk from Hanpokou. Belonging to the Academy of Science, this garden has exchange programs with Britain's Royal Botanical Gardens and the National Arboretum in Washington, DC. Here are 3700 varieties, including trees, flowers, grasses, and medicinal herbs on 740 acres of land. Started in 1934, it is the only subalpine garden of the ten botanical gardens in China. Tourists are free to wander through the greenhouses (tropical and subtropical plants), which are open daily from 7:30 a.m. to 6 p.m. Groups can get a guide. The most exotic plant here is the metasequoia tree, a species thought to be extinct and seen only in fossils until one was found in a primitive forest in west China and propagated here. A large specimen stands labeled by the driveway near the parking lot.

The **Three Treasure Trees** 三宝树 are said to be 1500 years old, but botanists say 500. They are nevertheless very impressive, the highest being 40 meters tall. One is a gingko and two are cryptomeria. A few meters away are the Yellow Dragon Pool and the Black Dragon Pool with waterfalls.

Pavilion for Viewing the Yangtze 望江亭 has another stunning view of the countryside below. At this point, the Yangtze River is about 15 km away. To the right, you can see the historic path up which vacationers used to be carried.

SHOPPING

Gulin 牯岭 , the only shopping area, was destroyed by fire in 1947 and then rebuilt. The arts and crafts stores sell porcelain dishes and statues made in Jingdezhen, 180 km away. Other good buys are cloud-mist green tea and watercolors of the mountain scenery. Locally made handicrafts are walking sticks and bamboo brush or pencil holders.

FOOD

Local delicacy—the Three Stones: stone frog, stone fish, and stone fungus.

HOTELS

Some of the buildings here are over 100 years old. Most are made of stone, with lots of space and high ceilings. The best hotel for business people is the Villa Village Hotel 179 Hedong Rd. 332900 2* says C.I.T.S. The Lushan Hotel is second. 446 Hexi Rd. 3*. All are modest with low standards.

Lulin Hotel (Lulin Fandian) • *Hunan Rd. 332900. 3*. Dist.A.P.40 km. Dist.R.W.40 km* • 1958; part renovated 1985. 240 beds for foreigners. Four stories. Farthest hotel from bus station (5 km); 3-minute walk to lake, 15-minute walk to botanical garden, and 20-minute walk to Hanpokou. From Gulin, go through tunnel and turn right. IDD, business center, no C.C. This is the best hotel.

Lushan Mansion (Da Sha) • *332900. 2*. 20-minute walk from bus station* • 1935; reconstructed 1985. This is No. 3.

C.I.T.S.: Lushan Hotel, 454 Hexi Rd., 332900; tel. 282497. Fax 282428.
C.T.S.: 113 Hexi Rd. 332900. Tel. 412667.

Z.M.Li

NANJING

(Nanking; Southern Capital) East China. SW part of Jiangsu province on the Changjiang (Yangtze) River, 4 hours by train or 1 hour by air (300 km) NW of Shanghai, or 16 hours by train (1¾ hours by air) SE of Beijing. Flights from Hong Kong, Nagoya, and 20 other Chinese cities. The 12 meter-wide Nanjing-Shanghai highway should be finished now. One can also go by ship from Shanghai. Nanjing is the capital of Jiangsu. Weather: Hottest: 40°C (rare)—August; coldest: ⁻7°C—January. Annual precipitation more than 1000 mm. Rain in summer. Urban population: 2.2 million. A good time to visit is late October to mid-November when the streets are lined with chrysanthemums.

Nanjing is important because of its historical relics and its beauty. It was settled 6000 years ago and was a walled city 2400 years ago. From A.D. 229 to 1421, it was intermittently the capital of the Eastern Wu (229–280 A.D.), Eastern Jin (317–420), Song (420–479), Qi (479–502), Liang (502–557), Chen (557–589), Southern Tang (937–975), Ming (1368–1421) and Taiping Heavenly Kingdom (1853–64). Many of the ancient relics in the present city are Ming, built by Zhu Yuanzhang (Chu Yuan-chang), first emperor of the dynasty (1368–99) whose reign name was Hongwu. After him, the capital was moved to Beijing, where his successors built the Forbidden City and were buried in elaborate tombs north of it.

In 1842, the Treaty of Nanking with England was signed here ending the First Opium War, and the city was declared an open port. On January 1, 1912, it became the capital of the Sun Yat-sen government and remained the Nationalist capital until April 5, 1912, when the capital was moved to Beijing. After a period of much confusion, Chiang Kai-shek unilaterally declared Nanjing the capital on April 18, 1927.

The Japanese captured Nanjing on Dec. 12, 1937, and massacred over 200,000 civilians in what is referred to as the Rape of Nanking. A museum was recently opened to commemorate this tragic event. The Nationalists moved their capital to Chongqing but returned to Nanjing after the Japanese surrender in 1945. Most buildings survived the war. The Communists took the city on April 23, 1949, and the capital was moved to Beijing. Nanjing is still the provincial capital.

Nanjing today is a beautiful city of broad avenues thickly lined with 240,000 sycamore trees. Central is the Drum Tower, with Zhongshan Road, the main shopping street, running south, northwest, and east, intersecting in the center of town. Part of Zhongshan Nan Road was roughly the old Imperial Way, open only for the emperor. The earlier dynasties were centered in this section of town. Xuanwu Lake dominates the northeastern sector. Above it to the east looms 450-meter Zijin (Purple Gold) Mountain. The magnificent Ming city wall snakes around most of the urban area.

Two thousand factories make metallurgical and chemical equipment, ships, telecommunication instruments, and synthetic fibers. The Zhong Xin Yuan silk factory manufactures brocade, and the Arts and Crafts Carving Factory works in ivory and wood.

Nanjing takes two days to see, but if you only have one day in the city itself, most important are the Sun Yat-sen Mausoleum, Linggu Temple, and Ming Tomb in the east part of the city, usually combined in a half-day tour. In the afternoon, you can choose from the Observatory (for the view), the museum, the Drum Tower, the Yangtze River Bridge or whatever you want from the following menu. The Zhonghua Gate and city wall, the Confucian Temple, Qinhuai River, and the Taiping Museum are close together.

*Sun Yixian (Sun Yat-sen) Mausoleum** 中山陵 (open daily) is on an 80,000-square-meter site. The building was built to be better than those of the emperors whom the father of the Chinese republic overthrew. Eight km from the Jinling Hotel, it is on the south side of Purple Gold Mountain, its *feng-shui* ideal. Dr. Sun (1866–1925) was buried here in 1929 in the rear of the hall (see "Milestones in Chinese History"). The mausoleum, 158 meters above sea level, has 392 steps and a 5-meter-high statue, and is well worth visiting.

Sun Yat-sen was born of peasant stock in Guangdong province, near Macao, in what is now called Zhongshan county, renamed after its most distinguished son. Zhongshan was Dr. Sun's honorific name.

Dr. Sun actually spent most of his life outside China, leaving home at the age of 12 to study at an Anglican school in Hawaii, where his older brother had settled. He studied medicine in Hong Kong and for a short time set up practice in Macao. He spent much of his life traveling in Europe and America, and living in Japan, writing and plotting against the Manchus and planning a government for China. His teachings have been slavishly followed in Taiwan, where he is almost worshiped. He is highly respected on the mainland, too.

An intriguing, complex man, Dr. Sun became a Christian early in life and, although he attacked missionaries as being imperialists, he admitted on his death bed to being a Christian still. He fought the Manchus because they could not rid the country of the foreign imperialists. After becoming president, he did make it a point to inform the first Ming emperor of what had happened!

Dr. Sun did not remain president for long. Because of the problems in uniting the country, he abdicated in 1912. The north was not willing to accept a southerner as head of state, he reasoned. He later accepted a post as director of railways for the country. At the same time, he flirted with socialism, coming under the influence of Russian advisers.

He was married first to a peasant woman and later to Soong Ching-ling, much against her father's wishes. The second marriage shocked the Christians but not most Chinese, who were used to the idea of several wives. Mme. Sun was the sister of Mme. Chiang Kai-shek of Taiwan. See also ''Shanghai'' and ''Zhongshan.''

Linggu (Valley of the Soul) Temple 灵谷寺 (open daily) is just an empty building, the only survivor of a whole complex of Buddhist structures, its statues destroyed during the Taiping war, when the Qing army slept here. Eight km from the Jinling Hotel, it was built originally in A.D. 513 by a Liang princess in memory of a famous monk. It was moved to its current location at the eastern foot of Zijin Mountain because the first Ming emperor wanted the original site for his own tomb. Without beams, it is reminiscent of medieval Europe because of its arches. Its eastern and western walls curve outward. Nearby is a nine-story pagoda built in the 1920s to complement the area around the mausoleum, 2 km to the NE. The pagoda can be climbed for a good view of this beautiful, wooded area. The new **Sun Yat-sen Museum** is nearby.

The **Xiaoling Mausoleum (Ming Tomb)** 明陵 is open daily; tel. 642990. This mausoleum of the first Ming emperor, Zhu Yuanzhang, and his empress (1398 and 1382 respectively) is not as impressive as those north of Beijing, but is worth a visit. The Sacred Way has over a dozen well-proportioned, larger-than-life-size mythical animals, four generals, and four ministers. The stone statues are beautiful. Most of the buildings were destroyed in the early days of the Qing, who overthrew the Ming dynasty. The mausoleum is 6 km from the Jinling Hotel.

Zhu Yuanzhang was an unemployed peasant and former Buddhist monk and beggar who fought his way to the throne and was a brilliant emperor.

The **Botanical Garden** 植物园 , with tropical and subtropical plants, is on one side of the Sacred Way.

Zijinshan (Purple Mountain), a.k.a. Bell Mountain 紫金山 dominates the northeastern skyline. The **Observatory** (tel. 642270) is on the west side and can be combined with a visit to Xuanwu Lake. This major research center of the Chinese Academy of Science was built in 1934 and is involved with space research such as manmade satellites. Tourists usually go there for the view and to see the copies of ancient instruments outside.

The armillary sphere (four dragons and spheres) was invented 2000 years ago in the Western Han and was used to locate constellations. The abridged armillary sphere (three dragons) was invented in the Yuan for the same purpose. Both these 500-year-old replicas were stolen by the Germans and French respectively in 1900. They were later returned. The gnomon column next to the abridged sphere was invented 3000 years ago and was used to survey the seasons and calculate the days of the year. It faces due south and north. In the large column is a small hole through which the sun shines at noon, casting an oval of light on the gauge below. Because of this instrument, the Chinese decided very early that there were 365¼ days a year.

Xuanwu Lake 玄武湖 is outside Xuanwu Gate, NE of the city (tel. 633154), 5 km from the Jinling Hotel. Twenty-five km in circumference, this lake is now used for recreation and fish farming. 1–2 meters deep, it was originally built in the fifth century, and several emperors have used it to train or review their navies and for private recreation. A black dragon was spotted here in the fifth century, so if you visit it on a dark and stormy night, you might want to look for it. You can walk from the railway station and take a ferry.

Jiangsu Provincial Museum (a.k.a. Nanjing Museum) 江苏省博物馆 (Zhongshan Dong Rd; tel. 641554. Closed Mondays) contains exhibits ranging from the era of Peking Man to revolutionary times in a traditional Chinese-style building. It was opened as a museum in March 1953. Three thousand items are on display. Among these are a 3000-year-old duck egg—genuine; the jade burial suit that was exhibited in America in 1973 (Eastern Han, from Xuzhou City, Jiangsu); a sixth-century Soul Pot covered with many birds, placed in a tomb so the birds could fly the soul of the deceased to paradise; maps of the early capitals in Nanjing from 229 to 589, so you can try to locate ancient landmarks in the modern city; a 20-meter scroll showing the inspection tour by Qing Emperor Kangxi (Kang-hsi) from Nanjing to Zhenjiang; the anchor from a British merchant ship lost in Zhenjiang; a photograph of a British-built electric company in 1882; a list of institutions set up by the

United States in China, with numbers of Chinese students and teachers and of foreign teachers. Located 4 km from Jinling Hotel.

The **Gulou (Drum Tower)** 鼓楼 is at the intersection of Zhong-shan Bei Road and Zhongyang and Beijing roads, in the center of the city. Built in 1382, it holds a 6-foot-diameter drum and an ancient giant stone tortoise carrying a stele added in the Qing, a report on the inspection tour of Qing Emperor Kangxi. (See *Drum Towers* in "What to See and Do.") Nearby is the Big Bell Pavilion.

Nanjing City Wall 南京城墙 is 12 meters high, 33.4 km in circumference, and from 7.62 to 12 meters thick. Built from 1368 to 1387, it once had 13,616 cannons on top. Roughly 10 km north-south by 5.62 km east-west, it is said to be the longest city wall in the world. The bricks were made in five provinces, and each is inscribed with the name of the superintendent and the brickmaster, plus the date made. The mortar was lime, tung oil, and glutinous rice paste. It was originally built with 13 gates, and 11 more were added. Cannot be missed.

The **Zhonghua Gate** 中华门 , on the south side, is the best gate to see. It has four two-story gates in succession (in case the enemy breaks through one), 12 tunnels, and room to garrison 3000 soldiers. One can walk along the top of the wall here.

Jiu Hua Hill (Monk Tang Pagoda) was originally built in the Song, about 1000 years ago, to keep the skull of Xuan Zhang (Hsuan-tsang), the monk who traveled to India in search of the Buddhist sutras and was immortalized in the novel *Pilgrimage to the Western World*. The skull of Xuan Zhang was buried in the southern part of the city, and was moved to Jiu Hua in 1962.

If you have more time or specialized interests:

Inside the city wall: **Qingliang Shan Park** was a lovely gathering place for painters and writers of old, on a hill overlooking the northern part of Nanjing near the university. It is on the main road to the Yangtze River Bridge. Among the writers was the author of the Nanjing-based classic novel *The Scholars*. A crematorium used to be in the area, and as a result few Chinese come here. It is a good place to get away from crowds.

The **Confucius Temple (Fuzimiao),** adjacent shopping center, hotel, and free market, are major tourist attractions, featuring Ming and Qing architecture and worth a visit. The Temple was originally built in 1034 A.D. as a place of sacrifice. Wars destroyed it many times and the current building is a post-Liberation reproduction. Moving wax statues of scholars in period dress demonstrates how examinations were written. Birds, fish and clothes sales. Nearby on the Qinhuai River is the former residence of famous Ming sing-song (courtesan) girl Li Xiang and one can rent boats (but the ride is short and the water dirty).

Originally built in the Ming dynasty, 600 years ago, the palace that now houses the **Taiping Museum**　太平天国历史博物馆　was rebuilt for Yang Xiuqing (Yang Hsiu-ching), eastern prince of the Taiping Heavenly Kingdom in the mid-19th century (tel. 623024). It now contains 1000 square meters of exhibits reflecting the: (1) background of the revolution; (2) uprising at Jintian village; (3) Nanjing as capital; (4) regulations and policies; (5) insistence on armed struggle; (6) resisting aggression; (7) safeguarding the capital; (8) continuing the revolution. Prominent inside is a plaque "in memory of the organizer and leader of the Ever Victorious Army, erected by Frederick Ward Post, American Legion, May 27, 1923." Frederick Ward was an American mercenary who fought against the Taiping and died in 1862.

Another relic of the Taipings well worth seeing is the **Tianwang Mansion (The Heavenly King's Mansion)** (292 Changjiang Rd. in the eastern part of the city). Open daily; tel. 641131. The palace was made for Hong Xiuquan (Hung Hsiu-chuan), the head of the Taipings, with materials from the Ming palace. After the 1911 Revolution, the Tianwang Mansion was used as the Presidential Residence.

The Ming Palace　明宫遗址 : These ruins are in the eastern part of Nanjing and can be seen in about five minutes. Built for the first Ming emperor from 1368 to 1386, this palace was copied in Beijing for the Ming palace there. The Forbidden City is about the same size. The palace was partially destroyed in 1645 by Qing troops, and what was left was pulled down to build the Taiping palaces. In 1911 only a gate was left standing, but in 1958 some of the relics were restored. From these you can get an idea of the original.

Meiyuan Xincun (Plum Blossom Villa)　梅园新村 : No. 30. Open daily, except Mondays; tel. 644743. Furniture, office, clothing, and photographs are as they were when Premier Chou En-lai headed the Communist delegation in its negotiations with the Nationalists (1946–47).

Shitoucheng (Stone City) of the Wu Dynasty　石头城 (north of the Hanzhong Gate, inside the western edge of the city wall) is open daily. After the Wu capital was moved here from Zhenjiang, this city, almost 2000 years old, was started by General Sun Quan on what was then the banks of the Changjiang River.

An appointment is needed to visit the **Chaotian (Worshiping Heaven) Palace** (east of Mochou Lake, inside the city wall at Yeshan (Smelting) Hill). Permission can be obtained from Nanjing Municipal Museum; tel. 641983. It is said that Fu Chai (Fu Tsai), king of Wu in mid-fifth century B.C. (see also "Suzhou"), created a special town for making steel swords here. In this city in A.D. 318, a prime minister of the Jin was urged by a geomancer to move the town because the energy emanating from the fire and metal was making the prime minister sick. Wang Dao moved the smelter and used the site as a garden. The smelter was put at its current site, SE of the Stone City.

The first emperor of the Ming dynasty had no such problems with fire and metal, and built a palace at Yeshan Hill for receiving homage from his subjects. In the 19th century, the palace was converted to a Confucian temple, currently the largest Confucian temple complex south of the Yangtze, and the home of the **Nanjing Municipal Museum南京市博物馆**. (Chongtiangong Jianye. Tel. 641983) Wax figures with costumes from six dynasties should be ready by now. Also in the city is a memorial hall to **Zheng He,** the Moslem eunuch who became one of China's most famous maritime commanders, making seven voyages to 30 countries of Asia and Africa from 1405 to 1433. His tomb is 10 km south of Nanjing. The English Corner is at the foot of Drum Tower Park, every Saturday 4–10 p.m.

Dr. Sun Yat-sen's Office in the same compound as Chiang Kai-shek's old headquarters is open to visitors.

Outside the city wall

Meiling Palace. About 3 km. outside the Zhongshan Gate. Also for fans of modern Chinese history, this 1930s building was the weekend home of Gen. Chiang Kai-shek and his wife from 1945 to 1949. Church services were held here, sometimes with the American ambassador. The ground floor is now a restaurant.

Yuhuatai (Rain-Flower) People's Revolutionary Martyr's Memorial Park 雨花台烈士陵园 is just south of the Zhonghua Gate, 5 km from the Jinling Hotel. Open daily; tel. 624003. This ancient battleground was later an execution ground used by the Japanese and warlords. Here the Nationalists killed 100,000 Communists and sympathizers from 1927 to 1949. Now a memorial park with exhibit hall and flower garden, it is known also for its multicolored agate pebbles.

Mochou (Sorrow-Free) Lake Park 莫愁湖 (outside the wall, SW of the city) contains several buildings from the Qing and a small 47-hectare lake. The white marble statue of Mochou is a local landmark. She was the good-hearted wife but submissive daughter-in-law who ended up killing herself, alas, because of her oppressive father-in-law. Open daily; tel. 623243.

The **Stone Engravings of the Southern Dynasties** can be seen any time. Scattered around the suburbs of Nanjing are relics of the Six Dynasties (222–589). Some of the 31 tomb sites (11 emperors and 20 nobles) are in the middle of a field off the main road. Many of the tombs are protected by distinctive pairs of stone mythical animals, pillars, or tablets, symbols of authority and dignity.

The **Southern Tang Tombs** 南唐二陵 are more than 30 km south of the city. Visitors can enter two to see old murals, reliefs, and coffins of the first two emperors of the Tang dynasty, Li Bian and Li Jing, who ruled over 1300 years ago. The tomb of the founder of that glorious dynasty is 21 meters long by 10 meters wide and at least five meters

high. The highly decorated coffins of the imperial couple are in the rear
under a chart of the stars and planets.

Day trips from Nanjing can be made to Zhenjiang and Yangzhou.
Also in the province are Changzhou, Suzhou, and Wuxi. See separate
listings. Also promoted is **Huai'an**—Zhou Enlai's birthplace, where there
is a Han pagoda, the Zhen Huai Tower, and a 70-bed hotel.

Of note too: **Lianyungang** on the Yellow Sea, the eastern end of
the train line from the Netherlands. About 300 km by road north of
Nanjing, this sprawling, open port city has an airport (connecting with
Beijing and Shanghai), hot spring, shell-carving factory, and 2000-year-
old rock sculptures. A 625.5-m-high mountain was the fictional setting
for the Monkey King, mischievous hero of the popular Qing novel *Pilgrimage to the West.* Guides can show you his birthplace, etc. Also has
a clinic for treating illnesses with beestings. Lots of canals and rivers.
The best **hotel** is the **Shenzhou Binguan.** (1 Yingzui Bei, Xugou,
222042. 3*. Telex 36912 LYSZH CN. Fax 310089. Five Swedish mod-
ules close to swimming beach. Nearer to port. C.C. IDD. B.C. H.K.J.V.
No USTV.) The second best is the **Tianranju Binguan.** (293 Hai Chang
Rd., Xinpu Dist. Telex 309066, closer to railway station (2 km). C.C.
(no Diners). USTV. B.C. IDD. Good restaurant linked with Beijing's
famous Donglaishun. Close to post office, and stores.) These hotels are
28 km apart. **C.I.T.S.** 26 Hailian Dong Rd. 222001. Tel./Fax 414043.

Nantong is for textile lovers: the **Textile Museum** (8 Wenfeng Rd)
is a reproduction of a 1900s factory and worth seeing; **Arts & Crafts
Printing & Dyeing Mill** (101 Renmin Xi Rd., tel. 6253, 7568) produces a batik-like "blue calico"; **Industrial Arts Research Institute**
has top quality embroidery. It also has three pagodas, clam-digging (in
season), a bird island (60 km away), and a March festival for whistling
kites (also made here).

Best **hotel,** the **Nantong Dajiudian.** (43 Qingniandong Rd. 226007.
Telex 36539 NTHNT CN. Fax 518996. Suburbs near Foreign Economic
Business Bldg. and textile museum. Dist. port 8 km. Dist. airport (1993)
40 km. C.C. 300 rooms. IDD. USTV due soon. B.C. Tennis.) Second
best, **Tiannan Hotel** (Dajiudian). (76 Renmin Xi Rd. 226005. 2*. Telex
365037 TNHTL CN. Fax 513519. C.C. Closer to port and city centre.
236 rooms. IDD. B.C.) Both have buses meeting ferries. **C.I.T.S.**
Building 8, Wenfeng Hotel, 5 Qingnian Dong Rd. 226007. Tel. 518023.
Telex 36519 NWFHL CN. Fax 510249.

This open port city (population 450,000) is west of Shanghai on
the north bank of the Yangtze, and reached by road from Wuxi and
Suzhou. Twice-a-day high-speed ferries from Shanghai's north suburbs
take 2–3 hours.

Xuzhou 徐州 in northwest Jiangsu. Planes from Shanghai and
Guangzhou. On two train lines. Han Dynasty Museum on the site of

Han Prince Chu's tomb (201–154 B.C.). Here they found the jade burial suit that once toured North America and 3000 terracotta horses and warriors 27–54 cm high. **South Suburb Guesthouse** (Nanjiao Binguan). (55 Heping Rd. 2*. Dist.A.P. 10; Dist.R.W.5 km. Telex 34077 XZSG CN.) **C.I.T.S.** 1 Pengcheng Rd. tel. 24842. Telex 368009 PMXZ CN.

Yixing, due west of Shanghai and Suzhou, on the west side of Lake Taihu is home of the famous purple clay pottery in Dingsu Factories and huge exhibition hall. Also known for its limestone caves. **Shanjuan Cave** 善卷洞 25 km sw of the city, was discovered about 2000 years ago. The 700 m walk takes about an hour. It has a 120-m-long underground river. The **Zhonggong Cave** 张公洞, 22 km sw of Yixing was the home of Zhang Daoling (one of the founders of Taoism) and Zhang Guolao (one of the Eight Taoist Immortals). 72 small, interconnected caves. 1 km walk up and down 1500 stone steps. **Tea plantation** 阳羡茶园 and **bamboo garden** 竹海. **Yixing Guest House** (Binguan). (1 Yichang Rd. 2*. Telex 34077 YXJSC CN. 104 rooms.) **C.I.T.S. and C.T.S.,** Yixing Guest House, 214200. Telex 34077 YXJSC CN. Tel. 702559, 702493.

For background on Nanjing, read Barry Till's *In Search of Old Nanking*.

CULTURAL PERFORMANCES:
The Nanjing Acrobatic Troupe has won international prizes.

SHOPPING
Made in Nanjing are "Yunjin (Figured) Satin" brocade, velvet tapestry and carpets, imitations of ancient wood and ivory carvings, silver jewelry, and paper cuts. Made in the province are inlaid lacquer (Yangzhou), purple sand pottery (Yixing), Huishan clay figures, fresh water pearls, silk underwear, batik (Nantong), and Suzhou embroidery. Store hours: 7 or 7:30 a.m.–7:30 or 8 p.m.; some open 24 hours.

Around the Confucian temple is a lively free market (jeans, fish, birds, back scratchers, etc.) with a good Bao Zi (see "Food") restaurant. On the nearby river, the flower girls used to solicit customers.

Friendship Store 友谊商店 (86 Zhongyang Rd. across from the Jinling; tel. 632802) can package and ship. One of the best in China. 8:30 a.m. to 5:30 (winter); to 6:30 (summer). Lots of shopping also in the **Jinling Hotel** and next door.

Ju Bao Zhai Antique Store (9 Hanzhong Rd., near Jinling Hotel, tel. 742550); antique stores at the Zhongshan Gate and provincial museum; **Sales Department of the Nanjing Handicraft Cooperative** (Zhongshan South Rd.; tel. 642613); **Jiangsu Cultural Relics Shop,** 321 Zhongshandong Rd., Nanjing; tel. 644701. **Nanjing Cultural Relics Shop,** 72 Taipingnan Rd.; tel. 543353. **Arts & Crafts**

Service 工艺美术服务部 31 Bei-jing East Rd.; tel. 634193, 634197);
Xinjiekou Department Store (3 Zhongshan South Rd.; tel. 641300);
Renmin (People's) Market (79 Zhongshan South Rd.; tel.
642766); **Foreign Languages Bookstore** 外文书店 Close to Xuanwu
Lake.

RESTAURANTS

Nanjing people say the recipe for Beijing roast duck originally was
from Nanjing, so you might want to try the Nanjing version. Among
the other local specialties are: salted duck, especially August Sweet-
Osmanthus duck, salted duck gizzard, roast chicken with coriander, salted
shrimps, casserole cabbage heart, Big Flat Pork Croquette (outside crisp,
inside soft), chrysanthemum-shaped herring, long-tailed shrimp and
squirrel-like mandarin fish. Restaurants in the top hotels are good. The
best disco is in the Jinling.

Maxiangxing Moslem Restaurant 马祥兴菜馆 ● *Gulou (Drum
Tower), Zhongshan North Rd.; tel. 633807.*

Dasanyuan Restaurant 大三元 ● *38 Zhongshan Rd.; tel.
641027* ● Guangdong.

Sichuan Restaurant 四川饭店 ● *171 Taiping South Rd.; tel.
642243, 643651.*

Luliuju Vegetarian Restaurant ● *Taiping Lu; tel. 643644* ● The
vegetarian Bao Zi are superb.

For good Western food: the Jinling and Nanjing hotels, especially
the first.

HOTELS

The top hotel is the Jinling. The rest are new or being renovated.
The best location downtown are the Central, Jinling, and Victory/Shen-
gli (75 Zhong Shan Rd., budget travelers only). For getting close to
China, there's the Mandarin Chamber and the Qing Huai Ren Chai (authentic old Chinese inn) smack in the Confucian Temple area.

Central Hotel ● *75 Zhong Shan Rd., 210005. Aiming for 4* Telex
34083. Fax 414194. Dist.A.P.12 km. Dist.R.W.10 km* ● Managed by
the Jinling Institute of Hotel Management. C.C. 1991. 10 stories, 354
rooms. USTV. IDD. Tennis, bowling, gym, sauna, pool.

Dingshan Hotel (Binguan) ● *90 Chahaer Rd., 210003. 3*. Telex
34103 DSHNJ CN. Fax 636929. On hill apart from the city. Dist.A.P.16
km. Dist.R.W.7 km* ● C.C. 1975, ren. 1993. Main building 8 stories,

126 rooms. IDD. B.C. Expects to replace three old Australian prefabs with 160-room building 1993.

Jinling Hotel (Fandian) • *Xinjiekou Square, 210005. 4*. Telex 34110 JLHNJ CN. Fax 714695. Dist.A.P.10 km. Dist.R.W. 10 km* • C.C. 1983, ren. 1990–91. 37 stories, 818 rooms. USTV due now. Hairdryers. Good shopping in hotel and neighborhood. IDD. Gym and sauna. Tanning machine. Pool. B.C. Dragonair. Reserve through Omni.

Mandarin Chamber Hotel (Zhuang Yuan Lou) • *9 Zhuang Yuanjing, Fuzi Temple, 210001. 3–4* quality. Fax 201876. Dist.A.P.12 km. Dist.R.W. 20 km* • On narrow street north of Confucius Temple. One can sit in fancy lobby and watch "old China" outside. Near street food market. C.C. 1991. Five stories, 120 rooms. Gym. IDD. B.C. Singapore J.V.

Nanjing Hotel (Fandian) • *259 Zhongshan Bei Rd., 210003. 3*. Telex 34102 NKHNK CN. Fax 306998. Dist.A.P.14 km. Dist.R.W. 5 km* • 1954, ren. 1984. Three buildings, 230 rooms. IDD. B.C. Currently building international club with dinner theatre and a 4* hotel with 180 rooms due 1993.

IMPORTANT ADDRESSES
Ambulance: tel. 633858.
Police: tel. 110.
C.I.T.S.: 202-1 Zhongshan Bei Rd. 210003. tel. 639013, Telex 34024 ITSNJ CN. Fax 308954.
CAAC 中国民航 : 52 Ruijin Rd. Tel. 643378 (domestic), 644410 (international), 408583 (airport).
C.T.S.: 313 North Zhong Shan Rd., 210003. Fax 685977. Tel. 771502, 302747.
C.Y.T.S.: tel. 803987, 53847.
Dragonair: Jinling Hotel, tel. 803987, 53847.
Jiangsu Travel and Tourism Bureau, and **Jiangsu Overseas Tourist Corp.,** 259 North Zhongshan Rd. 210003. Tel. 342328. Tel. JOTC 303262, 639013, JTTB. Tel. 638538. One of China's best agencies. Telex 34119 JTTBN CN. Fax 306002, 305568. (Sales and Promotion.) North American Dept., tel. 302275, 639013. J.T.&T. Fax 306002. Tel. 302275 Shanghai office, tel. 4712712 X5014.
Tourist Complaint Center and Hotline: 202–1 North Zhongshan Rd. Tel. 301221.

NANNING 南宁

South China. Capital of Guangxi Zhuang Autonomous Region, in the southwestern part of Guangxi, near the northeastern border of Vietnam. It is 7 hours by train from Guilin and trains from Vietnam should start soon. Can also be reached by air from 5 Chinese cities and Hongkong. Urban population is 900,000. Nanning has a subtropical climate, meaning great fruit, flowering trees, and mild, humid weather. Hottest—38°C; coldest—5°C. Annual precipitation 1300 mm, mostly May to September. It is worth visiting because of its national minorities, its karst caves, and medicinal herb garden.

Founded in 214 B.C. Nanning was the provincial capital from 1912 to 1936, and after 1949. It has a few industries.

The **Guangxi Museum** 广西博物馆 (Qiyi Rd.) is open daily, except Mondays and Fridays, 2:30–5:30 p.m. Botanical and zoological specimens, historical relics, and Taiping history. It also boasts the largest collection of bronze drums (over 300) in China. The 126.5-hectare **Nanhu (South Lake) Park** 南湖公园 in the SE has 1200 varieties of medicinal herbs, plus orchids and bonsai. The **Guangxi Botanical Garden of Medicinal Plants** 广西药用植物园 , 8 km from the city in the eastern suburbs, has 2100 kinds on 200 hectares. It also raises animals for medicinal purposes.

The **Yiling cave** 伊岭岩 , 32 km north in Wuming County, is much like a Guilin cave, with colored lights to highlight weird rock formations here that look like lions, a hen, and vegetables. Visitors usually walk 1100 meters. Outside is a pavilion built in the elaborate style of the Dong people.

For those interested in the customs of national minorities, visit a Zhuang village in Wuming County, and in Nanning, the **Institute of Nationalities** 广西民族学院 or Guangxi Minority Nationality College. The **Guangxi Art College** 广西艺术学院 teaches the art, music, and dances of the minorities. The **Ethnic Garden** displays real houses of the Zhuang, Yao, Miao, and Dong nationalities and a Dong bridge and drum tower. Arts and crafts are demonstrated and sold.

Twelve nationalities live in the region, of which the Zhuang form over one third. They are somewhat similar to the people of Thailand. The colorful Miao and Yao live here also. This makes Nanning a good place to look for handicrafts to study and buy.

The Taiping Heavenly Kingdom originated from **Jintian village* 272 km NE of the city. This was the most extensive peasant uprising in Chinese history. It started in 1851 and took over a large portion of the country with a capital in Nanjing. Its disruptions were largely responsible for the emigration of Chinese people from south China to America, Australia, and other parts of Asia. At the home of Wei Changhui, one of the leaders, weapons were made and hidden in a nearby trench and pond.

On the way to the Zhuang villages there's **Lingshui** 金田 in Wuming County, 46 km north of the city, with its relaxing 23°C lake in a hilly setting. **Guiping Xishan Hill** 桂平西山 , 248 km NE, has a marvelous view of the area.

The **Mount Hua Rock Paintings** are along the Ming River, 180 km away near the Vietnam border. Here one can take a boat trip to see primitive riverside rock paintings. Dances inspired by the paintings can be arranged. One can also watch local people pan for gold and visit the Longrui Nature Reserve, the only place in the world inhabited by rare white-headed langur monkeys and golden camellias. This is part of the Zuojiang Huashan Tourist Area.

Beihai is Guangxi's sea port, and one of the 15 Open Coastal Cities. In the Dong Autonomous Sanjiang County is the recently restored multi-pagodaed 64-meter-long Yongji Bridge in Dong architecture. **Liuzhou** is toward and closer to Guilin, with many Dong, Hui, Miao, Yao, and Zhuang nationalities and festivals. It has the **Liuhou Temple and Tomb** of the famous Tang writer who worked to free women from being bond slaves. There are also the **Dule Caves** (much like Guilin's) and the **Bai Lain Cave** whcrc Liujiang (Liuchiang) Man lived 20,000–30,000 years ago. The top hotel there is the **Liuzhou Grand (Binguan)** at 2 Longcheng Rd. 545001, with IDD and pool. **C.I.T.S.** and the **Liuzhou Tourist Bureau** are in the Liuzhou Hotel 545001; tel. 25669; telex 48575 GLFAO. For other destinations in Guangxi, see also Guilin under separate listing.

A good time to visit is during the Dragon Boat Festival (5th day of the 5th month), the Zhuang Song Festival (3rd day of the 3rd month), Lantern Festival (15th day of the 1st month), and Mid-Autumn Festival (15th day of the 8th month)—all on the lunar calendar. At the Song Festival, small groups of male and small groups of female singers compete with each other in wit, knowledge, and vocal quality. Then the boys chase the girls they like in order to continue the contest with more privacy. The festival also includes throwing embroidered balls and participating in dragon and buffalo dances. On the Western calendar, it's April 5, 1992, and Mar. 25, 1993.

Other festivals on the Western calendar include:

Song Festival (during Moon Festival). Lingsui Spring in Wuming County. Sept. 11, 1992, and Sept. 30, 1993.

Pan-wang Festival (Yao Nationality). Jingxiu Yao Autonomous Region, Nov. 9, 1992, and Nov. 28, 1993.

Lu-sheng Festival (Miao Nationality). Rongsui Miao Autonomous Region, Feb. 16–19, 1992, and Feb. 4–7, 1993.

Hua-pao (Firecracker) Festival (Dong Nationality). Shanjiang Dong Autonomous Region, April 5, 1992, and Mar. 25, 1993.

Dragon Boat races in Nanning, same dates as rest of China.

SHOPPING

Locally made are Zhuang brocade, bamboo, and pottery ware. The province also makes artistic shell, horn, and feather products, and stone carvings. Also produced are Xishan tea and Milky Spring Wine. Tourists can visit the silk factory. Locally grown are jack fruit, mango, almond, and longan.

Arts and Crafts Service 工艺美术服务部 (Xinhua Rd.; tel. 22779); **Foreign Languages Bookstore** 外文书店 (Minsheng Rd.; tel. 27033); **Friendship Store** 友谊商店 (Renmin Rd.; tel. 23480); **Nanning Antique Store** 南宁古物店 (Guangxi Museum, Gucheng Rd.; tel. 27810).

RESTAURANTS

The food here is much like neighboring Guangdong's: Cantonese. Please avoid eating endangered species.

HOTELS

C.I.T.S. says the top hotel is the Ming Yuan, then the Xi Yuan.

Xi Yuan Hotel (Fandian) • *Jiang Nan Rd. 530031.3*. Telex 48137* • 15 villas built from 1958 to 1985. No. 12 renovated 1986. 210 beds.

Ming Yuan Hotel (Fandian) • *Xinmin Rd. 530012.3* Telex 48143 MIYUH CN. Fax 38583* • 11 villas built from 1952 to 1985.

OTHER IMPORTANT ADDRESSES

Ambulance: tel. 120.
Police: tel. 110.
CAAC 中国民航 : 64 Chaoyang Rd. 530011; tel. 21459.
C.I.T.S. 中旅社 and **C.T.S.:** 40 Xinmin Rd. 530012; tel. 22042, 21041. Fax 20856. Telex 48142 CITSN CN. **Guanxi Tourism Administration:** tel. 25859. Write for list of interesting tour possibilities including forest preserves, Zhuang Nationality traditional medicine, hot sand

treatment, and dates of other festivals. Branch in Guilin, tel. 227298. Fax 227288.
Long distance operator: tel. 113.
Tourist Hotline: tel. 35301.

NINGBO (NINGPO) 宁波

East China. On the Zhejiang coast south of Shanghai, it can be reached by road from Hangzhou (4 hours), by plane from 9 Chinese cities and Hong Kong and by daily 11-hour ship from Shanghai (overnight best to save time). A hovercraft from Shanghai can make it in 5½ hours. Ningbo is on the Shanghai-Hangzhou railway line (slow).

A community of 600,000 people, Ningbo is known because some of the world's great ship builders and business people are from this area. It is also noteworthy for the oldest extant library in China and the home of the Goddess of Mercy.

The Ningbo area has been settled at least since 4800 B.C. Archaeologists found evidence of an advanced culture in the village of Hemudu in Yuyao County in 1973, and some scholars now claim the cradle of Chinese civilization was farther east than Henan and not confined to the Yellow River. The 6000–7000-year-old bone flute found in Hemudu is still playable. Inlaid-bone and wood-carving skills were known then.

Ningbo has been recorded since the Spring and Autumn period (700–476 B.C.). It has been a major port since the Tang, trading with Korea, Japan, and Southeast Asia. It was made a treaty port, open to foreign trade and residence, in 1842. After 1860, a French military detachment was stationed here. Ningbo was reopened as a port for foreign trade in 1979 for the first time in 30 years. This ice-free port is now one of the 15 Open Coastal Cities.

If you have only one day, see the library, one or two of the temples, and an arts and crafts factory.

The A.D. 1561 (Ming to Qing) *Tianyige Library 天一阁 is ½ km from the Overseas Chinese Hotel in the city. It still has more than 300,000 books. It started as a private library and now has in its more

400 · · · DESTINATIONS

modern extension next door over 80,000 rare books, mostly from the Ming, plus numerous stone tablets. Scholars can see these books upon request. The library is worth visiting for its simple elegance and its peaceful, tastefully designed gardens. This library was the blueprint for the other seven imperial libraries built during the Qing.

At the entrance to the library is a sign that says something like "This is not an amusement park. No fun inside. Keep out." Don't be intimidated by the blunt Ningbo manner. Note also the conversations of the man-in-the-street, which might sound like intense, bitter arguing.

The *Bao Guo Temple 保国寺 , built in 1013 (Northern Song), is the oldest extant wooden structure south of the Yangtze, and is in Yuyao, 20 km north of the Overseas Chinese Hotel. Unlike other temples, which have large beams for support, this one uses many small ones. The **Tianfeng Pagoda,** built in A.D. 695, was traditionally a place for scholars to gather to compose poems and enjoy the scenery. It is hexagonal, seven stories high, but not as beautiful as younger pagodas.

Both the **Tiantong Temples** 天童寺 , 35 km from the Overseas Chinese Hotel, and the **Ayuwang (King Asoka) Temple** 育王寺 , 30 km away, are east of the city. They were founded in the third century. The Tiantong is one of the largest temples south of the Yangtze, with over 700 halls, and some people feel it is more worth seeing than Hangzhou's Lingyin Temple. The Tiantong has sent many teachers to Japan and consequently attracts many Japanese visitors. It is the second holiest shrine of the Zen sect. Zen Buddhist statues are supposed to have deepset eyes looking at their noses as the nose safekeeps one's heart to avoid temptation. See if you can find any. Better still, try crossing your eyes when you feel tempted to sin.

The Ayuwang Temple has relics of Sakyamuni. The famous Buddhist monk Jianzhen (see "Yangzhou") once lived here after he failed in his third attempt to reach Japan in the Tang dynasty.

Visitors can also go to an **arts and crafts factory** (tel. 64617), 4 km from the Overseas Chinese Hotel. Also, the village of **Sanshiliu Wan,** 15 km from Xikou, specializes in *penjing,* the growing and selling of miniature trees.

Putuo Shan 普陀山 is the home of Guanyin (Kuan Yin), the Goddess of Mercy, and is one of the Four Sacred Buddhist Mountains. This 12.5-square-km island is reached by ship from Ningbo, a 2-hour trip offered four times a day. Direct ship also from Shanghai. On the way one passes the famous Zhaoshan-Qundao fishing ground with triangular fish nets, a most picturesque view, especially at sunset.

Putuo Shan has been a religious site since 847 A.D. It once had over 200 temples and nunneries, but the years and the Red Guards have done their worst, and 80 are now open. Those who remember hiking from innumerable nunneries to innumerable temples may be disappointed. No more tiny Buddhist statues inscribed with religious poems to help keep one single-mindedly devout line the narrow mountain paths. But one can still climb thousands of steps and hike through bamboo groves and along the rocky shore and beaches. Enough of the religious atmosphere remains for first-time visitors to enjoy, especially if you avoid the now-paved road, the buses and few taxis and have time for the hospitable and warm-hearted villagers.

Especially exotic (and noisy) is the **guesthouse** next to the Puji Temple, over a kilometer uphill from the ferry pier, where guests have been awakened early by chanting Buddhists. Rituals at 3 p.m. can also be seen from the upstairs windows. The best hotel is the 3* Xilei Xiao Zhaing, 316107. Fax 54937. Reservations through C.I.T.S. in Ningbo.

Visitors can also see the kowtowing pilgrims, forehead to ground every three steps, as they pay homage or ask special favors of this favorite deity. Especially touching are the sick and handicapped, carried on the backs of friends or family, who come to pray for healing. Devout Buddhists try to make a trip to Putuo at least once in a lifetime.

It is customary to purchase a yellow sack from one of the temples and, for a fee, have each temple rubber-stamp its seal on the sack to prove you've been there.

Putuo Shan is especially famous because repeated storms kept some Japanese worshipers from carrying away a statue of Guanyin from China. Near a cliff is the "Won't Go Temple," to commemorate the goddess's desire to remain in China.

SHOPPING

Made in the area are Mandarin coats, embroidery, bone and wood inlaid articles, bamboo articles, Ming-style furniture, colored clay models, handwoven carpets, blue porcelain, and straw mats.

Sesame seed and glutinous rice balls are served for breakfast. Also try dried longan fruit soup. Both are sweet.

HOTELS

C.I.T.S. says Asia Garden is best, then Ningbo Hotel, and third the Overseas Chinese Hotel.

Ningbo Asia Garden Hotel (Yazhou Huayuan Binguan) • *72 Mayuan Rd. 315010. 3*. Telex 37020 AGHZJ CN. Fax 362138, 366544. Dist.A.P.10 km. Dist.R.W.½ km.* • 1987, ren. 1991. 10 stories, 170 rooms. C.C., IDD, B.C. USTV.

Ningbo Hotel (Fandian) • *65 Mayuan Rd. 315000. 3*. Dist.A.P.5 km. Dist.R.W.1.5 km* • 1982; ren. 1987. 6 stories. 100 rooms. IDD. B.C.

Overseas Chinese Hotel (Hua Qiao Fandian) • *130 Liuting St. 315010. 3*. Telex 37001 NPHCM CN. Fax 364790. Dist.A.P.11 km, Dist.R.W.⁷/₁₀ km* • C.C. 1962; ren. 1990, 1992. 5 stories, 144 rooms. H.K.J.V. IDD. B.C.

Ambulance: tel. 366901.
Police: tel. 362934.
C.I.T.S. and **C.T.S.:** 65 Mayuan Rd., 315000; tel. 368690, 342391. Telex 37019 NPHCM CN. Fax 368390.
Ningbo Overseas Travel Co.: Asia Garden Hotel, tel. 664451. Fax 364481.
Ningbo Travel and Tourism: 51 Jiangxia Jia, tel. 367784. Telex 37020 AGH2J. Fax 64481.

QINGDAO (TSINGTAO)

North China. On a peninsula on the southern coast of Shandong province, 393 km east of the provincial capital Jinan by rail. 2-hour flight south from Beijing or north of Shanghai. Direct air connections with 19 Chinese cities. Air links with Hong Kong, Japan, Singapore, and Bangkok already exist or are due soon. It is on the Huanghai (Yellow Sea) and can also be reached by ship from Shanghai (26 hours) and Yantai, Guangzhou, and Dalian. Expressway from Yantai. The climate is temperate. Highest August average, 25°C; coldest January average, ⁻1.2°C. Annual precipitation, 715 mm. Population is 2 million. Good but crowded beaches.

Qingdao is an icefree port and summer resort, famous for its beer and mineral water. It should be put at the end of a hectic, tight schedule in summer.

Starting as a fishing village, Qingdao (pronounced Ching Dow) has been an important trading port since the seventh century. During the Ming, it was fortified against pirates. The Germans seized the area in 1897 in retaliation for the assassination of two German missionaries. Here they built a naval base and trading port, and protected them with at least 2000 men. The large number of Germans accounted for most of its architecture and its beer recipe.

In 1919, the Versailles Peace Conference confirmed Japan's 1915 seizing of the German territories in Shandong, including Qingdao. The Japanese stayed long enough to build huge cotton mills before they were forced to withdraw in 1937. During this period, the British built cigarette factories. The Japanese navy regained the city early in 1938, but not before a Chinese mob smashed the breweries, sending rivers of beer into the streets!

Qingdao's breweries were rebuilt, of course, and still produce the most popular Tsingtao Beer. Qingdao also bottles Laoshan mineral water from the mountains behind the city. The U.S. Navy was here in 1945. Full of hills and trees and red-tiled roofs, the city is very pretty. It also has 19 very intriguing national architectural styles, most from the imperialist past. It is now concerned about preserving the best of them. How many can you identify?

Qingdao is now the largest city and industrial center in Shandong. Its factories make diesel locomotives, automobiles, TV sets, textiles, and cameras. Its oceanic research institute is internationally famous. Huangdao District, on the west coast of Jiaozhou Bay, is the site of the new economic and technical development zone. Qingdao is one of the 15 Open Coastal Cities.

All of Qingdao's urban attractions can be covered in a day. A second day or two is needed for Laoshan Mountain if you enjoy hiking in exotic settings and want to see it all. Qingdao's 4 km of city beaches slope gently into the sea and are protected by four large bays east from **The Pier** 栈桥 (1891). The 440-meter pier is a good place to see the sunrise, and its Huilan Pavilion is Qingdao's most famous landmark. Southeast of the Pier and linked with the shore by a 700-meter-long dyke is **Xiaoqingdao (Little Qingdao Island)** 小青岛 .

The largest and best of the six city beaches is the **No. 1 Huiquan (Pearl Spring) Beach** 汇泉第一海水浴场 , with lifeguards, medical station and changing facilities. Be prepared to share any city beach with 100,000 other people in summer. They are open from early July to the end of September.

If you are worried about pollution, **Shilaoren** 石老人海滩 is 17 km east and should be less crowded.

Zhongshan Park 中山公园 is best seen when its 700 cherry trees bloom in April. It also has osmanthus, roses, and peonies. A Seaside Lantern Festival is held from July 1 to Sept. 1. Open daily, 6 a.m.–10 p.m. Tel. 279935.

Luxun Park 鲁迅公园 , with its many hilly paths, rocky hills, and old pine trees, has an excellent view of No. 1 beach, Xiaoqingdao, and the European buildings. The castlelike Museum of Marine Products is in this park. A good view can also be had from **Xiaoyu Shan (Little Fish Hill)** 小鱼山 , a tastefully designed park with a recent three-story pavilion, and three large ceramic screens showing the eight Taoist ferries crossing the sea, Pu Songlin's Universe, etc. Qingdao's nine other major peaks are similarly developed.

The **Qingdao Museum of Marine Products** 青岛水族馆 (tel. 284165) consists of a marine aquarium and an exhibition hall of specimens. The aquarium has 40 tanks with live marine animals, and an outdoor pond for seals. The badly designed exhibition hall has over 900 specimens and poor lighting, but a new one is in the works.

If you can borrow a bicycle, ride through the **Badaguan** area 八达关 , where the streets are named after the eight passes of the Great Wall and each street is lined with a different kind of blossoming tree: cherry, peach, or crape myrtle. Behind the streets are individually designed houses with spacious gardens, each one-of-a-kind with interesting features, a bit of old Europe. Some of these houses can be rented by the month with cooks and housekeepers. One of the most famous is at 18 Huanghai Road. Built in 1903 in the shape of a castle, with large blocks of granite, it was originally a hunting lodge for the German governor. Protected by Qingdao as a historical monument, the Stone House is now part of the Badashan Hotel.

The **Laoshan Mountains** 崂山 are roughly 40 km east of the city and can be reached by land or sea. The range is said to be the home of the Eight Taoist Immortals (genii, fairies). See "What Is There To See And Do." The boat trip gives an excellent view of the city.

You may have to choose one of three routes to tour Laoshan. On the South Route you cover the upper and lower Taiqing temples, Longtan Water Fall, and Dragon Well Falls. The North Route covers Shuilienbi (Water Fall Screen), Camel Head Rock, Fishscale Gorge, and Tsaoying Water Fall. The East Route covers Lion Peak (to see the sunrise), Fairy Bridge, Yuelong Cave, and Sheep Rock. A leisurely three-day trip would be ideal. 400-m-long chairlift.

Do not expect large temples. Many of the temples here are Taoist, with small buildings, small doorways, and small courtyards. The mystical Taoists apparently didn't want to be distracted in their meditative search for eternal peace, their communion with nature.

Laoshan is famous for the masculine shape of its mountains and its rushing waterfalls. It is full of legends. The highest peak, Mt. Laoding, is 1333 meters above sea level. The mountains extend over 386 square km and are full of granite canyons, grotesque crags, old temples, rivers, streams, and the Laoshan reservoir. The **Taiping (Great Peace) Taoist Temple** 太平宫 was founded in the Song. The biggest **Taiqing Taoist Temple** 太清宫 has over 150 buildings.

The **home of Qing writer Pu Songling** (1640–1715) 蒲松龄旧址 is open to the public. He lived in a very modest corner of the Taiping Temple. Pu wrote his famous *Strange Tales from a Lonely Studio* here. The trees he described are still standing.

An inscription about the visit of the first Qin emperor in 219 B.C. is also on the mountain. The builder of the Xi'an ceramic army searched for pills of immortality in this area.

Qingdao also has the **Qingdao Museum** 青岛博物馆 (Daxue Rd.; tel. 83762) open daily, except Mondays, 8:30 a.m.–5:30 p.m. in summer; 8:30 a.m.–4:30 p.m. in winter. The **Jimo Hot Spring** 即墨温泉 is 75 km NE, with water 90°C tempered to 38°C, said to be good for rheumatoid arthritis.

Annual beer festival in June. The Candied Haw (crab apple) Festival has attracted 500,000 people at the Haiyun Temple on the 16th day of the lunar new year. 18-hole golf course due soon.

SHOPPING

Shops are along Zhongshan 中山路 and Jiaozhou 胶州路 roads. Made locally are beautiful shell pictures, feather pictures, carpets, weaving, embroidery, and knitting. The shell products and embroidery are especially good buys. A large free market is on **Jimo St.** with clothes, handicrafts and bicycles for sale.

Qingdao Antique Store 青岛文物商店 (40 Zhongshan Rd.; tel. 84436); **Qingdao Arts and Crafts Shop** 工艺美术商店 (40 Zhongshan Rd.; tel. 228627).

RESTAURANTS

Seafood, of course! Abalone and prawns. Lots of sea cucumbers and scallops too. The food in the Overseas Chinese Hotel is very good.

Outside and to the right of the Dynasty Hotel is a market full of small restaurants. We enjoyed Steven's Shang Ge La Seafood Restaurant at #28 Huiquan Snack St., tel. 269698. We especially liked the Laoshan Fisherman's Banquet (minimum five people, 3 hours notice) at the Laoshan Hotel, National Highway 308, Laoshan Dist., tel. 496651.

Chunhelou Restaurant 春和楼餐厅 ●*Zhongshan Rd.; tel. 228482.*

HOTELS

The two top hotels with luxury standards are the Huiquan Dynasty (better) and the Haitian. The Huiquan is closer to the beach, sailboarding, the Foreign Trade Center and city center—with good Chinese food and slow elevators. The Haitian has a classier exterior and many return guests. The Badaguan is next with its own private beach.

For budget travelers, the Huanghai is better than the Overseas Chinese Hotel, but the Overseas Chinese Hotel is best for downtown shopping and architecture. Both are grubby with poor workmanship.

Badaguan Hotel (Binguan) • *19 Shanhaiguan, 266071. Telex 32224 BDGHL CN. Fax 336920. Dist.A.P. 30 km. Dist.R.W. 4 km. 20 buildings between 10 and 200 meters from swimming beach* • C.C. (no Diners). 1903, started by Germans. 1920s, additional villas by Japanese and Spanish. 1953 became hotel. 1988, main building (only one with IDD at front desk). Total 420 beds. Nos. 1, 5, 13, 17, and 18 for foreigners. Pool. Tennis. Gym. Bicycles.

Haitian Hotel (Dajiudian) • *39 Zhanshan Da Rd., 266071. 4*. Telex 321014 QDHTH CN. Fax 3717777. Dist.A.P. 25 km. Dist. R.W. 5 km. Dist. swimming beach 200 meters* • C.C. 1988–89. 40-story extension in 1992. 15 stories. 302 rooms. IDD. Tennis, pool, gym, bowling, B.C. USTV. Safe in every room.

Huanghai Hotel (Fandian) • *75 First Yanan Rd., 266003. 3*. Telex 43151 BOOTH CN. Fax 279795. Dist.A.P. 30 km. Dist. R.W. 4 km. Dist. beach 250 meters* • C.C. no Diners. 1979, ren. 1990. 21 stories. Best floors 10 to 19. 350 rooms. IDD. Claims it is able to get plane and train tickets where other hotels cannot. C.Y.T.S. and C.T.S. B.C. Gym.

Huiquan Dynasty Hotel (Huiguan Wang Chao Dajiudian) • *9 Nanhai Rd., 266003. 4* when extension completed. Fax 279220. Telex 32178 HQDTY CN. Dist.A.P. 35 km. Dist. R.W. 5 km. Across street from #1 swimming beach* • C.C. (no Diners). 1969, ren. 1989, 1992. 12 stories, 200 rooms. 1991–92, 23 stories, 300 rooms. IDD. B.C. USTV due soon. Korean Restaurant. Health center, bowling, pool, tennis and three-story penthouse suite due soon. Bicycles. Managed by Dynasty International. H.K.

Overseas Chinese Hotel (Hua Qiao Fandian) • *72 Hunan Rd., 266001. 2*. Telex 321129 OVSEA CN. Fax 270739. Dist.A.P. 40 km. Dist.R.W. 2 minute walk* • C.C. (no Diners). 1936. Ren. 1988. 5 stories, 62 rooms. C.T.S. B.C. Should have IDD now.

Stone Cliffs Beach Hotel (Shi Fang Binguan) • *Shilaoren Tourism Development Zone. 266071. 3*. Telex 32168 QSCBH CN. Fax 597052. Dist.A.P. 22 km. Dist.R.W. 17 km. Near Old Stone Man Rock* *on way to Laoshan* ● C.C. Book through UTELL. Sits on vein of gold. Take bus 104 from city. 1989. 3 stories, 168 rooms. Moslem restaurant related to Beijing's famous Donglaishun Restaurant. USTV. Japanese food. Tennis. Bicycles. B.C. Should soon have tennis, squash, sailboarding, pool, etc. Qigong. Cannot change travelers checks. Dirty beach.

OTHER IMPORTANT ADDRESSES

Ambulance: tel. 225000.
CAAC: 29 Zhongshan Rd.; tel. 283336, 270747, 286047.
C.I.T.S. 国际旅行社 : 9 Nanhai Rd. (tel. 279215) or Service Center, Huiquan Hotel (tel. 270830, 270691. Telex 32202 QCITS CN). Fax 270983.
C.T.S. 中旅社 : 31 Zhanshan Rd. 266071. Tel. 362021, 362095. Telex 32197 CTSOD CN. Fax 337185.
CYTS: Badaguan Hotel, tel. 362417, 361942.
Hospitals: If ill, you might find it more convenient to ask at your hotel for help. Failing that, try the **Qingdao People's Hospital** (Dexian Rd.; tel. 227625) or the **Qingdao Municipal Hospital** (Jiaozhou Rd.; tel. 26433, 24133).
Huang Hai Yin Dong School: 5 Nanhai Rd., 266071. Tel. 270438. Has sailboards (fan ban) for rent. Ask for Mr. Zhou Ben Liang.
Passenger Quay 客运码头 : Xinjiang Rd.; tel. 222940.
Police: tel. 119.
Qingdao Overseas Travel Corp: 9 Nanhai Rd., 266003, tel. 270830. Telex 32202 QCITS CN (Sales). Fax 270983.
Railway Station 火车站 : Tai'an Rd.; tel. 264971.

QINHUANGDAO 秦皇岛

(Chinwangtao) North China, northeastern tip of Hebei province on the Bohai Sea; one of China's busiest harbors. It is ice-free and is the port for a nearby oil field to which it is joined by a pipeline. The closest airport is at Shanhaiguan, 15 km away, with flights from Shanghai, Beijing, Guangzhou, etc. Train and upgraded highway from Beijing.

Originally a small village, Qinhuangdao was opened as a seaport in 1898 and became a base for foreign (especially British) shipping. In 1902 the British army also built a small pier. In 1904, contract workers from nearby East Mountain were recruited for South Africa. The railway was built in 1916. The current population is about 450,000. It is one of the 15 Open Coastal Cities, and includes Beidaihe.

The city is named after a legend. The Qin emperor is believed to have passed through here about 2200 years ago looking for pills of longevity. Suddenly he recognized a special tree described by his teacher. Surprised and afraid, he bowed to the tree and a branch bowed back.

Dong Shan (East Mountain) 东山 is where the Qin emperor searched for the pills and boarded his ships. There's a good view of the sea and the sunrise from here. Walk along the waterfront at night. A cruise boat goes to a fishing village at the mouth of the Xin Kai River and sometimes visitors can see the teams of fishing boats going out together, dragging the big nets between boats. In the old days, the fishermen used to sing to each other.

One can visit a shell-carving factory, the Sea God Temple, and the place where the Qin Emperor searched for longevity pills. Swimming beaches are at Dong Shan. Swimming also in the solar-energy swimming pool. For excursions from here, see "Great Wall" and "Beidaihe," the resort about 15 km south, and "Shanhaiguan," close to the place where the Great Wall meets the sea.

On May 1 is the "Go To Sea" festival.

SHOPPING

Grown locally are peaches, pears, sea cucumbers, and crabs (biggest in September–October). Made locally are pictures, lamps, ashtrays, etc., of shell. Also manufactured are mirrors, magnifying glasses, painted eggs, painted stones, butterfly and insect specimens, bird feather crafts, and necklaces of red beans (symbol of longing between lovers).

HOTELS

C.I.T.S. says the best hotels here are the Xinyi and the Asian Games Guest House. The Cindic is at Yingbin, 066000. 3*. Telex 271042 QHCHL CN. Fax 332253, but you can also stay in nearby Beidaihe.
Ambulance: tel. 120. **Police:** tel. 110, 119.
C.T.S.: 13 Guangming Rd. 066002; tel. 34269, 31426, 31634.
C.I.T.S.: 16 Jianshe St. 066000, tel. 335974, 333395. Telex 334765.
Qinhuangdao Tourism Bureau: Hohai Hotel 066000. Tel. 334394.

QUANZHOU 泉州

(Chuangchou) East China, 103 km north of Xiamen in Fujian, this ancient city was considered one of the two largest ports in the world by Marco Polo, who knew it as Zaiton or Citong when it exported silks and porcelain as far away as Africa. In the Song it had a population of 500,000. It declined because maritime trade was forbidden. Today, it is one of the 24 cities protected by the State Council as a historical monument. Its downtown area still has a great deal of slow-paced old China flavor plus charming touches of Moslem architecture. It also has the largest number of bicycle rickshaws I've seen in China (with sideseats) and the largest collection of Nestorian Christian and Manichaean relics. Weather: the hottest in July has been 32°C. Mild winters (no snow). Precipitation is 1400 mm, from July to September.

If you only have one day, C.I.T.S. recommends the Kaiyuan Temple, East and West Pagoda, Overseas Communication Museum, and Old God Rock in the morning. In the afternoon, the Grand Mosque, Wind-Shaken Rock, Holy Islamic Tombs, and Luoyang Bridge.

The **Kaiyuan Temple** is 1 km NW of the Overseas Chinese Hotel and dates from the Tang. The main hall has 100 heavy stone Greek-type columns. On top of 24 of these are gaudy part women/part birds, whose crowns appear to support the beams. These flying musicians are of gilded clay and are most unusual. Indian figures and Chinese dragons and tigers also decorate the temple. Look also for the 1000-armed, 1000-eyed Guanyin. Note the corners of the roof, the curled swallow tails, and the lively dragons that are distinctive aspects of Southern Fujian temple architecture.

Two large pagodas, the trademarks of the city, are on the temple grounds. These are the **East and West Pagodas**. The 48-meter-high **Zhenguo Pagoda** is east. Originally built of wood in 865, it was rebuilt of stone in 1238. The west **Renshou Pagoda,** 44 meters high, was originally built in 916 and rebuilt in 1228.

In the Song dynasty, this temple was home to over 1000 monks.

There is also the 9-story **Museum of Maritime Navigational History,** which houses relics from many religions, including Nestorian

Christian, Manichean, Hindu, and Islamic. Look for the Franciscan tombstone with a cross. It also has the remains of a 13th-century ship, 24 m long, found in Quanzhou Bay.

Old God Rock 老君岩 is 4 km from the city. This stone statue of Laotze/Laotzu, the founder of Taoism, is beautiful. 600 years old, he is about 5 meters high and grandfatherly, with a long beard.

At one time, 10,000 foreigners from Persia, Syria, and Southeast Asia lived in the southern part of the city. Most of them were Moslem. The ***Qingjing (Grand Mosque)** 清净寺 (Tushan St., ½ km from the O.C. Hotel), open daily, was built by local Moslems in 1009. One of the earliest mosques in China, it was copied from a mosque in Damascus and was renovated in 1310. It is one of the few mosques in eastern China with west Asian architecture, but unfortunately much of it is in ruins. But it is lovingly maintained. Arabic writing and west Asian arches point to its former glory. Inside is a small museum with text in English pointing out such events as Moslems fighting alongside Zheng Chenggong (Koxinga) and the continuing observance of customs like Ramadan, weddings officiated by an imam, and abstinence from eating pork. Three thousand Moslems still live on Tushan Street.

The **Islamic Tombs** 圣墓 are on Ling Shan Hill, outside the East Gate, 4 km from the city. They are protected by a Chinese-style pavilion. They could belong to two trader-missionaries who arrived in the city during the Tang. Koxinga prayed here before his fifth voyage to Southeast Asia. Arabic inscriptions.

A few steps away is the 50-ton **Wind-shaking Rock** 风动石 , an elephant-sized boulder that anybody can wobble. Honest!

In the neighborhood of the Luoyang Bridge is a stone-carving factory that makes Japanese lanterns, balustrades, temple pagodas, and photograph-like pictures. The stone columns of Chairman Mao's mausoleum in Beijing were cut here.

If you have more time, **Wanshan Peak** has some rare Manichaean relics. This religion, brought to China in the seventh century from Persia, was a combination of Zoroastrianism, Christianity, and paganism. At one time, St. Augustine was an adherent. On a stone tablet near the site of the monastery are inscribed the activities of the cult during the Song, when it was associated with Taoism. Behind the ruins is a circular Manichaean statue of a man.

Outside the south gate of Quanzhou about 13 km is the **Caoan Temple,** the only Manichaean temple left in China and the best preserved such temple in the world. There used to be temples in Xi'an and Luoyang as well, but the religion was persecuted in A.D. 843 and its leaders fled to Quanzhou. From here it spread along the east coast but died out in the Qing. This temple was first built in the Song and renovated in the Yuan. It has a 1.5-m-high carving of a Mani Buddha inside from 1339.

The **Heavenly Princess Palace** 天妃宫 and **Confucian Temple** are ½ km from the hotel. One hour by car from the city at the shore is the 1162-built five-story octagonal stone **Tower of the Two Sisters-in-law** 姑嫂塔 . The 21-meter-high structure was originally built as a navigational aid, but its name symbolizes the loneliness of the women left behind by the sailors and emigrants. The 161-acre **Overseas Chinese University** 华侨大学 is in the mountains east of the city. Its students are drawn from Southeast Asia, Hong Kong, and Macao.

The **Tomb of Zheng Chenggong (Koxinga)** 郑成功墓 is at Nan'an, about 25 km NW of Quanzhou. He was a pirate who allied himself with the defeated Ming forces in the mid-1600s, fighting the Manchus. With his fleet of 800 warships, this national hero successfully rid Taiwan of the Dutch.

SHOPPING

Embroidered blouses at the Friendship Store. Life-like artificial flowers. Also locally produced are stone carvings, woven bamboo, Dehua porcelain, Anxi Guanyin tea.

HOTELS

The two main downtown hotels are adequate and are neighbors. The Overseas Chinese Hotel should now be renovated and looking better than the Golden Fountain. New is the Quanzhou Hotel, 3*, closer to the Kaiyuan Temple.

Golden Fountain Hotel (Jinquan Jiu Dian) • *Baiyuan Qingchipan 362000. 3*. Cable 8888. Fax 224388* • 1965, ren. 1985. Lobby dark. Bit scruffy.

Overseas Chinese Building (Huaqiao Da Sha) • *Baiyuan Qingchipan 362000. Fax 224388* • 1951, ren. 1989. 12 stories, 221 rooms. C.C., IDD, limited hot running water.

C.T.S. 中国旅行 : Overseas Chinese Building, Baiyuan Rd. 362000; tel. 222192. Telex 93083 CISQI CN. Fax 223311.
C.I.T.S.: Jiuyi Rd. 362000; tel. 222749. Fax 212056.

QUFU 曲阜

(Chufu) North China. Southwestern Shandong province about 150 km south of Jinan. No airport. Reached by train to Yanzhou on the Beijing-Shanghai line and then by road for 18 km. It can also be reached by road from Jinan. It was believed that a railway would disturb Confucius' grave and its *feng shui*. A new railway station has opened closer to Qufu with trains only from Jinan. Population: 60,000.

Two days are minimal for this small, charming city, one day for the "three Kongs" (mansion, temple and forest), and one day for the tomb of Mencius, the birthplace cave of Confucius, and the Temple of Shao Hao. This is a good place for bicycling as it is relatively flat and has many interesting things to explore. At least a week for adventurous bicyclists.

The old city is centered around the Confucian monuments; the new city surrounds the old one.

The hometown and grave of Kong Fuzi (Master Kong), known to the west as Confucius, is one of the places to visit if you want to be immersed in old China. Take your time. Meditate in these beautiful, exotic surroundings. Read the *Analects of Confucius*. The discipline he advocates might be just what your hectic life lacks. Go back to the 17th century.

Confucius lived from 551 to 479 B.C. during the Spring and Autumn Period, a time of small warring kingdoms and political chaos. He was an itinerant teacher who preached that stability could be achieved by a return to the classics and the old Zhou dynasty rituals. He defined and promoted an already existing system of interpersonal relationships with its emphasis on responsibility and obedience.

His teachings were much like the rules of polite society anywhere: The virtuous or benevolent man does not lose his temper; the virtuous man thinks ill of people who criticize others in their absence, who talk badly of other people to make themselves look better, or who persist in promoting deceptions they know are false.

Confucius's virtuous man also did not concern himself with insignificant things, material gain, fame, or ambition. He was moderate in all things.

Confucius's ideas on government were far from democratic. People who do not hold office in a state should not discuss its policies, he said. He advocated that subjects be unquestionably subordinated to rulers, sons to fathers, younger brothers to older brothers, wives to husbands, younger friend to older friend. He was male chauvinism incarnate.

His philosophy was the official ideology in China for over 2000 years, promoted because it supported the oligarchical power structure. Filial piety was essential to the system, and its enforcement was supported by the state. If a child failed to care for his aged parents or was rude to them, the authorities would punish the child. Children owed their lives to their ancestors. They were obligated to respect and worship these people.

The philosophy deteriorated into a religion where descendents performed rituals to keep ancestral spirits happy, so the dead would influence the fortunes of the living.

Much Confucian influence is still felt in 20th-century Asia. One finds elements of his theories still stifling Chinese people everywhere. Confucius was behind the famous civil service system, which was based on the memorization of the classics and his analects. The imperial examinations and the arrogant, insular thinking did, however, outlive their usefulness. These stunted the development of modern China and were largely responsible for its poor defense against the 19th- and 20th-century imperialists. The civil service examination system was abolished in the early 1900s, and Confucius is now being studied dispassionately again.

In some family temples, food is still shared with ancestors, heads bowed and incense burned in worship especially during the Qing Ming Festival in spring, and the autumn equinox. And vestiges of the traditions surrounding the cult remain to this day, in spite of governmental discouragement—arranged marriages, marriages between two deceased people, or between one living and one deceased person, etc. This is not, however, as common as it was before Liberation. Rote memory is still the basis of much education, but hopefully this is changing today.

Confucius was born in Nishan, 35 km. southeast from his temple. He moved with his mother to Qufu after the death of his father, when he was three. His father was a general of the State of Lu. Qufu then was already old. It was the capital of a minor kingdom during the Shang (14th–11 century B.C.). The city is named "Winding City Wall" after the old wall built 3000 years ago. The current wall is Ming.

One fifth of the people in the city are surnamed Kong, and those in a direct line received state pensions for centuries (with no need to earn their living otherwise). Currently living are the 73rd–77th generations.

The Confucian monuments have been repaired and are now opened to tourists. They are in one part of the city and can be seen in a day.

The *Confucian Temple 孔庙 , occupying more than 20 hectares (about 50 acres), is the most important one in China and the largest in the world. First built in A.D. 478, it was rebuilt and enlarged to its present size during the Ming and Qing. Its gold-tiled roofs, its arches, red doors, and carved tile dragons are Ming. The two stone soldiers/generals over two meters tall near the gate are from the Han Dynasty (917–971). They once guarded a noble's tomb in another part of the city. Live egrets and cranes nest in the gardens here.

The **Dacheng Hall** is the main hall for paying homage to Confucius. Only the emperor could be carried over the carved dragons up to its door. The hall is over 31 meters tall and 54 meters wide, with the same appearance of some of the buildings in Beijing's Forbidden City which was copied from this temple. Important are the ten carved stone columns, two dragons and a pearl on each, slithering between clouds and a pearl. Note the set of ritual bronze bells, which are played on ceremonial occasions. (See also *Provincial Museum,* "Wuhan.")

The sage's birthday, **Sept. 28,** is currently celebrated with a re-enactment for tourists of the sacrificial ritual and homage by an emperor—in the hypnotic, slow movements and music of the times. It is part of the annual Confucian Cultural Festival late September and early October. Telephoto lens needed by photographers. Lucky are those who can get a blow-by-blow desription.

The ***Kong Family Mansion** 孔府 , has nine courtyards, over 400 rooms, and a garden, on 14 hectares. The gate in front is Ming. The Main Hall, Second Hall, and Third Hall were offices of the Duke of Yansheng, the 46th generation grandson who was made a noble by Emperor Renzong of the Song. These offices, with his desk under a yellow canopy and painted beamed ceiling, give authenticity to opera stage sets of the period. Ancient weapons, banners, and drums line the walls. The mansion was started in 1038.

Gifts to the family from emperors and high-ranking visitors include Zhou and Shang dynasty bronzes. Visitors would do well to read *In the Mansion of Confucius' Descendants* by Kong Demao and Ke Lan before arriving. From it you can get a feel for the human drama that took place here. Kong Demao, who is still living, was the daughter of the second wife of the Duke of Yansheng, her mother believed poisoned by the first wife. Her tale of being confined behind these walls is pathetic, but she was also party to great events as well as family misfortunes. Some photographs of the family are on display. The current Duke of Yansheng is said to be living in Taiwan. The old Kong Family Mansion

Hotel (first built in 1038 A.D.) and next to the family mansion, is expected to become an exhibition hall soon.

The **Confucian Forest,** 200,000 family tombs, reputedly the oldest and largest cemetery in the world. The trees were collected by disciples from all over the country. It is about 3 x 4 km. and has over 30,000 trees. Elaborately crafted gates, stone lions, and a stone-arched bridge punctuate the lovely greenness. Tall stone nobles and animals guard the gate to the *** Tomb of Confucius** 孔林 , a tumulus marked with stone tablets and fancy incense burners.

A small brick house, **Zi Gong's Hut,** stands nearby, originally built by one of the master's disciples, who lived in it for six years after Confucius's death, to show respect. **Lady Yu's Arch** was named after a daughter of Qing Emperor Qianlong, who was married to the then Duke of Yansheng. The title was hereditary until it was stopped by the Nationalistic.

Also in Qufu is a Sacred Way with stone animals and steles, the Temple of Yan Hui, the Temple of the Duke of Zhou, and the remains of the former capital of the State of Lu.

The tomb of Shao Hao, one of the five legendary rulers, is about 8 km. away. The Temple of Mencius, the later disciple who spread the teachings of Confucius to the rest of China, is 27 km. south of the city. Here is also a small museum, a temple to the mother of Mencius, and a hall for the wife of Mencius.

The birthplace of Confucius in Nisan should open soon as a museum and a theme park based on the six Confucian Arts is planned between the Forest and the Temple.

SHOPPING

Locally produced are wood carvings, stone rubbings, carpets and Nishan inkstones.

The Antique Store in the Mansion (tel. 5324) sells beautiful carved wooden beds and can ship them. A souvenir market is between the Queli Hotel and the Confucius Temple, and a market in Ming architecture is one block to the left as you leave the Queli Hotel. A small Friendship Store is on the same street as the Mansion.

HOTELS

The best hotel is the charming Queli, which has Western food, but needs work. It is the best location within walking distance of the Mansion, Temple, and shops. Ten-minute ride from the forest. Confucian food is not as salty as Shandong and each dish has a meaning, e.g., turtle for longevity. A genuine banquet used to have 400 courses.

Apricot Terrace Hotel (Xingtan Binguan) • *1 Donghua Nanmen/ 1 Xuequan Rd. 273100. 2*, aiming for 3. 3 km from the temple in the southern part of the city* • 1991–92. 4 stories. 300 rooms. Expects IDD soon. C.I.T.S., C.T.S. Needs much more work.

Queli Hotel (Binguan) • *1 Queli St. 273100.3*. Telex 39105 or 39106 BTHQF CN. Almost adjacent to the Temple of Confucius.* • 1986. Ren. 1992 or 1993. Exquisite Chinese architecture with courtyards and ponds. Two stories. 164 rooms. Striking murals and sculptures. Good furniture. Concerts of classical Chinese music if enough interested guests. Video of Confucian ceremonies on request. B.C. IDD soon. Good food.

Ambulance: tel. 120.
C.I.T.S. and **C.T.S.:** 1 Xue Quan Rd., 273100. Tel. 412492. Telex 39105 BTHQF CN. Fax 412022.
Qufu Tourism Bureau: tel. 412576.
C.T.S.: 2/F Nanjiao Hotel, Nanmenwai, Qufu 273100; tel. 412941.
Confucius Foundation: tel. 411850.
Police: tel. 110.

Z·M·Li

SHANGHAI (ABOVE THE SEA)

East China, on the north bank of the Huangpu River, 28 km from the (Changjiang) Yangtze River, on the east coast of China due west of the southern tip of Japan. Bordering on Jiangsu and Zhejiang provinces, it is about a 2-hour flight NE of Guangzhou and Hong Kong, and SE of Beijing. It is linked by air also with 53 other cities including Los Angeles, New York, Paris, San Francisco, Singapore, Toronto, Tokyo, and Vancouver, and by sea with Hong Kong and Kobe. From Shanghai are many land, water, and air services to other parts of China. Train to Hangzhou 3 to 4 hours; to Suzhou 1 hour. Sharing about the same latitude as Jacksonville, Florida, Shanghai's hottest temperature is 35°C in July–August; its coldest is ¯5°C in January–February. Most rain arrives in June. Population: 7.3 million. Very smoggy. Shanghai is sinking 5.6 mm a year.

This municipality, directly under the control of the central government, started out 5000 years ago as a tiny fishing village. It became a port in the 17th century. In 1840 its population was 500,000. In 1842 it was captured by the British, and although the Chinese paid a $300,000 ransom to keep it from being sacked, British soldiers and Chinese thieves looted it severely. The Treaty of Nanking of that year opened Shanghai to foreign trade and settlement. This led to its partition into British, French, and, later, Japanese concessions, which is still reflected in its downtown architecture. The British concession eventually became the International Concession, and all continued until the 1940s. Each of the concessions had its own tax system, police, courts, buses, and electrical wattage. A criminal could escape justice just by going from one concession to another.

Shanghai thrived as a port, trading principally in silk, tea, and opium. Most of the foreign trade was British and one fifth of all the opium reached China in fast American ships.

From 1853 to 1855, the walled section of Shanghai was seized by the Small Sword Society, a Cantonese-Fukinese secret society that wanted to restore the Ming dynasty and prohibit opium. It was helped in its struggle by some foreign seamen, but many other foreigners helped the Manchus regain the city. In 1860, the Taiping Heavenly Kingdom tried unsuccessfully to take Shanghai. In 1915 students and workers demonstrated here against the Twenty-One Demands of Japan. And in July 1921, the first Congress of the Communist Party of China was held here secretly.

In 1925, a worker striking for higher wages was killed at a Japanese factory. This led to a demonstration by workers and students in the International Settlement, during which the British police killed several demonstrators. A rash of nationwide anti-imperialist protests followed. In April 1927, Chiang Kai-shek ordered a massacre of the Communists here, and Chou En-lai barely escaped with his life. This period was the setting of Andre Malraux's famous novel *Man's Fate*.

In 1932, Shanghai resisted a Japanese attack for two months and made a truce. China appealed to the League of Nations and the United States, who did little to help. Japan attacked again in August 1937. The Nationalists fought back for three months before retreating to Nanjing and later to Chongqing. The American movie *Empire of the Sun* is set in this period and parts were shot in Shanghai. The Japanese stayed until 1945. In May 1949, the Communists took the city. During the Cultural Revolution, it was the scene of many intense political struggles, especially in January 1966.

Shanghai is now one of the 15 Open Coastal Cities, especially chosen for intensive economic development. It celebrated its 700th birthday in 1991.

Shanghai's cosmopolitan heritage is still reflected in its architecture and in the relative sophistication of many of its citizens. Its fashions and standards of products and services are more international than other Chinese cities, a result of its longer, more concentrated period of dealing with fussy foreigners. Its shopping is the best in the country.

Shanghai is one of the biggest ports and the largest city in China. Cruise ships dock almost at the foot of Nanjing Road. It is also still an important trading city and one of the biggest industrial cities. As an agricultural area, it is highly developed. Its rural counties are among the richest in the country, completely supplying the city. It grows two crops of rice and one of wheat each year. Its natives speak a dialect unlike that of Beijing and more akin to that of Hangzhou and Suzhou—only faster.

Not everybody likes Shanghai. It is a big, very crowded city that smells more of trade, commerce, and industry than ancient Chinese culture. The population density is 41,000 per square km, the highest in China. Its ancient relics are mainly outside the city. But it is exciting because its unique history is still reflected in its foreign buildings: the grandeur of the Bank of China lobby, the Greek columns of the customs house, the hybrid flavor of Sun Yat-sen's home. Do a lot of walking through this museum of 19th-century European and Japanese architecture. Look into the lobbies of the buildings along the Bund: Smile at the guard innocently and say "Just looking."

Shanghai is pleasant because the people are outgoing and lively. They are less reserved than those in Beijing. Making friends is easier here. Every Sunday morning in Renmin Park there is an English-speaking corner. Someone is sure to approach you to practice English. In about five parks, one can exchange postage stamps with other collectors, a good way to meet people. Shanghainese have been known for centuries for their quick wit, business talents, and efficiency.

Five days in Shanghai is sufficient to cover the important sights for you, but you have to make choices as there is enough for more. The following is a suggested itinerary.

Day 1: In the morning, the Yuyuan Garden, Huangpu Park, and a walk along the Bund, with lunch at the Peace Hotel; the Municipal Museum, Friendship Stores, Nanjing Road shops, or C.I.T.S. if you have to make bookings.

Day 2: The Jade Buddha Temple, with vegetarian lunch, Children's Palace, any of the modern history sites, and/or a workers' residential district or CAAC/China Eastern or C.T.S. for bookings, a look at the monumental new Shanghai Center, or the lovely Garden Hotel. (Ask Public Relations for a tour.)

On either of these days, you could substitute or try to squeeze in shopping, the zoo, a boat trip, an arts and crafts factory, the Shanghai Industrial Exhibition Hall, an antique or clothes market for shopping, or People's Square (and the nearby Huangpu Bird Market).

Day 3: The Botanical Gardens, Longhua Pagoda, Square Pagoda, carpet factory, and Zuibai Ci Pond. Take a picnic lunch with you if you want.

Day 4: Grand View Garden *(Dream of the Red Chamber)*. Restaurants there. She Shan Basilica.

Day 5: Jiading County and the Confucian Temple museum, Wuyi Garden (lunch), and Qiuxiapu.

On these last three days, you could also try to squeeze in a village or other rural enterprise. In the evening, try to see the Shanghai Acrobats or Shanghai Kunqu Opera (more melodic and graceful than Beijing Opera). For tickets, ask your hotel.

Huangpu Park 黄浦公园 is the oldest and smallest park in the city (Zhongshan Dong-1 Rd., across the bridge from Shanghai Mansions). Opened in 1868 by the British, next to the Suzhou and Huangpu rivers, this once displayed the infamous sign "No Dogs and Chinese Allowed." Now open from 5 a.m. to 10 p.m., even for foreign tourists.

*Yu Yuan Garden 豫园 (Yu Yuan Rd.; tel. 3260830, 3282465) is in the old Chinese part of Shanghai. Open 9–11:30; 1:30–5:30. I can't decide whether or not to recommend it if you are also going to see the gardens of Suzhou. It depends on how much time you have and how much you like gardens. This one is pretty good, but it is crowded. It was originally laid out between 1559 and 1577 by a financial official from Sichuan and now covers 20,000 square meters. About 100 years ago, a part was sold to merchants, and that is now the 98-shop **Yu Yuan Market,** once the busiest in the city. Here you can buy dressmaking patterns (six sizes in one pattern) and novelties, and watch *Jiao Zi* and other Chinese dumplings and pastries being made. The large new Old Shanghai Restaurant (at the parking lot) is famous. Some visitors have found the market fascinating. The area was the old Chinese district and the houses are pretty much the way they used to be. Very crowded.

From 1853 to 1854, the Yu Garden was used as the headquarters of the Small Sword Society, which staged an armed uprising and held part of Shanghai for 18 months. The pavilion opposite the exquisite stage is now a mini-museum.

Other points of interest: the top of Rockery Hill, which is an artificial mountain made with rocks carried from Jiangxi province. Until it was dwarfed by Shanghai's skyscrapers, this was the highest point in the city from which you could see and hear the Huangpu River nearby. The five dragon walls wind concentrically around the garden. Look for their heads. Note the unusually shaped doors, some like vases, and, of course, the lovely moon gate. Look for the **Pavilion to See the Reflection of the Water on the Opposite Side** (these names are really something!) and don't trip over the step-over doorways. The south side of the garden was for women; aristocratic women were usually kept out of sight of all but family members. Snack bar and antique store. (See also *Chinese Gardens* in "What Is There To See And Do?")

The excellent **Shanghai Municipal Museum** 上海市博物馆 (Henan Nan Rd.; tel. 3280160, 3262460). Open daily, 9 a.m. to 3:30 p.m. Closed holidays. Includes (on the ground floor) a demonstration of how the Shang bronzes were cast and what they looked like new (did you really think they drank out of those yucky green things?); a knife for beheading; a model of a 2000-year-old tomb, with skeletons of slaves buried alive so they could serve the departed master in the other world; a water vat used for refrigeration; 2000-year-old gilding on bronze; giant Ka drums. A revealing picture of ancient life can be seen on a bronze cowrie shell (money) container decorated with tigers climbing up the sides, a slave being bound for sacrifice, pigs being slaughtered, and two dead cows. On the second floor, a demonstration of how pottery was made from wicker baskets; an A.D. 618 polo game and three-color Tang camels. A well-designed display of ancient and contemporary porcelain arranged according to regional kilns helps the viewer understand the differences in clay, patterns, glazes, etc., of the various types. The collection of stone sculptures here is not as good as the one at New York's Metropolitan Museum.

On the third floor are murals of *fat* Tang ladies (fat was very fashionable then!); a horizontal scroll of life in 11th-century Kaifeng—look for the bride being carried in the sedan chair; and a collection of ancient calligraphy and paintings including a painting done by fingernail.

Jade Buddha Temple 玉佛寺 (170 Anyuan Rd., Puto District; tel. 2535745, or 2538805) is open daily, 8 a.m.–5 p.m., but closed for lunch. A good introduction to Buddhist temples, but nearby Suzhou has better and older ones.

The Jade Buddha Temple was founded in 1882 in the southern outskirts of Shanghai. The temple was bodily moved to Shanghai in 1918 and now occupies about two acres in the western part of the city.

Many monks live in this temple, and you might hear them singing or reading the scriptures. At your request and donation, monks will chant prayers for the well-being of your soul.

In the first hall, a 2.6-meter-high, gold-faced Wei Tuo, the military protector of the Buddhist scriptures, menacingly greets visitors. On each side are two temple guardians: the Eastern King, with a mandolin-like instrument, using music to defend and praise Buddha; the Southern King, with his dark, angry face, and sword; the Northern King, with a Chinese parasol; and the Western King, who ''looks after the whole world with penetrating eyes and carries a snake which is actually a net to catch converts.''

In the courtyard the incense burner made of iron and bronze, cast in 1922. The three largest figures inside the next parallel building are Sakyamuni (center), to his right the Amitaba Buddha (with lotus), and the Yuese Buddha, carrying the Buddhist wheel of law. Along the sides are the 20 guardians of heaven. Guanyin is centered behind the three main Buddhas. Note the very thin Sakyamuni, above, paying homage, and the 18 arhats.

On the second floor the seated 1.9-m-high Jade Buddha, carved from one piece of white jade in Burma, was brought to China in 1882. The shelves on both sides of the room contain 7240 volumes of Buddhist scriptures, printed in the Qing 200 years ago. They are similar to the book under the glass.

In another building is a Reclining Buddha, also of white jade. A good vegetarian restaurant, small antique store, a small museum and a newly founded Buddhist Academy with 100 students are also in this temple. See also *Buddhist Temples* in "What Is There to See and Do?" The **Jingan Temple** is tiny, eclectic, but conveniently located downtown. It looks and is relatively new, having been relocated several times. There is also the **Xiaotaoyuan Mosque** and the **Baiyunuan Taoist Temple** for those interested in religion.

Many group tours include a visit to a **Children's Palace.** These are after-school programs for 7–16-year-olds, much like community centers. Specially chosen children get extra opportunities to learn and practice art, sciences, music, sports, etc. Some of the 23 palaces in the city are in old mansions built by wealthy capitalists. A visit to one will not only give you a chance to learn something of the education of children but also to explore the buildings themselves.

Best set up for tourists is the Children's Palace at 64 Yan'an Road, tel. 2581850 (open Tuesday and Saturday afternoons after school hours for visitors but not all summer).

Children's Palaces were a project of Soong Ching-ling, the widow of Dr. Sun Yat-sen. Money is being solicited internationally for the Soong Ching-ling Foundation to continue and expand this work.

Modern Chinese history sites offer an opportunity to see the inside of some of those European houses. In addition, you can experience important facets of recent history. My favorite is the **former residence of Dr. Sun Yat-sen** (7 Xiangshan Rd., tel. 4372954). It is in the old French Concession, a large house by today's Chinese standards. Not open daily.

Once inside, you find that you have stepped back into the 1920s. The house was bought by Chinese-Canadians for the father of republican China for 16,000 pieces of silver. He lived here with his wife intermittently from 1920 to 1924, just before his death of cancer in 1925. His widow, Soong Ching-ling, lived in the house until 1937, when the war forced her to move to Chongqing.

Here, in 1924, Dr. Sun met Communist leader Li Dazhao (Li Tachao) publicly for the first time to work out Nationalist-Communist cooperation. Dr. Sun was much influenced by Marx and Lenin.

Besides the antiques, there are some old photographs, a 1920 China train map, Sun's medical instruments, clothes, and glasses. The railway map is significant because Dr. Sun was in charge of railways for a short time after he resigned as president. The house contains his library: a 1911 *Encyclopedia Britannica,* biographies of Bismarck, Cicero, Lincoln, and Napoleon in English, books in Japanese, and ancient works in Chinese. Because this is a shrine, no photos are allowed. (See also "Nanjing" for more about Dr. Sun.)

Museum and Tomb of Lu Xun (Lu Hsun) (Hongkou Park; tel. 6661181): museum open daily, except Sundays, 8:30 a.m.–4 p.m., except for lunch, and Tuesday and Thursday mornings. Tomb building opens daily, 8 a.m.–7 p.m. These are quite close to each other in the northern part of the city. Lu Xun (1881– 1936) was an author of short stories who wrote in the colloquial language about poor people, impoverished literati, and oppressed women. Chinese literature until then had primarily been about the wealthy elite, written in a snobbish literary style, too difficult for the masses to grasp. Although he was not a Communist, Lu Xun is considered a national hero. He died of tuberculosis in Shanghai.

The site of the First National Congress of the Communist Party of China 中国共产党第一次全国代表大会会址 (76 Xingye Rd.; tel. 3281177, 3285494) was the living room of a small rented house in the former French Concession. There, 12 representatives of the Party from all over China, including Mao Zedong, met secretly for four days starting on July 1, 1921.

Residence of Chou En-lai 周恩来故居 (73 Sinan Rd., tel. 4371775) was the Shanghai agency of the Communist Party in 1946 when efforts were being made at peace talks with the Nationalists.

Another relic from a previous era and still in use is the **Shanghai Industrial Exhibition Hall** 上海工业展览馆 (1000 Yan'an Zhong Rd.; tel. 2563037). Open daily, except Mondays, 8:30 a.m.–5 p.m., except for lunch breaks. Over 58,000 square meters of floor space with a display area of 20,000. Completed in 1955, with Soviet help, in the massive Soviet style, for trade exhibitions. Two large arts and crafts handicraft stores.

The **Shanghai Zoo** 上海动物园 (Hongqiao Rd.; tel. 4329775) is open daily, 7 a.m.–5 p.m. One of the better zoos in China. 70 hectares, 280 species. Pandas, rare Chinese birds, and Yangtze crocodiles.

If you wish to pay your respects to a very distinguished humanitarian and revolutionist, visit the beautiful white statue and **Tomb of Song Qingling (Soong Ching-ling)** 宋庆龄墓 in Wang Guo (International) Cemetery 万国公墓 (21 Lingyuan Rd.; Changning District near Hongqiao Rd.; tel. 4329034). The widow of the founder of republican China died in May 1981. Her parents, and the maid who served her for 52 years, are buried nearby. Do read *The Soong Dynasty.*

Soong Ching-ling was the sister of Mme. Chiang Kai-shek. She eloped with the already married Sun Yat-sen and was virtually disowned by her wealthy Christian father, up to that point a strong supporter of Dr. Sun. She was tolerated by her family and her powerful in-laws, although she was outspoken in her opposition to their exploitation of China. She was, after all, the widow of the widely respected father of the country. She chose to remain in China after Liberation, and worked to promote the welfare of the Chinese people.

The **Huangpu River boat trip** 黄浦江游船 is booked from the wharf near Huangpu Park at the foot of Beijing East Road. Tel. 3231662, 3211720. This 3½-hour, 60-km trip is usually offered as an option for prepaid tourists for additional payment and is available to individual travelers. It sails to the Changjiang (Yangtze) River at Wusong Kou, and back at 8:30 a.m. and 1:15 p.m. daily, with a 1½-hour night cruise at 7 p.m. during the summer. Important if you want to relax and see sailing junks and ships from all over the world on a muddy river with industries along its shores. On the return trip, however, are a magician and acrobatic show.

Renmin (People's) Square 人民广场 : 467 by 100 meters, 1951. Used for parades, ceremonial occasions, people-watching, and ball-playing. Also has a daily free market with flowers, *penjing* (miniature landscapes) and goldfish of many varieties. The Huang Pu Market is a block west. Open 7 a.m.–5 p.m.

The **Botanical Gardens** 植物园 (Longhua Rd.; tel. 4389413) is in the southern suburbs. Open daily, 8:30 a.m.–4:30 p.m. 70 hectares, 1954. Specializes in rock gardens and potted miniature trees, some several hundred years old.

Longhua Pagoda and Temple 龙华塔，寺 (tel. 4389997) is in the southern suburbs and can be combined with the Botanical Gardens and Songjiang County for a one-day trip. It is a noted scenic spot, the park formerly an execution grounds. It was originally built by Sun Quan of Three Kingdoms (222–280) for his mother. It was rebuilt several times, the latest in the early 1980s. It is considered the oldest temple in Shanghai district. Note the fine brick carvings on its walls. It has a small museum.

The brick and wood Song dynasty pagoda stands about 40 meters high, with seven stories. Festival days have attracted 50,000 visitors.

OUTSIDE OF SHANGHAI

Songjiang County 松江 has a history of 2500 years. It is about 40 km SW of the city and usually takes a full day to see. The rare **Square Pagoda** 方塔 in the Xingsheng Monastery (Sangong St., Songjiang) is 48.5 meters high. It was first erected in 1086–94 in the basic Song-dynasty style, with the tetragonal shape of the Tang. It still has some original brick and wooden brackets. During renovations in the late 1970s two Song murals of Buddha were uncovered, and from the pagoda's base, Song and Tang coins, bronze buddhas, and animal skeletons—offerings to atone for the sins of the deceased wife, probably of a nobleman. Its nine stories lean slightly seaward to compensate for prevailing winds.

The screen in front is the oldest brick carving in the area, erected in 1370 to keep evil spirits out of the Temple of the City Gods, which no longer exists. Very well preserved, the mythical animal on it is a *tuan,* greedily eating everything in sight. Note money in mouth. Other ancient relics have been assembled here from different parts of the county.

Also in Songjiang County is the **Zuibai Ci (Pond for Enjoying Bai's Drunkenness) Garden** 醉白池 , outside the West Gate of Songjiang town. First built in 1652 and expanded in 1958. The lotus flowers in the pond are said to date from the 17th century. Highlights include a stone engraving of 91 leading Songjiang citizens from the Ming and early Qing and a small museum. This can be skipped if your time is short, as can the oldest relic in Shanghai, the **Tang stone pillar** 唐朝 (A.D. 859). This 9.3-meter-tall carving, with some Buddhist inscriptions and carvings, just barely visible, is currently in the playground of the Zhongshan Primary School and subject to the carelessness of children at play. Songjiang is also noted for its fine embroidery and Moslem hats.

If you have an extra day, consider **Jiading County** 嘉定. It is 45 km NW of Shanghai and linked by a new superhighway. This should give you some time to also drop in at some prosperous villages along the way. At Nanxiang is the 6-hectare **Gu-Yi Garden,** tel. 6661246 where you can sample the famous steamed Nanxiang meat buns. First built in 1566 and renovated in 1746, it has two stone pillars inside over 1000 years old. The highly recommended **Qiuxiapu** is a 450-year-old classical garden, once belonging to a Ming officer. It gives *yin-yang* contrasts of stillness and liveliness, reality and dream, with 20 scenic spots in a small space.

The **Confucius Temple** 孔子庙 (Nan Da St., Chenxiangzhen, tel. 9532604) is one of the largest in South China. A major part of it is an interesting museum of local history, with maps showing how people migrated, an old fishing boat, and famous stone tablets relating to important events from the Ming. The temple itself was founded in 1219 and enlarged in the Yuan and Ming.

Another full day's excursion is to **Dingshan Lake,** tel. 2228228 X6071. 65 km north of Shanghai. The county itself dates from the Song and has many cultural relics, as well as a goldfish breeding farm and a pearl cultivation farm. Over 100 hectares of former farmland have been developed into a huge recreation complex with kite-flying contests in spring, 4000 plum trees (mostly for mid-March blossoms), 6 hectares of autumn-blossoming osmanthus trees, fishing and swimming areas, restaurants and hotels, and theme park. All the buildings are in tradi-

A scene from *Dream of the Red Chamber.*

tional southern Chinese architecture. If you look closely at the 47-meter-high pagoda here, you might discern that it is really a water tower.

The prime reason to go to the Dingshan Lake Scenic Area is to see the 11-hectare **Daguanyuan (Grand View Garden),** Shanghai's version of the setting of the popular Qing novel *The Dream of the Red Chamber.* Even if you haven't read this 1886-page novel, a visit is well worthwhile just to see this beautiful complex of pavilions, very tastefully decorated, some with genuine antique and/or real mahogany furniture. Each room is related to a scene from the tragic love story: the sickly heroine Lin Tai-yu's bedroom with medicine bottles, her harp, and her basket for burying flowers; spoiled, rich, but sensitive young hero Pao-yu's stunningly exquisite Happy Red Court, his books left in boxes because he didn't like to read; the Grand View Chamber, the living quarters for a visit home of the daughter who became an imperial concubine. See *Dream of the Red Chamber* under "What is There to See and Do?"

On the way back to Shanghai, you may want to visit **Zhujiajiao,** an obscure old village of white plaster row houses and narrow slate-paved streets along the ancient canal, where the masses seem to be living still in Red Chamber times. Also in Songjiang County, high on a hill beside the Academy of Science's Observatory, is a **Roman Catholic basilica** (Xu Jia Hui), looking most impressive but intriguingly and incongruously European, built in the 1920s. The observatory was also built by Jesuits in the 1860s. A Jesuit seminary is at the base of the hill. Stations of the cross line up the driveway.

Excursions can be easily made from Shanghai to Hangzhou, Ningbo, Putuo Shan, Suzhou, and Wuxi. The least crowded is very charming Ningbo. See separate listings.

After Hours: **Shanghai Acrobatic and Magic Troupe** (tel. 3274958): magicians, sword-swallowing, sometimes performing pandas, and juggling. Shanghai has high standards of music, art, and drama. It is a good place to sample the cultural life. **Shanghai Art Theatre** (tel. 2565544); **Shanghai Concert Hall** (tel. 3284383); **Grand Theatre** (tel. 2534260); **Beijing Theatre** (tel. 2581197); **Cathay Theatre** (tel. 4372549); **Renmin (People's) Theatre** (663 Jiujiang Rd.; tel. 3224509). There is also a drama club that performs Chinese plays in English. Ask the Hilton. A golf course is open near the airport.

The **Shanghai Art Salon of Film,** near the Jin Jiang Hotel, is a nightclub. The **Long Bar** at the Shanghai Center is a hangout of boisterous expatriate Americans. Some expatriates meet weekly at the Australian Consulate to celebrate T.G.I.F., and you might phone to see if you can join them. Popular hotel bars are on the third floor of the JC Mandarin, the third floor of the Garden, the fourth floor of the Sheraton, and the Silk Road in the Nikko. The best discos are at the Nikko, Sheraton, and Yangtze hotels.

Factories: Tourists might be interested in seeing and shopping in factories for jade carving, embroidery, woolen carpets, and tapestries.

SHOPPING

Produced in the city are jade, ivory, and whitewood carvings, lacquerware, needlepoint tapestries, silks, carpets, embroideries, gold and silver jewelry (especially filigree), artificial flowers, painted eggs, reproductions of antique bronzes, and cheap jogging suits. Big department and book stores are along Nanjing Road between the Peace and the Park Hotels, and along Huaihai Road. The Nanjing Road area is oppressively crowded, but it is getting classier. Jewelry prices here are generally the best in China.

Tailors are again available, but they take two weeks to three months to make anything and might not be aware of the latest Western fashions.

Shanghai Friendship Store 上海友谊商店 , one of the largest in China is north of the Peace Hotel at 40 Beijing Rd. East. Tel. 3234600. Open 9 a.m. to at least 9 p.m. Purchases can be crated and shipped. This store is on the grounds of the former British Consulate.

Selling antiques are the **#Friendship Store (Antique and Curio Branch)** 友谊商店古玩部 (694 Nanjing Xi Rd.; tel. 2539549) and the **#Shanghai Antique Store** 上海古玩商店 (194–226 Guangdong Rd.; tel. 3232144, 3212864. Good reproductions). Ask your hotel about the colorful antique markets.

For sportswear, the **Huating Market** is off Huaihai Rd. and another market is off Nanjing Dong Rd.

Shanghai Arts and Crafts Store 上海工艺美术商店 (190–208 Nanjing Xi Rd.; tel. 3276530).

Duoyunxuan (422 Nanjing Dong Rd.; tel. 3223410) is a highly specialized Chinese painting supplies store, where one can have scrolls mounted and buy top paintings and calligraphy.

Western-style "drug stores" (with no pharmacists) are in some of the hotels. **Caitongde Drugstore** (320 Nanjing Dong Rd.; tel. 3221160): traditional Chinese medicines; **Beijing Chinese Pharmacy** (760 Nanjing Dong Rd.; tel. 3222393); **Shanghai Jewelry and Jadeware Store** 438 Nanjing Dong Rd.); **Shanghai Arts and Crafts Trading Corp.** 上海工艺美术交易所 (1000 Yan'an Zhong Rd. 8:30 to 6 p.m. tel. 2790279 X2130). Two stores in the Exhibition Center.

See also Yu Yuan Market, above, for more proletarian souvenirs like folding scissors, chopsticks, wigs, fans, and crafts, and local snacks.

Foreign Languages Book Stores 外文书店 (390 Fuzhou Rd. 200001; tel. 3224109, 3223200) will mail books; **Shanghai #1 Department Store** (830 Nanjing Dong Rd.; tel. 3223344): city's largest; **Shanghai #10 Department Store** 上海第一 百货公司 (635 Nanjing Dong Rd.; tel. 3224466) second largest; **Shanghai Silk Shop** (592 Nanjing Dong Rd.; tel. 3224830) has silk from Shanghai, Jiangsu, Zhejiang, and other provinces.

Guan Long, on Nanjing Rd. near Jiangxi Rd. two blocks west of the Peace Hotel should be able to fix some broken cameras.

The **Shanghai Carpet Factory** is at 256 Cao Bao Rd.; tel. 4361713 (across from the Huaxia Hotel). **No. 1 Silk Printing & Dyeing Factory** (1133 Chang Ning Rd., 200051. Tel. 2519900, 2578766. Fax 2518977) is expensive compared to Suzhou, but selections and styles are good for ready-made garments. **The Li Hua Lace & Embroidery Store** (1932 Hushan Rd., near Jiao Tong University, tel. 4387378) has cheaper prices.

GETTING AROUND

Streets running east-west are named after cities and those running north-south after provinces.

Buses are incredibly crowded and subject to frequent breakdowns. You may also have to share taxis with other passengers, and it seems each group of passengers pays the fare from the point of departure. Shanghai also has mini-buses, taxi-vans, the price dependent on the number of passengers, and tiny Fiat taxis. Any complaints should be addressed to Shanghai Tourism Corporation and to the taxi company. Addresses in each taxi.

The first stage of the 14.4 km. subway will go from the railway station to Xinlonghua probably in 1993. Seven lines are planned to reach a total of 176 km. Stations will be back of the Garden Hotel and at the Sheraton. An elevated highway is being planned to circle the city.

Shanghai floods when it rains, so give yourself extra time to get around then, such as an extra hour to get to the airport from downtown.

RESTAURANTS

Shanghai food is sweeter, lighter, and prettier than other Chinese foods, with a delicate consistency. Every big hotel should be able to lay on a great banquet here. The hotel restaurants we've heard recommended most for western food are the Hilton's Atrium, the Sheraton's coffee shop, and the Continental Room at the Portman. Recommended also are the buffets at the Portman and the Chinese restaurant at the Jin Jiang Tower; the reasonably priced Japanese food at the Portman's Four Seasons; the Cantonese food at the Yangtze, and the Peach Garden Restaurant at the J.C. Mandarin. For Sichuan, there's the Jin Jiang Tower, the 12th floor at the Jin Jiang closed 9 p.m., and the City; for Shanghai, the 7th floor at the Peace.

Among the cheaper restaurants. I like the Chinese food at the Shanghai, the Hua Ting Guest House, the Shanghai Express at the Hilton, and the Park. Across from the Portman is the Xijiao Ting, popular with Asians. Budget travelers get a good view and good food at the Seagull's 2nd floor restaurant. Kentucky Fried Chicken is on the Bund beside the Dongfeng Hotel, across from the Park Hotel, and eventually nine other locations. Other restaurants visitors might like:

Friendship Restaurant • *Exhibition Center, 1000 Yanan Zhong Rd., tel. 2474078* • Hong Kong J.V. Uneven quality.

Golden Gate Restaurant • *73–77 Nan Hui Rd. (off Nanjing), tel. 2567859, 2567980* • Good Beijing duck. Reasonable prices.

Meilongzhen Restaurant • *1081 Nanjing Xi Rd., Lane 1081, No. 22.* • Tel. 2562718, 2551157.

Shangri-La Restaurant • *2/F Union Building, Yanan Dong Rd., tel. 3265381, 3265480* • Cantonese.

Wang Bao He Wine Shop • *603 Fuzhou Rd., tel. 3223673* • For crabs.

Windows on the World • *Ruijin Palace. 3rd, 4th & 27th Floors. 205 Maoming Rd. South* • Tel. 4336309, 4330808. Cantonese and Western.

Xin Ya Restaurant 新雅餐厅 • *719 Nanjing Dong Rd.; tel. 3206277.* • Cantonese.

HOTELS

Shanghai has an oversupply of hotel rooms and is still a buyer's market. Currently the best in the city are the luxury quality Hilton, the Garden, and the Westin. Also near the top are the Portman, the J. C. Mandarin, Sheraton Hua Ting, and Yangtze in that order. We also liked the Nikko Longbai, though it is far from town, and the Holiday Inn looks like a comfortable, fun place. The Sheraton is currently good value for money if you don't mind the less convenient location. The Jin Jiang Tower is the best of the Chinese-managed hotels and is good.

In the budget traveler range, our first choice is the Park, Peace, or Longman for the downtown location and atmosphere. The Ocean is also good, and central. Farther out, our choice would be the Shanghai for its good location and many services, the Huating Guest House, or the attractive Galaxy.

The **Bund** has been a good area for tourists, but it is now so crowded, and pickpockets are such a problem, that it is no longer fun to stay there. Do visit, but sleep in Ghetto no. 1. There you can see the *tai ji* people, bar hop, take a taxi to the Friendship Store or see the Peace Hotel jazz band.

If you want the Bund, the best hotel is the Peace, but for atmosphere, not service. The Peace, Seagull, and Shanghai Mansions there are the closest hotels to the Friendship Store. The Park is on the western edge of the Nanjing shopping area and should be considered by people more intersted in buying than sightseeing.

Hotel ghettos:

1) the best area for most business and tourist travelers, about 6 km from the Bund in a pleasant residential area have the Jin Jiang Hotel, Jin Jiang Tower, and Garden. These are close together within walking distance of shopping in the Jin Jiang Hotel and Huaihai Rd. The Hilton, Jing An, and Equatorial are clustered together. The Shanghai Hotel is nearby, close to the U.S. embassy. The Portman (in the Shanghai Centre), City (cheapest), and JC Mandarin are around the Shanghai Exhibition Centre with its two good tourist stores, and nearby CAAC/China Eastern, city hall, and China Travel Service. These three areas are within walking distance (about 3 km) of each other. The Shanghai Centre is the main international business centre and houses SIA and Northwest Airlines.

2) The growing Hongqiao Development Zone, 8 km from the airport and about 12 km from the Bund, has the International Trade Centre (ITC) with stores, an exhibition hall, some major economic government offices, and several good hotels: Westin, Yangtze, and Galaxy, in that order.

3) The Nikko-Airport-Cypress Hotels (in order of quality with Nikko best) are within two km of the airport. Frequent downtown shuttle buses.

4) The Sheraton Hua Ting-Hua Ting Guest House-Olympic area

(in order of quality with Sheraton best) are primarily recommended because of lower prices for good service. They are near the Indoor Stadium and the Caohejing high-tech area.

Between 1 and 2 is the new Holiday Inn. Between 2 and 3 are several small Chinese-run hotels, the best being the New Garden and then the Cherry Holiday. These are modest, somewhat out of the way; grubby but not bad. The Xi Jiao should be considered for the privacy but seems to be going downhill.

If you want to get into wholly Chinese neighborhoods, look for isolated hotels like the Novotel or the Holiday Inn. The Novotel, however, is too far out for tourists. Most hotels are American clones. If you want a feeling of old Shanghai, do consider the Peace, Park, or the Garden—all of which have some 1920s ambience.

Of the cheapest hotels, our first choice is the Seagull, with its fantastic location on the Bund or the Qian Nian Hui.

City Hotel (Chen Shi Jiu Dian) • *5–7 Shanxi Nan Rd. 200020. 3*. Telex 33532 SYTS CN. Fax 2550211. Managed by Chains International (Singapore)* • C.C. 1988–89. 304 small rooms. B.C. Soft beds. IDD. Sichuan and Cantonese food. Free airport pickup. USTV.

Cypress Hotel (Long Bai Fandian) • *2419 Hongqiao Rd., 200335. Telex 33288 CYH CN. Fax 2756739. Set in vast garden. Dist.A.P.2 km Dist.R.W.19 km* • C.C. 1982, ren. 1989. 165 rooms. China Eastern. B.C. Villas and apartments. IDD. USTV. Scruffy. Rundown. AT&T.

Galazy (Ying He Binguan) • *888 Zhongshan Xi Rd. 200051. Aiming at 4*. Fax 2750201. Telex 33176 SGHRD CN. Dist.A.P.9 km* • C.C. 1990–91. 35 stories, 844 rooms, soft beds. B.C. IDD. Sichuan and Cantonese food. Gym. bowling. Huating Group. Guests can use pool in nearby Rainbow Hotel. USTV.

Garden Hotel (Huayuan Fandian) • *58 Maoming Nan Rd., 200020. 5*. Fax 4338866. Telex 30157 GHSH CN. Dist.A.P.13 km. Dist.R.W.10 km* • 1989–90. 34 stories, 500 spacious rooms. Telephone jack by desk. Classy B.C. Garden. All-weather pool. Gym, tennis. IDD. USTV. Japanese and continental food. Hair dryers. Hotel Okura management. Member Leading Hotels of the World. AT&T. Executive floors.

Holiday Inn Yinxing (Yin Xing Jia Re Jiudian) • *338 Panyu Rd. 200052. Aiming for casual 4* atmosphere. Telex 30310 SFAC CN. Fax 2528545. Dist.A.P.8 km. Dist.R.W.12 km* • C.C. 1991–92. 534 rooms. Wide twin beds. Gym, indoor pool. B.C., kindergarten, IDD, tennis, USTV, non-smoking areas. Cantonese, Sichuan, and European food.

RMB restaurant. Children's playground with free nanny at lunch. Part of film art centre with 5 cinemas. Two executive floors.

Hotel Equatorial Shanghai (Gui Du Da Fandian) • *65 Yanan Xi Rd. 200040. Aiming for 4*. Fax 2581773. Beside Hilton. Emphasis on sports. Across street from Children's Palace* • C.C. 1991–92. 26 stories, 526 rooms. Thai, Japanese, Chaozhou, Sichuan, and Cantonese food. Indoor pool. Bowling. Gym. Tennis. Squash. IDD. Fast food alley. USTV. Executive floor. B.C. International Club. 1000 seat theatre. Korean Air and UPS offices. Managed by Equatorial International. Reserve through UTELL.

Hua Ting Guest House (Hua Ting Binguan #2) • *2525 Zhong Shan Xi Rd., 200030. 3*. Telex 30192 HTCHS CN. Fax 4390322 Dist.A.P.10 km. Dist.R.W.15 km* • C.C. Not to be confused with better neighbour, the Sheraton. 1987. Ren. 1990. 17 stories, 216 rooms. B.C. USTV. Slow elevators. IDD. Guests here can use facilities at Sheraton.

Jin Jiang Hotel (Jin Jiang Fandian) • *59 Mao Ming Nan Rd., 200020. Telex 33380 GRJJH CN. Fax 4331694. Dist.A.P.13 km. Dist.R.W.5 km* • C.C. 1929, ren. 1987, maybe 1994–95. Four buildings. About 18 stories. 677 rooms. IDD. B.C. Supermarket. Friendship Store. China Eastern and Dragonair. Central building best with only suites, then North 4*. South building dirty. USTV. Small TVs. AT&T.

Jin Jiang Tower (Xin Jin Jiang) • *161 Changle Rd. 200020. 5*. Telex 33652 FOJJT CN. Fax 4333265. Dist.A.P.14 km. Dist.R.W.3 km* • C.C. 1988–1990. 43 stories. 728 rooms with Chinese or western decor. Executive floor. B.C. IDD. Gym, outdoor pool, jacuzzi. Revolving restaurants. Korean barbecue, Italian restaurant. China Eastern. USTV. Year round outdoor pool. Poor bed lamps.

Longmen Hotel (Binguan) • *777 Heng Feng Rd., 200070, Aiming for 3*. Fax 6632004. Shanghai Railway Station complex* • C.C. 1990. 346 small rooms. 18th–21st floor for foreigners. USTV. B.C. Gym.

Nikko Longbai Shanghai Hotel (Re Hong Longbai) • *2451 Hongqiao Rd., 200335. 4*. Telex 30138 NHISH CN. Fax 2559333. Dist.A.P.2 km. Dist.R.W. 19 km* • C.C. 1987. 11 stories, 419 rooms. IDD. USTV. B.C. Golf center. Tennis, gym. Outdoor pool. Suburban setting. Cantonese and Japanese restaurants. Clinic. Managed by Nikko.

Ocean Hotel (Yuan Yang Binguan) • *1171 Dong Da Ming Rd., 200082. 3*. Telex 30333 OCETL CN. Fax 5458993. Dist.A.P.22 km. Dist.R.W. 9 km. One km east of International Passenger Quay* • C.C.

1988. 16 stories, 370 rooms. Executive floors. B.C. Gym. USTV. Sauna. Dim lights.

Park Hotel (Guoji Fandian) ● *170 Nanjing Xi Rd., 200003. 3*. Telex 339321 PARK CN. Fax 3276958. Dist.A.P.15 km. Dist.R.W.3 km. Near People's Park and Shanghai Acrobats* ● C.C. 1934. Ren. 1990. 24 stories, 210 rooms. IDD. Dim bedside light. USTV. Cantonese, Beijing food. B.C. Free airport shuttle.

Peace Hotel (Heping Fandian) ● *20 Nanjing Dong Rd., 20002. Requesting 4*. Telex 33914 BTHPH CN. Fax 3290300. Dist.A.P.19 km. Dist.R.W.5 km* ● C.C. 1929, ren. 1989–91. 11-story North Building (with famous 1920's jazz band) only part recommended. (Avoid South Building now.) 279 large harborview rooms. Exotic Indian Suite. USTV. IDD. Bit run-down and dark. Expects to take over the building next door and aim at 5* with gym, sauna, etc. After North Building upgraded, plans to improve South Building.

Portman Shangri-La (Poterman Jiu Dian) ● *Shanghai Centre, 1376 Nanjing Xi Rd., 200040. 5*. Telex 33272 PSH CN. Fax 2798999. Dist.A.P.14 km. Dist.R.W.5 km. Managed by Shangri-La International* ● C.C. 1990. 50 stories, 550 rooms each with 3 telephones. Japanese restaurant, grill room. B.C. Executive and non-smoking floors. IDD. USTV. Tennis, squash, putting green, gym. Indoor-outdoor pool. HK "drug store," supermarket. Clinic. Apartments, offices, theatre, exhibition hall.

Qian Nian Hui Hotel ● *123 Xizang Nan Rd. 200021. Aiming at 3*. Telex 33920 QNHSH CN. Fax 3201957. Near Bund and Yuyuan Garden* ● 11 stories, 165 rooms. IDD. B.C. Budget travellers only.

Seagull Hotel (Hai Ou Fandian) ● *60 Huangpu Rd., 200080. 2*. Telex 33603 SISC CN. Fax 3241263. Dist.A.P.20 km. Dist.R.W.3 km* ● 1985. Ren. 1990. 12 stories, 110 rooms. IDD in B.C. Great view of Bund. Modest. Grubby. Budget travelers only.

Shanghai Hilton International (Hilton Dajiudian) ● *250 Hu Shan Rd., 200040. 5*. Telex 33612 HILTL CN. Fax 2553848* ● C.C. 1988. 43 stories. 800 classy rooms each with three telehones. French, Cantonese and Sichuan cuisine. Teppanyaki. B.C. Clark Hatch gym. Indoor pool. Tennis. Squash. USTV. IDD. Non-smoking floor. Business studios. Executive floors. United Airlines. Can clean and cater. Train coach to Suzhou.

Shanghai Hotel (Shanghai Binguan) • *505 Wulumuqi Rd., 200042. 3*. Telex 33295 SHR CN. Fax 4331256. Dist.A.P.11 km. Dist.R.W.2 km* • C.C. 1983, ren. 1989. 23 stories, 552 rooms. B.C. China Eastern. Photo developing. Karakoke. Cantonese, Sichuan and Japanese food. Western breakfast for groups only. IDD. Gym. USTV. Post office.

Shanghai International Airport Hotel (Guoji Ji Chang Binguan) • *2550 Hongqiao Rd., 200335. Alming at 3*. Fax 2558393. Telex 30033 SIAH A CN. Dist.A.P.O.4 km. Dist.R.W.15 km* • C.C. 1988. 8 stories, 308 small rooms. Teppanyaki. IDD. Japanese J.V. USTV. Transit hotel. Massage. Clinic. B.C. China Eastern. Arranges city tours 3 times a day.

Shanghai J.C. Mandarin (Jing Chang Wen Hua) • *1225 Nanjing Xi Rd., 200040. 5*. Fax 2792314. Telex 33939 SJCMH CN. 6 km. from Bund* • C.C. 1990–91. 30 stories. 600 rooms each with 3 telephone jacks. IDD. Cantonese and continental cuisine. Clinic. B.C. Tennis, squash. Gym. All-weather pool. USTV. Managed by Singapore Mandarin International.

Shanghai Mansions (Shanghai Dasha) • *20 Suzhou Bei Rd., 200080. 3*. Telex 30173 SMH CNl Fax 3269778. Dist.A.P.25 km. Dist.R.W.3 km* • C.C. 1934, ren. 1991. 19 stories, 248 large rooms. Soundproof windows. IDD. B.C. Soft beds. Mostly groups. French, Russian, Yangzhou, Cantonese and Sichuan food.

Shanghai Olympic (O Lin Pike Julebu) • *1800 Zhong Shan Nan Er Rd., 200030* • Can use some facilities in adjacent Indoor Stadium. Telex 33413 SSSC CN. Fax 4396295. Three stories. 205 rooms. Gym. Squash. Budget travelers only.

Sheraton Hua Ting (Hua Ting Binguan #1) • *1200 Cao Xi Bei Rd., 200030. 5*. Telex 33589 SHHTH CN. Fx 2550830. Dist.A.P.10 km. Dis.R.W. 15 km.* Subway station due 1993 • C.C. 1986–87. Ren. 1990. 26 stories. 1008 rooms. IDD. Gym. 24-hr laundry. B.C. Indoor pool. Bowling. Tennis. USTV. Shuttle buses. Cantonese and Italian restaurants. 24 hr. American deli. Bicycles. Bowling. AT&T.

Westin Tai Ping Yang Shanghai (Tai Ping Yang Da Fandian) • *5 Zunyi Nan Rd., 200335. 5*. Telex 33345 PASHC CN. Fax 2755420, 2750643* • C.C. 1990–91. 578 spacious rooms. Non-smoking and executive floors. IDD. USTV. B.C. Bakery. Japanese and Italian food. AT&T. Bicycles. *Ofuro.* Gym. Tennis. Small outdoor pool. Classy. Guests can golf at 21-hole Shanghai Country Club. Shuttle bus.

Xi Jiao Guest House (Xi Jiao Binguan) • *1921 Hong Qiao Rd., 200335. Telex 3304 BTHHQ CN. Fax 4336641. Dist.A.P.5 km. Dist.R.W.11 km* • C.C. 1984. #2 and #3 villas ren. 1989. 7 buildings of 1–3 stories, 150 big rooms. Bit grubby and worn. IDD. B.C. Queen Elizabeth slept in suite in #7 villa (US$1000). Dark hallways. Huge garden. Lots of privacy.

Yangtze New World Hotel (Yangtze Jiang Da Jiudian) • *2099 Yanan Xi Rd., 200335. Requesting 4*. Fax 2750750. Telex 33675 YNWHR CN. Dist.A.P.8. km. Dist.R.W.10 km. Managed by New World International* • C.C. 1990–91. 34 stories, 570 rooms. Non-smoking and executive floors. B.C. Outdoor pool. Gym. Chaozhou and Cantonese food. IDD. USTV. Shuttle bus. Guests can use tennis, bowling, sauna facilities at nearby health club.

OTHER IMPORTANT ADDRESSES
Aeraflot: tel. 2558866.
Air France: tel. 255886 X221.
Ambulance: tel. 120.
AT&T-USA Direct: tel. 10811.
CAAC/China Eastern Airlines: 789 Yan'an Zhong Rd.; tel. 247225, 2471960 (international) Shanxi Nan Rd.; tel. 2475953, 2471805 (domestic). Also Cypress, International Airport, Jin Jiang, Jinan, Overseas Chinese, Sheraton, Peace, and Shanghai Hotels, and Ruijin Bldg.
China Eastern Airlines (Administration): tel. 2517555 X3061.
C.I.T.S. 中国国际旅行社 : 33 Zhongshan Rd. E1, 200002; tel. 4324960, 3217200 or 3214960. Telex 33022 TRMCO CN. Fax 3291949, and 66 Nanjing Rd. E. Telex 33277 SCITS CN. Fax 3291788. Tel. for train tickets 3217117, 3211244 X278; for plane tickets 3234067; travel arrangements 3210032; luggage 3232872; airport, tel. 4329327; railway station, tel. 3240319.
Consulate-General of Australia 澳大利亚领事馆 : 17 Fuxing Xi Rd., tel. 4374580, 4334604.
Consulate General of Britain: 244 Yongfu Rd., 200031; tel. 374569, 4330508. Fax 4333115.
Consulate-General of Canada: 4th Floor, Union Bldg., 100 Yan'an Dong Rd.; tel. 3202822. Telex 33608 CANAD CN. Fax 3203623.
Consulate-General of France 法国领事馆 : 1431 Huaihai Zhong Rd.; tel. 4377414, 4332639.
Consulate General of the Federal Republic of Germany: 151 and 181 Yongfu Rd., tel. 4336953. Fax 4714488.
Consulate General of Italy: 121 Wuyi Rd., tel. 524373-4.
Consulate-General of Japan 日本领事馆 : 1517 Huaihai Zhong Rd.; tel. 4362073, 4336639.

Consulate-General of Poland: 618 Jianguo W. Rd.; tel. 4370952, 4314998.

Consulate General of the Russia Federation: 20 Huangpu Rd., 200080; tel. 4558383. Telex 30220 SOUGC CN.

Consulate-General of the United States 美国领事馆 : 1469 Huaihai Zhong Rd.; tel. 4336880. Press and Cultural Affairs: 1375 Huaihai Zhong Rd.

C.T.S. 中国旅行社 : 104 Nanjing Xi Rd. 200040; tel. 3279112, 4338338. Telex 30183 CTSIR CHI. Head office: 881 Yanan Zhong Rd., 200040; tel. 2478888. Telex 33301 COTOS CN. Cable SCTS. Fax 2475521.

CYTS: 2 Heng Shan Rd., 200031; tel. 4331826. Telex 30241 CYTS CN. Fax 4335521, 4330507.

Community Church: Hengshan Rd.; tel. 4376576. Provides interpretors for services.

Dragonair: Jin Jiang Hotel; tel. 4336435, 2582582 X123. Fax 4334814; Airport 2558899 X5307.

Hong Qiao Airport 虹桥机场 : tel. 2537664, 2536530, 2518550.

Hospital for Foreigners: Hua Dong Yuen, 221 Yan'an Xi Lu, 6th floor; tel. 2563180. Near Shanghai Hotel; Sino-American Friendship Center, Shanghai First People's Hospital has the best equipment.

Information: 115.

Japan Airlines: Room 201, Rui Jin Bldg., 205 Mao Min Nan St.; tel. 4336337, 4336339.

Korean Airlines: Equatorial Hotel, tel. 2791688.

Northwest Airlines 西北航空公司 : Shanghai Centre; tel. 2798088, 2798100.

Huangpu River Sightseeing Service Station, Beijing Dong Rd. Wharf; tel. 3211098, 3255912.

Passenger Quay for Hong Kong: Book through travel agencies or China Ocean Shipping Agency,; tel. 3230970. Leaves 6 times a month from Wai Hong Qiao harbor (at Tai Pin Rd.). 400 berths each, 2½ days each way. Cheaper than flying, depending on class. See "Getting There."

Passenger Quay for Dalian, Qingdao, Ningbo, Chongqing, Wenzhou, and Hankou (Wuhan)

Passenger Quay for Japan 往神户（日本）码头 : Shanghai-Kobe ferry. 8500-ton ship; 600 passenger capacity. China Ocean Shipping Agency. See above. Leaves every 7 days. Trip 23 hours to Kobe, 47 hours to Osaka.

Railway Station 火车站 : tel. 3253030.

Shanghai Airlines: 555 Yan'an Rd., tel. 2550550, 2558558.

Shanghai Tourism Administration 上海旅游局 : 2525 Zhongshan Xi Rd. (Hua Ting Guest House) 200030; tel. 4390416 X2416, 4390630.

Fax 4391519. Telex 33022 TRMCO CN. (For brochures, list of desig-
nated tourist hotels, and complaints.)
Shanghai Tourism Corporation: 33 Zhong Shan Rd. (E1), 200002;
tel. 3217200. Telex 33411 SCITS CN. Fax 3291949. (Sales.)
Singapore Airlines: Shanghai Center, tel. 2798000.
Taxi Complaints: tel. 3232150.
Tourist Hot Line (for help with problems); tel. 4390630, 4391818.
Information line, tel. 3200200 for shopping, hospitals, etc. (in Chinese).
United Airlines: Hilton Hotel; tel. 2553333.
Specialized Reading (see also "Bibliography"):
Barber, Noel. *The Fall of Shanghai;* Pan Lin, *In Search of Old Shang-
hai.* Seagrave, Sterling. *The Soong Dynasty.* Very readable and reveal-
ing book about the Soongs, sons-in-law Gen. Chiang Kai-shek and Dr.
Sun Yat-sen, son T.V. Soong, reluctant premier and finance minister,
and their Soviet, gangster, and wealthy Christian, American, and Chinese
friends.

SHANHAIGUAN

North China. Northeastern Hebei province 20 km north of Beidaihe, is an important pass in the Great Wall. It can be reached
by air from Shijiazhuang, Beijing and Guangzhou, and is a three-
hour train ride from the capital.

Six km north is the **Meng Jiang-nu Temple,** which was built in
memory of another of China's chaste, almost supernatural heroines. Lady
Meng traveled on foot during severe winter months in search of her
husband, one of the hundreds of thousands of workers building the Great
Wall. Her deep sorrow and tears moved Heaven so much that the Great
Wall collapsed to reveal her husband's bones.

The temple was originally built in the Song dynasty, but the statues
were destroyed during the Cultural Revolution. They were restored in
the late 1970s in gaudy, crudely painted clay. But the view of the hills
to the north is interesting.

Six km from Shanhaiguan and about 40 km NE of Qinhuangdao is
Yansai Lake, a.k.a. Shihe Reservoir, an artificial lake created in 1974,
36 km by 200 meters. From the reservoir run 75 km of irrigation ditches,
an impressive network along the side of the mountain. A 1-hour boat
ride on the lake is breezy and restful.

Laolongtou (Old Dragon Head), the place where the Great Wall meets the sea, is also 4 km south of Shanhaiguan and was recently restored. Chenghai Tower on the seashore was built in 1579, and parts of the wall here are ruins in the sea. A temple to the Sea Goddess Mazu has been restored here.

Beijie Restaurant is 200 meters from the Great Wall at Shanhaiguan. Reservations are recommended.

See also "Beidaihe," "Qinhuangdao" and the "Great Wall."

SHANTOU 汕头

(a.k.a. Swatow and Chaoshan). South China. Northeastern Guangdong province. This port city and Special Economic Zone is 350 km by air north of Guangzhou, 10 hours by bus. It can also be reached by expressway from Shenzhen in 3 hours, soon, and ship from Hong Kong, ship from Shanghai, and road from Fujian. Flights currently from Hong Kong, Singapore, Bangkok, and 19 Chinese cities. Planned air connections with Japan and train with Guangzhou (1995). Shantou is the ancestral home of innumerable Chinese emigrants to South and Southeast Asia, Japan, and Africa. Many Chinese were also kidnapped from here and sent to Cuba in the late 1800s. Today about 15% of the population receives remittances from overseas. With the two municipal areas of Shantou and Chaozhou, and 11 counties, it has a population of about 10 million. The weather is mild, with an annual rainfall of 1400 to 2000 mm, mainly in the summer.

Shantou is famous for its port, which at one time was used by Europeans for the importation of opium to China. The district is also famous for its handicrafts. The Shantou Special Economic Zone is along the east and southeast coast of Shantou on both sides of Shantou harbor.

Among the attractions in **Chaozhou City** 潮州市 are: the **Kaiyuan Temple** 开元寺 , from the Tang dynasty (with its rare set of Buddhist sutras presented by a Qing emperor), **West Lake Park** 西湖 , the **arts and crafts factory,** and the **embroidery factory** 潮绣厂 . Across the **Xiangzi Bridge** is the **Han Wen-gong Temple** 韩祠 .

Chaozhou is a 2000-year-old town to which disgraced officers of the Tang were exiled, notably Han Yu, who objected to his emperor spending so much money on Buddhist structures. **Ling Shan Temple** (Tang) in Chaoyang County has a record of his dispute with the founder of the temple. Chaozhou is one of the Four Famous Ancient Towns, and still has Tang and Song architecture.

In **Shantou City** 汕头市 , 30 km south of Chaozhou, are: the **Arts and Crafts Exhibition** 工艺展览馆 and **Zhong Shan Park** 中山公园 , with its "gardens within gardens." To the east of Shantou is tiny **Maya Islet** 妈屿海滨浴场 7 km by ferry (2 or 3 times a day) with a temple to Sea Goddess Mazhu and the old British Customs House (now a hostel). Nanho here is the best beach in the area. Across the harbor is the **Jiaoshi Scenic Spot** 岩石风景区 . Nanho Island, with its good beaches, is three hours away by boat and near Taiwan's Jinmen (Quemoy).

Chaoyang County 潮阳县 , about 30 km south of Shantou, has two hills with Tang Taoist and Buddhist temples. In addition to the **Ling Shan Temple** 灵山寺 , there is the pagoda of **Wenguang Tower** 葫芦山 and much historical graffiti on **Gourd Hill** 文尖塔 by **West Lake.**

A globe on a tower at Shantou University marks the Tropic of Cancer.

SHOPPING

The area produces carpets, painted porcelain, jewelry, bamboo carvings, lacquer, lots of lace, and embroidery. It is also noted for its stone, shell, and gilded wood carvings. **Shantou Arts & Crafts** is on Seaside Sq.; tel. 74309, 74310.

HOTELS

The Shantou International is best. The Golden Gulf is 3*.

Longhu Hotel (Binguan) • *Yingbin Rd. 515041. 3*. Near the Bank of China, Customs House, and Longhu Park. Telex 45458 LHHTL CN. Fax 260708. Dist.A.P.12 km. In S.E.Z.* • C.C. 1984. Ren. 1991, three stories, 1987 seven stories; 237 rooms. IDD, gym, clinic. Small bathrooms. B.C.

Shantou International Hotel (Guoji Da Jiudian) • *Jin Sha Dong Rd. 515041. 4*. Telex 45475 STIH CN. Fax 252250. Dist.A.P.15 km. Dist.S.E.Z. 3 km* • C.C. 1988. 26 stories. 353 rooms. IDD, B.C. USTV, revolving restaurant. Planning gym. Lee Gardens International (H.K.)

Ambulance: tel. 120.
Police: tel. 110.
C.A.A.C.: 46 Shanzhang Rd.
C.I.T.S. Room 202, Peninsula Hotel. Jinsha Rd., 515041; tel. 241091, 240557. Fax 250033.

C.T.S. 中旅社 • *Shan Zhang Rd. 515031, tel. 33966, 52649. Fax: 52649;* 34 Huancheng Xi Rd., Chaozhou. 515600; tel. 732151.

SHAOGUAN 韶山

South China. In northern Guangdong near the Hunan, Jiangxi, and Guangxi borders. This city of over 360,000 people is on the Beijing-Guangzhou railway, with trains from Guangzhou, 220 km away. This area might be for people wanting to get off the beaten path, especially in winter, when other parts of China are too cold. It does have 310 frostfree days, with an annual rainfall of up to 2200 mm, mainly in the summer. Hottest temperature in summer could be 40°C; coldest in winter is an occasional ⁻4°C.

Shaoguan is an industrial and mining center. Although it is set on three rivers, the city itself is not pretty enough to be worth the tedious trip by hard-class train (no soft class available). The surrounding countryside, however, is a nice mix of anthropology and unusual mountain scenery. One can visit with some of the 130,000 Yao and Zhuang minority peoples.

The area was settled 120,000 years ago! Skull fossils have been found in Maba District, Qujiang County, dating from that period. The **Museum of Maba Man** can be visited 19 km south of Shaoguan, 2 km from Maba town. You can also tour the 1-km-long cave where the bones were found. Tel. (0751) 66955. Or you can take a white-water rafting trip at Pinshi.

Gufo (Ancient Buddha) Cave is 5 km SW of Lechang Town, 56 km north of Shaoguan City. It covers 10,000 square feet and has seven large "palaces," the widest related to the novel *Journey to the West.*

Tourists can also visit the 1400-year-old **Nanhua (South China) Temple** in Qujiang County, 24 km south of Shaoguan. This recently restored temple has a pagoda dating from the Ming and a statue of the Priest Huineng, the abbott in A.D. 677 who developed the Dhyana sect. During the Cultural Revolution, his bones were found inside the statue. Also in the temple are wooden arhats (Song) and a 5000-kg bronze bell

(Song). This, the largest temple in South China, is on 12,000 square meters of land.

HOTELS

Shaoguan city's Shaoguan Hotel is a centrally located high-rise while the Greenlake (a little better) is on the outskirts. All hotels here are just adequate.

Green Lake Villa Hotel (Bihu Shan Zhuang) • *Shahu Rd. 512028. Telex 45809 CITSG CN. Dist.A.P.35 km. Dist.R.W.6 km.* • Attractive, isolated setting. T.R. Hong Kong J.V. 1987–88. Two stories, 128 rooms. Limited IDD. C.C.(no MasterCard), bicycles.

Reception Center Hostel • *Biebi City, Ruyuan County. Dist.R.W.50 km. In fascinating mountain village, home of Yao people* • About 21 beds. No air conditioning. Fans and mosquito nets. Modest dorms, restaurant. No C.C. Used by bicycle tours.

Shaoguan Hotel (Binguan) • *162 Jie Fang Rd. 512000. Near shopping and park. Dist.A.P.30 km* • No C.C. Hong Kong J.V. 1988. 16 stories, 150 rooms. No IDD.

C.I.T.S.: Green Lake Hotel, Shahu Rd. 512000. tel. 6231.
C.T.S.: 27 Xidi Zhong Rd. 512000; tel. 3108, 4323. Guangzhou office; tel. 663488 X921.
Shaoguan Tourist Corporation: Fengdu Rd. North; tel. 84718.

SHAOXING 绍兴

(Shaohsing) East China, in Zhejiang province. 60 km from Hangzhou by train or road, 3 hours from Ningbo.

This 2000- to 3000-year-old town is best known for its wine, but it was also the birthplace of China's most famous pre-Liberation writer, Luxun (Lu Hsun). Some of his stories, notably *The Story of Ah Q,* were set in this town, and a highly recommended but very sad 1982 movie was made of the Ah Q novella here. Literary types should pay a visit to his former residence and the **Luxun Memorial Hall** 鲁迅纪念馆 .

Shaoxing is also known for its lovely canals and **East Lake** 东湖, alive with boats of all descriptions. Especially striking are its distinctive foot boats, the oars worked by feet. Highly recommended is a trip by these boats onto the lake and into the caves cut out of the lake's quarried cliffs to see the hanging gardens, and go under arched bridges to old temples—a good way to see what Shaoxing has to offer. Boat trip also to ancient **Keqiao,** 12 km from Shaoxing, in places following a 5-km stone towpath.

Shaoxing is famous throughout China for its distinctive opera. It is less formal, full of emotion, action, and audience-pleasing lyrics, gorgeous costumes, and flashy sets. All parts played by women.

Shaoxing is an ancient city. The tomb of the Xia dynasty founder is in the south suburbs at the base of Mt. Kuaiji. Whether or not the third century B.C. pioneer in irrigation and flood control was/is in **Yuwang Miao** is anyone's guess. In any case, he died in Shaoxing during a visit. The name *Shaoxing* means "gathering place"; for example, of the people celebrating the miraculous engineering feats of Emperor Yu.

Also of interest are the **Orchid Pavilion** 兰亭 , dating back to the fourth century, and the **Shen Family Garden** 沈园 , which commemorates the meeting between Song dynasty lovers. **Jianhu Lake** 鉴湖 , first dredged in the second century, covers more than 200 square km. The home of the early 20th century female revolutionist **Qiu Jin** is open as a museum. **Premier Chou En-lai,** though born in Jiangsu province, was brought up in this city and you can visit his home.

If you want to visit East Lake, Yuwang Miao, Lan Ding (Orchid Pavilion), Luxun's home and museum, Qiu Jin's home, and stroll about the town, you need at least two full days. You could also ask about the story of the scholar writing with a brush made of mouse whiskers. Tours can visit a home for the aged.

Shaoxing is attractive because it still has many houses, streets, canals, and boats hardly changed from centuries ago. Much time can be spent walking around in this time warp.

Changes have been made, however, like the addition of a local television station, and the lovely sycamore and plane trees lining the streets. The **Second Hospital** 第二医院 was the former mission hospital. Near it was an old pagoda.

Writes one former missionary child of his early life in Shaoxing, "I used to play among the ruins of an old temple there and with a child's carelessness and disdain for the familiar, pretend it was something seemingly far more exotic and romantic: a Mayan temple!"

Ted Stannard also says, "In my childhood, Shaoxing's streets and lanes were almost all paved with great rough-hewn but well-worn flagstones. Where they balanced unevenly across hidden drains beneath the thoroughfares, they would sometimes tip and sound hollowly underfoot or rickshaw wheel. Only a few blocks of the midtown shopping area had asphalt paving before World War II. I can still remember the sensation of silent floating when my bicycle reached that stretch . . . I never saw a car in Shaoxing until the Japanese occupation brought in charcoal-burning army trucks, and in the late forties after the war, the mayor installed barrier posts at all the principle entry-ways to the city to keep out all cars except his own.

''Today the main arterials are asphalt-paved, and many streets widened by filling in canals or tearing out the shops or homes that had lined them. Trucks, cars, and those uniquely Chinese farm tractors ply the streets side-by-side with man-hauled carts, cycles, and pedestrians. But step off into any side-street or lane and you are back in timeless China, threading your way between high-walled compounds and across algae-clogged canals on flagstones worn by centuries of footsteps.

''Marco Polo walked these streets, along the lacework of canals that led him, in his journals, to liken Shaoxing (and Suzhou) to Venice. The canals drain a lowland area reclaimed from the sea centuries ago by a hydraulic engineer who succeeded where his father had failed (at the cost of his head, thanks to a popular imperial theory of incentives), and went on to become the Emperor Yu. A local saying credits him with saving the people of Shaoxing from being fishes.

''The **Yuwang Temple** is in moderately good repair, despite some damage during the Cultural Revolution. It has a series of courtyards and steep stairways to the main temple where a gigantic figure of the emperor peers down benignly upon those who visit. Off to one side outside this temple is a pavilion sheltering an ancient stone linga, taller than any man, with a small hole piercing its tip. . . . Childless women would try to toss a pebble or coin through the needle's eye as a fertility charm.''

SHOPPING

Shaoxing wine, of course, brewed with 2000 years' experience. Visitors frequently stop in at the **Xian Heng Wine Shop,** 44 Luxun Rd., tel. 33619, named after a Luxun short story. Also locally made are lace, felt hats, paper fans, silk, porcelain, bambooware, and ink stones. **Shaoxing Antique Store,** Jiefang Nan Rd., tel. 533574.

HOTEL

Shaoxing Hotel (Binguan) • *9 Huanshan Rd., 312000. 3*. Dist.A.P.67 km. Dist.R.W.3 km* • 1950s. 2 and 3 stories. 115 rooms. Renovated 1988; 85 additional rooms and pool. The dining hall is an old family temple. This is the best hotel.

Ambulance: tel. 522919.
Police: tel. 533058.

C.I.T.S. and **Shaoxing Tourism Bureau:** 20 Fushan Xi Rd. 312000.
C.I.T.S., tel. 533252, 536672. S. T. B., tel. 536674, 536670. Fax
535262. Wine-tasting tours.
C.T.S.: Huanshanxi Rd.; tel. 533252.
Tourist Hotline: tel. 533252, 536672.

SHENYANG 沈阳

(Formerly Mukden) Northeast China. Capital of Liaoning province, which borders on Korea. 1¼ hours by air NE of Beijing.
Flights from Hong Kong, Irkutsk, Khabarousk, and 33 Chinese
cities. Also reached by train and expressway from Dalian. Weather:
Hottest in August, averaging 23.8°C: coldest in January, ⁻20°C.
Rain mainly June to August. A lot of air pollution. Population:
urban about 4.6 million, with Manchus the largest group.

With a recorded history of over 2000 years, Shenyang was the
Manchu capital from 1625 until 1644. After that, the Qing capital moved
to Beijing. Shenyang is the biggest industrial city in this region, which
was formerly Japanese-held Manchuria. The Mukden Incident on September 18, 1931, a surprise attack on the Chinese army stationed here,
marked the beginning of Japanese aggression in China.

Shenyang today is a cultural center also, with institutions of higher
learning and research. It is the home base of the Shenyang Acrobats,
among China's best.

If you only have one day, C.I.T.S. suggests the Imperial Palace,
North Tomb, Zoo, and open market.

The 19-year reigns of Nurhachi/Nulhachi and Huangtaiji (Huang
Tai Chi) were enough to build the very impressive ***Imperial Palace
阳故宫** , from 1625 to 1636, now restored to its original gaudy splen-
dor. In an area of almost 60,000 square meters, it is also one of the
best museums in China. Although this palace has a lot of Han influence,
look for Mongolian and Manchu-style touches.

The most impressive section is the eastern one, with its octagonal
Dazheng Dian (Hall of Great Affairs) and Shiwang Ting (Pavilions of
Ten Princes). Does the Beijing Palace have such dragons on its pillars,

and the yurtlike design? The hall was used for important ceremonies and meetings with top officials. Huangtaiji commanded his military forces and political business from the Chongzheng Dian (Hall of Supreme Administration). At the back of this hall is a road to the Fenghuang Lou (Phoenix Tower) and the Qingning Gong (Palace of Pure Tranquillity). The Manchu leaders lived in the Qingning Gong, which is the most distinctively Manchu.

In the western section is the Wenshuo Ge (Hall of Literary Source), especially constructed for the *Complete Library of the Four Treasures* of Qing Emperor Qianlong. No signs in English.

The *Beiling (North) Tombs 北陵 (a.k.a. Zhaoling), north of the city, are of Huangtaiji and his wife Borjigid (Poerhchichiteh). Huangtaiji was the son of Nurhachi. Begun in 1643, the tombs were completed in 1651. Hours are from 8:30 a.m. to 4:00 p.m. (summer) and from 10 a.m. to 3 p.m.. (winter). The **Dongling (East) Tombs** 东陵 (a.k.a. Fuling), are of Nurhachi and his wife Yihnaran. During the Ming, Nurhachi unified the tribes, became ''khan'' in 1616, and made Shenyang his capital in 1625. Also of interest is the **Shenyang Steam Locomotives Museum** 沈阳火车博物馆 Sujiatun Jiwuduan, Sujiatun District (8 a.m. to 4 p.m. in summer and 10 a.m. to 3 p.m. in winter), and an overnight in **Tieling Village** with a peasant family. If you're interested in modern history, ask about visiting Marshall Zhang Shi's Mansion, south of the imperial palace.

The 40-square km **Qianshan Mountain Park** 千山公园 is 130 km south. At Yixiang, about 250 km west of the city is *Fengguo Temple,** dating from the Liao and said to be the second largest temple in China. Does anyone dispute that? Also of interest in the province are Anshan and Dalian (375 km from Shenyang). See separate listings. Ask also about the Xin Le Neolithic museum on the site, near the entrance to the Friendship Hotel in Shenyang. One can also visit the border area at **Dandong** where you can boat on the Yalu River (famous for those who know about the Korean War), and visit the King of Medicine Temple on Feng Huang (Phoenix) Hill, a visit to which should cure you of all ills.

In Dandong is the Yalu Jiang Hotel (Dasha), 87 Jiuwei Rd., 118000. Built 1987. 176 rooms. **C.T.S.,** Dandong Hotel, tel. 27721.

SHOPPING

Produced in the province are diamonds, ginseng, sable, and carvings of jade, agate, jet, and amber. Also produced are ceramics, feather patchwork, the musical instrument *zheng,* shell carvings and pictures.

RESTAURANTS

Local delicacies include monkey head mushrooms, available at the **Lumingchun Restaurant,** 2 Nanjing Nan St., tel. 27721. One of the best restaurants is the **Xin Lu Yuan** in the Huasha Hotel (tel. 665552) for Shandong and northeast food.

Laobian Dumpling Restaurant 辽宁大厦 ● *13, Section 2, Bei Shichan St., tel. 721819* ● Dumplings with various fillings.

HOTELS

The best hotel seems to be the Zhongshan, then the Phoenix, third the Rose or the 3* Jincheng.

The Phoenix is 10 to 15 minutes' walk to the tomb, which is open from 6 a.m. until 10 p.m. The Rose, Zhongshan, and Liaoning hotels are near the railway station.

Liaoning Hotel (Binguan) ● *97 Zhongshan Rd. 110001, 3*. Telex 80083 LNH CN. Fax 339103. Dist.A.P. 27 km. Dist. R.W. 1 km. Next to giant statue of Chairman Mao in center of city* ● 1927, Ren. 1990. Four stories. 77 rooms. Lots of charming 1920s ambience.

Phoenix Hotel (Fenghuang Fandian) ● *109 Huanghe Nan St. 110031. 3*. Fax 731713. Telex 80045 FHFD CN. Fax 665207. Dist. A.P. 18 km* ● 1984. 15 stories. 360 rooms. Sauna. C.C.

Rose Hotel (Da Jiudian) ● *21 Zhongjie Rd. 110011. 3*. Telex 80084 SHYRH CN. Fax 449546. Dist.A.P. 24 km. Dist.R.W. 4.5 km* ● 162 rooms.

Zhongshan Hotel (Da Sha) ● *65 Zhong Shan Rd. 110011. 3*. Telex 804088 SYZSB CN. Fax 339189. Dist.A.P. 23 km. Dist.R.W. 1 km* ● 1990. 208 rooms.

CAAC: 31 Zhonghua Rd., Section 3; tel. 364089.
C.I.T.S. 中国国际旅行社 ：113 Huanghe Nan St. 110031; tel. 664796. Fax 664772. Telex 80081 CITSS CN. Can book trains to U.S.S.R. and D.P.R. Korea.
C.T.S.: 189 Shifu Rd., tel. 229373. Fax 229372.
CYTS: tel. 722971, 227706.
U.S. Consulate: 41 Lane 4, Section 5, Sanjing St., Heping District; tel. 290038, 290000, Telex 80011 AMCS CN. Shenyang also has a Korean and a Japanese consulate.
Liaoning Overseas Tourist Corporation: 1 North Huanghe St., 110031. Tel. 600276, 600778. Telex 804065 LNTB CN. Fax 600897. Tours go from here to Korea and Russia.
Liaoning Tourism Administration: 113 Huanghe Nan Rd. 110031; tel. 466326, 464650. Fax 660415.

Ambulance: Tel. 120.
Police: Tel. 110.

SHENZHEN 深圳

(Shumchun) South China. On the Hong Kong border, this is a
Special Economic Zone reached by air from at least 4 Chinese
cities and hopefully 17 more. A hefty departure tax of ¥ 110 must
be paid, even on domestic flights. Huangtian Airport is 32 km
west of the city. Shenzhen is joined to Quangzhou by road and a
yet-to-be-completed six-lane superhighway. A new railway line
connecting Shenzhen to Beijing is due in 1997. Hong Kong currency is freely used, and hotel prices are quoted in it. You can
obtain a 5-day visa at the Hong Kong border or a longer one for
all of China. "Hong Kong time" is used here, which could be
different from the rest of China.

Urban Shenzhen (pop. 700,000 + temporary laborers) is about 7
km by 10 km, spreading mainly east and west from the railway station
and its 1987-built Customs House, which touches the border. Only travelers on the through-express trains now cross the famous old covered
bridge.

Fast electric trains zip between Kowloon Station and Lowu on the
Hong Kong border. The section from Shenzhen to Guangzhou is electrified and takes 2 hours, although you might end up at the wrong railway station in Guangzhou. Shenzhen is building an international airport.

At press time, no Hong Kong taxis were allowed into Shenzhen,
but city buses ran at least twice a day. Trains are the fastest and most
convenient transport. Hong Kong buses take tourists on day trips, or
connect with Shenzhen buses for other destinations in Guangdong or
Fujian. Taxis are hard to get here.

The main resorts are in the suburbs, or toward Shekou, which is
29 km west. Two resorts have amusement park rides, the biggest at the
Honey Lake Country Club (Dist.R.W.8 km), boasting the longest roller
coaster ride (2 km) in the world. Its monorail is 4.5 km long.

The day trippers see China's largest, wealthiest Special Economic

Zone, and its greatest concentration of skyscrapers. They might see the reservoir that supplies half of Hong Kong's water supply. Greater Shenzhen has no historical monuments save the modest grave of the last Song emperor, who fled here to escape the Mongols (in Shekou). But it does have **Splendid China** (Jinxiu Zhong Hua). This is a theme park of 29 hectares with over 80 of China's top tourist attractions in miniature, including the Great Wall, a Suzhou garden, the Terracotta Warriors, and three Yangtze gorges. It is highly recommended (but not in the rain) as a super-deluxe catalog. We urge you to take a guide as no explanations are in English. Very photogenic, it is between Shenzhen and Shekou, next to the Shenzhen Bay Hotel, and is great for children too. Newly opened is the Folk Culture Villages next to the miniatures. This is a 180,000-square-meter exhibition of 24 life-size minority villages, with demonstrations of handicrafts, cooking, and three shows a day of dances and songs of all 56 nationalities. Evenings have a parade with perhaps a costume show, wedding processions, and carnival. Both can be reached by bus from the Shenzhen train station. Tours can be booked through C.T.S. in Hong Kong.

During the summertime *litchi (lichee)* season, tourists also come here to pick this sweet fruit. The tour price usually includes all-you-can eat and 2.5 kg to take home. A Lichee and Fine Food Festival takes place the end of June and early July.

Shekou has 50-minute hovercraft service with Hong Kong four times a day. A retired cruise ship, the **Minghua/Sea-World,** is now moored in the bay, providing 239 small hotel rooms. There is also an exhibit of the **Qin Dynasty Terracotta Warriors.**

From the higher floors of the Forum Hotel one can see Hong Kong's Sheung Shui, a neat switch after the decades of tourists getting a peek at China from Hong Kong.

Shenzhen has 125 hotels and resorts suitable for foreigners. In the city itself, the most convenient for business people is the flashy Century Plaza (close to the International Trade Center—ITC) and the classier Forum (next to the Customs House). Both are good. The Nanhai in Shekou is a little far for business people, but beautiful, and the best for tourists. Less convenient for business people is the Oriental Regent, and then the Guang Dong, but they are progressively cheaper. The Bamboo Garden is more for budget tourists.

China's first McDonald's is in Shenzhen.

Bamboo Garden Hotel (Zhu Yuan Binguan) • *Dong Men Bei Rd. 518003. 3*. Telex 420390 BGH CN. Fax 533138. Dist.R.W.4 km. Dist.ITC 1 km* • Attractive suburban setting. C.C. 1981, ren. 1991; addition 1989. Four stories, 170 rooms. Bowling, clinic, B.C. HKTV. H.K.J.V. Large rooms, no drawers, soft beds, small bathrooms.

Century Plaza Hotel (Xin Du Jin Dian) • *Kin Chit Rd. 518000. 4*. Fax 234060. Telex 420382 CPHTL. Fax 8106466. Walk to ITC* • C.C. 1987. 24 stories, 427 rooms. Executive floor, B.C. Pool, health club. Citibank on premises. IDD, soft beds, large bathrooms. Japanese restaurant. Managed by Pacifica International. AT&T.

Forum Hotel Shenzhen (Fulian Jiudian) • *67 Heping Rd. 518000. Reservations Fax 201700. Telex 420199 Forum CN.* • U.S. reservations Forum Hotels International. 1990. 28 stories. 538 rooms. IDD. B.C. Beijing, Continental, and Japanese food. Non-smoking floors. HKTV. Pool. Health club.

Shangri-La Hotel • *East side, Railway Station, Jianshe Rd., 518001. Fax 589878* • 1993. 556 rooms. Pool. B.C. Clinic.

Outside Shenzhen City

Marina Ming Wah • *Gui Shan Rd., Shekou. 2*. Fax (755) 686668 Telex 420886 MARMW CN. Dist.A.P.25 km. Dist.R.W.30 km* • C.C. 1992. 85 rooms. IDD. Hairdryers, B.C. Tennis. gym. Jogging track. Outdoor pool. Free ferry shuttle. Clinic. Swiss-Belhotel Management H.K.

Nan Hai Hotel (Da Jiudian) • *Shekou 518069. 5*. Telex 420879. Fax 692440. Dist.R.W. 30 km* • Managed by Miramar Group (H.K.). In residential area near town. C.C. 1985. 11 stories. 396 rooms. B.C. Tennis. Mini-golf, pool, disco. Ideal for honeymoons. Bicycles.

C.I.T.S.: tel. 229403, 229402.
C.T.S.: Overseas Chinese Hotel 518010; tel. 518001. Or Baoan Rd. 518003; tel. 240890.
C.Y.T.S.: tel. 253695.
Shenzhen International Travel Service: 2/F, Block A, Nanyang Mansion, Kin Chit Rd.; tel. 227511, 227510, 236903. Telex 420306 SZTGC CN. Cable 0595. Fax 36903.
Shenzhen Tourism General Corporation: 3/F, The Tourist Centre Mansion, Ying Chun Rd., 518001. Tel. 255742, 252236. Fax 255741. Telex 420486 SZTGC CN.

SHIJIAZHUANG 石家庄

(Shihchiachuang, Shihkiachwang) North China. The capital of Hebei province, a few hours by train south of Beijing, Shijiazhuang is on the main line to Guangzhou, east of the Taihang Mountains on the Hebei Plain. It is linked by air with six other cities. With a population of over 900,000, it is primarily an industrial city.

Shijiazhuang is of importance to Chinese revolutionary history as the burial place of the Canadian who became a Chinese hero. Dr. Norman Bethune 石求恩医生 , the son of a Gravenhurst, Ontario, clergyman, arrived in China in 1938 to help the Communist Eighth Route Army in its fight against the Japanese. Working almost in the front lines, he died of blood poisoning on November 12, 1939, in Huangshikou village, Tangxian county, in Hebei. That year, Chairman Mao wrote a much publicized article, pointing him out as an example of "utter devotion to others without any thought of self." He became known to every schoolchild, and statues were made of him all over the country. A Canadian feature film, *Bethune—the Making of a Hero* is highly recommended.

In Shijiazhuang is the **Bethune International Peace Hospital** 求恩国际和平医院 , first set up in 1937 in the Shanxi-Chahar-Hebei Military Area and moved here in 1948. Dr. Bethune is buried in the western part of the **North China Revolutionary Martyrs' Cemetery** 华北军区烈士陵园 , where there is also the Bethune Exhibition Hall and the Memorial Hall for Revolutionary Martyrs. The city also has the **Hebei Provincial Exhibition Hall and Museum** 省展览馆 .

Visitors can see a cotton mill and a free market. Foreign professionals dealing with criminals have visited a prison and a court here.

Shijiazhuang is also known for the ***Zhaozhou (Anji) Bridge*** 赵州安济桥 , still serviceable, although it was built between A.D. 605 and 610. About 2000 meters north is the ***Yongtong*** (Smaller Stone Bridge) built between 1190 and 1195, and 32 meters long. In the town of Zhengding, 15 km north, is the ***Longxing Buddhist Temple*** 隆兴寺 (Song dynasty), with a bronze 20-meter-high Buddha and the **Rongguo Mansion.**

Spectacular is **Cangyan Hill** 苍岩山, 70 km SW, full of pointed peaks and dramatic cliffs. Fuqing Buddhist temple is on a bridge first built in the Sui.

Ninety km from the city is ***Xibaipo Village** 西柏坡 , Pingshan County, the now relocated site of the 1948 headquarters of the Communist Party Central Committee.

An unusual pagoda is at the ***Kaiyuan Temple** in **Dingxian,** about 75 km NW of Shijiazhuang. Dating from the Eastern Wei 540 A.D., this 11-story, 84-meter-high structure has eight sides, two overlapping squares. Ask about the Song Dynasty tunnels lined with bricks, found in Yonqing County, an underground Great Wall.

Also in the province are Beidaihe, Chengde, Handan, Qinhuangdao, Shanhaiguan, Tangshan, and Zunhua. See separate listings.

SHOPPING

Locally made are painted-on-the-inside snuff bottles, white marble carvings from Quyang County, and Liuling wine. Elsewhere in the province are made golden-thread tapestry (Zhuoxian), shell crafts (Qinhuangdao), horse saddles (Zhangjiakou), ink slabs (Yishui), woven straw (Chengde), Handan ceramics, and Tangshan porcelain.

HOTELS

Hebei Guest House (Binguan) • *23 Yucai Rd. 050011. 3*. 20 km from airport.*

C.I.T.S. 国际旅行社 : 1 Fuqiang St.; tel. 44319.
C.T.S.: 22 Yucai Rd., 050011. Tel. 016766, 014570.
CYTS: tel. 615961 X2230, 34166.
Hebei Tourism Administration and **Hebei Overseas Tourist Corporation:** 22 Yucai St. 050021; tel. H.T.A. 614319; tel. O.T.C. 614766. Fax 615368. Telex 26275 HBITS CN.
Tourist Hotline: tel. 614239.

▌SILK ROAD

This term was first used by a German author in the 19th century and is still used because it is so apt. Silk was the main commodity carried along the caravan routes between Cathay and Europe. It dazzled the eyes of Marco Polo, who traveled here in 1275. Bales of silk have been found in ancient tombs along the way: it was that highly valued.

Informal trade between China and West Asia goes back over 2000 years. In 138 B.C. (Han), Emperor Wudi sent his emissary Zhang Qian (Chang Ch'ien) on missions westward to get help to fight the Huns. Zhang returned 13 years later, having been imprisoned most of that time by hostile tribes, but he fired the emperor's interest in trade. The Han emperors encouraged trading caravans with imperial protection and the building of beacon signal towers. From then on, the routes flourished periodically until the 14th century, especially in the Tang. It declined because sea-going ships were able to trade more efficiently and because of hostilities along the land routes.

Trade was mainly in high-value or easily transported goods. The Chinese exchanged silk, tea, and seeds for peach and pear trees. They also exchanged skills, such as iron-, steel-, and paper-making. They received grapes, pomegranate and walnut trees, sesame, coriander, spinach, the Fergana horse, alfalfa, Buddhism, Nestorianism, and Islam.

Goods were exchanged along the route especially with India and West Asia. A few items even reached Rome. The road went west from Xi'an along the Weihe River valley, Hexi Corridor, Tarim Basin, Parmirs (in Soviet Asia), Afghanistan, Iran, Iraq, and Syria. It was about 7000 km long. (2700 km within China). Northern and southern routes divided at Dunhuang on either side of the Taklamakan/Takelamagan Desert.

Many Arab and Persian merchants settled in Xi'an and even as far east as Yangzhou. Some of the cities on the Silk Road are open to foreigners, and tourists find themselves in a world of onion-domed mosques, bazaars, oasis, grapes, Soviet and Turkish faces, embroidered caps, and languages their national guides cannot understand. Spontaneous dancing and singing, uncontrolled by Han reserve, make people here delightful. Visitors are frequently asked to join in and contribute to the festivities.

Tourists find giant rock carvings and murals, some of the best in the world. They can explore earthen-walled ghost cities, the western end of the Great Wall, old tombs, Lama temples, and look for mummies. They can figure out how and what the beacon towers communicated. They can learn how water is channeled to make this desert flourish. They can buy carpets, jade goblets, jewelled daggers, and musical instruments.

But the Silk Road is not Turkey, Pakistan, or Afghanistan. It is China, an ingredient that makes this area of mixed cultures special and worth the hardships.

Tourists in this area must be fit and adventurous. It is not for the finicky and inflexible. While good hotels exist, there are few luxury standards here. Do not expect IDD, convenient hotel money changing, good plumbing, air conditioning, or a constant flow of electricity. Many visitors get sore throats and upset stomachs. Careful travelers should take their own chopsticks and bowl, even on the tourist track, and avoid food that is not cooked thoroughly on the spot. The area is extremely dry and cold even on summer nights. Long train and bus rides through the desert are not comfortable. Tourist buses, but not trains, are air-conditioned. But buses have broken down in the desert and the coolest retreat has been the shade of a rock or a sand dune—if you're lucky. You should be prepared for delays and be pleasantly surprised if they don't happen. While waiting, think about the peasants and herdsmen who struggled to raise crops and animals here while the spring or autumn sandstorms howled mercilessly. Think of the sand smothering the crops. Think of the caravans passing through. What did the camels and traders do when they couldn't see a foot ahead of them?

You should have the foresight to carry your own liquid refreshments and something to protect your nose and eyes from dust. Also imperative for travel here is an inflatable pillow to cushion bumpy roads, a strong flashlight for caves, a flask for water, and if you want to buy a carpet, a folding bag with lock. Try to plan your trip for the Sunday bazaar in Kashi.

The government is in the process of upgrading services in this area. By the time you go, planes may be flying into most of the cities on the route. Paved roads might reach the most important cave temples.

As you travel around, try to pick out the characteristics of the different nationalities. See if you can identify people from their facial features and their distinctive dress. Among the groups along the Silk Road are the Kergez, Han, Huns, Huis (Moslems), Kazaks (not related to Cossacks), Kirghiz, Manchus, Mongols, Russians, Tarjiks (Tajiks), Tartars, Turfans, Uzbeks, Uygurs (Uighurs), and Xibos.

You might be taken to some minority villages and left to fend for yourself. Prepare some questions about lifestyles, schooling for nomads, number of children, handicrafts and courtship customs. Do lots of reading beforehand. Many guides know nothing about these people. On the other hand, one of our highlights was stopping spontaneously on spotting a nomad yurt by the road, and being invited in for a look.

If you don't want to risk spoiling your trip with diarrhea, read about how to avoid upset stomachs in "Food." Do not eat anything from the local markets. The meat beyond Xi'an is mainly mutton. Wise is the traveler who says something like "I would love to try it, but it doesn't agree with me. Thank you anyway," when handed a glass of mare's milk buzzing with flies. The well-meaning tribesman in his yurt is not going to appreciate the pain you will go through later. Don't drink it because you "don't want to hurt his feelings." You are the one who will suffer!

Conference Travel of Canada and China RailExpress Travel Service have very deluxe train tours. Several agencies have less elegant land tours. Regular charter flights during the April–July tourist season have served Dunhuang, Jiayuguan, Lanzhou, and Xi'an. Kashi and Dunhuang cannot be missed.

Read William Dalyrymple's *In Xanadu, A Quest,* about his 1986 trip here and Peter Hopkin's *Foreign Devils on the Silk Road* about archaeological raids here in the early 1900s. There are many books on China's national minorities.

See "Xi'an," "Dunhuang," "Kashi," "Lanzhou," "Turpan," and "Urumqi."

SUZHOU (SOOCHOW)

East China. Yangtze basin, Jiangsu province, about 1 hour (86 km) west by train from Shanghai and 219 km SE of Nanjing. Infrequent air connections with Beijing, Foshan, and Shenzhen. Expressway from Shanghai due soon, with 45-minute trip from Shanghai airport. Direct bus from Hangzhou 170 km in 3.5 hours. March 15–Nov. 15. Weather: Hottest—36°C (usually 1 or 2 days late July, early August); coldest—end of January, averaging 0° to 7°C. Snow once or twice a year. Rain: May–July. Population: almost 700,000 in the old city.

Suzhou was founded by He Lu, King of Wu, as his capital in 514 B.C. It is one of China's oldest cities. Iron was smelted here more than

2500 years ago and silk weaving was well developed in the Tang and Song. Marco Polo visited in the latter half of the 13th century. During the Ming, textile manufacturing flourished. From 1860 to 1863, 40,000 troops of the Taiping Heavenly Kingdom controlled the area. During the Japanese occupation, the Jiangsu provincial puppet government headquartered in the Humble Administrator's Garden.

The people here speak the Wu dialect, which is similar to that of Shanghai, only with softer tones and more adjectives. Industries include the manufacturing of TV sets, wristwatches, chemicals, electronics, and instruments. Tourists would probably want to see the **factories** where artisans weave and print silk, make sandalwood and silk fans, and create one of the four most famous embroideries in China. Musical instruments are also made here. The **villages** raise silkworms, jasmine flowers for tea, shrimp, and tangerines, and are therefore particularly good to visit. The old city proper is under state protection as a historic and cultural treasure. No new factories can be built in the old city, and existing factories that pollute are being moved out to the suburbs.

The walled city is about 3 by 5 km and is crisscrossed by many canals. The western and southern moats are actually part of the famous Grand Canal (A.D. 610). The city wall was built in 514 B.C. and remnants, including three gates, remain. Also remaining is one of the eight water gates, now topped by a watchtower and museum.

Suzhou is one of the prettiest towns in China, its streets thickly lined with plane trees and its tiny whitewashed houses of uniform design. Unlike many other Chinese communities, the Japanese war inflicted little damage here. It is known primarily as a cultural and scenic city, similar in this respect to Japan's Kyoto. Its classical gardens are among the best in China.

The main street, Renmin (People's) Road, runs north-south; Jingde and Guanqian roads (actually linking) run east-west, meeting with Renmin almost in the center of the city. Many of the buildings were redecorated for Suzhou's 2500th birthday in 1986.

If you only have one day, C.I.T.S. suggests two of the gardens, Tiger Hill, one handicraft factory, and a boat trip.

Shizilin (Shih Tzu Lin; Lion Forest) Garden 狮子林 Dong Bei (Northeast) St., 4 km from the Nanlin Hotel, was built in 1350 during the Yuan and so named because the teacher of the monk who built it lived on Lion Rock Mountain. Some of the rockeries are shaped like lions. Six acres: compact. Guides say that it was once owned by the granduncle of the American architect I. M. Pei. Notable are the maze inside the rockeries at the entrance and the rocks, some carved and then weathered in Lake Tai (Taihu) for scores of years. The rock structure above the stone boat was a waterfall, which in the early days was hand-poured.

Exquisite is the Standing-in-Snow Study, so named because a student once went to visit his teacher there and, too polite to awaken him, stood patiently in the snow.

Changlang Ting (Gentle Wave or Surging Wave) Pavilion 沧浪 (Renmin Rd.) is 1 km from the Nanlin Hotel. About two acres, it is the only garden that is not surrounded completely by a view-blocking wall. A pond lies outside and can be enjoyed from a View-Borrowing Pavilion. A hall houses 125 steles with the images of 500 sages, dating from the kingdom of Wu to the Qing. Carved in relief in 1840, the deeds of each one are confined to 16 poetic characters. The garden, one of the oldest in the city, was founded in 1044 (Song) by the poet Su Tzu-mei. In the Yuan and early Ming, it was a Buddhist nunnery.

Look for the set of dark brown furniture made from mahogany tree roots that look like chocolate-covered peanuts. This garden is not as spectacular as the others, so if you're short on time, skip it.

Yi (Joyous) Garden 怡园 (Renmin Rd.) was built by a Qing official and, at 100 years, it is the newest. It has taken the best of all the gardens, concentrating them into about an acre. The rockeries are from other older gardens. The dry boat is an imitation of the one in the Humble Administrator's.

*Liu (Lingering) Garden 留园 (Liuyuan Rd., 6 km from the Nanlin Hotel) was originally built in 1525 (Ming). The 8-acre garden consists of halls and studios in the east sector, ponds and hills in the central, and woods and hills in the western section. In late autumn, these woods are red. Look through some of the 200 different flower windows at the scene beyond. You are in a living picture gallery. A huge 5-ton, 6-meter-high rock from Lake Tai stands in the eastern section.

Wangshi (Master of Nets) Garden 网师园 (Shiquan St., ½ km from the Nanlin Hotel), originally built in 1140 (Southern Song), is one of the best. The Metropolitan Museum of Art in New York City has reproduced the Peony courtyard as the Astor Chinese Garden Court. This garden is very pretty, especially when decorated with colorful palace lanterns for the **Clasical Night Garden** in summer when tourists rotate among the pavilions to hear musicians and storytellers, and to see folk dancers. Don't miss this charming experience.

*Zhuozheng (Humble Administrator's) Garden 拙政园 (Dong Bei St., 5 km from the Nanlin Hotel) is the largest in Suzhou. It was laid out in 1522 (Ming) by a humble administrator (a dismissed official) and later split into three after the owner lost it gambling. The largest and most open of the gardens, three-fifths water, is reminiscent of the water country south of the Yangtze. Almost all buildings are close to water. If you only have a short time, visit the central part. Fragrant Island there is a two-story stone ''dry boat'' complete with gangplank, ''deck,'' and ''cabin.'' The Mandarin Duck Hall has blue windows and classical furniture, with live ducks in a cage at the side of the hall. A garden blooms within a garden. A covered walkway in the western section follows the natural contours of the land. Look also for the Little Flying Rainbow Bridge, the Pavilion of Expecting Frost, and the Pavilion of Fragrant Snow and Azure Clouds.

Note also the Lingering and Listening Hall for listening (of course) to the raindrops on the lotus leaves. Who else but the aristocratic Chinese constructed buildings just for something like that! Ramps instead of stairs make one wonder about wheelchairs back then. Look for the wood carving and the cloud designs on the glass. A 200-year-old miniature pomegranate tree is included in the excellent collection of *penjing-bonsai.*

*Hu Qiu (Tiger) Hill 虎丘 (9 km from the Nanlin Hotel) is important. The 45-acre site is NW of the city outside the moat. The grounds were an island many years ago, but now they are about 100 km from the East China Sea. It was originally called Hill of Emergence from the Sea. Named Tiger Hill because a white tiger appeared here at one time, the entrance (the head), the pagoda (the tail), and what is in between considered the back of the tiger. On the right after entering is the Sword Testing Rock which He Lu, King of Wu, was supposed to have broken in the sixth century B.C. On the left is a large magic rock. If the stone you throw stays on top, you will give birth to sons—so beware! On the right is a pavilion with red characters, the Tomb of the Good Wife, a widow sold by the wicked brothers of her deceased husband to another man. Forced to be a courtesan, she committed suicide.

Here is also where Fu Chai, King of Wu, is said to have built a tomb for his father, He Lu, in the early fifth century B.C., after which the tomb builders were slaughtered to keep the location a secret. Hence, no one is sure if this is indeed the right place. If you look carefully, you can still see the red of the blood on the large flat rock. Oh, come on!

The tomb of He Lu is believed to be beyond the moon gate. In 1956, unsuccessful attempts were made to enter it. The foundation of the pagoda started to protest. Inside are supposed to be 3000 iron and steel swords. You can see the cave, blocked by large, cut stones, from the bridge to the pagoda. Is it or isn't it the 2500-year-old tomb? The two holes on the bridge were for hauling up buckets of water.

The Tiger Hill Pagoda, known also as Leaning Tower of Suzhou, was built originally in the 10th century A.D. (Northern Song). It caught fire three times, and its wooden eaves burned up. The latest repairs were made in 1981, when its foundation was strengthened. At 47.5 meters high, it tends to tilt to the northwest. Pilgrims used to climb the 53 steps here on their knees. Note the Indian arches.

The **Grand Canal Boat Tours** 大运河游船 go from (1) the Panmen Water Gates, the Wumen Arch Bridge and Ruiguang Pagoda eastward along the city wall, and to the Precious Belt Bridge with its 53 arches: 60 minutes; (2) Suzhou to Wuxi, 45 km in 3 hours. Some group tours are met with a dragon boat at the train station and cruise to their hotels. Avoid the front seats.

If you have more time: The **Beisi (North Temple) Pagoda** at the north end of Renmin Road, is nine stories and 76 meters high, the tallest pagoda south of the Changjiang River, first built in the 10th century.

Han Shan (Cold Mountain) Temple 寒山寺 , 10 km west of the Nanlin Hotel, was the home of two Tang monks, Han Shan and Shide. To the right of the central, gold Sakyamuni Buddha is Wu Nan, the young disciple who wrote the sutras; the older man is disciple Ja Yeh. The original bell was stolen by Japanese pirates but replaced with a bell cast about 100 years ago as a gift from Japan. Originally built in the Liang dynasty (sixth century), the current buildings are Qing.

C.I.T.S. organizes special excursions to hear the bronze bells here on midnight Dec. 31, New Year's eve. If one hears the bells chime 108 times on this night, one should have few troubles in life! Monks chant and pray for guests. Lion and dragon lantern dances. Open 7 p.m. to 1 a.m. on this occasion.

Xiyuan (West Garden) Temple 西园 (Liuyuan Rd.) is also very beautiful. Near the Han Shan Temple, it is the largest group of Buddhist buildings in Suzhou. It was originally built in the 16th century but was destroyed by fire, and rebuilt in 1892.

The ceiling in the main building is magnificent—bats (happiness) and cranes (long life) as in Beijing's Forbidden City. The central Buddhas are seven meters tall, including base and mandala. Behind the Buddhas to the right is the Bodhisattva of Wisdom, with a crown on his head. To the left is the Bodhisattva of Universal Benevolence.

The 500 arhats here are worth studying, each face so real, expressive, profound, individual. Outstanding is the crazy monk, who can look sad, happy, or wry, depending on the angle at which you see him. Gilded on modeled clay, each statue is larger than life. But can you find any women? Enjoy those incense burners. At the time of the Great Leap Forward (1958–60) and backyard furnaces, they were supposed to be smelted. But the C.I.T.S. director said no!

Look also for the five-colored carp and giant soft-shelled turtles in the pond in the back garden.

The 16 colored arhats in the **Zijin (Purple Gold) Nunnery** are older (Song) and said to be better than those in the West Garden Temple. The **Twin Pagodas** 双塔寺 , almost in the middle of Suzhou, are known as the big and small "brushes" (used by Confucius for writing). They were built in the Song in honor of the sage.

The **Xuan Miao Guan (Mysterious Wonder Taoist Temple)** in the middle of the city has been described as the tallest, most magnificent temple in the area and probably in China. Do you agree? Three giant, gilded sculptures of the founders of Taoism dominate. Originating in the Jin (A.D. 265–420), the temple's current central Sanqing Hall was built in the Southern Song.

The **Confucius Temple** 孔庙 looks very big and impressive and is now the Stele Museum of Suzhou. Inside are hundreds of steles.

Lingyan (Divine Cliff) Hill 灵岩, 14 km west of the city, is very important to Buddhists. It is topped by a seven-story pagoda, probably Qing. The pagoda is at the site of the palace built by Fu Chai, King of Wu, for his beautiful queen, Xi Shi. A Buddhist college is in the 25-meter-high Lingyan Temple. At the foot of the hill is the ancient town of Mu Tu, founded during the Wu.

The **Suzhou Embroidery Research Institute** 苏州刺绣研究所 is not a factory. It trains young people to do embroidery, develops new embroideries (new stitches, new materials; for example, human hair), and creates masterpieces in thread for places like Beijing's Great Hall of the People.

The **Suzhou Museum** (Dongbei St.) was the site of the official residence of a Royal Prince of the Taiping troops. First built in 1860.

Theatrical, Musical Instruments, Embroidery, Silk, and Folk Custom Museums have opened. Most are in or near the North Pagoda Temple and are worth a visit. The theatrical museum is in the fancy old Shaanxi Provincial Guild Hall in the south of the old walled city. The folk arts museum has a piece with Prince Charles and Princess Diana back to back. A Silk Festival takes place in early September.

SHOPPING

Inkstones, brushes, jewelry, embroideries, silks, taditional musical instruments, antiques, iron reproductions of ancient relics, excellent prints of Suzhou, and reproductions of some of the arhats are available. This is one of the best places to buy sandalwood fans (always smell them to be sure) and rubbings. The **Suzhou Silk Garments Factory** has a 20-minute show of ancient and modern clothes and a wide selection of garments for sale. You should be able to get a 15% group discount. 46 Lu Jia Xiang, 215001. Tel. 771278, 772231. Other silk factories have demonstrations of how silk is made. **#Suzhou Cultural Relics Shop,** Leqiao, Renmin Rd., tel. 773851. **Handicraft Trade Centre,** 568 Renmin Rd. (near pagoda), tel. 771180.

Suzhou Sandalwood Fan Factory: 58 Dong Bei St. 215000; tel. 774982. **Friendship Store** 友谊商店 : 504 Renmin Rd., tel. 773524, 225218. 9:30 a.m. to 8 p.m. Other stores, 7:30 or 8:30 a.m.–6 or 7 p.m. **Mahogany Carving Factory,** tel. 772883. **Jade Carving Factory,** tel. 771869.

The best hotel here for tourists is the Bamboo Grove because of its garden architecture and location within the city wall. The best for business people is the Aster, west of the city wall in the new business district close to the exhibition hall. The Bamboo Grove has bigger rooms.

Bamboo Grove Hotel (Zhu Hui Fandian) • *Zhu Hui Rd., 215006. Aiming for 4*ᵗʰ. *Telex 363073 BGH SZ. Fax 778778. South of the Master of Nets Garden* • C.C. Lee Garden International management. 1990–91. 5 stories. 3 connecting buildings. 384 rooms. IDD. Gym. Sauna. Bicycles. Clinic. B.C. Executive floor, pool and USTV due soon.

Nan Lin Hotel (Fandian) • *20 Gun Xiu Fang, 215006. Telex 363063 NLHSZ CN. Fax 771028. Dist.R.W.10 km. Walk to Master of Nets Garden* • 1986. Ren. 1991. 3*. San Shiu Lou (main building), 7 stories, 212 rooms. IDD soon. B.C., Clinic. Great garden. Generally run-down. Dark.

Nanyuan Guest House (Binguan) • *249 Shi Quan St., 215006. 3*. Telex 363075 NYHSZ CN. Fax 778806* • C.C. (no Diners). Built before 1929, ren. 1990. 4 buildings. 120 rooms. Chinese furniture. Pool. IDD. B.C. Huge garden. Musty.

New World Aster Hotel (Yadu Dajiudian) • *156 Sang Xiang Rd. Aiming for 4*. *Fax 731838. Dist.R.W.6 km* • C.C. New World International Management. 1991. 29 stories, 410 rooms. Glitzy. Free shuttle. Outdoor pool and bowling soon. Clinic. B.C. Food Street with Cantonese, Chaozhou and Suzhou snacks.

Suzhou Hotel (Fandian) • *115 Shi Quan St., 215006. 3*. Telex 363002 SZTLX CN. Fax 771015. Dist.R.W.7 km* • C.C. 1992. 7 stories. 174 rooms. Clinic. B.C. 1958 building being renovated with IDD in rooms, gym, sauna and pool. Due 1993.

Suzhou Xucheng Hotel (Dasha) • *No. 120, Sanxiang Rd., 215004. 3*. Telex 363037 XCHSZ CN. Fax 731520. Close to Aster and more for budget business people. Dist.R.W.4 km* • 1989. Ren. 1992. 16 stories, 280 rooms. IDD. Clinic. B.C. Bit scruffy and dark.

OTHER IMPORTANT ADDRESSES

C.I.T.S. and **C.T.S.:** Suzhou Hotel, 115 Shiquan Rd. 215006. C.I.T.S. tel. 234646, 223063. C.T.S. tel. 321240, 224908. Telex 363028. SZCTS CN. Fax 773593.
CAAC 中国民航 : 192 Renmin Rd.; tel. 222788.
CYTS: tel. 222498, 221467.
Railway Booking Office: 203 Guanqian St.; tel. 226462, 224646.

Railway Station Information Service: tel. 772831.
Telephone Information: tel. 114.
Ambulance: tel. 222853.
Police: tel. 110.

TAI'AN 泰安

North China. About 80 km south of Jinan, the capital of Shandong, the closest airport. Access by road or rail usually combined with a visit to Qufu, 80 km away. Hottest time (36–37°C) briefly July and August; coldest December and January, minus 10°C. The annual precipitation is 700 mm, mainly from July to September. It is about 10°C colder at the top of the mountain. The best time to climb is from April to October, but one can climb all year round except in inclement weather. Urban population over 250,000.

Tai'an is where you go to ascend **Mt. Tai (Taishan)** 泰山 , one of China's Five Sacred Mountains. It is a 2.5 billion year old mountain, one of the oldest in the world. In ancient times, emperors came here to offer sacrifices to Earth and to Heaven. If they went up the mountain, they were probably carried up, and visitors today have the same choice by bus or taxi. If you have only one day, you can be driven halfway up to the **Zhongtian (Middle Celestial) Gate** 中天门 . Then you can take the 2078-meter-long suspended cable car almost to the top at **Nantian (Southern Celestial) Gate** 南天门 between 7 a.m. and 7 or 8 p.m. (no service during high winds.) From the top of the cable car to the summit at an altitude of 1,545 meters are 500 more steps. You can lunch at the hotel near the summit and then return to see the **Daimiao (Temple)** and a free market.

The longer, more satisfying way is to climb (at least one way) because the mountain has 30 old temples and 66 well-documented scenic spots, including beautifully carved memorial arches, Han dynasty cypress trees, white water, breathtaking views of forests and crags, and a stone pillar that looks suspiciously like a lingam. If you do it the hard way, you are following in the footsteps of Confucius!

The top can be reached in 5 or 6 hours on foot through the Path of

Eighteen Bends. Important to note are the 7000-plus stone stairs, each carefully placed by human labor! Like an almost vertical Great Wall! And they are not narrow! It is difficult to get lost. The stairs are very steep and in some places difficult to climb. The **Temple of Azure Clouds** is over 970 years old (Song). Note the bronze or iron roof ornaments, rafters, bells, and tiles of the main hall, made of metal to endure the severe mountain storms. Inside are nine huge gilt statues. Can you imagine having to carry these and the bronze Ming tablets up here! The summit is at **Tianzhu Feng (Heavenly Pillar Peak)**天柱峰, a.k.a. Yuhuang Ding (Jade Emperor Peak).

The **Tomb of Feng Yuxiang (Feng Yu-hsiang)** 冯玉祥墓 may be of interest to students of modern Chinese history. This was the famous "Christian General" who fought with the Nationalists against the Japanese and baptized his men with water hoses. His tomb is at the east end of the Dazhong Bridge, downhill from the Dragon Pool Reservoir. He is known more for his eccentricity than his military successes.

The 72 visiting emperors used to offer their sacrifices at the **Daimiao (Temple to the God of Taishan)** 岱庙, close to the Taishan Guest House at the base. On special occasions like the climbing Festival, a reenactment of the rituals as performed by Song Emporer Zhengzong have been presented and should not be missed at the impressive Daimaio. The **Tian Kuang Hall** 天贶殿, which is the main hall, has a mural 3.3 by 62 meters, painted in the Song, showing the pilgrimage of Song Emperor Zhenzong here. It includes 570 to 657 figures. (Count them!) This hall was built in A.D. 1009 and is considered one of the three eminent halls of China.

FESTIVALS

During the third or fourth lunar month, there is a festival on the summit. September 9–12 is the mountain climbing competition.

SHOPPING

Carpets and baskets are made locally. Peaches, walnuts, chestnuts, and dates are grown.

HOTELS

At the foot the best are the Overseas Chinese (better) and the Taishan Guest House. The best in the city is the Shenqi on the summit. If your schedule is tight and there is a strong wind threatening to cancel the cable car, better stay down below.

Taishan Guest House (Binguan) ● *Daizong Fang, Hongmen, 271000. 3☆. Telex 397005 TSTA CN. Fax 333837. Dist.R.W.4km* ● Ren. 1989. 5 stories, 111 rooms. Gym. Clinic.

Taishan Overseas Chinese Hotel (Huaqiao Dasha) • *Dongyue St. 271000. 3*. Fax 228171. Dist.R.W.3 km* • C.C. (No Diners). 1990. 14 stories, 204 rooms. Cantonese food.

Shenqi Hotel (Binguan) • *10 Tian St., 271000. 3*. Fax 223837* • C.C. About 2 km upward from top of cable car. 1991. Two stories, 102 rooms. IDD. Sauna. Great view. Seven restaurants, traditional medicine banquet. Clinic. Cantonese and Sichuan food. Sauna.

C.I.T.S. 中国国际旅行社 and **Taian Tourism Bureau:** 46 Hongmen Rd. 271000, above Dai Temple and the Taishan Arch; tel. 333259, 337020. Telex 397005. Fax 333837.
C.T.S.: tel. 338371.
Ambulance: tel. 334161, 334432.
Police: tel. 110.

TAISHAN 台山

(Cantonese, Toishan; Toishanese, Hoishan) South China. This place should not be confused with Taishan, the mountain in Shandong farther north, listed under Tai'an. Taishan is a county on the southern coast of Guangdong province, 146 km SW of Guangzhou and about 80 km, as the crow flies, west of Aomen (Macao). Taichen can be reached by road from Guangzhou in about 3 hours. A fast way to go there from Hong Kong is the 4-hour ferry to Guanghoi, and then bus or taxi. Weather: Subtropical. August is the hottest month, with a mean temperature of 28°C; January is the coldest, with a mean of 14°C. The annual precipitation is about 2000 mm, mostly from April to August. It can be very humid in summer. From this county many Chinese left their families for the Chinatowns of the United States and Canada. Many families here live off remittances. Population 980,000. See "Special for Overseas Chinese."

Visitors can go to a local market, visit cottage industries like embroidery, artistic ceramics, bamboo weaving, etc., or explore a village.

Near the Overseas Chinese Hotel is a statue of Chen Yu Hi   ,
a Chinese-American who returned to China to start in 1906 the first
railway line by a private company in China; 100 km. long, it was used
from 1912 to 1942 when it was destroyed by the Japanese. The old
railway station still standing nearby is patterned after one in Seattle at
the time. There is also a museum.

Taishan still retains a lot of its old over-the-sidewalk architecture
and charm. But things are changing.

On the outskirts of town is a 7-story Ming pagoda. **Stone Flower
Mountain** 石花山 , one of Taishan's eight scenic attractions, is about
2 km NE of the town, with an artificial lake and weird rock formations.

Shang Chuan Island's **Fei Sa Beach** 飞沙里 is about 64 km south
of Taichen, plus a 40-minute boat ride. It has 4 km of beach and clear
water. The inns there are not yet up to standard. Nearby are the St.
Francis Xavier Church 沙勿略墓 where the Jesuit died in 1552 (he
was buried in Goa), and a primeval forest inhabited by 3000 monkeys.
To the east is **Zhongshan County,** birthplace of Dr. Sun Yixian (Sun
Yat-sen).

Basically, the attractions are rural, of interest mainly to Overseas
Chinese looking for their roots, and other visitors wanting a restful ex-
posure to south China. It does not have magnificent temples and palaces.

FESTIVALS

Taichen has a unique festival (9th day of the 9th lunar month.)
During the Qing, a young scholar, angry that he could not get a state
post, buried his poems and articles in a tomb on one of the mountains.
Then he became successful. Ever since, people have been visiting the
tomb for luck.

RESTAURANTS

Taishan food is basically the same as Cantonese, but there are some
dishes that are unique, like mud fish, steamed minced pork with salted
egg, and peanuts fried with water chestnuts.

HOTELS

The top hotel is the Taishan, then the Garden, but don't expect
much. The postal code for the town is 529200.

Huaqiao (Overseas Chinese) Mansion ● *1, Tong Ji Rd., Taichen.
Cable 3307. Dist. bus station 1 km. Central near shops, sports field,
and man-made lake. ●* 1975; ren. 1988, 1990. Four stories, 66 rooms.
C.C., C.T.S. Budget travelers only.

Garden Hotel (Yuanlin Jiu Dian) • *529200. Dist. bus 1 km. Attractive garden-style hotel on edge of man-made lake at base of mountain* • C.C. 108 rooms. Hot spring water in all rooms. C.I.T.S. H.K.J.V. IDD. HKTV.

Stone Flower Mountain Inn (Shihua Shan Lu Guan) • *529200. Stone Flower Mountain, northeast edge of Taichen, in garden, beside mountain reservoir. Dist. bus station 1 km.* • No C.C. 7 buildings. 24 rooms. No meals except for groups. No carpets or room telephones. Slow if any laundry service. Local rural architecture. Mosquito nets. Fans.

In spite of crude facilities, many foreigners like this charming hotel because of its setting and closeness to the Chinese people. Living conditions here are actually better than in most Chinese homes where hot water never comes out of a tap. The Inn has classes for foreigners and local people, and free use of bicycles. Foreign students can teach English at the Inn to save money on expenses. Write Mr. Feng Yuan Chao at the Taishan Tour Co.

Taishan Hotel (Binguan) • *529200. 3*. Fax 22683.* • C.C. 1989–91. 12 stories. 80 small rooms. HKTV. IDD. B.C.

Ambulance: tel. 25824.
Police: tel. 110. **Fire:** tel. 119.
C.T.S. 中旅社 : 1 Tong Ji Rd. 529200; Tel. 24768.
Taishan Bureau of Travel and Tourism and **Taishan Tour Co.** • 19 Stone Flower Overseas Chinese Village, Huan Bei St., 529200. Tel. 25847, 29999.

An inexpensive minibus leaves the hotels for Guangzhou early in the morning.

太 原

TAIYUAN

North China. In the center of Shanxi province, of which it is the capital, Taiyuan is over an hour's flight SW of Beijing, and 2½ hours north of Guangzhou. Flights from 19 other cities. One can also arrive by train from Beijing, Xi'an, Zhengzhou, Hohhot, and Datong, etc. The hottest temperature is 35°C for a few days in August. The coldest is ⁻14°C in January. Annual precipitation is 400 mm from July to September. Altitude: 800 meters. Population is 2.05 million.

The city was founded in the Western Zhou (1066–771 B.C.) Because of its strategic location, it was the site of many wars, changing hands five times between A.D. 396 and 618. It was a silk center under the Sui and has been growing grapes for a thousand years. Although it used to be a highly cultured city with many architectural wonders, the wars and modern industry have changed its complexion.

Taiyuan is most famous for the **Jinci Temple** 晋祠 , 25 km SW of the city at the foot of Xuanweng Mountain. One source says it was started in the Northern Wei (386–534) in memory of the second son of King Wu of the Western Zhou. The Jin Temple was renovated, with additions, in 1102 (Northern Song). Female statues in temples, aside from goddesses, are very rare in China. Was this second son a lush? A son much pampered by women? Are the women here to continue indulging him in the after-life?

Alas, no! Centuries ago, Shanxi was very short of water. Sea and water deities have usually been female. In Shanxi a spring was found near Jinci, so people started worshiping Shuimu (Mother of Water). The maids-in-waiting and the mermaids were her retinue.

The temple is the oldest wooden structure in the area and is charming. In the **Shengmu (Sacred Lady Hall)** 圣母殿 are 43 dusty, life-size clay figures, 30 of these court maids-in-waiting, all lithesome, each different in expression, and still retaining much color. They were made in the Song.

Uphill from the Jinci about 40 minutes by road, the Tianlong Shan (Mountain of Celestial Dragon) has a little temple with four *lohan* and 24 small caves with many old, damaged statues.

The **Chongshan Monastery** 崇善寺 in the city itself is believed to have been a Sui palace once. Only part of the original (Tang) monastery is standing, and part of that is the Shanxi Provincial Museum. The monastery is famous for its ancient 1000-handed, 1000-eyed Goddess of Mercy. It, along with the two other bodhisattvas are eight meters tall. The beams and ceiling are quite remarkable. During the Sino-Japanese War, a bomb went through the ceiling without exploding, and the repair work is still visible. It is 3 km from the Yingze Hotel.

Next door is the **Shanxi Provincial Museum** 山西省博物馆 . Museum #1 has a vast collection of neolithic artifacts. So far, 200 paleolithic and 500 neolithic sites have been unearthed in the province, plus over 500 tombs and other ancient ruins. The museum is closed on Mondays.

Provincial Museum #2 is considered more important than Museum #1. It is at the site of the Chunyang Palace on the west side of May 1 Square. The palace itself was built between 1573 and 1619, and renovated in the Qing. It contains 20 exhibition halls with ceramics, bronzes, carvings, lacquer, calligraphy, embroidery, books, and other documents unearthed around the province. There is also a huge coal museum.

The **Shuangta Temple**, a.k.a. the Yongzuo Monastery, has twin pagodas, symbols of Taiyuan, 8 km from the Yingze Hotel. The pagodas were built in the Ming and are over 50 meters high. They are octagonal and built of carved bricks. Inside the monastery are exhibitions of old coins, pottery, etc., and a corridor with 207 stone tablets of Ming calligraphy.

In Shanxi province are also a great number of important historical monuments; 70 km southwest is the **Qiao Family Compound** and **folk museum,** originally the home of a wealthy Qing merchant. This is highly decorated with carvings. In the southern tip is *Yong Le Palace 永乐宫 in **Ruicheng County,** with 400-meter-long Yuan dynasty murals, artistically beautiful. From it, one can also study social and architectural history. Nearby in **Yuncheng County** is the **Guan Di Temple,** founded in the Sui and completely renovated in the Qing. **Pingyao** 平遥 , about

100 km SW of Taiyuan, is a well-preserved ancient city with 6.7 km of city walls, and shops and homes untouched since the Ming and Qing.

At **Hongdong,** about 200-km SW of Taiyuan, is the ***Guangsheng Temple,** listed as Yuan and Ming. It has excellent colored ceramic figures and frescoes. An intricate, stunning collection of about 1000 lively Buddhist and animal figures over 300 years old is at the **Xiaoxitian (Miniature Western Paradise),** NW of Guangsheng Temple and north of Xixian county town. These are also worth a visit. Be prepared to climb and crane your neck. Take a flashlight and binoculars.

***Dingcun** 丁村 paleolithic ruins are in Xianfen county, roughly 25 km SW of Hongdong. Also in this area is a Han (nationality) folk museum, with 19 Ming and Qing courtyards, the oldest built in 1593. **Houma,** another 50 km SW of Linfen, is a Jin site from the Eastern Zhou. A low but spectacular (depending on the season) waterfall is at **Hukou** on the Yellow River, northeast of Dingcun. Guesthouses are at Yuncheng City. One could spend a fruitful month exploring this province alone! Much of the Chinese collection in Toronto's Royal Ontario Museum is from Shanxi.

See "Datong" for the Yungang Grottoes, the Great Wall, Wutai Mountain, Sakyamuni Pagoda, and the Huayan and Shanhua Monasteries. See "Hengshan" for the Mid-Air Temple.

SHOPPING

Locally made are fur coats, including rabbit and wild rat(!) skin, gold and lacquer inlaid crafts, reproductions of ancient ironware, black-glazed porcelain, Junco brand carpets, Fen Chiew wines, vinegar, fine glassware, lacquerware, jade carving, and brass and copperware (especially fancy charcoal-burning hot pots). Grown locally are dates, pears, persimmons, walnuts, and wild jujubes.

There is a **Friendship Store** (tel. 440593); Taiyuan also has an antique shop, arts and crafts shop, bazaars, and department stores.

RESTAURANTS

Shanxi people love noodles and vinegar-flavored dishes. The **Jin Yang Restaurant** (1 Binzhou Rd., tel 442710) is known for Shanxi food, especially noodles and Shanxi duck. **Cooks' Training Centre** (16 Food St., tel. 228772) has special cakes. **Qingheyuan Restaurant** has Mongolian hot pot and mutton. Five hundred-meter-long Food Street, in the southern part of the city, has 46 food shops and restaurants.

HOTELS

Avoid the Airport Hotel!

Shanxi Grand Hotel ● *5 South Xin Jian Rd. 030001; telex 282037 SGHTL CN. Fax 443525. 3*● 1989. 168 rooms. Better.*

Yingze Hotel ● *51 Yingze St. 030001. 2* 17 km from airport* ● 1976; renovated 1984. 596 beds. Telex room.

Ambulance: tel. 440025
Police: tel. 110
CAAC 中国民航 : 38 Yingze St.; tel. 442903.
C.I.T.S. 中国国际旅行社 : Room 112, Yingze Hotel 030001; tel. 441155 telex 28009 ITSTY CN. Fax 441155.
C.T.S.: Yingze Guest House, tel. 443377; telex 28001 ITSTY CN.
CYTS: tel. 447106.
Shanxi Prov. Tourism Administration: No. 5 Wun Yun Lane, 030001. Tel. 227201, 447525. Complaints and suggestions.
Shanxi Overseas Tourist Co.: fax 442923.

TANGSHAN 唐山

North China, NE of Tianjin in Hebei province. Tangshan was almost completely destroyed by an earthquake in 1976; 240,000 people were killed. Much has since been rebuilt, and it is back in business as an industrial center noted for porcelain. It is not a tourism center but a museum about the earthquake can be visited. C.I.T.S. is in the Tangshan Hotel, Jianshe Bei Rd., 063000. Tel. 22210 X 534. Fax 28612.

TIANJIN 天津

(Tientsin; Ferry to the Imperial Capital) North China. 1.5 hours (120 km) By train SE of Beijing, 70 km from the Bohai Sea. Joined by superhighway to Beijing. On the Beijing-Shanghai and the Beijing-Harbin railway lines. Flights from Hong Kong and 9 Chinese cities. Ships from Inchon (Korea), Kobe (Japan), Dalian, Yantai, Qingdao, and Shanghai (708 nautical miles). Coldest: January, ‾6°C; hottest: July, 40°C. Annual precipitation averaging 600 mm, mostly June–August. Urban Population: 3.34 million. China's third largest city.

Tianjin is more of a gateway to elsewhere than a tourist destination in itself, though interest in the Last Emperor has brought tourists here. It is a port city, the largest commercial seaport in North China. One of the treaty ports open to foreign trade by the Opium Wars, it is now one of China's biggest industrial centers and one of the 15 Open Coastal Cities. It has China's first free trade zone. It was also the home of the Last Emperor from 1925 to 1931.

It is mainly for business travelers but in between appointments, there are things to do in addition to golf. For tourists, it is worth a two-day stop, one for city attractions and one for excursions outside. Resident foreigners say it is a good place to live because the people are friendlier and more polite than in Shanghai and Beijing, and the sightseeing is less crowded. Many of Beijing's foreign residents drive the two hours to Tianjin on weekends for a change of pace.

Tianjin was a trading post in the 12th century during the Jin. It developed as a port in the Yuan. During the Ming (1404), city walls were built and the city was called Tianjinwei by the Duke of Yen, who crossed the Haihe River here on a military expedition. After the Grand Canal opened in 1412, inland commerce and Tianjin's fortunes improved. A city wall was built about this time, and an imposing old fort once stood at the confluence of the three rivers.

Tianjin was invaded by the British and French in 1858. In June of that year the Treaty of Tientsin was signed. Christian missionaries were given freedom of movement, and the Chinese were forced to guarantee the protection of missionaries because "the Christian religion as professed by Protestants and Roman Catholics inculcates the practices of virtue, and teaches man to do as he would be done by.'' In 1860 British and French troops from Tianjin marched on Beijing. They forced the Qing rulers to ratify the Treaty of Tientsin and burned down the Summer Palace. The resulting Treaty of Peking opened Tianjin and nine other ports to foreign trade.

Nine countries eventually controlled over 3500 acres of this city: Britain (with over 1000 acres), France, Germany, Japan, Russia, Italy, Belgium, Austria, and the United States. The concessions lasted from 20 to 80 years and, as in Shanghai, left the Chinese some very interesting old European architecture as well as bitter memories. The Treaty of Peking also forced the Chinese to permit French missionaries to own or rent property anywhere, and further helped to inflame smoldering anti-Christian and anti-foreign resentment.

Many of these feelings resulted from what the Chinese saw as Christian arrogance, which insisted that the Christian God was the only true God. Added to this were cultural misunderstandings. Quite a few Chinese actually believed that the children in Catholic orphanages were either eaten by nuns or ground up for medicine. The French Catholics did pay money for female babies (to keep them from being killed). By 1870 the atmosphere was so tense that after the French consul fired at a minor Chinese official, the consul was immediately hacked to death. Ten nuns, two priests, and another French official were also brutally killed in what is now known as the Tientsin Massacre, or what the Chinese prefer to call the Tientsin Revolt. The tragedy might not have happened if all Christian missionaries had refused to become arms of western imperialism.

In 1976 it was severely damaged by an earthquake centered in nearby Tangshan.

Tianjin today, like Beijing and Shanghai, is a municipality directly under the central government. It has eight urban and four rural districts and five suburban counties. Its factories make Flying Pigeon bicycles, Seagull watches, petrochemicals, textiles, diesel engines, etc. The Dagang Oil Field is 60 km away. Tourists would probably be interested in seeing its arts and crafts factories. Its counties grow walnuts, chestnuts, dates, Xiaozhan rice, and prawns. Cultural presentations here sometimes include traditional opera, Beijing Opera, Tianjin ballet, acrobats, and puppets.

The city proper sprawls on both sides of the Hai River. The area immediately SW of Jiefang (Liberation) Bridge was formerly French. The section south of that, around the Astor Hotel, was formerly British. Liberation Road was Victoria Road. It is smoggy with industries, of interest primarily to fans of old European architecture, modern history, and handicrafts.

There is enough in the city for over 2 days depending on your interest. The **Dabei (Grand Mercy) Temple** (Tianwei Rd., near the Grand Canal) is the city's biggest Buddhist temple, founded in 1656 (Qing). The **Grand Mosque** (Dafeng Rd., near the Grand Canal) was built in 1644 (Qing). The **Tianjin History Museum** 天津厂史博物馆 (4 Guanghua Rd.; tel. 414660) contains exhibits on the ancient and revolutionary histories of Tianjin, and has some bronzes, jade, paintings, and calligraphy.

The **Tianjin Arts Museum** (77 Jiefang Bei Rd.; tel. 382484) has sculptures and other traditional works of art from ancient times. The **Tianjin Museum of Natural History** 自然博物馆 (Machangdao, Hexi Dist.; tel. 318031) has fossils of mammoths and dinosaurs.

The **Friendship Club** 友谊俱乐部 (268 Machang Dao) was built in 1925. It is open to both Chinese and foreigners. Formerly the Tientsin Club, it reeks of Britain in the early 1900s, with beautiful, high mahogany paneling and a drab, dismal interior. There are billiards, badminton, tennis, four bowling lanes, a 1300-seat theater, a 600-seat banquet hall, and a ballroom with an "elastic" wooden floor. (Real springs are beneath it.) Swimming is in a 33°C mineral-water pool.

Ningyuan Park is in the classic Chinese style. Originally built for Cixi, the Qing Empress Dowager, it is on 54 hectares. Its Beijing Restaurant specializes in roast pork with sesame seeds.

The **Zhou Enlai (Chou En-lai) Museum** 周恩来纪念馆 is in the western part of the city, south of the Grand Mosque. The former premier studied at Nankai Middle School here from 1913 to 1917, and briefly at Nankai University (1919), where he led student uprisings before going to France in 1920. Tel. 222703.

Near **Food Street** is **Ancient Culture Street** 古文化街 in Qing dynasty style, and an A.D. 1326 **Temple of the Sea Goddess.** But it is nothing like Beijing's Liulichang or Nanjing's Confucian Temple area. We found nothing much to buy (except in its well-stocked antique shop). Do let us know if this has changed. But festivals are held on Ancient Culture St., with stilt and dragon dances and special exhibits: ask C.I.T.S. for the dates of the Spring Festival, the Folk Art Show Competition, the Harvest Celebration, and the Workers' Cultural Season.

On the last Sunday of October every year is the International Marathon.

The **Theater Museum** is a "must" for theatre lovers. The building itself is a gem in the gaudy south China style, a guild hall for Guangdong merchants built in 1907. 31 Nanmennei St., Nankai Dist. Tel. 253443, 255017.

The **Catholic Cathedral** is next to the International Market. We found a French-speaking person inside who showed us around. Well worth the effort. Tel. 701929.

The Last Emperor Pu Yi lived in the **Zhang Yuan Garden** and the **Jing Yuan Garden,** and was an honorary member of the **Tientsin**

Club (now the Friendship Club). No other Chinese were allowed to be members then.

Factories

Tianjin is a good place to visit arts and crafts factories.

The **No. 2 Carpet Factory** (Jie Fang South Rd., He Xi District. Tel. 282113) is one of the biggest carpet factories here, and makes Junco-brand carpets. Carpets have been made for more than 100 years in Tianjin, thick carpets of pure wool, with no synthetics. Knots are made by hand, either 70 rows per square foot (ordinary) or 120 rows (refined). Embossing is also done by hand. Washing in a chemical solution adds gloss.

Visitors allergic to dust or wool should avoid carpet factories.

Tianjin Painted Sculpture Workshop (202 Machangdao, Hexi Dist.; tel. 319866); **Tianjin Special Handicrafts Factory** (116 Hongxing Rd., Hedong Dist.; tel. 242172, 43475); **Yangliuqing New Year Picture Society** (111 Sanheli, Tonglou, Hexi District; tel. 314843). New year's pictures of deities, like the Kitchen God, who informed Heaven of what happened during the year in the family were put up traditionally each lunar new year. These pictures are much brighter and more cheerful than traditional Chinese art.

Silk carpets are made in Wuqing county, about 28 km north.

EXCURSIONS FROM TIANJIN

Beidaihe seaside resort, 3½ hours NE by train—see separate listing.

Beijing—see separate listing.

Chengde—see separate listing.

Qing Tombs, about 3 hours' drive NE. See "Zunhua."

***Dule (Temple of Solitary Joy)** 独乐寺 , 120 km north, about 2 hours' drive, is in the western part of **Jixian city** and can be combined with a trip to Panshan Mountain and the Great Wall in one day. It was founded in the Tang. Its Guanyin (Goddess of Mercy) Hall and the Gate to the Temple were rebuilt in A.D. 984 (Liao). The magnificent Guanyin Hall, 23 meters high, is the oldest existing multistoried wooden structure in China. The 16-meter-high, 11-headed goddess is one of the largest clay sculptures in China. The mythical animals at the gate are the oldest extant *chiweis* in China!

The **Yuyang Guesthouse** 渔阳宾馆 is a 104-room hotel in Jixian. 1980. Chinese food, but Western breakfasts. Fourteen courtyards.

The **Panshan (Screen of Green) Mountain** 盘山 (about 100 km north of Jixian County City in Tianjin Municipality) has been a mountain resort since the Tang. Highest peak is 1000 meters above sea level, on top of which is a pagoda said to contain a tooth of Buddha. Famous for its scenery, unusual rocks, and pines. It also has a lake. Its 70

Buddhist temples were burned by the Japanese during World War II. Some of the buildings have been replaced or renovated.

The **Great Wall** in Jixian County should have a museum by now and a hotel. See also "Great Wall."

SHOPPING

The main shopping streets are Binjiang Dao and Heping Road. Made in Tianjin are wool carpets, painted clay figurines by Master Zhang, New Year pictures, porcelain vases, tablecloths, accordians, cloisonne pens, soccer balls, basketballs, kites, and inlaid, lacquered furniture.

Friendship Store 友谊商店 (264 Binjiang Dao, Heping Dist.; tel. 251637): All of the above, plus jewelry, jade, ivory, fur coats, and hats, suede coats, padded silk jackets, men's suiting, shell work, cloisonne, carved lacquer, screens, inlaid chests, cork and boxwood carvings. Shipments can be made internationally; **Tianjin First Friendship Store** (21 Youyi Rd., Hexi Dist.; tel. 319073, 334505). This store has almost everything imaginable on four stories but it is not exceptional. Also ships purchases, tailors, arranges certificates of origin, mail orders, and books tickets for trains, ships, and airplanes; **Painted Sculpture Studio** (270 Machang Dao; tel. 36203); **Quanyechang Emporium** (290 Heping Rd.; tel. 703771); **Wenyuange Antique Store** (263 Heping Rd.; tel. 703450); **Yangliuching New Year's Picture Studio:** Good prices for scrolls, reproductions, and prints. See factory, above; **#Tianjin Cultural Relics Co.**, 161 Liaoning Rd., tel. 701461. Branches in Friendship Hotel, and Astor Hotel.

We found the **International Market** too crowded, confusing, and its goods badly displayed. But some shoppers might thrive in it.

RESTAURANTS

The Nanshi Food Street has three stories of shops, restaurants, wine shops, and tea houses. The food here is from all over China and abroad, and includes typical Tianjin snacks such as *goubuli* (steamed meat dumpling), *erduoyan* (fried cake), and *shibajie* (deep-fried dough twist).

HOTELS

The top luxury-class hotels here are the Hyatt, Sheraton, and Crystal Palace with the cheaper, older Friendship Hotel still popular with business people on a budget. The new Geneva Hotel (30 Youyi Rd., 3☆) is in the World Economic Trade and Exhibition Centre (TWTC).

The Hyatt and the Friendship have good locations for business people within walking distance of government offices and foreign trade corporations. The Astor and Tianjin First are almost adjacent to the Hyatt and are also a cheaper, less luxurious alternative.

The Sheraton, Crystal Palace and InterTech are close together with the state guest house in the south suburbs, with more space and greenery, and nearer TWCC, C.I.T.S., and Friendship Store. These are also closer to the development zone and harbor.

In Tanggu, next to the Economic and Technology Development Region, there is a swimming beach. The best hotel appears to be the Victory.

Astor Hotel • *33 Taier Zhuang Rd. 300042. 3*. Telex 23266, 23268 ASHTL CN. Dist.A.P.30 km. Dist.R.W.4 km. On Haihe River.* • C.C. Hong Kong management, British built. 1900, Expanded in 1924, ren. 1992. Old wing, where Dr. Sun Yat-sen and President Hoover slept, has 93 big rooms. Old flavor. 1987 wing looks good. 7 stories, 120 rooms. IDD. B.C. For budget travelers.

Crystal Palace Hotel (Shui Jing Gong Fan Dian) • *Youyi and Binshui Rd., 300016. 4*. Fax 310591. Telex 23277 TCPPH CN. By East Lake. Dist. A.P.17 km. Dist. R.W.8 km.* • 1987–88. 7 stories, 346 rooms. 7-story lobby. Striking, ultra modern palacial architecture deserves a visit. Built in five sections to withstand earthquakes. Beautifully set coffee shop. IDD, C.I.T.S. Health club. Pool. Skates for rent. Non-smoking floor. Art deco decor in rooms. C.C., bicycles, B.C.

Friendship Hotel (Youyi Binguan) • *94 Nanjing Rd. 300040. Telex 23265 TFH CN. Fax 310372. Dist.A.P.22 km. Dist.R.W.4 km.* • C.C. 1977. 9 stories, 209 rooms. Should have IDD now. B.C.

Hyatt Tianjin (Kai Yue Fandian) • *198 Jiefang Bei Rd. 300042. 4*. Telex 23270 HYTJN CN. Fax 311234. Dist.A.P.20 km. Dist.R.W.3 km. On bank of Haihe River.* • Primarily business travelers. C.C., bicycles. USTV. 1986, ren. 1990. 19 stories, 420 rooms. IDD. B.C. Health center. Non-smoking area in coffee shop. Regency Club. Cantonese and Japanese food.

InterTech Hotel (Kejizixun Da Sha) • *25 Youyi Rd., He Xi District 300201. 2* or 3*. Telex 23332 ISTCC CN. Fax 319391. Dist.A.P. 10 km. Dist. R.W. 5 km* • C.C. 1987. 8 stories, 100 small but adequate rooms. Apartments. IDD. B.C. USTV due soon. For budget travelers only.

InterTech is a business consulting agency.

Sheraton Tianjin Hotel • *Zi Jin Shan Rd., He Xi Dist. 300042. 4* Telex 23353 SHTJH CN. Fax 318740. Dist.A.P. 15 km. Dist.R.W. 8 km. Near free market, Yanyuan Gardens, Friendship Club* • C.C. 1987. 6 stories, 282 rooms. Bicycles. 6-story atrium lobby. B.C. Unlike other hotels, reservations held only until 4 p.m. Gym, pool.

Tianjin First Hotel (Diyi Fandian) • *158 Jie Fang Rd. 300040. 2*. Telex 23265 TFH CN. Fax 313341. Dist.A.P.14 km. Dist.R.W.4 km.* • No credit cards. Built 1924 as Talati Hotel and still has original elevator alongside new Otis. Newer 1987 section has better rooms. 6 stories, 98 rooms and 20 suites. Mainly for budget travelers. IDD.

Victory Hotel (Shengli Binguan) • *11 Jin Tang Rd., Tanggu Dist. 3*. Telex 23375 TJYH CN. Fax 984470, 984270. Dist.A.P.30 km. Dist.R.W. 1 km* • 1987. 15 stories, 298 rooms. C.C. (no Diner's), IDD, B.C. H.K.J.V. Pool, tennis, bowling, gym, sauna.

OTHER IMPORTANT ADDRESSES
AT&T: Tianjin Phone Center.
Airport 飞机场
CAAC 中国民航售票处 : 242 Heping Rd.; tel. 704045, 705888.
C.I.T.S.: 22 Youyi Rd., 300074. Tel. 312619, 314831. Telex 23281 TJITS CN. Fax 312619. Phone for sub-branches in hotels.
C.T.S.: 22 Youyi Rd., 300074. Tel. 318974. Telex 23281 TJITC CN. Fax 312619. 198 Jiefang Rd.; tel. 318974. Telex 23265 TFH CN.
CYTS: tel. 809814.
Tianjin International Golf Club: Northwest, Tianjin Airport, tel. 249391.
Tianjin Tourism Bureau, 18 Youyi Rd., 300074. Tel. 318812. Telex 23281 TJITS CN. (Complaints.)
Tourism Hotline: tel. 318814 (day); 318812 (night).
Xingang (New Harbor) 新港 : 50 km from Tianjin. Has Friendship Store, hotel, and Seamen's Club. Accessible by train or road.

TURPAN 吐鲁番

(Turfan). Northwest China. Northeast Xinjiang province, roughly 198 km SE of the capital Urumqi. It can be a 3-day tour by road or train from the capital and should include Gaochang, Jiaohe, the Baziklic Caves, Astana Tombs, Imin Minaret and Karez Wells. It can also be reached from Lanzhou by road or rail. An airport, 90 km away, is planned. Weather: The hottest in China! Turpan is in the Turpan Basin, which is known as ''the oven.'' Temperatures reach over 40°C in summer. Rainfall averages 16.6 mm a year, and in very dry years, it has been 4 mm. Strong winds blow more than 30 days a year. The hot air from the basin and cold air from the north create violent storms. In winter, people could wear fur coats in the morning, light clothes at noon, and dine in the evenings around hot stoves. The temperature has hit −17°C in January. For summer nights, one needs a sweater. It is an area of extremes. Weather people and geographers would love it. The best time to visit is late May–Oct. Sandstorms April and early May. The lowest point of the basin is Aydingkol Lake, its water surface 154 meters below sea level. It is second only to the Dead Sea as the lowest body of water in the world. Nearby is Bogda Mountain with an altitude of 5445 meters. **But wait! Don't stop reading!** Some of the people who have been there say the dust and the plumbing are worth it! Population 200,000, mostly Uygurs.

Turpan was once an oasis on the Silk Route. An oasis? Yes, an oasis! It existed then and now because of subterranean water from the 2000-year-old **Karez wells** 坎儿井. During the Western Han (206 B.C.–A.D. 24), soldiers were sent to develop agriculture here. Some sources say the technology for the wells came from Shaanxi province. Other historians say farther west, as the word is Persian. In any case, the wells are most common in Turpan and nearby Hami, to the east.

In spring, snow from the Tianshan Mountain melts, and this water flows into the Turpan Basin. While a lot of this evaporates, some water does soak into the ground and is stored in vast natural underground reservoirs reached by sloping channels tapped in turn by the wells. You can see the desert dotted with lines of wells.

Modern irrigation methods based on these wells have transformed Turpan into an agricultural area. Californians, and anyone else who has made deserts produce food, should be fascinated. Cultivated here are grain, grapes, cotton, and the famous Hami melons. Grapes have grown here for 2000 years. The vineyards are north of the city. The wooden huts with the holes are for drying the September-harvested seedless raisins in the hot, dry air. Ask to see the drying process. Hami melons are much in demand. They have a sweet perfume somewhat like face powder, with the texture of cantaloupe and taste of honeydew.

Turpan is also a good place to experience the different cultural minorities. **Uygur (Uighur)** 维吾尔族 and **Hui** 回族 nationalities live here with the Han.

The dry climate has meant the preservation of historical monuments. The area has many ancient tombs, Buddhist grottoes, and the ruins of ancient cities.

The ghost city of ***Gaochang** 高昌故城 , 40 km SE of Turpan, was capital of the State of Gaochang (500–640) and reached its peak in the ninth century, with a population of 50,000. Try to imagine it then. It was on the Silk Road and flourished from the first century B.C. to the 14th A.D., during which the first king of Gaochang married the Sui emperor's daughter and Gaochang was captured by Mongolians. Here were once 30 to 40 monasteries! The buildings were made of mud bricks and are now without roofs. Take a donkey cart if it's too hot to walk. Did it only decline with the Silk Road?

Eight km from Gaochang are the **Astana Tombs** 阿斯塔娜古墓, dating from the third century to about the eighth A.D. This is where 500 mummies, plus their belongings, were found, along with 2100 documents and books. Take a flashlight. Visitors routinely see only a couple of Tang mummies in a dark room. Where are the others? The dry weather preserved the bodies with still discernable eye lashes and eyeballs. Was Astana the Uygur capital? Astana means capital in Uygur.

*Jiaohe (a.k.a. Yarkhoto, and possibly Yaerhu) 交河故城 , 10 km west of Turpan, existed from the second century B.C. to the 14th A.D. Its mud brick buildings are better preserved than Gaochang's and were encompassed in an area 1.65 km × 0.3 km. It also had a population of 50,000. In the northwestern part are temple ruins with the remains of Buddhist images. There is also a rare brick Buddhist temple. Do take a donkey cart as the walk is long. Different in structure from Gaochang, the city was carved out rather than built. It was abandoned in the Ming for lack of water.

The 37-meter-high **Imim Minaret** 额敏塔 ,(1778) stands 2 km east of Turpan, its geometric patterns in the Uygur style. However, its smooth inverted-cone shape with rounded top is reminiscent of those towers south of New Delhi on the road to Agra. The ***Pazikelik (a.k.a. Baziklic, Bezeklik) Thousand-Buddha Caves** 柏孜克里克千佛洞 are

16 km NE of Turpan by dusty road on a cliff of the Flaming Mountains. About 80 of the grottoes are still intact but in poor condition, destroyed by looters, earthquakes, and archaeologists. Many of the murals were taken to the Berlin Museum in Germany and destroyed by bombs during World War II. (Read *Foreign Devils on the Silk Road*.) Faces were mutilated by Moslems. They were built over a period of 1400 years, starting in the Southern and Northern Dynasties (A.D. 420–550). Dunhuang's are more interesting and younger, but it is good to compare the two. The **Flaming Mountains** 火焰山 themselves are historical, so named because the incessant sun is supposed to make the red rocks seem on fire from a distance. Perhaps this happens at sunset just in the classic tale *Pilgrimage to the West*. In that story, the monkey king pushes a hot brick from the furnace of one of the Taoist immortals to stop Monk Xuanzhang from going to India. The mountains are 100 km long and 10 km wide, their highest peak 800 meters above sea level. Unless you know the story, this is just another set of hills and may not be worth a special stop. They are between the Caves and Turpan, in the hottest part of the depression.

Turpan also has a salt lake and therapeutic hot sands. It grows grapes with a 15 to 20% sugar content, among the best in China. Grapes grow almost everywhere, along streets and beside private homes. A 2.5-km grape corridor is between the center of the city and the Imam Minaret. Grape festival Aug. 20. Small museum near Turpan Hotel. The train station is 45 km from town at Daheyan.

The **Oasis** is the better hotel, with air conditioning, but neither is well-maintained.

Oasis Hotel (Liuzhou Binguan) • *41 Qinian, 838000. Telex 1696* • Terrible plumbing. Food not bad but cold. Our tablecloth was not changed for six meals, even though soiled.

Turpan Tourist Hotel (Binguan) • *Qingnian Rd. 838000. Dist.A.P. 30 min.* • 1986. 5 stories. Uygur staff.

C.I.T.S. and **C.T.S.:** Oasis Hotel, tel. 2907. Fax 22768. Telex 79133. TFBTH CN.

URUMQI 乌鲁木齐

(Urumchi) Pronounced Oo-roo-*moo*-chi. Northwest China. This capital of Xinjiang (Sinkiang) Uygur Autonomous Region, an area one sixth of China's total, borders on the Soviet Union and Mongolia. It can be reached by plane from Beijing (over 3 hours), Lanzhou (3 hours) and Shanghai (4½ hours). Flights also from Istanbul, Sharjah, Alma Ata Kazakhstan, and 24 Chinese cities. It can be reached by train from Xining and Lanzhou, but from the Qinghai capital, it is about 1600 km. The Beijing-Urumqi express covers almost 4000 km, the longest train ride in China. A railway to the Soviet Union via Altay Mountain pass should be ready in 1992. Urumqi is at an altitude of 650 to 910 meters and is surrounded by mountains. Weather: Hottest in August, 40.9°C. Coldest in December, ‾41.5°C. However, the coldest in August has been .5°C. Pack for cold summer nights. In May and June, the coldest has been ‾8.9°C and ‾4.2°C! Consider yourself warned. Maybe you can use the weather as an excuse to buy a fur jacket! The annual precipitation is 200 mm. There is snow between November and March. The best time to visit is May–September. Population: 1.3 million urban, mainly Uygurs (Uighurs), but also Hans, Kazaks, Mongolians, and Huis. The city has 13 nationalities, the province 47.

Urumqi dates from the Han, but its attractions are its people and the scenery. It has been described as an ugly Russian-looking city. **Tianshan (Heaven Mountain)** 天山 and **Lake Tianzi (Heavenly Lake)** 天池 , 115 km south of the city, is about 1980 meters above sea level and colder than Urumqi. We had snow in early May. Take something extra for warmth, especially if you want to climb. Tianzi has beautiful scenery but the boat trip on the lake could have been missed as nothing different could be seen. Our visit to a minority yurt was not well planned. No spiel. The lake is 5 square km and 100 meters deep. An ancient **glacier** 冰山 , about 100 meters thick, 2 km by 5 km, sprawls near ice caves and valleys. But visitors are frequently too cold to stay to explore. This area might look like the Rockies or Switzerland. But did you ever see a yurt and prancing camels near Lake Louise?

About 75 km south of Urumqi is the **Nanshan Pasture** 南山草原 —mountains, valleys, fountains, waterfalls, and cypress and pine trees. The pasture is in Kazak country (not related to Cossacks). Horseback riding, mountaineering, and digging for valuable ginseng roots are listed among the attractions. Here, if you are lucky—or unlucky—you might find a game of polo played with an initially live goat instead of a ball! Shades of Afghanistan! You might be able to dine and/or sleep in a yurt. Barbecued mutton drowned by tea with mare's milk has been offered to some groups. Here it is impolite to show the soles of your feet.

In the city itself, one usually visits the nine-story **Hong Ding Shan Ta (Red Hill Pagoda)** 江顶山塔 , founded in the Tang, the current building finished in 1788. From the design of the pagoda here, you should be able to see a resemblance to Indian stupas. This is about a 5-minute stop. The excellent **Xinjiang Museum** 新疆博物馆 has a collection of historical relics of the various nationalities living in the region. Exhibits include gold Roman coins, silver Persian coins, and other relics of the Silk Road. One hall contains murals; another displays 3200-year-old mummies. A special new exhibition hall displays ancient artifacts and the customs of 12 minorities in Xinjiang. The museum is good for 2 hours. Titles are in Chinese and English!

The **National Minorities Palace** 少数民族官 is good for its museum with costumes of the different groups, as well as a shop.

One of the highlights of Urumqi is the **Free Market/Bazaar** 自由市场 , which is near the hotel. You should find handicrafts there. Don't forget to haggle over prices! And close your eyes to the tempting fruit, ''bing'' pancakes, and spicy and delicious shish-kebobs there, unless you can see them being cooked. Tourists before you have gotten sick from eating from these stalls.

The different minority groups make for an interesting city. The Uygurs controlled NW China during the Tang. In A.D. 788, a Tang princess married a Uygur khan, by no means a love match. In subsequent years, Chinese silk and sugar were exchanged for Uygur horses and furs. Uygur cavalry often helped the Tang. Strangely enough, the Uygurs were the main supporters of the Manichaean religion (see ''Quanzhou''). The power of the Uygurs declined after their capital was sacked by the Kirghiz of Western Siberia. In 842, a food shortage turned the Uygurs into very aggressive raiders and China retaliated with force and the execution of Uygurs in Xi'an.

Other Important Destinations in Xinjiang: This is a huge region, the largest in China. It is much less populated than other parts of China, as a great deal of it is desert and mountain. Two cave temples are at **Baicheng** 拜城 and **Kuqa,** almost halfway in between Kashi and Urumqi. Kuqa has an airport. The ***Kezil/Kerzil Thousand Buddha Grottoes** at Kuqu are from the Han and have 236 grottoes. Xinjiang has at least

8 important groups of grottoes. Tour agencies also have land tours to Tibet and Pakistan.

For other caves and tourist attractions in the region, see "Silk Road," "Turpan," and "Kashgar." Ask about the Corban Festival, the Moslem New Year, with its songs, dances, horse races, courtship rituals on horseback, wrestling, and lamb snatching.

SHOPPING

Urumqi is just about the best place on the Silk Road to shop for minority handicrafts. These include carpets, decorated daggers, jewelry, embroidered caps, jade carving, embroidery, musical instruments, and fur and leather articles. Hand-knotted wool carpets in Persian designs are especially good buys but are probably cheaper in Pakistan. The Overseas Chinese Hotel has a good shop.

Urumqi General Carpet Rug Factory 乌鲁木齐地毯厂 (64 Jinger Rd.; tel. 25825, 53293). **Musical Instrument Factory** (Jiefang Rd.; tel. 23284). **Xinjiang Antique Store** (Jiefang Rd.; tel. 25161). **Jade Sculpture Factory** (jasper, topaz, crystal, Hotan jade; 68 Renmin Rd.; tel. 24528, 27897). **Urumqi Foreign Trade Carpets Factory** (14 Li Yu Shan Rd.; 830000.; tel. 416338, 412544.) Do ask about the handicrafts bazaar. The Friendship Hotel had a very nice, but small, mounted, autographed prints of camels.

FOOD

Local specialties include roast whole goat or sheep, kebabs, thin-skinned steamed buns with stuffing, fried rice (eaten with bare hands), deep-fried *nang,* mare's milk, and dried sour cheese. Local fruits include seedless white grapes, pears, Hami melons, apples, and raisins. The meat in Xinjiang is mainly mutton, because Moslems do not eat pork.

HOTELS

The best should be the Holiday Inn downtown. There is supposed to be a 3* Grand Hotel and the World Plaza Hotel somewhere but it wasn't found. The Overseas Chinese Hotel is downtown and not too bad. Backpackers stay at the Hongshan Hotel. Except for the joint-venture hotels, don't expect much.

Friendship Guesthouse (Youyi Binguan) • *Yan'an Rd., 830001. 2*. Fax 267791. Dist. A.P.28 km. The other side of town. Dist.R.W.8 km* • C.C. Large garden. Isolated. Two buildings. 1982 ren. 1992. 2 stories, 150 rooms. B.C. Needs work.

Holiday Inn Urumqi (Xinjiang Jia Ri Da Jiudian) • *53 Xinhua Bei Rd., 830002. Aiming for 3*. Telex 79161 XJGHP CN. Fax 217422.*

Dist.A.P.20 km. Dist.R.W.6km ● C.C. 1992. 25 stories, 383 rooms. Should have IDD, B.C., Moslem, Sichuan and Cantonese food, English pub, gym and sauna. Also solarium, Jacuzzi, golf simulator, tennis, USTV, and rooms for wheelchair travelers.

C.I.T.S. 中国国际旅行社 : 51 Xinhua Bei Rd. 830002; tel. 225913; telex 79108 CITSU CN. Fax 210689.
C.T.S.: 47 Xinhua Nan Rd. 830001; tel. 267238, 261130; Telex 79164 BOOTH CN. Fax 267131. Tours to Alma Ata and Tashkent.
CAAC: 62 Youhao Rd., tel. 77942, 78351.
CYTS: 227172, 2274380.
Xinjiang Overseas Tourist Corp.: 32 Xinhua Nan Rd. 830002; tel. 23782. Telex 79027 XJTC CN. Fax 78691.
Mountaineering: 72 Renmin Rd.; tel. 27072.
See also ''Silk Road.''

WEIFANG 潍坊

North China. Almost in the center of Shandong province, it is noted for its international kite festival (the first 5 days in April) every year, its unique kite museum and home stays. Twice weekly air connection with Beijing, more during the festival. Urban population 400,000.

There are Buddhist relics from the Sui and Tang dynasties here, and a 7.5 meter high stone ''Longevity'' character, the biggest such character in China, carved over 500 years ago. In **Shanwang** , southwest of the city, 18-million-year-old prehistoric fossils have been found. The **Shanwang Paleontological Museum** there has 10,000 specimens. Tourists can live with farming families in Shijiazhuang village.

But kites are the main draw and they are fun. One can visit the kite and woodblock print-making village of **Yangjiabu** to watch the process and see professional adult kite fliers testing their goods. One can buy a kite and learn flying techniques from the champions. One can explore the kite museum with room after room of the world's best kites from 350 m. long centipedes to tiny matchboxes that fly.

The festival itself draws 300,000 spectators. One should book early or go on a tour to ensure transportation and hotel. Chinapac (Canada) has had tours. Contestants have come from England, Germany and Holland.

Students of modern history might be interested in the Second Middle School, a little over a kilometer from the Weifang Hotel. This was once the Weihsien Concentration Camp. British, Canadian, and American prisoners of the Japanese there in the 1940s included Eric Liddell, the hero of the movie *Chariots of Fire*. A gold medalist in the 1924 Olympics for winning the 400 meters, this Scottish athlete refused to race on Sundays. He later became a Congregational missionary in China and died of a brain tumor in 1945. He was buried near the prison camp six months before the end of the war. Look for the seven-foot-high memorial stone in Chinese and English. Some of the original prison-missionary buildings are still standing.

A visit here might also be a good opportunity to see a school, and this one is typical, with few funds for construction, library, or teaching equipment. This school was founded by American Congregationalists in 1883, burned down by troops in 1901, and rebuilt with Boxer indemnity funds in 1918. Telephone foreign affairs office, 236901, or a travel agency, for appointment.

One of the food treats here is fried scorpions or cicadas, actually quite tasty. I've eaten three of each. Honest!

SHOPPING

Made locally are woodblock prints, kites, lacquer furniture inlaid with silver, cotton toys and bronze imitations.

The Weifang and Yuan Fei Hotels are neighbors, both near parks, a reconstructed Qing wall, fascinating decibel counter, and kite museum. Both have good food, but maintenane problems. Higher prices during festival. Dist.A.P.8 km. Dist.R.W.2.5 km.

Weifang Guest House (Binguan) • *131 Shengli St., 261041. 2*. Telex 324203 FAOWF CN* • No C.C. 1978. Back building for foreigners 1981, rcn. 1985 and maybe 1989. 2 stories, 23 rooms. Garden. High ceilings. Bicycles. No IDD. Dorms.

Yuan Fei Hotel (Dajiudian) • *127 Shengli St., 261041. 3*. Telex 324202 YFHWF CN. Fax 223840* • 21 stories. 225 rooms. AmEx and MasterCard only. Macao J.V. Quite good but needs work. USTV. Business center. Qigong. Has charming Chinese room with *kong* at no extra charge. This is the better hotel.

Ambulance: 236016.
Police: 236411.
C.I.T.S. and **C.T.S.:** 33 Shengli St., 261041 Tel. 233854, 224766. Telex 324203 FAOWF CN. Fax 233854.
Weifang Tourism Bureau: 125 Shengli 261041; tel. 226901. Fax 238688. (Complaints, etc.)

WEIHAI 威海卫

A.k.a. Wei-hai-wei North China. Northern Shandong province on the Bohai Sea 95 km east of Yantai and NE of Qingdao. Urban population 230,000. Hottest 28° C August; coldest minus 12° January. 70 mm. rain mainly August. This off-the-beaten track family vacation city can be reached by road or rail (soon), flights from Beijing and Jinan. Ferry from Dalian and Inchon, Korea.

Weihai was developed in the Ming because of its excellent harbor. Some of the funds to strengthen the navy base here were squandered by Empress Dowager Cixi on her Summer Palace in Beijing. In 1894, the Japanese won a naval battle here and occupied the city. From 1898 to 1930, it was a British naval base on a 25-year lease, and was used to keep an eye on the Russians at Port Arthur (now Dalian), 100 km north. The British tutor of the Last Emperor Reginald Johnson (remember Peter O'Toole?) was the British administrator here. For the American navy and other imperialists, it was a summer resort with good beaches. Today it is still a beautiful little open-port city off the tourist track, with small but good beaches and hot springs. Natives are proud of its appearance and cleanliness. There has been a rule that no two buildings downtown should look alike.

Liugong Island (3 sq. km.) has a navy museum with incredible Qing navy dress uniforms and models of ships. Wax figures of the men who fought the Japanese in 1895 are in the former headquarters. In Weihai you can also find factories that produce carpets, leather goods, embroidery, artificial fur, etc.

One can drive to the easternmost tip of China at Chengshan Gap where the Yellow Sea meets the Bohai Sea. Not much to see except a marker and fishing village. **Yuanya** fishing village, 5 km from Weihai, is open for overnight home stays.

HOTELS

There are no fancy resorts here. The Dongshan Hotel overlooking a beach and fishing village, has no air-conditioning and few other services, but are adequate for families. They are surrounded by interesting old European houses. The Weihaiwei Mansion is in the city and is better for business people.

Dongshan Hotel (Binguan) • *27 Dong Shan Rd., 264200. 2*. Fax 224764. Dist.A.P.42 km. Dist.city center 12 km* • No C.C. 1980, ren. 1989. 3 buildings, 2 and 3 stories, 84 rooms. #2 building best and closest (50 meters) to beach. High ceilings, thin drapes, big bathrooms.

Weihaiwei Mansion (Dasha) • *82 Haigang Rd. 264200. 3*. Telex 327216 WMNWH CN. Fax 232281. Dist. port 100 meters. Dist.A.P. 30 km* • H.K.J.V. C.C. (No Diners) 1990–91. 17 stories. 153 rooms IDD. Tennis (across street). B.C. Clinic. Long, narrow rooms. Hot spring water and USTV.

Ambulance: tel. 223017
Police: tel. 110
C.I.T.S. and **C.T.S.:** 27 Heping Rd., 264200, tel. 223616, 225147. Telex 327205 FAOWH CN. Fax 231152.
Tourist Hotline: tel. 225149, 223616.
Weidong Ferry Co. (to Korea): tel. 5510470.
Weihai Tourism Bureau, 67 Tonyi Rd., 3F, 264100. Tel. 223616.

WUHAN

Southwest China, 18 hours by train south of Beijing and 18 hours north of Guangzhou. The capital of Hubei province can also be reached by ship, or by air from 40 cities including Hong Kong. Weather: Hottest—39°C (July and August); coldest—⁻5°C (January and February). Annual precipitation 1200 mm, mainly February to May. Population: 6.3 million, the fifth largest in China.

Wuhan, the capital of Hubei, is really three cities **Hankou (Hankow) 汉口 , Hanyang 汉阳 , and Wuchang 武昌**, separated from each other by the Changjiang (Yangtze) and Han rivers, and joined by bridges. It is the most important site of the republican revolution, and is noted for its industries, its ancient chime bells, and as a gateway to the Wudang Mountains and Yangtze Gorges.

The city itself dates from the 11th century B.C. (Shang). The city wall in Hanyang, no longer standing, was first built in the Han, almost 2000 years ago. The Wuchang wall was built during the Three Kingdoms (220–265), by Sun Chuan, King of Wu, and can still be seen at the **Small East Gate 小东门** . Hankou and Hanyang were originally one city, but in the 15th century, the Han River changed its course. It has been an important port for at least 2000 years.

Several foreign nations forced concessions here after the Opium War, and some of the architecture still reflects old Europe. Wuchang is especially famous because on October 10, 1911, the first victory of the

Sun Yat-sen revolution against the Manchus took place here, although Sun himself was absent. Wuhan became the headquarters of the left wing of the Nationalist party. In 1923, the Communists led a successful railway workers' strike.

The city was liberated in May 1949. The three cities merged administratively shortly afterward. During the Cultural Revolution, it experienced some of the heaviest fighting between factions.

Wuhan is the home of the huge Wuhan Iron and Steel Works. Other industries include metallurgy, machine building, and electronics.

The **Museum of Hubei Province** 湖北省博物馆 displays some of the world's most exciting recent archaeological discoveries. In 1978, 7000 articles were excavated from the **Zenghouyi Tomb,** located just outside of Suizhou city. Dating from the Warring States period 2400 years ago, the tomb of Marquis Yi of Zeng contained bronzes, weapons, lacquer, musical instruments, gold, and jade. The contents were found in water in which oxidized copper was accidentally dissolved. This saved most of the pieces from decay. Some of the lacquer is still preserved in water that shows the original brilliant red at its best.

Most important in the find is a complete set of 65 ritual bells of different sizes. When struck, they emit a perfect 12-tone system covering five octaves. Each bell also has two tones depending on where it is struck, a quality that has not yet been found in any other bell anywhere else in the world. In addition, the name of the tone and the date were inscribed on each bell in both the Zeng and Chu scripts. The two languages side by side here are as valuable to linguists as the Rosetta stone.

The bells were a gift from the king of Chu. Since their reigns overlapped by only a few years, the technology to produce them must have been at an astoundingly high level. Not only are their tones precise, they were probably cast in a short length of time. The heaviest is 203.6 kg and 1½ meters high. Imagine pouring hot metal into a mold that size! And of the exact amount to produce the prescribed tone!

Ritual bells were only played for ceremonies, not for pleasure. Only aristocrats and royalty were allowed to possess them, and only in certain numbers. Reproductions have been played for visitors, who have heard *Jingle Bells* as well as ancient Chinese music. They sound crisper than other bells because of the bosses.

Students of modern Chinese history must visit the site of the first victory of the republican revolution, on Shouyi Road in Wuchang. There, revolutionists accidentally exploded some ammunition, and this point of no return started the lightning that led to the takeover of the city. A statue of Dr. Sun Yat-sen dominates the front of the **Hubei Military Government Building** 武昌起义军政府旧址（红楼） , now the 1911 Revolution Memorial Hall. Republican troops broke through the **Qiyi Men (Uprising Gate)** 起义门 and seized Wuchang. Originally named Zhonghe Gate, the Qiyi Gate is one of the 10 original gates of Wuchang.

If you have more time the 45-meter-high, seven-story **Hongshan Pagoda** 洪山宝塔 in Wuchang dates from the Yuan (1279). The **Guiyang Temple (of Original Purity)** 归元禅寺 , started at the end of the Ming over 300 years ago, is the most important Buddhist temple in the city, and one of the 10 biggest in China. It contains 500 clay arhats, each life-size, distinctive, and 250 years old.

The five-story, 51-meter-high, **Huang He Lu (Yellow Crane Tower)** 黄鹤楼 , first built in A.D. 223 on top of the Yellow Swan riverside rock, inspired many famous poets, including Li Bai. It was destroyed by nature or war and rebuilt several times. It was reconstructed and expanded on its present site on Snake Hill starting in 1981. The design is based largely on the Qing version that lasted from 1868–84, but is 20 meters taller. It also has elements of the previous versions, pictures of which are inside. The tower gives a good view of the Yangtze and the city. Elevator. Each floor has a guide.

The poets were inspired by the legend of the wine shop on the original site. Here, the owner used to give free wine to an old man who drew a picture of a yellow crane on the wall in gratitude. After the old man left, the crane came to life and danced for the customers, and the owner became rich. When the old man returned decades later, he mounted the crane and flew off into the sky.

Nearby are the White Tower, the Tablet Corridor, and gardens. Wuhan will be rebuilding 20 historical buildings in the vicinity.

The **Wudang Mountain** 武当山 is important as a Taoist center, with an impressive collection of religious buildings. It is the home of the Wudang style of martial arts. Mostly built in the Ming, it includes eight palaces, two temples, 36 nunneries, and 62 grotto temples, all along a 30-km-or-so mountain path. The highest of its 72 peaks, Tianzhu, is over 1600 meters. On top is the *****Golden Hall** (Yuan and Ming) of gilded copper. Wudang needs 5 days and is not as strenuous as other mountains. New hotels are at the foot.

The museum at the *****Ancient Copper Mine in Tonglushan** 古铜矿铜绿山 Daye county, has been described by a Canadian metallurgist as "incredible." One hour by road from Wuhan, it takes another half hour to explore. It is now an open pit with mining tools, shaft, ropes, and baskets, started in the Zhou about 3000 years ago. Nowhere else in the world at the time was mining technology so far advanced.

Wuhan is also planning a 200 meter-long street halfway up Sheshan Hill, with old-style shops and attendants in period dress selling souvenirs and local products. Some fans might be interested in watching kick boxing in Canzhou, nearby.

For other destinations in the province see "Gezhouba" and "Yangtze

Gorges.'' From Wuhan, one can take a regular ferry or one of the luxury tourist ships through the Yangtze Gorges to Chongqing. See separate listings.

CULTURAL EVENTS

Noteworthy are the Wuhan Acrobatic Troupe, Beijing Opera Troupe of Wuhan, the Wuhan Song and Dance Drama Troupe, and, of course, the Zenghouyi Chime Bells. All of these have performed abroad.

SHOPPING

Made locally are gold and silver jewelry, lacquerware, carpets, shell carvings, carved turquoise, boxwood carving, feather fans, colored pottery, jadeware, and paintings.

Hubei Antique Shop 武汉古玩店 (Provincial Museum, East Lake Scenic Spot Area; tel. 75336); **Wuhan Antiques and Curios Store** 汉古玩店 (1039 Zhongshan Ave., Hankou; tel. 21453); **Wuhan Carpet Weaving Mill** (14 Hankou Ruixiang Rd.; tel. 22803, 22003): this factory can be visited; **Wuhan Emporium** (208 Liberation Thoroughfare; tel. 52991); **Wuhan Friendship Store** 友谊商店 (Liberation Thoroughfare, Hankou; tel. 25781 and 25794); **Wuhan Service Department of Arts and Crafts** 工艺美术店 (Minshen Rd., Zhongshan Ave., Hankou; tel. 53478).

RESTAURANTS

Among the well-known Hubei dishes are: mianyang three steamings of fish, pork, and chicken; grilled meats of five kinds of poultry; fish balls soup with egg white in the shape of the Three Gorges; stir-fried sliced pork kidney in phoenix-tail shape; fried boneless eel; braised wild duck in brown sauce; steamed catfish; lotus seeds with white fungus in sweet soup.

HOTELS

C.I.T.S. says the top hotel is the Qingchuan (needs work), then the Jianghan, and thirdly the Yangtze (tops for business travelers). All need more work.

Holiday Inn Wuhan • *Jie Fang Ave.* • probably 1993. 407 rooms. Bowling, pool, health center, C.C. Should be best when open.

Jianghan Hotel (Fandian) • *211 Shengli St., Hankou 430014. Telex 40150 HBIAN CN. Fax 514342. Dist. A.P. 28 km. Dist. R.W. 1 km* • Old European architecture. B.C., IDD.

Qingchuan Hotel (Fandian) • *88 Ximachangjie, Hanyang. 430050. 3*. Telex 40134 HBQC CN. Fax 564964. Dist.Wuchang A.P.15 km. Dist.Hankou A.P.10 km* • C.C. 1984; ren. 1991. 24 stories. 300 rooms. On hill above Yangtze. View of Yellow Crane Tower. IDD, B.C.

Yangtze Hotel (Da Jiudian) ● *539 Jiefang Da Dao, Hankou 430030. 3☆. Telex 40204 YGHTE CN. Fax 554110. Dist.A.P. 25 km. Dist.R.W. 15 km. Near government trading offices.* ● C.C. 1987, ren. 1992. 8 stories. 205 rooms. IDD. Should have health center now, karaoke, and night club. B.C., H.K.J.V.

IMPORTANT ADDRESSES
CAAC 中国民航 : 209 North Liji Rd., Hankou 430030; tel. 51248.
C.I.T.S. 国际旅行社 : 48 Jianghan Yi Lu, Hankou; tel. 25018 and 24109. Telex 40211 CITWH CN.
C.T.S. 中旅社 : 1365 Zhongshan Ave., Hankou 430014; tel. 321666. Fax 511074, or 2 Chezhan Rd., Hankou; tel. 514378. Yangtze cruise branch, tel. 21161 or 356721.
CYTS: tel. 813729, 812912 X530.
Hubei Tourism Administrative Bureau 湖北省旅游局 : 1365 Zhongshan Ave., Hankou 430014; tel. 512657, 25552. Telex 40133 HBHTY CN.
Hospitals: In case of emergency, try your hotel first if convenient. Otherwise: **No. 1 Hospital, Wuhan Medical College** 武汉医学院附一院 : :389 Liberation Thoroughfare; tel. 51171.
　　No. 2 Hospital, Wuhan Medical College 武汉医学院附二院 : 130 Liberation Thoroughfare; tel. 54191.
Wuhan Port Passenger Transport Station 武汉港客运站 : Yianjiang Ave., Hankou; tel. 53875.
Wuhan Tourist Corp.: Yangtze Hotel, tel. 556473.

WUXI 无锡

(Wusih) East China. Between the northern shore of Lake Taihu and the Yangtze River, in southern Jiangsu province, this industrial and resort city also straddles the ancient Grand Canal. It is less than an hour by train from Suzhou, and 80 km west of Shanghai. It is a 2-hour flight south of Beijing. The urban population is 1 million. Weather: Hottest—in July, 38°C; coldest—in January, ⁻4°C. Annual precipitation 1056 mm, mainly in June.

Wuxi is one of the oldest cities in China, founded over 3000 years ago, during the Zhou. After deposits of tin became depleted, its name was changed to Wuxi, meaning "no tin." Contrary to its image of a placid, sail-filled lake, Wuxi has the fifth highest industrial output in China. But it is known as a beauty spot, with classical Chinese gardens and a famous lake from which many of the best gardens get their rockery. Notable are the **Liyuan (Li Garden)** 蠡园 and **Meiyuan (Plum Garden)** 梅园 . The Liyuan has a "thousand-steps veranda," with 89 windows on the inside wall. At the Meiyuan, the plum blossoms are best seen in the early spring. In 2235-square-km **Lake Tai** 太湖 is the **Yuantouzhu (Turtle Head) Islet** 鼋头渚 , with a bridge, temple, and pavilions. Also on Turtle Head Islet, one of the sets at the Tang Cheng TV Studio is open to tourists. The Tang palace with guards dressed in period uniforms and armed with swords and spears is a good stop for photos. Don't waste time at the "Journey to the West" exhibition adjacent. It is not that well done. On Hu Gui Shan are a few wild monkeys.

The Liyuan is close to the Shuixiu and Hubin hotels; the Taihu Hotel is close to Meiyuan and Yuantouzhu.

Historical sites include **Xihui Park** 锡惠公园 , west of the city, with its **Tianxia Di'er Quan (Heavenly Second Spring)** 天下第二泉 (Tang), **Jichang (Garden to Entrust One's Happiness) Garden** 寄畅园 , and the **Longguang (Dragon Light) Pagoda** 龙光塔 (great view), both from the Ming. Jichang Garden is one of the best-known South China gardens, uniting the distant hills with the intimacies within the walls. A copy of this garden is in the Summer Palace in Beijing. Bells ring at midnight "for luck" December 31 at the **Kaiyuan Temple.**

Wuxi is also a silk-producing center, the hills around it filled with mulberry trees. Tourists can see the local **silk industry,** from silkworm-rearing through the printing and dyeing process at a silk factory. There are the **Hui Shan Clay Figures Factory** 惠山泥人厂 boat trips with lunch on Lake Tai and trips on the **Grand Canal** 大运河. One can take a 15 km cruise in Wuxi itself. A trip across Lake Tai, can also involve a tour of **Huzhou** 湖州 (ancient writing brush factory) before you go to Hangzhou.

Visits can be arranged to **Huaxi Village** 1½ hours away for demonstrations of ancient farming and village life. A good time to visit is the Mid-Autumn festival, with lots of colored lanterns, moon cakes, an evening cruise on the lake and, one hopes, a full moon. New is the Artist Palace from the classic novel *Pilgrimage to the West,* and hopefully, an aquarium.

Excursions can be made to nearby (69 km) **Yixing** purple sandware porcelain factory and caves, and to **Jiangyin** 江阴 (home of Ming dynasty scientist and traveler Xu Xiake). Jiangyin and Huaxi village can be combined in one day's sightseeing. Trips also can be arranged to

Changzhou, Zhenjiang, Yangzhou, Suzhou, Nanjing, and Shanghai. See separate listing.

SHOPPING

Locally made and good are clay figurines, embroidery, freshwater pearls, pearl face cream, and silk. Made in the province are porcelain and Yixing pottery. No. 1 Silk Spinning Mill has a display of silkworms. Garment prices reasonable. The clothes at the No. 3 Silk Spinning Factory seemed too expensive.

The Friendship Store here is good with an antique store beside it. 28 Liangxi Rd., 214062. Tel. 668915. Wuxi Antique Store, 466 Chungshan Rd., tel. 26520.

Festivals the Lake Tai Arts Festival takes place for one week with folk dancing, singing. Cherry and Pottery festivals in April.

RESTAURANTS

Local specialties include ice fish, spareribs, deep-fried eel, crabs, and shrimp.

HOTELS

The best is the Wuxi Grand, the second best the Milido; both are downtown, and convenient for business people. Tourists can walk to the canal. Close to shopping. But the best choice for tourists is either the hilltop Jing Ming Lou at the Taihu Hotel or the Lakeside right beside Lake Taihu. The Jing Ming Lou has a good view of the lake with singing birds. The Lakeside is next to Li Garden. Long walk to town. A cheaper, adequate downtown hotel is the Liangxi at 63 Zhongshan Rd.

Lakeside Hotel (Hubin Fandian) • *Hubin Rd., Li Yuan, 214075. 3*. Telex 362002 WXHB CN. Fax 202637. Dist.A.P.23 km. Dist.R.W.12 km. Dist.City Center 4 km* • 1976–78. Ren. 1987. 10 stories. 186 modest, comfortable rooms. B.C., pool. IDD. USTV. Clinic. B.C.

The neighboring **Shuixiu Hotel** under the same management should now be renovated to 3-star standard.

Milido Hotel (Dajiudian) • *2 Liangxi Rd. 214061. 3*. Telex 362029 WMLD CN. Fax 200668. Dist.Lake Taihu 4 km* • C.C. 1987–88. H.K. management. 1987–88. Ren. 1991–93 floor by floor. 9 stories, 251 rooms. Pool. B.C., IDD. Clinic. Gym and USTV soon.

Taihu Hotel (Fandian) • *Mei Yuan, 214064. Telex 362021 WTUH CN. Fax 602771. Dist.A.P.26 km. Dist.R.W. 14 km. 30-minute walk to lake* • C.C. (no Diners). 1991, Jing Ming Lou. Aiming for 3*. 90 rooms. B.C. USTV and pool due soon. IDD. H.K.J.V. Cheaper rooms next door. We hope this building can keep its initial high standards. The Taihu itself has never practiced good maintenance.

Wuxi Grand Hotel (Dajiudian) • *1 Liangqing Rd. 214061. 4*. Telex 362055 WXGHL CN. Fax 200991. Dist.A.P.22 km. Dist.R.W.4 km* • C.C. 1988–89. 20 stories, 342 rooms. Pool, gym, B.C. Japanese, Cantonese and Sichuan food. C.I.T.S. and C.T.S. IDD. USTV. Pan Pacific management. Cheaper west building.

OTHER IMPORTANT ADDRESSES

Ambulance: tel. 226119.
Police: tel. 226842.
C.I.T.S. and **Wuxi Tourism Administration:** 7 Xin Sheng Rd., 214002; tel. 200416. Telex 362025 WCITS CN. Fax 201489. Complaints to Xu Jierong, Wang Bosheng.
C.T.S. 59 Chezhang Rd. 214005; tel. 223613, 221906. Fax 202743. Telex 362038 WXCTS CN.
China United Airlines tel. 221323.
CYTS: tel. 666829, 660262 X287.
Wuxi Municipal Tourism Bureau No. 1 Qing Yang Rd. Tel. 226618.

XIAMEN

(Hsiamen, Amoy) East China. SE coast of Fujian (Fukien) province, over 200 km across the straits from Taiwan, but 2½ km from Quemoy (Jinmen/Kinmen), the Nationalist-held island. Xiamen can be reached by air, sea or air-conditioned bus from Guangzhou and Hong Kong. The passenger ships *Gulangyu* and *Jimei* sail every Tuesday and Friday between Hong Kong and Xiamen, a journey of 17 hours. Direct trains from Nanjing and Shanghai. Weekly ship from Taiwan. It is a 1½-hour flight SW of Shanghai and 1 hour flight NE of Guangzhou. It is also linked by air with 28 other Chinese cities and Hong Kong, Jakarta, Manila, Penang, and Singapore. Weather: hottest—38°C, July–Aug.; coldest—minus 4°C, Feb. Annual precipitation is 1206 mm, mainly from May to July. Population: urban 370,000.

Xiamen was the homebase of General Zheng Chenggong (Cheng Cheng-kung), a.k.a. Koxinga, who repelled the Manchu invaders for a while and then rid Taiwan of the Dutch in 1662. Xiamen was a relatively minor trading port until it was seized by the British in 1839. In 1842, the Treaty of Nanking allowed foreigners to build residences and warehouses here. For many years, especially in the late 1950s, both explosives and propaganda shells have been lobbed to China from Quemoy, off the SE coast of Xiamen.

Xiamen is part of a 131-square-km. Special Economic Zone.

While the national language is also spoken, local people here speak the Xiamen Dialect/Fukienese, which is different from both Cantonese and Mandarin. Fukienese is also spoken by the majority of people on Taiwan.

If you only have one day for sightseeing, take in Gulangyu, South Putuo Temple, and hurry through Jimei.

The southeastern part of the city contains the downtown shopping area, the **botanical gardens** 万石植物园 (where among the tropical and subtropical plants is a redwood tree brought by then U.S. President Richard Nixon). Also in this area are the South Putuo temple, Xiamen University (built by Tan Kah Kee in 1921), and the ferry pier to Gulangyu. Staying at the Lujiang Hotel is convenient to these places.

The 1000-year-old **Nan Putuo (South Putuo) Temple** 南普院 is named after Putuo Island, the home of the Goddess of Mercy. Most of the current buildings are from the 1920s and 1930s, but the tablets, scrolls, sculptures, bells, etc., were made in the Song and Ming. On the lotus base of the statue of Buddha is carved the biography of Sakyamuni, and the story of the monk Xuanzang who went to India. The eight 3-meter-high ''imperial tablets'' in Mahavira Hall tell about the Qing suppression of an uprising and are written in Manchu and Chinese. Most famous is the stunning, three-faced, multiarmed statue of Guanyin. A festival is held here New Year's Eve.

Behind the temple is **Five Old Men Peaks,** which can be climbed for a good view of the Taiwan Straits. The famous Chinese writer Lu Xun taught at **Xiamen University** 厦门大学 in 1926–27 and a five-room memorial hall on his life is here. He helped to found the **Museum of Anthropology** 人类博物馆, with exhibits from prehistoric man to the Qing, and relics from the national minorities. Look also for the Australian boomerang and the 700-year-old Japanese sword.

At the foot of Five Old Men Peaks is the **Overseas Chinese Museum** 华侨博物馆 , outlining the contributions of natives who emigrated overseas.

One can charter a tour boat around the islands.

Gulangyu (Drum Wave) Island 鼓浪屿 is 1.7 hilly square km., seven minutes across the ''Egret River'' by ferry. Pop. 25,000. Formerly the foreign ghetto, it is good for another half day unless you want to hike or go swimming too. It has the best beach (Gangzi Hou), frangipani, flame trees, magnolias, and other heavily scented trees, and tiny shops. A very charming collection of old mansions built for foreigners have now been converted into guesthouses. Gulangyu is a car- and bicycle-free resort area, great for children and relaxing. It is cleaner and more prosperous-looking than the fishing villages of Hong Kong's outlying islands, to which it bears some resemblance. Staying here, however, makes it difficult for hectic sightseeing and shopping unless a special ferry to the guesthouses is laid on. The dominating new statue is of Koxinga. Gulangyu has two small museums, two churches, and a temple.

A high percentage of music lovers live here and you will probably hear strains of Bach and Verdi floating on the breeze. The island has a concert hall, which is especially good for chamber music groups.

Everyone *must* climb 90-meter-high **Riguang Yan (Sunlight Rock)** 日光岩 , the highest peak here, for the view and the story of the two devoted egrets, the male killed by a greedy, unromantic goshawk. Also here is the **Lotus Flower Nunnery** (a.k.a. Sunshine Temple), the camp where Koxinga stationed his men, and **Zheng Chenggong Memorial Hall** 郑成功纪念馆 , with souvenirs of his life, including a history written by a Dutchman about the fall of Taiwan/Formosa. The city museum is nearby. The **Shuzhuang Garden** was built by a Taiwan resident who moved here after the Japanese took over that island in the late 1890s. Unlike most gardens of China, it incorporates the sea into its design. ''The garden is in the sea and the sea is in the garden.'' One can rent sailboards near the ferry pier.

Jimei, 2.83 square km, is worth an hour and is over 10 km north of downtown. It is reached by a 2.8-km granite causeway from Xiamen Island, built in 1953–55, and is on the road to Quanzhou. Eighty percent of the 23,000 people here have relatives abroad. On Jimei is a most interesting monument built by an Overseas Chinese philanthropist, Tan Kah Kee, who made his money from rubber, rice, and pineapples in Singapore. **Turtle Garden** 鳌园 , built in 1950, is an encyclopedia in stone, full of pictures of the things Mr. Tan wanted to teach people: factories, machinery, exotic animals, Chinese literature, history, and culture. How many scenes can you identify? His elaborate tomb is typically horseshoe-shaped. His biography is in pictures around the tomb.

Nearby is the huge **Jimei Middle School,** one of many which he also financed. Here, mainly Overseas Chinese students from all over the world come to study. For those curious about the man, a tiny museum nearby also shows pictures of his life.

EXCURSIONS

In the vicinity of Xiamen, closer to Fuzhou, is the tomb of Koxinga. Reached by road is the historical city of Quanzhou. See separate listing.

SHOPPING

Locally made are Caiza silk figures, lacquer thread–decorated vases, colored clay figures, and bead embroidery. You may want to try the *Yupi* peanuts, the *gongtang* crisp peanut cakes, dried longan fruit, and preserved olives. Locally grown are longan, litchis, peanuts, sugarcane, and, of course, rice. The main shopping street is Zhongshan Road.

Xiamen Antiques and Curios Store 厦门文物店 (211 Zhongshan Rd.; tel. 23363); **Friendship Store** 友谊商店 (tel. 23817, 24385); **Tourist Shopping Center** (103 Si Ming Bei Rd.; tel. 20133); **Lacquer Thread Sculpture Factory** 漆绒雕厂 (tel. 20329); **Arts and Crafts Factory** 工艺美术厂 (tel. 24784).

Also open is the Donghai Shopping Center, Zhongshan Bei Rd. (tel. 21094).

RESTAURANTS

Fujian food is much like Cantonese, and heavy on seafoods, of course, with some distinctive dishes. See ''Food'' for recommended local dishes. Hotels have the best food.

HOTELS

Fujian is particularly busy with Taiwan visitors. Reservations are recommended. The top hotel is the Xiamen Mandarin. The Holiday Inn and the Plaza should compete with it for top spot after they are open fully.

Though run down, the Lujiang is good for tourists, located in old Amoy on the harborfront. The Xiamen is isolated on a hilltop downtown and provides privacy and peace. The Xindeco is recommended for budget business people. On Gulangyu, the Gulong looks the best. New hotels for backpackers near railway station.

Gulong Hotel ● *14 Huasheng Rd., Gulongyu 361002. Fax 30165. Near beach ●* Gym. Karaoke. Night club.

Holiday Inn Harbourview ● *12–8 Zhen Hai Rd. 361001. Telex 93138 HIHXM CN. Fax 236666. Dist.A.P. 13 km. Dist.R.W. 7 km ●* C.C. 1992. 22 stories, 367 rooms. IDD. Clinic. B.C. Non-smoking and executive floors.

Lujiang Hotel (Binguan) ● *54 Lujiang Rd. 361001. 3✫. Fax 224644. Telex 93024 LUTEL CN. Dist.A.P.12 km. Dist.R.W.5 km. Walk to Hong*

Kong ferry pier, ferry to Gulangyu, and shopping • 1961, some ren.
1989. 6 stories. C.C. Hong Kong management. IDD. No sports facilities. Large rooms. Pleasant but shabby. Night club. B.C.

   Xiamen Mandarin Hotel • *Huli District 361006. 4☆. Dist.A.P.7
km, Dist.R.W.11 km. Telex 93028 MANDA CN. Fax 621431.* • Upon a
hill, surrounded by factories. C.C. 1984; 3 stories, 74 rooms. 1988; 7
stories, 133 rooms, 22 two-story villas. Conference hall, sauna, jacuzzi,
health club, French restaurant, pool, bowling, tennis, shuttle bus to city.
IDD, H.K.J.V. but no connections with Mandarin International Hotels
Ltd.

   Xiamen Plaza • *908 Xia He Rd. 361004. Fax 558899. Dist.A.P.
9 km* • 1991. 380 rooms. IDD. Fax machines for rent. B.C., outdoor
pool, patisserie. Managed by Manila Hotel. International.

   Xindeco Hotel (Jiudian) • *Xing Rong Rd., Huli Dist. 361006. Telex
93027 INFRM CN. Fax 621814. Dist.A.P.5 km. Dist.R.W.6 km* • Near
government trade offices. T.R., C.C. Hong Kong/CYTS J.V. 1988; 12
stories, 128 large rooms. IDD, B.C., gym, pool. USTV. Some rooms
should have direct computer hookup to business satellite.

OTHER IMPORTANT ADDRESSES

C.I.T.S. 中国国际旅行社 : 7 Hai Hou Rd., 3/F; tel. 225277, 220848.
Fax 31832. Telex 93063 XMITS CN. Head office: Zheng Xing Man-
sion, 15th floor, Hubin Bei Rd. 361012; tel. 51825. Fax 51819. Telex
93148 ITSXM CN, or for FITs 93063 XMITS CN. Service Counter at
Lujiang Hotel: tel. 225277, 220846, 31832.
C.T.S. 中旅社 : Overseas Chinese Bldg., 70–74 Xin Hua Rd. 361003;
tel. 222053, 225602. Telex 392428 CTSXM. Fax 31862.
CYTS: 4 Bai Jia Cun Rd.; tel. 220017, 220019. Fax 220024.
CAAC 中国民航 and **Xiamen Airlines:** 230 Hubin Nan Rd.; tel.
225942, 225902 X394, 225802 (airport).
Dragonair: tel. 225398, 225433. Fax 225034.
Ferry Quay 轮渡码头 : Lujiang Rd.; tel. 221336. Ferries to Gulan-
gyu every 5–15 minutes.
No. 1 Hospital of Xiamen 厦门第一医院 : Zhen Hai Rd.; tel. 222280.
Ticket Office for Ships to Hong Kong: Dongwen Rd.; tel. 222517.
Xiamen International Airport 厦门国际机场 : Gao Qi; tel. 220630
(for flight times).
Xiamen Railway Station 火车站 : Wuchun; tel. 222812.
Xiamen Tourism Bureau: 3/F, 7 Haihou Rd.; tel. 225557, 225355.
Zhongshan Hospital South Hubin Rd., tel. 226596, 225468.

XI'AN

(Sian; Western Peace) Northwest China. 1¾-hour flight or about 22-hour train ride SW (1165 km) of Beijing; 8-hour train ride west of Luoyang. Air routes with 40 cities now include Hong Kong and in the future with Japan, Singapore, and Bangkok. Check with C.I.T.S. about summer plane charters with Tianshui, Lanzhou, and Yinchuan. Capital of Shaanxi province on the Guanzhong Plain, it borders on the Loess Plateau to the north and the Qinling Mountains to the south. Altitude: 400 meters. Weather: Hottest—40°C—July; coldest—⁻14°C in January. Rain all year round, but especially July through early September. Annual precipitation 550–770 mm. Fog in winter might affect plane flights. Population: inside wall 3 million.

Next to Beijing, Xi'an is the best city to visit in China, especially if you are interested in ancient Chinese history, traditional culture, and archaeology. It is one of the 24 historical cities protected by the State Council and, unfortunately, has been sinking due to lack of water.

Just to glimpse all it has to offer takes a full week. To savor Xi'an slowly, to study it deeply, reading about Empress Wu and her lover-protector-henchman while sitting in the shadow of a Tang pagoda—or even reading about that crafty fictional Tang detective Judge Dee, two giant silk-flower petals sticking sideways out of the back of his magisterial cap—even that kind of depth could take months.

Ancient Xi'an is the setting for many Chinese operas, their sweet young heroines waving flowing ribbon sleeves and their flag-pierced generals galloping away to battle amid the clash of cymbals. Here the real camels, caravans, and traders were involved in the exchange of silver, furs, horses, and sesame for Chinese silk and porcelain. Here that egomaniac of an emperor ordered the burning of all books except those he liked, and demanded that his subjects create an army of life-size soldiers so he could maintain his empire after his earthly death.

Xi'an was the capital intermittently for 1183 years and 11 dynasties, including the Zhou (of the ritual bronzes), the Qin (of the Great Wall and ceramic army), the Han (of the jade burial suits), the Sui (of the Grand Canal), and the Tang—ah, the Tang! This city was the center of China's world from the 11th century B.C. to the early 10th A.D. Commerce on the Silk Road thrived west of here to the Mediterranean and beyond. (See "Silk Road.") Thousands of foreigners lived in the Western Market then.

In spite of the occasional invasions and sackings by rebels and tribesmen, Xi'an, then named Chang'an (Everlasting Peace), reached its highest peak in the Tang, the population then almost two million. It was one of the largest cities in the world, with walls measuring 36 km in circumference. It declined because of late Tang debauchery and corruption, the eunuchs ruling the court and increasingly powerful governors-general controlling the provinces. In 906, the last of the Tang emperors allowed one of his generals to take complete charge while he enjoyed his lady love. Xi'an rolled downhill from there on, following the fortunes, also, of the Silk Road. We highly recommend Cooney and Alteri's novel, *The Court of the Lion,* about this period.

A short-lived peasant regime made Xi'an a capital again in the 17th century, but it never regained its past glory. Xi'an did, however, continue to be a tourist resort and destination for religious pilgrimages because of its Buddhist roots. In 1900, when the Empress Dowager fled the international force sent to rescue the foreign legation from the Boxers, she went to Xi'an.

During the Xi'an Incident, Generalissimo Chiang Kai-shek was kidnapped. One of Chiang's own officers thus forced him to cooperate with the Communists against the Japanese. (See 1936 in "Milestones in Chinese History.") After Chiang agreed to his captors' demands, the Communists set up a liaison office here, which is now the ****Museum of the Eighth Route Army** 八路军西安办事处博物馆 . On May 20, 1949, the Communists took over the city.

Today, Xi'an is a textile and manufacturing center. It also produces Chinese and Western medicines, and airplanes. It is an educational center, with about 20 colleges, universities, and research institutes.

Xi'an Jiaotung (Communications) University is the best known, and one of the 11 "super-key" universities in the country.

Xi'an's agricultural areas grow cotton, maize, wheat, vegetables, pomegranates, and persimmons. Many houses and walls have been made of loess soil mixed with straw. If cared for properly and protected with bricks on top, mud walls can last 100 years. Cheap too! But today many farmers are rebuilding in brick.

The walled city is laid out in the classic Chinese style in a rectangle, most streets parallel, the bell tower almost in the center. If you only have one day, try to see the Qin Army Vault Museum, Bronze Chariots, Banpo Village, the Big Wild Goose Pagoda, the Provincial Museum, the Bell Tower, and the City Wall and gates. If you've never seen a Chinese-style mosque, try to fit in the Great Mosque too. This is a very rushed itinerary. Be aware that many taxi drivers here do not use their meters. Settle on a price before you get in. Judge distance by the size of the city wall.

The standard 3-day tour is:

—Qin Tomb and Terracotta Warriors, Bronze Chariots, Huaqing Hot Spring, and Banpo Neolithic Village.

—Qianlong Tomb, 75 km west of Xi'an.

—Shaanxi Provincial Museum, Big Wild Goose Pagoda, Bell and Drum Towers, and the Great Mosque.

If you have more than three days, you might want to sightsee according to geographical groupings.

In Xi'an and its immediate vicinity: Wild Goose Pagodas, Bell Tower, Drum Tower, City Wall, Great Mosque, Xi'an Stele Museum, Shaanxi Provincial History Museum, Xianqing Palace Park, Banpo Museum, Memorial Museum of the 8th Route Army, Xi'an Film Studio.

West and South of Xi'an: Chariot and Horse Pits, Xiangjiao Temple, Xiangji Temple, Qinglong Temple, Temple of Du Fu, Cao Tang Temple, Peasant Painting of Hu County.

East of Xi'an: Huaqing Hot Springs, Qinshihuang's Tomb and Army, Bronze Chariots and Horses.

North and Northwest of Xi'an: Xianyang Museum, Maoling, Zhaoling, and Qianling tombs. Famen Temple. International airport.

THE ESSENTIALS

*The Museum of Emperor Qin's Terracotta Army 秦俑坑博物 馆 (30 km NE of the city) is the most spectacular and important place to visit here because of its 2180-year-old painted-ceramic army of more than 8000 soldiers buried to "protect" the tomb of the first Qin emperor. Slides of reasonable quality can be purchased at the souvenir shops. You can take **photos** here in one designated spot for a price on special occasions like the Asian Games. If you exceed your agreed limit, there is a fee or fine if you are caught, ¥300 to ¥800, payable to the museum. Get a receipt.

The relics were discovered in 1974 by local peasants digging a well. A sign near the entrance shows where the well was dug. The terracotta army is a puzzle because the emperor left no record of its existence. It would be hard to hide a project of this magnitude! Excavation started in 1976. A permanent building protects the army and tourists from most of the elements, and visitors are able to walk around the periphery of the once-buried relics. If you look carefully, you might see signs of oxidation and the loss of original colors.

There are three vaults. **No. 1,** opened to the public in 1979, is 62 by 230 by 5 meters deep. Most of the army was found facing east, toward the tomb, 1½ km away. The soldiers were in lines of roughly 70 across and 150 deep, separated by 10 partition walls and 11 corridors.

The men are hollow from the thigh up and made in two parts; they are 1.78–1.87 meters tall. The soldiers in front hold crossbows; also in front were bells and drums. Charioteers hold their hands out before them as if clutching reins. The horses originally wore harnesses with brass ornaments and have been identified as a breed from Hechu in Gansu. Officers can be distinguished from soldiers by their clothing and armor. Are every one of the 2,000 faces here different? Judge for yourself.

Researchers believe that kilns were built around the molded figures (probably two horses at a time) and destroyed after firing. There are remains of 30 wooden chariots.

In separate buildings are **Vault No. 2,** which contains about 1400 cavalrymen, archers, charioteers and infantrymen. **Vault No. 3** has 64 officers and was probably the "command post." The extra payment is worth it.

Near the main museum is a smaller building with two of the 20 **bronze chariots** found. These are also outstanding and can be seen at close range.

***Tomb of Emperor Qinshihuang (Chin Shih Huang-ti)** 秦陵 is in Lintong County. The first emperor of the Qin Dynasty, the builder of the Great Wall, and first unifier of the Chinese nation, lived from 259 to 210 B.C. and became king of Qin at age 13. What he achieved in so short a reign is incredible, and it is no wonder that he searched his empire for pills of longevity. Over 700,000 people worked on his tomb recorded through history as a deep and magnificent underground palace begun in 246 B.C., when he was 14 years old.

Preliminary explorations at this site have started, and so far archaeologists believe that the tomb has not been robbed, and that the ancient records are correct. "Rivers of mercury" probably flow through it. Lack of money and technology has postponed the excavation of this extremely important tomb. At press time, all that can be seen is a tumulus 6 km in circumference and 40 meters high, covered with pomegranate trees.

The **Huaqing Hot Springs** 华清池 , the *site of the Xi'an Incident, have been so overshadowed by modern events that their ancient history is frequently overlooked. They are at the base of Lishan Hill, 30 km NE of Xi'an. Huaqing has been an imperial resort for the last 3000 years, its most famous tenants Emperor Xuanzong (Hsuan-tsung), the last Tang emperor, and the woman blamed for his downfall, his favorite concubine Yang Guifei (Kuei-fei). The influence of Yang Guifei and her relatives at court caused much dissatisfaction. In 755, an adopted son of hers rebelled, and the emperor's troops refused to fight as long as she remained alive. The Japanese say she escaped to Japan. The Chinese say she was strangled, and troops rode out to victory over her dead body. The emperor lived on even though they had vowed to die together. Promises! Promises!

The imperial couple used to winter here because it was warmer than Xi'an. They bathed in the Jiulong (Nine Dragons) Hot Spring and the Guifei Hot Spring. And now, so can you! You pay very little for a 40-minute soak in 43°C mineral water (sodium, sulfur, and magnesium), said to be good for rheumatism and skin disorders. You can see Yang Guifei's personal bath. The current buildings are post-Liberation in the old Tang style.

You can also trace the flight from his bedroom of Chiang Kai-shek, the Chinese Nationalist leader, as he panicked at the sound of gunfire at 5 a.m. on a cold December morning in 1936. He left behind his false teeth and wore only one shoe. A pavilion today marks the spot up the hill where he was captured.

The ***Dayan (Big Wild Goose) Pagoda** 大雁塔 of the Da Chi Eng Temple, along with the Little Wild Goose Pagoda in Jianfu Temple, are the most famous pagodas in China because of their age and their important historical connections. They are not, however, the most beautiful or spectacular. The bigger pagoda was built to house the sutras brought back from India in A.D. 652 (Tang) by the famous monk Xuanzang (Hsuan-Tsang). It was probably named in memory of the temple in India where the monk lived, on a goose-shaped hill. Or it could have acquired its name because some monks were starving and Buddha, in the form of a wild goose, dropped down close to them. The monks, being vegetarians, refused to eat it.

The pagoda has seven stories, 248 steps, and a great view from the top. In adjoining Da Cien Temple (A.D. 647) are painted-clay statues of 18 lohan (Ming), most with strong Indian rather than Chinese features.

While both pagodas are historical monuments protected by the State Council, only a stop at one is really necessary.

The **Xi'an Stele Museum** is in an old (Qing and Ming) Confucian temple and its extensions north of the South Gate. It is of primary interest to calligraphers. The museum also has the most important *collection of steles in China, with over 1000 from the Han through the Qing, including 12 Tang engravings of the Confucian classics. These have been used by centuries of scholars to copy and study for content as well as calligraphy.

Important here is the seventh-century Nestorian stele, written in Syriac with a cross at the top. You really have to search for it in this forest, but it is a rare piece of Christian history, the commemoration of the establishment of the church in Xi'an. In the late 1980s before the opening of the new provincial museum, the stele was in the second pavilion of steles at the back of the museum, the first stele on the left. Look for the cross at the top. Rubbings of this and other steles can be obtained in the souvenir shop. The Nestorian sect started in the fifth century but was declared heretical by Rome in A.D. 431. The sect flourished in west Asia, but relics have also been found in Quanzhou.

The **Shaanxi Provincial History Museum** is outside the south wall near the Garden Hotel in a Tang-style building. The collection is one of the best in China and covers the period from the Zhou to the end of the Tang. It has many outstanding pieces, all labeled in English and Chinese. Among them: (1) an eighth-century B.C. stone drum, believed to be the earliest stone tablet in China, with writing (about a hunting expedition); (2) a bronze gate hinge from the Qin; (3) the standardizations of weights, measures, and currency by the first Qin emperor; (4) a wooden model of a bronze seismograph (eight dragons) from the first or second century B.C.; (5) giant stone carvings, the largest from the eastern Han, including a life-size rhinoceros and ostrich (inspired by live animals given as tribute). Four of the bas-reliefs of horses from the Zhaoling tombs are on one of the walls. Two others are said to be in Philadelphia. (6) Gold- and silver-inlaid dishes and ancient Byzantine and Persian coins found in the Western Market. A most recent and very celebrated find is the 62 cm-high Gilded Bronze Horse, from the 2000-year-old tomb of Han Emperor Wu Di.

The *Bell Tower was first built in 1384 (Ming) in another location, and moved here 200 years later. It has been renovated several times. Three sets of eaves weaken "the force of the rainfall," and actually only two stories are here. The tower is 36 meters tall. The furniture is gorgeous (Qing) and the very fancy traditional ceiling is Ming. From the second story you can see all four gates of Xi'an. Parking is impossible.

The nearby **Drum Tower** is also impressive and contains a large antique store, where paintings, porcelain, and jade can be purchased. The tower was built in 1384 and is original. Drums were beaten about 800 times in 10 minutes before the city gates were closed for the night.

The *Great Mosque 大清真寺 , the largest in Xi'an, is on a back street north of the Drum Tower. It was founded as a mosque in 742 (Tang), but the present buildings are mainly Ming, with some subsequent construction. The buildings are a good example of the Sinification of foreign architecture right down to the bats, dragons, unicorns, marbletop tables, and mother-of-pearl-inlaid furniture. The Great Hall (Ming) is, however, more west Asian, the writing Arabic, the arches and flowers more like Istanbul or Baghdad. Shoes must be removed. Prayers are said five times a day. Moslems first came here from Xinjiang and Guangzhou, and they founded this mosque with encouragement from the Tang emperors. Today in Xi'an, 14 other mosques and this one serve 60,000 or so Moslems here. See also ''What Is There to See and Do?''

Banpo (Panpo) Museum 半坡博物馆 , in the eastern suburbs of the city, is the actual archaeological site of a 6000-year-old neolithic village. The site covers 50,000 square meters, of which the museum encloses 3000. There you see living quarters, one of the oldest pottery kilns in the country, and a graveyard.

The museum encompasses a communal storage area, moat, graveyard (skeletons under glass), and fireplaces. In the museum are also a bow drill, barbed fish hook, clay pots, and pottery whistle believed to be the earliest musical instrument in China. Among its other artifacts are hairpins, stone axes, and a pot with holes in the bottom, probably used as a steamer. Its narrow-necked, narrow-based water jugs, with two handles, look surprisingly like amphoras also used by the ancient Greeks and Romans! Is there a connection? The exhibits are also labeled in English.

This culture is believed to be matrilineal (1) because of the burial customs. Most of the 174 graves had one skeleton each; the few graves that contained more than one skeleton had no male-female couples; (2) the women gathered wild food at first while the men hunted. After the women discovered how to plant seeds, land became valuable and it was passed on from mother to daughter; (3) because of the burial system (with no couples), scientists concluded that there were no fixed marriages. Besides, did neolithic people know where babies came from? (4) the village consisted of one big house in the center for old and young, and smaller houses for visiting males. The men kept their belongings in their native villages, where they were later buried.

As agriculture developed, men started pursuing it too. As surpluses grew (and probably the basic principles of physiology were discovered), fixed families started. In later neolithic gravesites in Gansu, male skeletons were found lying straight, females leaning toward them. Since the women were bound, they were probably buried alive with him. So much for early women's lib!

Now, what is *your* theory?

*Maoling, on a plateau north of the Wei River, 40 km NW of Xi'an, has more than ten tombs, small grassy pyramids, about 46.5 meters high. The main tomb is that of the fifth Han emperor, built 139–87 B.C. According to records, it contains a jade suit with gold threads (seems to be a Han fad), and, in a gold box, more than 190 different birds and animals, jade, gold, silver, pearls, and rubies. The other identified tombs are of the emperor's favorite concubine Madame Li; ***General Ho Qubing,** who fought the Xiongnus/Huns, and strengthened the dynasty from the age of 18 until he died of disease at 24!; General Wei Qing; his horse breeder Jing Min Ji, who remained faithful even after Jing's tribe was defeated by the emperor; and General Ho Guang.

Some of the earliest and, therefore, most primitive massive stone carvings, originally placed in front of the tombs, can be studied here. Look for the horse stomping a Hun aristocrat. Each stone has a few lines added to the natural shape of the rock. Also in the museum are Han artifacts found by local peasants, including an irrigation pipe and ceramic animal figures. Near Maoling is the **Xianyang Museum,** containing 3000 painted terracotta warriors and horse figures from the Western Han (206 B.C.–A.D 24). They are each between 55 and 68 cm high, and artistically better than the Qin Army.

Also near Maoling is the **Tomb of Yang Guifei, 杨贵妃墓**, the beautiful, tragic imperial concubine. Women have taken earth from here to put on their faces, hoping it will make them equally beautiful.

Xingjiao Temple (a.k.a. Xiangjiao Temple), about 25 km east of the Renmin Hotel, is on a sylvan hillside, which, with a little mist, could look like the lonely setting of the famous Japanese movie *Rashomon*. The place oozes with atmosphere, although the buildings are recent. It was founded by Tang Emperor Gaozong in A.D. 669, but destroyed and rebuilt several times. The remains (at least some of them) of monk Xuan Zhang, who first walked to India "day and night" and brought back the sutras, are buried in the small, five-story pagoda here. About 20 monks are in residence.

The ***City Wall** was built from 1374 to 1378 (Ming), probably with material from the old Tang wall, which by then had decayed: 3.4 (north-south) by 2.6 km (east-west); 12 meters high. The walls follow the boundaries of the Tang imperial city. The gates open to the public are the imposing **Ximen (West) Gate 西城门**, **South Gate,** and soon the **East Gate.** The wall, gates, and moat are being restored. Six new gates have been added to the original four to facilitate the flow of traffic. A small section of the south wall can be seen in its original Tang dynasty state. You can walk on top of the south wall, and eventually all of it.

IF YOU HAVE MORE TIME OR SPECIALIZED INTEREST:

The **Xian Film Studios** is worth a visit if only for the magnificent reproduced Qin palace used for the strongly recommended Sino-Canadian movie "The First Emperor." Also book. Other exhibits as well. Has own modest, grubby hotel too. 70 Xi Ying Rd., Tel. 711158. Fax 711585. Telex 700213 FCHTL CN.

The **Kaiyuan Men Gate** was the starting point of the Silk Road and is now marked with a huge recent photogenic statue. West of city.

*__Qianling__ 乾陵 Tomb of Tang Emperor Gaozong (Kao-tsung) and the Empress Wu, 79 km from Xi'an: She was as ruthless and outrageous as Qing Empress Dowager Cixi, but a more successful ruler. He died in A.D. 683 and she in 705. This unexcavated tomb is 75 km NW of the city, a worthwhile full day's excursion that can include other tombs as well. While earlier tombs were built to create their own artificial hills on the plains, the Tang tombs were built into existing hills. This one is 400 meters high, 1049 meters above sea level.

Approaching the hill, one passes statues of horses and ostriches, and 10 12-feet-high guardian figures holding swords. Then on the left are the life-size statues of guards, tribal heads, and foreign diplomats who paid their respects at the funeral. The 61 statues are now without heads, alas; look for names on their backs. One is labeled Afghanistan. The wall around the tomb is 4470 meters. Some of the minor tombs in the neighborhood are excavated, and visitors can go underground to see the coffin and fine murals of court scenes in the tombs of **Princess Yong-tai** and **Prince Yide.**

Although many of the structures at Qianling were destroyed in the war at the end of the Tang, the museum here contains about 4000 pieces.

*__Zhaoling__ 昭陵 , 70 km NW of Xi'an, is the tomb of the second Tang Emperor Taizong. It is built against a mountain near Liquan. The 20,000-hectare cemetery contains 167 minor tombs (children, wives, generals) and took 13 years to build. A small museum with Tang pottery, stone tablets, and murals can be visited. This tomb is not worth visiting unless you can read classical Chinese. The six famous bas-reliefs of the emperor's favorite horses in the Provincial Museum came from here. One is now in the university museum in Philadelphia.

If you're tired of tombs by now, head SW of Xi'an to **Huxian County Town** 户县 . Here you can visit the Huxian Peasant Painting Exhibition Hall. Some of the 2000 painters in the county have also exhibited abroad these recordings of their everyday lives and achievements in gay colors.

About 15 km away is the thatched-cottage **Caotang Temple** 草堂室 (Tang), where Indian monk Kumarajiva Jiumoluosi translated the sutras into Chinese. He died in A.D. 413 and was buried here in 855. The current buildings are recent, with a fine rose garden. Japanese Buddhists have presented a modern wooden statue of the monk.

The 2-meter-high stupa has some elaborate carvings and, from a well in the ground, a cloud used to come out at dawn, travel to Xi'an, and return at evening, said the guide. But this hasn't happened since the Cultural Revolution!

The **Horse and Chariot Pit** 车马坑, Zhangjiapo, Chang'an county, can be combined with Huxian county for a half-day tour. It is the burial site of two chariots, six horses, and one slave (11th century B.C.— Western Zhou) and is the best of seven such pits found. It is of special interest to archaeologists.

Back around town, the ***Small Wild Goose Pagoda** 小雁塔 , outside the south wall, is 45 meters high and was constructed of brick in A.D. 684. Thirteen stories high, it is minus two of its original stories, destroyed during earthquakes in 1444. This is all that remains of the great Da Jianfu Temple, so important in the Tang.

The ruins of ***Daming Palace,** built in A.D. 634 (Tang), are now in cultivated fields and can't really be seen.

Other sights include the **Qinglong Temple,** in the Tang-dynasty Chang'an city in the southern suburbs at Tian Lumiao. Six famous Japanese monks were initiated into Buddhism here between A.D. 794 and 1192, and links with Japan still exist.

The **Louguan Taoist Temple** has now been restored. It is beyond Huxian, about 70 km west of Xi'an. It is said to be the place where Lao Tzu, founder of Taoism, taught. The temple has resident monks and makes traditional medicines. The setting and especially the entrance gate are very fine. A big yearly fair is held here.

Binxian County 彬县 is about 130 km NW of the city, and is a two-day trip. It is famous for its caves of Tang Buddhist statues, the largest about 25 meters tall. Recent renovations with German help.

***Huangling County:** Tomb of the Yellow Emperor. See "Yan'an."

Huashan Mountain 华山 , 150 km east of Xi'an, peaks to 2100 meters. Cable cars and a small hotel are being built. Until then, it is mainly for serious climbers because of its 80-degree cliffs (there *are* iron chains to hang on to) and a "1000-foot-long Flight of Stone Steps." One also squeezes through the "100-foot-long Gorge." Famous as one of the Five Sacred Mountains, it is dotted with old temples.

Also in Shaanxi is "Yan'an." See separate listing.

Several new sites are being or have been opened. **Hanzhong,** 45 minutes by air from Xi'an or 14 hours by train, dates from the Three Kingdoms' period. It has the earliest tunnel in China (40 meters long) and the tomb of Zhuge Liang, Prime Minister of Shu (See also Chengdu.)

Famen Temple, 法门寺 120 km from Xi'an, can be included in a one-day trip along with the Qianling Tomb, and a small but extremely valuable museum of ancient Zhou bronzes in Shaocheng Village where they were excavated (9 km from Famen). These are near **Baoji,** on the old Silk Road.

Famen Temple is extremely important because it houses a finger bone of Prince Gautama, the founder of Buddhism whose statue is in every Buddhist temple in China and who lived in the 5th century B.C. Unfortunately a tourist town has been built around this shrine. This and loud rock music has destroyed the mystical atmosphere but the museum is worth the trip. While tourists will not normally be shown this rare relic, they can see some of the treasures that were buried with it. Among the over 900 pieces are well preserved gold-inlaid ceremonial vessels, ancient glass and jade, gilt Buddhas, jewelry, gold walking stick, gold chain basket, fake ''bones'' of jade—the largest group of Tang artifacts found since 1950. They were gifts from Tang Emperors Yi Zong and Xi Zong. Empress Wu donated gilded embroidery with threads finer than those made today. Titles in English in the air-conditioned museum.

The temple was founded in the Han Dynasty, 2000 years ago. The bone and the treasures found with them were re-discovered in the 1980s during repairs to one of the pagodas here. Additional payment to visit the vault under the reconstructed pagoda is overpriced at ¥10.

In **Tongchuan City,** Yao Xian county, 200 km north of Xi'an are the ruins of ancient celadon kilns and workshops. A museum should be open there now. Yao Xian county also has a grotto with 40 Ming statues, the largest 11 meters tall.

Xi'an also has an **English Corner** Sunday mornings at the Foreign Language Institute.

SHOPPING

The main shopping area is east of the Bell Tower on Dong Da Ave. Most stores are open 7 or 9 a.m.–8 or 9 p.m. Made locally or in the province are: rubbings, reproductions of three-color Tang camels and horses, Qin Army soldiers, and murals. Also made are inlaid lacquer, cloisonne, stone and jade carvings, gold and silver jewelry, peasant paintings, silk embroidery (South Shaanxi), and celadon. Cloisonne seems cheaper in Shanghai and Beijing than here.

C.I.T.S. suggests you start haggling at ½ the first asking price with all private merchants.

You will also find cheap reproductions of the Terracotta Warriors. Some of these are not kiln-dried and are extremely breakable. The better quality is usually found in government-approved stores.

200 meter long Tang Dynasty style street with food and souvenirs can be found near the Big Wild Goose Pagoda.

At stalls outside many tourist attractions, you will find red cotton vests with appliqued snakes, scorpions, lizards, and pandas. These are very popular with tourists. At about ten yuan, they are the cheapest in

China here. The yucky bugs are to frighten away the evil spirits. But do you want to wash them?

Xi'an Friendship Store 友谊商店 (Nanxin St., near Dong Da St.; tel 228301); **Xi'an Arts and Crafts** (almost opposite the Friendship Store on Nanxin St.); **Xi'an Cloisonne Factory** (9 Yanta Rd.; tel. 52547 prices higher than Beijing); **Arts & Crafts Studio** (next door at 19 Yanta Rd.); **Phoenix Embroidery Factory** (33 East Rd. 710005; tel. 227689, 221473); **Xi'an Antique Store** (Drum Tower; tel. 17187); **Xi'an Jade Carving Workshop** (173 Xi-1 Rd.; tel. 222570); **Xi'an Special Arts and Crafts Factory** (138 Huancheng Xi Rd.; tel. 228891). **Arts and Crafts Factory** (90 km outside Xi'an near Qianling). Makes Tang and Buddhist art reproductions.

Also **Xi'an Luxury Friendship Store** (No. 5 Building, South St.; tel. 221450, 224789). **#Shaanxi Cultural Relics Store,** (Shaanxi Provincial Museum, tel. 713691). **#Xi'an Cultural Relics Shop** (375 Dong Dajie. Tel. 715874).

RESTAURANTS

Xi'an food is similar to that of Beijing: somewhat bland. Its famous local dishes are crisp fried chicken or duck, and dried fish shaped like grapes. A typical Moslem dish is Yang Rou Pao Mutton Soup. Much of its food has been inspired by imperial tastes. Two celebrated wines are made here—one thick and sweet with the appearance of milk. Served hot, Chou Jiu wine inspired Tang poet Li Po, who drank 1000 cups and wrote more than 100 poems. The other wine is Xifeng Jiu (55% alcohol), one of the Eight Most Famous Wines in China. For some local dishes, see "Food." Most hotels have good Chinese food, but only joint ventures have good Western food.

The popular *jiaotze* dumpling restaurant De Fachang near the Bell Tower serves over a hundred different kinds of dumplings, which all seem to taste the same. The hygiene needs work here and in the popular Qingya Zhai Moslem Restaurant on Eastern St. Big night food markets are near the Xi'an and New World Xi'an hotels. In season, try the persimmons, which are not stringent like American ones.

Dongya Restaurant 东亚饭店 ● *46 Luoma Shi; tel. 717396, 28410* ● Suzhou.

Tang Dynasty Theatre Restaurant ● *39 Changan Rd., across from the Xi'an Hotel; tel. 711633, 711655* ● Cantonese. Expensive by Chinese standards, but clean.

Night Life Tang Dynasty Theatre Restaurant. Across from the Xi'an Hotel. Programs usually include classical Tang Dynasty dances. Disco afterwards, maybe to 2 a.m., free to dinner guests. Hong Kong management. Tang Theater Restaurant, Xian Garden Hotel. French food, classical Chinese programs. Tel. 711111. Bar at Xian Hotel favorite of locals. Some outdoor bars in gardens by city wall in summer. Groups can arrange a fireworks display. Ask about the powerful Shaanxi drum dances.

HOTELS

The overabundance of hotel rooms here has meant a price war. Individual budget travelers should telephone around after arrival to the joint ventures for the best deals.

The top hotels are the Golden Flower and the Sheraton. The Hyatt is third. The Xidu and the Lee Gardens are new and should be very good too. We've been expecting the Novotel and Sofitel to open for some time now. They might or might not be by the time you get there. The Tang Cheng and Xi'an are the best of the Chinese-managed hotels, and are also adequate.

The best location for tourists who like exotic surroundings is inside the city wall. But traffic jams are common and the air is not fresh. The Bell Tower and New World have the best location across the street from the historic Bell Tower and within walking distance of the Friendship Store, the South Gate, Xi'an Stele Museum, the Drum Tower and Mosque. The Sofitel and Novotel have the second best, close to the bus station, city square and Friendship Store in the northeast part. The Hyatt and New World are also inside the wall, both within walking distance of impressive gates.

The only hotel with Chinese garden architecture is the attractive Xi'an Garden.

The Xidu, Golden Flower, Holiday Inn, and Jianguo are all outside, east of and relatively close to the city wall.

The Xi'an Hotel is outside, but relatively close to the south city wall. Also south but farther from the wall is the Garden. The Dynasty snuggles up to the outside of the west wall. Some hotels might not yet have all facilities listed.

For budget travelers, we recommend the Jianguo Inn, Dynasty, and Xi'an. Do not confuse the Dynasty Hotel (cheap), the Grand New World (formerly the New World Dynasty), and the New World Hotel (cheap).

The airport in Xianyang is 40 km est and it takes about an hour to get to the city. On the way, look for the Xin burial tumuli (pointed top) and Han (rounded top).

Bell Tower Hotel Xi'an (Zhong Lou Fandian) • *Southwest corner of Bell Tower, 710001. 3*. Telex 70124 XABTH. Fax 718970. Dist.R.W.4 km* • C.C. 1985; ren. 1987. Holiday Inn management. 7 stories, 320 rooms. Apartments. Best view from odd-numbered rooms.

Shanghai Airlines. IDD. Bicycles. Small lobby. B.C., C.I.T.S. BBQ buffet. Gym. USTV.

Golden Flower Hotel (Jinhua Fandian) • *8 Chang Le Road West, 710032. 4*. Telex 70145 GFH CN. Fax 335477. Dist.R.W.3 km* • Book through UTELL or SARA. C.C. 1985 wing, 7 stories. 1990 wing, 11 stories. Total 498 rooms and suites (including apartments with kitchenettes). IDD, health club, indoor pool, grill room, B.C. Executive floor. Non-smoking floor.

Grand New World Hotel (Gu Du Da Jiu Dian) • *48 Lian Hu Rd. 710002. 4*. Telex 70156 XDHTL CN. Fax 719754, 714222. Dist.R.W.4 km* • New World Hotels International. C.C. 1989–90. 14 stories, 502 rooms. IDD. Non-smoking floor. Dim sum. Unusual but good color schemes. Gym. Food Street. B.C. Pool. Tennis. Library. Deli. Acupuncture. 1200-seat theatre. Bicycles. Karaoke.

Holiday Inn Xi'an (Shenzhou Jia Ri Jiu Dian) • *No. 8, South Section, Huang Cheng East Rd., 710048. Aiming for 3*. Telex 70043 COLT CN. Fax. 335962. Dist.R.W.8 km* • C.C. 1989, 13 stories, 355 rooms. IDD. Fitness center. B.C. 7th floor non-smoking. Cakeshop. Pool. C.I.T.S.

Hyatt Xian (Efang Gong) • *158 Dong Da St. 710001. Aiming for 3*. Telex 70048 AFPH CN. Fax 716799. Dist.R.W.2 km* • On busy commercial street. T.R., C.C. 1990. 8, 10 and 12 stories, 404 classy rooms. Attractive Japanese windows in some rooms. B.C. IDD. Regency Club. Gym. 2 rooms for wheelchair travelers. Disco. Tennis and steam bath due soon. Sauna has TV. 20-ft. Jacuzzi.

Jianguo Hotel (Fandian) • *20 Jin Hua Nan Rd. 710048. 3*. Telex 700209 XAJGH CN. Fax 335145. Dist.R.W.4 km* • T.R., C.C. 1989–90. 6 stories. 740 large rooms. Hair-dryers. 30% of rooms have balconies opening onto garden. Non-smoking floor. IDD. Pool. Gym. B.C. USTV. C.I.T.S., C.T.S. This hotel, which is not related to the Jianguo in Beijing, seems to be going downhill. The **Jianguo Inn** here has 160 smaller, cheaper rooms and a cafeteria.

Lee Gardens Hotel • *8 Laodong Nan Rd. Southwest of walled city near Northwest Technical University* • C.C. 1992. Eight stories. 296 rooms. IDD. Cantonese restaurant. Store has Tang reproductions. Executive floor. Clinic.

New World Hotel (Xin Shi Jie Jiudian) • *5 Nan Da St. 710002. 3*. Telex 70042 NWH CN. Fax 716688. Dist.R.W. 4 km* • Chains International Hotels management. 1988. 6 stories, 138 small rooms. IDD. Business services available. Disco. Low quality facilities. Chains International (H.K.) management.

Sheraton Xian Hotel (Xilaidun Da Fandian) • *12 Feng Gao Xi Rd., West Suburb, 710077, 4*. Residential area. Two km west of West Gate. Telex 70032 GAHL CN. Fax 742983.* • C.C. 1991. 16 stories, 480 rooms. Executive floor. Indoor pool. Health complex. Grill room. Non-smoking floors. Disco. B.C. USTV. IDD. Tennis and clinic due soon.

Tang Cheng Hotel (Binguan) • *3 South Ling Yuan Rd. 710061. 3*. Fax 711041. Telex 70013 TCH CN* • C.C. 1986–87. 11 stories, 406 rooms. IDD. C.I.T.S.

Xi'an Hotel (Binguan) • *36 North Section, Chang'an Road, 710061. 3*. Telex 70136 XAHTL CN. Fax 711796. Dist.R.W.10 km* • Near C.I.T.S. and the Small Wild Goose Pagoda. C.C. 1982, ren. 1988. 14 stories, 286 rooms. 1987 building, 14 stories, 264 rooms. IDD. Bicycles. Gym. Pool. B.C.

Xian Garden Hotel (Tang Hua Binguan) • *4 Dong Yan Yin Rd., Da Yan Ta, 710061. 4*. Telex 70027 GAHTL CN. Fax 711998. Theatre restaurant and a small but interesting Tang dynasty museum open evenings (no titles in English.) Dist.R.W. 14 km* • C.C. 1988. 4 stories, 301 rooms. Japanese restaurant. Fast food shop. IDD. Small TVs and bathrooms. Rooms for wheelchair travelers. C.I.T.S. Managed by Lalaport Japan.

Xidu Hotel (Xidu Dasha) • *15 Chang Lok Rd. 710032. Dist.R.W.3 km* • Dynasty Group management. 1991. 26 stories, 500 rooms.

OTHER IMPORTANT ADDRESSES

CAAC: tel. 42264.
China International Travel Service: 32 Changan Bei 710061. Tel. 711455 (24 hours). Telex 70115 CITSX CN. Fax 711453. Also books charter flights to Hong Kong. Branches in many hotels.
China Northwest Airlines/CAAC: tel. 42264. Branches People's, Qindu, and Xi'an hotels.
China Travel Service and Overseas Chinese Travel Service: 272 Jiefang Rd. 710004. Tel. 712557, 712658. Fax 714152. Telex 70148 CTSSP CN. For Xi'an branch, tel. 711760.

CYTS: 48–90 Hong Yin Rd., 710068. Hong Ying Rd. Tel. 712179, 27296. Fax 719356.

Hospitals:

C.I.T.S., above, has a clinic.

Shaanxi Provincial People's Hospital: Huangyancun; tel. 51331.

Western Capital Hospital: near Golden Flower Hotel; tel. 33174 X71265, 332971.

Railway Station 火车站 : Jiefang Rd.; tel. 26911. **C.I.T.S.** nearby in Jiefang Hotel, tel. 713329 X237.

Shaanxi Tourism Administration: tel. 711489, 711337, and **Shaanxi Overseas Travel Corp.** (sales): tel. 711526, 711660, both at 15 Chang'an Bei Rd., 710061. Telex 700201 OTCSX CN. Fax 711660. Complaints to Office of Excellent Service at STA.

Tourism Hotline: tel. 711480.

XINHUI

(Hsinhui; Cantonese, Sunwai) South China. This county, about 80 km SW of Guangzhou in Guangdong province, is in the heart of fan-palm country, from which many Chinese emigrated to America and Australia. Every spare inch seems to have these trees, whose leaves are woven into baskets, fans, and mats. The county seat, **Huicheng,** has a population of about 110,000 and is about a two-hour air-conditioned bus ride from Guangzhou, or a three-hour boat ride from Hong Kong or an overnight boat ride from Guangzhou, both to Jiangmen, and then a half-hour bus ride to Xinhui.

Visitors can see the fan-palm factory or relax on very pretty Guifeng Mountain on which is Yuhu (Jade) Lake. A Tang dynasty temple, destroyed during the Japanese war, is being rebuilt on the mountain. In another direction from the city and 7 km away, a magnificent old tree called **Birds' Paradise** is home at night to thousands of cranes and egrets and is best seen at dusk. A small museum is across from the Guifeng Guest House.

In the area also is the **Yutai Temple** (Tang), and the **Zhenshan**

Pagoda. In the southeastern part of the county 40 km. away is the **Yamen Fort,** a modest building used by the Qing administrators, and the remains of **Ciyuan Temple,** recently renovated, first built in the Ming by a famous poet. It commemorates some Song generals who fought heroically to the death.

The Overseas Chinese Association in Xinhui organizes free 20 day summer camps for people with roots in the county. Classes in calligraphy, history, traditional medicine, etc.

Aside from the woven palm products, this county is noted for its dried Mandarin orange peel used in soups and congee. (The best smell strongly of oranges.)

HOTELS

The Xinhui Hotel appears to be the best followed closely by the Kui Yuan but neither is outstanding. Both are centrally located and about 10 km. from the port in Jiangmen.

Kui Yuan Hotel (Binguan) • *15 Zhong Xin Rd. 529100. On main street near shopping.* • C.C. 1987–88. 15 stories, 198 rooms. Hong Kong J.V. Should have IDD and telex now. Major credit cards.

Xinhui Hotel (Jiudian) • *Zhi Zheng Bei Rd. Zhong 529100. 3*☆.
• C.C. 21 stories, 150 rooms. Revolving restaurant on top wobbles.
C.T.S. and C.I.T.S.: Guangzhou Guest House, 15 Gankou Rd., Beimen, 529100. tel. 663176.
Overseas Chinese Association: tel. 663589.
Xinhui Tourist Bureau: Beimen 529100; tel. 662422.
Ambulance: tel. 662129, 662480.
Police: tel. 110.

XINING   西宁

Northwest China. Capital of Qinghai (Tsinghai) province. A little over 6 hours by small plane from Beijing (three stops), or 55 minutes NW from Lanzhou. The highway to Lhasa is now asphalted, the highest highway in the world. The railway joins Xining with Golmud in the western part of the province and also with Lanzhou and Xi'an, eastward. Currently being built is a 1200-km line from Golmud to Lhasa. When it is finished, it should be one of the most spectacular train rides in the world. Qinghai is the source of both the Yellow and Yangtze rivers and has a lot of hydroelectric power. It is rich in aluminum, coal, and oil. Weather: Hottest—less than 32°C in July and August; coldest—⁻16°C in January and December. Annual precipitation is 450 mm in July and August.

This province has only recently opened to tourists. A one-day visit to Xining can include the Taer Lamasery, Dongguan Mosque, and North Mountain Temple. The *Taer Monastery 塔尔寺 (Ming), the center of the yellow-hat sect of Tibetan Buddhism, is at Huangzhong, about 30 km from the Xining Guest House and the Qinghai Hotel. Built in 1397 (or 1577, depending on the source), it is worth a visit. Its kitchen has three bronze cauldrons that are said to cook 13 cattle at one time to serve 3600 people. Ask why meat is served in this Buddhist monastery! In the winter, frozen butter, two meters high by 26 meters long, is sculptured into Buddhist scenes and displayed on the 15th day of the lunar New Year. It also has 20,000 religious paintings and embroideries. C.T.S. has a branch in the monastery.

The **Dongguan Mosque** 东关，清真寺 , one of the biggest in Northwest China, was built in 1380 and is 2 km from the Xining Guest House. The **North Mountain Temple** 北禅寺 is also 2 km from the hotel.

Qinghai Lake 青海湖 (China's largest saltwater lake) is 3196 meters above sea level and is 130 km from the capital. A bird sanctuary, **Bird Island** 鸟岛 , is about 350 km away from Xining. The 8-square-km island attracts 100,000 migrating geese and gulls each summer and autumn, and has bird-watching pavilions and Tibetan-style hotels.

About 60 km east is the *Qutan Temple (Ming). Also in the vicinity is the 6282-meter Ma Qing Gang Re Mountain.

The province has wild antelope, yak, donkeys, camels, lynx, deer, and pheasant, all protected.

Golmud 格尔木市 is a new industrial city in the Gobi Desert, in the west of the province. It has a population of 130,000, is 800 km from Xining, and is a trans-shipment point for Tibet. Between Xining and Golmud is the Salt Bridge and Salt Pond. **Golmud Hotel** modest but adequate. See ''Lhasa.''

The province is huge, covering one thirteenth of China, and is in the Qinghai-Tibet Plateau. It has less than four million people, mainly Han (60%), the rest Tibetan, Hui, Mongolian, Kazak, Sala, and Tu. Many of these are nomadic herdsmen. Ninety-six percent of its land is pasture for 22 million horses, yak, and sheep. Livestock breeding has been practiced here for 4000 years, and cow dung is used for fuel. Half of China's yak and one third of all the world's yak are in Qinghai.

Times are changing however: recently, a 3500 gm gold nugget was found, and a gold rush is on. The national government is focusing its economic development on the NW region. Pastureland is now contracted to herdsmen for 30 years, thus encouraging the users to manage it more wisely. Bonuses are given in some counties for families who send children to school, not an easy task for nomads. The government is building railways and highways.

SHOPPING

Good buys are handicrafts made by the minorities.

HOTELS

Qinghai Hotel (Binguan) ● *20 Huang He Rd. 810001. Cable 0524. Dist.A.P.30 km. Dist.R.W.3 km. Near government trade offices and tourist shopping* ● 1989. 23 stories, 270 rooms. Clinic, sports center, business and conference centers.

Xining Guest Hotel (Binguan) ● *215 Qiyi Rd. 810000. Dist.A.P. 12 km. Dist.R.W. 4 km* ● 1957; ren. 1985. 400 rooms. Main tourist hotel.

C.I.T.S. and **C.T.S.** 国际旅行社 : 215 Qiyi Rd. 810000. tel. 23901. **Qinghai C.T.S.** and **Qinghai Tourism Bureau:** 57 Xi Ave. 810000; tel. 42721. Telex 70053 CIPSX CN. Fax 42721.
C.Y.T.S.: tel. 76339.

YAN'AN 延安

(Yenan) Northwest China. Flight connections with Xi'an, Tai-yuan, and Beijing. 8½ hours by road or rail north of Xi'an. Northern Shaanxi in the Loess Plateau. Weather: Hottest—35°C in July; coldest—⁻25°C in January. Rainy season: August–September. Altitude 800–1000 meters. During the rainy season, planes may be postponed or canceled. Urban population: 50,000.

Yan'an was a small administrative town 1000 years ago. In 1936 it had a population of 3000. It became the most important Communist revolutionary site in China in January 1937 after the end of the Long March. The Communists chose to settle here because of the rugged mountain terrain, a wise choice because the Nationalists failed to dislodge them for 10 years. Here, the Communists trained leaders, developed policies, organized the peasants, and planned strategy against the Nationalists and Japanese. In 1945 the population was 100,000. Chiang Kai-shek finally succeeded in capturing the city without a fight in March 1947 and held it until April 1948, while Mao Zedong (Mao Tse-tung) went on to take the whole of China.

Today Yan'an is primarily of interest to revolutionists and students of modern history and architecture. For others it has only a Tang pagoda famous primarily because of the revolution, and a tiny cave of 10,000 Buddhas. This is an interesting off-the-beaten-path destination now.

The city, clinging to the mountainside, stretches along both sides of the Yan River and the South and Dufu streams. The soil is loess, excellent for construction. Most of the area houses are quonset-hut-shape "caves," either freestanding or dug into a mountain. They are said to be cozy and dry in the winter and cool in the summer. Many buildings have been converted to brick as income increases.

The city is now largely industrial. Nearby are oil wells and coal mines. Meter-high mounds of huge black chunks of coal piled haphazardly in the streets are a little startling.

The middle school rates a visit insofar as it was started after the Long March, whose leaders visited often to oversee the curriculum. Now it is like any other school. See also "Milestones in Chinese History."

Yan'an Revolutionary Memorial Hall 延安革命纪念馆 : This excellent museum has a giant map outlining the route of the Long March in neon. Titles are in English and Chinese. Exhibits also include a fascinating model of tunnel warfare, Communist bank notes, and Chairman Mao's horse (stuffed).

Residences of Chairman Mao 毛主席旧居 are also museums, furnished as simply as they were then, all of them ''caves'':

(1) Foot of Fenghuang (Phoenix) Hill 凤凰山麓 : January 1937–November 1938. Here Mao wrote his important articles on ''contradiction'' and ''protracted war.'' The photo in front of the cave was taken in 1937, just after Zhou Enlai (Chou En-lai), who lived nearby, returned from settling the Xi'an Incident. Mao left this cave because of Japanese bombing.

(2) Yangjialing 杨家岭 : November 1938–January 1943. The auditorium was the site of several party Central Committee meetings and a national congress (1945), delegates risking their lives to come from and return to Nationalist-held areas.

(3) Zaoyuan (Date Orchard) 枣园 : January 1943–end of 1945. The Secretariat was close by. The lilac tree in front was planted by Mao. On his desk is the first iron bar made in the local foundry. He exercised his hand with the bar to avoid writer's cramp. From here Zhou Enlai flew to Chongqing to negotiate with Chiang, an American-instigated effort to avoid civil war.

(4) Wangjiaping 王家坪 : January 1946–March 1947. Headquarters of the Eighth Route Army. Dances were held in the garden. The civil war resumed, and here Mao argued with his military commanders about withdrawing from Yan'an in the face of an enormous Nationalist campaign in March 1947.

Baota (Precious Pagoda) 宝塔（延安宝塔） a.k.a. Yan'an Pagoda: 44 meters, nine stories; 1300-year-old (Tang) building. Can be climbed.

Wangfo Dong (Cave of the 10,000 Buddhas) 万佛洞 is right in town below the pagoda and relatively close to Wangjiaping. It dates from the Song and Jin. Most of the Buddhas are tiny; some are in good condition. The cave was used to house the printing presses of the Central Committee.

Liu Lin Village has been documented by visitors as far back as the '60s. Read Jan Myrdal's *Report from a Chinese Village* if you want to compare progress then and now.

Huangling County 黄陵 , just about halfway on the road between Xi'an and Yan'an, 4 hours' drive from each. Huangling makes an interesting break and, for ancient Chinese history buffs, is a very important stop. There is a hotel, built mid-1980s.

The ***Tomb of the Yellow Emperor Xuan Yuan:** 3.6 meters high and 50 meters in circumference, originally built in the Han but moved here to its present site in the Song. The Yellow Emperor is the legendary ancestor of the Chinese people believed to have lived about 2000 B.C. The tomb is at the top of Qiaoshan (hill), 1 km north of Huangling town. At the base is Xuan Yuan temple. Of its 63,000 cypress trees, one is said to have been planted by the Yellow Emperor himself. It is the largest known ancient cypress in China. In front of the tomb is the Platform of Immortality built by Emperor Han Wu (156–87 B.C.) to announce his victory over his enemy and to pray for longevity. The temple of Xuan Yuan was built in the Han. The throne stands in the middle with information about Xuan's life on both sides. In ancient times, travelers had to dismount from their horses and pay respect to their First Ancestor as they passed by.

The **Cave Temple of a Thousand Buddhas** (Tang) is halfway up Ziwu Hill in the western part of Huangling county.

Ask about performances of the Waist Drummers and the Ankle and Wrist Drummers. Ask also about China's second largest waterfall, 210 km from Huangling County on the Yellow River, and the **Mausoleum of Hua Milan,** the warrior woman who inspired Maxine Hong Kingston's famous book.

See "Food" for local dishes.

HOTELS

Yan'an Guest House (Binguan) • *56 Yanan St. 716000. Dist.A.P. 10 km.* • 1965; ren. 1980. 3 stories. 168 rooms.
CAAC: Dong-guan Airport; tel. 3854.
C.T.S. and C.I.T.S.: 106 Yanan Ave., 716000; tel. 2589.
See also "Jinggang Shan" and "Shijiazhuang."

YANGTZE GORGES 长江三峡

(a.k.a. Yangzi or Changjiang River Gorges) The boat trip through the gorges and on the great river itself to or from Chongqing is highly recommended not just for its relaxed sightseeing of spectacular scenery but also for its history. Do bring binoculars, a telephoto lens if you're a camera bug, and reading material. The scenery includes sheer cliffs rising up to 400 meters on either side of narrow, rushing water, mountains up to 1000 meters, old towns cut by slender lines of stone steps, and a mountain lined from top to bottom with a pagoda. The Yangtze River is also a busy highway, but one rarely sees sailboats or tow paths being used. The river is now being harnessed even more for flood control, irrigation, and hydroelectric power.

A controversial dam, planned with Canadian help, has been considered. If built, it would displace up to a million people, raise the water level about 175 meters, and destroy the dramatic effect of the gorges. In 1989, the decision was postponed for five years. In 1991, the idea was resurrected.

Guides will tell you stories of the Three Kingdoms, but do bring your own history books along, or a copy of *The Sand Pebbles* or John Hersey's *A Single Pebble*. Probe International's *Damming the Three Gorges* is an environmental group's readable critique of the feasibility study of the proposed dam. Van Slyke's *Yangtze, Nature, History and the River* also describes the foreigners who lived here, and the Three Kingdoms. The *Romance of the Three Kingdoms* has been translated into English, and the names of the heroes of this great military story will keep coming up almost anywhere you go in central China. If you don't have a guide with you, maybe the steward or cook can point out landmarks, or get a tourist map. The Yangtze was also central to the foreign merchants, gunboats, and missionaries in the late 1800s and early 1900s, but guides will not give you much information about this embarrassing period.

There are several ways of sailing the Gorges. The cheapest are the **passenger ferries,** where tour groups get first crack at the top second-class accommodations with a lounge and the best view. Second-class has two bunks. No one gets private toilets, baths, or air conditioners. Individual travelers with second-class tickets might even get downgraded to third, fourth, or fifth class, where you share a room with an increasing number of people, or sleep in hallways. You might get bumped off the boat entirely by tour groups. Try for an outside cabin. The inside ones can get pretty stuffy in summer, and you might find other passengers gambling noisily on the floor outside your room.

Stops are prescheduled and not necessarily at tourist sites like Shibaozhai, nor can you be sure your ship will get close enough to get a photo of that lovely 11-story pagoda unless you have a lens at least 200 mm long. But you only pay for passage to where you want to get off. And, by ferry, you can get closer to Chinese people, and experience with them the loudspeakers blaring announcements at 6 a.m. and queues for showers. After all, didn't you come here to meet the people?

Ferries can be booked through travel agencies, or directly at the pier a couple of days ahead of time.

Currently, more expensive air-conditioned ships for tourists ply the Yangtze from April 1 to Dec. 1, and can be booked through tour agents. On these you are isolated from Chinese people, but these **tourist ships** are more comfortable.

Itineraries differ depending on which way you are going—up- or downriver, and which ship you book, and are usually between Chongqing and Wuhan (longer), or Yichang.

Most tourists go downstream, but some travelers have gone upstream and prefer having the extra day to relax and a ship almost entirely to themselves. Some, but not all, have been given the scheduled day trips.

Stops might include climbing hundreds of stairs, part of the lifestyle.

The ships include the *Bashan* (one of the fanciest), leased by Abercrombie and Kent. Pacific Delight and Canada Swan can book the newer and bigger *Yangtze Paradise*. Other ships are not as fancy. In fact, older ships tend to get rundown. These tourist ships stop for sightseeing at some but not all of the following: Lake Dongting, Fengdu, Fengjie, Jingzhou, Jiujiang, Lushan, Shashi, Shibaozhai, Wanxian, Yichang, Yueyang, and Yunyang. The highlight for many tourists is the day trip up the three little gorges on the Daning River, where they can see wild monkeys and suspended coffins. Do make sure you can stop there before you book.

The services of these tourist ships include guide-interpreter, double rooms with private baths, laundry, doctor, currency exchange, post and telegraph, beauty salon, library, lounge (with evening movies), a bar, Western food, and a store—none of which the public ferries have. Depending on class, you would be lucky to get a seat for eating on a passenger ferry.

The quality of the ships differ; they are owned by different companies. Do not expect the *Love Boat* with a social convener. There is usually a captain's dinner, and a final dance (to ancient music, so bring your own cassettes). Some ships have smelly toilets. Most have picture windows so you can enjoy the view from your cabin. Few have working swimming pools. Some have been delayed by repairs and gone through one of the gorges after dark or during meal times. If this happens to you, we urge you to insist on a car to see anything missed due to the fault of the ship, or take your food and eat out on deck.

Meanwhile back at the **public ferry,** which operates all year round, going downstream from Chongqing to Wuhan, which is the best way to go—faster—the trip takes two nights on board ship and three days on the water. The ferries stop at towns along the way for a few minutes up to several hours. Take your own soap and towel. Each ferry has about 24 second-class cabins. None have much privacy. It is better, if you are on a ferry, to ride only to Chenglingji (Yueyang) because the stretch between Yichang and Wuhan, a whole day's ride, isn't all that interesting. After a day of sightseeing around Dongting Lake (Candice Bergen was a missionary there in *The Sand Pebbles*—see "Yueyang"), you can go on to Changsha or Wuhan by train.

Ferry Downstream —Day 1: Leave Chongqing early (about 7 a.m.). Note white pagoda on north bank at Changshou. At about 3 hours out, Fuling. At 8½ hours out, Zhongxian. At 10 hours out, look for **Shibaozhai (Precious Stone Village),** a.k.a. Shibao Block, on the north bank, with its 11-story Qing pagoda. It is built on a limestone rock hill, Yuyin Shan (Jade Seal Hill), that rises to 160 meters above the river. In the main temple are statues of Liu Bei, Zhuge Liang, Guan Yu, and Zhang Fei, historical personages. Three of these swore oaths in a peach orchard to support each other. They are immortalized in *The Romance of the Three Kingdoms.* Emperor Liu Bei, who led an unsuccessful army to avenge the death of Guan Yu, retreated here and died of sorrow.

At 12½ hours, overnight stop at 2000-year-old **Wanxian,** the site of one of the first successful assertions of Chinese power against the imperialist gunboats during the Northern Expedition. There was a lot of shooting here in the late 1920s. Tourists climb about 85 steps to the 700,000-population town for a silk factory and store.

Day 2: The ship leaves early (about 2:30 a.m.), depending on the current, to reach the first gorge 4½ hours later, at daylight. Near the entrance on the north bank is a two-story pavilion with red lacquer columns, which marks the beginning of the gorges. On the south side of Kui Men Gate are two stone towers and five Chinese characters, which mean "The Kui Men Gate is an unmatched pass."

The **Qutang (Chutang) Gorge** is 8 km long and takes about an hour to pass through. It is the "most imposing" of the gorges, only

100–150 meters wide. Prepare for a very windy passage, as the wind as well as the water is funneled between the cliffs.

The **Wuxia (Wuhsia),** or just Wu Gorge, starts 30 minutes after you leave the Qutang. It is 44 km long and takes about 1½ hours to pass through. Look for the Twelve Peaks Enshrouded in Rain and Mist, of which you can see six on the north bank and three on the south. Of these, the Peak of the Goddess is the highest, at over 1000 meters. It has a tall stone column on top that looks like "a strongly built young woman gazing from high up in the sky at the waterway down below." Look for a tablet-shaped rock with six Chinese characters meaning "The Wu Gorge boasts craggy cliffs," said to be written by a prime minister of the Shu Kingdom in the third century. Ask also about Xiang Xi (Fragrant Stream), where a lady-in-waiting of a Han emperor dropped her pearls accidentally. The water here is said to be "limpid and fragrant" as a result.

About 20 minutes after leaving the Wuxia Gorge at the town of Badong, pomelos, oranges, and persimmons are for sale on shore, if in season. Look for a temple high on a hill. You are now in Hubei province.

About 1 hour from Badong is the 75-km-long **Xiling (Hsiling) Gorge,** which takes about 1½ hours to pass through. It is the longest and most treacherous of the three. Thirty minutes beyond the entrance, on the south side, is Kuang Ming village, with a large temple, Huang Ling Miao. Then comes Five Sisters Peaks, Three Brothers Rocks, and the Needle. This is the area considered for the largest dam in the world. Then you go through the locks of **Gezhouba** dam, where you might stop and see a good model of the project, which includes a 2561-meter-long and 70-meter-high dam, two power stations, a silt discharge gate, a reservoir, a flood-discharge gate, and a channel for migrating fish. Nearby **Yichang** has an airport and the relatively good Three Gorges Hotel with C.I.T.S., tel. (0717) 223255, fax 224446. C.Y.T.S. is tel. 25251. Yichang is an industrial city in the plains. This is the end of the spectacular scenery. From here read or get to know some of the 500 other passengers. If you stay on board, you arrive late afternoon the next day in Wuhan.

Fengjie was the capital of the state of Kwei during the Spring and Autumn Period (722–481 B.C.), the time of Confucius. The tomb of Liu Bei's wife is here. See *Romance of the Three Kingdoms.* The ancient wall and gate still stand. Fengjie is near the western entrance to the gorges. **Fengdu** has statues of demons and hell. Not as kitschy as Hong Kong's Tiger Balm Gardens. A real village is nearby that might satisfy you more. The Qing Ming festival celebrated here is special.

Jingzhou has a well-preserved 2000-year-old mummy, an ancient gate, walls from the Three Kingdoms period (A.D. 220–265), Ka Yuan Taoist Temple from the Tang (now also a museum), and Tai Hui Temple from 1393 A.D., factory for thermos bottles and bedspreads, and a museum. C.I.T.S., Jingzhou, Jiangling, 434100. Tel. 67999, 66429. Telex 416014 ZBTH CN. Fax 67261. C.T.S.: tel. 20155, 24895.

Shashi is a centuries-old trans-shipment port, opened to foreign trade in 1895. Over 2000 years old, it has the Zhanghua Temple (Ming) and a gate built by Guanyu of the Three Kingdoms. Airport. C.T.S. tel. 2325.

If you miss the boat at any of your stops, travel agents can arrange transport for you to catch up. Some tourists on cruises have been able to drive to see the gorges by land, a rewarding experience.

GEZHOUBA

Southwest China, in Hubei, is the new town (1970s) where tour boats pass through the locks on the Changjiang (Yangtze) River, 3 km downstream of the Three Gorges and about 1 km upstream of Yichang. The biggest multipurpose water conservancy project on the river, it includes a 2561-meter-long and 70-meter-high dam, two power stations (2.715 million kwh capacity), a silt-dischrage gate, a reservoir, a flood-discharge gate, and a channel for migrating fish. Completed in 1988, 21 generators should be able to produce 14.1 billion kwh annually. The difference in water level is about 20 meters. Visitors can see a working model.

YANGZHOU 揚州

(Yangchow) East China. 20 km north of the Yangtze on the Grand Canal in Jiangsu province, Yangzhou is almost 2500 years old and famous for its gardens and pavilions. Because of its location, it was a very prosperous port after the Sui emperors had the canal built. In the Tang dynasty, it was the residence of over 5,000 foreigners. One of Prophet Mohammed's descendants is buried here, and in 1282 Marco Polo is said to have spent three years as inspector. Yangzhou's wealth declined with that of the canal, and by the Qing, it was famous only as an imperial resort city. It is one of the 36 historical and cultural cities protected by the State Council. It is one of the nicest cities, with lots of old Chinese architecture and a relaxed atmosphere. (All new buildings must be in traditional Chinese styles and industries in the suburbs.) It can now be reached by ferry and bus from Zhenjiang on the south shore, 2 hours by expressway from Nanjing, or by boat along the Yangtze or the Grand Canal. An international airport is planned for 1995 between Yangzhou and Nanjing. Currently, one uses the Nanjing airport 120 km away. The closest railway is in Zhenjiang. Its population is 400,000. Its hottest temperature is 34°C in July–August; its coldest is −2°C in January–February. Annual precipitation is about 1000 mm, mainly from June to September.

If you only have one day in Yangzhou, the 2½-hour Emperor Qian Long's boat tour, which includes:

—**Shouxi (Slender West) Lake** 瘦西湖 , in the NW suburbs, 4.3 km long and surrounded by lovely, peaceful scenes: curled-roof pavilions, the Five Pavilion Bridge, and the imposing White Dagoba (Qing), all packaged in the north and south Chinese garden styles. At the Diaoyutai (Fishing Terrace), Qing Emperor Qianlong is supposed to have fished once. He sounds like a good politician. The Five Pavilion Bridge was built on the occasion of his visit. It is best seen on the night of a full moon, when 15 moons are supposed to reflect from the water under the arches, a Chinese puzzle that must be seen.

—The **Daming Temple** 大明寺 , was founded in the fifth century. An impressive arch commemorates a famous nine-story pagoda that used to be here but was destroyed by fire in 843. The Daming has 18 three-meter-high carved Buddhist statues.

—The **Jian Zhen Memorial Hall** 鉴真纪念堂 , near Daming Temple, built in 1973 to commemorate the 1200th anniversary of the death of Monk Jian Zhen. It, too, is lovely in spite of its youth; it is a copy of the Toshodai Temple in Nara, Japan. This abbot of Daming Temple persisted in going to Japan to teach Buddhism in spite of five unsuccessful efforts and his blindness. He succeeded at age 66. Because he and his disciples also introduced Tang literature, medicine, architecture, sculpture, and other arts to Japan, he is highly honored in that country, where he died and is buried. An over-1000-year-old statue of Jian Zhen, now a national Japanese treasure, was brought back for a visit ''because it looked homesick.''

Along the way, one can also see a delightful potted landscape garden, and the 24-Maid Bridge. All these places can be seen on foot or by bus, but a boat is more fun. In the afternoon, there's a lacquerware, jade-carving or paper-cutting factory, and shopping.

—The **Yangzhou Museum** 扬州博物馆 , small, informal, and pleasant. The Marco Polo Hall was opened recently. The Italians sent a bronze lion, the symbol of Venice. Curiously, there are two Italian tombstones on display, one possibly a woman's, dated 1342 and 1344.

—The **Geyuan Garden** 个园 (Qing), started as a private garden and later the home of the Ye Chun Poet's Society in the Qing. It is full of gnarled rockeries, moon gates, bamboo, latticed doorways, wavy walls, and real picture windows. The rockeries are built around a spring-summer-autumn-winter theme. Do these inspire you, too, to poetry?

—The **Heyuan Garden** 何园 (Qing), in the SE part of the city close to the Geyuan, typical of Yangzhou's gardens. The Arabic-styled **Tomb of Puhaddin** is on the east bank of the Grand Canal, near the Heyuan. Built in the 13th century, it contains the remains of this 16th-generation descendant of Mohammed, the founder of Islam. Puhaddin (Burhdn Al-Dan) came to China as a missionary in the Southern Song. The 700-year-old **Xianhe (Crane) Mosque** is one of the four most famous in China, and was built between 1265 and 1275. It is worth a visit. Open daily except Fridays; tel. 44963. A Han tomb has recently opened 4 km away.

If you have more time, Yangzhou has five kilometers of canals, a seven-story pagoda, and **Guang Ling,** a classic book publishing house, the only place in China where you can see the Song Dynasty printing process.

Festivals: Food Festival in autumn. Unusual boat festival in Qintong 60 km away during the Qing Ming. The Daming Temple bells bring luck to those who hear them midnight, Dec. 31.

Day trips can be arranged to go from here to Zhenjiang and Nanjing; there are longer excursions along the canal.

SHOPPING

Locally made are lacquerware, red lacquer carving, jade carving, velvet flowers, paper cuts, and silk lanterns. At the paper-cutting factory, a master craftsman can cut lacy paper chrysanthemums for you. Yangzhou also exports potted landscapes, miniature trees and mountains.

Friendship Store (454 Guoqing Rd. North; tel. 223032, 223715 with adjacent antique stores. **Yangzhou Antique and Curio Store** (1 Yanfu Rd; tel. 224987.) Antiques, arts, and crafts.

RESTAURANTS

Thousand-layer oily cake may sound awful, but it is delicious. People also go to Yangzhou from Nanjing just for the dumplings. Both the Yangzhou and Xiyuan hotels can reproduce a banquet from the novel *Dream of the Red Mansion*. (The author's father lived here.)

HOTELS

The best located for tourists are the Xi Yuan and Yangzhou, with good gardens and within walking distance of the museum and tourist stores. The Yangzhou has more services and liveliness. Both had dirty carpets. The Qiong Hua seems to be the best equipped and better located for business people. Whether it can maintain its initial high quality is a question.

Qiong Hua Hotel (Dasha) • *3 Pi Fang St., 225001. 3☆. Telex 364022 YZQBD CN. Fax 231079. Dist. city hall and trade offices 2 km. Dist. He Garden 200 m* • C.C. 1991–92. Four adjoining buildings, 22 stories, 150 rooms. IDD. B.C. Dorm. Gym, pool, and tennis soon.

Xi Yuan Hotel (Fandian) • *1 Fengle Shang St., 225002. 2☆. Fax 233870* • C.C. 1976, ren. 1990. 210 beds for foreigners. No western breakfast. IDD from lobby only. No elevator in five story building. B.C.

Yangzhou Hotel (Binguan) • *5 Fengle Shang St., 225002. 3☆. Telex 364018 YZHTL CN. Fax 343599* • C.C. 1985. Ren. 1988. 9 stories, 150 rooms, B.C. gym, pool. IDD. Elevator.

C.I.T.S.: 1 Upper Fengle St., 225002 tel. 345746, 348925. Telex 364001 YZTLR CN. Fax 233870.
C.T.S.: Xiyuan Hotel; tel. 343804, 344888 X377. Telex 34075 YZHTL CN.

CAAC   : Zhenyuan Hotel, Sanyuan Rd.; tel. 24619.
CYTS: tel. 344844, 342619.
Ambulance: tel. 43506, 340790.
Police: tel. 110.
Yangzhou Tourism Administration: 1 Fengle Shangjie 225002.

YANTAI 烟台

A.k.a. Zhifu (Chefoo, Cheefoo) North China. On the northern coast of Shandong province, about 250 km NE of Qingdao by train or 5-hour superhighway. It can be reached by plane from 4 Chinese cities. It can also be reached by ship, and by direct 16-hour train from Beijing and Shanghai. Weather: Coldest—⁻10°C in January; hottest—28.3°C in July and August. Annual precipitation about 700 mm in June.

Inhabited almost 2200 years ago, this fishing village was visited by the first Qin emperor early in its existence. That egomaniac really got around! In 1398, during the Ming, a military post was set up, and beacon towers built for transmitting messages. Yantai means "smoke tower."

Yantai was opened to foreign trade in 1862. It was a summer resort for the U.S. Navy's Yangtze Patrol (with White Russian bar girls). The China Inland Mission operated a school here for missionary children; the buildings now are used by the Chinese Navy. Yantai's harborside area and Chaoyang Street still reflect the old architecture. Yantai Hill once housed 10 foreign consulates.

Yantai is one of the original Coastal Cities recently opened to trading and accelerated industrial development. The urban population is now over 780,000.

Today, Yantai is an important ice-free port that has received international cruise ships. It also claims one third of China's prawn catch, and one tenth of its total aquatic harvest. It farms prawns, abalone, scallops, and jelly fish. It grows peanuts (one fifth of China's crop), cherries, grapes, and apples, and grows and cans white asparagus. It mines one quarter of China's gold. The closest mine is about 80 km from the city.

Yantai is one of the prettiest little cities in China, nestled between the sea and, on three sides, gentle hills. Many of its buildings are topped with orange tiles, and some are of rose-colored stone. It does not have the depressing look of neglected structures that many Chinese cities unfortunately have. It has a cheerful atmosphere of vitality and prosperity. Off the main tourist track, it is more for relaxed family sightseeing and swimming than hectic tourism.

Penglai Pavilion 蓬莱阁 is the most important tourist attraction here and is 83 km NW of the city, past the Yantai Economic and Technology Development Zone. A visit to Penglai can take a day.

Penglai Pavilion was a favorite place for centuries of scholars and poets, for it was from here, legend says, that the Eight Taoists Immortals flew across the seas. After getting drunk, each tried to compete with the other using his-her own treasure. (See *Attributes of the Eight Taoist Genii* in "What Is There to See and Do?") Some people say they flew to Japan, fighting on the way with the dragon king of the sea. A Japanese legend speaks of seven fairies. But some people say these fairies achieved immortality or arrived in paradise. Myths vary. The pavilion was first built in the Northern Song (1056–63) and extended in 1589. The buildings themselves cover 19,000 square meters.

From the Penglai Pavilion, mirages have been seen on the calm summer surface of the sea by many people. A recent one was in 1988. C.I.T.S. says a video was made and can only be seen in Penglai. Let me know what it looks like. Natives have conflicting opinions about the ideal conditions for mirages, but they seem to be summer and autumn with the east wind blowing shortly after a gentle rain, between 2 and 3 p.m. The mirage is of a high mountain, an island or old city, which some people believe to be Dalian or Korea across the straits.

The pavilion with the tables and chairs has a chair of longevity. If people sit on it, they will live a long time. It was in this room that the immortals had their party! Oh, come on!

Movies about the Taoist immortals have been shown regularly on television. Ask about them, at your hotel. A good Hong Kong one is the *Eight Immortals Cross the Sea*. One should realize that these mythical people were each from different periods of history—but legend says they did get together during the Song! Fairies can do anything!

Among the other buildings nearby are the Temple of the Sea Goddess Tian Hou, a Taoist temple, and the Wind Protection Hall, where lighted matches will not blow out even if the wind is from the north. Important is the room full of calligraphy by a famous Ming calligraphist who lived here for three years waiting unsuccessfully to see a mirage. Let that be a lesson to you!

The *Penglai Water Town (a.k.a. Beiwocheng), immediately to the south of the pavilion, was built as a fortress, particularly against Japanese pirates. The Song and Ming navies trained here, and the Ming expanded the defenses. Intriguing is the water gate. In the old days, pirates were lured inside and the gate closed behind them. Then, after the water level rose, the gate was opened and the dead pirates flushed out. Originally built in 1376, the gate was rebuilt in 1596.

A replica of the Ming town **Dengzhou** 登州 , including an old-style bazaar, is on the way from the bus stop to the pavilion. Two recently built Ming warships take visitors for rides.

On special occasions, spear-carrying guards in Ming dress, waving dynastic flags, stilt and boat dancers, and firecrackers enliven the gateway and market.

The **Eight Immortals Palace** is a nearby exhibition with moving figures of these famous mythological people. It can give you some background, but it's not Disneyland.

Also important to see in Yantai is the **Museum** 烟台博物馆 (2 Yulan St.; tel. 222520). Open daily, except Mondays, in the middle of town. It is in a gaudy Fujian-style guild hall with a temple dedicated to the sea goddess. The beautifully restored building was constructed from 1884 to 1906 in Fujian, and brought in three sections here. Note the jawbone of a whale and the remains of a giant sea turtle. A statue of the goddess, destroyed during the Cultural Revolution, has been replaced in wax. The museum has a few relics from 8000 B.C. to more recent times, with labels in English. It can be seen in 40 minutes. Antique store on premises.

Pleasant to visit is the 600-year old white **Yuhuang (Jade Emperor) Temple,** at 70 meters above sea level, with a good view of the city. The temple building is original, the tower built in 1984, and the memorial arch in 1876. A 600-year-old white pomegranate tree here still bears fruit. Nearby is another garden, ''Little Penglai,'' inspired by the real one to the north.

A visit to the **Zhang Yu Wine Company** 张裕葡萄酒厂 and the **Woolen Embroidery Factory** 绒绣厂 are also recommended if you are interested. The wine-making and the embroidery date from imperialist days, the needlepoint probably taught by missionaries. Some of the patterns are European. The woolen embroidery of China's mountains in Chairman Mao's Mausoleum in Beijing was made here.

If you have more time: On **Yantai Hill,** a lighthouse was built on top of a Ming dynasty beacon tower. It has a good view of the harbor.

Yangma Dao (Horse Racing Island) (a.k.a. Elephant Island, because of its shape) is 1 hour by road away. Here the first Qin emperor raised horses and visited three times. A 4-km horse-racing track with bleachers opened in 1985, but no gambling at this time. The best hotel seems to be the Yangmadao or the Minzhu but don't expect much.

Yantai has two bathing beaches in the city proper: **No. 1 Bathing Beach** 海水浴场 , in central Yantai, and **No. 2 Bathing Beach** farther east (tel. 5440). Both have all facilities. C.I.T.S. here claims that Yantai has no sharks, but rival summer resort Qingdao does! The swimming season goes from June to early September.

Yantai is a pioneer in **home-stay** programs "for tourists bored by temples." Visitors can pay to live very comfortably in the relatively substantial homes of rich peasants or fishermen, and learn about life in the countryside (usually two days and one night). Visitors can also sail with fishermen.

By Chinese standards, some of the rural villages here are incredibly wealthy, and a visit will explain why. **Xiguan Village** 西关村 , 23 km away, is one of the places where you can spend the night with a family (usually part of a package, and not cheap).

Kongtong Isle 崆峒岛 is 4.5 nautical miles off Yantai, and visitors can see a fishing village here. Lots of wild rabbits.

See also "Weihai," "Qingdao," and "Jinan."

SHOPPING

Riesling wines, vermouth, Gold Medal Brandy, lace, tablecloths, straw weaving, wooden-framed clocks, and partially completed woolen needlepoint pieces (very cheap). The best selection is the Arts and Handicraft Service Counter at Nan Da Ave. but it's limited. Try the factories and department stores. For the Zhangyo/Changyo Wine Co., tel. 222029.

FOOD

Seafood, of course! Shandong food is not peppery hot or overly sweet. Lots of garlic, onions, and salt. Yantai people say that Beijing duck originated when two indigent Yantai peasants went to Beijing and found a dead duck on the road. Improvising an earthen oven, they cooked the duck. An official happened by, liked the smell, and asked for a taste. Pleased, he presented the dish to the emperor, who rewarded the official and the poor peasants. See Shandong section under "Food" for some dishes. The best restaurant seems to be the Zhifu Hotel, but ignore the dirty tablecloths.

HOTELS

Hotels here have all been rundown. There are water shortages in summer. The top were the Yantai and the Zhifu. The Yantai is closer to town than the Zhifu and has smaller rooms. The Zhifu is closest to swimming and has a cozier atmosphere. It has been the favorite of resident foreigners. The 1991 3* Asian Hotel is downtown and could be better.

The Cheefoo has the most historical setting at one end of the bund and next to Yantai Hill where the foreign consulates were. In its beautiful suites (with the cigarette burns in the stained carpets), its magnificent dining room with its 15-meter ceiling (once used as a church), and its 1870 bowling alley, one does get a feeling of faded imperialist grandeur. The airport is 25 km from town.

Yantai Hill Guesthouse (Yantai Shan Binguan) • *34 Haian Rd., 246001. Fax 246313. Dist.A.P.25 km. Dist.R.W. 2 km* • T.R., C.C. Two buildings for foreigners. The **Cheefoo Club** was the former British Consulate. Late 1800s. 1913 became hotel. Ren. 1988, 3 stories, 19 rooms. No elevators. Suite 1201 and 1203 face the bund. 1201 has own wide balcony. Double rooms are adequate. The **Seaview Restaurant,** 1988. 3 stories, 38 rooms. IDD. Poorly-maintained dining room.

Yantai Hotel (Dajiudian) • *Eastern Suburbs, 264001. 3*. Fax 248169. Dist.A.P. 25 km. Dist.R.W.8 km. Dist.#2 beach 1.5 km* • Amex and MC. Hong Kong J.V. 1989. 8 stories, 183 rooms. IDD. Low hallway ceilings. Dim sum.

Overseas Chinese Hotel • See C.T.S. below. For backpackers only.

Zhifu Hotel (Zhifu Binguan) • *1 Ying Bin Rd., 264001. 3*. Telex 32561 ZFHYT CN. Fax 248289. Dist. A.P.23 km. Dist.R.W. 8 km. Dist.#2 beach 500 meters* • C.C. 1981, ren. 1988. 6 stories. 115 rooms. IDD. Business center.

OTHER IMPORTANT ADDRESSES
Ambulance: tel. 222436, 222137.
Police: tel. 110.
C.I.T.S. 国际旅行社 : 17–2 Yuhuang Ding Xi Rd., 264000; tel. 245626. Telex 32524 ITSYT CN. Fax 247387. Contact Yantai Tourism Bureau here for brochures or complaints.
C.T.S. 中旅社 : 30 Huanshan Rd. 264001; tel. 224431. Telex 32566 OCGYT CN. Fax 246124.
CAAC 中国民航 : Airport. Southern suburbs; tel. 226605, 241406. Ticket office: 6 Dahaiyang Rd.; tel. 245908.

YINCHUAN 银川

Northwest China. Capital of the Ningxia (Ningsia) Hui Autonomous Region, which lies between Inner Mongolia and Gansu on the north central border of China. It is linked by air with Beijing, Lanzhou, and Xi'an. It is also linked by train with Beijing and is on the Lanzhou-Baotou line. Yinchuan is in the northern part of the province, a few km west of the Huanghe (Yellow) River. It is in the middle of a mesh of irrigation canals in the plains, but close to mountains and classic sand deserts. Weather: In the province the coldest temperature ranges from $^-13°C$ to $^-7°C$ in January; the hottest is 17°C to 26°C in July. Very little rain. Sandstorms, which blow hard in spring and autumn, mean having to take a cover for your nose and eyes.

Yinchuan has only recently been opened to tourists, and whoever goes there has to be adventurous. It is not as far from Beijing as the Silk Road, but the weather is severe, and it is still in the early stages of being developed for tourists.

Ningxia was inhabited 30,000 years ago, and 8000-year-old neolithic relics have also been found here. It was home to the Yong and Di tribes in the Western Zhou. The first Qin emperor conquered the tribes and connected parts of the Great Wall here. He sent thousands of men to settle and defend this area.

Ningxia was close enough to the trade routes for Persian coins to be found in its Northern Wei tombs. It exists because parts have been irrigated by the Yellow River for the last 2000 years. Its fight against the relentless sands is admirable, and visitors from areas like California should be especially interested in how the Chinese here manage. A great deal of the region is covered by the Liupan Mountains, through which the Long March passed in 1935.

Ningxia Hui Autonomous Region was founded in 1958, and many people were moved here from other parts of China in the '60s during the Cultural Revolution. Today, it has many national minorities, including the Huis (31.7%), Mongolians, Manchus, Turfans, and others. The provincial population is 3.89 million.

Ningxia now produces rice, wheat, melons, fruit, and the black hairlike moss called *facai*. The region exports coal and also produces petroleum, mica, asbestos, and lime.

Yinchuan (formerly Xingqing) was founded in the Tang and had a variety of other names until 1947. It was the capital of the Western Xia during the early part of the Song (1038) when it was known as Xing-qing. The Xia kings reigned for about 190 years, but the dynasty was destroyed by Genghis Khan. Very little is known about the Western Xia, the rulers of the Tangut/Qiang people.

Today, 400,000 people live in the urban part of Yinchuan, about 20% Huis, Moslem descendants of those who came 700 years ago to develop this region.

Of importance to visitors is the **Chengtian Monastery Pagoda** 承天寺宝塔 , built in A.D. 1050 (Western Xia) and renovated in the Qing. Like many of the area's pagodas, it is unusually plain. The old **Tanglai Canal** 唐徕古渠 (Tang) and **Hanyan Canal** 汉延古渠 (Han) should be seen as examples of ancient irrigation efforts. Note the old water-wheels. The **South Gate Mosque** 南关清真寺 is recent, with an on-ion dome. The **Zhongda Mosque** 中大寺 is more in the Chinese style.

The **Tongxin Mosque** 同心清真寺 is from the early Ming and was repaired in the Qing. It is one of the largest mosques in the region. The imposing **Jade Emperor Pavilion** 玉皇阁 (Ming) is good for photographs, with its delicate towers, as is the unusual **Drum and Bell Tower** 钟鼓楼 . The *Haibao (Sea Treasure) Pagoda (a.k.a. North Pagoda)** 海宝塔 is also unusual, a naked structure without fancy eaves, and appearing more like a strange sort of Masonic temple. Dating from the early 5th century, it was destroyed by an earthquake but rebuilt in the 18th century in its original style. It is 1 km north of the city.

The **Twin Pagodas at Baizi Pass on Mt. Helan** 拜寺口双塔 and the **Western Xia Mausoleum** 西夏王陵 are at the base of Mt. Helan, 25 km southwest of Yinchuan. The mausoleum is rather crude and of interest primarily to people keen on history. In treeless surroundings, it has a stark kind of primitive beauty. The founder of the Western Xia kingdom built over 70 tombs, most as decoys.

The remains of the nine imperial tombs can be visited. Archaeologists believe that octagonal glazed-tile pagodas once stood by each tomb. For atmosphere, tourists can visit at night when the tombs are illuminated and accompanied by ancient music. The tomb of Li Yuan-hao the dynasty's founder can be entered.

Adventurers can also take rides on the river on rafts buoyed by inflated sheep skins. How many of your friends at home have ever, ever done that! Normal watercraft are also available. At **Qingtongxia** 青铜峡 south of the city, is a gorge and an impressive dam. Nearby on a barren hill, the mysterious 108 white dagobas are arranged in the shape of a triangle in 12 rows from one to 19 in odd numbers. The smallest one is about six feet and three arm-spans around. They are Buddhist structures from the 13th and 14th centuries, apparently built to ward off the ''108 human frustrations.''

The city also has a **museum** 博物馆 and a Russian Orthodox Church. The Guyuan grottoes, the mosque in Tongxin county, the Kangji Buddhist Pagoda in Tongxin County, and the Wanshou Pagoda (the latter two both dating from A.D. 1038 to 1227) are among the attractions renovated for Ningxia's 30th anniversary in 1988.

Also in the region: **2000-year-old rock paintings on Helan Mountain** 贺兰山古石画; the ruins of the **Great Wall** 长城 (Warring States: 475–221 B.C.) are mainly earthen mounds, no stone. Especially important are the ***Buddhist grottoes on Mt. Xumi** (a.k.a. Sumeru) 须弥山 in Guyuan County. They are Northern Wei to the Tang (A.D. 618–907) and have a 19-meter-tall bust of Buddha rising from the floor of a cave. In the south of the province, these caves are impressive, although many of their 300 statues are damaged. Unless they have been recently built, few, if any, sidewalks and stairs connect the 132 caves. This cave temple covers an area 1 by 2 km and the trip is rugged.

The **Gao Temple,** in Zhongwei County in the western part of the province, is striking because of its sandy monotone. A temple for Confucianism, Buddhism, and Taoism, it also has statues of the Jade Emperor, the Holy Mother, and Guan Yu, the god of War. These point to the eclecticism of Chinese religion. Multipurpose temples of this broad range, however, are rare.

SHOPPING

The region produces sheepskin garments, licorice root, Helan inkstone carvings, rugs, and blankets.

Food is mainly Moslem (mutton, no pork). Corn on the cob and oil sticks (like long donuts) are delicious.

HOTELS

Helan Shan Hotel • *Wei Si Rd. 750021. 2*.*

Ningxia Hotel (Binguan) • *5 Gongyuan St. 750001. 2*.*

CAAC: 14 Minzu Bei St.; tel. 2143.
C.I.T.S. and **C.T.S.:** 150, Jiefang Xi St. 750001; tel. 22265, 33720; telex 750065 NX FAXO CN or 70191 TBNXY CN. Fax 44308. C.T.S., 4th floor, tel. 44485.
Ningxia Tourist Bureau: 117 Jiefang Xi St., 750001. Tel. 22265.
Police: tel. 114.
Tourist Hotline: tel. 44485.

YUEYANG 宜兴

(Yoyang, Yochow) South China. On the north shore of Lake Dongting 洞庭湖 in northern Hunan, just south of the Yangtze, 2000 year old Yueyang is sometimes a side trip from Changsha, 160 km south. It is also close to the mother of all dragon boat races.

Yueyang Tower 岳阳楼 was first built in a.d. 716 in the Tang as a place for officers to train the navy. The site was a Warring States military burial ground. The tower was destroyed and rebuilt many times, the latest time in 1867 in the original Tang style. At that time it became the west gate of the city. It is made of wood, is 19 meters high, and covers 240 square meters. One of the eight Taoist genii—Lu Tung-pin, with the supernatural sword—was a Tang scholar who became a priest after failing the imperial examinations. He is said to have magically saved the original tower from collapsing. He is also said to be responsible for the creation of the long, silver-white fish in Lake Dongting. On the right of the tower is the Drunk Three Times Pavilion, named after the occasions Lu became drunk here; on the left is the Fairy Plum Pavilion, named because a stone slab with imprints was found under the foundation during renovations in the Ming. The main tower is now a museum.

Tourists have also visited a fishing village and the annual lotus flower festival.

Junshan Island 军山岛 , 15 km west across the lake, has 72 hills on 247 acres of land. The highest hill has a celebrated view of the 740,000-acre lake, which is one of the settings of the novel and movie *The Sand Pebbles*. The island grows the famous Junshan Silver Needles Tea, many species of bamboo, and a tree with red leaves on one side and green on the other. It is a bird-watcher's paradise. The island also abounds in myths, so expect your guide to tell you many of the stories as you sip tea made from Liu Yi well water. Try to imagine the time during the Song when 10,000 troops were stationed here.

As for the dragon boats, in 278 B.C. in the nearby Miluo River, Qu Yuan, the great patriotic poet, drowned himself in protest against the destruction of the State of Chu. Ever since, Chinese people have commemorated this tragic event with the races. Some believe the boatmen were originally hurrying to feed the fish before the fish could eat Qu Yuan!

HOTELS

The Yueyang Hotel • *26 Dongting Bei Rd., 414000* • Seems to be the best.

C.I.T.S. and **C.T.S:** Yunmeng Hotel, 25 Chengdong Rd. 414000; tel. 22482, 24498.

ZHAOQING 肇庆

(Chaoching) East China. About 110 km west of Guangzhou on the west bank of the Xijiang River, Zhaoqing is famous for its scenery and Duan inkstones. It can be reached by ship or bus from Hong Kong or Guangzhou or by a railway from Guangzhou and soon direct trains from Shenzhen. The population is about 200,000. The weather is subtropical, with an annual precipitation of 1599 mm, mainly from April to August.

Seven Star Crags, 七星岩 so named because they appear placed like the seven stars of the Big Dipper, has been described by one tourist as "prettier than Hangzhou." The mountains are very much like those of Guilin, including caves with grotesque limestone formations and an underground stream for boat riding. Seven Star Crags (or Cliffs) is like a potted miniature garden.

Known since ancient times, Zhaoqing was the home for six years of the Italian Jesuit missionary Matteo Ricci, 利玛窦 his first in China. He lived in "Shuihing" in the 1580s. While no one knows exactly where Ricci's house was, an educated guess places it between the boat landing and the Ming pagoda in the old city by the river. The district here has a Song dynasty gate with houses that look like they haven't changed since Ricci's time. The earthen wall circles the old city and can be walked or cycled for an interesting experience. Zhaoqing was also one of the starting points of the Northern Expedition in 1926, and was not really developed as a resort until 1955. Then, 460-hectare Star Lake was created for irrigation, fish breeding, and scenery. Walkways, bridges, and lights were set up in the caves.

The seven crags are named Langfeng (Lofty Wind), Yuping (Jade Screen), Shishi (Stone Chamber), Tianzhu (Pillar of Heaven), Chanchu (Toad), Shinzhang (Stone Palm), and Apo (Hill Slope). The biggest cave is at the foot of Apo Crag and can be entered by boat. If you hit the rocks at Music Instrument Rock, you get different musical notes. Zhaoqing also boasts the **Baiyun (White Cloud) Temple,** built in the Tang (618–907) and the **Chongxi, Wenming, and Xufeng pagodas. Qingyun Temple** is at the middle of 1000-meter-high Dinghu (Tripod) mountain, 18 km NE of Zhaoqing. You could also look for the **Yuejiang Tower,** and the **Water and Moon Palace,** from the Ming. These were damaged during the Cultural Revolution but are now renovated.

The mountain, which is a nature preserve, has a 30-meter-high waterfall on its NW side.

The **Xinghu Amusement Park** is near Xinghu Lake and the Memorial Arch in town. The city also has restaurants, swimming pools, and an art gallery. Golf is planned.

SHOPPING

In addition to the famous inkstones, locally made are ivory and bone carvings, sandalwood fans, paintings, straw products, umbrellas, and jewelry. Ginseng Beer is made here. **Guangdong Zhaoqing Duanxi Factory of Famous Ink Stones** (Gongnong Rd.; tel. 23975. Cable 4551). A good-sized shopping center juts out into the lake near the Overseas Chinese Hotel.

HOTELS

The best hotel by the lake is the Songtao. In town, it's the Overseas Chinese Hotel. 100 km. from closest airport in Foshan; 130 km. from the airport in Guangzhou.

Locust Flower Hotel (Furong Binguan) • *Kang Le Bei Rd. 526022* • New building 1991.

Songtao Hotel (Songtao Binguan) • *Seven Star Crags, 526020. 3☆. Telex 44386 STHZQ CN. Dist. bus station 4 km by road, 2 km by boat across the lake. Dist. river port 6 km. Hotel is across lake from city in park.* • C.C. Ren. 1985. Attractive but not luxury class garden-style hotel between two of the crags (one 90 meters high). 3 and 4 stories. 211 rooms. Good stores. Should have pool now. IDD, B.C. H.K.J.V.

Overseas Chinese Hotel (Huaqiao Dasha) • *90 Tianning 526040. 3*. Telex 44629 HQHZQ CN. Fax 233637. Dist. R.W. 4 km. Near bus station, stores, night market, and lake.* • 1987–88 complete renovations. 239 rooms. B.C. IDD.

C.I.T.S.: tel. 222758.
C.T.S. 2–3 Arch St. East, tel. 225351, 225813 and 90 Tianning Bei Rd. 526000; tel. 22952.
Guangdong Zhaoqing Tourist Trade Development General Corp.: 53 Qixingyanpaifang Dongjie 526040; tel. 223952, 224627.
Recommended reading: *The Wise Man from the West—Matteo Ricci and His Mission to China* by Vincent Cronin.

ZHENGZHOU 郑州

(Chengchow) Northwest China. On both the Beijing-Guangzhou and the Shanghai-Xi'an railway lines, this capital of Henan province is also a 2-hour flight south of Beijing. It can also be reached by air from 23 other Chinese cities and Hong Kong. It is about 20 km south of the Yellow River on the main railway line between Luoyang and Kaifeng. In the province, the coldest average temperature is ⁻10°C in January; the hottest is 27°C in July. Annual rainfall is 500–900 mm, especially July through September. Population: urban 1.7 million.

Zhengzhou is historically important as one of the first cities to be built in China. This was during the Shang dynasty 3500 years ago. It is also important because of its proximity to Shaolin Monastery, known to every *kung fu* fan. Zhengzhou is a good place to start a driving tour (avoiding hours of waiting in airports). In one week you can also cover Mangshan, Dengfeng, Luoyang, Kaifeng, Anyang, the Song Tombs and some countryside at your own pace.

For historians, Zhengzhou has one of the best museums because Henan was a big part of the cradle of Chinese civilization. It was in Anyang that the oracle bones with one of the first Chinese writings were found. The capitals of the Eastern Zhou, Han, Wei, Jin, Northern Song,

Tang, and Liang were in this province. At least one of the capitals and possibly four of the five other capitals of the Xia dynasty were also in this province. The Xia was China's first dynasty, and until recently was clouded in legend, traditionally dating from the 16th century B.C. China's first Buddhist temple, the Luoyang Grottoes, and the earliest astronomical observatory are also located here.

Zhengzhou was the site of the February 7th Beijing-Hankou Railway Workers' General Strike of 1923, part of a larger workers' movement for better wages and conditions. Over 100 railroad workers were killed. The strike is commemorated with a modern 14-story double pagodalike clock tower in February 7th Square, built in 1971.

If you only have one day in Zhengzhou, you have a hard choice to make. One day is only time for sightseeing along the Yellow River, **Mangshan Mountain** 邙山 (31 km from the International Hotel). There is time also for the Provincial Museum and nearby Shang palace ruins and old city walls.

Dahecun Village 大河村 , a 5000-year-old site for Yangshao and Longshan neolithic cultures and Shang ruins, is NE about 12 km and can also be included.

Mangshan/Yellow River Scenic Area is an interesting but tacky theme park on the south shore. 150-meter statues of two Xia dynasty kings are being built. Fortune-telling by computer (in Chinese). Chinese wedding procession. Autographs on 2 × 4 ft. stone tablets of the Lieut. Governor of Kansas and you—if you want to pay. Good view of the river.

Songshan Mountain 嵩山 is about 75 km SW of Zhengzhou in **Dengfeng County** 登封层 and takes two days. It stretches more than 60 km east to west. The highest peak is 1512 meters above sea level. It is one of China's Five Sacred Mountains, and emperors came here to worship. During the Southern and Northern Dynasties (a.d. 420–589), 72 temples and monasteries flourished here.

Hotels in Dengfeng County town are modest and might not have heat or 24-hour hot water. The best is the Songshan Guest House, an acceptable base if you want to spend three or four days bicycling. Let us know if the promised roadside signs in English are up.

Songshan is the home of *Shaolin Monastery 少林寺 , world famous because of the popularity of China's martial arts. Here is where one of the better kung-fu movies was filmed in the early 1980s. If you have a chance, see *Shaolin Monastery*. This Hong Kong-China production should make ancient China seem more vivid to you.

Shaolin was first built in A.D. 495–496 and became famous because 13 fighting monks from here supported the first Tang emperor. (There is a famous story about a group of monks from Shaolin involved in a conspiracy against the Manchus, but they were from a lesser-known Shaolin Monastery in Fujian.)

At this Shaolin temple 13 km NW of Dengfeng County town, you can see the depressions in the floor worn by generations of monks practicing martial arts. (The Shaolin Martial Arts Training Center (Wu Shu Guan) is close to the temple, and exhibitions can be arranged. Classes too with instruction in Chinese. Some differences in style with western kung fu. Wushu Festival in September. The hostel here is Chinese standard, spartan, 20 rooms.) Among the murals and frescoes are some of 500 arhats (Ming), but also some depicting fighting monks. At one time, 2000–3000 monks lived here. The ***Ta Lin (Forest of Pagodas)** 塔林 is the largest group of memorial pagodas in China. A cemetery for abbots, it has over 240 miniature pagodas grouped here, dating from the Northern Wei.

Northwest of the temple is a cave where the sixth century Indian missionary Bodhidharma, was reputed to have spent nine years in meditation before achieving Nirvana. He was the founder of Chan Buddhism, more popularly known as Zen, and is frequently depicted in art in his robes, crossing the Yangtze River standing on a reed.

The 43-meter-high ***Songyue Pagoda** 嵩岳寺塔 at **Fawang Temple** 法王寺 is the oldest proven extant pagoda in China, 4 km. from Dengfeng. Built of brick in about A.D. 520 (Northern Wei), it is also unusual because it has 12 sides and is curved like an Indian *sikhara* tower. It is of extreme importance to those studying pagoda architecture. The **Songyang Shuyuan (Songyang Academy of Classical Learning)** 嵩阳书院 at the foot of the mountain has two cypress trees said to be over 3000 years old, each measuring 12 meters in circumference. The school was one of the four imperial academies preparing students for the imperial examinations.

Zhongyue Miao (Central Mountain Temple) 中岳庙 , at the base of Taishi Peak and 4 km east of Dengfeng County, was founded in the Qin and moved here in the Tang. It has four feisty 3½-meter-high iron figures (Northern Song) guarding it, whom children pat ''to gain strength.'' One of the earliest Taoist temples, it is huge, the largest extant monastery in the province. It was enlarged during the Qing, along the lines of the Forbidden City in Beijing. The ***Taishi Tower** 太室阙 is from the Eastern Han. One can climb to the top of Huanggai Peak for an overall view of the 400 or so buildings and the 300 Han cypresses. 10-day temple fairs occur during the third and tenth lunar months.

The ***Shaoshi Tower** 少室阙 and the ***Qimu Tower** 启母阙 , also on the mountain, are from the Eastern Han too. The ***Astronomical Observatory** 观星台 was built early in the Yuan, based on a Zhou dynasty concept. It is the oldest in China. It was able to prove that the earth revolved around the sun once every 365.2425 days, 300 years before the Gregorian calendar. 14 km. from Dengfeng County town. China's first astrological museum is nearby.

A search for the first Xia capital, China's oldest dynasty, has been centered in Dengfeng County, ½ km west of the town of **Gaocheng 告城** at **Wangcheng Gang (Royal City Mound) 皇城岗** . This site is not usually included in a tour, but people interested in archaeology might ask about it. Uncovered have been city walls, skeletons (probably of slaves, buried alive in a foundation pit), wine vessels, bronze fragments, and ceramic pots. However, Wangcheng Gang was found to be of a later date (5th century B.C.).

Across the river and ½ km NW of Gaocheng is another site where the earliest bronze vessels in the province were found and carbon-dated to 2000 B.C. This is now thought to be the earliest Xia capital. These sites are about 40 km SW of Zhengzhou.

Also SW of Zhengzhou, but closer to the city, are the **Han Tombs at Dahuting (Tiger-hunting) Pavilion 打虎亭村汉墓** in **Mixian County 密县** . They are worth a short stop for their paintings and stone carvings. Between Luoyang and Zhengzhou is the ***Gongxian County Cave Temple,** dating from A.D. 517 (Northern Wei) to Song, some of its 7743 Buddhist sculptures in an excellent state of preservation. They are not as big or as impressive, though, as Luoyang's, but they are certainly worth a look.

The ***Song Tombs,** 65 km west of Zhengzhou and also in Gongxian, are from the Northern Song, when that illustrious dynasty had its capital in Kaifeng. They are impressive for their huge stone guardians, among them foreign envoys wearing turbans. The tombs themselves have so far proved less spectacular than those of the later Ming and Qing emperors and are spread over an area 15 km long. They were built in a much shorter time than those of their successors, and without the personal supervision of the emperor who was going to reside there. One of the imperial tombs is expected to be opened in the near future.

Gongxian was also the home county of Tang poet Du Fu (Tu Fu). **Du Fu's Native Place,** the cave where he was born, has been embellished with brick walls and can be visited. The famous three-color Tang porcelain (horses, camels) of which you see reproductions in every Friendship Store in the area, were first made in a kiln at **Xiaohuangye.** One can also visit the 300-year-old **Manor of Landlord Kang Baiwan** for a good insight into how the aristocracy lived then. Just imagine yourself living here as a servant! In what did you cook? Where did the sewage go? The cave dwellings in this county are fantastic.

In Yanshi county are the ruins of a capital of the early Shang dynasty, at least 3000 years old, one of the earliest, largest, and best-preserved ancient cities.

In the province, there's also Kaifeng (70 km away), Luoyang, and Anyang. For destinations close by in Shanxi province, across the Yellow River, see ''Taiyuan.'' For Hebei province, see ''Shijiazhuang.''

SHOPPING

Made here are reproductions of three-color Tang porcelain figures, jade and lacquerware, calligraphy and paintings. It's a good place to buy Chinese writing brushes, paper, inkstones, and inkbars. Made in the province are also Jun porcelain and embroidery from Kaifeng. The Friendship Store is at 96 Erqi Bei Rd., north of People's Park. Tel. 22406. **#Henan Cultural Relics Shop,** 4 Jinshuidadao, tel. 555347.

RESTAURANTS

C.I.T.S. says the best is at the Regent Plaza Hotel, 114 Jinshui Rd., tel. 556600, and the Guangzhou Restaurant, 97 Erqi Bei Rd., tel. 25588.

HOTELS

The best is the International.

International Hotel (Guoji Fandian) • *114 Jinshui Rd. 450003. 3☆. Dist.R.W.8 km near the government office and trading corp.* • 1982. Ren. 1989. 240 rooms. Pool. Gym. IDD.

Ambulance: tel. 551553.
Police: tel. 110.
C.I.T.S. and **C.T.S. 国际旅行社** : 15 Jinshui Rd. 450003; tel. 552072. Fax 552273, 557705. Telex 46041 CITSZZ CN.
CAAC 中旅社 : 38 North Feb. 7 Rd.; tel 25496 (international), 24339 (domestic).
CYTS: tel. 551374, 552191.
Henan Travel and Tourism Bureau and **Henan Provincial Tourist Corp.:** 16 Jinshui Rd., 450003. **H.T.T.B.:** tel. 557880, 552879. Telex 46056 FAOHN CN. Fax 557705. **H.P.T.C.:** 26367, 26351. Telex 46081 CITSY CN. Fax 552273.
Tourist Hotline: 552484.

ZHENJIANG 湛江

(Chinkiang, Chenchiang, Chenkiang: to pacify the river) East China, in central Jiangsu province, where the Grand Canal meets the south bank of the Yangtze. About 1 hour by train (63 km) east of Nanjing, and about 4 hours (220 km) NW of Shanghai. The closest airports are at Changzhou and then Nanjing. It is a historic old city, its streets lined with plane trees, some of its houses small and whitewashed like Suzhou's, others black brick with courtyards. It is bound on three sides by hills and on the north by the Yangtze River. Weather: Coldest—⁻5°C from the mid to the end of January; hottest—38°C, July and August, with breezes from the Yangtze. Annual precipitation 1000 mm, mainly in July. Population: 470,000.

Zhenjiang was founded in the Zhou. It boasts 2500 years of history, including seven as capital of the Eastern Wu (third century), when it was called Jingko (entrance to Nanjing). In the Qin dynasty (221– 206 B.C.), 3000 prisoners were sent here to build canals and roads. Many battles were fought in the area and the city is mentioned in *The Romance of the Three Kingdoms.*

During the Yuan, Zhenjiang was visited by Marco Polo. The first British missionaries arrived in the 17th century. Toward the end of the First Opium War, it was the only city that strongly resisted the imperialists. After that failed, however, about 1000 foreigners, mainly merchants and missionaries from Britain, Germany, and the United States lived here. The foreigners left their mark on some of the architecture.

In 1938, Marshall Chen Yi's New Fourth Army was stationed about 50 km away, and some skirmishes with the Japanese took place in the area. In April 1949, the British warship H.M.S. *Amethyst,* while rescuing British citizens upriver, was caught in the crossing of the Yangtze by the People's Liberation Army and held for over three months here. The captain refused to cooperate or admit his ship fired first. Under cover of a passing passenger boat, the *Amethyst* finally escaped.

The American Nobel and Pulitzer Prize-winning author Pearl Buck (1892–1973) grew up here, studied in what is now the Zhenjiang Second Middle School (founded 1884) and taught here (1914–17), a total of 18 years. In the past, China criticized her for being "imperialist" and ignored her writings. In the 1950s, U.S. senator Joseph McCarthy accused her of being a Communist. Zhenjiang and sister city Tempe, Arizona, have renovated one of her homes as the Sino-U.S. cultural exchange center for the 100th anniversary of her birth. It is for the study of foreign missions, her books, and cultural exchanges. It would appreciate copies of her books, *Good Earth, Imperial Women, Dragon Seed, My Several Worlds,* etc. Hsu Heping of C.I.T.C. Can show you where Buck's mother is buried (now a warehouse with a few surviving European tombstones) and arrange visits with some of her old students.

Today, Zhenjiang has 500 factories and mines, and makes industrial chemicals, textiles, silk, and paper (from rice stocks) for export.

If you only have one day, C.I.T.S. suggests Jinshan Hill, Jiaoshan Island, the museum, and the Thousand-Year-Old Street. Tiny **(Xiao Matai Jie)** street, which is 4 km from the Jinshan Hotel, has an unusual Song or Yuan stupa built above the sidewalk, but until it is cleaned up and organized better for tourists, I can't recommend it.

Jiao Hill 焦山 (150 meters high) on Jiao Shan Island is less than ½ km from the city (13 km from the Jinshan Hotel). Up 250 steps is a magnificent view of the Yangtze—all three of Zhenjiang's hills have magnificent views of the Yangtze—and one can see the place where the *Amethyst* was held. What would you have done if you were captain?

Back at the base of Jiao Hill, you can look at the **Battery,** which was used against the British in 1842. Also below is a garden with steles of many calligraphers, including that of the father of modern calligraphy, Wang Hsi-chih of 1500 years ago. At the loquat orchard and the **Din Hui Buddhist Temple** most of the Ming statues were destroyed by the Red Guards. The existing statues were made in 1979.

Jinshan (Golden Hill) 金山 , 1 km from the Jinshan Hotel, looks better from afar than close up. The temple here was first built 1500 years ago (Jin) and rebuilt several times since, a victim of lightning, fire, and weather. The current pagoda was finished in 1900 with animal carvings, in time for the Empress Dowager Cixi's birthday. It reflects her crude tastes. Seven stories tall, 30 meters high, it is easier climbing up the 119 steps than down because of the shallow steps.

But there are some fun **caves,** all the more interesting because of the presence in one of the white, ghastly-looking, life-size figure of the monk Fa Hai, and in another the two beautiful women said to be the White Snake and the Blue (sometimes Green) Snake, both fairies. The cave is said to reach Hangzhou!

The story of the Snakes is also the plot of a famous Beijing opera. Briefly, the several-thousand-year-old White Snake from Mount Emei (the Blue Snake is the maid) becomes a beautiful woman and goes to

Hangzhou. There at the Tuanqiao (the Bridge of Breaking Up), she falls in love with a scholar, and eventually the two marry. The White Snake, using her magic powers, takes money from a government official to build a house, but because the official's seal is still on the money, the young man is arrested and ordered beaten for theft. The White Snake again uses her magic so that whenever her husband is beaten, the official's wife feels the pain. Consequently, the young man is expelled to Zhenjiang. After his arrival, the monk master Fa Hai, jealous of their happiness, tries to separate the couple, but the White Snake floods the area, including Jin Shan temple. They are reunited at the Tuanqiao. The unrelenting monk master retaliates by imprisoning the White Snake under the Leifeng pagoda in Hangzhou. There she is rescued by the Blue Snake. The White Snake, her husband, and her son are reunited and live happily ever after.

This is a popular Chinese tale and a study of the significance of its symbolism and the psychology of its popularity could keep a folklorist busy for years.

Museum: Housed in the former British consulate building next door to the former Southern Baptist Convention buildings. It is 4 km from the Jinshan Hotel. Its permanent collection includes an anchor from the British ship *Amethyst* and a land lease dated 1933 referring to the "former British Concession lot." A tiny silver coffin found under the nearby Iron Pagoda contains two gold coffins and the ashes of a Buddhist saint. Charming is the Song porcelain pillow in the shape of a sleeping child. No titles in English, but a new exhibition hall is due in 1994.

If you have more time, the **Bei Gu (North Consolidated) Hill,** 9 km from the Jinshan Hotel, is the site of the temple where Liu Pei, hero of *The Romance of the Three Kingdoms,* was married to the sister of Sun Chuan. After he died, his wife mourned for him at the pavilion on top of the hill now called Mourning over the River Pavilion. On this hill also is an 11th-century Iron Pagoda (Northern Song), originally nine stories high. Struck by lightning several times, it was repaired in 1960 and now has only its first, second, fifth, and sixth stories.

There is **Maoshan,** 60 km southwest, one of the birthplaces of Taoism. Temple fairs are the 15th of the second lunar month, the 18th of the third, and the 3rd of the tenth lunar months annually. Zhenjiang has the **Sericulture Research Centre** at the China Agricultural Science Academy (6 km away), and a **Silk Garment and Prop Factory** for fancy old-style garments for theatres and films.

Zhenjiang also offers **boat tours** on the Yangtze and the Grand Canal and a **Children's Palace** (6 km away). Annual events include the Dec. 31 bell tolling for luck at the Jinshan Temple.

Yangzhou is 25 km away by road and ferry across the Yangtze. **Yixing** is 150 km away. See separate listings.

SHOPPING

Dashikou 大市口 is Zhenjiang's main shopping area. Zhenjiang's factories make elaborate palace lanterns and are famous for their "crystal" meat and vinegar. Also made in the city are silk, jade carvings, paper cuttings, and silk birds. Arts and Crafts at 8 Huancheng Rd., tel. 225512.

RESTAURANTS

A local specialty is crab cream bun, a steamed meat pastry. Make a hole first and slurp out the soup inside. Food here is concerned with fragrance, shape, and color, and is neither too sweet nor too salty. You might find your hors d'oeuvres looking like butterflies, peacocks, or fans. Everything can be dipped in vinegar.

Tongxinglou Restaurant 同兴楼饭店 • *218 Zhongshan Rd.; tel. 222842. No parking.*

Yanchun Restaurant • *Renmin St.; tel. 231615.*

HOTELS

The Jinshan is the better hotel, but the renovated Runzhou/Zhenjiang Binguan/Grand Yangtze (the name was not settled at press time) could be better. The Jinshan is in the western suburbs close to the Jinshan Temple; the Runzhou etc. is downtown close to the Pearl Buck home.

Jinshan Hotel (Jiudian) • *1 Jinshan Xi Rd. 212002. Telex 360025 ZJJSH CZ. Fax 234530. Dist.R.W. 5 km* • C.C. Bldgs. #1–3, 2✩, #4, 3✩. New building due soon, then tearing down #1–3. 1979; ren. 1990. 143 rooms. IDD, B.C. China Eastern booking office. #4 had dim reading lamps, but was fine. Pool, tennis, theaters, dance halls.

Runzhou (Fandian) etc. • *92 Zhong Shan Xi Rd., 212002. Aiming for 3✩. Fax 236425. Dist.R.W. 300 meters* • C.C. 1963, ren. 1992. 6 stories, 128 rooms. IDD. B.C. Gym and pool due soon.

Ambulance: tel. 221612.
Police: tel. 110.
CAAC: 38 Bei Erqi Rd.; tel. 24339.
C.I.T.S. 中国国际旅行社 : 25 Jianking Rd. 212001; tel. 233287, 237538. Telex 360025 ZJJSH CN. Fax 233084. Ask for Pearl Buck specialist, Hsu Heping.
C.T.S.: 401 Zhongshan Xi Rd. 212001; tel. 231663.
CYTS: tel. 31451, 21649.

Zhenjiang Foreign Affairs Offices: 141 Zhendong Rd. 212001; tel. 221867, 233231 (complaints).

ZHONGSHAN 中山

(Chung Shan) South China in Guangdong province. Close to the Portuguese colony of Macao, across the Pearl River delta south of Hong Kong, this city can be directly reached by 1½-hour Hovercraft from Hong Kong at least 4 times a day, or via Macao. It is 90 km. (2 to 4 hours by road, depending on the traffic) SW of Guangzhou.

A 1-day tour from Hong Kong usually includes a visit to the former residence of Dr. Sun Yixian (Sun Yat-sen) 孙中山故居 in **Cuiheng** village 翠亨村 . The house was designed by the father of the Chinese republic himself and is a blend of Spanish and local style. The Sun Yixian Memorial Middle School is a couple hundred meters away. Tourists have taken lunch in **Shiqi** 石岐 and visited the Long Rui Village before returning to Macao or Hong Kong, or going on to other places in the area.

For more about Dr. Sun Yat-sen see Nanjing.

Shiqi (Shekki, Shekket) is the cultural, economic and political center of Zhongshan City which has 25 urban and rural districts. The urban population of Shiqi is 170,000. It is in water country, full of intriguing waterways begging to be explored. It has a lot of activity, and new buildings. We experienced a traffic jam in downtown Zhongshan! Yet the water, the age-old river boats, reminds one of a much smaller, old Bangkok.

In the center of the city are floating restaurants (one of them a smaller version of Hong Kong's Jumbo), and a night market with fancy awnings.

Visas for the whole of China can be obtained at the port about 10 km. from Shiqi in 15 to 20 minutes. Instant camera available.

The **Zhongshan (Chung Shan) Hot Spring Golf Club** 中山温泉 高尔夫球会 is close to the Zhongshan Hot Spring Resort. The 18-hole, par 72 golf course was designed by the Palmer Course Design

Company, named after Arnold Palmer. For those coming from abroad, the club can arrange visas. The address is: Sanxiang Commune, Zhongshan City; tel. 24019; cable: 3306; telex: 44828 CSHS CN. In Hong Kong, telephone 5–8335666, 5–8335723. In Macao, tel. 71702. Bookings also from major hotels in Guangzhou.

SHOPPING

Made locally are straw handicrafts, clothing, embroidery, and sequinned articles.

HOTELS

The top hotels in Zhongshan District City: #1 Zhongshan International; #2 Fu Hua; #3 Hot Spring; #4 Cuiheng. Reservations recommended weekends and Hong Kong holidays. The Fu Hua and Zhongshan International are close together at the bridge in the center of Shiqi near the night market and floating restaurants.

Cuiheng Hotel (Binguan) • *Cuiheng Village 528454. 3*. About 29 km southeast of Shiqi; 24 km from Zhongshan ferry port. Across road from post office and bus station, and a couple hundred meters from the home of Dr. Sun Yat-sen.* • 1988. Very modern looking hotel, with hotel's Rolls Royce parked in front. 3 stories, 242 rooms. Villas. Pool. Health center planned. Wax museum on hill behind hotel. Amusement park.

Fu Hua Hotel (Jiudian) • *1 Fuhia Rd., Shiqi, 528401. 4*. Telex 426006 CTSZS CN. Fax 828678. 15 km from Zhongshan port. Opposite bus station.* • 1986. 19 stories, 242 rooms. H.K.J.V. Revolving restaurant on roof. Exterior elevator. B.C. IDD. Bowling. Lounge open to 2 a.m.! Separate building for sports.

Zhongshan (Chungshan) Hot Spring Hotel (Wenquan) • *Shanxiang Township 528463. 3*. Telex 44828 CSHS CN. 20 km. NW. of Macao. 37 km. south of Shiqi.* • C.C. 1980. 15 villas. H.K.J.V. Isolated rural setting next to golf course. Attractive garden style. Major credit cards. Ren. 1987. 400 rooms. Shooting gallery. Horses. Children's playground. Two swimming pools. IDD to Hong Kong. Should have fax and business center.

Zhongshan International Hotel (Guoji Jiudian) • *Zhongshan Rd. No. 1, Shiqi 528401. 4*. Telex 426002 ZSIH CN. Fax 824735.* • 1986, ren. 1988. C.C. 22 stories. 369 rooms. First-class well maintained modern hotel in the center of the city. Revolving restaurant. B.C. Good quality stores. IDD.

C.I.T.S. Zhongshan Rd. No. 1, Shiqi 528401; tel. 822243 or 824788. Telex 426002 ZSIH CN. Fax 824736.
C.T.S Zhongshan Rd., West Suburb, Shiqi 528401; tel. 22034. Telex 44782 CTSZS CN. Fax 28678.

ZHUHAI 珠海

South China, Guangdong Province. Adjacent to the Portuguese colony of Macao across the Pearl River delta southwest of Hong Kong, this Special Economic Zone can be directly reached by ferry from Hong Kong or Shekou, and by road via Macao. It is a 2-hour drive from Guangzhou if no traffic jams. Otherwise, 4 to 5 hours. Sometimes helicopter to Taishan. 3-day visa can be acquired upon arrival without photos, and can be extended in Zhuhai (photos needed). An international airport is planned.

Zhuhai says it is one of the five largest tourist destinations in China with visitors mainly from Hong Kong and Macao, but also many from abroad.

In the vicinity are the Lenzan cave and the birthplace of Dr. Sun Yat-sen. Also in the vicinity is the Banyan Cave with a temple, and beaches. The best beach is at Juizhou Islet 九洲岛 , an area now being developed with a 2-km-long cable car, an old style fishing village, bird garden and motor boats. It should be ready in 1992 or so. The sea water is generally very murky in this region.

Also an 18-hole golf course and international trade and exhibition center.

See "Zhongshan." The urban population is 160,000.

Zhuhai International Golf Club 珠海高尔夫球场 /**Pearl Land Amusement Park** 敎育街自由市场 are adjacent, over 30 minutes north of the city. The amusement park is huge and has an 1.8 km. roller coaster, and a 36-seat, 4-abreast ferris wheel. The golf club has a restaurant, Japanese-style bath, visa service, and cheap pick-up at Zhuhai port on the border. Bookings can be made at Japan Golf Promotion Co. Ltd., Room 1009, Gloucester Tower, The Landmark, 11 Pedder St., Hong Kong. Tel. 5–262325.

HOTELS AND RESORTS

Zhuhai has at least 83. The Zhuhai Resort, Shijing Shan and Garden are close together near the large Jiuzhoucheng Shopping Center , Zhuhai International Trade and Exhibition Center , and small amusement park, about 2 km. from the Zhuhai dock. They are about 3 km. from the Gong Bei Palace, 5 km. from the Macao ferry pier and a 20 minute drive to Pearl Land and the golf club.

Reservations needed weekends, July–August and Hong Kong holidays.

Gongbei Palace Hotel (Gongbei Binguan) • *Shuiwan Rd., Gongbei District 519020. Telex 45638 GBPHC CN. 10 min. walk from Customs House at Macao border.* • 1984. C.C. Very attractive garden-style hotel with villas. 290 rooms. B.C. Gym. Pool. Beach. H.K.J.V.

Shijing Shan Tourist Centre (Lu You) • *1 Jingshan Rd. 519000. Telex 45617 SCST CN. Fax 332582.* • 1981, ren. 1988. Garden style. 115 rooms. Shooting gallery, boating, tennis, pool. IDD. No business center, but this hotel has ties with the exhibition center.

Zhuhai Holiday Resort (Dujiachun Jiu Dian) • *Shi Hua Shan, 519015. 4*. Telex 456230. Fax 332036. On waterfront* • C.C. 1986, ren. 1991. 10 stories, 462 rooms. 87 villas. IDD. HKTV. B.C. Tennis. Bowling. Outdoor pool. Roller skating. Horses, archery, go-karts.

Zhuhai Hotel (Binguan) • *Zhuhai Shi 519000. 4*. Telex 456218 ZHRT CN. Fax 332339* • 1983. Hong Kong and Macao J.V. C.C. Attractive garden-style hotel with villas. Well maintained. Three stories, 283 rooms. IDD. Stop-smoking and male-fertility clinics. B.C. Tennis. Pool.

C.I.T.S. • Zhuhai Resort, Jingshan Rd.; tel. 332822. Telex 45637 CITS CN. Fax 332339. Hong Kong office tel. 3686181. Macao tel. 566622. Guangzhou tel. 669900 X1283.
C.T.S.: 4 Shuiwan Rd., Gongbei 519020; tel. 885777 or Binnan Rd., Xingzhou 519000; tel. 886849. Fax 888456.

Zhuhai Travel Service Corporation • Binhai Rd., Gongbei, Zhuhai, 519000. Tel. 885376, 885902.

ZIBO 淄博

North China. In Shandong, on the Beijing-Shanghai express-train route, it can also be reached by air via Jinan. Zibo is near **Linzi,** the capital of Qi (859–221 B.C.), where 150 ancient tombs have yielded 600 sacrificed horses, bronzes, crossbows, and bronze coins from that era. A new museum in the Qi style has been put at the site of the Qi capital. Zibo itself makes good porcelain, artistic pottery and glassware, and silk. C.I.T.S.: Zibo Guest House, 189 Zhongxin Rd. 255000; tel. 225341, 223341. C.T.S.: Chengguan Bei St. 064200; tel. 225341, 222920.

ZUNHUA 遵化

(Tsunhua) North China. Hubei province, about 125 km NE of Tianjin and 135 km east of Beijing but most people go there from Beijing. It takes 3 or 4 hours to get there because the road is congested with donkey and horse carts, and creeping tractors.

Among the imperial Qing tombs at nearby **Dongling** (Eastern Tombs) are those of Qianlong (Chien Lung) at Yuling. Qianlong is the emperor who snubbed Britain's envoy. He is buried with his five wives. A devout Buddhist, his tomb is covered with religious statues and sutras in Indian, Tibetan, Chinese, Manchurian, and Mongolian.

The tombs of Empress Dowager Cixi (Tzu Hsi) and Empress Ci'an are together at **Dingdongling.** The Empress Dowager was the fascinating, outrageous, scheming, brilliant, scandalous but short-sighted woman who built the Summer Palace in Beijing. Her tomb, covered with phoenixes deliberately and arrogantly placed *above* the dragons (symbolizing the emperor), was completed in 1881 and renovated in 1895, with an additional 4590 taels of gold as decoration. She died in 1908. Both mausoleums can be entered. The carving is more elaborate than that in the Ming tombs, with Buddhist sutras (in Tibetan and Sanskrit) and figures inside. You can see an exhibition of her clothes, utensils, and photos. Her tomb was robbed in 1928 by a Nationalist warlord who used explosives to open it. He stripped over 500 pearls off her clothes.

Like the Ming tombs, there is also an animal-lined Sacred Way, the figures here smaller but more elaborately carved. It seems each dynasty tried to outdo its predecessors, the Ming being more elaborate than the Song (see "Zhengzhou"). The tombs of the emperors and empresses have yellow glazed roofs. Those of persons of lesser importance have green roofs.

The attendants here are dressed in Qing imperial costumes with eye-catching Manchu hats, and high heels attached to the center of their shoes. Some heels are in the shape of vases or bells.

Another word of warning: No decent bathrooms nor running water exist except in the guesthouse in the courtyard to the right of Qianlong's Tomb.

The **Xiling (Western Tombs),** 120 km SW of Beijing at **Yixian** are not as illustrious. The 14 mausoleums hold the remains of Emperors Yongzheng (Tailing), Jiaqing (Changling), Daoguang (Muling), and Guangxu (Chongling), plus the usual retinue of wives and children. Visitors can enter Chongling, the last royal tomb in China, but it has no funeral objects as it was robbed.

C.T.S.: Government Building, Chengguan Bei St. 064200; tel. 2920.

SPECIAL FOR OVERSEAS CHINESE

And Anyone Else Who Wants to Help

Overseas Chinese who speak no Chinese should take C.I.T.S. or C.T.S. tours if they are interested primarily in getting the best accommodations and facts in English while sightseeing. If you want to be treated more like family, sometimes taking second place to foreign guests, but getting cheaper rates, go on a Chinese-speaking tour. If you want to learn about China, try to find a family, especially yours, to live with.

I have gone to China all three ways. Emotionally it's a strain, because with a C.I.T.S. group, I get annoyed at the higher prices and furious with foreigners joking about *my* people. With one C.T.S. Hong Kong group, our tour director had a lot of *guanxi,* and we were met not just by a guide, but by the manager of C.T.S., and given the same rooms as Foreign Friends for cheaper prices. Our trip down the Yangtze was a riotous floating poker game, interrupted only by glances at the Three Gorges. I missed much of the commentary because it was all in Cantonese and Mandarin, but we had a ball!

With relatives, I learned more about China than any of the group tours, but in a different way. The first time we met, they pointed out a long-forgotten photograph on the wall of my Canadian family taken 20 years before. My aunt knew everyone by name. Until I started planning a trip to China, I didn't know she existed. In her home, I saw how a six-course meal could be cooked in one wok in one hour. I learned how politeness smooths over a multitude of sins, all ignoring my embarrassing encounter with a naked nephew who was bathing behind a screen in the kitchen (there was nowhere else to bathe). On the streets they pointed to the strange-looking foreigners, *my* fellow Westerners, who had then just started to invade Xinhui. I didn't learn much about the history of the city, but I sure learned a lot about Chinese people and myself.

I think people of Chinese ancestry in particular should visit China. If you feel this bicultural conflict as many of us do, it would be good to explore the Chinese part of your roots. If nothing else, it will help you understand your parents, your grandparents, and your great-grandparents. It might even help you understand things about yourself.

In my father's village in Taishan, I was shocked to learn he had been born in a mud house. I found the watch towers where he used to look out for bandits, and imagined him riding the water buffalo. My grandfather's grave was a simple mound. I expected something more elaborate, considering the money my father said he sent back to the village.

I highly recommend a visit to your ancestral village. Even if you have no relatives there, at least you can look around and see how you would have lived if your ancestors had not emigrated. If you find relatives, you might find your name, if you're male, in a family history book. Part of my novel *Beyond the Heights* is about this experience, which can be traumatic.

But you don't have money to take expensive presents? Don't be silly! People outside China send back presents to family partly to show off. They also send because they feel a strong family obligation. People in China ask for expensive luxury presents like Omega watches because they want to keep up with the Wongs. Remittances have supported a few idlers. If you don't want to contribute to idleness and foolish pride, don't give an expensive gift.

So what do you think will happen if you don't take them a video? Do you think your relatives are going to be rude to you? Of course not. If they ask, tell them you couldn't afford it. My relatives were pleased with the U.S.$20 watch I took in once, especially after I showed them the U.S.$16 Timex I wore myself. Making friends and learning about China are much more important.

You should take some presents, of course. You'd take a bottle of wine to a hostess in the United States, wouldn't you? In China, you and your F.E.C.s are in a privileged position. You could accompany aunts, uncles, and cousins to the Overseas Chinese store and buy them what they want, in exchange for R.M.B. Then you could use the R.M.B. to treat them to dinner at a restaurant, a nice gesture, especially if you're staying with them.

You may find you have nothing in common with Chinese people. On the other hand, you may find that you do. You may have no feelings of obligation to help, dismissing their comparative poverty as their, not your, bad luck. So be it. At least you went and had a look.

For those who do feel pangs of conscience, I think you should be sensitive to opportunities to help. They would trust you more than any other foreigner and would be less reticent to ask you for help.

You can teach—simple skills like English and the principles of democracy. You can teach swimming! Imagine my surprise at finding that no one in my village knew how to swim! You can inspire them with technical advances in your home country, drawing pictures if you can't speak the language.

Developing industries and markets have high priority, and never before have the opportunities been so ripe. Every rural village in Guangdong and Fujian seems to be building a hotel for visiting relatives. And restaurants! You may be asked your opinion. The handicraft industry, especially tourist souvenirs, is flourishing. They need ideas on cottage industries that would appeal to foreigners.

New enterprises no longer need approval from Beijing, and you could help them with foreign exchange and expediting imports of machinery and materials from abroad. But do read something about appropriate technology, spare parts, and maintenance before you do. Photocopy machines have lain idle for years because no one knew how to fix them. You may want to set up a joint venture as many other Overseas Chinese and compatriots have done. Ethnic Chinese investors get special tax treatment and duty-free import privileges.

Paying for education is also important. Tuition fees now will have to be paid for most college programs, ranging from ¥50–¥150 per semester. Completely self-financing students could pay ¥1000 to ¥2000 a year. The tuition for a two-year European-accredited MBS program costs about ¥13,000 RMB at the China-EC Management Institute in Beijing. Government schools have been free, but a very small percentage of students have been able to qualify. Private schools, including universities, have now sprung up, but fees are needed, of course. These are much cheaper than schools in your home country, and may be more relevant to China's needs. You might be interested in setting up a scholarship fund for people from your ancestral village. I discovered that no one from my father's village had ever gone to university in China. You may want to invest in a private school yourself. Or stay and teach. Of course, living in China takes a special kind of person, one with a great deal of patience and, particularly, a good sense of humor. It is not easy for someone used to Western affluence and efficiency to adapt to Chinese standards, but many do.

Sponsoring a Chinese student to study abroad is also helpful, but only if the student returns to apply his knowledge in China. Nothing is really solved if the student sends back only foreign exchange to an increasingly greedy family. China needs scientists and technicians *in China.*

Help to emigrate is of debatable value. China cannot modernize if her best brains leave the country.

SPECIAL FOR BUSINESS PEOPLE

Advice: Trading with China is not like trading with other countries. As one trade official put it, "If you want to play in the Chinese sand pile, you have to play by Chinese rules."

These rules are much too complicated to put into a travel guide. There are lots of books, business guides, and experienced people to give advice. But to get you started: Trading with China is done primarily through foreign trading corporations, a list of which can be obtained from a Chinese mission. Joint ventures are negotiated through the Ministry of Foreign Economic Relations and Trade (MOFERT).

People who know say:

1. It is possible sometimes for a member of a tour group to get a business appointment.

2. Don't come with the attitude, "We're going to liberate the Chinese." These aren't Chinese laundrymen you're talking to. They'll ask you questions like "Why did you reduce the number of your employees from 500 to 200 last year?" Be prepared. The Chinese know b.s. when they hear it.

Do your homework before you go to China. Visit Chinese trade fairs in North America. Talk with trade officials in the Chinese consulates, your state, provincial or federal trade offices, and China trade councils. Find out about government feasibility studies, trade missions, and funding programs. Question people who are doing business in China.

You could sound out the trade department of your own consulate or embassy in China about your plan, find out about your competition, and ask for some direction on how to proceed.

3. The Chinese want specific proposals. Don't give them general statements. However, whatever proposal you make will be extensively discussed. Do not quote rock-bottom figures. The Chinese like to negotiate.

4. Be patient. If you lose patience, you've lost the negotiating battle.

5. Keep accurate notes. The Chinese do. But no tape recorders. The Chinese use interpreters even though they can speak good English. There is plenty of time to make notes. Record who is present, dates, and what was said. Later the Chinese may say to you, "On such a date you said . . . Why are you now saying . . . ?"

6. There is no need to take your own interpreter—too expensive. Chinese interpreters are competent.

7. A Memorandum of Understanding means two parties have identified a field where there is reason to believe there are grounds for possible future negotiations, which, if exploited should lead to a possible contract. It is not a contract, even if it mentions prices.

Trade consultant Kees de Zwager of Gates to China puts it this way: "A Letter of Intent confirms that the parties have met and some prospect exists for a continuation of talks. This letter is not to be taken lightly, as the Chinese might refer to it later.

"A contract is a starting point for further negotiations and is the next step on the road. The negotiating process is continuous. This is an ancient Chinese tradition. One negotiates daily even after all is settled."

8. If the Chinese give you a welcoming banquet, you should return a banquet. Get advice from your embassy.

9. Gifts must be modest: an appointment calendar or a small calculator or some useful novelty. Cash is out because it could be interpreted as corruption.

10. The atmosphere in China among foreign traders is very informal and friendly. Fairs are among the best places to get advice from fellow traders unless you happen to meet a competitor. They are also good places to establish contacts with Chinese officials, and working with trusted partners is how the Chinese prefer to do business.

Says Kees de Zwager, "The Canton Trade Fair is good for new traders to China. What they can see and achieve in three days would otherwise take six weeks of travel in China. The fair represents 30 provinces. Other fairs are provincial or regional. The Canadian Embassy adds that information about fairs can be obtained from Chinese commercial missions abroad, the China Council for the promotion of International Trade (CCPIT), and the organizers.

Says de Zwager, "But the Canton Trade Fair is not a good place to buy because many fair-goers are tourists and the prices are not the best. But one can make contacts and appointments.

"One must be aware in China, business is not done through strangers."

11. Your host unit in China can book you a hotel, arrange for transportation to meet you upon arrival if you wish, and book tickets for your next destination. You must tell your unit what class of hotel you want or you might be booked into something you don't want. Your host unit should be able to get you a corporate hotel discount.

Do not expect decisions to be made as quickly as elsewhere. You may need two or three visits as an introduction to show the sincerity of your interest.

12. Do take a pile of your business cards preferably with a Chinese translation on the flip side. It would also be helpful to take a one-page introduction of your company in Chinese. Exchanging cards with both hands is now part of the ritual when people meet for business.

13. China has been improving its communications and constructing industrial buildings, especially in the Special Economic Zones and 15 Coastal Cities. IDD telephone communications, luxury hotels, international airports, branches of foreign banks, new labor regulations, tax breaks, and decentralized decision making have been among China's efforts to encourage foreign investment. Recently, however, the Communist Party has strengthened its control again.

14. Spouses can come along on a business trip but are not usually included in business functions like banquets. Many spouses should be left in big cities where there is more for them to do, rather than going to tiny communities with dumpy hotels and no English. But this depends on the spouse.

15. Remember that the Chinese are primarily interested in technology transfers with minimal amounts of foreign exchange spendings. They are interested in counter-trade (with payment in Chinese products) and export markets for Chinese products. They prefer that earnings be reinvested in China. They are looking for the training of Chinese personnel, and joint-venture investments.

16. It could take up to two years before you have any results, so you must budget enough for product development. If a project is big, it could take three to five years.

17. If you are buying from China, be prepared for possible problems with quality control, on-time delivery, and Chinese factories making over-runs for sale to others.

18. You might find that hiring a China trade consultant is a more efficient way for you to do business with China.

Best News Sources on Trade with China: *Asian Wall Street Journal* (daily); *South China Morning Post* (Hong Kong daily); *Asian Wall Street Journal Weekly; Far Eastern Economic Review* (weekly). The U.S. Commerce Department has a National Trade Data Bank. The U.S.-China Business Council has published a list of database vendors in its Nov./ Dec. 1991 *China Business Review.*

Very Helpful: ''China Trade Report'' (monthly), *Far Eastern Economic Review; The China Business Review* (bimonthly), U.S.-China Business Council; *Business China* (bimonthly); *China Briefing* (quarterly and free), Hongkong Shanghai Banking Corporation; *Amcham*

Magazine (of the American Chamber of Commerce, Hong Kong); *China Trader,* and *China Daily.*

Also Helpful: *Economic Reporter,* English Supplement; *China's Foreign Trade; China Phone Book and Address Directory.*

Books: *China,* Business Profile Service. The Hong Kong and Shanghai Banking Corporation, Hong Kong; anything from the U.S.-China Business Council. Note especially *U.S. Investment in China* (1990) and *China,* by Robert Delfs and Thomas D. Gorman, published in Hong Kong by the Far Eastern Economic Review. Susan Goldenberg's *Hands Across the Ocean: Managing Joint Ventures with a Spotlight on China and Japan,* Roderick Macleod's *China, Inc.: How to do Business with the Chinese;* Jim Mann's *Beijing Jeep: The Short, Unhappy Romance of American Business in China;* Scott Seligman's *Dealing with the Chinese.*

Trade Councils: Established in 1973, the U.S.-China Business Council is a private, not-for-profit membership association of more than 300 American firms engaged in trade and investment with the People's Republic of China. The Council's primary objective is the promotion and facilitation of bilateral economic relations, and its activities include delegations, seminars, and briefings on various topics related to trade with China. Other services provided member firms include practical business assistance, advice on the development and expansion of their trade with China, and up-to-date information through the resources of its library in Washington, DC, and offices in Beijing.

    The Canadian equivalent is the Canada-China Trade Council, "founded in 1978 as a federally incorporated non-profit organization to serve as the private sector link between Canadian companies doing business in China and counterpart Chinese organizations. . . . Council members represent a broad spectrum of Canadian industry and service, and range from companies first exploring the Asian Pacific markets to those who have their own offices in China. . . . CCTC's Beijing Office is one of the largest Canadian commercial presences in China . . ." and ". . . offers a practical and cost-effective alternative to opening a company office in China, utilizing shared infrastructure and experience."

    The British equivalent is the Sino-British Trade Council.

    For Australian and other business addresses, see "Important Addresses."

    See also *Individually as a Business Person* in "The Basics" and "Introduction."

Useful Phrases

These are designed so you will be able to communicate with people who speak only Chinese. In most cases you need only point to the Chinese and you will get a "yes" (shi de) or "no" (bu shi) answer or a reassuring smile or an attempt to look up an answer from this book.

Read through the phrases at your leisure so you will know what is available. If you think you need other phrases, get a Chinese-writing friend to do them for you.

Pinyin romanization is courtesy of Miss Zhou Dayan of the Beijing Tourism Administration.

Numbers refer to tones: 1 for high; 2 for rising; 3 for a low falling and rising tone; 4 for falling. Words without numbers are neutral. The correct tone is essential. To avoid misunderstandings, point out the phrases in this book to the people with whom you want to communicate as you try to say them.

See "Quick Reference" for the pronunciation of this romanization.

TRAVEL

Arrivals

I am looking for the interpreter who is supposed to meet me.

我正在找一位翻译，他是来接我的。
Wo zheng zai zhao yi wei fan yi, ta shi lai jie wo de.

He is from ———. 他是＿＿＿＿＿＿的人。
Ta shi———ren.

C.I.T.S.	中国国际旅行社。	Zhong guo guo ji lu xing she
the Foreign Ministry	外交部	Wai jiao bu
Foreign Trade Corporation	外贸公司	Wai mao gong si
Academy of Sciences	科学院	Ke xue yuan

All-China Sports Federation 中华全国体育总会
Zhong hua quan guo ti yu zong hui

Committee for Cultural Relations with Foreign Countries
对外文委
Dui wai wen wei

Chinese People's Association for Friendship with Foreign Countries
对外友协
Dui wai you xie

People's Institute for Foreign Affairs
中国人民外交学会
Zhong gua ren min wai jiao xue hui

When do I get my passport back?
什么时候能将护照还给我？
Shen me shi hou neng jiang hu zhao huan gei wo?

Where do I get my checked luggage?
我托运的行李在那里取？
Wo tuo yun de xing li zai na li qu?

That bag is mine. Please give it to me.
那个手提包是我的。请递给我。
He ge shou ti bao shi wo de. Qing di gei wo.

Is there someone here who can carry my bag for me?
有没有人可以帮我拿手提包？
You mei you ren ke yi bang wo na shou ti bao?

Please call a taxi for me.
请代我叫一辆出租汽车。
Qing dai wo jiao yi liang chu zu qi che.

How long will it take for the taxi to get here?
出租汽车要多久才能到达这里？
Chu zu qi che yao duo jiu cai neng dao da zhe li?

minutes 分钟   hours 小时
fen zhong   xiao shi

Is there a bus I can take to the city?

3 4 2 1 4 4 1
Ycu jin cheng de gong gong qi che ma?

How can I get to the city?

我怎样可以到城里去？

3 3 4 3 3 4 2 3 4
Wo zen yang ke yi dao cheng li qu?

City Travel

Do you have a map of this city in English?

你有一张这个城市的英文地图吗？

3 3 4 4 4 2 4 1 2 2
Ni you yi zhang zhe ge cheng shi de ying wen di tu ma?

. . . with city bus routes? 有公共汽车路线图的？

3 1 4 4 1 4 4 1
You gong gong qi che lu xian tu de?

I want to go to ———.

我要去 ———。

3 4 4
Wo yao qu ———.

China International Travel
Service 中国国际旅行社

1 2 2 4 3 2 4
Zhong guo guo ji lu xing she

CAAC office 中国航空公司

1 2 2 1 1 1
Zhong guo hang kong gong si

Bank of China 中国银行

1 2 2 2
Zhong guo yin hang

hotel 旅馆

3 3
lu guan

hovercraft terminal 气垫船终点站

4 4 2 1 3 4
qi dian chuan zhong dian zhan

train station 火车站

3 1 4
huo che zhan

ferry terminal 渡船码头

4 2 4 1
du chuan ma tou

airport 飞机场

1 1 3
fei ji chang

bus station 公共汽车站

1 4 4 1 4
gong gong qi che zhan

商业中心（像为北京设计的）

shang ye zhong xin

Guangzhou (Canton)
Export Commodities Fair 广州出口商品交易会

guang zhou chu kou shang pin jiao yi hui

Where can I get a ———? 我在哪里可以叫／乘 _____?

wo zai na li ke yi jiao/cheng ———?

taxi 一辆出租汽车

yi liang chu zu qi che

bicycle rickshaw 三轮车

san lun che

subway 地下铁道列车

di xia tie dao lie che

motorscooter 摩托车

mo tuo che

city bus 市内公共汽车

shi nei gong gong qi che

About how much would it cost? 大约要多少钱？

Da yue yao duo shao qian?

City Bus

What number city bus do I take to go from here to ———?
我从这里到_____应该乘那一路公共汽车？

Wo cong zhe li dao ——— ying qai cheng na yi lu gong gong qi che?

Please show me where I can get that bus.
请告诉我在那里上车。

Qing gao su wo zai na li shang che.

Across the street?
过街？

Guo jie?

This side?
这一边？

Zhe yi bian?

Please tell me where I get off for ———.
请告诉我到_____去应该在那儿下车。

Qing gao su wo dao ——— qu ying gai zai nar xia che?

Do I need to change to another bus?

我要不要换车？

<small>3 4 2 4 4 1</small>

Wo yao bu yao huan che?

What number?

几路？

<small>3 4</small>

Ji lu?

Taxi

Please drive more slowly.

请开的慢一些。

<small>3 1 4 4 1</small>

Qing kai de man yi xie.

Please drive faster.

请开的快一些 。

<small>3 1 4 4 1</small>

Qing kai de kuai yi xie.

Please wait for me.

请等我一会。

<small>3 3 3 4 4</small>

Qing deng wo yi huir.

I will be about ——— minutes.

我要耽搁＿＿＿＿分钟。

<small>3 4 1 1 1 1</small>

Wo yao dan ge ——— fen zhong.

How much does it cost for you to wait?

等我得付多少钱？

<small>3 3 3 4 1 3 2</small>

Deng wo dei fu duo shao qian?

An hour?

一小时？

<small>1 3 2</small>

Yi xiao shi?

Where will you wait?

你在哪里等我？

<small>3 4 3 3 3 3</small>

Ni zai na li deng wo?

I want to be sure there is a taxi for me early tomorrow morning at ——— o'clock.

我要确定能在明天早晨＿＿＿点种叫到一辆出租汽车。

<small>3 4 4 2 4 1 3 1 2 3 1</small>

Wo yao que ding neng zai ming tian zao chen ——— dian zhong

<small>4 4 2 4 1 1 1</small>

jiao dao yi liang chu zu che.

Could you order a taxi for me for that time?

你能为我订一辆那个时候要的出租汽车吗？

Ni neng wei wo ding yi liang na ge shi hou yao de chu zu che ma?

Buying a Ticket (see also Permission)

I want to buy a ticket to go to ———.

我要买一张到_____去的车票。

Wo yao mai yi zhang dao ——— qu de che piao.

One-way	单程		Return	来回
	dan cheng			lai hui

Can I make the return reservation now?

现在我能订回来的票吗？

Xian zai wo neng ding hui lai de piao ma?

I want to go ———. 我要在_____走。

Wo yao zai ——— zou.

in the morning	早晨		in the afternoon	下午
	zao chen			xia wu
in the evening	晚上		today	今天
	wan shang			jin tian
tomorrow	明天		the day after tomorrow	后天
	ming tian			hou tian
next week	下星期		earlier	早一些
	xia xing qi			zao yi xie
later	晚一些		as soon as possible	尽早地
	wan yi xie			jin zao de
soft class	软席		hard class	硬席
	ruan xi			ying xi
berth	卧铺		seat	座位
	wo pu			zuo wei

What times does it leave?

什么时候开车？

Shen me shi hou kai che?

What time does it arrive?

什么时候到？

Shen me shi hou dao?

Where does it leave from?

车从哪儿开出？

^{1 2 3 1 1}
Che cong nar kai chu?

Please write that address here.

请你把地址写在这里。

^{3 3 3 4 3 3 4 4 3}
Qing ni ba di zhi xie zai zhe li.

What time should I be there?

我应该在什么时候到那里？

^{3 1 1 4 2 2 4 4 4 3}
Wo ying gai zai shen me shi hou dao na li?

How much is it?

多少钱？

^{1 3 2}
Duo shao qian?

Do you have a schedule in English?

你有一个英语时间表吗？

^{3 3 2 4 1 3 2 1 3}
Ni you yi ge ying yu shi jian biao ma?

Cancellations

Do you think someone might cancel a ticket later?

你想等一等会有人退票吗？

^{3 3 3 4 3 4 2 4 4}
Ni xiang deng yi deng hui you ren tui piao ma?

Could I take his place?

能把他的位子给我吗？

^{2 3 1 4 3 3}
Neng ba ta de wei zi gei wo ma?

When should I try again?

我应该什么时候再来问？

^{3 1 1 2 2 4 4 2 4}
Wo ying gai shen me shi hou zai lai wen?

Can I exchange this reservation for another time?

我能把订的这张票换一个别的时间的吗？

^{3 2 3 4 4 3 1 2 4 4 2 2 1}
Wo neng ba ding de zhe zhang piao huan yi ge bie de shi jian de ma?

Is there a service charge?

要付服务费吗？

^{4 4 2 4 4}
Yao fu fu wu fei ma?

I would like to cancel this ticket and get a refund.

我想把这张票退掉。

^{3 3 3 4 1 4 4 4}
Wo xiang ba zhe zhang piao tui diao.

If I wait here, is there a possibility I can get a ticket?

如果我等在这里，有可能买到一张票吗？

Ru guo wo deng zai zhe li, you ke neng mai dao yi zhang piao ma?

Someone may not show up.

可能有人不来。

Ke neng you ren bu lai.

It is an emergency.

这是一个紧急情况。

Zhe shi yi ge jin ji qing kuang.

(For waiting list, see Hotel section of this chapter.)

Private Car

Checkpoint　检查站

Jian cha zhan

Do you have permission to pass here?

你有通行证吗？

Ni you tong xing zheng ma?

I didn't know we needed permission.

我不知道我们需要办通行证。

Wo bu zhi dao wo men xu yao ban tong xing zheng.

I didn't see a sign.

我没有看见牌子。

Wo mei you kan jian pai zi.

We are only sightseeing.

我们只是在观光。

Wo men zhi shi zai guan guang.

We are traveling from ——— to ———.

我们是从＿＿＿＿旅行到＿＿＿＿。

Wo men shi cong ——— lu xing dao ———.

We are lost.

我们迷路了。

Wo men mi lu le.

Could you please tell me how to go from ——— to ———?

请告诉我从＿＿＿＿到＿＿＿＿怎么走。

Qing gao su wo cong ——— dao ——— zen me zou.

How far is it from here?

从这里去有多远？

Cong zhe li qu you duo yuan?

Please mark where we are now on this map.

请在地图上把我们现在所在的地方做个记号。

Qing zai di tu shang ba wo men xian zai suo zai de di fang zuo ge ji hao.

Please draw a map for us.

请给我们画个地图。

Qing gei wo men hua ge di tu.

here

这里

zhe li

there

那里

na li

Do you have a telephone?

你有电话吗？

Ni you dian hua ma?

We are ———. 我们是。_____。

Wo men shi ———.

diplomats 外交官

wai jiao guan

guests of the China International Travel Service

中国国际旅行社的客人

zhong guo guo ji lu xing she de ke ren

Overseas Chinese 华侨

hua qiao

foreign experts 外国专家

wai guo zhuan jia

Where can we find a(n) ———? 哪里有_____？

Na li you ———?

gas station? 加油站

jia you zhan?

restaurant? 饭馆

fan guan?

lavatory? 厕所

ce suo?

hotel? 旅馆
lu guan?

English-speaking person? 会说英语的人
hui shuo ying yu de ren?

Please circle the location on this map.

请在这个地图把那个位置圈一下。
Qing zai zhe ge di tu ba na ge wei zhi quan yi xia.

Permission

Is permission necessary?

需不需要先申请？
Xu bu xu yao xian shen qing?

Do I need permission to come back to this city?

再回这个城市我还需要先申请吗？
Zai hui zhe ge cheng shi wo hai xu yao xian shen qing ma?

Where do I get permission to go there?

到哪里办申请？
Dao na li ban shen qing?

Please write that address down here.

请把地址写在这里。
Qing ba di zhi xie zai zhe li.

Alien Permit

Where is the office of the Security Police? I want to get permission to go to the following cities:

公安局在哪里？我要申请到以下几个城市去：
Gong an ju zai na li? Wo yao shen qing dao yi xia ji ge cheng shi qu:

When? 什么时候？
Shen me shi hou?

Passport? 护照？
Hu zhao?

What hotel are you staying in? 你住在哪一个旅馆？
Ni zhu zai na yi ge lu guan?

Who invited you to China? 谁邀请你来中国的？
Shui yao qing ni lai zhong guo de?

Come back tomorrow.	请明天再来。 Qing ming tian zai lai.
Come back in two days.	两天后再来。 Liang tian hou zai lai.
What time?	什么时间？ Shen me shi jian?
Is there any charge?	要付钱吗？ Yao fu qian ma?

Departures (see also City travel)

Is it time to board yet?

还不该上车吗？
Hai bu gai shang che ma?

Which platform?

哪一个站台？
Na yi ge zhan tai?

Which coach?

哪一辆车箱？
Na yi liang che xiang?

Where is the ———?

——————在哪里？
——— zai na li?

waiting room	侯车室 hou che shi	
schedule in English	英语时间表 ying yu shi jian biao	
restaurant	餐馆 can guan	
retail store	商店 shang dian	
ticket	车／船 (car) che / (boat) chuan /	passport 护照 hu zhao

(plane ticket) fei ji piao 飞机票
customs declaration form

海关报税单

hai guan bao shui dan

foreign exchange receipt

外汇兑换收据

wai hui dui huan shou ju

identification badge

身份证章

shen fen zheng zhang

Lost and Found

I have lost my ———,

我的_____丢了。或：我找不到我的_____。

Wo de ——— diu le huo : zhao bu dao wo de ———.

spouse	丈夫／妻子	luggage	行李
	zhang fu / qi zi		xing li
tour group	旅行团	watch	手表
	lu xing tuan		shou biao
glasses	眼镜	wallet	皮夹子
	yan jing		pi jia zi
umbrella	伞	camera	照像机
	san		zhao xiang ji
purse	钱包	tape recorder	录音机
	qian bao		lu yin ji
typewriter	打字机	shoe	鞋
	da zi ji		xie
luggage wheels	推行李的小车	package	包裹
	tui xing lide xiao che		bao guo

Have you seen it? 你看见了吗？

Ni kan jian le ma?

Is there a lost-and-found here? 这儿有失物招领柜吗？

Zher you shi wu zhao ling gui ma?

If someone finds it, could you 如果有人找到了，

Ru guo you ren zhao dao le,

please mail it to me at this address? 请寄到这个地址给我。

^{3 4 4 4 4 4 3 3 3}
qing ji dao zhe ge di zhi gei wo.

HOTEL

General Information

Where do I register? 我在哪儿登记？

^{3 4 3 1 3}
Wo zai nar deng ji?

I have a reservation for today. 我已经订了今天的房间。

^{3 3 1 1 1 1 2 1}
Wo yi jing ding le jin tian de fang jian.

single 单人房   double 双人房   suite 套房

^{1 2 2}   ^{1 2 2}   ^{4 2}
dan ren fang   shuang ren fang   tao fang

——— persons   个人

^{4 2}
———ge ren

cheapest   最便宜的   whatever is available

^{4 2 4}
zui pian yi de

most expensive   最贵的   不管有什么都行

^{4 4}   ^{4 3 3 2 1 2}
zui gui de   bu guan you shen me dou xing

old wing   老厅   in between 中间的

^{3 1}   ^{1 1}
lao ting   zhong jian de

private bath or shower 私人浴室或淋浴   new wing 新厅

^{1 2 4 4 4 2 4}   ^{1 1}
si ren yu shi huo lin yu   xin ting

air-conditioned   有冷气的   not air-conditioned 没有冷气的

^{3 3 4}   ^{2 3 3}
you leng qi de   mei you leng

⁴
qi de

better view   看出去风景较好的。

^{4 1 4 3 3 3}
kan chu qu feng jing jiao hao de

Can I wait in the lobby until a room is available?

我在前门大厅等到有房间空出来行不行？

^{3 4 2 2 4 2 4 2 1 2 2}
Wo zai qian men da ting deng dao you fang jian kong chu lai xing

^{4 2}
bu xing?

Please put me on the waiting list.

请把我的名字登记上。

^{3 3 3 2 3 1 4 4}
Qing ba wo ming zi deng ji shang.

I will check with you tomorrow morning.

明天早上我再来问。

Ming tian zao shang wo zai lai wen.

I would like to make a reservation for a future date.

我想订一个房间。

Wo xiang ding yi ge fang jian.

I am looking for a friend.

我在找一个朋友。

Wo zai zhao yi ge peng you.

Please show me the registration forms so I can find his room number.

请将登记本给我查一下他的房间号数。

Qing jiang deng ji ben gei wo cha yi xia ta de fang jian hao shu.

His nationality?

他的国籍？

Ta de guo ji?

Is there someone to carry my bags to my room?

有人帮我把行李拿到房间里去吗？

You ren bang wo ba xing li na dao fang jian li qu ma?

Where is ———?

_____ 在哪儿？

——— zai nar?

barber shop	理发店
	li fa dian
hairdresser	理发师
	li fa shi
masseur	按摩师
	an mo shi
bank	银行
	yin hang
post office	邮局
	you ju
cable office	电报局
	dian bao ju

Telex 用户电报
yong hu dian bao

clinic 诊疗所
zhen liao suo

retail store 零售商店
ling shou shang dian

bar 酒吧间
jiu ba jian

coffee shop 咖啡馆
ka fei guan

When does it open? 什么时候开门?
Shen me shi hou kai men?

When does it close? 什么时候关门?
Shen me shi hou guan men?

Do you have ————? 你有＿＿＿＿吗? Where? 在那里?
Ni you ———— ma?　　　　　Zai na li?

ping-pong 乒乓
ping pang

billiards 台球
tai qiu

badminton 羽毛球
yu mao qiu

racket 拍子
pai zi

bird 羽毛球
yu mao qiu

net 球纲
qiu wang

volleyball 排球
pai qiu

swimming pool 游泳池
you yong chi

hot spring 温泉
wen quan

nearby park for jogging 附近可供步行锻练的公园
fu jin ke gong bu xing duan lian de gong yuan

scales for weighing luggage 秤行李用的磅秤
cheng xing li yong de bang cheng

Chinese newspaper
中国报纸
zhong guo bao zhi

typewriter
打字机
da zi ji

meeting room for ——— people
——— 人开会用的会议室
——— ren kai hui yong de hui yi shi

professional photographer
职业摄影师
zhi ye she ying shi

simultaneous translation equipment
同声翻译设备
tong sheng fan yi she bei

interpreter
翻译
fan yi

movie projector 放影机
fang ying ji

35 mm. 35毫米
san shi wu hao mi

8 mm. 8毫米
ba hao mi

super 8 超8
chao ba

slide projector 幻灯机
huan deng ji

tape recorder	录音机	
	lu yin ji	
spool	录音胶带	
	lu yin jiao dai	
cassette	暗盒	
	an he	
8-track	八声道	
	ba sheng dao	
microphone	扩音机	
	kuo yin ji	
megaphone	传声筒	
	chuan sheng tong	
refrigerator	冰箱	
	bing xiang	
freezer	致冷器	
	zhi leng qi	

What is the rental price?

租金多少？

Zu jin duo shao?

Can you organize a cocktail party for ——— people?

你能为＿＿＿人安排一个鸡尾酒会吗？

Ni neng wei ——— ren an pai yi ge ji wei jiu hui ma?

Please show me the room.

请你让我看看那个房间。

Qing ni rang wo kan kan na ge fang jian.

How much for hors d'œuvres and canapes?

小吃多少钱？

Xiao chi duo shao qian?

How much for liquor?

酒多少钱？

Jiu duo shao qian?

How much if we supply our own liquor and you supply the ice and glasses, waiters, and bartender?

我们带自己的酒，你供应冰块、玻璃环、服务员和酒

Wo men dai zi ji de jiu, ni gong ying bing kuai, bo li bei, fu wu

吧间招待员，要多少钱？

yuan he jiu ba jian zhao dai yuan, yao duo shao qian?

What is your cable address?

你的电报挂号是什么？

Ni de dian bao gua hao shi shen me?

What is your telephone number?

你的电话号码是什么？

Ni de dian hua hao ma shi (shen me?) duo shao?

Dining Room

Where is the dining room?

餐厅在哪里？

Can ting zai na li?

Chinese food

中餐

Zhong can

Western food

西餐

xi can

upstairs?

楼上

lou shang?

downstairs?

楼下

lou xia?

What time does it open? close? 餐厅什么时候开？关？

Can ting shen me shi hou kai? guan?

Laundry

If I give you my laundry now when will it be done?

如果我现在把要洗的东西给你，什么时候可以洗好？

Ru quo wo xian zai ba yao xi de dong xi ge ni, shen me shi shou

ke yi xi hao?

I must have it by tomorrow morning. I am leaving at ———.

我明天早上一定要。我＿＿＿＿点钟动身。

Wo ming tian zao shang yi ding yao. Wo ——— dian zhong dong shen.

Where is my laundry? I gave it to the attendant yesterday and he promised to have it done now. 我交去洗的东西在哪里？

Wo jiao qu de dong xi zai na li?

我是昨天交给服务员的，他答应我现在可以洗好。

Wo shi zuo tian jiao gei fu wu yuan de, ta da ying wo xian zai ke yi xi hao.

man's	男人的	nan ren de
woman's	女人的	nu ren de
child's	小孩的	xiao hai de
shirt	男式衬衫	nan shi chen shan
trousers	长裤	chang ku
blouse	女人衬衫	nu ren chen shan
underpants	内裤	nei ku
undershirt	内衣	nei yi
socks	短袜	duan wa
dress	衣裙	yi qun
pajamas	睡衣	shui yi

tie	领带
	ling dai
suit (man's)	西装
	xi zhuang
dry cleaning	干洗
	gan xi

I am leaving this morning.　　　我今天早上走。
　　　　　　　　　　　　　　　Wo jin tian zao shang zou.

I don't have anything else to wear.　我没有别的衣服可穿了。
　　　　　　　　　　　　　　　Wo mei you bie de yi fu ke chuan le.

I need it today.　　　　　　　　我今天要。
　　　　　　　　　　　　　　　Wo jin tian yao.

I need it right now.　　　　　　我现在就要。
　　　　　　　　　　　　　　　Wo xian zai jiu yao.

Rooms

There are mosquitoes in this room. Can you give me an incense coil to burn?

这个房间里有蚊子。你能给我一盘蚊香吗？

Zhe ge fang jian li you wen zi. Ni neng gei wo yi pan wen xiang me?

Do you have a mosquito net?

你有蚊帐吗？

Ni you wen zhang ma?

extra blanket?

你还有毯子吗？

Ni hai you tan zi ma?

Please give me some hot water in a thermos.

请给我一暖瓶热水。

Qing gei wo yi nuan ping re shui.

I need enough hot water for a bath.

我需要足够洗一个澡的热水。

Wo xu yao zu gou xi yi ge zao de re shui.

Please bring me ———. 请给我拿＿＿＿＿来。

Qing gei wo na ——— lai.
3   3   3   2

ice	冰	beer	啤酒	tea	茶
	bing 1		pi jiu 2 3		cha 2
orange soda	橘子汽水	Coke	可口可乐	glasses	玻璃杯
	ju zi qi shui 2 4 3		ke kou ke le 3 3 3 4		bo li bei 1 1
cup	杯子	towel	毛巾	soap	肥皂
	bei zi 1		mao jin 2 1		fei zao 2 4
clean	干净的	fan	电风扇／扇子		
	gan jing de 1 4		dian feng shan / shan zi		

Something is broken in my room. 我房间的＿＿＿＿坏了。

Wo fang jian de ——— huai le.
3   2   1   4

toilet	厕所	light	电灯
	ce suo 4 3		dian deng 4
telephone	电话	chair	椅子
	dian hua 4 4		yi zi 3
bed	床	air conditioner	冷气机
	chuang 2		leng qi ji 3 4 1
fan	电风扇	mosquito net	蚊帐
	dian feng shan 4 1 4		wen zhang 2 4
television	电视机	radiator	暖气
	dian shi ji 4 4 1		nuan qi 3 4

There isn't enough heat. 不够热

Bu gou re.
4   4   4

This is dirty. 这个不干净

Zhe ge bu gan jing.
4   4   4   1   4

Could someone fix it immediately?

能叫人立刻来修吗？

Neng jiao ren li ke lai xiu ma?
2   4   2   4   4   2   1   0

No. 不能   Yes. 能   I will try. 我试试看

bu neng.   neng.   wo shi shi kan.
4   2   2   3   4   4   4

I will ask my director.

我问一下主任。
Wo wen yi xia zhu ren.

Can I get a discount on my room if it is not fixed before I leave?

如果在我离开以前没有修好，我是否可以少付房钱？
Ru guo zai wo li kai yi qian mei you xiu hao, wo shi fou ke yi

shao fu fang qian?

Can I have a hot water bottle?

能给我一个热水袋吗？
Neng gei wo yi ge re shui dai ma?

Telephones

How do I get an outside line on the telephone?

我怎样打外线电话？
Wo zen yang da wai xian dian hua?

Please telephone this person and ask him/her to meet me at the hotel at
——— o'clock. My name is ——— and my room number is ———.

请你给这个人打一个电话，让他／她在＿＿＿点钟到
旅馆来找我。我叫＿＿＿＿住在＿＿＿＿号房间。
Qing ni gei zhe ge ren da yi ge dian hua, rang ta zai ———

dian zhong dao lu guan lai zhao wo. Wo jiao ——— zhu zai ———

—— hao fang jian.

I would like to make an international telephone call.

我想和国外通一个电话。
Wo xiang he quo wai tong yi ge dian hua.

I would like to call long distance in China.

我想打个中国国内的长途电话。
Wo xiang da ge zhong guo guo nei de chang tu dian hua.

Can I take it in my room?

我能在我房间里接吗？
Wo neng zai wo fang jian li jie ma?

Can I pay for it with a credit card?

我能用信用卡付款吗？
Wo neng yong xin yong ka fu kuan ma?

collect call

收话人付款的长途电话。
Shou hua ren fu kuan de chang tu dian hua.

FOOD

Banquets 宴会

(Arrangements can be made at service counter at hotel.)

Can you recommend a good restaurant for me?

你能推荐一家好的餐馆吗？

Ni neng tui jian yi jia hao de can guan ma?

One noted for good food, moderate prices. I don't care what it looks like.

一家菜闻名，而价钱公道的，我不在乎餐馆的样子如何。

Yi jia cai wen ming er jia qian gong dao de. Wo bu zai hu can guan de yang zi ru he.

One noted for beautiful surroundings and good food.

一家环境优美，菜又好的餐馆。

Yi jia huan jing you mei, cai you hao de can guan.

Could you please make a reservation for me for ——— people at ——— each. The chef can decide the menu.

请你代我订_____人一桌的菜。每人_____元的。菜单由厨师决定。

Qing ni dai wo ding ——— ren yi zhuo de cai. Mei ren ——— yuan de. Cai dan you chu shi jue ding.

Yes, I understand we have to pay extra for drinks.

对，我知道喝的要另外算。

Dui, Wo zhi dao he de yao ling wai suan.

Can we bring our own bottles of liquor?

我们能自己带酒吗？

Wo men neng zi ji dai ju ma?

Is it possible to include one dish of ——— for that price?

这个价钱能不能有个_____菜？

Zhe ge jia qian neng bu neng you ge ——— cai?

Please make the reservation for ——— o'clock.

请代我订在＿＿点钟。

Qing dai wo ding zai ——— dian zhong.

today

today	今天	jin tian
tomorrow	明天	ming tian
the day after tomorrow	后天	hou tian

Please write down the name and address for the taxi driver.

请将名字和地址写给司机。

Qing jiang ming zi he di zhi xie gei si ji.

Hotel Dining Rooms and Other Restaurants

I am in a hurry. 我有急事，请你快一点

Wo you ji shi, qing ni kuai yi dian.

Please bring me ———. 请给我＿＿＿＿＿＿。

Qing gei wo ———.

a bowl of noodle soup	一碗汤面	yi wan tang mian
fried noodles	炒面	chao mian
fried rice	炒饭	chao fan
an assortment of meat dumplings	肉馅饺子／馄饨	rou xian jiao zi / hun tun
a dish of meat	一盘肉菜	yi pan rou cai

anything that can be
prepared quickly　　　任何快餐都行
　　　　　　　　　　　4　2　4　1　1　2
　　　　　　　　　　ren he kuai can dou xing

I would like a Chinese breakfast.　我要一份中式早餐
　　　　　　　　　　　　　　　3　4　14　1　4　3　1
　　　　　　　　　　　　　Wo yao yi fen zhong shi zao can.

rice congee	大米粥	baked buns	烧饼
	4 4		1 3
	da mi zhou		shao bing
pickles	泡菜	oil sticks	油条
	4 4		2 2
	pao cai		you tiao
salted eggs	咸蛋	dim sum	点心
	2 4		3 1
	xian dan		dian xin
peanuts	花生米	soy milk	豆浆
	1 1 3		4 1
	hua sheng mi		dou jiang
tea	茶		
	2		
	cha		

I would like a Western breakfast.　我要一份西式早点
　　　　　　　　　　　　　　　3　4　14　1　4　3　3
　　　　　　　　　　　　　Wo yao yi fen xi shi zao dian.

fruit or juice	水果或水果汁		
	3 4 3 3 4 1		
	shui guo huo shui guo zhi		
toast or buns	烤面包或小园面包		
	3 4 1 4 3 1 3 1		
	kao mian bao huo xiao yuan mian bao		
eggs	鸡蛋	butter	黄油
	1 4		2 2
	ji dan		huang you
bacon or ham	咸肉或火腿	coffee	咖啡
	2 4 3 3 3		1 1
	xian rou huo huo tui		ka fei
jam	果酱	milk	牛奶
	3 4		2 3
	guo jiang		niu nai
sugar	糖		
	2		
	tang		

If you have a menu in English, please bring it.

如果你有英语菜单，请拿给我看一看。

Ru guo ni you ying yu cai dan, qing na gei wo kan yi kan.

What do you recommend that is good but not expensive?

你可以介绍什么好而又不贵的菜吗？

Ni ke yi jie shao shen me hao er you bu gui de cai ma?

What is the specialty of this restaurant?

这里的特菜是什么？

Zhe li de te cai shi shen me?

Please bring enough food for one person.

请你给够我一个人吃的饭菜。

Qing ni gei gou wo yi ge ren chi de fan cai.

Please bring enough food for all of us. Total cost no more than ———
per person.

请你给够我们大家吃的饭菜，每人不超过_____。

Qing ni gei gou wo men da jia chi de fan cai, mei ren bu chao guo
———.

Please bring me one order of ———.

请你给我一份_____。

Qing ni gei wo yi fen ———.

beef	牛肉 niu rou	vegetables	蔬菜 shu cai
chicken	鸡 ji	celery cabbage	芹菜 qin cai
pigeon	鸽子 ge zi	green beans	青豆 qing dou
goose	鹅 e	green onions	葱 cong
pork	猪肉 zhu rou	bean sprouts	豆芽 dou ya
fish	鱼 yu	bamboo shoots	竹笋 zhu sun
crab	螃蟹 pang xie	water chestnuts	荸荠 bi qi

lobster	龙虾 long² xia¹	watercress	水芹菜 shui³ qin³ cai⁴
shrimp	虾 xia¹	cabbage	白菜 bai² cai⁴
sea cucumber (or slug)	海参 hai³ shen¹	mushrooms	蘑菇 mo² gu¹
bean curd	豆腐 dou⁴ fu	cloud's ears (fungus)	银耳 yin² er³
Beijing (Peking) duck	北京鸭 beijing³ ¹ ya¹	pine nuts	松子 song¹ zi³
duck	鸭子 ya¹ zi		
monkey	猴子 hou² zi	cashews	枧如树果 ru² shu⁴ guo³
snake	蛇 she²	peanuts	花生 hua¹ sheng¹
dog	狗 gou³	walnuts	核桃 he² tao²
frogs' legs	蛙腿 wa¹ tui³	eggs	蛋 dan⁴
civet cat	香猫 xiang¹ mao¹	caviar	鱼子 yu² zi³
turtle	甲鱼 jia³ yu²	hors d'œuvre	小吃 xiao³ chi¹
lotus seed	莲子 lian² zi³	black or yellow bean	黑或黄豆 hei¹ huo³ huang² dou⁴
heart	心 xin¹	gizzard	胗 zhen¹
liver	肝 gan¹	kidney	腰子 yaozi¹

brains	脑 3 nao	spareribs		2 3 pai gu
hocks	蹄膀 2 3 ti bang	tongue		2 she
steak	牛排 2 2 niu pai	fillet (boneless)		3 1 liji
slices	肉片 4 4 rou pian	balls		2 wanzi
soup	汤 1 tang	stomach		3 du zi
minced	剁碎的 4 4 duo sui de	shark's fins	鱼翅 2 yu chi	
bird's nest	燕窝 4 1 yan wo			
stir-fried	快炒 kuai chao	roasted	烤 3 kao	
deep-fried (in batter)	炸(裹鸡蛋面) 2 3 1 4 zha (guo ji dan mian)	cooked in wine	酒焖的 jiu men de	
poached	烫熟的 4 4 tan shu de	barbecued	烧烤 1 3 shao kao	
steamed	蒸的 1 zheng de	baked	烘烤 1 3 hong kao	
fried in paper	包纸炸的 1 3 4 bao zhi zha de	baked in mud	泥烤 2 3 ni kao	
scrambled	炒 3 chao	baked in salt	盐烤 2 3 yang kao	
boiled (hard)	煮（老的） 3 3 zhu (lao de)	boiled (soft)	煮（嫩的） 3 4 zhu (nen de)	
sweet and sour sauce	糖醋汁 2 4 1 tang cu zhi			
hoisin sauce	甜面酱 2 4 4 tian mian jiang	bland	淡的 4 dan de	

oyster sauce	牡蛎酱 3 4 4 mu li jiang	no salt	无盐的 2 2 mi yan de
soy sauce	酱油 4 2 jiang you	sour	酸 1 suan
mustard	芥茉 4 jie me	spicy hot	麻辣 2 4 ma la
hot pepper	辣椒 4 1 la jiao	sweet	甜 2 tian
plum sauce	梅子酱 2 2 mei zi jiang	no sugar	无糖 2 2 wu tang
sesame oil	芝麻油／香油 1 2 2 1 2 zhi ma you / xiang you	salty	咸 2 xian
peanut oil	花生油 1 1 2 hua sheng you	1000-year-old eggs	皮蛋 2 4 pi dan
coriander	芫荽 2 1 yan sui	white rice	白米饭 2 3 4 bai mi fan
honey	蜂蜜 1 4 feng me	ginger	姜 1 jiang
salt	盐 2 yan	garlic	蒜 4 suan
vinegar	醋 4 cu		
canned	罐头的 4 2 guan tou de	fresh	新鲜的 1 1 xin xian de
sweet cakes	甜饼 2 3 tian bing	apples	苹果 2 3 ping guo
bananas	香蕉 1 1 xiang jiao	oranges	橘子 2 ju zi
apricots	杏子 4 xing zi	plums	李子 3 li zi
olives	橄榄 3 3 gan lan	kumquats	金橘 1 2 jin ju

pomelo	柚子	lichees	荔枝
	you zi		li zhi
pineapple	菠萝		
	bo luo		

What kind of tea do you have?

你们有什么茶？

Ni men you shen me cha?

jasmine	茉莉花茶	lung ching	龙井茶
	mo li hua cha		long jing cha
woo lung	乌龙茶	bo ni	普洱茶
	wu long cha		pu er cha
chrysanthemum	菊花茶	ginseng	人参茶
	ju hua cha		ren shen cha
milk (hot)	热牛奶	milk (cold)	冷牛奶
	re niu nai		leng niu nai
unsweetened	未加糖的	soft drink	饮料
	wei jia tang de		yin liao
beer	啤酒	Coca Cola	可口可乐
	pi jiu		ke kou ke le
red wine	红酒	fruit juice	果子汁
	hong pu tao jiu		guo zi zhi
white wine	白酒	fermented mare's milk	发酵的马奶
	bai pu tao jiu		fa jiao de ma nai
mao tai	茅台酒		
	mao tai jiu		
mineral water	矿泉水	buttered tea	油茶
	kuang quan shui		you cha
cold drinking water	冷开水	cocoa	可可
	leng kai shui		ke ke

This tastes terrible. Please bring me something else.

这个很难吃／喝。 请给我来点别的。

Zhe ge hen nan chi / he. Qing gei wo lai dian bie de.

Enough! 够了！

      Gou le!

We cannot eat any more. Please cancel the other dishes!

我们吃不下了，请把别的菜取消罢！

Wo men chi bu xia le. Qing ba bie de cai qu xiao ba!

Western food

西餐

Xi can

bread	面包	hot dog	热狗
	mian bao		re gou
sandwich	三文治	hamburger	面包夹牛肉饼
	san wen zhi		mian bao jia niu rou bing
ice cream	冰淇淋	popsicle	冰棍
	bing ji ling		bing gun

Please write down the name of this dish so I can order it again.

请将这个菜名写下来，我以后好再要。

Qing jiang zhe ge cai ming xie xia lai wo yi hou hao zai yao.

I am a strict vegetarian. I would like to order a dish of only vegetables, cooked in vegetable oil. What do you recommend?

我是一个真正的素食者。我想要一个素油炒的蔬菜。你能给我介绍几个这样的菜吗？

Wo shi yi ge zhen zheng de su shi zhe. Wo xiang yao yi ge su you chao de shu cai. Ni neng gei wo jie shao ji ge zhe yang de cai ma?

I am a Moslem. I do not eat pork or anything cooked in lard. What do you recommend?

我信伊斯兰教。我不吃猪肉或猪油烧的东西。你有什么我可以吃的呢？

Wo xin yi si lan jiao. Wo bu chi zhu rou huo zhu you shao de dong zi. Ni you shen me wo ke yi chi de ne?

I am a diabetic. I cannot eat anything with sugar in it.

我有糖尿病，我不能吃任何有糖的东西。

Wo you tang niao bing. Wo bu neng chi ren he you tang de dong xi.

TELEPHONE (see also Hotel Telephones)

Finding a Public Telephone

Please show me where I can find a telephone.
请告诉我哪里有电话？
Qing gao su wo na li you dian hua.

How much for using the telephone?
打一次电话多少钱？
Da yi dian hua duo shao qian?

Can you find out the telephone number for ———?
你能帮我找一找 _____ 的电话号码吗？
Ni neng bang wo zhao yi zhao ——— de dian hua hao ma ma?

the China International Travel Service in this city?
这里的中国国际旅行社？
zhe li de zhong guo guo ji lu xing she?

the CAAC office in this city?
这里的中国航空公司？
zhe li de zhang guo hang kong gong si?

someone who speaks English?
会说英语的人。
hui shuo ying yu de ren?

Please telephone this person. I want to talk to him.
请给这个人打一个电话。我要和他说话。
Qing gei zhe ge ren da yi ge dianhua. Wo yao he ta shuo hua.

I want to make ———. 我要一个_____。
Wo yao yi ge ———.

a long-distance call in China 中国境内的长途电话。
zhong guo jing nei de chang tu
dian hua.

an international telephone call 国际长途电话。
guo ji chang tu dian hua.

Can I take the call in my room?
我能在我房间里接吗？
Wo neng zai wo fang jian li jie me?

Can I pay for it with a credit card?

我能用信用卡付款吗？

Wo neng yong xin yong ka fu kuan me?

collect call

收话人付款的长途电话。

Shou hua ren fu kuan de chang tu dian hua

How long will it take?

要多久可以接通？

Yao duo jiu ke yi jie tong?

EMERGENCIES

If Lost

Help! 救命！

Jiu ming!

Excuse me. 对不起。

Du bu qi.

I am lost. Which way to this
address?

我迷路了，到这个地址去走那一条路？

Wo mi lu le, dao zhe ge di zhi qu zou na yi tiao lu?

the closest hotel?

最近的旅馆在哪里？

Zui jin de lu guan zai na li?

the nearest English-speaking person?

在哪个最近的地方可以找到会说英语的人？

Zai na ge zui jin de di fang ke yi zhao dao hui shuo ying yu de ren?

Can you ask someone to take me there?

你能叫人带我去吗？

Ni neng jiao ren dai wo qu ma?

I am very tired.

我很累。

Wo hen lei.

Please don't push me.

请不要推我。

Qing bu yao tui wo.

Where can I find a telephone?

哪里有电话？

_{3 3 3 4 4}
Na li you dian hua?

Embassies

Please contact the embassy of ———.

请你和_____大使馆接个电话。

_{3 3 4 3 3 1 4 4 4}
Qing ni he ——— da shi guan jie ge dian hua.

I will speak to them on the telephone.

我要和他们说话。

_{3 4 2 1 1 4}
Wo yao he ta men shuo hua.

Please tell their representative to come here.

请告诉他们的代表到这儿来。

_{3 4 4 1 4 4 4 4 2}
Qing gao su ta men de dai biao dao zher lai.

Australia	澳大利亚 _{4 4 4} Ao da li ya
Belgium	比利时 _{3 4 2} Bi li shi
Britain	英国 _{1 2} Ying guo
Canada	加拿大 _{1 2 4} Jia na da
France	法国 _{3 2} Fa guo
India	印度 _{4 4} Yin du
Indonesia	印尼 _{4 2} Yin ni
Italy	意大利 _{4 4 4} Yi da li
Japan	日本 _{4 3} Ri ben
Malaysia	马来西亚 _{3 2 1 4} Ma lai xi ya

Mexico

墨西哥

4 1 1
Mo xi ge

Netherlands

荷兰

2 2
He lan

New Zealand

新西兰

1 1 2
Xin xi lan

Pakistan

巴基斯坦

1 1 1 3
Ba ji si tan

Philippines

菲律宾

1 4 1
Fei lu bin

Portugal

2 2 2
Pu tao ya

Singapore

新加坡

1 1 1
Xin jia po

Spain

西班牙

1 1 2
Xi ban ya

The Federal Republic of Germany

德意志联邦共和国

4 4 4 2 1 4 2 2
De yi zhi lian bang gong he guo

Switzerland

瑞士

4 4
Rui shi

Thailand

泰国

4 2
Tai guo

U.S.A.

美国

3 2
Mei guo

Miscellaneous Emergencies

Stop, please.

请停下来。

3 2 4 2
Qing ting xia lai.

I need a lavatory. Please show me the closest one.

我需要上厕所。请告诉我最近的一个在哪里。

3 1 4 4 4 3 4 3 4 4 1 4 4 3 3
Wo xu yao shang ce suo. Qing gao su wo zui jin de yi ge zai na li.

women's 女人的 （如指厕所则是：女厕男厕）
nu ren de (ru zhi ce suo ze shi) nu ce nan ce

men's 男人的
nan ren de

Stay away! 站开点！
zhan kai dian!

Danger! 危险！
wei xian!

Run away! 跑开！
pao kai!

Follow me! 跟着我！
gen zhe wo!

Please hurry! 快些！
kuai xie!

air attack 空袭
kong xi

air-raid shelter 防空洞
fang kong dong

boat sinking 船在沉
chuan zai chen

Fire! 失火了！
shi huo le!

Explosion! 爆炸了！
bao zha le!

Earthquake! 地震了！
di zhen le!

Get outside, away from falling debris.
到外面去，躲开掉下来的碎砾。
Dao wai mian qu, duo kai diao xia lai de sui li.

Riot! 暴动！
bao dong!

accident 意外。
yi wai

flood   水灾。

shui zai

Please call someone who speaks English.

请叫一位能说英语的来。

Qing jia yi wei neng shuo ying yu de lai.

Please call the China International Travel Service.

请叫中国国际旅行社的人来。

Qing jiao zhong guo guo ji lu xing she de ren lai.

Medical Emergencies

Is anyone hurt?   有人受伤吗？

You ren shou shang ma?

Is there someone here who can help us?

这里有那一位能帮助我们吗？

Zhe li you na yi wei neng bang zhu wo men ma?

Please ask people to stand back and give us some air.

请你叫人们靠后站，使我们能吸到些空气。

Qing ni jiao ren men kao hou zhan, shi wo men neng xi dao xie
kang qi.

Please call a doctor.

请叫一位医生来。

Qing jiao yi wei yi sheng lai.

Please bring ———. 请你拿_____来。

Qing ni na ——— lai.

blanket   一床毯子

yi chuang tan zi.

stretcher   一个担架

yi fu dan jia

oxygen   氧气

yang qi

ice   冰

bing

splints   夹板

jia ban

bandages   绷带
             1   4
             beng dai

drinking water   喝的水
             1   3
             he de shui

Stop the bleeding.   止血
             3   3
             Zhi xue.

Call an ambulance.   叫救护车来
             4   4   4   1   2
             Jiao jiu hu che lai.

Get him to a hospital.   送他去医院
             4   1   4   1   4
             Song ta qu yi yuan.

Hurry.   快！
             4
             Kuai!

Help him breathe.   帮助他呼吸
             1   4   1   1
             Bang zhu ta hu xi.

A bone caught in the throat.   喉咙里卡了一根骨头。
             2   2   3   3   1   1   2
             Hou long li qia le yi gen gu tou.

Help him lie down.   帮他躺下。
             1   1   3   4
             Bang ta tang xia.

Raise his head.   把他的头抬起来。
             3   1   2   3   2
             Ba ta de tou tai qi lai.

Lower his head.   把他的头放下去。
             3   1   2   4   4
             Ba ta de tou fang xia qu.

Raise his feet.   把他的脚抬起来。
             3   1   3   2   3 2
             Ba ta de jiao tai qi la.

Give heart massage.   给他按摩心脏。
             3   1   4   2   1   4
             Gei ta an mo xin zang.

Give mouth-to-mouth resuscitation.   做口对口的呼吸急救。
             4   3   4   3   1   1   2   4
             Zuo kou dui kou de hu xi ji jiu.

Get him cool.   让他凉快凉快。
             4   1   2   2   4
             Rang ta liang kuai liang kuai.

Fan him.   给他扇一扇。
             3   1   1   1   1
             Gei ta shan yi shan.

appendicitis	阑尾炎
	lan wei yan
bleeding	流血
	liu xie
Broken bone. Do not move it.	骨头断了，不要挪动。
	Gu tou duan le. Bu yao nuo dong.
burn	烧伤
	shao shang
diabetic	糖尿病
	tang hiao bing
drowned	淹了
	yan le
drunk	喝醉了
	he zui le
epileptic fit	癫痫发作
	dian xian fa zuo
heart attack	心脏病发作
	xin zang bing fa zuo
high fever	高烧
	gao shao
insect bite	虫咬了
	chong yao le
poisoned	中毒了
	zhong du le
snake bite	蛇咬了
	she yao le
stroke	中风
	zhong fang
vomit	呕吐
	ou tu

Medical (see also Medical Emergencies)

Where can I find a doctor to treat this ———?

在哪里能找到一位医生治这_____?
Zai na li neng zhao dao yi wei yi sheng zhi zhe ———?

itch	痒	yang
pain here	这儿痛	zher tong
bleeding here	这儿流血	zher liu xie
common cold	受凉感冒	shou lian gan mao
diarrhea	腹泻	fu xie
cough	咳嗽	ke sou
headache	头痛	tou tong
fever	发烧	fa shao
difficulty in breathing	呼吸困难	hu xi kun nan
hives	荨麻疹	xun ma zhen
sore throat	喉咙痛	hou long tong
acupuncture	针刺治疗	zhen ci zhi liao
compress	纱布垫	sha bu dian
injection	打针	da zhen
soak	浸湿	jin shi

bandage	用绷带包扎
	yong beng dai bao zha
Go to the hospital.	去医院
	Qu yi yuan.
How long bed rest?	要卧床多久？
	Yao wo chuang duo jiu?
When can he continue on his journey?	他什么时候可以继续旅行？
	Ta shen me shi hou ke yi ji xu lu xing?
What is his temperature?	他的体温是多少？
	Ta de ti wen shi duo shao?
What is that in Fahrenheit?	华氏多少度？
	Hua shi duo shao du?
Is it a high fever?	体温高吗？
	Ti wen gao me?
Is it normal?	正常不正常？
	Zheng chang bu zheng chang?

Dental

dental	牙齿的。
	ya chi de
I have a pain here.	我这儿痛。
	Wo zher tong.
I think I have lost a filling.	我想我有一个牙齿的充填物掉了。
	Wo xiang wo you yi ge ya chi de chong tian wu diao le.
Can you give me a temporary filling?	能给我临时补一下吗？
	Neng gei wo lin shi bu yi xia ma?
Please do not pull out the tooth.	请不要把那个牙拔掉。
	Qing bu yao ba na ge ya ba diao.
Please pull out this tooth.	请把这个牙拔掉。
	Qing ba zhe ge ya ba diao.

Can you give me something to ease
the pain?

你能给我什么止痛的药吗？

Ni neng gei wo shen me zhi tong de
yao me?

Pharmacy (see also Medical)

traditional Chinese herbal medicine

中国草药

zhong guo cao yao

Western medicine

西药

xi yao

allergy to antibiotics

对抗生素过敏

dui kang sheng su guo min

aspirin

阿司匹灵

a si pi ling

insulin for diabetic

治疗糖尿病的胰岛素。

zhi liao tang niao bing de yi dao su

How many teaspoons a day?

一天服几匙？

Yi tian fu ji shao?

How many times a day?

一天服几次？

Yi tian fu ji ci?

How many pills?

几丸？

Ji wan?

For how long?

服多久？

Fu duo jiu?

How much water?

多少水？

Duo shao shui?

Boil and drink like tea?

熬后像喝茶一样喝下去吗？

Ao hou xiang he cha yi yang he
xia qu ma?

All of it?

全喝吗？

Quan he ma?

With sugar?

加糖吗？

Jia tang ma?

Is it bitter?	苦不苦？ 3 3 Ku bu ku?
Any more injections?	还要打针吗？ 2 4 3 1 Hai yao da zhen ma?
aphrodisiac	催欲剂 1 4 4 cui yu ji
ginseng	人参 2 1 ren shen
sea horse	海马 3 3 hai ma
pearl	珍珠 1 1 zhen zhu
sleeping pill	安眠药 1 2 4 an mian yao
snake	蛇 2 she
insects	昆虫 1 2 kun chong
herb	草药 3 4 cao yao
mineral	矿石 4 2 kuang shi
animal	动物 4 4 dong wu
deer horn	鹿角 4 3 lu jiao

WEATHER

What is the temperature today?
今天的温度是多少？
1 1 1 4 4 1 3
Jin tian de wen du shi duo shao?

Is it hot? 今天热吗？
1 1 4
Jin tian re ma?

cold 冷
3
leng

rainy 有雨
3   3
you yu

snowing 下雪
4   3
xia xue

sunny 晴
2
qing

Do I need to take a ———? 我需要带_____。
3 1 4 4
Wo xu yao dai ———?

coat 一件外套
1 4   4 4
yi jian wai tao

sweater 一件毛衣
1 4   2 1
yi jian mao yi

umbrella 一把伞
1 3 3
yi ba san

swimming suit 游泳衣
2   3   1
you yong yi

suntan lotion 一瓶防晒油
1 2 2 4 2
yi ping fang shai you

RENTALS

Where can I rent a ———? 哪里可以租_____?
3 3 3 3 1
Na li ke yi zu ———?

bicycle 一辆自行车
1 4 4 2 1
yi liang zi xing che

rowboat 一条划艇
1 2 2 3
yi tiao hua ting

tennis racket 一个纲球拍
1 4 3 2 1
yi ge wang qiu pai

car (with driver) 一辆有司机开的汽车
1 4 3 1 1 1 4
yi liang you si ji kai de qi che

How much for an hour? 多少钱一小时？
Duo shao qian yi xiao shi?

a day? 一天？
yi tian?

deposit? 押金多少？
ya jin duo shao?

I will return in about ——
hours. 我大概在＿＿小时后送还。
Wo da gai zai —— xiao shi hou song huan.

CONVERSATIONS

Courtesies

hello! 你好！Ni hao!
Good-bye! 再见！Zai jian!
I'm sorry. (or) Excuse me! 对不起（或）请原谅！Dui bu qi (or) Qing yan liang!
Please 请 Qing.
Thank you. 谢谢你！Xie xie ni.
You're welcome. 不客气。Bu ke qi.
Yes. 是。Shi de.
No. 不是。Bu shi.
Maybe. 可能。Ke neng.
Wait awhile. 等一会。Deng yi hui.

Please tell me how to say this in Chinese.
请告诉我这个用中国话怎么说。
Qing gao su wo zhe ge yong zhong guo hua zen mo shuo.

Please say it again slowly.
请再慢一些说一遍。
Qing zai man yi xie shuo yi bian.

Would you feel offended if I gave you a small token of my appreciation?
如果我送你一件小纪念品以表示我的谢意，你会不会不高兴？
Ru guo wo song ni yi jian xiao ji nian pin yi biao shi wo de xie yi, ni hui bu hui bu gao xing?

It is not necessary.
你不需要这样做。
Ni bu xu yao zhe yang zuo.

But you have been so kind and I feel I will be indebted to you for the rest of my life.

但是你对我这样好，使我觉得此生欠了你很大的情份。

Dan shi ni dui wo zhe yang hao, shi wo jue de ci sheng qian le ni hen da de qing fen.

It is not convenient.

我不便接受。

Wo bu bian jie shou.

In that case, I will not feel offended.

如果是这样的话，我就不会不高兴了。

Ru guo shi zhe yang de hua, wo jiu bu hui bu gao xing le.

Meeting Strangers (Please have someone fill in the blanks beforehand in Chinese.)

Hello.

I am sorry, I do not speak Chinese.   对不起，我不会说中文。

Dui bu qi, wo bu hui shuo zhong wen.

I speak English.   我说英文。

Wo shuo ying wen.

My name is ———.   我的名字是_____。

Wo de ming zi shi ———.

I am from ———.   我是_____人。

Wo shi ——— ren.

I am in China for ——— weeks.   我要在中国_____周。

Wo yao zai zhong guo dei ——— zhou.

——— months.   _____个月。

——— ge yue.

I arrived ———.   我是在_____到的。

Wo shi zai ——— dao de.

I expect to leave ———.   我预定在_____离开。

Wo yu ding zai ——— li kai.

Please write that down and I will have someone translate it later.

请把它写下来，以后我再找人翻译。

Qing ba ta xie xia lai, yi hou wo zai zhao ren fan yi.

I am visiting ——, ——, ——, ——, ——, and ——.

我将到＿＿＿＿ ＿＿＿＿ ＿＿＿＿

Wo jiang dao —— ——

＿＿＿＿ ＿＿＿＿ ＿＿＿去观光。

—— —— ——

qu quan guang.

Where do you work?

你在哪里工作？

Ni zai na li gong zuo?

| | factory | 工厂 |
| | | gong chang |

commune 公社
gong she

hospital 医院
yi yuan

office 办公室
bang gong shi

restaurant 饭馆
fan guan

transportation 运输部门
yun shu bu men

hotel 旅馆
lu guan

school 学校
xue xiao

cultural organization 文化机构
wen hua ji gou

government organization 政府机构
zheng fu ji gou

I am a —————.

我是一个_____

Wo shi yi ge ———

(profession)

（职业）

(zhi ye)

Do you work in this city?

你在这个城市工作吗？

Ni zai zhe ge cheng shi gong zuo

ma?

Where were you born?

你出生在哪里？

Ni chu sheng zai na li?

How many children do you have?

你有几个孩子？

Ni you ji ge hai zi?

Are they all in school?

他们都进学校了吗？

Ta men dou jin xue xiao le ma?

How old are they?

他们多大？

Ta men duo da?

How much money do you make a
month?

你一个月赚多少钱？

Ni yi ge yue zhuan duo shao

qian?

How much do you pay for rent?

你的房租多少？

Ni de fang zu duo shao?

for food?

你吃饭花多少钱？

Ni chi fan hua duo shao qian?

What hours do you work?

你什么时间上班和下班？

Ni shen me shi jian shang ban he

xia ban?

Do you have any relatives in my
country?

你有亲属在我的国家吗？

Ni you qin shu zai wo de guo jia ma?

Do you have any friends in my
country?

你有朋友在我的国家吗？

Ni you peng you zai wo de guo jia ma?

How many years of schooling have
you had? 你曾在学校读过多少年书？

Ni ceng zai xue xiao du guo duo shao nian shu?

How much time have you spent doing manual labor in the countryside?

你下乡干体力劳劲的时间有多久？

Ni xia xiang gan ti li lao dang de shi jian you duo chang?

When was the last time, and for how long?

你最后一次是什么时候去的，去了多久？

Ni zui hou yi ci shi shen me shi hou qu de, qu le duo jiu?

Especially for People with Chinese Relatives

I am very happy to meet you.

见到你我很高兴。

Jian dao ni wo hen gao xing.

Could you join me for a meal?

你能和我一起吃饭吗？

Ni neng he wo yi qi chi fan ma?

For tea? 你能和我一起喝茶吗？

Ni neng he wo yi qi he cha ma?

In the hotel? 我们在旅馆里吃好吗？

Wo men zai lu guan li chi hao ma?

Then follow me. 那么，咱们去吧！

Na me, zan men qu ba!

In a nearby restaurant? 到附近的饭馆去吃好吗？

Dao fu jin de fan guan qu chi hao ma?

Do you know of a good place? 你知道有什么好饭馆吗？

Ni zhi dao you shen me hao fan guan

ma?

Please lead the way, but you are my
guest. 请你带我去，不过让我请客。

Qing ni dai wo qu, bu guo rang wo qing ke.

Could you please order? 你点菜好吗？

Ni dian cai hao ma?

Anything you like. 随便什么你喜欢吃的菜都行。
Sui bian shen me ni xi huan chi de cai dou xing.

I don't know how to do it in
Chinese. 我不知道怎样用中国话说。
Wo bu zhi dao zen yang yong zhong guo hua shuo.

Not too much. I don't like to waste
food. 不要点太多菜。我不愿意浪费。
Bu yao dian tai duo cai. Wo bu yuan yi lang fei.

Did you know my father? 你认识我的父亲吗？
Ni ren shi wo de fu qin ma?

Did you know my grandfather? 你认识我的祖父吗？
Ni ren shi wo de zu fu ma?

Have you visited my ancestral
village lately? 你最近去过我的家乡吗？
Ni zui jin qu guo wo de jia xiang ma?

How is it? 那儿怎么样？
Nar zen me yang?

Poor? 挺穷吗？
Ting qiong ma?

Prosperous? 富裕吗？
Fu yu ma?

Far away? 很远吗？
Hen yuan ma?

Just getting along? 还过得去吗？
Hai guo de qu ma?

Can you take me there for a short
visit? 你能带我去看一看吗？
Ni neng dai wo qu kan yi kan ma?

One of your children? 你的孩子？
Ni de hai zi?

Can you help me make
arrangements? 你能帮我安排吗？
Ni neng bang wo an pai ma?

As soon as possible. 愈快愈好。
Yu kuai yu hao.

When I get back from my tour. 我参观回来的时候。
Wo can guan hui lai de shi hou.

Should I make the application now? 我要不要现在就申请？
Wo yao bu yao xian zai jiu shen
qing?

Tomorrow? 明天？
ming tian?

I am sorry I know so little about
you. 我很遗憾对你不够熟悉。
Wo hen yi han dui ni bu gou shu xi.

What do you do for entertainment? 你参加什么娱乐活动？
Ni can jia shen me yu le huo
dong?

sports	运动？ yun dong?	movies?	看电影？ kandian ying?	
parks?	去公园？ qu gong yuan?	visiting friends?	看朋友？ kan peng you?	
no time	没有空？ mei you kong?	television?	看电视？ kan dian shi?	

How many ration coupons do you
get for a month for ———? 你一个月有多少_____？
Ni yi ge yue you duo shao ———?

肉票 rou piao	meat		公斤 gong jin	kg.
粮票 liang piao	grain		斤 jin	catties
布票 bu piao	cotton cloth		米 mi	meters
油票 you piao	cooking oil		两 liang	ounces

肥皂　　soap
2　4
fei zao

块　　bars
4
kuai

Is it sufficient for your needs?　它够不够？
1　4　4　4
Ta gou bu gou?

Do you have ———?　你有＿＿＿＿吗？
3　3
ni you ——— ma?

a bicycle　　一辆自行车
1　4　4　3
yi liang zi xing che

a sewing machine　　一架缝纫机
1　4　2　4
yi jia feng ren ji

a television set　　一个电视机
1　4　4　4　1
yi ge dian shi ji

a fan　　一个风扇
1　4　1
yi ge feng shan

a radio　　一个无线电
1　4　2　4　4
yi ge wu xian dian

your own kitchen　　一个自已的厨房
1　4　4　3　2　2
yi ge zi ji de chu fang

a refrigerator　　一个冰箱
1　4　1　1
yi ge bing xiang

a gas stove　　一个煤气炉
1　4　2　4　2
yi ge mei qi lu

Where is the closest school to your house?　离你家最近的学校在哪里？
2　3　1　4　4　2　4　4　3　3
Li ni jia zui jin de xue xiao zai na li?

primary　　小学
3　2
xiao xue

middle　　中学
1　2
zhong xue

Do your children walk to school?
你的孩子是不是步行去学校？
3　2　4　2　4　4　2　4　2　4
Ni de hai zi shi bu shi bu xing qu xue xiao?

Do your children take a public bus?

你的孩子是乘公共汽车去吗？

₃ ₂ ₄ ₂ ₁ ₁ ₄

Ni de hai zi shi cheng gong qi che qu ma?

How much does it cost for ———? _____是多少钱？

₄ ₁ ₃ ₂

——— shi duo shao qian?

tuition 学费

₂ ₄

xue fei

room and board 膳宿费

₄ ₄ ₄

shan su fei

university 大学

₄ ₂

da xue

How many people are there in your household who make money?

你们家里有几人赚钱？

₃ ₁ ₃ ₃ ₃ ₂ ₂

Ni men jia li you ji ren zhuan qian?

How much money did you all make last year?

去年你们全家的收入是多少？

₄ ₂ ₃ ₂ ₁ ₄ ₄ ₁ ₃

Qu nian ni men quan jia de shou ru shi duo shao?

Do you have any savings?

你们有储蓄吗？

₃ ₃ ₃ ₄

Ni men you chu xu ma?

How much did you spend for ———?

你（你们）_____化多少钱？

₃ ₃ ₁ ₁ ₃ ₂

Ni (ni men) ——— hua duo shao qian?

clothing 穿

₁

chuan

food 吃

₁

chi

rent 房租

₂ ₁

fang zu

entertainment 娱乐

₂ ₄

yu le

transportation 交通

₁ ₁

jiao tong

medical expenses　医药
yi yao

per month?　一个月？
yi ge yue?

per year?　一年？
yi nian?

May I see your house?
我能看看你的房子吗？
Wo neng kan kan ni de fang zi ma?

How many people sleep here?
多少人睡在这里？
Duo shao ren shui zai zhe li?

Where do they all sleep?
他们都睡在哪里？
Ta men dou shui zai na li?

Who does the cooking?
哪一位烧饭？
Na yi nei shao fan?

Who takes care of the children while you are working?
你上班的时候，谁照顾孩子？
Ni shang ban de shi hou, shui zhao gu hai zi?

Do you have a clinic with a full-time doctor nearby?
你们附近有没有一个长驻大夫的诊所？
Ni men fu jin you mei you yi ge chang zhu dai fu de zhen suo?

How much does it cost for a visit if you are sick?
每看一次病要付多少钱？
Mei kan yi ci bing yao fu duo shao qian?

Do you get your salary if you are sick and cannot work?
如果你病了不能上班，工资是不是照发？
Ru quo ni bing le bu neng shang ban, gong zi shi bu shi zhao fa?

How much does it cost per day in the hospital?
住院一天要多少钱？
Zhu yuan yi tian yao duo shao qian?

How many days maternity leave does a woman get with pay?
有工资的产假是多少天？
You gong zi de chan jia shi duo shao tian?

If she is nursing her baby, how many hours with pay does she get a day to feed it? 如果自已照顾婴儿，不扣工资的喂奶时间一天有几小时？

Ru guo zi ji zhao gu ying er, bu kou gong zi de wei nai shi jian yi tian you ji xiao shi?

How many years of school have you had? 你上过几年学？

Ni shang guo ji nian xue?

primary	小学	xiao xue
middle	中学	zhong xue
university	大学	da zue
technical school	技术学校	ji shu xue xiao
on-the-job training	在职训练	zai zhi xun lian

Please forgive me if I am asking too personal questions,

如果我的问题太冒昧，希望能得到你的谅解。

Ru guo wo de wen ti tai mao mei, xi wang neng de dao ni de liang jie,

but I am very curious about the way of life in China.

但是我很想知道中国的生活情况。

Dan shi wo hen xiang zhi dao zhong guo de sheng huo qing kuang.

Are you happy here?

你在这里幸福吗？

Ni zai zhe li xing fu ma?

Do you like the government?

你喜欢这个政府吗？

Ni xi huan zhe ge zheng fu ma?

Do you want your children to study abroad?

你想让你的孩子到国外去读书吗？

Ni xiang rang ni de hai zi dao guo wai qu du shu ma?

I think I can help you.

我想我可以帮你的忙。

Wo xiang wo ke yi bang ni de mang.

I am sorry I cannot help you.

很抱歉，我不能帮你的忙。

Hen bao qian, wo bu neng bang ni de mang.

It is very expensive to travel abroad.

出国路费很贵。

Chu guo lu fei hen gui.

It is very expensive to go to school abroad.

到国外读书要化很多钱。

Dao guo wai du shu yao hua hen duo qian.

I am not wealthy.

我不是一个富裕的人。

Wo bu shi yi ge fu yu de ren.

Especially for Villages

What is the name of this ———? 这个_____叫什么？

zhe ge ——— jiao shen me?

How many people are in this ———? 这个_____有多少人？

zhe ge ——— you duo shao ren?

commune	公社？
	gong she
production brigade	生产大队？
	sheng chan da dui
production team	生产队？
	sheng chan dui
live here	在这里生活。
	zai zhe li sheng huo
work here	在这里工作。
	zai zhe li gong zuo

How much money did you make last year?

你去年的收入是多少？

Ni qu nian de shou ru shi duo shao?

Can a woman make the same amount as a man if she does the same job—like drive a truck?

男女是否同工同酬？例如驾驶卡车。

Ran nu shi fou tong gong tong chou? Li ru jia su ka che.

How big is your private vegetable plot?

你的蔬菜自留地有多大？

Ni de shu cai zi liu di you duo da?

(1 hectare = 15 mou; 1 mou = 10 fen)

Do you raise for your own use ———?

你饲养的＿＿＿是给自己吃的吗？

Ni si yang de ——— shi gei zi ji chi de ma?

    pigs   猪

                  zhu

    poultry 鸡

                  ji

Did you raise enough meat to sell some on the free market?

你饲养的家畜和家禽除自己食用，还有没有多余的拿到自由市场去卖？

Ni si yang de jia chu he jia qin chu zi ji shi yong, hai you mei you duo yu de na dao zi you shi chang qu mai?

Did you sell vegetables on the free market?

你在自由市场卖过蔬菜吗？

Ni zai zi you shi chang mai guo shu cai ma?

If so, how much money did you make selling your surplus?

你卖了多少钱？

Ni mai le duo shao qian?

Your household?

这是你的家吗？

Zhe shi ni de jia ma?

How many earners are there in your household?

你家里有几口人？

Ni jia li you ji ge ren zhuan qian?

How many people are there in your household?

你家里有几个人赚钱？

Ni jia li you ji kou ren?

Is there anyone here who speaks English?

这里有人会说英语吗？

Zhe li you ren hui shuo ying yu ma?

Can I meet them?

我能见见他们吗？

Wo neng jian jian ta men ma?

Are your grown-up children living in this village?

你的成年子女住不住在这个村里？

Ni de cheng nian zi nu zhu bu zhu zai zhe ge cun li?

If you are sick and unable to work, does the commune take care of you?

如果你病了不能工作，公社照顾你吗？

Ru guo ni bing le bu neng gong zuo, gong she zhao gu ni ma?

Your family? 你家里的人？

Ni jia li de ren?

What if you have no family? 如果你没有亲属怎么办？

Ru guo ni mei you qin shu zen me ban?

Is there a pension when you get too old to work?

你们有养老金吗？

Ni men you yang lao jin ma?

Do you still have ———? 你们还有＿＿＿＿吗？

Ni men hai you ——— ma?

ancestral tablets	祖宗牌位	zu zong pai wei
ancestral temple	祖庙	zu miao
ancestral family book	家谱	jia pu

Do you decorate the graves during the Qing Ming still?

你们清明还去上坟吗？

Ni men qing ming hai zu shang fen ma?

Is this pond for fish? 这是养鱼池吗？

Zhe shi yang yu chi ma?

ducks? 这是养鸭池吗？

Zhe shi yang ya chi ma?

May I see your ———? 我能看看你们的_____吗？

Wo neng kan kan ni men de ——— ma?

composting techniques 堆肥技术

dui fei ji shi

irrigation system 灌溉系统

guan gai xi tong

old watchtower 老的守望塔

lao de shou Wang ta

retail store 零售店

ling shou dian

tractor 拖拉机

tuo la ji

school 学校

xue xiao

house 房子

fang zi

private plot 自留地

zi liu di

pigs 猪

zhu

source of drinking water 饮水源

yi shui yuan

latrine 厕所

ce suo

clinic—for family planning 诊所——负责节育的

zhen suo—fu ze jie yu de

motorized water pumps 机器水汞

ji qi shui beng

Who takes care of the children while you work?

你工作的时候谁照顾孩子？
³ ¹ ⁴ ² ⁴ ² ⁴ ²
Ni gong zuo de shi hou shui zhao gu hai zi?

What is the name of that ———? _____叫什么？

⁴ ²
——— jiao shen me?

tree 那棵树
⁴ ¹ ⁴
na ke shu

vegetable 那种菜
⁴ ³ ⁴
na zhong cai

building 那幢房子
⁴ ⁴ ²
na zhuang fang zi

Please write down the name here in Chinese so I can have it translated later.

请用中文把名字写在这儿，以后我再让人翻译。
³ ⁴ ¹ ² ² ³ ² ³ ⁴ ⁴ ³ ⁴ ³ ⁴ ⁴
Qing yong zhong wen ba ming zi xie zai zher, xi hou wo zai rang
² ¹ ⁴
ren fan yi.

Especially for Factories

How many people work here?

有多少人在这儿工作？
³ ¹ ³ ² ⁴ ⁴ ¹ ⁴
You duo shao ren zai zher gong zuo?

Salary range a month, i.e., lowest-highest?

最高和最低的月工资是多少？
⁴ ¹ ² ⁴ ¹ ⁴ ¹ ⁴ ¹ ³
Zui gao he zui di de yue gong zi shi duo shao?

How much do most workers make?

大多数工人的收入是多少？
⁴ ¹ ⁴ ¹ ² ¹ ⁴ ¹ ³
Da duo shu gong ren de shou ru shi duo shao?

What is the age range?

最年轻和最老的工人的年纪有多大？
⁴ ² ¹ ² ⁴ ³ ¹ ² ⁴ ³ ¹ ⁴
Zui nian qing he zui lao de gong ren de nian ji you duo da?

How long does it take to make one of those?

做一个那样的东西需要多长时间？
⁴ ² ⁴ ⁴ ⁴ ¹ ¹ ⁴ ¹ ³ ² ² ¹
Zuo yi ge na yang de dong xi xu yao duo chang shi jian?

days	天	tian[1]
months	月	yue[4]
weeks	星期	xing[1] qi[1]
cooperative?	合作社？	he[2] zuo[4] she[4]?
state-owned?	国有的？	guo[2] you[3] de?

Where do you get your raw materials? 你的原料是从那里来的？
Ni de yuan[3] liao[2] shi[4] cong[4] na[2] li[4] lai[2] de?

Where do you sell most of your products? 你的产品大多在那里出售？
Ni de chan[3] pin[3] da[3] duo[4] zai[3] na[3] li[1] chu[3] shou[4]?

Do you have a store where I could buy something like this?
你们有出售这样产品的商店吗？
Ni men[3] you[3] diu[3] shou[3] zhe[4] yang[4] chan[4] pin[2] de shang[3] dian[3] ma?

How old are you?
你多大岁数啦？
Ni duo[3] da[1] sui[4] shu[4] la[4]?

How many years have you worked here?
你在这里工作几年啦？
Ni zai[3] zhe[4] li[4] gong[3] zuo[1] ji[4] nian[3] la[2]?

How much money do you make a month?
你一个月赚多少钱？
Ni yi[3] ge[1] yue[4] zhuan[4] duo[4] shao[1] qian[3]?

How many hours do you work a week?
你一星期工作多少小时？
Ni yi[3] xing[1] qi[1] gong[1] zuo[1] duo[3] shao[1] xiao[3] shi[3]?

Do you live in factory-provided housing?
你住在厂里给的房子吗？
Ni zhu[4] zai[3] chang[4] li[3] gei[3] de fang[3] zi[2] ma?

How much rent do you pay?

房租多少？

Fang zu duo shao?

How many years of training have you had to do this?

你经过多少年的训练才能做这个工作？

Ni jing guo duo shao nian de xun lian cai neng zuo zhe ge gong zuo?

It is interesting.　很有趣

Hen you qu

beautiful.　漂亮

piao liang

very difficult.　很难

hen nan

SHOPPING

For Daily Necessities

What do you recommend for ———?

_____ 你说吃什么好？

——— ni shuo chi shen me hao?

motion sickness　晕船（晕车）

yun chuan (yun che)

Do you have any ——?　你有_____吗？

ni you ——— ma?

aspirin　阿司匹灵

a si pi ling

toothpaste　牙膏

ya gao

toothbrush　牙刷

ya shua

razor　剃刀

ti dao

razor blades　剃刀刀片

ti dao dao pian

toilet tissue	卫生纸 4 1 3 wei sheng zhi	
mild soap	咸性不大的肥皂 2 4 4 4 2 4 xian xing bu da fei zao	
hand soap	肥皂 2 4 fei zao	
laundry detergent	洗衣粉 3 1 3 xi yi fen	
shampoo	洗头水 2 2 3 xi tou shui	
sanitary napkins	卫生巾 4 1 1 wei sheng jin	
sanitary belt	卫生带 4 1 4 wei sheng dai	
ball-point pen	圆珠笔 2 1 3 yuan zhu bi	
notebook	笔记本 3 4 3 bi ji ben	
letter-writing paper	信纸 4 3 xin zhi	
airmail paper	航空信封 2 1 4 1 hang kong xin feng	
envelopes	信封 4 1 xin feng	
foreign film	外国胶卷 4 2 1 3 wai guo jiao juan	
something to cover this	可以包扎这个____的东西。 3 3 1 1 4 4 1 ke yi bao zha zhe ge ——— dong xi	
cut		伤口 1 3 shang kou
blister		水疱 3 4 shui pao

something to keep my shoe from hurting

有什么东西可以防止我的鞋子把这儿磨疼。

you shen me dong xi ke yi fang zhi wo de xie zi ba zher mo teng

an antiseptic ointment or cream

消灾药膏或软膏

xiao zai yao gao huo ruan gao

menstrual cramps

月经痛

yue jing tong

Mending

Where can I get this mended?	这个在什么地方可以修理？ Zhe ge zai shen me di fang ke yi xiu li?
How soon will it be finished?	多快能修好？ Duo kuai neng xiu hao?
Can it be done faster?	能够快一些吗？ Neng gou kuai yi xie ma?
I will have it done later.	我以后再修。 Wo yi hou zai xiu.
Please do it now.	请你现在就修。 Qing ni xian zai jiu xiu.
How much will it be?	要多少钱？ Yao duo shao qian?

You may not be here when I come to get it. Please write down here what I should ask for.

我来取的时候你可能不在。请将我要取的东西写在这儿。

Wo lai qu de shi hou ni ke neng bu zai. Qing jiang wo yao qu de dong xi xie zai zher.

Shopping in General

Please show me on the map where there is a ———.

请指给我看地图上哪里是＿＿＿＿＿＿。

Qing zhi gei wo kan di tu shang na li shi ———.

Please take me to a ———.

请带我到一个_____去。

^{3 4 3 4 1 4} ⁴

Qing dai wo dao yi ge ——— qu.

Please point the way to a ———.

请指给我看到_____怎么走。

^{3 3 3 3 4 4} ^{3 3}

Qing zhi gei wo kan dao ——— zen me zou.

How many blocks is it?

要过几条街？

^{4 4 3 2 1}

Yao guo ji tiao jie?

left	左面 ^{3 4} zuo mian
right	右面 ^{4 4} you mian
department store	百货商店 ^{3 4 1 4} bai huo shang dian
foreign-language bookstore	外文书店 ^{4 2 1 4} wai wen shang dian
cloth store	布店 ^{4 4} bu dian
Arts and Crafts Store	手工艺品商店 ^{3 1 4 3 1 4} shou gong yi pin shang dian
Friendship Store	友谊商店 ^{3 2 1 4} you yi shang dian
Chinese traditional medicine store	中国药店 ^{1 2 4 4} zhong guo yao dian
antique store	古董铺 ^{3 3} gu dong pu
more expensive	更贵一些的 ^{4 4 1 1} geng gui yi xie de
less expensive	便宜一些的 ^{2 1 1} pian yi yi xie de
bigger	大一点的 ^{4 1 3} da yi dian de

smaller

小一点的

xiao yi dian de

Do you have others the same as this?

你还有这样的东西吗？

Ni hai you zhe yang de dong xi ma?

Different color?

不同颜色的？

Bu tong yan se de?

Different design?

不同图案的？

Bu tong tu an de?

How old is this?

这个有多少年了？

Zhe ge you duo shao nian le?

Will I be able to take it out of China?

我能把它带出中国吗？

Wo neng ba ta dai chu zhong guo ma?

What dynasty?

什么朝代的？

Shen me chao dai de?

Can you wrap it so it won't break when I mail it?

能不能把它包好免得会在邮寄时打破。

Neng bu neng ba ta bao hao mian de hui zai you ji shi da po?

Where can I have this wrapped and shipped?

哪里可以包装及运出这个？

Na li ke yi bao zhuang ji yun chu zhe ge?

I'm sorry, I don't have ration coupons.

很抱歉我没有布票。（粮票、工业券）

Hen bao qian wo mei you bu piao. (liang piao, gong ye quan)

I was told I didn't need ration coupons.

人家告诉我我不需要给布票。

Ren jia gao su wo wo bu xu yao gei bu piao.

Will you be getting more within the next three days?

三天之内你们会有更多的来货吗？

San tian zhi nei ni men hui you geng duo de lai huo ma?

Can it be washed in soap and water without damage?

这能用肥皂和水洗吗？

Zhe neng yong fei zao he shui xi ma?
^{4 2   2   2 4 2   3 3}

Should it be dry-cleaned?

需要不需要干洗？

Xu yao bu xu yao gan xi?
^{1 4   4 1 4   1   3}

Arts and crafts—also for Sightseeing

What is it made of? 这是用什么东西做的？

Zhe shi yong shen me dong xi zuo de?

bamboo	竹子 zhu zi	marble	大理石 da li shi
bone	骨头 gu tou	metal alloy	合金 he jin
brick	砖 zhuan	mother-of-pearl	螺母 luo mu
bronze	铜 tong	palm straw	棕榈章 zong lu zhang
carved	雕刻的 diao ke de	(for baskets and mats)	（编篮子和席子用）
celadon	青瓷 qing ci		(bian lan zi he xi zi yong)
ceramic	陶瓷 tao ci	paper	纸 zhi
clay	泥 ni	pearl	珍珠 zhen zhu
cloisonné	景泰兰 jing tai lan	plastic	胶料 jiao liao
coconut	椰子 ye zi	rattan	藤 teng
coral	珊瑚 shan hu	rayon	人造纤维 ren zao xian wei

cotton	棉花 mian hua	rice husks	谷壳 gu ke
dough (flour mixture)	揉面 rou mian	rice paper	宣纸 xuan zhi
eiderdown	绒毛 rong mao	satin	缎子 duan zi
enamel	搪瓷 tang ci	silk	丝 si
filigree	金丝 jin si	silver	银子 yin zi
glass	玻璃 bo li	soapstone	皂石 zao shi
glaze	釉料 you liao	stone	石头 shi tou
iron	铁 tie	turquoise	松石 song shi
ivory	象牙 xiang ya	wire	铁丝 tie si
gold	金子 jin zi	wood	木头 mu tou
jade	翡翠 fei cui	wool	羊毛 yang mao
lacquer	漆器 qi qi	animal	动物 dong wu
lapis lazuli	青金石 qing jin shi	vegetable	蔬菜 shu cai
leather	皮子 pi zi	mineral	矿石 kuang shi
malachite	孔雀石 kong que shi		

What is it? (Animate objects)

这是什么？

zhe shi shen me?

banyan tree

榕树

rong shu

bird

鸟

niao

bodhisattva (Lohan)

岁汉

luo han

Buddha

佛

fo

camel (two-humped)

骆驼（双峰）

luo tuo (shuang feng)

cypress tree

柏树

bai shu

dragon

龙

long

(five-toed imperial)

五爪金龙

wu zhao jin long

dromedary (one-humped)

单峰骆驼

dan feng luo tuo

emperor

皇帝

huang di

empress

皇后

huang hou

fairy

仙女

xian nu

god

神

shen

goddess

女神

nu shen

goddess of mercy

观音

guan yin

flames	火焰 huo yan
horse	马 ma
imperial family	皇室 huang shi
lion	狮子 shi zi
leaders	领袖 ling xiu
Mao Tse-tung	毛泽东 Mao Ze Dong
Chou En-lai	周恩来 Zhou En Lai
lotus	莲花 lian hua
Lu Hsun (author)	鲁迅（作家） Lu Xun (zuo jia)
mandarin	橘子 ju zi
monkey	猴子 hou zi
mountains	山 shan
mountains of Kweilin	桂林的山 gui lin de shan
mythical animal	神兽 shen shou
peach	桃子 tao zi
phoenix	凤凰 feng huang

poet

诗人
shi ren

revolutionary hero

革命英雄
ge ming ying xiong

Soldier Lei Feng

战士雷锋
Zhan Shi Lei Feng

Dr. Norman Bethune

白求恩大夫
Bai Qiu En Dai Fu

revolutionary theme

革命题材
ge ming ti cai

e.g., episodes on the Long March 如长征组歌
ru chang zheng zu ge

scales of the dragon

龙鳞
long lin

scholar

学者
xue zhe

temple guardian

庙祝
miao zhu

tiger

老虎
lao hu

tortoise

龟
gui

What language?

哪一国文字？
Na yi guo wen zi?

ancient Chinese	中国古文 zhong guo qu wen	Mongolian	蒙文 meng wen
Arabic	阿拉伯文 a la bo wen	Sanscrit	梵文 fan wen
Chinese	中文 zhong wen	Tibetan	藏文 zang wen
Manchu	满族文 man zu wen		

(Inanimate objects)

What is it?	这是什么？ Zhe shi shen me?
bell	钟、铃 zhong, ling
Buddha's footprint	佛的脚印 fo de jiao yin
chariot	战车 zhan che
cooking utensil	炊具 chui ju
cosmetic box	化妆品盒 hua zhuang pin he
costumes—theatrical	戏装 xi zhuang
drum	鼓 gu
fan	扇子 shan zi
food-serving utensils	餐具 can ju
funeral objects (buried with deceased)	陪葬品 pei zang pin
gong	锣 luo
house	房子 fang zi
incense burner	香炉 xiang lu
inkstand	墨水台 mo shui tai
jar	坛子 tan zi

jewelry	手饰 shou³ shi⁴
jug	盂· yu²
mask—theatrical	戏台用面具 xi⁴ tai² yong⁴ mian⁴ ju
mirror	镜子 jing⁴ zi
moon	月亮 yue⁴ liang⁴
musical instrument	乐器 yue⁴ qi⁴
ornament	装饰品 zhuang¹ shi⁴ pin³
paperweight	纸镇 zhi³ zhen⁴
pearl (flaming usually)	夜明珠 ye⁴ ming² zhu¹
pillow	枕头 zhen³ tou
poem	诗 shi¹
by Chairman Mao	毛主席的诗 mao² zhu³ xi² de shi¹
snuff bottle	鼻烟壶 bi² yan¹ hu
spirit screen	招魂幡 zhao¹ hun² fan¹
toilet box	梳妆盒 shu¹ zhuang¹ he²
tool	工具 gong¹ ju⁴

toy	玩具	wan ju
vase	花瓶	hua ping
water buffalo	水牛	shui niu
weapon	军器	jun qi
wheel of the law	法轮	fa lun
wine goblet	酒杯	jiu bei
yin-yang symbol	太极图	tai ji tu
calligraphy	书法	shu fa
carving	雕刻	diao ke
copy	抄本、摹本、复制品	chao bei, mo bei, fu zhi pin
drawing	画	hua
embossing	浮雕	fu diao
embroidery	刺绣	ci xiou
engraving	雕刻	diao ke
etching	蚀刻	shi ke
fresco	壁画	bi hua

handmade

手工的
shou gong de

ink

墨水
mo shui

machine-made

机制的
ji zhi de

original

原本
yuan ben

print

印刷
yin shua

rubbing

摹拓
mo ta

scroll

卷轴
juan zhou

sculpture

雕塑品
diao su pin

sketch

速写
su xie

watercolor

水彩
shui cai

woodcut

木刻
mu ke

woven photograph

丝织像
si zhi xiang

hand loom

手织机、纺车
shou zhi ji, fang che

Paying

How much does that cost?

那个多少钱？
Na ge duo shao qian?

Please write down that price here.

请你将价钱写在这儿。
Qing ni jiang jia qian xie zai zher.

That's too expensive.

太贵了。

Tai gui le.

How about half the price?

半价怎么样？

Ban jia zen me yang?

How much then?

那样是多少钱？

Na shi duo shao qian?

yuan/kwai/renminbi

元／块／人民币

yuan / kuai / ren min bi

mao (1/10 of a yuan)

毛（1／10元）

mao (1/10 yuan)

fen (coin)

分（硬币）

fen (ying bi)

Do you know how much that is in U.S. money?

你知道合成美金是多少？

Ni zhi dao he cheng mei jin shi duo shao?

Please bring my bill.

请把帐单给我。

Qing ba zhang dan gei wo.

Do I pay you or the cashier?

我把钱付给你还是付给出纳员。

Wo ba qian fu gei ni hai shi fu gei chu na yuan?

I am leaving early tomorrow morning. Can I pay the bill tonight?

我明天一早就走。我可以不可以在今晚付帐？

Wo ming tian yi zao jiu zou. Wo ke yi bu ke yi zai jin wan fu

zhang?

May I have a receipt, please?

能给我一个收据吗？

Neng gei wo yi ge shou ju ma?

Can I pay with ———?　我能用＿＿＿＿付款吗？
　　　　　　　　　　Wo neng yong ——— fu kuan ma?

a Bank of China traveler's check　中国银行的旅行支票
　　　　　　　　　　　　　　zhong guo yin hang de lu
　　　　　　　　　　　　　　xing zhi piao

a foreign traveler's check
　　　　　　　　　外国旅行支票
　　　　　　　　　wai guo lu xing zhi piao

a personal check
　　　　　　　私人支票
　　　　　　　si ren zhi piao

a company check
　　　　　　　公司的支票
　　　　　　　gong si de zhi piao

a credit card
　　　　　　　信用卡
　　　　　　　xin yong ka

BUILDINGS

What is the name of this place?
这个地方叫什么名字？
Zhe ge di fang jiao shen me ming zi?

Please write it in Chinese.
请把它用中文写下来。
Qing ba ta yong zhong wen xie xia lai.

What was it before Liberation?
解放前这个地方是做什么用的？
Jie fan qian zhe ge di fang shi zuo shen me yong de?

What dynasty was it built in?
它是那个朝代建造的？
Ta shi na ge chao dai jian zao de?

What date?
什么年代？
Shen me nian dai?

How high is it?　它有多高？
　　　　　　　Ta you duo gao?

stories?　　　　　　　多少层？
　　　　　　　　　　duo shao ceng?

meters?	多少公尺？
	duo shao gong chi?
Can I get a closer look?	我能走近一些看看吗？
	Wo neng zou jin yi xie kan kan ma?
Can I go inside?	我能进去吗？
	Wo neng jin qu ma?
What direction is it?	这是什么方向？
	Zhe shi shen me fang xiang?

north	北	bei		south	南	nan
east	东	dong		west	西	xi

ancient?	古代的？
	gu dai de?
minorities?	少数民族的？
	shao shu min zu de?
imperial?	宫殿式的？
	gong dian shi de?
modern?	现代的？
	xian dai de?
post-Liberation?	解放后的？
	jie fang hou de?
revolutionary?	革命的？
	ge ming de?
for children?	为孩子的？
	wei hai zi de?
for workers?	为工人的？
	wei gong ren de?
Is it religious?	是不是宗教性的？
	Shi bu shi zong jiao xing de?
ancestral	祖先的
	zu zian de
atheistic	无神论的
	wu shen lun de

Buddhist	佛教的 ²　⁴ fo jiao de
Christian	基督教的 ¹　¹　⁴ ji du jiao de
Confucian	孔教的 ²　⁴ kong jiao de
Lamaist/Tibetan	喇嘛的／西藏人的 ³　　　¹　⁴　² la ma de / xi zang ren de
Moslem	伊斯兰教的 ¹　¹　²　⁴ yi si lan jiao de
Taoist	道教的 ⁴　⁴ dao jiao de
Is it any of these?	它是这其中的一种吗？ ¹　⁴　⁴　²　¹　　¹　³ Ta shi zhe qi zhong de yi zhong ma?
air-raid shelter	防空洞 ²　¹　⁴ fang kong dong
apartment building	公寓 ¹　⁴ gong yu
aqueduct	沟渠 ¹　² gou qu
aquarium	水族馆 ³　²　³ shui zu guan
archaeological site	考古现场 ³　³　⁴　³ kao gu xian chang
bridge	桥 ² qiao
cemetery	公墓 ¹　⁴ gong mu
church	教堂 ⁴　² jiao tang
cinema	电影院 ⁴　³　⁴ dian ying yuan

dagoba (Indian stupa)	舍利子塔（印度神龛） she li zi ta (yin du shen kan)
democracy wall	民主墙 min zhu qiang
drum or bell tower	鼓或钟楼 gu huo zhong lou
exhibition hall	展览馆 zhan lan guan
fort	堡垒 bao lei
factory	工厂 gong chang
garden	花园 hua yuan
gate	大门 da men
hotel	旅馆 lu guan
house	房子 fang zi
kiln	窑 yao
library	图书馆 tu shu guan
military camp	军营 jun ying
moat	护城河 hu cheng he
monastery	寺 si
monument—commemorative	纪念碑 ji nian bei

mosque	清真寺 _{1 1 4} qing zhen si
museum	博物馆 _{2 4 3} bo wu guan
observatory	天文台 _{1 2 2} tian wen tai
office building	办公大楼 _{4 1 4 2} ban gong da lou
pagoda	塔 ₃ ta
palace	皇宫 _{2 1} huang gong
park	公园 _{1 2} gong yuan
pavilion	馆、楼阁 _{3 2 2} guan, lou ge
playground	操场 _{1 3} cao chang
restaurant	饭馆 _{4 3} fan guan
resort	胜地 _{4 4} sheng di
school	学校 _{2 4} xue xiao
primary	小学 _{3 2} xiao xue
middle	中学 _{1 2} zhong xue
university	大学 _{4 2} da xue
shipyard	船坞 _{2 1} chuan wu

shrine	神龛	shen kan
sports stadium	运动场	yun dong chang
stele	石碑	shi bei
grave	墓	mu
historical event	历史性的	li shi xing de
poem	诗	shi
subway	地下铁道	di xia tie dao
temple (ancestral or Taoist)	庙	miao
theater	戏院	xi yuan
tomb	墓	mu
train station	火车站	huo chen zhan
wall	墙	qiang
watchtower	瞭望台	liao wang tai
water tower	水塔	shui ta
zoo	动物园	dong wu yuan

May I take a photo of you?

我能给你拍张照片吗？

Wo neng gei ni pai zhang zhao pian ma?

Please smile.

请微笑。

Qing wei xiao.

Can I have a photo of you and me together?

我能和你合拍一张照片吗？

Wo neng he ni he pai zi zhang zhao pian ma?

I would like to show my friends what nice people there are in China.

我想让我的朋友看看在中国有多么友好的人。

Wo xiang rang wo de peng you kan kan zai zhong guo you duo me
you hao de ren.

I would like to show my friends who cannot visit China what things
look like here. 我想让我那些不能来访问中国的朋友看看
中国是什么样子。

Wo xiang rang wo na xie bu neng lai fang wen zhong guo de peng
you kan kan zhong guo shi shen me yang zi.

Could you please take my photo in front of this place with my camera?

请用我的照像机给我在这里拍一张照。

Qing yong wo de zhao xiang ji gei wo zai zhe li pai yi zhang zhao.

It is all set. Just press here. 都对好了，你只要在这里按一下。

Dou dui hao le. Ni zhi yao zai zhe li an
yi xia.

Closer. 靠近一些。   Back up. 退后一些。

Kao jin yi xie.   Tui hou yi xie.

I'm sorry, I don't have any more film.

对不起我没有胶卷了。

Dui bu qi, wo mei you jiao juan le.

I'm sorry, I didn't know I couldn't take photographs here.

对不起，我不知道不许在这儿拍照。

Dui bu qi, wo bu zhi dao bu xu zai zher pai zhao.

May I have my camera back?

能将我的照像机还给我吗？

Neng jiang wo de zhao xiang ji huan gei wo ma?

Where can I get film developed?

哪里可以冲洗胶卷？

Na li ke yi chong xi jiao juan?

Black and white?

黑白的。

Hei bai de?

Color slides?

彩色幻灯片？

Cai se huan deng pian?

Color prints?

彩色照片？

Cai se zhao pian?

Do you cut the film and mount the slides?

你们切装幻灯片吗？

Ni men qie zhuang huan deng pian ma?

How much for each print?

印一张多少钱？

Yinyi zhang duo shao qian?

How long will it take?

要多长时间？

Yao duo chang shi jian?

What size film do you have?

你们有几号胶卷？

Ni men you ji hao jiao juan?

Do you have any foreign film?

你们有外国胶卷吗？

Ni men you wai guo jiao juan ma?

ENTERTAINMENT

Is there a good cultural presentation on now in this city?

现在这里有没有一个好的文艺节目在上演？

Xian zai zhe li you mei you yi ge hao de wen yi jie mu zai shang yan?

movie	ballet
电影	**芭蕾舞**
dian ying	ba lei wu

acrobats	杂技 2 4 za ji	traditional opera	京戏 1 4 jing xi
play	话剧 4 4 hua ju	martial arts	武术 3 4 wu shu
puppet	木偶戏 4 3 4 mu ou xi	concert	音乐会 1 4 4 yin yue hui
Chinese	中国的 zhong guo de	foreign	外国的 4 2 wai guo de
English subtitles	英文字幕 1 2 4 4 ying wen zi mu	sports competition	运动比赛 4 4 yun dong 3 4 bi sai

Where can I buy tickets? 在哪里买票？
4 3 3 3 4
Zai na li mai piao?

What is the address?
什么地方？
2 4
Shen me di fang?

I would like tickets ———. 我要_____票。
3 4   4
Wo yao ——— piao.

for today. 今天的。
1 1
jin tian de.

for tomorrow. 明天的。
2 1
ming tian de.

for the day after tomorrow. 后天的。
4 1
hou tian de.

What are the times? 有那些时间的？
3 3 1 2 1
You na xie shi jian de?

How much do the best seats cost? 最好的座位多少钱一张？
4 3 4 4 1 3 2
Zui hao de zuo wei duo shao qian
1
yi zhang?

Do you have seats close to the stage so I can take photographs?
有没有靠近舞台可以让我拍照的位子？
3 2 3 4 3 3 1 3 4 4
You mei you kao jin wu tai ke yi rang wo pai zhao de wei zi?

How about an aisle seat?

侧厢的座位怎么样？

Ce xiang de zuo wei zen me yang?

Is the theater air-conditioned?

戏院有冷气吗？

Xi yuan you leng qi ma?

Is the theater heated?

戏院有暖气吗？

Xi yuan you nuan qi ma?

What time is the performance over?

演出什么时候完？

Yan chu shen me shi hou wan?

Will you be my guest?

我请你看好吗？

Wo qing ni kan hao ma?

Can you buy the tickets for me?

你能代我买票吗？

Ni neng dai wo mai piao ma?

Where will I meet you?

我们在哪里碰头？

Wo men za na li peng tou?

What time?

什么时候？

Shen me shi hou?

I have to cancel my tickets.

我得退票。

Wo dei tui piao.

Can I have my money back?

能把钱退给我吗？

Neng ba qian tui gei wo ma?

Would you like to use my tickets instead?

你愿意要我的票吗？

Ni yuan yi yao wo de piao ma?

Can we go backstage to meet the performers?

我们能去后台看看演员吗？

Wo men neng qu hou tai kan kan yan yuan ma?

I must tell you how very much I enjoyed the performance.

我一定要告诉你我是多么欣赏你的演出。

Wo yi ding yao gao su ni wo shi duo me xin shang ni de yan chu.

I hope someday you can come to perform in my country.

我希望有一天你能来我的国家演出。

Wo xi wang you yi tian ni neng lai wo de guo jia yan chu.

May I touch your costumes?

我能摸摸你的戏装吗？

Wo neng mo mo ni de xi zhuang ma?

May I touch your musical instruments?

我能摸一摸你的乐器吗？

Wo neng mo yi mo ni de yue qi ma?

May I take a photograph with you?

我能和你合拍一张照片吗？

Wo neng he ni he pai yi zhang zhao pian ma?

Can you show me how this works?

你能告诉我这个怎么用？

Ni neng gao su wo zhe ge zen me yong?

How much training have you had?

你受过多久的训练？

Ni shou guo duo jiu de xun lian?

At what age did you start?

几岁开始的？

Ji sui kai shi de?

Will you be giving another performance here?

你在这里还将再演出一次吗？

Ni zai zhe li hai jiang zai yan chu yi ci ma?

When?

什么时候？

Shen me shi hou?

Will it be the same?

还是这个节目吗？

Hai shi zhe ge jie mu ma?

Where is there a dance party in this city?

这个城市里什么地方有午会？

Zhe ge cheng shi li shen me di fang you wu hui?

When? What day and time?

什么时候？那一天？几点钟？

Shen me shi hou? Na yi tian? Ji dian zhong?

How much does it cost?

多少钱？

Duo shao qian?

MISCELLANEOUS

Colors

red	红色	hong se	blue	蓝色	lan se
orange	橙色	cheng se	purple	紫色	zi se
yellow	黄色	huang se	black	黑色	hei se
green	绿色	lu se	brown	褐色	he se

Directions

near	近	jin	far	远	yuan
up	上	shang	down	下	xia
above	上面	shang mian	below	下面	xia mian
inside	里面	li mian	outside	外面	wai mian
right	右	you	left	左	zuo
center	中间	zhong jian			

Months of the Year

January	一月 _{1 4} yi yue		July	七月 _{1 4} qi yue
February	二月 _{4 4} er yue		August	八月 _{1 4} ba yue
March	三月 _{1 4} san yue		September	九月 _{3 4} jiu yue
April	四月 _{4 4} si yue		October	十月 _{2 4} shi yue
May	五月 _{3 4} wu yue		November	十一月 _{2 1 4} shi yi yue
June	六月 _{4 4} liu yue		December	十二月 _{2 4 4} shi er yue

Days of the Week

Sunday	星期天 _{1 1 1} xing qi tian		Thursday	星期四 _{1 1 4} xing qi si
Monday	星期一 _{1 1 1} xing qi yi		Friday	星期五 _{1 1 3} xing qi wu
Tuesday	星期二 _{1 1 4} xing qi er		Saturday	星期六 _{1 1 4} xing qi liu
Wednesday	星期三 _{1 1 1} xing qi san			

Today, Yesterday, and Tomorrow

today	今天	jin tian
yesterday	昨天	zuo tian
tomorrow	明天	ming tian

Seasons

spring	春	chun		summer	夏	xia
autumn	秋	qiu		winter	冬	dong

Terms and Names

attendant (term used for room boy, waitress)	服务员	fu wu yuan
interpreter (term used for guide)	翻译	fan yi
cadre (also leading member)	干部	gan bu
management committee	管理委员会	guan li wei yuan hui
party member	党员	dang yuan
Communist Party of China	中国共产党	zhong guo gong chan dang
Politburo	政治局	Zheng Zhi Ju
State Council	国务院	Guo Wu Yuan
peasant	农民	nong min
worker	工人	gong ren
People's Liberation Army	中国解放军	Zhong Guo Jie Fang Jun
Four Modernizations	四个现代化	Si Ge Xian Dai Hua
agriculture	农业	nong ye
national defense	国防	guo fang
technology	技术	ji shu

science	科学 ke xue
Is there a campaign on now?	现在有运动吗？ Xian zai you yun dong ma?
Chairman Mao	毛主席 Mao Zhu Xi
socialism	社会主义 she hui zhu yi
dictatorship of the proletariat	无产阶级专政 wu chan jie ji zhuan zheng
democratic centralism	民主集中制 min zhu ji zhong zhi
Gang of Four	四人帮 Si Ren Bang

Numbers

one	一	yi	eleven	十一	shi yi
two	二	er	twelve	十二	shi er
three	三	san	twenty	二十	er shi
four	四	si	twenty-one	二十一	er shi yi
five	五	wu	thirty	三十	san shi
six	六	liu	forty	四十	si shi
seven	七	qi	fifty	五十	wu shi
eight	八	ba	hundred	百	bai
nine	九	jiu	thousand	千	qian
ten	十	shi	ten thousand	万	wan

MILESTONES IN CHINESE HISTORY

The Chinese interpret history in Marxist terms, pointing out that dynasties fell primarily because of peasant unrest and uprisings. Roughly, this is how they see history (here with place names in the new spelling and historical names in the old). See "Quick Reference" for new spellings of dynasties.

c. 1,000,000–4000 years ago—primitive society.
c. 21st century–476 B.C.—slave society. Slave holders owned all the means of production including slaves captured in wartime. Slaves were killed and buried with their deceased owners supposedly to continue their work of servitude in the afterworld.
475 B.C.–A.D. 1840—feudal society. While slaves were kept after the end of the 5th century, slave holders ceased to own all the means of production. A new class of landowners found that giving slaves some freedom resulted in better production. Land was contracted to them as serfs in return for a large part of the harvest. If the serf did not produce, the fields were contracted to someone else. The transition to feudal society took place in the Warring States period, and after 476 B.C. slaves were no longer sacrificed.
1840–1919—semi-colonial and semi-feudal society. Pure feudalism ended with the Opium Wars and the advent of foreign domination. In 1919 the May 4th Movement marshaled anti-imperialist and nationalistic sentiments.

The Chinese also call *1912–1927* the period of the First Revolutionary War, which failed when Chiang Kai-shek betrayed the revolution and massacred the Communists. They also consider this war a failure because of the divisions within the Communist Party itself.

August 1927–July 1937 was the Second Revolutionary War, a period of armed struggle against the Nationalists and the warlords from the first armed Communist uprising to the beginning of the Japanese war.

In July 1937 the Japanese invaded China and there was some attempt at cooperation between the Communists and Nationalists again. After the Japanese surrender in 1945, the civil war resumed. That war and the semi-colonial and semi-feudal society ended with Liberation in 1949. Now is the socialist society.

With earlier dates approximations, the milestones are:
c. 8,000,000 years ago—Ramapithecus (Lufeng, Yunnan).
c. 1,000,000 years ago—Yuanmou Man.

c. 600,000–700,000 years ago—Lantian Man.
c. 400,000–500,000 years ago—Peking Man. (See Zhoukoudian under "Beijing.")
c. 20,000–30,000 years ago—Liuchiang Man (Guangxi), Hotao Man (Inner Mongolia), and Upper Cave Man (Zhoukoudian).
c. 5,000–7,000 years ago—Lungshan Culture (Shandong) and Yangshao Culture (Henan). (See "Xi'an"—Banpo Museum.)

Dynastic dates overlap because different dynasties controlled different parts of China at the same time. Eastern and Western usually refer to periods of the same dynasty with different capitals, e.g., Changan or Luoyang. Northern and Southern Sung refer to the Kaifeng and Hangzhou capitals.

c. 21st–16th centuries B.C.—HSIA: beginning of slave system; irrigation and flood control work; rudimentary calendar; earliest form of writing. (Some scholars now say the first writing dates from 2300 B.C.); bronzes (a.k.a. Xia).

c. 16th–11th centuries B.C.—SHANG: earliest glazes, wine, and silk; highly developed bronze casting primarily of ritual vessels; jade handles on swords and spears; ivory cup inlaid with jade; iron; cowry shells used for money; trade outside of China; development of writing; ancestor worship; divination by tortoise shells; beginning of cities (Zhengzhou and Anyang). Celadon.

c. 11th century–771 B.C.—WESTERN CHOU and 770–249 B.C.—EASTERN CHOU: welded bronze; flat building tiles; first lacquer; copper coins; crossbows; walled cities; elaborate rituals and music using jade as well as bronze vessels. (a.k.a. Zhou.)

770–476 B.C.—SPRING AND AUTUMN PERIOD: warring states fighting for power; Confucius preached a return to the Chou rituals and tried to stabilize society by insisting on obedience to the emperor, father, husbands, older brothers, etc. Beginnings of feudalism; cylindrical tile sewer pipes; iron implements and oxen for plowing; steel; metal spade-shaped coins; knowledge of multiplication tables, mathematics, astronomy; medicine.

475–221 B.C.—WARRING STATES: transitional period to feudalism; *Master Sun's Art of War* written; Taoism, Mohism, and Mencius; first large scale irrigation and dams including erosion control; iron farm tools widely used; mining; use of arch in tomb and bridge building; discovery of magnets; carpenter's saw, plane, and square; manure for fertilizer; salt production; medical diagnosis through feeling the pulse; the first books on astronomy.

221–206 B.C.—CHIN: unification of China for the first time; building of Great Wall; standardization of weights and measures; strict legal code; unification of currency; standardization of writing; first clay burial figures; the burning of all historical records except those dealing with the Chin, medicine, and agriculture; the execution of some scholars. (a.k.a. Qin.)

206 B.C.–A.D. 220—EASTERN AND WESTERN HAN: water wheel, windmill, the first plant-fiber paper, seismograph, water-powered bellows for smelting; first important Chinese medical text; the first armillary sphere; the discovery that moonlight comes from the sun; the use of general anaesthesia in surgical operations, and acupuncture and moxibustion; jade burial suits and gold-coated bronze; Szuma Chien, China's first historian.

2nd century B.C.—14th century A.D.—The Silk Road: The Chinese exchanged silk, tea, iron and steel, knowledge of deep-well digging, paper making, peach and pear trees. They received grapes, pomegranate and walnut trees, sesame, coriander, spinach, the Fergana horse, alfalfa, Buddhism, Nestorianism, and Islam. Trade was with India, West Asia, and even Rome, and the main stops in China west from Xi'an were Lanzhou, Wuwei, Dunhuang, north through Turpan or south through Ruoqiang. Arab and Persian traders settled in Xi'an and Yangzhou (Yangchow).

A.D. 68—First Buddhist temple built by Emperor Han Ming-ti in Luoyang.

220–265—THREE KINGDOMS (Wei, Shu, and Wu): development of a water pump, celadon, and ships big enough to carry 3,000 men.

265–420—WESTERN AND EASTERN TSIN and 420–589—SOUTHERN (Sung, Chi, Liang, Chen) and NORTHERN (Wei, Chi, Chou) DYNASTIES: first arched stone bridge, widespread use of celadon, two crops a year. Northern Wei dynasty started Buddhist statues at Luoyang and Datong.

581–618—SUI: built the Grand Canal (2,000 km. long), ships up to 70 meters long, and an arched stone bridge still in use today (Zhaoxian county, Hebei).

618–907—TANG: one of China's most prosperous and culturally developed dynasties; three-color glazes, snow-white fine porcelains, inlaid mother-of-pearl, gold and silver, wood-block printing, fine silks, the weaving of feathers; water wheel and adjustable curved-shaft plow; attempt at land reform; the most prosperous period of the Silk Road and the opening of a special office for foreign trade in Guangzhou, a city where a mosque was built by Arab traders; cultural expansion—Tang princess took Buddhism to Tibet; Chinese monks took Buddhism to Japan and Korea (Kyoto is modeled on Xi'an); Chinese monk Hsuan Tsang went to India 629–645 to obtain Buddhist sutras. Chinese travelers also went to Persia, Arabia, and Byzantium; Tang poets still the most famous. Look for fat faces in paintings and sculptures—they are most likely Tang.

907–960—FIVE DYNASTIES (Liang, Later Tang, Later Tsin, Later Han, Later Chou): a transitional warring period.

916–1125—LIAO: controlled Inner Mongolia and part of southern Manchuria; invaded China and occupied Beijing; built extant 66.6-meter wooden pagoda, Ying Xian, Shaanxi.

960–1279—NORTHERN AND SOUTHERN SUNG: another of the most prosperous and culturally developed dynasties; first paper money, moveable type, compass, gunpowder, rocket-propelled spears; fine porcelains; red lacquer; the development of acupuncture and moxibustion; progress in mining and metallurgy; Hangzhou, then known as Qinsai, was the largest, richest city in the world. (a.k.a. Song.)

1038–1227—WESTERN HSIA: controlled today's Gansu and western Inner Mongolia.

1245—Franciscan friars arrived at Inner Mongolia.

1115–1234—KIN (a.k.a. CHIN): captured Beijing and controlled Kaifeng, the Wei River valley, Inner Mongolia, and northwestern China.

1271–1368—YUAN (a.k.a. Mongol): water clock; improved cotton spinning and weaving; developed blue-and-white and underglaze red porcelain; cloisonne; controlled all of today's China and areas north and east including Moscow, Kiev, Damascus, Baghdad, and Afghanistan.
*1275–92—*Marco Polo visited China, serving in court of Kublai Khan.

1368–1644—MING: imported corn, potato, tobacco, peanut, sunflower, tomato (seeds that is) from America; refined blue-and-white porcelain; polychrome porcelain; sea links with Malacca, Java, Ceylon, East Africa; opium first introduced as a narcotic.
*1513—*First European to south China—Jorge Alvares of Portugal.
*1557—*Macao "lent" to the Portuguese.
*1582—*First Christian missionary, Matteo Ricci, S.J., to Macao and then in *1601* to Beijing.
*1623—*Dutch colony in "Formosa," a.k.a. Taiwan—until 1662.

1644–1911—CHING (a.k.a. Manchu): made some of the best porcelains in early part of dynasty; had to cope most with foreign powers; Cheng Chengkung, a.k.a. Koxinga, drove out Dutch from Taiwan; expanded into Russia, Korea, Vietnam, Burma, Sikkim at first, but later lost a great deal of territory. (a.k.a. Qing)
*1683—*Taiwan became part of China.
*1757—*All foreign trade in south confined to Chinese trading associations (Cohongs) in Guangzhou (Canton). Families of foreign traders live in Macao.
*1784—*First U.S. trading ship, *Empress of China*—Guangzhou.
*1793—*First British mission—Lord Macartney.
*1807—*First Protestant missionary, Robert Morrison of Britain.
*1830—*First U.S. missionaries.
*1839—*Chinese attempted to stop opium trade. Burned 20,000 chests near Guangzhou, more than half one year's trade.
*1840–42—*Opium War, mainly over freedom to trade with China and of course British objection to the government's opium policy. Britain needed to sell China opium to balance trade. British forces with French help seized a few cities along the coast and threatened Nanjing. The Chinese gave in, ceding Hong Kong to Britain and opening to foreign trade Guangzhou (Canton), Xiamen (Amoy), Fuzhou (Foochow), Ningbo (Ningpo), and Shanghai. This was the beginning of the foreign exploitation of a militarily weak, and badly-led China until 1949. Also involved were Germany, Italy, Japan, Belgium, Russia and the U.S.
*1841—*Uprising of people of Sanyuanli, Guangzhou, against the foreign imperialists.
*1844—*Treaty of Wang-hsia. First U.S. treaty with China.
*1844—*Emperor agreed to tolerate Christian churches.
*1848–50—*Chinese emigration to America and Australia started.
*1851–64—*Taiping Heavenly Kingdom, a rebellion against the Manchus led by a Christianity-inspired Cantonese who believed himself the younger brother of Jesus Christ. Starting in January 1851 in Jin Ting Village, Guangxi. This was the largest peasant movement in Chinese history. At one time or another it occupied most of China, including Zhejiang (but not Shanghai), Guilin, Suzhou,

and almost Chongqing. It established a capital at Nanjing for eleven years. It was defeated in part by a foreign mercenary army led by a British officer Charles Gordon, known as Chinese Gordon, who was later killed in the Sudan.

1856–60—Second Anglo-Chinese War, a.k.a. Arrow war, and more unequal treaties. British took Kowloon.

1860—British and French sacked Beijing, burned down Summer Palace.

1870—China started to send thirty students a year to U.S. to study. Students also to Britain and France.

1870—Tientsin Massacre of French missionaries (see ''Tianjin'').

1885—French took Vietnam (then a tributary state of China) and turned over Taiwan and Pescadores to China.

1895—Sino-Japanese War. Japan took Taiwan, the Pescadores, and the Liaoning peninsula from China.

1898—Britain leased area north of Kowloon and about 235 islands around Hong Kong for 99 years.

1898–1908—The Kuang Hsu Emperor kept under house arrest by Empress Dowager Tzu Hsi for defying her and passing reforms that attempted to modernize China.

1899—''Open Door'' notes on China, whereby the U.S. unilaterally declared that foreign powers should not cut up China into colonies, that all nations should be free to trade with China. Only Britain bothered to reply, but because of these notes, China looked for a while to the U.S. as its only foreign friend.

1900—Boxer Rebellion, a.k.a. the Rebellion of the Society of the Righteous and Harmonious Fists, a reaction, at times encouraged by the Manchu Empress Dowager, against the increasing foreign domination of China. Attacks on foreigners and Chinese Christians. (See ''Beijing.'') Foreign powers, including the Americans, responded by capturing Beijing, sacking it, and forcing another humiliating treaty on China.

1904—Russian-Japanese War fought on Chinese soil. A year later southern Manchuria taken by Japanese.

1908—Death of Empress Dowager. Succeeded by two-year old Pu-yi.

April 1911—Most important of several small abortive attempts by Dr. Sun Yat-sen against the Qing. Huanghuagang Insurrection, Guangzhou.

October 10, 1911—First victory of Sun Yat-sen's republican revolutionists following an accidental explosion in one of their bomb factories. Hankou.

January 1, 1912—Dr. Sun Yat-sen declared provisional president of the Chinese Republic, with its capital at Nanjing.

1912—Outer Mongolia with Russian help declared independence from China.

1913—Yuan Shih-kai elected president of the new republic.

August 27, 1914—Japan declared war on Germany. Under guise of attacking German concession at Kiaochow Japanese troops gained foothold in China, also taking over naval base at Qingdao (Tsingtao).

1915—Yuan agreed to many of Japan's Twenty-one Demands. Much protest. More protest after Yuan proclaimed himself emperor.

June 11, 1916—Death of Yuan in Beijing of heart attack. Warlords controlled country.

1917—China sent coolies to France to dig trenches along Western Front.

1919—Versailles Treaty concluding World War I. Japanese kept gains in China. Western powers retained their pre-war concessions.

May 4, 1919—Student demonstrations against the Versailles Treaty mark the beginning of the nationalistic and cultural upsurge known as the *May Fourth Movement*, the training ground for many Communist revolutionaries.

July 1, 1921—Founding of the Chinese Communist Party in Shanghai with Russian Communist help, although the Soviets, for tactical reasons, preferred to support Sun Yat-sen.

1923—Sun Yat-sen agreed to cooperate with Russian and Chinese Communists. Chiang Kai-shek sent to Moscow for military training. Mikhail Borodin and General Vassily Blucher arrived as advisers. Communists were allowed to join the Nationalist Party as individuals. Sun Yat-sen could not be sure of help from Britain and America.

1924—Chiang Kai-shek established Whampoa Military Academy, Guangzhou, with Chou En-lai in charge of political indoctrination. The Soviet Union voluntarily gave up privileges and concessions in China and recognized Outer Mongolia as part of China.

March 12, 1925—Dr. Sun died of cancer in Beijing.

May 30, 1925—Demonstrations in the International Settlement in Shanghai.

1926—Northern Expedition started out led by Generalissimo Chiang Kai-shek and Whampoa-trained officers with Communist cooperation and Soviet supplies. It attempted to unify China, wrest control from the warlords, and fight the unequal treaties. The Nationalists aimed for support from merchants, landlords, and warlords; the Communists concentrated on the peasants and urban proletariat.

March 1927—The Northern Expedition took Nanjing.

April 12, 1927—Chiang purged Communists in Shanghai. Chou En-lai escaped. Chiang later killed Communists in other cities.

August 1, 1927—Nanchang Uprising. Founding date of the Chinese Red Army.

April 18, 1927—Chiang declared Nanjing his capital.

September 8, 1927—Autumn Harvest Uprising led by Mao. Miners from An-yuan, some students, peasant cadres, and a peasant militia set out to take Changsha. Ill-prepared, they withdrew to Jinggang Shan (Chingkang Mountains), Jiangxi (Kiangsi), where they met up with the army from the Nanchang Uprising and established the first Chinese soviet, distributing land to the peasants in the area.

June 4, 1928—Nationalists took Beijing, renaming it Peiping (Northern Peace).

1930—Communists unsuccessfully attacked Nanchang and Changsha. Chiang retaliated with three "extermination" campaigns which almost succeeded against Jinggang Shan.

September 18, 1931—Japanese invaded Manchuria and set up puppet government under Pu-yi. Chiang returned to Nanjing to head the defense. With no international help available, Chiang accepted a humiliating truce in 1933.

1933—Chiang renewed attack on Communists on Jinggang Shan with a "scorched earth" policy.

October 16, 1934—The Communists, aware they could no longer hold their base on Jinggang Shan, started out with 80,000 troops on what is now known as the *Long March*. It was not until they arrived three months later in Xunyi (Tsunyi), Guizhou (Kweichow), that they decided on northern Shaanxi as their goal, since that was the only Communist base big enough. In addition, there was the added incentive of being able to fight the Japanese invaders in that area. At that meeting also, Mao Tse-tung took over as leader of the March.

From Xunyi, the march continued in spite of Nationalist bombs and persistent Nationalist pursuers. The major battles were fought at Loushan Pass (February 1935) and Luting suspension bridge over the Tatu River, which forward units had to cross on its three chains under fire, the enemy having ripped up most of the wooden floor boards. There were uninhabited grasslands, snow-capped 16,000-foot mountains, and hostile tribesmen. Edgar Snow gives a good account of the march in *Red Star Over China*. Some of the important battles have been immortalized in ivory or porcelain.

During the Long March, the original Central Army was joined by other Communist armies. It officially ended in Wuqi in northern Shaanxi on October 20, 1935. For the original marchers now reduced to 8,000, including thirty women, it had been a journey of 12,500 kilometers.

From Wuqi, the Communists eventually moved to Bao An where Edgar Snow visited them and researched his classic book. The move to Yan'an was made in January, 1937 (see ''Yan'an'').

1934—Chinese Communists declared war on Japan but Chiang concentrated on eliminating the Communists.

1936—Xi'an Incident. Chiang kidnapped by one of his own officers at Huaqing Hot Spring and forced into a wartime coalition with the Communists against the Japanese.

July 7, 1937—Marco Polo Bridge Incident. Killing of Japanese soldiers near Beijing set off *1937–45* war between Japan and China. Japan occupied most urban areas. Chiang moved capital to Hankou and finally to Chongqing (Chungking). Western powers remained neutral. Many warlords with their private armies rallied in fight against Japanese. Badly armed, the warlords were destroyed.

Although Nationalists blocked supply routes, Communist Eighth Route Army and New Fourth Army waged guerrilla warfare against Japanese, engaged in political and economic work among peasants, and developed strategy, discipline, and plans for takeover of rest of China. (See ''Yan'an.'')

1938—Canadian surgeon Dr. Norman Bethune joined Eighth Route Army and died the following year of blood poisoning while operating without antiseptics. Because of his skills at improvisation and selfless devotion to duty, Bethune later became a Chinese national hero. (See ''Shijiazhuang.'')

December 7, 1941—The U.S. declared war after Japan's attack on Pearl Harbor. It increased aid to Chiang via the Burma Road until 1942, and then via transport planes over the Himalayan ''hump'' to Chongqing and Kunming. U.S. tried to reconcile Mao and Chiang against the Japanese.

1943—Treaties with U.S. and Britain abolishing concessions and extraterritorial rights. At the Cairo Conference, Chiang promised to make more effort to fight Japan; Roosevelt and Churchill promised more military aid and China's repossession of Manchuria, Taiwan and the Pescadores after Japan's defeat.

February 1945—Yalta Conference declared Outer Mongolia to be independent, Manchuria to be under Russian sphere of influence.

August 6 & 9, 1945—U.S. dropped atomic bombs on Hiroshima and Nagasaki, Japan. Russia invaded Manchuria.

August 14, 1945—Japanese surrender. Lin Piao, leading Communist Army, advanced into Manchuria to receive Japanese surrender. Chou En-lai and Mao Tse-tung met with Chiang in Chongqing.

October 1945—Nationalists and Communists clashed in Manchuria.

November 1945—Chongqing talks broke off. U.S. President Truman ordered end of all aid to Nationalists, because the U.S. would otherwise be involved in a civil war. Civil war continued. Communists advanced because of severe inflation, Nationalist government corruption, breakdown of law and order, mass Nationalist troops defections, and the Communists' exemplary work in winning the hearts and minds of the peasants.

October 1, 1949—Known as *Liberation*. Chairman Mao proclaimed the birth of the People's Republic of China from the Gate of Heavenly Peace in Beijing. Later Chiang and troops and officials loyal to him fled to Taiwan. Refugees flooded Hong Kong. Communists tried but failed to take offshore islands of Matsu and Quemoy across from Taiwan.

December 1949—Mao visited Moscow.

February 1950—Sino-Soviet Treaty of Friendship and Alliance.

1950—Trials started against landlords. Two million people believed executed. Social reforms instigated. Remolding of intellectuals.

January 5, 1950—Britain resumed diplomatic relations.

1950–1953—Land reform. .15–.45 acres per peasant.

1950–51—Campaign to assert control over Tibet opposed by Khamba tribesmen. People's Liberation Army (PLA) took Tibet, September 1951.

1950—North Korea invaded south. In October, Chinese forces joined North Koreans after United Nations and South Koreans counterattacked north of 38th parallel border and threatened China.

In China, many foreign missionaries, teachers, and scholars jailed and then expelled as imperialist spies. China accused U.S. of poison gas and germ warfare and circulated maps showing American bases surrounding China. U.S. and Canada decided against resuming diplomatic relations.

1951—Americans began an embargo which wasn't lifted until the 1970s.

1953—China started to use Hong Kong and Macao as trading centers and sources of foreign exchange.

1954—Chiang signed mutual defense treaty with U.S.; French defeat and beginning of U.S. involvement in Indochina.

1954–55—Countryside reorganized into cooperatives with pooling of labor and land.

1955—Bandung Conference of nonaligned nations of Asia and Africa to continue "struggle against imperialism and colonialism" and to assert idea of peaceful coexistence. Attended by Chou En-lai.

1955—Khamba rebellion in Tibet.

1956–57—*Hundred Flowers Movement*. Free expression of opinion temporarily encouraged.

1957—*Anti-Rightist Campaign*. Public criticism and jailing of "Rightists," many of whom were not released until 1978.

1958–60—*Great Leap Forward*. Mobilization of masses to increase production; communes established; backyard furnaces smelted scrap metals. Mao resigned presidency to concentrate on this campaign, which apologists claim succeeded because it mobilized the masses. In 1979 the Chinese leadership admitted it was an economic disaster.

August 1958—Chinese attempted to capture Quemoy. Russia refused to give help, except to threaten retaliation if the Americans intervened. Nationalist air force outfought the Communists.

1959—Mao accused Russians of being revisionists, or giving in to capitalism and to nuclear blackmail. Chinese rejected Russia's offer of nuclear weapons in exchange for bases in China. Dalai Lama fled to India.

June 1960—Bucharest Conference. Rift between Russia and China became extremely bitter.

1959–62—Period of extreme economic difficulties due to "natural calamities." Some scholars also blame bad planning. Government insisted on repaying Russians for military aid immediately.

August 1960—Khrushchev ordered end of all Soviet aid to China. Advisers left many unfinished projects and took the plans back to Russia.

1962—Liu Shao-chi became president. Mao chairman of the Communist Party.

October 1962—India asserted control of disputed border territory. China sent punitive invasion force into India. It defeated the Indians and then unilaterally announced ceasefire in November and withdrew.

1963—China started to supply Hong Kong with fresh water.

October 1964—First atomic bomb exploded at Lop Nor testing grounds in Xinjiang (Sinkiang).

1964—Chiang Ching, wife of Mao Tse-tung, started campaign to make culture serve the revolution. Traditional Peking opera abolished. From this time until her downfall, only eight revolutionary operas allowed, all written by committees.

November 1965—Publication of article instigated by Mao in a Shanghai daily *Wen Hui Pao* brought the Cultural Revolution into the public eye for the first time.

May 25, 1966—First important "Big Character Poster" put up at Beijing University.

July 29, 1966—Chairman Mao swam the Yangtze River at Wuhan (9 miles) to show he was still powerful.

August 18, 1966—First of many Red Guard rallies in Tian Anmen Square, Beijing, in support of Chairman Mao with PLA Commander Lin Piao at his side. Schools closed so that students could travel and learn how to make revolution. From this time until the end of the Cultural Revolution, much violence took place; the British embassy was sacked (August 22, 1967) by a group of extremists called the May 16th Detachment, which also took over the Foreign Ministry and the media at the same time.

The *Great Proletarian Cultural Revolution* was started by Chairman Mao to regain lost power, an attempt to return to his ideals of the Chinese Communist revolution. Supporters of "revisionism" as propagated by President Liu Shao-chi had been promoting, among other things, an intellectual elite and an urban base. One big quarrel was over which incentives to use to increase production: bonuses versus pure political idealism. Liu wanted bonuses. (He was to succeed in 1978.)

Chairman Mao had always taught that the workers and the peasants, not the intellectuals, are the basis of the Chinese revolution. So as Mao regained his power with Red Guard and army help, many party cadres were sent to May Seventh Cadre Schools to be reeducated in the "correct" political thinking by learning to respect and love physical labor. Police chiefs pounded beats; doctors swept floors to help them identify with the masses and understand their problems. Officials who took privileges like personal use of office cars and the acceptance of "gifts" were violently attacked.

Red Guards, riding free on the trains and sleeping in school dormitories while fed by the municipalities, traveled around the country taking part in revolutionary movements such as the "Four Olds." In this, they physically destroyed many religious statues, buildings, ancestral tablets, and opposed many of the old virtues like long life, happiness, and personal wealth. They changed the names of streets and parks from old dynastic names to "The East Is Red" and "Liberation," stripped some women of their tight trousers (it was the style then), and cut off long "bourgeois" hair. They sought to eliminate "old ideas, old culture, old customs, and old habits." They also attacked elements of foreign influence. They believed all these were obstacles to completing the course of the revolution. Deng Xiaoping was denounced. Liu was deposed in 1968 and has since died. He was officially rehabilitated in 1979.

1967—Communist-inspired riots in Macao and Hong Kong.

1969—Border clashes with Soviet Union. Schools reopened with emphasis on "more red than expert." Students were chosen for university, after they completed at least two years of manual labor, by fellow peasants and workers according to level of political consciousness—how well they knew Maoist theory and how enthusiastic and selfless they were in serving the people.

1970—First Chinese satellite launched.

1971—U.S. Secretary of State Dr. Henry Kissinger and U.S. table tennis team visited China. Lin Piao accused of plotting to overthrow Mao, killed in plane crash while fleeing to Soviet Union. Death announced in 1973. China took United Nations seat from Taiwan. Canada resumed diplomatic relations.

1972—President Richard Nixon's historic visit.

1973—Campaign criticizing Lin Piao and Confucius. Deng Xiaoping rehabilitated and became Vice-Premier in charge of planning.

1974—Chinese aided Frelimo guerrillas in Mozambique and Angolan guerrillas against Portuguese. Asserted control in Paracel Islands. One million Soviet troops along border. Russian tanks within 600 miles of Beijing. Deng Xiaoping announced Three Worlds policy in speech of United Nations.

1975—Death of Chiang Kai-shek in Taiwan.

January 1976—Death of Premier Chou En-lai. Succeeded by Teng Hsiao-ping (Deng Xiao-Ping) as acting premier.

April 1976—Tian Anmen incident (see "Beijing"). Supporters of Chou put wreaths on monument honoring former premier. Chiang Ching, Mao's wife, ordered removal. Clash ensued. Deng blamed.

July 1976—Tangshan earthquake. China refused all outside help.

September 9, 1976—Death of Mao Tse-tung. Hua Kuo-feng succeeded.

October 6, 1976—Gang of Four arrested. *The Gang of Four*, along with Lin Piao, are blamed for many of the country's ills. They are Chiang Ching, widow of Chairman Mao, and three leaders from Shanghai who rose to prominence during the cultural revolution.

1977—Split with Albania, for many years China's only ideological friend.

August 1977—Deng completely rehabilitated. Resumed previous posts.

1978—Democracy walls flourished for four months.

1979—The U.S. and China resumed full diplomatic relations. Because of continued Vietnamese "armed incursions" Chinese forces invaded Vietnam. Border clashes since then. Government bans posters critical of Communists. See "Local Customs."

January 1, 1980—First of series of new laws on crime and judicial procedures officially came into effect.

1980–81—Multicandidate county-level elections.

1980—Zhao Ziyang succeeded Hua Guo-feng as premier. Leaders tried to improve living standards and eliminate "left deviation, i.e. over-rigid and excess control of economic system, the rejection of commodity production, and the mistaken attempt to transfer prematurely the ownership of all enterprises to the state." Admitted financial deficit. Began economic reassessment and retrenchment. Banned all Democracy Walls. Wei Jingsheng, one of the leaders, sentenced to 15 years' imprisonment.

December 1980—Pan-Am flew first direct U.S.-China flight in 30 years.

1981—Chinese officials stated that Mao Tse-tung's contribution to China outweighed his mistakes. China modified the commune system, making the family the basic economic unit, and diminished the role of the Communist Party in just about every aspect of life. Chiang Ching (Jiang Qing) and one other member of the Gang of Four were given suspended death sentences following trials the previous November. Hua Guo-feng, Mao's chosen successor, was replaced by Hu Yaobang as Chairman of the Communist Party.

1982—The United States agreed not to increase arms sales to Taiwan; British Prime Minister Margaret Thatcher visited Beijing to discuss Hong Kong's future.

China announced centralized economic controls only for some essential commodities, and gradual changes in prices based on market forces. The Chinese fiancee of a French diplomat was arrested (and later released).

1983—Beijing ordered the round-up of 50,000 criminals and executions of 10%, in its campaign against the increase in crime. Public sentencing rallies, marches of condemned criminals through the streets, and posting of photos of executed prisoners continued the following year.

U.S. Defense Secretary Caspar Weinberger visited, and permitted the sale of some U.S. military technology to China. The United States grant of political asylum to a visiting Chinese tennis player disrupted cultural and sports exchanges between the two countries. Hijackers forced a CAAC plane to fly to Seoul. Marriages between most Chinese and foreigners were now permitted with one month's notice. The campaign against "spiritual pollution" (immoral foreign influences) was vigorously pursued and gradually slowed down.

Record harvests along with a sharp increase in cash crops, encouraged the continuation of the new economic policies. All state-owned companies were ordered to make a profit and pay taxes.

1984—another abundant harvest, the fourth in a row. Foreign exchange reserves hit a record high, and China went on an importing spree. The Cultural Revolution was denounced completely. The Communist Party booted out thousands of leftists. Intellectuals started being sought out and encouraged to contribute to modernization. The Italian correspondent for *Der Spiegel* was expelled.

Factories became independent, making their own production and marketing decisions. An American demographer reported 250,000 female infanticides in China since 1979. U.S. President Ronald Reagan visited. China protested the release to Taiwan of Chinese hijackers imprisoned in Seoul.

Britain and China agreed on Hong Kong's future: It will all revert back to China in 1997. Deng proclaimed a one-country, two-systems policy in dealing with Taiwan and Hong Kong.

The Communist Party spelled out its plan for the next three to five years and explained "socialism with Chinese characteristics." China started drafting up bankruptcy laws. The chronic shortage of electricity continued.

1985—The riot following China's loss to Hong Kong in a soccer match in Beijing left 30 policemen hurt, 25 vehicles damaged, and 127 arrested. Two-hour lunch breaks were reduced to one hour for factory workers.

Nine aging members of the Politburo resigned to make way for younger leaders. Over one million elderly party members also resigned. President Li Xiannian visited the United States and Canada. Unauthorized resale of imported motor vehicles in Hainan Island created a big corruption scandal. Such shopping sprees helped to deplete foreign exchange reserves, and restrictions again were imposed for a few months.

1986—Taiwan negotiated release of its cargo plane hijacked to Canton. Sweden became the first customer for China's satellite launching service. China joined the Asian Development Bank. Some government-owned factories allowed to issue stock.

A Shenyang factory declared the first case of bankruptcy since Liberation. Queen Elizabeth II visited. First stock market since Liberation opened in Shanghai. The government announced that all new factory workers would be under limited contracts instead of lifetime assignments. In addition, the government also started a federal unemployment insurance and pension scheme.

1987—Student demonstrations for more freedom led to the resignation of leaders advocating "bourgeois liberalization." This included the Communist Party general secretary. University students were given improved teaching of Marxist-Leninist theories, trips to the countryside and factories, and military training. Two foreign heroin smugglers were executed in Kunming.

Chinese student Yang Wei, who studied in the U.S., was sentenced to two years imprisonment for conducting "demagogical propaganda for counter-revolutionary ends." He was reported as being involved with the demonstrations, the Chinese Alliance of Democracy, and the journal *China Spring*.

Demonstrations by Tibetans in Lhasa for the separation of Tibet from China resulted in the closing of Tibet to all foreign tourists except those in prepaid tours. Some foreigners expelled from Tibet.

Taiwan permitted its citizens to visit the mainland. Many tearful, dramatic reunions took place between family members who had not seen each other since Liberation. Mail, telegram, and telephone service also resumed.

China Travel Service official sentenced to death for "illegal sales of foreign exchange and motor vehicles." Shortages of pork, beer, and grain.

Three AIDS deaths so far in China; one a foreigner, one an Overseas Chinese; and one a child who had been given a transfusion of imported blood.

1988—China opened the rostrum on the Gate of Heavenly Peace to tourists. Hainan became 31st province. First visit of Chinese foreign minister to Moscow since 1957. A few relatives from China visited Taiwan. US$35 billion foreign debt. Cut-back on non-capital enterprises to control inflation. More demonstrations for independence in Tibet. Ugly demonstrations against African students, especially in Nanjing.

1989—40th anniversary of the founding of the People's Republic of China. Death of Panchen Lama. 39-hour visit of President Bush to China. More demonstrations and martial law in Lhasa. At least 12 killed. The Dalai Lama offered to allow China to keep troops in Tibet and oversee its foreign affairs. He was awarded the Nobel Peace Prize.

In Beijing, the death of Hu Yaobang set off student demonstrations and hunger strikes for democracy and the end to corruption. These continued relatively unopposed by the government for a month and a half and attracted up to a million supporters. Demonstrations in other cities as well. The first Sino-Soviet summit in thirty years was disrupted. Martial law in some sections of Beijing was declared. Some students refused to leave Tiananmen Square. In early June, the army tried to take back control in spite of the opposition of citizens. An estimated 300 to 3000 people were killed. Rioters burned 450 military vehicles, police cars and public buses.

Many foreigners were evacuated. The government denied any killings in Tiananmen Square. Those killed were "ruffians and criminal elements taking advantage of the turmoil." It said the students needed political education and sent another batch to the army. Everywhere students and workers were set to studying the government's version of the "counter-revolutionary rebellion." Student leaders were arrested. Rioters were executed in Shanghai and Beijing. A youth was arrested for trying to place a wreath in the square. A debated number of people were jailed for "counter-revolutionary crimes" like spreading "rumors" or destroying state property. Zhao Ziyang was placed under house arrest for supporting the students and revealing state secrets. Jiang Zemin was named secretary-general of the Communist Party.

Around the world, thousands of protestors marched, especially in Hong Kong. Some foreign governments imposed economic sanctions (most since withdrawn). They made it easier for Chinese students to stay abroad. Some of the student leaders took refuge in foreign missions. The most prominent was astrophysicist Fang Lizhi, who lived for almost a year in the U.S. embassy before being allowed to leave safely for the U.S.

Tourism almost stopped. The World Bank suspended all loans, but has since resumed them. Some foreign businesses withdrew. Chinese abroad set up the Front for Democratic China in France. Because of these and the Nobel Peace Prize, China accused foreign governments of interfering in its internal affairs. Amnesty International said at least 500 people were executed for offenses related to the demonstrations and counter-revolutionary activities.

Premier Peng Li announced a "planned and market economy" and the continuation of the open policy.

China admitted to over 1 million children born in spite of population control regulations. 112% increase in railway fares, the first in 35 years.

1990—China relatively back to normal. Again austerity, political education, and restrictions on press freedom and students going abroad. 12 Roman Catholic bishops arrested because of their secret Vatican ties. Martial law was lifted in Beijing and Lhasa. The 4th national census officially counted 1.16 billion people including Taiwan, Hong Kong, and Macau, an annual increase of 17 million and more than expected. China denied foreign reports that it had exceeded 1.4 billion. The hijacking of a Chinese plane concluded in a collision with two other planes in Guangzhou and the deaths of 127 people. Inflation was held down to 2%, compared to 17% in 1989.

China supported the United Nations resolution for economic sanctions against Iraq's invasion of Kuwait and lost an estimated US$2 billion in trade, transport, and civil aviation, plus debts owed by Iraq. It abstained from voting on the resolution to use all necessary means as it preferred a peaceful solution.

The Asian Games was an organizational success but did not attract the large numbers hoped for. Taiwan and other Asian tour groups helped to bring up 1990 tourism figures to about 95% of 1988 levels.

1991—China's first nuclear power plant started operating in Zhejiang province, 100 km southeast of Shanghai. Heaviest floods in 40 years hit 18 provinces. Premier Li Ping visited U.N. China counted 8 AIDs victims since 1985 and 607 HIV positives (mainly in Yunnan). Soviet Union collapsed. China made friends with all her neighbors. Increased relations with Taiwan. Chiang Ching/ Jiang Qing committed suicide. China's leaders talked of a 5-day work week by the year 2000. Tourist arrivals exceeded 1988 figures. *Wall Street Journal* estimated a potential 110 million floating population. China cut back on free health care and subsidies to state corporations and on food prices.

The US accused China of using convict labor in exports and squabbled over the protection of intellectual property. China achieved an international trade surplus including a US$10 billion surplus with U.S.

Annual per capita income in Beijing ¥2300.

1992—The first section of the Shanghai subway, and the Euro-Asia Bridge railway line from Rotterdam to Lianyungang should be completed.

1993—The first section of Shanghai's subway due to open.

1997—Hong Kong to return to China, July 1.

1999—Macao, which is currently Portuguese, to return to China.

See also ''Introduction.''

IMPORTANT ADDRESSES AND INFORMATION

SOME CHINESE MISSIONS ABROAD

Telephone

Australia
Embassy of the People's Republic of China
15 Corinthian Drive
Yarralumla, Canberra, A.C.T. 2600
Consulates General in Sydney and Melbourne

Canada
Embassy of the People's Republic of China (613) 234–2706
515 St. Patrick St. 234–2682
Ottawa, Ont., K1N 5H3

Consulate General of the People's Republic of China
240 St. George St.
Toronto, Ont., M5R 2P4 (416) 964–7260

Consulate General of the People's Republic of China (604) 736–3910
3380 Granville St.
Vancouver, B.C. V6H 3K3

England
Embassy of the People's Republic of China (01) 636–5726
49–51 Portland Pl.
London, W1N 3AG.

France
Embassy of the People's Republic of China 361005
11, Ave. Georges V 361096
75008, Paris 361097

Japan
Embassy of the People's Republic of China
4-33, Moto-Azabu 3-chome (03) 403–3389
Minato-ku, Tokyo 403–3380

Malaysia
Embassy of the People's Republic of China
229, Jalan Ampang
Kuala Lumpur   428495

Nepal
Embassy of the People's Republic of China   411740
Baluwater, Kathmandu, Nepal   412589

New Zealand
Embassy of the People's Republic of China
2–6 Glenmore St.
Wellington

Philippines
Embassy of the People's Republic of China
2038 Roxas Blvd. (Visa Office), Metro Manila   57.25.85
or 4896 Pasay Rd., Dasmarinas, Metro Manila   86.77.15

Singapore
Office of the Commercial Representative of the People's Republic of China
70–76 Dalvey Rd.
Singapore 1025   7343360

Thailand
Embassy of the People's Republic of China
57 Rachadapisake Rd.   2457037
Bangkok   2457044

U.S.A.
Embassy of the People's Republic of China
2300 Connecticut Ave., N.W.   (202) 328–2517 (visa)
Washington, DC 20008   (202) 328–2500 (chancery)

Consulate General of the People's Republic of China
104 S. Michigan Ave., Suite 1200
Chicago, IL 60603   (312) 346–0288

Consulate General of the People's Republic of China
3417 Montrose Blvd.   (713) 524–4311
Houston, TX 77066   (713) 524–0778

Consulate General of the People's Republic of China
501 Shatto Place
Suite 300   (213) 380–2507
Los Angeles, CA 90020   (213) 380–2506

Consulate General of the People's Republic of China
520 12th Ave.   (212) 330–7409
New York, NY 10036   (212) 279–4275

Consulate General of the People's Republic of China
1450 Laguna St.   (415) 563–4857
San Francisco, CA 94115   (415) 563–4885

China National Tourist Offices
55 Clarence St., 11 fl., Sydney NSW 2000, Australia; tel. 299–4057. Fax 290–1958.
4 Glentworth St., London NW1, England; Fax (071) 4875842
Office du Tourisme de Chine, 51 rue Sainte-Anne, Paris 75002, France.
Fremden verkehrsamt der Volksrepublik China, Ilkenhans Strasse 6, 6000 Frankfurt/M, 50.
6/F Hamamatsu Building, 1–27–13, Hamamatsu-cho, Minato-ku, Tokyo, Japan
Lincoln Building, 60 E. 42nd St., Suite 3126, New York, N.Y. 10165, U.S.A.; Fax (212) 599–2892; tel. (212) 867–0271; night 247–0769.
333 West Broadway, Suite 201, Glendale, CA 91204; tel. (818) 545–7504; night 247–1398. Fax 545–7506

TOUR ORGANIZERS AND TRAVEL AGENTS
Canada

Bestway Tours & Safaris, 203–1774 West 5th Ave., Vancouver, B.C. V6K 2G3; tel. (604) 732–4686, (800) 663–0844. Fax: (604) 732–9744.
Canada Swan International Travel Ltd., Park Square, 107–5701 Granville St., Vancouver, B.C. V6M 4J7. Tel. (604) 266–3300, (800) 663–2111. Fax: (604) 266–8867.
China Travel Service (Canada) Inc., 556 W. Broadway, Vancouver, B.C. V52 1E9, tel. (604) 663–8727, (800) 663–1126. Fax (604) 873–2823.
Chinapac International, Suite 2, 1955 West Broadway, Vancouver, B.C. V6J 1Z3. Tel. (604) 731–1693, (800) 661–8182. Fax (604) 731–1694.
Conference Travel of Canada, 95 St. Clair Ave., West, Ste. 1108, Toronto M4V 1N5. (416) 922–8161, 1–800–387–1277 (Ont.-Que.), 1–800–387–1488 (rest of Canada). Fax (416) 922–7365.
Tour East Holidays, 4040 Finch Ave. East, Suite 100, Scarborough, Ont. M1S 4V5; tel. (416) 292–8855, (800) 263–2808. Fax (416) 292–9877.

China (See also Beijing)

China International Travel Service, Corporate Headquarters, 103 Fuxingmen-nei Ave., Beijing, 100800; tel. 6011122. Telex 22350 CITSH CN. Fax 6012013, 5122068.
China RailExpress Travel Service, Block 3, Multiple Service Bldg., Beifengwo Rd. Haidan Dist., Beijing, 10038; tel. 326350, 3264140. Telex 222224 YTSRB CN. Fax 3261824.
China Travel Service and Overseas Chinese Travel Service, Head Office, 8 Dong Jiao Min Xiang, Beijing 100005. Tel. 5129933, 5129539. Telex: 22487 CTSHO CN. Fax 5129008.

China International Sports Travel Co., No. 1 Pan Jia Yuan Rd., Chao Yang Dist., Beijing 100021. Tel. 7716478, 7716490 or 4, Tiyuguan Rd., Beijing, 100061; tel. 7017366. Fax 7017370.
CYTS Tours Corp., 23B Dong Jiao Min Xiang, Beijing 100006. Tel. 5127770, Fax 5120571. Telex 20024 CYTS CN.

Hong Kong

China International Travel Service (H.K.), 6th Fl., Tower II, South Seas Centre, 75 Mody Rd., Tsimshatsui, Kowloon. Tel. 7325888. Telex 38449 CITC HX. 1018 Swire House, 11 Chater Rd. C. Tel. 8104282. Fax 7217154
China Travel Service (H.K.), Head Office; C.T.S. House, 78–83 Connaught Rd. C., Hong Kong. Tel. 8533533. Telex 85222 HCTSF HX. Fax 5419777 Branches: 77, Queen's Rd. C., Hong Kong. Tel. 5252284, 5236222. *Branches:* 27–33, Nathan Rd., 1/F (entrance on Peking Rd.), Kowloon. Tel. 7211311. (Open Sundays and holidays.) Hung Hom Railway Station, Kowloon, tel. 3–330660. Branches in Bangkok, Frankfurt, Jakarta, Los Angeles, London, Manila, Paris, San Francisco, Singapore, Sydney, Tokyo, and Vancouver.
CYTS Hong Kong, 11/F, Energy Plaza, 92 Granville Rd., Tsimshatsui East, Kowloon. Tel. 7212398. Fax 7217596.
China Youth Travel, Rm. 606, Wing On House, 71, Des Voeux Road, C., Hong Kong. Tel. 5259075. Telex 61679 YOUTH HX. Fax 8106063.
Hong Kong Student Travel Ltd., Room 833–835 Star House, Tsimshatsui, Kowloon. Tel. 7303267. Branch: Room 901 Wing On Center Bldg., 26 Des Voeux Rd. Central. Tel. 8107272. Fax 7219407. Telex 52988 ACSTB.
Jin Jiang Travel (HK) Ltd., Room 1810–1811, Wing On House, 71 Des Voeux Rd. Central. Tel. 8680633, 5265651. Fax 7452881.
Time Travel Services, Block A, 16/fl., Chung King Mansion. Tel. 7239993, 3666222. Telex 37670 TRVEL HX. Fax 7395413.
The Travel Advisers Ltd., Room 1006, 10/F, Silvercord, Tower One, 30 Canton Rd., Tsimshatsui, Kowloon. Tel. 3698321. (Across from Marco Polo Hotel.) Fax 3751078.

Macao

C.I.T.S. Zhuhai Branch, 6A–4C, R/C Rua de Sacadura Cabral. Tel. 566622.

Misc.

Helen Wong's Travel, 1st floor 806–808 George St. Sydney NSW 2000, Australia. Tel. (02) 281–6606, (008) 252760. Fax (02) 281–6630.
Yangrima Travels, P.O. Box 2951, Kathmandu, Nepal. Tel. 227627. Fax: 977–1–227628. Telex 2474 SUMTRA NP. Uses Sherpa guides and own equipment in Tibet.
Globetrotter Tours (NZ), P.O. Box 6145, 86 Symonds St., Auckland, New Zealand. Fax (09) 773–75.
Hann Overland, 2 Ivy Mill Lane, Godstone, Surrey RH989H.

Sitara Travel Consultants (pvt) Ltd., Sitara Lodge, 163-A, Bank Road, P.O. Box 63 Rawalpindi, Pakistan. Thos. Cook & Sons, P.O. Box 24, Auckland, New Zealand.
Trans-Himalaya, 30 Hanover Rd., London NW10 3DS, UK (land tours in Tibet).

U.S.A.

Abercrombie and Kent, Tel. 1–800–323–7308. In Illinois, call (708) 954–2944. Fax (708) 954–3324.
Arunas Travel Co., 125–10 Queens Blvd., Suite 2305, Kew Gardens, New York, 11415–1512. Tel. (718) 520–1134, (800) 473–4735. Fax (718) 575–1741. Telex 6791044 ARUNAS. Fax: (212) 808–9332.
Asian Pacific Adventures, 826 South Sierra Bonita Ave., Los Angeles, CA 90036. Tel. (213) 935–3156. Fax (213) 935–3156.
Avia Travel, 5429 Geary Blvd., San Francisco, CA, 94121. Tel. (415) 668–0964. (800) 950–2842. Fax (415) 386–8519. (Cheaper airfare.)
Backroads Bicycle Touring, 1516 5th St., Berkeley, CA 94710–1740. Tel. (415) 527–1555. Fax (415) 527–1444.
CET, 1110 Washington St., Lower Mills, Boston, Ma., 02124. Tel. 1–800–225–4262. Fax (617) 296–6830.
China International Travel Service (GD), 138B, World Trade Center, San Francisco, CA 94111. Tel. (415) 362–7477, 1–800–362–3839. Fax (415) 989–3838.
China Master Agent Program, and **China Tourism Council,** P.O. Box 2881, Reston, VA 22090. Tel. (703) 715–3050. Fax (703) 648–1523.
Elderhostel, 75 Federal St., Boston, MA 02110–1941. Tel. (617) 426–8056.
Euro-Asia Express, 475 El Camino Real, #206, Millbrae, CA 94030. 1–800–782–9624, 1–800–782–9625. Fax (692–7489). For cheaper air fares.
InterPacific Tours International, InterPacific Plaza, 111 East 15th St. New York, N.Y. 10003. Tel. (212) 953–6010, (800) 221–3594. Fax (212) 953–0350.
Kuo Feng Corporation, 396 Broadway, Room 200, New York, N.Y. 10013. Tel. 1–800–233–8687, (212) 966–8463; 166 Geary Blvd., San Francisco, CA 94108.
Mountain Travel—Sobek, 6420 Fairmount Ave., El Cerrito, CA 94530-3606. Tel. 1–800–227–2384; (415) 527–8100. Fax (415) 525–7710.
Orient Flexi-Pax Tours, 630 Third Ave., New York, NY 10017. Tel. U.S. 1–800–545–5540; Canada 1–800–843–6635. Fax (212) 661–1193.
Pacific Delight Tours, Inc., 132 Madison Ave., New York, NY 10016. Tel. 1–800–221–7179. (Offices also in Los Angeles, and Minneapolis). Fax (212) 532–3406.
Sino-American Tours, 37 Bowery, Confucius Plaza, New York, N.Y., 10002. Tel. (212) 925–6424, 1–800–221–7982. Fax (212) 925–6483.
U.S. China Travel Service, Inc., Main Office, 212 Sutter St., 2nd floor, San Francisco, CA 94108. Tel. (415) 398–6627, 1–800–332–2831, 1–800–553–8764. Also 223E, Garvey Avenue, Suite 138, Monterey Park, CA 91754. Tel. (818) 288–8222.

CHINA FRIENDSHIP ASSOCIATIONS

Australia-China Society, 2nd Floor, 4 Tattersalls Lane, Melbourne, Victoria, Australia 3000. Tel. 66638827.

Federation of Canada-China Friendship Associations, 26 Grand Cedar Ct., Stittsville, Ont., K2S 1C8. Tel. (613) 836–6923. Fax (613) 741–3330.

Society for Anglo-Chinese Understanding, 152 Camden High St., London, NW1, England.

New Zealand-China Friendship Society, c/o Mrs. N. W. Goddard, 82 Evans Bay Parade, Wellington 1, New Zealand.

U.S.-China Peoples Friendship Association, National Office, 306 W. 38 St., Rm. 603, New York, NY 10018-2903. Tel. (212) 643–1525. Tours Office, 1322 Helmsman Way, Sacramento, CA 95833. Tel. (916) 925–1006. Fax (916) 925–7455.

FOR SCHOLARS, STUDENTS, TEACHERS, FOREIGN EXPERTS, AND EXCHANGES

Canada

Association of Universities and Colleges of Canada, 151 Slater St., Ottawa, Ont. K1P 5N1. Tel. (613) 563–1236. Fax (613) 563–9745.

China Desk, Canadian Council of Churches, 40 St. Clair East, Toronto, Ont., M4T 1M9.

Canadian Executive Service Organization, Operations Centre, Suite 2000, 415 Yonge St., Toronto, Ont. M5B 2E7. Tel. (416) 596–2376.

Canadian International Development Agency, 200 Promenade du Portage, Hull, Quebec K1A 0G4.

China Educational Exchange, c/o Mennonite Central Committee, 134 Plaza Drive, Winnipeg, MB R3T 5K9. Tel. (204) 261–6381.

Exchanges Section, Academic Relations, **Department of External Affairs,** 125 Sussex Drive, Ottawa, K1A OG2. Tel. (613) 996–4527. Fax (613) 992–5965.

Ontario-Jiangsu Educational Exchange, Room 200H, Administrative Studies Bldg., York University, 4700 Keele St., North York, Ont., M3J 1P3. Tel. (416) 736–5784.

World University Service of Canada, China Programme, P.O. Box 3000, Station C. Ottawa, Ont. K1Y 4MTS. Tel. (613) 798–7477. Fax 798–0990.

China

Chinese Educational Association for International Exchange, 37 Damucang Hutong, Beijing.

Foreign Experts Bureau, Friendship Hotel Beijing, 100873 or P.O Box 300, Beijing, 100086. It is quicker to write directly to the Office of the President or the Foreign Affairs Office of the school where you wish to teach, as the Foreign Experts Bureau is primarily a central clearing house.

Misc.

Education Office, **British Council,** 65 Davies St., London W1Y 2AA, U.K. Tel. 01–499–8011. Fax 01–493–5035.
Great Britain-China Centre, 15 Belgrave Square, London SW1X 8PG.
United Nations Volunteers, Palais des Nations, CH–1211 Geneva 10, Switzerland. Fax (41 22) 798 85 70.

U.S.A.

American Institute for Foreign Study, 102 Greenwich Ave., Greenwich, CT 06830. Tel. 1–800–727–AIFS, (203) 863–6106. Fax (203) 869–1173.
China Educational Exchange, 1251 Virginia Ave., Harrisonburg, VA 22801. Tel. (703) 434–6701. Fax 434–5556.
Committee on Scholarly Communication with the People's Republic of China, National Academy of Sciences, 2101 Constitution Ave., NW, Washington, DC 20418. Tel. (202) 334–2718. Fax (202) 334–1774.
Council for International Exchange of Scholars (CIES), 3400 International Drive, N.W., Suite M-500, Washington, D.C. 20008–3097. Tel. (202) 686–4023. Fax (202) 362–3442.
East Asian & Pacific Affairs, United States Information Agency, Washington D.C. 20547. Tel. (202) 619–5839. Fax (202) 619–6684.
International Education Programs, U.S. Department of Education, 400 Maryland Ave., S.E., ROB 3, Room 3082, Washington, DC 20202.
International Executive Service Corp., P.O. Box 10005, Stamford, Conn. 06904. Tel. (203) 967–6000.
National Association for Foreign Student Affairs, 1875 Connecticut Ave., N.W. Suite 1000, Washington, D.C. 20009–5728. Tel. (202) 462–4811. Tel. (202) 462–4811.
National Committee on U.S./China Relations, 777 United Nations Plaza, New York, NY 10164. Tel. (212) 922–1385.
United Board for Christian Higher Education, 475 Riverside Drive, New York, 10115. Tel. (212) 870–2608.
Teach-in-China Program, U.S.P.F.A., P.O. Box 387, Union City, GA 30291.
WorldTeach, Harvard Institute for International Development, One Eliot St., Cambridge, MA 02138. Tel. 495–5527.

Canada

Air China, Unit 15, 131 Bloor St. W., Toronto, Ont., M5S 1R1; 1040 West Georgia St., Vancouver, B.C. V6B 4H1.
Amnesty International, 130 Slater St., Ste. 900, Ottawa, Ont., K1P 6E2.
Bank of China, 100 Yonge St., Suite 1005, Toronto, Ont. M5C 2W1.
Canada-China Trade Council, Suite 310, 133 Richmond St. W., Toronto, Ont. M5H 2L3.
Cheefoo Schools Assoc., P.O. Box 147, 260 Adelaide St. East, Toronto, Ont., M5A 1N0. Tel. (416) 467–4820.
Convention Administrator, Canadian Wildlife Service, Environment Canada, Ottawa, Ont. K1A OH3.

Customs and Excise, Revenue Canada, Travellers Division, Connaught Bldg., Ottawa, Ont., K1A 0L5. Tel. (613) 954–6373. Fax (613) 954–1765.
External Affairs, East Asia Trade Division, Ottawa, Ont., K1A 0G2.
IAMAT International Association for Medical Assistance to Travellers, 1287 St. Clair Ave. W., Toronto, Ont., M6E 1B8.
On Board Courier Services, 10105 Ave. Ryan, Dorval, Quebec H9P 1A2. Tel. (514) 633–0740 or Toronto (416) 675–1820 or Vancouver (604) 276–0206.

China

Amity Foundation, 17 Da Jian Yin Xiang, Nanjing. Tel. 649701. Fax 741053.
China Daily, 15 Huixin Dongjie, Chaoyang Dist., Beijing 100029. Foreign Liaison Office, tel. 4224488 X3212.
Travel China, room 2109, 9A Jianguomennei Ave., Beijing 100740. Tel. 5136287. Fax 5122096.

For other addresses in China, see each city under "Destinations," especially "Beijing," "Guangzhou," "Shanghai," and "Shenyang."

England

Air China, 41 Grosvenor Garden, London SW1W OBP.
China Travel Service (UK) Ltd., 24 Cambridge Circus, London WC2H 8HD. Tel. (01) 836–9911. Fax (01) 836–3121.
Sino-British Trade Council, 5/F, Abford House, 15 Wilton Rd., London SW1V 1LT.

Hong Kong

American Chamber of Commerce, 1030 Swire House. Central Hong Kong. Fax 8101289.
Asian Wall St. Journal, G.P.O. Box 9825, Hong Kong.
Australian Trade Commission, 24/F, Harbour Centre, 25 Harbour Rd., Wan Chai, (G.P.O. Box 820), Hong Kong. Tel. 8331133.
Bank of China, 2A Des Voeux Rd. Central, Hong Kong. Tel. 8266888.
Canadian Chamber of Commerce, 13/F, One Exchange Square, 8 Connaught Pl., G.P.O. Box 1587, Tel. 5244711.
Canadian Commission, Box 11142, GPO, 11/14 F, Tower I, Exchange Square, 8 Connaught Rd., Hong Kong. Tel. 8104321.
China Phone Book Co. Ltd., GPO Box 11581, Hong Kong.
China Travel Press, 2204 C. C. Wu Bldg., 302–308 Hennessy Rd., Wanchai. Tel. 5752270.
Dragonair, 12/F, Tower 6, China Hong Kong City, 33 Canton Rd., Tsimshatsui, Kowloon. Tel. 7383388. 1843–1844 Swire House, 11 Chater Rd., Central. Tel. 8108055. Telex 45936 DRAGH HX. Fax 7360833.
Far Eastern Economic Review, G.P.O. Box 160, Hong Kong.
Hong Kong Bank China Services, Level 13, 1 Queen's Rd. C. Hong Kong.
Hongkong China Liaison Office, Board of Global Ministries, The United Methodist Church, 2 Man Wan Rd., C–17, Kowloon. Tel. 7601129.

Hong Kong Tourist Association, 35/F Jardine House, 1 Connaught Place, Connaught Rd. Central. Tel. 8017111. Fax 8104877. Represented abroad by offices in Auckland, Barcelona, Chicago, Frankfurt, London, Los Angeles, New York, Paris, Rome, Osaka, San Francisco, Singapore, Sydney, Tokyo, and Toronto.
South China Morning Post, G.P.O. Box 47, Hong Kong.
United States Consulate, 26 Garden Rd., Hong Kong. Tel. 5239011.
Visa Office, Ministry of Foreign Affairs of the People's Republic of China in Hong Kong. 5/F, Lower Block, 26 Harbour Rd., Wanchai. Tel. 5–744163. 9 a.m.–noon and 2–5 p.m. daily. Saturdays 9 a.m.–noon.

Misc.

China Southwest Airlines, Kathmandu. Tel. 411302, 416541.
Vol Libre, Images, Aventures, Impasse Treileet, 34000 Montpellier France. Fax 67 52 74 64. (Contact Gilles Santantonio on paragliding in China.)

U.S.A.

Air China, 45 E. 49th St., New York, NY 10017; 51 Grant Ave., San Francisco, CA 94108; 2500 Wilshire Blvd., Los Angeles, CA 90057.
Amnesty International, 322 Eighth Ave., New York, NY 10001.
Asia Watch, 485 Fifth Ave., New York, NY 10017–6104. Tel. (212) 972–8400. Fax (212) 972–0905.
Asian Wall St. Journal Weekly, 200 Liberty St., New York, NY 10281.
Bank of China, 410 Madison Ave., New York, NY 10017.
China Books and Periodicals, 2929 24th St., San Francisco, CA 94110 (retail and mail orders).
China Daily Distribution Corp., 15 Mercer St., Suite 401, New York, NY 10013.
China Eastern, 2500 Wilshire Blvd. Suite 100, Los Angeles, CA, 90057. Tel. (213) 384–2703. Fax (213) 384–6103; 299 N. Dantno Ave., Room 211, Arlington Heights, IL 60004. Tel. (708) 670–8264. Fax (708) 670–0642.
Europ Assistance Worldwide Services/Travel Assistance International, Suite 400, 1133 15th St., N.W., Washington, D.C. 20005. Tel. (202) 331–1609. Fax (202) 331–1588.
Frandon Enterprises, 511 North 48th, Seattle, WA 98103. (For lead-testing kits).
IAMAT (International Association for Medical Assistance to Travelers), 417 Center St., Lewiston, NY 14092.
International SOS, Tel. (215) 244–1500, 1–800–523–8930 (U.S.A.), 1–800–441–4767 (Canada). Fax (215) 244–9617. Telex 831598 ISOS PHA.
Mongolia Society, Inc., 321–322 Goodbody Hall, Indiana University, Bloomington, IN 47405.
National Council of Churches, China Program Administrative Committee, 475 Riverside Dr., 6/F, New York, NY 10115.
Now Voyager (Courier Service), 74 Varick St., Suite 307, New York, NY 10013. Tel. (212) 431–1616.

U.S. Dept. of Commerce, China Desk, room 2317, Washington, D.C. 20230. Tel. (202) 377–3583.
United States Customs Service, Public Information Division, P.O. Box 7407, Washington, DC 20229.
U.S. Dept. of State, Bureau of Consular Affairs, Washington, D.C. 20520. (202) 647–0254. Fax (202) 647–0256.
U.S.-China Business Council, 1818 N St. NW, Suite 500, Washington, D.C. 20036/5559. Tel. (202) 429–0340. Fax (202) 775–2476.

CHINA IDD DOMESTIC TELEPHONE CODES

When dialing from outside China, use the number 86 for China and then the domestic code. When dialing in China, use "0" before the code.

Anshan 412; Anyang 372; Beidaihe 335; Beijing 1; Changchun 431; Changsha 731, Changzhou 519; Chaozhou 7681; Chengde 314; Chengdu 28; Chongqing 811.

Dalian 411; Dandong 415; Datong 352; Dunhuang 9473; Emei 833; Foshan 757; Fushun 413; Fuzhou 591; Guangzhou 20; Guilin 773; Guiyang 851; Haikou 898; Handan 310; Hangzhou 571; Harbin 451; Hefei 551; Hohhot 471; Huangshan 559; Jiangmen 7682; Jilin 432; Jinan 531; Jingdezhen 798; Jinggangangshan 7060; Jiujiang 792; Jiuquan 937.

Kaifeng 378, Kaiping 7658; Kashi 998; Kunming 871; Lanzhou 931; Lhasa 891; Liangyungang 518; Luoyang 379; Lushan 7010; Maanshan 555; Nanchang 791; Nanjing 25; Nanning 771; Nantong 513; Ningbo 574.

Qingdao 532; Qinhuangdao 335; Quanzhou 595; Qufu 5473; Sanya, 7605; Shantou 754; Shanghai 21; Shaoguan 751; Shaoxing 575; Shenyang 24; Shenzhen 755; Shÿiazhung 311; Shunde 7653; Suzhou 512; Taian 538; Taishan 7657; Taiyuan 351; Tianjin 22; Tianshui 938; Urumqi 991.

Weifang 536; Weihai 5451; Wuhan 27; Wuxi 510; Wuzhou 772; Xiamen 592; Xian 29; Xinhui 7656; Xining 971; Xuzhou 516; Yanan 911; Yangzhou 514; Yantai 535; Yichang 717; Yinchuan 951; Yueyang 730; Zhanjiang 759; Zhaoqing 758; Zhengzhou 371; Zhenjiang 511; Zhongshan 7654; Zhuhai 756; Zhangzhou 596; Zibo 533; Zigong 813.

CHINESE CUSTOMS REGULATIONS

Upon entrance every tourist is requested to fill in a Baggage Declaration in duplicate to be handed in to Customs.

Articles for personal use carried by a tourist including foodstuffs to be consumed during the trip, 2 bottles of wine (not exceeding 750 grams each) and 400 cigarettes may be imported duty free. Wristwatches, recorders (including multi-purpose combination sets), cameras and cinecameras for personal use may be imported but may not be transferred or sold privately and are to be taken out of the country at the time of exit. Gifts for friends and relatives or articles carried on behalf of others are to be declared to the Customs.

Tourists should retain the duplicate copy of the baggage declaration issued by the customs at the entry port. Upon exit tourists should fill in the blanks for exit declaration which is to be submitted to the customs for inspection.

Invoices for purchases made in China in reasonable quantities for personal use should be produced to the customs upon exit. Shipped goods are exportable with the export permit which is obtained upon application.

Import of the following articles is prohibited:

(1) Arms, ammunition and explosives of all kinds;

(2) Radio transmitter-receivers and principal parts;

(3) Renminbi;

(4) Manuscripts, printed matter, films, photographs, gramophone records, cinematographic films, loaded recording tapes, video-tapes, etc. which are detrimental to China's politics, economy, culture and ethics;

(5) Poisonous drugs, narcotics and opium, morphia, heroin, etc;

(6) Animals, plants and products thereof infected with or carrying disease germs and insects pests;

(7) Insanitary foodstuffs and germ-carrying foodstuffs from infected areas; and

(8) Other articles the import of which is prohibited by state regulations.

Export of the following articles is prohibited:

(1) Arms, ammunition and explosives of all kinds:

(2) Radio transmitter-receivers and principal parts;

(3) Renminbi and securities, etc. in RMB;

(4) Foreign currencies, bills and securities in foreign currencies (with the exception of those allowed to be taken out);

(5) Manuscripts, printed matter, films, photographs, gramophone records, cinematographic films, loaded recording tapes, video-tapes, etc. which contain state secrets or which are otherwise prohibited export;

(6) Valuable cultural relics and rare books relating to Chinese revolution, history, culture or art;

(7) Rare animals and rare plants and their seeds;

(8) Precious metals and articles made thereof, jewelry, diamonds and ornaments made thereof (with the exception of those which have been brought in and declared to the Customs); and

(9) Other articles the export of which is prohibited by state regulations.

Overseas Chinese with foreign passports can import, duty-free, to be left in China on one's first visit each year, one of an item worth ¥200 to ¥1000 RMB such as a TV, washing machine, refrigerator, or motorcycle, or any five of the following worth ¥50 to ¥200: bicycle, sewing machine, fan, radio, typewriter, electronic organ, electric kettle. Also a "reasonable amount of clothing." A Chinatown or Hong Kong travel agent specializing in Overseas Chinese tours can give you more details.

Duty if levied, is high. You might pay ¥600 on a Rolex watch; ¥275 on a Chinese-made 12–15-inch color television, ¥350 on a similar foreign-made one. If you don't want to pay the duty, leave the item with Customs and pick it up on the way out.

BIBLIOGRAPHY

Ahrens, Joan Reid and Malloy, Ruth Lor. *Hong Kong Gems and Jewelry*. Hong Kong: Delta Dragon, 1986.

Austin, Alvyn J. *Saving China—Canadian Missionaries in the Middle Kingdom, 1888–1959*. Toronto: University of Toronto Press, 1986.

Barber, Noel. *The Fall of Shanghai*. New York: Coward-McCann and Geoghegan, Inc., 1979.

Barr, Pat. *To China with Love—the Lives and Times of Protestant Missionaries in China, 1860–1900*. New York: Doubleday & Co., Inc., 1973.

Bauer, E. E. *China Takes Off—Technology Transfer and Modernization*. Seattle: University of Washington Press, 1986.

Behr, Edward. *The Last Emperor*. Toronto: General Paperbacks, 1987.

Booz, Elizabeth, B. *Tibet*. Hong Kong: Shangri-la Press, 1986. Lincolnwood, IL: Passport Books.

Booz, Patrick R. *Yunnan*. Lincolnwood, IL: Passport Books, 1987.

Bredon, Juliet. *Peking*. Shanghai: Kelly and Walsh, Ltd., 1931; Hong Kong: Oxford University Press. 1982.

Buck, Pearl S. *The Good Earth*. New York: J. Day, 1977.

Buckley, Michael, and Samagalski, Alan. *China—A Travel Survival Kit*. Victoria and Berkeley: Lonely Planet.

Cao, Xuegin. *A Dream of Red Mountains,* abridged version. Huang Xin Qu. Beijing. Foreign Language Teaching and Research Publishing House.

Catchpool, Brian. *A Map History of Modern China*. London: Heinemann Educational Books Ltd., 1977.

Chen, Jack. *A Year in Upper Felicity*. New York: Macmillan, 1973.

Chen, Jerome. *Mao and the Chinese Revolution*. Oxford, 1976.

Chen Yuan-Tsung. *The Dragon's Village*. New York: Pantheon, 1980.

Coonay, Eleanor and Alteri, Daniel. *The Court of the Lion*. New York: Avon Books, 1989.

Coye, Molly Joel, etc., editor. *China, Yesterday and Today*. New York: Bantam Books, 1984.

Cronin, Vincent. *The Wise Man from the West, Matteo Ricci and His Mission to China*. London: Collin, Fount Paperbacks, 1984.

Dalrymple, William. *In Xanadu, A Quest*. William Collins Sons & Co., London. Toronto. 1989.

Daubier, Jean. *A History of the Chinese Cultural Revolution*. New York, Toronto: Vintage Books, 1974.

Dawson, Raymond. *Imperial China*. New York: Pelican Books, 1976.

Er Si, etc. *Inside Stories of the Forbidden City*. Beijing: New World Press, 1986.

Fairbank, John K. *The United States and China*. Cambridge: Harvard University Press, 1983.

Fitzgerald, C. P. *The Tower of Five Glories—A Study of the Min Chia of Ta Li, Yunnan.* West Point, CT: Hyperion Press, 1973.

Fleming, Peter. *Bayonets to Lhasa.* New York: Oxford University Press, 1985.

Gargan, Edward A. *China's Fate—A People's Turbulent Struggle with Reform and Repression. 1980–1990.*

Gernet, Jacques. *Daily Life in China on the Eve of the Mongol Invasion. 1250–1276.* Stanford, Ca.: Stanford University Press, 1973.

Goede, William. *Love in Beijing and Other Stories.* Dunvegan, Ont: Cormorant Books, 1988.

Goldenberg, Susan. *Managing Joint Ventures With a Spotlight on China and Japan.* Harvard Business School Press, 1988.

Gu Hua. *A Small Town Called Hibiscus.* Beijing: Panda Books, 1983.

Guisso, R.W.L. and Pagani, Catherine. *The First Emperor of China.* Toronto. Stoddart Publishing, 1989. In the U.S. Birch Lane Press, New York.

Haldane, Charlotte. *The Last Great Empress of China.* New York: Bobbs-Merrill, 1965.

Han Suyin. *The Crippled Tree.* New York: Bantam, 1972. *A Mortal Flower.* London: J. Cape, 1966. *Birdless Summer.* New York: Putnam, 1968.

Harrer, Heinrich. *Seven Years in Tibet,* London: The Adventure Library, Rupert Hart-Davis, 1957; London: Granada, 1984.

Hersey, John A. *A Single Pebble.* Chicago and Montreal: Bantam Books, 1961.

Hinton, William. *The Great Reversal—The Privatization of China, 1979–1989.* Monthly Review Press, New York. 1990.

Hopkirk, Peter. *Foreign Devils on the Silk Road.* New York: Oxford University Press, 1989.

Latsch, Marie-Luise. *Peking Opera as a European Sees It.* Beijing: New World Press, 1980.

Li Nianpei, *Old Tales of China—a tourist guidebook to better understanding of China's stage, cinema, arts and crafts.* Beijing: China Travel and Tourism Press, 1981.

Li Xueqin, *The Wonder of Chinese Bronzes.* Beijing: Foreign Languages Press, 1980.

Liang Heng and Shapiro, Judith. *Son of the Revolution.* New York: Vintage Books, 1984.

Lin Yutang. *Moment in Peking.* New York: John Day, 1939.

Ling, Ken. *The Revenge of Heaven.* New York: G.P. Putnam's Sons, 1972.

Lo Kuan-chung. *Three Kingdoms.* Robert Moss, trans. & ed. New York: Pantheon, 1976.

Macleod, Roderick. *China, Inc. How to do Business With the Chinese.* New York: Bantam Books, 1988.

Malloy, Ruth Lor. *Beyond the Heights.* Hong Kong: Heinemann Educational Books Ltd. (Asia), 1980.

McCawley, James D. *The Eater's Guide to Chinese Characters.* Chicago and London: The University of Chicago Press, 1984.

McKenna, Richard. *The Sand Pebbles.* Greenwich, Conn.: Fawcett, 1962.

Medley, Margaret. *A Handbook of Chinese Art.* New York: Icon Ed., 1974.

Richardson, Hugh E. *Tibet and Its History.* Boston and London: Shambala, 1984. Random House distributor.

Ryder, G., ed. *Damming the Three Gorges*. Toronto: Probe International, 1990.

Salzman, Mark. *Iron and Silk*. New York: Random House, 1986.

Seagrave, Sterling. *The Soong Dynasty*. New York and Sydney: Harper & Row.

Shipton, Diana. *The Antique Land*. Oxford University Press. Hong Kong, 1987.

Snow, Edgar. *Red Star Over China*. New York: Penguin, 1977.

Spence, Jonathan. *To Change China: Western Advisers in China. 1620–1960*. Boston, Toronto: Little, Brown, 1969.

Sullivan, Michael. *The Arts of China*. Los Angeles, Berkeley, London: University of California Press, 1977.

Tsao Hsueh-Chin. *The Dream of the Red Chamber* (Hung Lou Meng). New York: The Universal Library, Grosset & Dunlop, 1973.

Turner-Gottschang, Karen, etc. *China Bound—A Guide to Academic Life and Work in the PRC*. Washington, DC: National Academy Press, 1987.

UNESCO. *Tibet and the Chinese People's Republic: A Report to the International Commission of Jurists by its Legal Inquiry Committee on Tibet*. Geneva: International Commission of Jurists.

U.S. Government. *Post Report on China*. Government Printing Office, Washington, DC.

Van Slyke, Lyman P. *Yangtze. Nature, History and the River*. Reading, MA: Addison-Wesley: 1989.

Warner, Marina. *The Dragon Empress: The Life and Times of Tz'u-Hsi, Empress Dowager of China, 1835–1908*. New York: Macmillan, 1972.

White, Theodore. *In Search of History*. New York: Warner, 1978.

Williams, C.A.S. *Outlines of Chinese Symbolism and Art Motives*. New York: Dover Publications, 1976.

Witke, Roxanne. *Comrade Chiang-Ching*. Waltham, MA: Little, Brown, 1977.

Woodcock, George. *The British in the Far East*. New York: Atheneum, 1969.

Wu Zuguang. *Peking Opera and Mei Lanfang*. Beijing: New World Press, 1981.

Yang Gang. *Daughter*. Phoenix Books, Foreign Language Press, Beijing. 1988.

———. *Doing Business in Today's China*. The American Chamber of Commerce in Hong Kong.

———. *Zhonghua Renmin Gongheguo Fen Sheng Dituji*. (Atlas of China). Beijing: Xinhua Shudian, 1971.

———. China City Guide Series. Beijing: Travel and Tourism Press. 1983. Guides of Beijing, Guangzhou, Guilin, Hangzhou, Kunming, Nanjing, Shanghai, Taiyuan, Tianjin, Xiamen, etc.

QUICK REFERENCE

Official Chinese Holidays

January or February	Spring Festival/New Year, the date depending on lunar calendar (3 days).
May 1	Labor Day
October 1 and 2	National Day, celebrating the founding of the People's Republic of China in 1949.

In addition, the following are celebrated with special programs, but offices and schools are open.

March 8	International Working Women's Day
March 12	Tree-planting day, south China
April	Tree-planting day, north China (first Sunday)
May 4	Youth Day (May 4th Movement)
June 1	Children's Day
July 1	Founding Day of the Communist Party of China
August 1	Founding Day of the People's Liberation Army
Sept. 10	Teacher's Day
Sept. 27	World Tourism Day. Celebrated by different cities in turn. Special events 1993, Henan province, see Zhengzhan.

The Chinese also celebrate several other traditional holidays. The Lantern Festival is the last day of the old lunar new year celebrations. The Dragon Boat races commemorate the untimely death of an upright official. Originally, the boats raced to feed the fish so they wouldn't eat him! (But no one thinks of that now.) The Mid-Autumn Festival celebrates the most beautiful full moon of the year.

Check with C.I.T.S. about special events related to the festivals (not necessarily on the specified day). Daylight-savings time about the second Sunday in April until 2nd Sunday in September.

Some major festivals are listed here. For regional festivals, please look up individual destinations like Weifang (for the kite festival), Kunming (for the Water-splashing Festival and Third Moon Market), and Guiyang for festivals of the nationalities. Be aware that the dates for same festivals might not be decided until the last minute, especially in Tibet. On the other hand, festivals might be cancelled without much warning.

Since the dates for the traditional festivals fluctuate (like Easter) according to the lunar calendar, the Western equivalents are:

Old Spelling	*Pinyin*	*Province in Pinyin*
AMOY	Xiamen	Fujian
CHANGCHOW	Changzhou	Jiangsu
CHANGSHA	Changsha	Hunan
CHAOCHING	Zhaoqing	Guangdong
CHENGCHOW	Zhangzhou	Fujian
CHENGCHOW	Zhengzhou	Henan
CHENGTEH	Chengde	Hebei
CHENGTU	Chengdu	Sichuan
CHIAYUKUAN	Jiayuguan	Gansu
CHINGHUNG,	Jinghong,	Yunnan
HSISHUANG PANNA	Xishuangbanna	
CHINGKANG		
MOUNTAINS	Jinggang Shan	Jianxi
CHINGTECHEN	Jingdezhen	Jianxi
CHINGKIANG (also		
Chenkiang)	Zhenjiang	Jiangsu
CHINWANGTAO	Qinhuangdao	Hebei
CHIUCHUAN	Jiuquan	Gansu
CHIUHUA		
MOUNTAINS	Jiuhua Shan	Anhui
CHUFU	Qufu	Shandong
CHUNGKING	Chongqing	Sichuan
FOOCHOW	Fuzhou	Fujian
FASHAN (also Fatshan)	Foshan	Guangdong
HAIKOW	Haikou	Guangdong
HANGCHOW	Hangzhou	Zhejiang
HANTAN	Handan	Hebei
HOFEI	Hefei	Anhui
HSINHUI (also Sunwai)	Xinhui	Guangdong
HSILINHOT	Xilinhot	Nei Monggol
HSINHSIANG	Xinxiang	Henan
HSUCHOW	Xuzhou	Jiangsu
HUHEHOT	Hohhot	Nei Monggol
IHSING (also Yising)	Yixing	Jiangsu
KIANGMEN (also		
Kongmoon)	Jiangmen	Guangdong
KIRIN	Jilin	Jilin
KIUKIANG	Jiujiang	Jiangxi

KUNGHSIEN	Gongxian	Henan
KWANGCHOW (also Canton)	Guangzhou	Guangdong
KWEILIN	Guilin	Guangxi
KWEIPING	Guiping	Guangxi
LHASA	Lhasa	Xizang (Tibet)
LANCHOW	Lanzhou	Gansu
LIENYUNKANG	Lianyungang	Jiangsu
LIUCHOW	Liuzhou	Guangxi
LOSHAN	Leshan	Sichuan
LOYANG	Luoyang	Henan
MOKAN MOUNTAINS	Mogan Shan	Zhejiang
MT. OMEI	Emei Shan	Sichuan
NANKING	Nanjing	Jiangsu
PAOTOW	Baotou	Nei Monggol
PEHTAIHO (also Peitaihe)	Beidaihe	Hebei
PEKING	Beijing	
SHAOHSING	Shaoxing	Zhejiang
SHASHIH	Shashi	Hebei
SHIHCHIACHUANG (also Shihkiachwang)	Shijiazhuang	Hebei
SHIHHOTZU	Shihezi	Xinjiang
SIAN	Xi'an	Shaanxi
SOOCHOW	Suzhou	Jiangsu
SWATOW	Shantou	Guangdong
TACHAI	Dazhai	Shanxi
TACHING OIL FIELD	Daqing Oil Field	Heilongjiang
TAKANG OIL FIELD	Dagang Oil Field	Tianjin
TALIEN	Dalian (also Luda)	Liaoning
TATUNG	Datong	Shanxi
TIENTSIN	Tianjin	
TSINAN	Jinan	Shandong
TSINGTAO	Qingdao	Shandong
TSUNGHUA	Conghua	Guangdong
TSUNHUA	Zunhua	Hebei
TUNHUANG	Dunhuang	Gansu
TURFAN	Turpan	Xinjiang
TZUPO	Zibo	Shandong
URUMCHI	Urumqi	Xinjiang
WANHSIEN	Wan Xian	Sichuan

WEIFANG	Weifang	Shandong
WUSIH	Wuxi	Jiangsu
YANGCHOW	Yangzhou	Jiangsu
YENAN	Yan'an	Shanxi
YENTAI	Yantai	Shandong
YOYANG	Yueyang	Hunan

DYNASTIES-pinyin (old spelling)

夏 Xia (Hsia) c. 21st–16th century B.C.
商 Shang (Shang) c. 16th–11th century B.C.
西 Western Zhou (Chou) c. 11th century–771 B.C.
春 周 Spring and Autumn Period 770–476 B.C.
战 秋 国 Warring States Period 475–221 B.C.
秦 Qin (Chin) 221–206 B.C.
西 汉 Western Han (Han) 206 B.C.–A.D. 24
东 汉 Eastern Han (Han) 25–220
三 国 The Three Kingdoms 220–265
魏 Wei (Wei) 220–265
蜀 Shu (Shu) 221–263
吴 Wu (Wu) 222–280
西 晋 Western Jin (Tsin) 265–316
东 晋 Eastern Jin (Tsin) 317–420

南 北 朝 Southern and Northern Dynasties 420–589

夏商西春战秦西东三魏蜀吴西东南南	周秋国 汉汉国魏蜀吴晋晋北朝	朝 宋齐梁陈 朝北东西北北		

Southern and Northern
Dynasties 420–589
Southern Dynasties 420–589
Song (Sung) 420–479
Qi (Chi) 479–502
Liang (Liang) 502–557
Chen (Chen) 557–589
Northern Dynasties 386–581
Northern Wei (Wei) 386–534
Eastern Wei 534–550
Western Wei 535–556
Northern Qi (Chi) 550–577
Northern Zhou (Chou) 557–581
隋 Sui (Sui) 581–618
唐 Tang (Tang) 618–907
五 代 Five Dynasties 907–960
辽 Liao (Liao) 916–1125
宋 Song (Sung) 960–1279

北宋	Northern Song (Sung)	960–1127
南宋	Southern Song (Sung)	1127–1279
西夏	Western Xia (Hsia)	1038–1227
金	Jin (Kin)	1115–1234
元	Yuan (Yuan)	1271–1368
明	Ming (Ming)	1368–1644
	Hongwu (Hung Wu)	1368–1399
	Jianwen (Chien Wen)	1399–1403
	Yongle (Yung Lo)	1403–1425
	Hongxi (Hung Hsi)	1425–1426
	Xuande (Hsuan Teh)	1426–1436
	Zhengtong (Cheng Tung)	1436–1450
	Jingtai (Ching Tai)	1450–1457
	Tianshun (Tien Shun)	1457–1465
	Cheng Hua (Cheng Hua)	1465–1488
	Hongzhi (Hung Chih)	1488–1506
	Zhengde (Cheng Teh)	1506–1522
	Jiajing (Chia Ching)	1522–1567
	Longqing (Lung Ching)	1567–1573
	Wanli (Wan Li)	1573–1620
	Taichang (Tai Chang)	1620–1621
	Tianqi (Tien Chi)	1621–1628
	Chongzhen (Chung Cheng)	1628–1644
清	Qing (Ching)	1644–1911
	Shunzhi (Shun Chih)	1644–1662
	Kangxi (Kang Hsi)	1662–1723
	Yongzheng (Yung Cheng)	1723–1736
	Qianlong (Chien Lung)	1736–1796
	Jiaqing (Chia Ching)	1796–1821
	Daoguang (Tao Kuang)	1821–1851
	Xianfeng (Hsien Feng)	1851–1862
	Tongzhi (Tung Chih)	1862–1875
	Guangxu (Kuang Hsu)	1875–1908
	Xuantong (Hsuan Tung)	1908–1911

HOW TO PRONOUNCE CHINESE LETTERS

Following is a table of the Chinese phonetic alphabet showing pronunciation with approximate English equivalents. Letters in the Wade-Giles system are in parentheses.

"a" (a), a vowel, as in far;

"b" (p), a consonant, as in be;

"**c**" (ts), a consonant, as in "ts" in its; and

"**ch**" (ch), a consonant, as in "ch" in church, strongly aspirated;

"**d**" (t), a consonant, as in do;

"**e**" (e), a vowel, as "er" in her, the "r" being silent; but "**ie**," a diphthong, as in yes and "**ei**," a diphthong, as in way;

"**f**" (f), a consonant, as in foot;

"**g**" (k), a consonant, as in go;

"**h**" (h), a consonant, as in her, strongly aspirated;

"**i**" (i), a vowel, two pronunciations:
    1) as in eat
    2) as in sir in syllables with the consonants c, ch, r, s, sh, z and zh;

"**j**" (ch), a consonant, as in jeep;

"**k**" (k), a consonant, as in kind, strongly aspirated;

"**l**" (l), a consonant, as in land;

"**m**" (m), a consonant, as in me;

"**n**" (n), a consonant, as in no;

"**o**"(o), a vowel, as in "aw" in law;

"**p**" (p), a consonant, as in par, strongly aspirated;

"**q**" (ch), a consonant, as "ch" in cheek;

"**r**" (j), a consonant pronounced as "r" but not rolled, or like "z" in azure;

"**s**" (s, ss, sz), a consonant, as in sister; and "**sh**" (sh), a consonant, as "sh" in shore;

"**t**" (t), a consonant, as in top, strongly aspirated;

"**u**" (u), a vowel, as in too, also as in the French "u" in "tu" or the German umlauted "u" in "Muenchen";

"**v**" (v), is used only to produce foreign and national minority words, and local dialects;

"**w**" (w), used as a semi-vowel in syllables beginning with "u" when not preceded by consonants, pronounced as in want;

"**x**" (hs), a consonant, as "sh" in she;

"**y**" used as a semi-vowel in syllables beginning with "i" or "u" when not preceded by consonants, pronounced as in yet;

"**z**" (ts, tz), a consonant, as in zero; and "**zh**" (ch), a consonant, as "j" in jump."

—from *China Reconstructs,* March 1979

CELSIUS-FAHRENHEIT CONVERSION TABLE

Centigrade (Celsius)		Fahrenheit
−40°		−40°
−20°		− 4°
0°	Freezing Point	32°
10°		50°
20°		68°
30°		86°
40°		104°
50°		122°
60°		140°

70°	158°
80°	176°
90°	194°
100°	Boiling Point 212°

To convert Fahrenheit to Celsius subtract 32, multiply by 5, and divide by 9. To convert Celsius to Fahrenheit multiply by 9, divide by 5, and add 32.

To convert kilometers to miles, multiply by 6 and divide by 10.

MILE-KILOMETER CONVERSION TABLES

Miles	Kilometers	Kilometers	Miles
1	1.6093	1	.621
2	3.2186	2	1.242
3	4.8279	3	1.863
4	6.4372	4	2.484
5	8.0465	5	3.105
6	9.6558	6	3.726
7	11.2651	7	4.347
8	12.8744	8	4.968
9	14.4837	9	5.589
10	16.093	10	6.21
20	32.186	20	12.42
30	48.279	30	18.63
40	64.372	40	24.84
50	80.465	50	31.05
60	96.558	60	37.26
70	112.651	70	43.47
80	128.744	80	49.68
90	144.837	90	55.89
100	160.93	100	62.1
200	321.86	200	124.2
300	482.79	300	186.3
400	643.72	400	248.4
500	804.65	500	310.5
600	965.58	600	372.6
700	1126.51	700	434.7
800	1287.44	800	496.8
900	1448.37	900	558.9
1000	1609.3	1000	621.

(Prepared by Linda Malloy)

WEIGHTS AND MEASURES

China uses both the metric system and the Chinese system

1 gong-jin (kilogram)	= 2.2 pounds
1 jin or gun (catty)	= 1.33 pounds = .604 kg.

1 dan (picul) = 100 catties	= 133 pounds or 60.47 kg.
1 mi (meter)	= 39.37 inches
1 gong li (kilometer)	= .6 mile = 1 km.
1 li (Chinese mile)	= .3106 mile = ½ km.
1 mu	= .1647 acres
1 hectare	= 2.471 acres = 10,000 sq. meters
100 hectares	= 247.1 acre = 1 sq. km.
259 hectares	= 1 sq. mile

LEADERS

In early 1992, Li Peng was premier, Deng Xiaoping was usually described as "leader" or "elder statesman," and Jiang Zemin was general secretary of the Communist Party. Yang Shangkun was president.

GLOSSARY.....................................

arhats—Buddhists who have attained Nirvana.

bodhisattvas—Buddhist saints who have attained Nirvana but have returned to help others. See "What Is There to See and Do?"

CAAC—formerly China's only airline. See "Getting Around." Here used collectively for former CAAC regional airlines.

cadre—in Chinese *kanpu*, meaning "core element." Any person who plays a leadership role.

C.I.T.S.—China International Travel Service.

C.T.S.—China Travel Service (the travel agency for Overseas Chinese and Compatriots).

dagoba—similar to an Indian stupa, a bell-shaped tower under which is buried a Buddhist relic or the ashes of a monk.

Dist. A.P.—distance airport.

Dist. R.W.—distance railway station.

F.E.C.s—Foreign Exchange Certificates.

F.F.—Foreign Friend

feng-shui—literally, wind and water. Geomancy. The belief that the placement of buildings in relation to water, and the contours of the land, affects the fortunes of the people who live in or near them; in the case of tombs, the placement affects the fortunes of the descendants.

Food Street—term usually used for fast food, cheaper Chinese restaurants.

guanxi—connections. See "Local Customs."

H.K.—Hong Kong

J.V.—joint venture; a business arrangement involving several parties. China has entered into many joint ventures with foreign businessmen.

lohan—the Chinese word for *arhat*. or Buddhist Saint.

Luxingshe—the Chinese name for C.I.T.S.

Manchu—the group from northeast China who ruled China under the dynasty name *Qing*.

Distances Between Main Tourist Cities

(Shortest distance between cities by rail in kilometres)

	Beijing	Shanghai	Tianjin	Guangzhou	Nanning	Changsha	Shaoshan	Wuchang	Nanjing	Wuxi	Suzhou	Hangzhou	Jinan	Qingdao	Xi'an	Kunming	Chengdu	Chongqing	Zhengzhou	Shijiazhuang	Dalian	Shenyang	Changchun
Shanghai	1462																						
Tianjin	137	1325																					
Guangzhou	2313	1811	2450																				
Nanning	2565	2063	2702	1334																			
Changsha	1587	1187	1724	726	978																		
Shaoshan.	1718	1216	1855	755	1007	131																	
Wuchang	1229	1534	1366	1084	1336	358	489																
Nanjing	1157	305	1020	2116	2368	1492	1521	1229															
Wuxi	1334	128	1197	1939	2191	1315	1344	1406	177														
Suzhou	1376	86	1239	1897	2149	1273	1302	1448	219	42													
Hangzhou	1651	189	1514	1622	1874	998	1027	1356	494	317	275												
Jinan	494	968	357	2284	2536	1558	1689	1200	663	840	882	1157											
Qingdao	887	1361	750	2677	2929	1951	2082	1593	1056	1233	1275	1550	393										
Xi'an	1165	1511	1302	2129	2381	1403	1534	1045	1206	1383	1425	1700	1177	1570									
Kunming	3179	2677	3316	2216	1501	1592	1503	1950	2982	2805	2763	2488	3119	3512	1942								
Chengdu	2048	2353	2185	2544	1829	1920	1831	1887	2048	2225	2267	2542	2019	2412	842	1100							
Chongqing	2552	2501	2689	2040	1325	1416	1327	1774	2552	2729	2771	2312	2523	2916	1346	1102	504						
Zhengzhou	695	1000	832	1618	1870	892	1023	534	695	872	914	1189	666	1059	511	2453	1353	1857					
Shijiazhuang	283	1266	420	2030	2282	1304	1435	946	961	1138	1180	1455	298	691	923	2865	1765	2269	412				
Dalian	1238	2426	1101	3551	3803	2825	2956	2467	2121	2298	2340	2615	1458	1851	2403	4417	3286	3790	1933	1521			
Shenyang	841	2029	704	3154	3406	2428	2559	2070	1724	1901	1943	2218	1061	1454	2006	4020	2889	3393	1536	1124	397		
Changchun	1146	2334	1009	3459	3711	2733	2864	2375	2029	2206	2248	2523	1366	1759	2311	4325	3194	3698	1841	1429	702	305	
Harbin	1388	2576	1251	3701	3953	2975	3106	2617	2271	2448	2490	2763	1608	2001	2553	4567	3436	3940	2083	1671	944	547	242

Mongol—the group of people from north China who ruled China under the dynasty name *Yuan*.

neolithic—pertaining to the Stone-Age period in which man developed pottery, weaving, and agriculture, and worked with polished stone and metal tools.

penjing—the art of growing miniature trees and plants. Similar to Japanese *bonsai*.

P.L.A.—People's Liberation Army (currently being reorganized).

pinyin—the new system of romanizing the Chinese language now adopted as official.

pusa—the Chinese word for bodhisattva or Buddhist Saint, higher level than lohan.

qigong—Chinese yoga. Health and healing through breathing exercises and magnetism.

ren.—renovated.

R.M.B.—*ren min bi*—people's money, one of the terms used to refer to Chinese currency. R.M.B. is not the same as F.E.C., above.

stele—a large stone tablet used to commemorate an event, a life, or an important piece of writing.

Wade-Giles—the most commonly used of the old systems of romanizing the Chinese language.

W.C.—water closet. Toilet.

wok—a large, round pan fitted into a stove for cooking.

work unit—every salaried worker belongs to one of these.

X—telephone extension

¥—yuan, similar to a dollar. See "Budget."

Names of People in *pinyin* and Wade-Giles

Pinyin	*Wade-Giles*
Bainqen Lama	Panchen Lama
Cixi	Tzu Hsi, (Tsu-hsi, Qing Empress Dowager)
Deng Xiaoping	Teng Hsiao-ping
Feng Yuxiang	Feng Yu-hsiang (general)
Guan Yu	Kuan Yu (Three Kingdoms)
Guo Moruo	Kuo Mo Ruo
Hua Kuofeng	Hua Guo-feng (former Party chairman)
Jiang Jieshi	Chiang Kai-shek
Jiang Qing	Chiang Ching (widow of Mao Tse-tung)
Lin Biao	Lin Piao
Liu Shaoqi	Liu Shao-chi (former president)
Mao Zedong	Mao Tse-tung
Sun Yixian	Sun Yat-sen (father of republican China)
Xuan Zhang	Hsuan-tsang (Tang dynasty monk)
Yuan Shikai	Yuan Shih-kai (2nd president of China)
Zhong Shan	Chung Shan (the honorific name of Dr. Sun Yat-sen)
Zhou Enlai	Chou En-lai (former premier of China)
Zhu Yanzhang	Chu Yuan-chuan (first Ming Emperor)

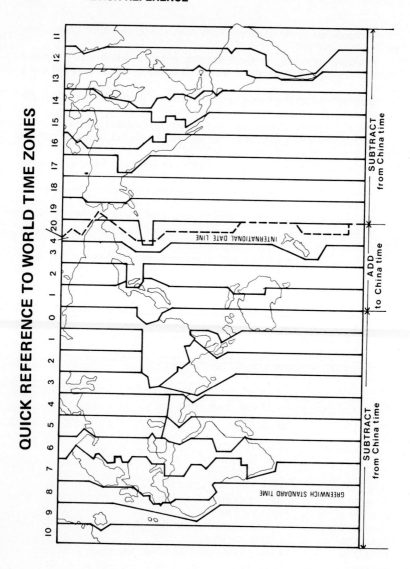

QUICK REFERENCE TO WORLD TIME ZONES

All of China is in one time zone. At 8 a.m. in China the time is 1 a.m. in West Germany or 7 a.m. in Singapore. The time in China is 13 hours later than in the eastern United States. For example, 8 a.m. in China is 7 p.m. Eastern Standard Time, or 6 p.m. Daylight Savings Time, the *previous* day in New York City.

BUDGET AND HOTEL QUICK REFERENCE

HOW MUCH MONEY SHOULD YOU TAKE TO CHINA?

Be aware that (a) only a few credit cards are accepted only by the larger and more expensive hotels and some restaurants, and stores for foreign visitors. Cash advances cost 4%. See "Important Addresses and Information." Find out before you go the latest regulations regarding credit card usage in China from your credit card company; (b) personal checks are not generally accepted, but some can be cashed at the Bank of China with some credit cards; (c) companies and embassies established in China can pay by check if known to the person cashing the check; (d) it takes five banking days to cable money to you in China, assuming everyone knows his job and has your passport number; (e) you might ask your embassy to cash a personal check, but I wouldn't count on it.

These all mean, of course, that you should take enough **cash or traveler's checks.** Cash brings a slightly lower foreign exchange rate than traveler's checks, leaving you with less money. But you might be able to haggle better with U.S. dollars in cash.

For current foreign exchange rates, check business newspapers, your local bank, or *China Daily*. For rates at press time, see below.

Prepaid travelers booking through a travel agent usually have to pay the full price of the tour prior to their arrival in China. You may have to pay extra at the end of your trip. A final accounting is tallied toward the end of the tour. If there are to be additional expenses, you are usually consulted during the trip. For example, flights delayed by weather might mean an option of paying for an additional day or cutting out another part of the tour.

Many travel agencies cover any small additional costs themselves rather than antagonize their clients. On the other hand, you might get some money back.

So how much money should you take to China?

Read ahead and then budget in addition to the price of your China tour:

¥ _____ (a) at least ¥500 per week for "unforeseen circumstances" that one hopes won't happen. How much would it cost if you lost your passport and had to spend a couple of extra nights in a hotel in Shanghai?

¥ _____ (b) for "optional tours" that might mean you would otherwise be wandering around the city alone.

¥ _____ (c) for whatever you want for shopping. It's painful to resist buying things you've watched being made, especially if you know they are more expensive at home; don't forget film and film processing (if you can't wait to do it before you get home).

¥ _____ (d) if you socialize a lot and enjoy buying a round of drinks in the evening.

¥ _____ (e) if you take people out to dinner.

¥ _____ (f) for laundry, cheap at modest hotels; more at international standard hotels.

¥ _____ (g) for a massage at a modest hotel barber shop, or for about ¼ of that at a public bath house.

¥ _____ (h) for a barber or hairdresser.

¥ _____ (i) for miscellaneous extras—overweight luggage, telephone calls, medical expenses, postage, photography, etc.

After you total this up, add about 20%, and you should have sufficient.

¥ _____ Total.

Pay-as-you-go travelers should budget in addition to the above:

¥ _____ (j) for a hotel room (one or two people). The highest prices are for luxury, international standard hotels. The lowest prices listed are for adequate but crude accommodations, almost always with private bath in the smaller cities. In the larger cities you may have to book an expensive hotel room.

¥ _____ (k) for food and drinks.

¥ _____ (l) for transportation (between and inside cities), permits, etc. Count on airport tax each time you leave China. Less energetic people tend to use taxis more, and could spend a maximum of ¥190 a day on taxis.

¥ _____ (m) for entrance fees to most tourist attractions.

¥ _____ (n) bus or boat tours

¥ _____ (o) C.I.T.S. charges.

¥ _____ (p) entertainment

¥ _____ (q) unforeseen circumstances like currency fluctuations, medical treatment, and price changes. Give yourself ample. Be sure you are covered by medical insurance.

¥ _____ **Grand Total.** Now figure out what that comes to in your own currency.

You should calculate 10% to 40% less on hotels and transportation if you're good at arguing.

Those who want to save money have to take much more time, and not care about the highest available standards of cleanliness and comfort.

If you go on your own, save first **before** going to China. Look for bargain airfares. Haggle with managers in travel agencies and airline offices (especially Air China, CAIL, KAL, PAL, SIA, and CAL). You have nothing to lose but your pride. Read the youth travel columns in newspapers. Talk to backpackers about cutting costs. Find out about flying as a courier. Check out travel agents in local Chinatowns. What about the train from London to Beijing via Moscow?

Or how about the special air rates between London and Hong Kong for British citizens? Or excursion fares? Across the Pacific, check out Euro Asia Express or Avia Travel. Look into tour prices from Canada. How about via Manila? C.I.T.S. and CAAC discount from December 1 to March 31 on some routes and tours. Hotels too.

Let the Chinese pay your way, or at least part of it. Go as a **teacher or foreign expert,** or while you are in China offer to teach at a school for a few months. The Chinese will hire qualified teachers more readily if you pay your own airfare to get there, and will give you a modest bit of pocket money besides, and possibly travel discounts. You'll get a much less superficial experience than as a tourist, and teaching can be very satisfying.

Organize your own tour group. In a group of 15 persons (sometimes 10), inclusive service in China is free for one to two travelers, and airlines might give one free seat.

In China

At each **hotel,** do not be afraid to *ask* if there are cheaper rooms. If the clerk says no, keep trying every day, or try other hotels. The Chinese might offer you the most expensive for your own comfort as well as for the higher revenue. Rooms on the uppermost floors are usually more expensive. *Argue* pleasantly. Tell the clerk you're a student (if you have your card), or a foreign expert (even if you've just given *one* lecture). Many hotels have dorms with up to 30 or 40 beds in a room for about ¥20 and up. Try hostels. Share rooms with friends, as most rooms cost the same for one guest as for two. As hotels in big cities are more expensive, stay away from the center of the city. Or take anything you can get for the first night, and then look around.

Book **hard-class train.** You might like it. If not, you can frequently upgrade your accommodations, if space is available, by paying more.

Travel with an Overseas Chinese friend and book through **C.T.S. Avoid** travel agents if you can.

Do not assume that the Chinese are giving you anything free. Always ask, "What is the charge?"

Go by **public bus or boat.** Some of these aren't bad. Some are filthy and noisy. See "Jiangmen" for one kind of boat. Some buses are air-conditioned and reasonable. The price difference between the regular ferry and the luxury tour boats on the Yangtze River is considerable. So are the standards of comfort and privacy. See "Yangtze Gorges."

Eat in bun or noodle shops or at market stalls. These cost considerably less than hotel restaurants and some of them are clean. One backpacker spent 2½ months in China eating cheaply at market stalls and never got sick. But others aren't so lucky.

Avoid tourist restaurants. Invite one of the young people trying to practice English on you to take you to a restaurant where ordinary people eat.

If you're traveling only a few kilometers by **taxi,** it may be cheaper to have your taxi wait than to hire a car by the day or the half-day. Ask about waiting time and maximum distances for the day rate.

Ask your hotel service desk or C.I.T.S. if a **tour bus** you can join goes to the tourist attractions. For one or two people, this may be cheaper than taking taxis. You might try to hitch free rides with tour groups. Or try to interest other individual travelers in sharing taxis or minibuses. How about renting a bicycle?

Stay with friends or relatives. Courtesy demands you take them presents, but this could be anything from a bag of fruit, candy, or cookies, to a video or refrigerator. See *Gifts* in "What to Take" and "Special for Overseas Chinese."

Foreign hitchhikers have traveled around China successfully, sleeping in hostels for local Chinese (after much persistent pleading), sometimes for less than ¥1 a night. (Take your own bedding and don't be surprised at bedbugs.)

Travel during low tourist season. The south is pleasant in the wintertime.

Search out backpackers, who are usually happy to exchange travel tips. Look for them in dormitories at hotels like the Bei Wei in Beijing, and the Chungking Mansions in Hong Kong.

RECENT PRICES

These are listed primarily to help you plan. Since the mid-1980s, China has been allowing market forces to set prices, and many of the following will go up or down. Yes, some prices might go *down* 10 to 50% in winter. Prices depend on supply and demand. Budget travelers should shop around for everything.

These prices will also help you avoid being ripped off by China's new class of private enterprisers, with whom you are expected to haggle over prices. Do start at one-quarter of the asking price and see what happens when you feign lack of interest, and don't pay more than you would in a government fixed-price store.

Most quotes here are FEC unless otherwise specified. Most hotels mentioned are top hotels.

Note that tourist hotels are usually paid in F.E.C.s.

10% service and 3 or 5% sales tax are added to bills in some joint venture restaurants and hotels.

Some establishments have two sets of prices—the higher for R.M.B.; the lower for F.E.C. This might change in 1993 if the FEC is phased out.

Always check your change and tab. Store clerks and waitresses might not be accurate.

Your highest prices are usually in the big cities, especially Beijing. Guangzhou is cheaper. The more expensive the hotel, the higher the cost of other services like laundry, food and hair cuts. US$1 = HK$7.8.

Businesses are named here to give you some options. Mention does not necessarily mean endorsement.

Collected in late 1991 and early 1992, prices listed here are subject to inflation, but they should give you an idea of what to expect if you add about 10–15%. In 1991, backpackers were able to manage on US$12 a day for room, food, and local transportation, so don't let the high figures scare you. Dormitory accommodations averaged ¥15 a night.

The black market rate is roughly ¥1 FEC to ¥1.10 RMB, but unless you are staying a long time we urge you to avoid it. It fluctuates and, especially after a devaluation of the yuan, is not worth fooling around with. It is subject to sleight-of-hand artists.

AIR FARES

Cheapest air fares from North America found so far: One Canadian dollar is roughly US$.85. Add US$18 tax for flights from the U.S., Can.$40 to each Canadian flight. Be sure to ask about special conditions, like advance payment, open return, restricted departure days. Maybe your own travel agent can match these prices.

International—economy-class return fare:
Los Angeles-Beijing March, 1992. Avia. US$1039.
New York-Beijing, May, 1992. InterPacific. $1372.
San Francisco-Beijing. May 1992. Euro-Asia. US$1215.
Toronto-Beijing March 1992. China Swan. Can. $1010.
Toronto-Beijing June, 1992. Conference Travel. As low as Can.
$1150.
Vancouver-Beijing return March, 1992. China Swan. Can. $800.
Domestic—one-way economy:
Beijing-Guangzhou ¥695; —Lhasa ¥1200; —Shanghai ¥420; Xi'an
¥370; —Urumqi ¥1005.
Guangzhou-Hangzhou ¥385; —Qingdao ¥660; —Urumqi —¥1360.
Hong Kong—one-way:
Beijing HK$1850; —Shanghai HK$1290; —Guangzhou HK$400.

AIRPORT TAX IN CHINA

¥60 for international and Hong Kong except from Shenzhen, which
charges ¥110 even for domestic flights.

BUSINESS CENTERS

Rental electric typewriter ¥25 per hour. Photocopy 50–80 fen
per page. Exhibition Centre Hotel.

Photocopy 50 fen per page. Domestic telex 1 minute ¥3; telex to
U.S. at ¥23 a minute. Minimum 3 minutes. Rental typewriter free. Qilu
Hotel, Jinan.

Printing 100 business cards ¥25–50 depending on speed. Portman
Shangri-La. Don't expect international standards.

CLINICS

Sometimes just the cost of medicines, otherwise cheap. Hospitals
could cost up to ¥300 a day.

COMMUNICATIONS

Here, too, you should shop around.

Fax to U.S., ¥24.80 a minute. Three-minute minimum, plus ¥18
first page, ¥6 each additional page. Shangri-La Hotel (Beijing).

At the Exhibition Centre Hotel, a fax cost ¥24.90 per minute to
Canada, ¥17.70 per minute to the U.S. Three-minute minimum, plus
¥6 per page plus 20%.

Expensive joint venture hotels like the Shangri-La, Traders, Palace, and Garden (Shanghai) charge .50 for **local telephone calls,** usually free.

Travelers on a budget would do well to check hotel service charges
on **long distance telephone calls** before calling. Those calling collect

or with an AT&T calling card or on a USA Direct telephone might find prices cheaper, especially for calls over three minutes. The local Telephone and Telecommunications office could be cheapest.

IDD: ¥22.50 per minute to U.S. and Canada, Qilu Hotel, Jinan.

Postage: Airmail letter ¥2 for 10 gm., ¥2.50 for 20 gms., ¥4.40 for 30 gms.; airmail postcard ¥1.60 to North America. Registration ¥3. Express ¥100 up to 500 gms. Cost of posting one 3'x5' wool carpet by surface from Kashi in farwest China to the U.S. ¥150 including registration.

Courier Service: UPS Shanghai to U.S. First 500 gms., ¥175; every additional 500 gms., ¥55. Goods needs export license and invoice.

FOOD AND BEVERAGES

Breakfast buffet: *Beijing:* Shangri-La and Holiday Inn Crowne Plaza ¥48. Tianping Lee Garden US$10. Chang Fu Gong ¥52. Tianlun Dynasty ¥50. Peace Hotel ¥35. Holiday Inn Lido ¥40; *Guangzhou:* White Swan ¥38; *Guilin:* Holiday Inn ¥42; *Shanghai:* Portman Shangri-La US$12, JC Mandarin ¥53.

Chinese and continental breakfasts are always cheaper. At the Shangri-La, Chinese breakfast is ¥30. At the New World Aster (Suzhou), Suzhouese Set Breakfast was ¥6 (congee, preserved vegetable, meat bun and tea.) Cantonese Set Breakfast was ¥8 (fried noodles, spring roll and tea.

Set dim sum breakfast, famous Banxi restaurant (Guangzhou) ¥15 per person for 12 or 13 dishes.

Many hotels like the Garden, Holiday Inn, and China in Guangzhou, the Tianlun Dynasty, Holiday Inn Lido and Jing Guang New World in Beijing, and the Yangtze and Hilton in Shanghai have **cheaper Chinese restaurants** or Food Streets. These are cleaner than locally run restaurants. One can get fried noodles or rice for ¥7.50–¥18 and filling congee for ¥6–¥14.

You can find much cheaper food if you go native. Meals in the Dai section of Jing Hong and in local restaurants in Yangshuo were less than ¥10 (including ¥1.50 for a liter of beer). You can fill yourself from ¥1 to ¥5 in stalls at street markets, which might or might not be clean.

Western Food: Pete's Place, **Exhibition Center Hotel.** Appetizers ¥20–25; soups ¥10–12; main courses ¥30–90; salads ¥12–29; sandwiches and omelettes ¥21–30; pasta ¥25–40; pizza ¥30; desserts ¥8–15; beverages ¥6–12; soft drinks ¥8–10; beer ¥10–13; aperitifs ¥19; cocktails ¥20.

Qilu Hotel, Qufu. Soup ¥4–4.50; appetizers ¥12–14; salads ¥6–16; sandwiches & burgers ¥10–15; entrees ¥12–25; egg and pasta ¥7–18; desserts ¥2.50–3.

Minim's de Paris (Beijing), not gourmet but filling. Set meals ¥60 and 70. Salads ¥35; pepper steak ¥28; charcoal grill ¥30. Roast turkey ¥25.

Holiday Inn Guilin Bake Sop, entrance outside hotel. 90 fen for a croissant.

The best western restaurant in Shanghai seems to be at the **Hilton.** It has cold appetizers ¥22–46; hot appetizers ¥18–32; soups ¥11–13; salads ¥14–28; sandwiches ¥22–39; burgers ¥29; international entrees ¥28–59; oriental entrees ¥19–57; desserts ¥17–21; cakes ¥14, 15. Ice cream ¥15; beverages ¥11–18; house wine by the glass ¥18.

Fancy Chinese Banquets: ¥40 per person (minimum 5 people). Highly recommended Fisherman's Dinner, Laoshan Hotel, Qingdao.

The Guangzhou Overseas Tourist Corporation suggests ¥90–100 each for a special banquet. (It budgets ¥30 and up for a regular meal for tour groups.) The **Royal Garden** (Guilin) says ¥70 per head (table of 10) includes snake and turtle. The **Guishan** (Guilin) has one for ¥488 (10 people) including suckling pig. The **Universal** can provide a Cantonese banquet for ¥250 a table.

Bar: Beijing International—cocktails ¥23–30; aperitif ¥20; sherry and port ¥22–23; whiskey ¥25–80; gin and vodka ¥27–28; rum ¥25–28; cognac ¥38–80–900; liqueur ¥23–25; beer ¥8–14; soft drinks ¥10. **Room mini-bar, Palace Hotel** (Beijing). Tiny bottles. Spirits ¥35–45; wines ¥49; champagne ¥285; beer ¥18 and 22; soft drinks and juices ¥16–24; Mars bar or Toblerone ¥20; mixed nuts or cashew nuts ¥15.

Beijing International Hotel, Chivas Regal, Black Labele, Old Parr ¥50; Martell Cognac V.S.O.P. ¥30; Remy Martin VSOP ¥28; martini ¥22; vodka ¥20; Four Roses ¥18; Canadian V.O. ¥16; Campari ¥15; sodas ¥9 and 12; beer ¥9 and ¥15.

LAUNDRY

	Huiquan Dynasty (Qingdao)	Portman Shangri-La (Shanghai)
Undershirt	2.00	5.00
Trousers	5.00	20.00
Shirt	3.50	18–22.00
Underpants	2.00	5.00
T-Shirt	2.50	14.00
Dress	5.00	28.00
2 pc. pyjamas	4.00	16.00
Skirt	5.00	22.00+
Handkerchief	1.50	4.00
Socks	1.50	5.00

Drycleaning: two-piece suit ¥40 at **Portman Shangri-La,** ¥30 at **Shangri-La** (Beijing), and ¥16 at the **Exhibition Centre Hotel** (Beijing).

If laundry prices are too high, go buy underwear and even dress shirts for not much more, sometimes less.

LUGGAGE STORAGE

Most frequently free. A few hotels and airports charge ¥1–3 per day depending on size of bag, but in many hotels, it's free.

RECREATION

Shangri-La Hotel (Beijing), karaoke bar ¥65 per person. Private karaoke room ¥1500 minimum for whole evening. Squash ¥20 an hour. Swimming pool free for hotel guests, ¥35 for outsiders.

Qilu Hotel (Jinan); tennis ¥30 an hour daytime, ¥45 an hour after dark. Use of 10-piece gymnasium ¥10. Billiards ¥30 per hour.

Guishan Hotel, (Guilin); 11-piece gym ¥20, massage ¥55 an hour.

SALARIES

Attendants in many hotels make about ¥300 basic a month plus about ¥50 bonus; **Liuhua Hotel** (Guangzhou) pays them ¥400 average a month. Doctors take home ¥250 a month. An American teacher is paid ¥30 RMB an hour teaching English in a 4-star hotel in Guilin. Performing musicians get about ¥35 a night.

The per capita annual income in Guangdong, the highest in China is ¥1143 for farmers and ¥2530 for urban and township residents.

SHOPPING

Many U.S. name-brand garments are made here, and overruns and seconds are on sale. The street markets are cheapest if you haggle. One in Beijing had Ann Klein silk blouses for ¥100, good patterned silk skirts for ¥110 (but local expatriates insisted *they* could have paid ¥90). Late 1991 silk bomber jackets were ¥60–80 at the Huating Market in Shanghai. They were selling in Friendship Stores for ¥150 (Guangzhou) and ¥260 (Beijing). And silk dress shirts in many solid colors were going for ¥85–100.

Last winter, down jackets were about ¥110; 3/4 length down coats ¥165–195; men's cashmere sweaters were ¥200 to 550; cashmere jackets ¥750; and cashmere coats ¥1440. Silk sweaters ¥150 and up. Two-Piece long silk underwear ¥68–100. Handmade patchwork comforters were about ¥300. All in the Friendship Store, Beijing.

Good buys in antiques made since 1796 if you're careful. Tiny brass hammers with certificates saying they were 150 years old were marked at ¥150 each at the antique store near the Lijiang Hotel, (Guilin) but after some discussion they sold for ¥75. The first asking price at a nearby free market for the same was ¥10 to ¥37 with no certification. So do look around.

Haggling in markets in general should start at something ridiculously low like 25%.

SIGHTSEEING

Entrance fees to tourist attractions usually ranged from 50 fen to ¥10. Sometimes there were additional fees of about ¥10 to see something special inside; for example, to get into the grounds of the **Temple of Heaven** is only 50 fen, but entrance fees to some buildings inside were ¥2 and ¥5 in addition.

To go up to the Rostrum at **Tiananmen Gate** where Mao proclaimed the People's Republic of China costs ¥30.

Day tours to the **Great Wall** and **Ming Tombs** range from ¥12 for Chinese-speaking people to ¥150 for only one person with an English speaking guide including lunch from the big hotels. The more people in the group, the cheaper it usually is. Still, it was ¥40 with English-speaking guide from the Qiaoyuan, Longtan, and Xinqiao Hotels (for backpackers).

City tour—¥180 each, minimum two people; one-day Zhaoqing ¥200 each minimum two. Baiyun Hotel (Guangzhou).

Li River Cruise, booked from hotel ¥175. Guilin. Includes lunch and bus 45 minutes to quay and return from Yangshuo to Guilin.

A **two-hour cruise** on Taihu lake in Wuxi could cost ¥10 per person in a group tour.

TIPPING

This is not officially allowed, and some attendants will refuse tips. For porters in hotels ¥1–1.50 each bag or ¥3–5 per load, depending on the quality of the hotel. Porters at train stations have set fees.

Guides would like tips, and travel agents encourage the giving of tips so service will be better. One Canadian travel agency suggest ¥20 per day per guide (or driver) per tourist. I think this should be a maximum, as it almost equals a salary.

TRANSPORTATION

Airport Transfers arranged through hotels: Beijing: US$38 for China World and Traders; ¥120 Minzu Hotel, ¥196 Shangri-La. Guilin: Royal Garden ¥70. Shanghai: Hilton ¥61. CAAC bus from airport to town much cheaper (about ¥5).

Bicycles: Beijing ¥25 a day, Exhibition Centre Hotel. ¥10 for 5 hours, Minzu Hotel. ¥5–¥10 per day, Beijing Tourism Administration.

Public Buses within Beijing 10 fen to ¥1.50 depending on distance; subway 50 fen anywhere. Buses Hong Kong–Xiamen US$43,

Hong Kong–Zhaoqing $38. (Travel Advisers, H.K.); Kunming-Dali ¥27 (Camellia Hotel). Tourist buses Suzhou-Hangzhou ¥60.

Cable Car Taishan ¥12 oneway.

Canoe ¥15 per person per day. Yangshuo.

Donkey Carts have to be negotiated beforehand. Roughly ¥1 per km per ride.

Pedicabs have to be negotiated beforehand. Roughly ¥1 per km per ride.

Taxi in Beijing, with a flagfall of ¥12 and ¥2.00 per km, it was very expensive for short trips. From the Sheraton to the Beijing International is now ¥20 by taxi. Still some ¥1 and ¥1.60 per km taxis, but also some ¥3 per km. Check before you get in.

In Guangzhou, flagfall could be ¥4.20, ¥4.60, or ¥4.80 depending on the per km rate ¥1.20, ¥1.40 or ¥1.60 respectively. In Shanghai, most taxis start at ¥14.40 for ¥1.60 per km. A few are cheaper.

Parking in front of CAAC in Beijing, ¥5 an hour.

Gasoline ¥2 a litre, ¥8 a gallon in Beijing.

Trains Hong Kong–Guangzhou express US$36. (Travel Advisers, H.K.) **#3 Beijing–Moscow,** second class ¥821, first class ¥1150 and deluxe class ¥1320. Leaves Wednesdays. Takes 5 days. (C.I.T.S.) **#19 Beijing–Moscow** via Shenyang. second class ¥794, deluxe ¥1268. Leaves Tuesdays. 6 days. (C.I.T.S.) **Beijing–Guangzhou** soft sleeper ¥563, hard ¥296; –Shanghai soft ¥459, hard ¥241; –Urumqi soft ¥849, hard ¥446; –Xi'an soft ¥347, hard ¥182. **Guangzhou–Hong Kong** soft class express train ¥117. (Night boat ¥111, 2–4 to a cabin). **Guilin–Guangzhou** soft class sleeper on tourist train ¥180. 15 hours. ¥150 plain. Guilin–Hong Kong flight ¥680 or HK$1000. Always full. Shanghai-Suzhou soft seat about ¥15.

TRAVEL AGENTS

Booking train ¥6, booking plane ¥5. Qilu Hotel, Jinan.

Booking train ¥30 a ticket. Palace Hotel: ¥15 a ticket Shanghai Hilton. For reconfirming plane tickets, hotel ticketing services seem to be better than government travel agents. Prices for services by travel agents range considerably depending on each city.

Service fees of travel agencies range widely depending on cities. A guide for two people for an 8-hour day ranges from ¥40 to ¥100. Booking a train can range from ¥5 to ¥40.

Guide/interpretor ¥100 a day for one guest plus ¥10 each additional person; booking plane ticket ¥25; reconfirming plane ticket ¥15; booking train ¥20. CITS Beijing.

All-inclusive tours from North America:

14 days from Vancouver from Can. $1739–2195 depending on season. Shanghai, Suzhou, Qufu, Tai'an, Jinan, Beijing. Chinapac.

10 days from U.S. West Coast, Beijing, Xian, Shanghai from US$1499, winter departures. Orient Flexi-Pax Tours.

All-inclusive tours booked in Asia:

25 days Beijing–Urumqi, one-way surface. US$2710. 8 days Hong Kong–Lhasa US$189. Weekly departures.

10 days, Hong Kong, Xian, Beijing, Shanghai, Guilin, H.K. US$1673. The Travel Advisers (Hong Kong).

17 days Hong Kong, Guangzhou, Guiyang, Kaili, Rongjiang, Guilin. $2816. Air from U.S. about $1210. Asian Pacific Adventures.

8 days drive/fly back—Kathmandu–Lhasa–Kathmandu. US$900. Fly both ways $1025. Includes transportation, only breakfasts in all hotels, entrance fees. Visas extra. Yangrima Trekking & Mountaineering (Kathmandu).

VISAS

Visas from a Chinese consulate: Can.$50. U.S.$10.

C.I.T.S. (Hong Kong) HK$150 (within 3 working days); HK$320 (within one working day) for U.S. citizens.

Mongolian Transit Visa US$24. Russian Visa $58 (takes 3 weeks). The Travel Advisers (Hong Kong).

HOTELS

Prices are quoted in F.E.C.'s, H.K., or U.S. dollars depending upon the information received from hotels. F.E.C. prices are lower than R.M.B. prices. Surcharges of 10 to 15% could be added in some hotels. (Some of these hotels include these taxes in the quoted price.) Payment however is usually made in F.E.C.'s, but this might change soon.

The agency from whom you book your hotel should be able to tell you the latest price, but don't count on it unless the hotel is top international standard. Agents have trouble getting information too.

Please note that the telephone numbers are the latest we could possibly obtain. In the late 1980s, China has been in the process of upgrading its telephone service, and therefore changing many of its telephone numbers.

Hotel prices have been bouncing since mid-1989. Even at press time, some hotels were making readjustments. Until prices stabilize with higher hotel occupancies, do expect fluctuations and price wars. If in doubt, contact the hotel and haggle. The following prices should be considered maximums for rooms. Few guests pay these prices. Most get at least 10% discount upon asking. The prices in parenthesis are recent discounts. All prices are subject to change.

I regret that we could not get all hotel prices. We write to every one of them, but some do not answer. Some like to keep their prices flexible and secret. * indicates 1991 prices where I could not get more recent ones. These will give you a general idea of what to expect.

$ means US$ unless otherwise specified. Most beds in a dorm for backpackers range from ¥10 to ¥20. *One US$ = $7.8 HK.*

	telephone	*rate in F.E.C.s.*	*page*
Anshan:			
Anshan	514066		184
Shengli	27991, 27911		185
Anshun:			
Hongshan	23454		298
Anyang:			
Anyang	23575	+18.75 group rate	186
Baotau:			
Baotau	26612	*$20	188
Qingshan	24615		188
Beidaihe:			
Beidaihe Hotel for Diplomatic Personnel	441287	*$20	190
Jinshan	41678	¥80–180	190
Beijing:			
Beijing	5137766	$60–100 ($50–90)	216
Beijing Airport Movenpick	4565588	$48 (10%)	217
Beijing Grace	4362288	$75–120 ($45–60)	217
Beijing International	5126688	$95	217
Beijing-Toronto	5002266	$80–90 (10%)	217
Bei Wei	3012266	¥110–160	217
Chang Fu Gong	5125711, 5125555	$110–140 (20%)	217
China World	5052266	$150 ($75)	217
Diaoyutai	866250, 8031188	$140	217
Exhibition Center	8316633	$35–65	217
Fragrant Hill	285256	$70 (20–30%)	
Friendship	8498888	$40–60 ($20–60)	218
Grand Hotel	5137788	$150–170 (20%)	218

Great Wall Sheraton	5005566	$110–135 (35%)	218
Guang Hua	5018866	¥150 (20%)	
Haoyuan	5125557	¥100–220	218
Holiday Inn Crowne Plaza	5133388	$120–130 (3rd night free)	218
Holiday Inn Lido	5006688	$120–130	219
Hong Kong-Macao	5012288	$100–140 ($45)	
Huadu	5001166	¥190 (170)	219
Jianguo	5002233	$90 (83)	219
Jing Guang New World	5018888	$110–180 (60–100)	219
Kunlun	5003388	$110–135 (85–110)	220
Landmark	5016688	$29 (26)	220
Longtan		¥68	220
Ming Yuan	654931 X3095	¥100	220
Minzu	6014466	¥195–240	
New World Tower	5007799	$85 ($52)	220
Overseas Chinese Hotel	4016688		220
Palace	5128899	$105–155	220
Parkview Tiantan	7012266, 7012277	$70–90 ($40–45)	
Peace	5128833	$98 (70)	220
Qiaoyuan	1338861	¥60–80	221
SAS Royal	4081893	$100–110	
Sara	513666	$140–160	221
Shangri-La	8412211	$130–180 (59–89)	
Summer Palace	2581144	¥100	221
Rainbow	3012266	$30–50 (25–35)	
Tianlun	5138888	$70	222
Tianping	5158855	$100–120 (20%)	222
Traders	5052277	$120 (50)	
Xinqiao	5128925	$240 (20%)	222
Youth Hostal	4015882	$25–30	
Changchun:			
Changbaishan	883551, 882003		228
Nanhu	883571		228
Provincial Chunyi	37917		228
Changsha:			
Huatian	442888	*$50–100	233
Lotus	401888	*¥120–140	233

Shaoshan	2127	*¥50	
Xiangjiang	468888	*¥110–120	233
Changzhou:			
Jiang Nan Chun	603666	¥140	234
Changzhou Grand	602641, 609988	$45	234
Chengde:			
Diplomatic Missions	221970, 221984		
Qiwanglou	223528	*$45–55	239
Yunshan	226161-2	*¥220	239
Chengdu:			
Chengdu	444112, 443312	*$40–50	245
Jinjiang	582222	$40–50 (30–40)	244
Minshan International	583333	*¥211	245
Sichuan	661115		
Sichuan College of Education	53981 X19		
Chongqing:			
Congqing Binguan	354491, 49901	¥140	249
Chongqing Fandian	49301	$35 (27)	
Holiday Inn Yangtze	483380	$65	249
Shaping Grand	663194, 663293	¥140	252
Renmin (People's)	351421	¥140	249
Yuzhou	811829	*¥100–150	250
Dali:			
Dali		¥18–60	
Dalian:			
Banchuidao	235131, 272533	$50	252
Furama	230888	$125 (80)	252
Holiday Inn	808888	$75–85	253
International	238238	$65	252
Regent	282811	$60–70 (40–50)	253
Nanshan	238751		253
Datong:			
Datong G.H.	532476		257
Yungang Hotel	521601	*$30–38	257
Dazu:			
Dazu		¥90–100	259
Beishan		¥90–100	259
Dunhuang:			
Dunhuang	2415, 2538	¥130	262
Solar Energy	2312, 2306	$35–40 ($20)	262

Emei:

Hong Zhu Shan	33888	*$20–40	263

Foshan:

Foshan	353338, 367923		265
Golden City	357228	HK$380–450	265
Overseas Chinese	223828	HK110–230	265
Rotating Palace	2856722		
Xiqiao	56799		

Fushun:

Friendship	22181	*¥138	267
Fushun	24481	*¥50	267

Fuzhou:

Donghu	557755		270
Foreign Trade Centre Hotel	550154	$70	270
Hot Spring	551818	*$40–52	270
Lakeside	539888	$80	270

Guangzhou:

Bai Yun	3333998	(H)$75; (L)¥178	284
China	6666888	(H) $190; (L)$90	284
Dong Fang	6669900	(H)$100–175; (L)$65–105	284
Garden	3338989	(H)$190–210; (L)$85–100	284
Guangdong Victory	8862622	(H)¥215–(L)¥132	284
Guangzhou	3338168	(H)$65–(L)$25	284
Holiday Inn City Center	7766999	(H)$190–200; (L)$100–140	285
Holiday Inn Riverside	7779709		285
Hotel Equatorial	6672888	(H)$180–200; (L)$75–90 (45–55)	285
Landmark	3355988	(H)$140; (L)$75–85 (40%)	285
Liu Hua	6668800	(H)¥336–350; (L)¥150–165	285

Parkview Square	6665666	(H)$140–180; (L)$45–90	286
Plaza Canton	4418888	(H)$130–140; (L)$70–80	285
Ramada	7772988	$95–115 (50%)	
White Swan	8886968	(H)$180; (L)$90	286
Youth Hostel	8888251		286
Guilin:			
Dangui (Osmanthus)	334300, 332261	¥156	293
Garland	332511	$45–50 (20%)	293
Gui Shan	443388	$90–100 (30%)	293
Holiday Inn Guilin	223950	$90–100 (20%)	293
Hotel Universal	228228	$32–49	294
Li River	222881		294
Park	228899	$70–90	294
Plaza	442488	$80–85 (50–60)	294
Ronghu (Banyan)	223811	$55 (20%)	294
Royal Garden	442411	$85–105 (50%)	293
Sheraton Guilin	225588	$90–100 ($60)	294
Windsor Seven Stars	442311	$55–70	
Yangshuo	2260	¥60	294
Guiyang:			
Huaxi	551129	¥50–180 (40–64)	298
Park	622888	*¥120	298
Plaza	626285	*¥120	298
Haikou:			
Haikou Hotel	72266, 72221		301
International Financial Centre	73088, 74099	*$36–85	301
Haikou Tower	72990, 73962	*$30–44	301
O.C. Hotel	72776	*$43	301
Handan:			
Handan	25911		302
Hangzhou:			
Dragon	554488	$100–110 (95–105)	309
Friendship	777888	$65	309

Huangang	771324	*¥180	309
O.C. Hotel	23401	*¥155–137	309
Shangri-La	777951	$100–110 (72–108)	309
Wanghu	771024	$40–60	309
Xin Qiao	776688		310
Zhejiang	25601, 777988	*$23–37	310
Harbin:			
Friendship Palace	418001		313
International	31441, 33001		313
Peace Village	220101		313
Swan	220201	*¥160–260	313
Hefei:			
Anhui	331100		315
Anhui Friendship	336948, 331707		315
Daoxinglou	252548	*$45	315
Jianghuai	52221	*$25	315
Luyang	331133	*$45	315
Hohhot:			
Inner Mongolia	664233	*$24	321
Zhaojun	662211	*$30	322
Huangshan:			
Beihai (North Sea)	2555	*$61	324
Cloudy Valley	2444		323
Jade Screen	2385, 2330	*¥120	324
Taoyuan (Peace Spring)	2295		324
Xihai	2200, 2555		324
Jiangmen:			
Crystal Palace	373288	*HK$318–368	325
Donghu (East Lake)	333611	*¥102–445	325
Jiayuguan			
Changcheng	25233	$25	327
Jiayuguan	26258	$25	327
Jilin:			
Milky Way	241780		328
Xi Guan	243141		328
Jinan:			
Minghu	556688	¥180	332
Pearl	615111	$40	332
Qilu	47961	¥175–225	332
Shandong Teachers University	643711	$11	332
Jingdezhen:			
Jingdezhen Binguan	225954, 225953		334
Jingdezhen Fandian	222301		334

Jinghong:

Jinghong		*¥24–26	
Xishuangbanna	2524, 2969	¥60–110	345
Banna Building		¥28	

Jiujiang:

Nanhu	225041, 225042		334

Kaifeng:

Dongjing	33313	$18.75 group	338
Kaifeng	25188, 23901		338

Kashgar:

Kashgar	2367, 2368	¥88	340
Qiniwak		¥70	341
Seman	2129, 2060	¥70	341

Kunming:

Camelia	23000	¥78	345
Golden Dragon	33104, 33015		345
Green Lake	22192, 23514		345
Kunming	22063, 23918	¥140	345

Lanzhou:

Lanzhou	28321, 22985	*¥120–180	352
Jincheng	27931	¥198	352

Leshan:

Jia Zhou	22301, 22419		354
Jiu Ri Reng	2850		354

Lhasa:

Banak Shol	23829		364
Holiday Inn Lhasa	22221, 32221	$46–74	364
Kirey	23462		364
Sunlight	22227		
Tibet	24966, 23738	*$34–46	364

Lianyungang:

Shenzhou	310080, 310088	¥140–160	
Tian Ran Ju	51688	¥154–198	

Liuzhou:

Liuzhou Grand	23854	*¥60–90	

Luoyang:

Friendship	22111, 22689	*$39	368
Garden	21682, 22651	*¥120	381
Peony	413690	$30 group	381

Lushan:

Lulin	282100, 282424		384
Lushan Hotel	282932, 282060		
Lushan Mansion	282860, 282160		384

Nanjing:

Central	400888, 400666	$60–80	394
Dingshan	801868	$49	394
Jingling	742888, 741999	$80–120	395
Mandarin Chamber	202555, 202988	$48	395
Nanjing	634121	$50	395
Victory	648181	¥120	395

Nanning:

Ming Yuan	28923		398
Xi Yuan	29923		398

Nantong:

Nantong	518989	¥260–340
Tian Nan	518151	¥140

Ningbo:

Asia Garden	366888	$55 (45)	401
O.C. Hotel	363175	*$26	402
Ningbo	366334	*¥100	401

Qingdao:

Badaguan	364822, 364888		406
Haitian	371888	$90–110	406
Huanghai	270215		406
Huiquan	279279, 279215	$78–88	406
O.C. Hotel	286738	*¥165–215	406
Stone Cliffs	597888	¥300	406

Quanzhou:

Golden Fountain	225078		411
O.C. Hotel	222192	*¥80–90	411

Qufu:

Apricot Terrace	411539		416
Queli	411303	$60	416

Sanya:

Sanya International Hotel	73068, 74041

Shanghai:

Cherry Holiday Villa	2758350		431
City	2551133	$75–95 (48)	431
Cypress	2558868	$40	431
Equatorial	2791688	$110	431
Galaxy	2755888	$45 (10%)	431
Garden	4331111	$125–165 (100)	431
Holiday Inn Yinxing	2528856, 252871	$70–130 (50%)	431
Hua Ting	4391818, 4391380	$36	432
Jin Jiang	2582582	$45–65 (10%)	432

Jin Jiang Tower	4334488, 471235	$75–100	432
Longman	6623700	$40–45	432
New Garden	4329900		432
Nikko Longbai	2559111	$100–110 ($77)	432
Novotel Shanghai	4701688		
Ocean	5458888	$60–85 (20%)	432
Olympic	4391391	¥220	433
Park	3275225	¥177–250	433
Peace	3211244	$45–56 (15%)	433
Portman	2798888	$105–145 (72–98)	433
Qianhe	4700000		
Qing Nian Hui	3261040	¥170–210	433
Seagull	3251500	¥170–175	433
Shanghai	4712712	$50 (20%)	433
Shanghai Hilton	2550000	$120–155 (100)	433
Shanghai International Airport	2558888, 2558866	$50 (39)	434
Shanghai JC Mandarin	2791888	$125–185 ($75)	434
Shanghai Mansions	3246260	¥240 (15%)	434
Sheraton Hua Ting	4396000	$65–95	434
Westin	2758888	$100–120 (20%)	434
Xiqiao	4328800	$80 (10–20%)	435
Yangtze	2750000	$85–130	435
Shantou:			
International	251212	*$68–87	439
Longhu	260706	$72 (48)	439
Shaoguan:			
Green Lake Villa	74887	*$25	441
Jin Yuan Villa	668800	*¥70	441
Shaoguan	81870, 81871	*¥70	441
Shaoxing:			
Shaoxing	35881		443
Shenyang:			
Phoenix	466507	¥220	446
Rose	449941	¥220	446
Zhongshan	333888	$60–	446
Shenzhen:			
Bamboo Garden	533138	*HK$290	448
Century Plaza	220888	*HK$500–750	449

Guang Dong	228339	*HK$390–430	449
Forum	236333	*HK$560–770	449
Marina Ming Wah	689968	HK$400–620	449
Nan Hai	692888	*HK$420–850	449
Shangrila	561188		
Shenzhen Bay	770111	HK$450–550	449
Shijiazhuang:			
Hebei	615961	¥80–180	451
Suzhou:			
Bamboo Grove	225601	$70–100	460
Nanlin	227651, 224641	$45–54	460
Nanyuan	227661	$50–65 (35–50)	
New World Aster	731888	$85–95	459
Suzhou	224646	¥208	460
Xucheng	331928	$36–40	460
Tai'an:			
O.C. Hotel	228112	¥180 (160)	462
Taishan	334694, 224694	¥120–170	463
Shenqi	223827, 333866	¥260 (220)	463
Taishan (Guangdong):			
Garden	23148, 25668		464
Stone Flower Mountain	25834	*$5	465
Taishan	26888	*¥118	465
Taiyuan:			
Taiyuan Grand	443901	*¥167–185	
Yingze	443211	*$31–35	469
Tianjin:			
Astor	311688	*$65	474
Crystal Palace	310567	*$70–80	474
Friendship	310372-3	*$45	475
Hyatt Tianjin	318888	*$80–100	475
InterTech	319115	*$25–30 (20–25)	475
Sheraton Tianjin	343388	*$75–85	475
Tianjin No. 1	316438	*¥210	475
Victory	985833	*$45	475
Turpan:			
Oasis	22491	¥100–152	490
Turpan	22025		479

Urumqi:

Friendship	268088, 267512	¥120–150 (110)	482
Holiday Inn Urumqi	225157, 217077	$70–85	482
O.C. Hotel	267970, 24406, 70530		

Weifang:

Weifang	222981		484
Yuan Fei	226901	¥120–170	484

Weihai:

Dongshan	222712	*$40	486
Weihaiwei	232542	$51 (39)	486

Wuhan:

Jianghan	21253, 23998		490
Qingchuan	411141, 444361	*$30–40	490
Yangtze	562828	$53–69 ($42)	491

Wuxi:

Hubin	668812, 603824	$40–45 (35–60)	493
Liangxi	226812	¥120	493
Milido	665665	$50	493
Taihu (Jing Minglou)	607888	$50	493
Wuxi Grand	666789	$60 (55)	494

Xiamen:

Gulong	225280		497
Holiday Inn Harbor View	220313, 236592	US$95–150	497
O.C. Hotel	225602	$49	497
Lujiang	222922	$35–54	497
Xiamen Mandarin	623333	$65–95	498
Xiamen Plaza	558888		
Xindeco	621666	*$61–77	498

Xi'an: lots of jivi hotels in $30–50 range

Bell Tower	29201, 718760	$50–60 (45–55)	511
China Merchant	718988	*$50–75	
Dynasty	712718	*$60–85	
Golden Flower	332981	*$90–110	512
Grand New World	716868	$100–120 (80–100)	512
Holiday Inn Xi'an	721882, 334280	¥390	512
Hyatt Xi'an	712020	*$130–190	512
Jianguo	338888	$65 (50)	512
Lee Gardens	741370	$60–80	512
Merchants	718988		512
New World	719988	*$55–95	513

Sheraton Xi'an	741888	$90–650 (69–450)	513
Tang Cheng	711165, 54171	$216	513
Tang Hua Garden	711111	$105–125	513
Xi'an	711351	*$30–35	513
Xidu	715118		
Xinhui:			
Kui Yuan	664801		515
Xinhui	663700		515
Xining:			
Qinghai	44365		517
Xuzhou:			
Nanjiao	22371, 38980	¥133–177	
Yan'an:			
Yan'an	213122		520
Yangzhou:			
Qiong Hua	231321	US$42–46 ($31–38)	528
Xiyuan	344888	¥140	528
Yangzhou	342611	¥150	528
Yantai:			
O.C. Hotel	224431, 246919		533
Yantai	248468	¥180–240	533
Yantai Shan	224491, 224493	¥160	533
Zhifu	248422	¥160–180	533
Yinchuan:			
Ningxia	45131		536
Yinchuan	23053, 22615		536
Yixing:			
Yixing	702811, 702383	*¥105	538
Yueyang:			
International Bldg.	24811	*¥100	538
Zhaoqing:			
Locust Flower	226688		539
O.C. Hotel	232952		540
Songtao	24412		539
Zhengzhou:			
International Hotel	556600	$26.25 group rate	544
Regent Plaza	28046		544
Zhenjiang:			
Jinshan	232970	$30	548
Runzhou	231055, 226061	$35 (28)	548

Zhongshan:

Cuiheng	824091, 824077		549
Fu Hua	822034		550
Kinghua	824688		
Zhongshan Hot Spring Resort	822811		550
Zhongshan International	824788	*HK$338– 380	550

Zhuhai:

Garden	332568, 333968		552
Gongbei Palace	886833		552
Shi ching Shan	333518		
Zhuhai Holiday Resort	332038	HK$368 (250)	552
Zhuhai Hotel	333718, 332973		552

Zibo:

Zibo	213341

HOTEL CHAINS AND SOME NORTH AMERICAN TOLL-FREE NUMBERS

Forum Hotels International: 1–800–327–0200
Hilton International: 1–800–268–9275
Holiday Inn: 1–800–HOLIDAY
Hyatt International Corp.: 1–800–228–9000; 1–800–233–1234
Leading Hotels of the World: 1–800–223–6800
New World Hotels International: 1–800–227–5663 (U.S.)
Movenpick-Radisson Hotels: Runzhou
Nikko: 1–800–645–5687
Novotel/Sofitel: 1–800–221–4542
Okura: (NY) (212) 755–0733, (LA) (213) 388–1151
Omni: 1–800–THE OMNI
Par Pacific: 1–800–327–8585
Peninsula Group: SABRE SR13132
Preferred Hotels: 1–800–323–7500
Ramada Worldwide Reservations: In the U.S., 1–800–228–2828; Canada, 1–800–268–8998
SAS: see UTELL below
SARA: see UTELL below or 1–800–432–7272
Shangri-La International: 1–800–359–5050
Sheraton International: 1–800–325–3535
Steigenberger: 1–800–223–5652
Swiss-Belhotel: 1–800–553–3638 (U.S. only)
Swissôtel: 1–800–637–9477.
Swissair Nestle Swissotel: 1–800–637–9477
Westin: 1–800–228–3000

HOTEL RESERVATION AGENCIES IN NORTH AMERICA

Orient Hotel Reservations: Sino-American Tours, 1–800–221–7982. New York State Tel. 212–925–6424. SABRE direct access Y/TUR/QSA. Fax 212–925–6483.
UTELL U.S.: 1–800–44UTELL.

FINANCES

Not all foreign banks and financial institutions have relations with the Bank of China. To avoid inconvenience, always ask if their services can be used in China.

Only some **foreign currencies** are accepted for exchange in China. These are: Australian dollar (A$), Austrian schilling (Sch), Belgian franc (BF), Canadian dollar (Can$), Danish krone (DKr), West German mark (DM), French franc (FF), Japanese yen (¥), Malaysian dollar (M$), Dutch guilder (fl.), Norwegian krone (NKr), Singapore dollar (S$) Swedish krona (SKr), Swiss franc (SF), pound sterling (£), US dollar (US$) and Hongkong dollar (HK$).

Not all **credit cards** are acceptable in China. Some can be used to pay for a limited number of hotels, obtain cash, and pay for purchases in a few designated stores, with a 4% surcharge. Currently accepted are Federal Card, Visa/MasterCard, American Express, Diner's Club, Million Card, Great Wall, and JCB Card. Payment can also be made with Renminbi Travelers Letter of Credit bought with foreign currencies, drafts and other payment instruments in convertible currencies issued by the Bank of China branches in London, New York, Los Angeles, Toronto, Singapore, Luxembourg and Hongkong and the banks maintaining accounts in convertible Renminbi with the Banking Department, Bank of China, Head Office.

Some travelers, however, have found Letters of Credit difficult to convert into F.E.C.s.

The only **traveler's checks and money orders** accepted are issued by foreign banks that have concluded payment arrangements with the Bank of China. These are:

Rafidain Bank, Baghdad, Iraq. T/C	US.$, £
Arab Bank Ltd., Amman, Jordan. T/C	US.$ £
The National Bank of Australasia Ltd., Melbourne, Australia. T/C	Australian Dollar
Bank of New South Wales, Sydney, Australia. T/C	Australian Dollar
Australia & New Zealand Banking Group Ltd., T/C	$, $A
Commonwealth Trading Bank of Australia, Sydney, Australia. T/C	$, $A
MITSUI-THOMAS COOK T/C	Japanese Yen

Hankyu Express International Co. Ltd., "VISA" T/C	Japanese Yen
Yamaguchi Bank Ltd., "VISA" T/C	Japanese Yen
The Bank of Tokyo, Ltd., Tokyo. T/C	US.$, Yen
The Sumitomo Bank Ltd., "VISA" T/C, Tokyo	Yen
The Fuji Bank, Ltd., Tokyo. T/C	Yen
Barclays Bank International Ltd., "VISA" T/C and International Money Order, London	£, US.$
Lloyds Bank Ltd., London. T/C	£
Standard Chartered Bank Ltd., London. T/C	£, US.$
The Royal Bank of Scotland Group T/C, London	£
Grindlays "VISA" T/C, London	£
National Westminster Bank Ltd., London. T/C	£
Thomas Cook & Sons Ltd., London. T/C	£, US.$, Can.$, A$
The Hongkong & Shanghai-THOMAS COOK T/C	Hongkong Dollar
Standard DM. T/C Issued by 30 German Banks	Deutsche Mark
Societe Francaise Du Cheque De Voyage S.A. T/C	French Frs.
Societe Generale THOMAS COOK T/C	French Frs.
Swiss Bankers T/C, Berne, Switzerland.	Swiss Frs.
Banque Bruxelles Lambert, Brussels T/C	Belgian Frs.
Societe Generale De Banque, Brussels T/C	Belgian Frs.
Algemene Bank Nederland N.V., Amsterdam T/C	Florin
Amsterdam-Rotterdam Bank N.V., Amsterdam T/C	Florin
Nederlandsche Middenstandsbank N.V., Amsterdam. T/C	Florin
Norwegian T/C	Norwegian Krone
The Royal Bank of Canada, Montreal. World Money Order	Can.$, US.$
Bank of America, San Francisco, T/C	US.$
Citicorp, New York, T/C	US.$
Manufacturers Hanover Trust Co., New York, International Money Order	US.$
American Express Co., New York. T/C	US.$, £, F.frs., Can.$, Yen, DM, S.frs.
First National Bank of Chicago "VISA" T/C, Chicago	US.$
Republic National Bank of Dallas, Texas. T/C	US.$

CURRENCY

Chinese money is called Renminbi (RMB)—people's money. The Chinese dollar, known as the *yuan* (or *kuai*) equals 10 *jiao* or 100 *fen*. Yuan notes are in denominations of 10, 5, 2, and 1. The smaller jiao notes are 5, 2, and 1. The coins are 5, 2, and 1 fen.

F.E.C.s are Foreign Exchange Certificates with which you must pay for tourist hotels and some tourist restaurants and shops. These are being phased out.

Foreign exchange rates fluctuate. There is also a slight variation for cash or traveler's checks. Please consult your bank, Bank of China, or the *China Daily*.

The following chart will give you a rough idea of Chinese equivalents. If you cannot find the exchange rate in effect when you go, draw up your own table so that you can convert easily.

IF YOU END UP WITH A LOT OF UNWANTED RMB

The future of the FEC is in flux. If it has been phased out by the time you get to China, the following will not apply.

Most places frequented by tourists take only FEC. One diplomat said Chinese authorities even refused to cremate a dead foreigner unless paid in FEC. And even some post offices are asking for FEC.

Try to avoid collecting a lot of RMB in change, especially if you're on a quick trip or a group tour where you won't have a chance to spend it. **Keep a lot of small change in FEC handy.**

If you want to use up RMB (as opposed to FEC), use it in taxis, free markets, non-tourist approved stores, and offer it to pay for food in restaurants, even hotel restaurants. Many hotel restaurants now take RMB at the price quoted in the menu.

It is not illegal for foreigners to possess RMB, although some places might charge you extra for paying in RMB. Discuss this (cheerfully, please!) with the clerk, as in "But I don't see a sign that says I have to pay in FEC" or "That's all I have." You may or may not get away with it, depending on your timing. Sometimes the government has a campaign insisting that foreigners pay in FEC; sometimes clerks forget about it.

Some stores with prices quoted in RMB give discounts for FEC.

If you still have RMB left over when you leave China, you could leave it with friends or relatives, or as a charitable donation (at a temple), or to the Amity Foundation (13 Da Jian Yin Xiang, Nanjing). Amity is a Christian social welfare group serving all Chinese, not just Christians.

Another possibility is the Soong Ching-Ling Foundation. This foundation helps children in China. Also, some airports have a box for the Chinese Red Cross.

DOLLAR TO YUAN CONVERSION TABLE

If you want a handy chart to show you Chinese currency equivalents with your money, enter the current exchange rate into column **C** by multiplying the rate with the number in column **A.** Column **B** contains the Feb. 1992 U.S. dollar rate as an example.

BUYING YUAN

A *Your Currency*	B *Yuan (Jan.)*	C *Current Rate*
1	5.45	
2	10.90	
3	16.35	
4	21.80	
5	27.25	
6	32.70	
7	38.15	
8	43.60	
9	49.05	
10	54.50	
20	109.00	
30	163.50	
40	218.00	
50	272.50	
60	327.00	
70	381.50	
80	436.00	
90	490.50	
100	545.00	
200	1090.00	
300	1635.00	
400	2180.00	
500	2725.00	
600	3270.00	
700	3815.00	
800	4360.00	
900	4905.00	
1000	5450.00	

In Feb. 1992, the exchange rates in RMB yuan as printed in *China Daily* were:

Currency		Per	Buying	Selling
Australia	Dol	100	407.15	409.19
Austria	Sch	100	49.08	49.32
Belgium	Fr	10,000	1,675.74	1,684.14
Canada	Dol	100	465.00	467.33
Denmark	Kr	100	88.93	89.38
Deutsche	Mk	100	344.94	346.67
Dutch	Fl	100	306.58	308.12
Finnish	Mk	100	127.52	128.16
France	Fr	100	101.21	101.72
Italy	Lira	10,000	46.29	46.52
Japan	Yen	100,000	4,293.78	4,315.30
Norway	Kr	100	87.87	88.31
Singapore	Dol	100	332.68	334.35
Sweden	Kr	100	95.63	96.10
Swiss	Fr	100	385.88	387.82
U.K.	Pound	100	999.11	1,004.12
USA.	Dol	100	544.37	547.09
HK	Dol	100	69.92	70.27
Macao	Dol	100	67.89	68.23

MAPS

The People's Republic of China
(old spelling)

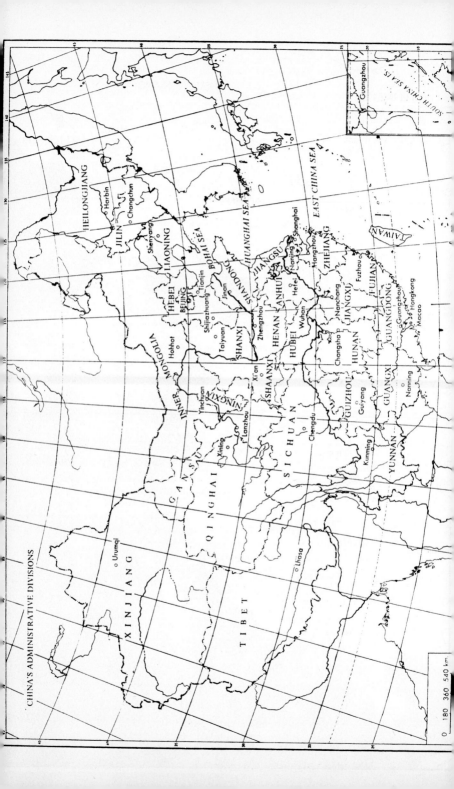

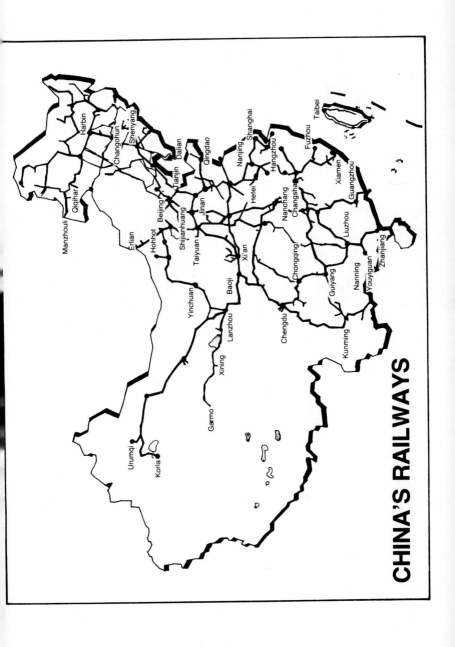

CHINA'S RAILWAYS

Xuzhou

JIANGSU

ANHUI

Yangzhou

Nanjing

Zhenjiang

Hefei

Changzhou

Wuxi

Yixing

Suzhou

Yangtze River

Shanghai

Hangzhou

SHANGHAI

Huangshan

Shaoxing

Ningbo

ZHEJIANG

Fuzhou

FUJIAN

Quanzhou

Zhangzhou

Xiamen

**EAST CHINA
TOURIST REGION**

Z.M. Li

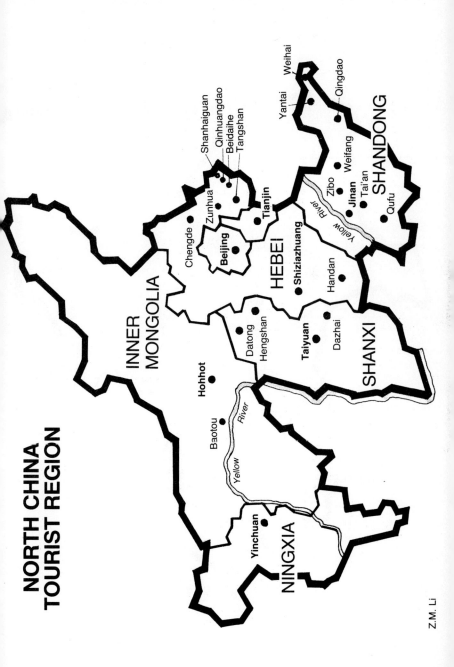

NORTH CHINA
TOURIST REGION

INNER MONGOLIA

Chengde

Zunhua

Beijing

Tianjin

Shanhaiguan
Qinhuangdao
Beidaihe
Tangshan

HEBEI

Shiziazhuang

Handan

Yellow River

Zibo

Weifang

Jinan

Tai'an

Qufu

SHANDONG

Yantai

Weihai

Qingdao

Datong

Hengshan

Taiyuan

Dazhai

SHANXI

Hohhot

Baotou

Yellow River

Yinchuan

NINGXIA

Z.M. Li

NORTHEAST CHINA
TOURIST REGION

HEILONGJIANG

● Daqing

Harbin
●

JILIN

Changchun **Jilin**
●   ●

Shenyang
●

Fushun
●

LIAONING

● Anshan

● Dalian

Z.M. Li

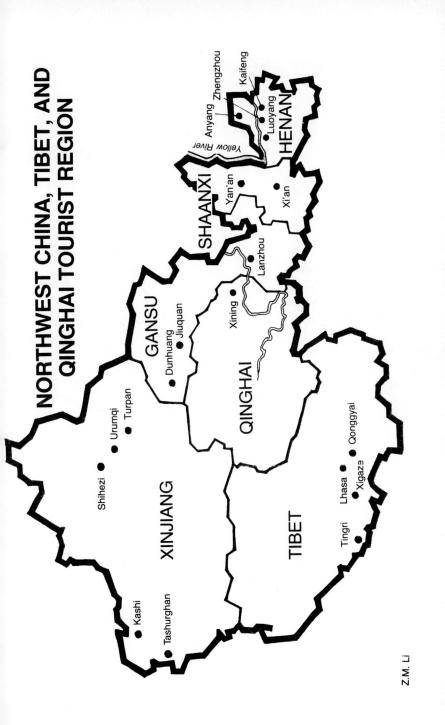

NORTHWEST CHINA, TIBET, AND QINGHAI TOURIST REGION

Z.M. Li

Jiujiang

Lushan

Jingdezhen

Yueyang

HUNAN **Changsha**

Nanchang

JIANGXI

Shaoshan

Hengshan

Jinggang
Mountains

Guilin

Liuzhou

Shaoguan

GUANGDONG

Shantou

GUANGXI

Wuzhou

Foshan

Conghua

Zhaoqing

Guangzhou

Guiping

Xiqiao

Shekou

Nanning

Jiangmen

Shenzhen

Taishan

Hong Kong

Xinhui

Zhuhai

Zhongshan

Zhanjiang

**SOUTH CHINA
TOURIST REGION**

Haikou

HAINAN

Sanya

Z.M. Li

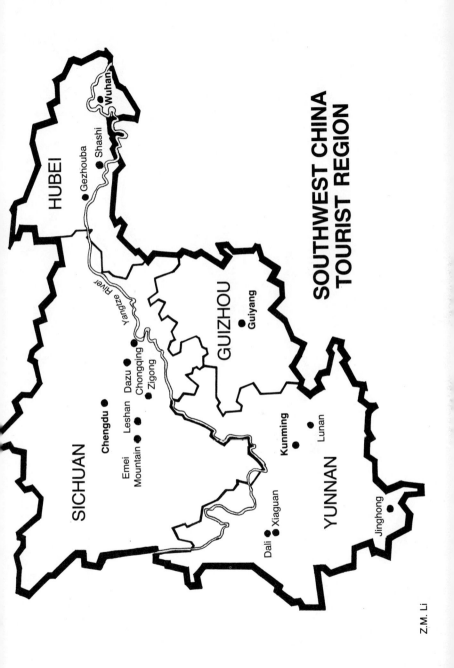

SOUTHWEST CHINA
TOURIST REGION

HUBEI

• Gezhouba

Shashi

Wuhan

Yangtze River

SICHUAN

Chengdu •

Leshan Dazu

Emei • Chongqing

Mountain • Zigong

GUIZHOU

Guiyang
•

Kunming
•

Lunan
•

YUNNAN

Dali •
• Xiaguan

Jinghong
•

Z.M. Li

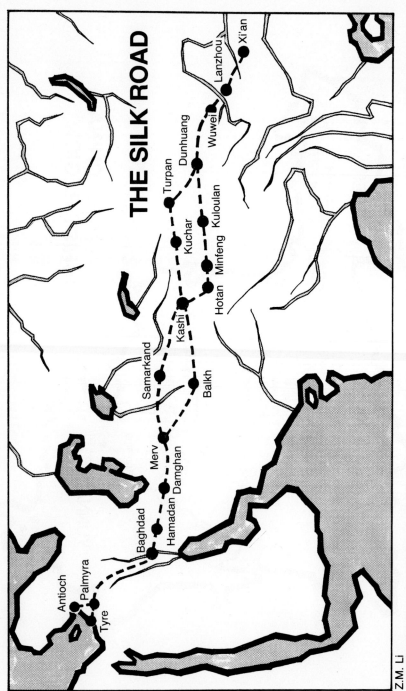

THE SILK ROAD

Xi'an
Lanzhou
Wuwei
Dunhuang
Turpan
Kuchar
Kuloulan
Kashi
Minfeng
Hotan
Samarkand
Balkh
Merv
Damghan
Hamadan
Baghdad
Antioch
Palmyra
Tyre

Z.M. Li

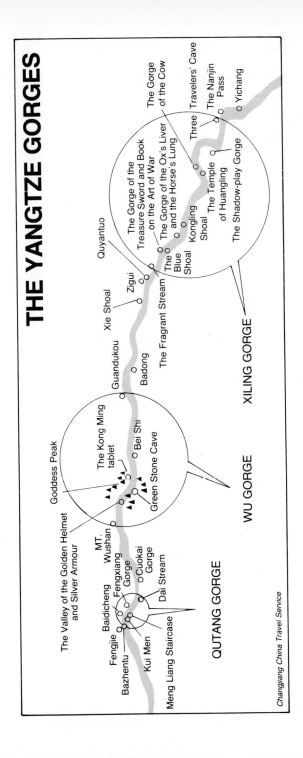

THE YANGTZE GORGES

The Valley of the Golden Helmet
and Silver Armour

Goddess Peak

The Kong Ming
tablet

○ Bei Shi

Guandukou

Green Stone Cave

MT.
Wushan

Fengxiang
Gorge

Baidicheng

○ Cuokai
Gorge

Badong

Xie Shoal

Zigui

Quyantuo

The Gorge of the
Treasure Sword and Book
on the Art of War

The Gorge of the Ox's Liver
and the Horse's Lung

The Gorge
of the Cow

Three Travelers' Cave

The Nanjin
Pass

Fengjie

Kui Men

Dai Stream

The Fragrant Stream

The
Blue
Shoal

Kongling
Shoal

The Temple
of Huangling

The Shadow-play Gorge

Yichang

Bazhentu

Meng Liang Staircase

QUTANG GORGE

WU GORGE

XILING GORGE

Changjiang China Travel Service

BEIJING

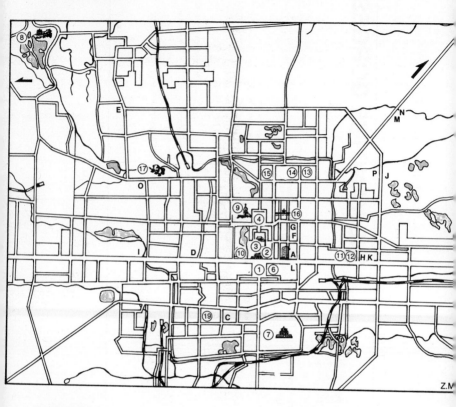

Z.M

Tourist Hotels

A. Beijing/Grand
B. Xin Qiao
C. Qianmen
D. Minzu
E. Youi [Friendship]
F. Peace/Palace/Taiwan
G. Sara/Tianlun/Holiday Inn Crowne
H. Jianguo Hotel
I. Yanjing Hotel
J. Great Wall Sheraton, Liangma
K. Toronto-Beijing/China World/Traders
L. Chongwenmen Hotel
M. Yanxiang/Grace
N. Holiday Inn Lido
O. Xiyuan Hotel
P. Huadu Hotel and Kunlun

Of Interest to Visitors

1. Tian Anmen [Gate of Heavenly Peace]
   Square
2. Tian Anmen Gate
3. Forbidden City and Palace Museum
4. Coal Hill Park
5. Great Hall of the People
6. Museums of the Chinese Revolution
   and Chinese History
7. Temple of Heaven
8. Summer Palace
9. Beihai Park
10. Zhongnanhai (Chung Nan Hai)
11. International Club
12. Friendship Store
13. Lama Temple
14. Temple of Confucius
15. Drum Tower
16. CAAC
17. Beijing Zoo
18. Beijing Library
19. Niujie Mosque

CHANGSHA

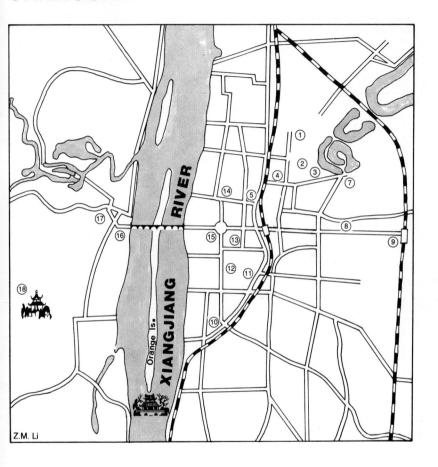

Z.M. Li

1. Hunan Provincial Museum
2. Martyrs' Park
3. Hunan Guest House
4. Hunan Exhibition Hall
5. Xiangjiang Guesthouse
6. Friendship Store
7. Yongyuen Hotel
8. Lotus Hotel
9. Railway Station
10. Hunan No. 1 Normal School
11. Tianxin Park
12. Huangxing Rd.
13. Jiefang Rd.
14. Zhongshan Rd.
15. Hunan Embroidery Building
16. Huatian Hotel
17. Fenglin Hotel
18. Aiwan Pavilion

CHENGDU

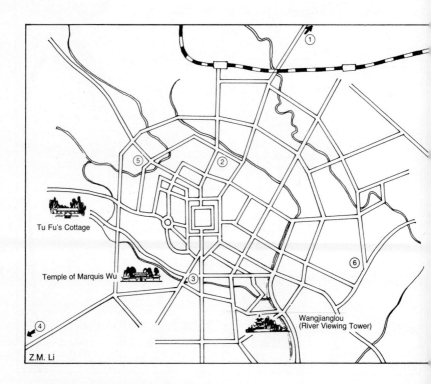

Tu Fu's Cottage

Temple of Marquis Wu

Wangjianglou
(River Viewing Tower)

Z.M. Li

1. **To Zoo and Divine Light Monastery**
2. **Wenshui Monastery**
3. **Jinjiang and Minshan hotels**
4. **To Leshan and Emel Shan**
5. **Tomb of Wang Jian**
6. **Chengdu Hotel**

CHONGQING

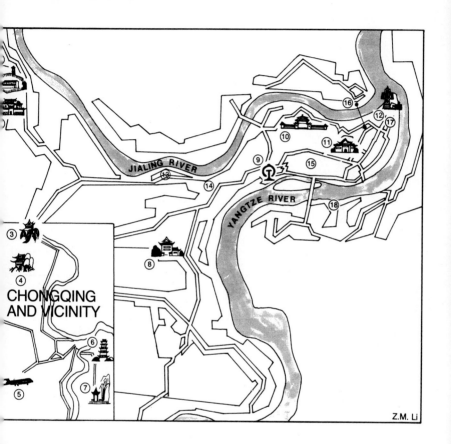

Z.M. Li

1. Jiatse Cave
2. Bai Gong Guan
3. North Hot Spring Park
4. Chingyun Park
5. Airport
6. South Hot Spring Park
7. South Mountain Park
8. Yuzhou Guest House
9. Railway Station

10. People's Guest House
11. Chongqing (Bingguan) Guest House
12. Chaotianmen Wharf
13. Hongyancun (Red Crag Village)
14. Eling (Goose Neck Park)
15. Loquat Hill
16. Cableway
17. Chongqing (Fan Dian) Hotel
18. Holiday Inn

DATONG

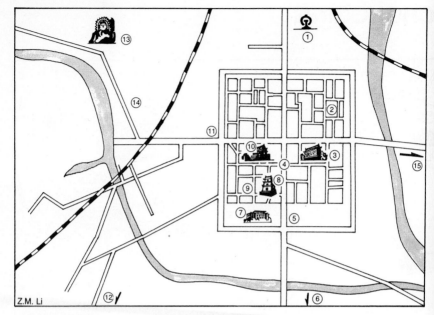

Z.M. Li

1. Railway Station
2. Municipal Carpet Factory
3. Nine Dragon Screen
4. Drum Tower
5. Yungang Guest House
6. Airport
7. Datong Guest House
8. Shanhua Monastery
9. Brassware Factory
10. Huayan Monastery
11. Red Flag Bazaar
12. To Wooden Pagoda, Yingxian County
13. Yungang Caves
14. Guanyin Hall
15. To Temple in Mid-air

GUANGZHOU

1. National Peasant Movement Institute
2. Memorial Gardens to the Martyrs of the 1927 Guangzhou Uprising
3. Mausoleum of the Seventy-two Martyrs at Huanghuagang
4. Guangzhou Zoo
5. Zhenhai Tower
6. Dr. Sun Yat-sen Memorial Hall
7. Temple of the Six Banyan Trees
8. Guangzhou Cultural Park
9. Guangzhou Trade Center
10. C.I.T.S.
11. CAAC
12. Friendship Store
13. Huai Sheng Mosque a.k.a. Guang Ta Monastery
14. Nanfang Department Store
15. Zhoutouzui (Ship Quay)
16. Qingping Free Market
17. Guangxiao Temple
18. Cathedral of the Sacred Heart
19. Folk Arts and Crafts Hall (Zhen Family Temple)

Hotels

A. Dong Fang (Tung-fang) and China Guanzhou
B. Guangzhou
C. Liu Hua
D. Landmark
E. Novotel
F. Holiday Inn City Centre
G. White Swan
H. Baiyun and Garden (opposite)

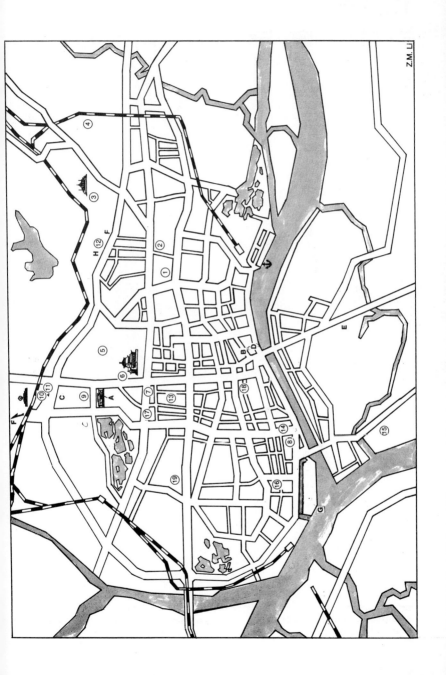

GUILIN

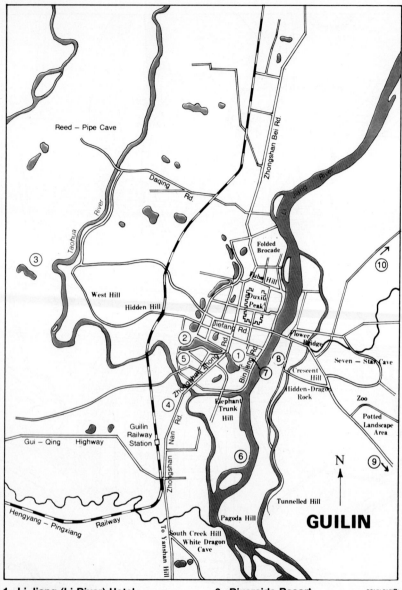

1. Li Jiang (Li River) Hotel
2. Ronghu Hotel
3. Jiashan Hotel
4. Osmanthus Hotel
5. Holiday Inn
6. Riverside Resort
7. Sheraton
8. Guishan
9. to Pine Garden
10. to Ming Tomb

ROMY PARIÑA

HANGZHOU

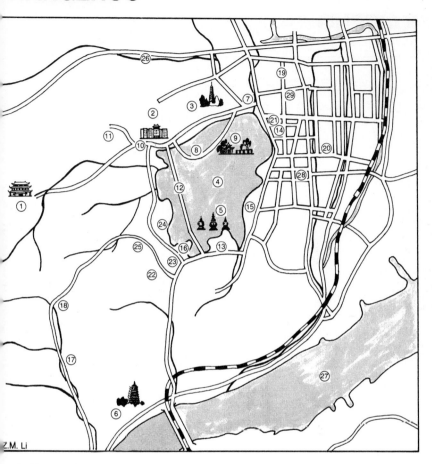

1. Lingyin Temple
2. Shangri-La Hotel
3. Baochu Pagoda
4. West Lake
5. Three Pools Mirroring the Moon
6. Six Harmonies Pagoda
7. Children's Palace
8. Baidi Causeway
9. Autumn Moon on Calm Lake
10. Temple of Yue Fei
11. Jade Spring
12. Sudi Causeway
13. Nanshan Rd.
14. Hubin Rd.
15. Liulangwenying Park
16. Huagang Park
17. Nine Creeks and Eighteen Gullies
18. Dragon Well
19. Yan'an Rd.
20. Jiefang Rd.
21. Overseas Chinese Hotel
22. Huajiashan
23. Huagang Hotel
24. Xihu Hotel
25. Zhejiang Hotel
26. Dragon Hotel
27. Qiantang River
28. Friendship Hotel
29. Wanghu Hotel

Z.M. Li

KAIFENG

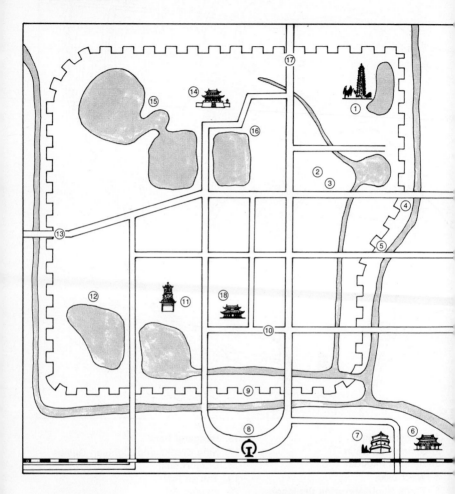

1. Iron Pagoda
2. Dongjing Hotel
3. Painter's Studio
4. Caomen Gate
5. Songmen Gate
6. King Yu's Terrace
7. Pota Pagoda
8. Railway Station
9. South Gate
10. Kaifeng Guest House
11. Yanqing Taoist Temple
12. Baofu Pit
13. West Gate
14. Dragon Pavilion
15. Yangjia Lake
16. Panjia Lake
17. North Gate
18. Xiangguo Monastery

KUNMING

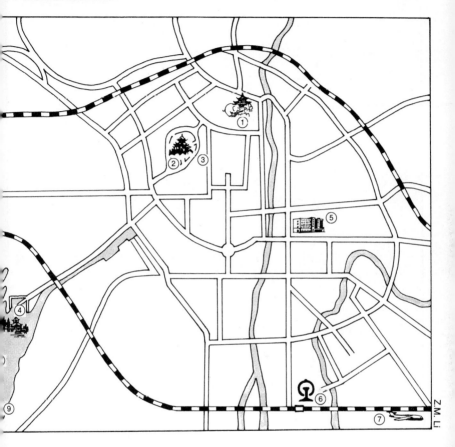

1. **Yuantongshan Mountain**
2. **Zhui Hu (Green Lake) Park**
3. **Green Lake Hotel**
4. **Daguan Lou (Grand View Pavilion)**
5. **Kunming Hotel and C.I.T.S.**
6. **Railway Station**
7. **To Airport**
8. **Dianchi Lake**
9. **To Western Hills**
10. **Golden Dragon Hotel**

NANJING

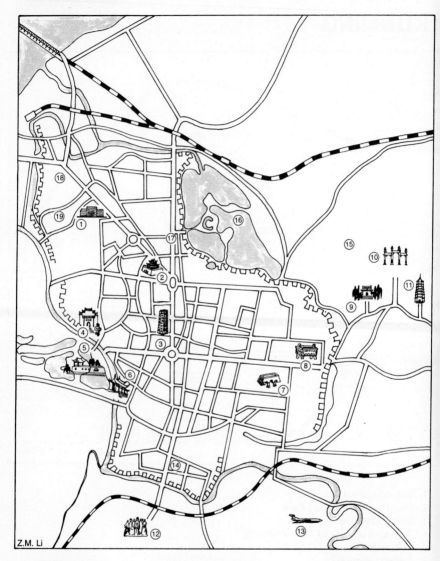

Z.M. Li

1. Nanjing Hotel
2. Drum Tower
3. Jinling Hotel
4. Stone Citadel
5. Mochou Park
6. Chaotian Palace
7. Wuchao Gate and
   Ming Palace ruins
8. Nanjing Provincial
   Museum
9. Ming Tomb
10. Sun Yat-sen Mausoleum
11. Linggu Pagoda
12. Yuhuatai Mausoleum
13. To Airport
14. Taiping Museum and
    Confucian Temple
    Market
15. Observatory
16. Xuanwu Lake
17. Friendship Store
18. Shuangmenlou Hotel
19. Dingshan Hotel

QINGDAO

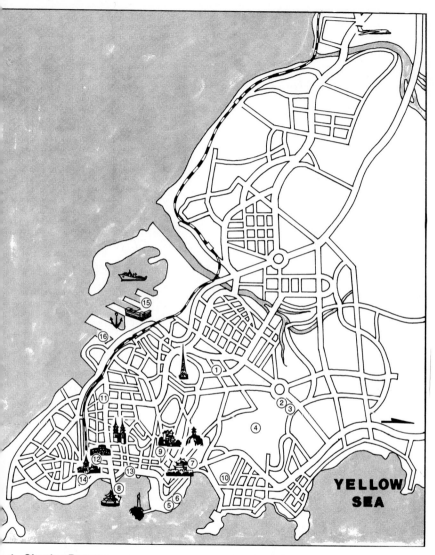

1. Qingdao Brewery
2. Embroidery Factory
3. Jade Carving Factory
4. Zhongshan Park
5. Luxun Park
6. Qingdao Museum of Marine Products
7. Qingdao Museum
8. Pier

9. Haitian Hotel
10. Huiquan Dynasty
11. Zhongshan Rd.
12. Huaqiao (Overseas Chinese) Hotel
13. Zhanqiao (Pier) Guesthouse
14. Railway Station
15. Youyi (Friendship) Hotel
16. Passenger Quay

URBAN SHANGHAI

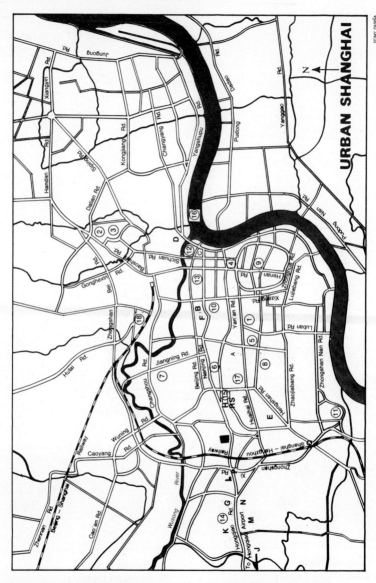

1. Site of the First National Congress of
   the Communist Party of China
2. Museum and Tomb of Lu Xun
3. Lu Hsun's Former Residence
4. Shanghai Municipal Museum
5. Former Residence of Dr. Sun Yat-sen
6. Shanghai Exhibition Centre/ Shanghai
   Centre/Portman/City/JC Mandarin
7. Jade Buddha Temple
8. Shanghai Art and Handicraft
   Research Studio
9. Yu Yuan Garden
10. People's Square
11. Lung Hua Pagoda
12. Friendship Store
13. Main Shopping area

SUZHOU

TAIYUAN

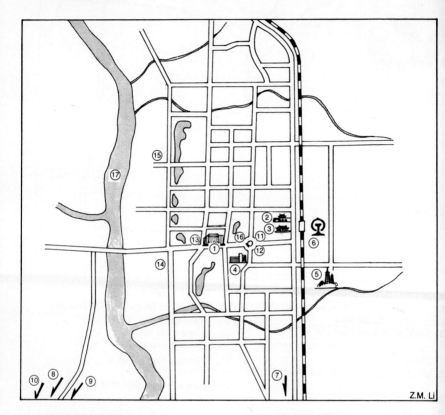

Z.M. Li

WUHAN

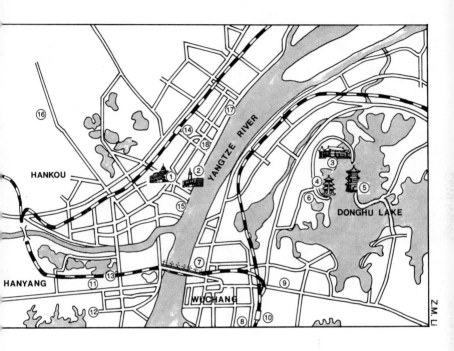

1. Xuangong Hotel
2. Wuhan Customhouse
3. Changtian Lou (Long Heaven Tower)
4. Qingchuan Hotel
5. Huguang Ge (Lake Scenery Pavilion)
6. Hubei Provincial Museum
7. Yellow Crane Tower on Snake Hill
8. Qiyi (Uprising Gate)
9. Hongshan Hill

10. Wuchang Railway Station
11. Hanyang Railway Station
12. Guiyang Temple
13. Platform of the Ancient Lute
14. Hankou Railway Station
15. Passenger Quay
16. Airport
17. Shengli Hotel
18. Jianghan Hotel

ANCIENT XI'AN

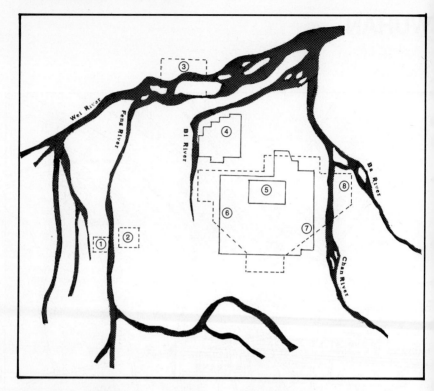

Locations in different historical periods

1. W. Han—Fengjing
2. W. Han—Haojing
3. Qin—Xianyang
4. Han—Changan
5. Ming and Qing—Xi'an
6. Sui—Daxing
7. Tang—Changan
8. Xi'an today

XI'AN

1. Shaanxi Stele Museum
2. Big Wild Goose Pagoda
3. Little Wild Goose Pagoda
4. Bell Tower
5. Drum Tower
6. West City Gate
7. Great Mosque
8. Holiday Inn Shenzhou
9. New World Xi'an
10. Renmin, Novotel, and Sofitel
11. Friendship Store
12. Zhonglou (Bell Tower) Hotel
13. Garden Hotel
14. Hyatt Hotel
15. Golden Flower Hotel (Jinhua)
16. Jianguo
17. Sports Hotel
18. Tangcheng Hotel
19. XI'an (Xiaoyanta Hotel)
20. Scarlet Bird Hotel

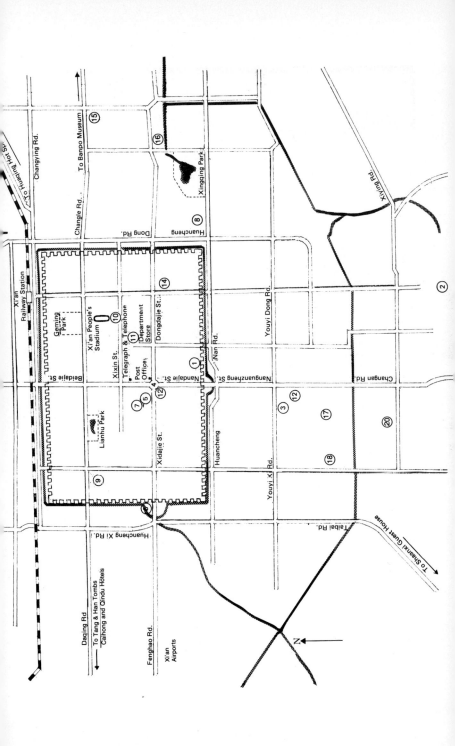

INDEX